Criminal Law in Canada

CASES, QUESTIONS, AND THE CODE

Seventh Edition

Criminal Law in Canada

CASES, QUESTIONS, AND THE CODE

Seventh Edition

Simon N. Verdun-Jones

School of Criminology
Simon Fraser University

NELSON

NELSON

Criminal Law in Canada: Cases, Questions, and the Code, Seventh Edition

by Simon N. Verdun-Jones

VP, Product Solutions, K–20:
Claudine O'Donnell

Director, Qualitative Publishing:
Jackie Wood

Publisher:
Leanna MacLean

Marketing Manager:
Sydney Pope

Content Manager:
Helena Ng

Photo and Permissions Researcher:
Natalie Barrington

Production Project Manager:
Shannon Martin

Production Service:
SPi Global

Copy Editor:
Karen Rolfe

Proofreader:
SPi Global

Indexer:
SPi Global

Design Director:
Ken Phipps

Post-secondary Design PM:
Pamela Johnston

Interior Design:
Diane Robertson

Cover Design:
Colleen Nicholson

Cover Image:
LdF/Getty Images

Compositor:
SPi Global

Printed and bound in the United States of America
1 2 3 4 22 21 20 19

For more information contact
Nelson Education Ltd.,
1120 Birchmount Road,
Toronto, Ontario, M1K 5G4.
Or you can visit our Internet site at nelson.com

Library and Archives Canada Cataloguing in Publication

Title: Criminal law in Canada : cases, questions, and the code / Simon Verdun-Jones (School of Criminology, Simon Fraser University).

Names: Verdun-Jones, Simon N. (Simon Nicholas), author.

Description: Seventh edition. | Previously published: Toronto, Ontario: Nelson Education, 2015.

Identifiers: Canadiana 20190149094 | ISBN 9780176724412 (softcover)

Subjects: LCSH: Canada. Criminal Code. | LCSH: Criminal law—Canada—Textbooks. | LCSH: Criminal law—Canada—Cases. | LCGFT: Textbooks.

Classification: LCC KE8809 .V47 2019 | LCC KF9220.ZA2 V47 2014 kfmod | DDC 345.71—dc23

ISBN-13: 978-0-17-672441-2
ISBN-10: 0-17-672441-9

This book is dedicated to Dr. Ardashes Avanessian,
without whom it would not have been possible.

"Honour a physician with the honour due unto him for the uses which ye may have of him: for the Lord hath created him."

Ecclesiasticus, Ch. 38, verse 1

BRIEF CONTENTS

CONTENTS

PREFACE FOR STUDENTS

For many people, the prospect of studying a legal textbook may be somewhat daunting. Practitioners of the law tend to employ a dense and opaque form of technical language that is alien to those who have not been the beneficiaries of a law school education and on-the-job training in law offices and the courts. However, *Criminal Law in Canada: Cases, Questions, and the Code* is designed to be user-friendly to readers who require a broad and reasonably detailed understanding of the criminal law but do not intend to join the legal profession in the near future.

To make the study of criminal law as user-friendly as possible, this textbook makes considerable use of the *case method* of studying law. In other words, it seeks to discuss the general principles underlying Canadian criminal law in the context of specific cases decided by the courts. Each chapter contains not only a statement of the relevant principles of law but also a discussion of the facts of decided cases and significant extracts from the judgments of the courts. This case-oriented approach is intended to equip the reader to apply the general principles of Canadian criminal law to the kinds of concrete factual situations they may encounter in everyday life or read/hear about in the media or online. The quotations from the judgments delivered in decided cases should provide some degree of insight into the legal method of analysis judges use to deal with the harmful or potentially harmful events that occur in real life and represent an infringement of Canadians' fundamental values.

Provided the reader progresses step by step through the book, there should be no difficulty in understanding the basic concepts that underlie Canadian criminal law. It is hoped that each chapter of the book will gradually increase the reader's knowledge of the basic principles of Canadian criminal law so that, by the end of the book, all the "pieces of the puzzle" will fit neatly together in the reader's mind. Provided the reader is patient and thorough, the study of criminal law should prove to be a rewarding challenge that need arouse none of the fears so frequently associated with it.

Associated with the case method is the inclusion in the textbook of a series of problems, or "Study Questions," that appear at the end of each chapter. Most of these problems are based on relatively uncomplicated fact patterns and are designed to prompt the reader to devise legal solutions by applying the legal principles discussed in the preceding chapter. These problems may well serve as the basis for classroom debate or for discussion within less formal student study groups. By working through the study questions in each chapter, the reader should not only acquire a more comprehensive understanding of criminal law but also find it easier to remember the information learned. When the problems are discussed in the classroom or in groups, the experience should also prove to be enjoyable and stimulating.

Over and above the use of the case method, some noteworthy features of this textbook should advance the objective of making the learning experience both agreeable and informative. There are 48 diagrams (figures) designed to assist the reader's comprehension of legal principles and rules and assist in the preparation for examinations, quizzes, and tests. Furthermore, in each chapter, there is a box intended to provide an in-depth focus on a specific case or issue raised in the chapter. It is suggested that readers undertake online research that will expand their knowledge of the cases and/or issues discussed in the 12 boxes: this research will assist in stimulating classroom and small-group discussions. Finally, each chapter contains eye-catching illustrations drawn by Greg Holoboff. These illustrations, coupled with their respective captions, provide a valuable and memorable insight into the most important legal principles discussed in the textbook.

An extensive glossary will also facilitate the reader's understanding of the most important of the technical terms used in the textbook. It is always a good idea to consult the glossary if the reader is seeking a brief definition or explanation of what might, on first acquaintance, appear to be a complex and indecipherable concept. Furthermore, the appendix provides a very brief overview of the system of criminal courts in Canada. The information in the appendix may help the reader comprehend the various steps that a case may take from trial through to a final appeal.

Finally, readers are strongly urged to supplement their study of this book with an in-depth exploration of some of the leading criminal cases that have been decided by Canadian courts. A closer study of some of the critical cases that have helped shape the contemporary body of Canadian criminal law will certainly add new—and valuable—dimensions to the task of understanding the vital issues that confront Canadian courts on an ongoing basis. A very good resource is the website of the Canadian Legal Information Institute (www.canlii.org/en). This website provides easy access to decisions of the Supreme Court of Canada and, in particular, the *Supreme Court Reports*, which include lengthy headnotes summarizing the decisions in a manner that enables readers to quickly grasp the important legal issues raised therein. The website also enables readers to review the complete judgments of nearly all of the cases discussed in this textbook, whether the decisions were made in appellate courts (other than the Supreme Court of Canada) or in trial courts.

PREFACE FOR INSTRUCTORS

The seven editions of this book have all been informed by the author's lengthy experience with the challenging task of teaching criminal law to students who, for the most part, do not intend to enter the legal profession. This book was designed to meet the very specific needs of these particular students. Law school textbooks are not appropriate because the depth of their coverage goes far beyond the needs of such students, who would also tend to perceive them as somewhat "dry." Paradoxically, other criminal law textbooks in Canada, although they were specifically written for non-lawyers, are far too general in their approach and do not provide sufficiently detailed information about the law for these students. Indeed, many of these students will be required to acquire a broad and reasonably sophisticated understanding of criminal law in order to carry out their future duties in various professions related to the criminal justice system (probation, police, and parole officers, court workers, forensic mental-health professionals, etc.) and related systems (such as social work and mental health). The prime objective of the first edition of *Criminal Law in Canada: Cases, Questions, and the Code* was to meet the requirements of these students, and this objective has remained constant right up to the current, seventh, edition.

One of the most effective methods of teaching criminal law to criminology, criminal justice, or law and security students is the *case-oriented approach*, in which students are encouraged to study not only the general principles of criminal law but also the specific details of decided cases. By combining the study of general principles with a close analysis of specific cases, students learn to apply these principles of criminal law to concrete, factual situations that arise in everyday life or to situations that they may encounter in their professional lives. This book unequivocally adopts the case-oriented approach to the study of criminal law. Individual decided cases are discussed in considerable detail and there are significant extracts from the opinions of judges. It is hoped that this approach will more adequately meet the needs of students who seek to acquire a working knowledge of Canadian criminal law and, at the same time, render the study of law somewhat more palatable. Indeed, reading real-life "stories" should be an inherently appealing task for those students who are seeking employment in the criminal justice system or in closely related areas, such as mental health and social work.

As part of the case-oriented approach, a number of study questions have been included at the end of each chapter. These are specifically designed to encourage students to test the extent to which they have absorbed the major principles of law covered in each substantive chapter. However, it is important to recognize that the questions are not intended to be particularly complex or difficult; if they were, they would not serve the function of permitting the average student to test their understanding of the major principles covered in the chapter. In the author's experience, answering the study questions is a necessary first step in the student's assimilation of the principles of criminal law and should be followed by more complex problem-solving exercises that draw together a number of different topics and encourage the student to see the criminal law as a whole rather than as a series of separate compartments. It usually takes a few weeks before students are ready to tackle these more complex exercises; instructors might wish to delay their use until students have completed at least the first three chapters of the book.

NEW TO THIS EDITION

The seventh edition retains the basic structure of the sixth edition. The seventh edition brings the criminal law up to date, including more than 60 new cases decided since the writing of the sixth edition and covers important legislative changes made to the *Criminal Code* since the previous edition.

In addition, each chapter was modified to update a box that focuses on the issues raised by a particular case or a specific topic that will stimulate student discussion. It is suggested that student discussion of the cases and/or topics will be enhanced by encouraging them to search for contemporary Internet coverage of the cases discussed in the 12 boxes. This process will also enable them to develop their research skills and enrich classroom or small-group discussions. In addition, 12 new illustrations, specifically produced for this book by Greg Holoboff, were added to provide strong visual images that underscore critical legal principles discussed in the text.

The most dramatic changes to the *Criminal Code* include the enactment of provisions that permit "medical assistance in dying" (MAID): Bill C-14, as assented to on June 17, 2016. These are discussed in Chapter 3. The legislation represented the response of the Parliament of Canada to the decision of the Supreme Court of Canada in *Carter v Canada (Attorney General)* (2015). The amendments to the *Criminal Code* permit medical practitioners and nurse practitioners, in certain closely defined circumstances, to both assist suicide and carry out active euthanasia with respect to suffering patients whose "natural death has become reasonably foreseeable." The Box in Chapter 3 explores the legislation in some depth and raises potential questions about its constitutionality in light of the Supreme Court's judgment in *Carter*. The Box should provide the basis for some spirited student discussion.

An important series of legislative changes to the *Criminal Code* were enacted by *An Act to amend the Criminal Code (offences relating to conveyances) and to make consequential amendments to other Acts*, S.C. 2018, c. 21. The Act made significant changes to the law relating to impaired driving and being in care or control while impaired as well as to the various offences associated with dangerous and impaired driving. In addition, the legislation made some noteworthy reforms to the *Criminal Code* provisions relating to the law of consent in the context of charges of sexual assault as well as removing some reverse-onus clauses from a number of *Criminal Code* sections. The relevant provisions of this very recent legislation have been incorporated into the seventh edition.

Another critically important amendment to the *Criminal Code*, which is highlighted in the seventh edition, is the amendment to Section 232 (S.C. 2015, c. 29, s. 7). This amendment sharply limits the availability of the defence of provocation as a defence to a charge of murder. In order to qualify for the defence, the accused must now show that the conduct of the victim would constitute "an indictable offence" that "is punishable by five or more years of imprisonment." The significance of this change is discussed in Chapter 10. The question of whether the defence should be abolished because of its frequent association with domestic violence should engage students in some basic questions about legal and social policy.

Among the important recent decisions by the Supreme Court of Canada that are discussed in this edition are:

- *Canada (Attorney General) v. Bedford* (2013), which provides an example of the importance of the Canadian *Charter of Rights and Freedoms* and the power of the courts to strike down legislation that infringes *Charter* rights and is not justifiable under Section 1 of the *Charter*.
- *R. v. Borowiec* (2016), in which the Supreme Court provided a detailed analysis of what it called "a particularly dark corner of the criminal law, the law of infanticide."
- *R. v. Buzizi* (2013), *R. v. Cairney* (2013), and *R. v. Pappas* (2013), which examined critical aspects of the defence of provocation.
- *Carter v. Canada* (Attorney General) (2015), which struck down the ban on physician-assisted suicide and led to the enactment of the medical assistance in dying legislation described above.
- *R. v. D.L.W.* (2016), in which the Supreme Court reasserted the principle that "Parliament is presumed to intend that true crimes have a subjective fault component."
- *R. v. Flaviano* (2014), in which the Supreme Court affirmed an important decision by the Alberta Court of Appeal, concerning the application of section 273.2(b) of the *Criminal Code*, which requires the accused person who claims mistaken belief in consent as a defence to a charge of sexual assault to "take reasonable steps" to ascertain that the complainant was consenting.
- *R. v. George* (2017), in which the Supreme Court analyzed the application of section 150.1(4) of the *Criminal Code*, which requires an accused person who claims an honest mistake as to the age of the

complainant with respect to a charge of sexual interference or sexual assault, to show that they took "all reasonable steps to ascertain the age of the complainant."

- *R. v. Hutchinson* (2014), an extremely important case in which the Supreme Court articulated the nature of the "voluntary agreement of the complainant to engage in the sexual activity in question" [s. 273.1(1)] and the circumstances in which fraud may vitiate such consent under s. 265(3)(c).
- *La Souveraine, Compagnie d'assurance générale v. Autorité des marchés financiers* (2013), a case in which the Supreme Court reviewed the nature of the defence of due diligence with respect to a charge of a provincial regulatory offence.
- *R. v. Lloyd* (2016), which provides an example of the Supreme Court using the *Charter* to strike down a mandatory minimum sentence [section 5(3)(a)(i)(D) of the Act, S.C. 1996, c. 19].
- *R. v. Riesberry* (2015), in which the Supreme Court reviewed the nature of fraud under section 380 of the *Criminal Code*.
- *R. v. Simpson* (2015), a case in which the Supreme Court defined the nature of the "colour of right" defence.
- *Wilson v. British Columbia (Superintendent of Motor Vehicles)* (2015), in which the Supreme Court examined the nature of regulatory offences in contrast to true crimes.

The seventh edition also includes important appellate and trial cases decided in other courts between 2013 and 2019.

The seventh edition contains an extensive glossary, which students should be encouraged to consult because it frequently provides answers to the most basic questions that they may have following their first acquaintance with new—and sometimes challenging—material. It is strongly recommended that students also read some of the most significant cases discussed in this book. Ideally, they should read at least one or two cases in their original form (perhaps through the Canadian Legal Information Institute's website, **canlii.org**, which is easily accessible online and includes the *Supreme Court Reports*, which include headnotes that greatly facilitate beginning students' appreciation of the important and relevant legal issues raised in decisions of the Supreme Court).

ABOUT THE NELSON EDUCATION TEACHING ADVANTAGE (NETA)

The **Nelson Education Teaching Advantage (NETA)** program delivers research-based instructor resources that promote student engagement and higher-order thinking to enable the success of Canadian students and educators. To ensure the high quality of these materials, all Nelson ancillaries have been professionally copy edited.

Be sure to visit Nelson education's **Inspired Instruction** website at **http://www.nelson.com/inspired** to find out more about NETA. Don't miss the testimonials of instructors who have used NETA supplements and seen student engagement increase!

Assessing Your Students: NETA Assessment relates to testing materials. **NETA Test Bank** authors create multiple-choice questions that reflect research-based best practices for constructing effective questions and testing—not just recall but also higher-order thinking.

INSTRUCTOR RESOURCES

All instructor ancillaries for this title are provided on the Instructor Companion Site at **http://www.nelson.com/site/crimlawincanada7e**, giving instructors the ultimate tool for customizing lectures and presentations.

Combined NETA Instructor's Manual and Test Bank: This resource was written by Tamara O'Doherty, Simon Fraser University. It is organized according to the textbook chapters and addresses key educational concerns, such as typical stumbling blocks students face and how to address them. Other features include key ideas or concepts that students should grasp; common misconceptions or difficult topics to help instructors address them through lectures, out-of-class work, or in-class activities; instruction on how to engage students; and activities to connect and bridge concepts, reveal misconceptions, and further understanding of key concepts.

ACKNOWLEDGMENTS

The various editions of this textbook have been wonderfully informed by the numerous generations of excellent students with whom I have had the privilege of exploring criminal law over more than 40 years. Their enthusiasm and creative support have encouraged me to continue writing for them, and their constructive criticism has greatly assisted me in the preparation of the seven editions of this textbook.

In addition, I owe a profound debt to my colleagues, both graduate students and faculty members, at the School of Criminology at Simon Fraser University who have contributed directly and indirectly to many aspects of the seventh edition. In particular, I would like to recognize Neil Boyd, Danielle Brown, Tiana Gaudette, Soraya Janus, David MacAlister, Tamara O'Doherty, and Marsha-Ann Scott.

I would like to move a very special vote of thanks to Greg Holoboff who created the superb original illustrations for this textbook. Greg consistently managed to produce visual images that perfectly demonstrated the application of legal principles that I asked him to illustrate. He has certainly proved that a picture can very well be worth a thousand words.

Finally, but by no means least in terms of importance, there are a number of individuals who played an important role in the production of this textbook. I have greatly enjoyed my lengthy association with Nelson Education. Special recognition is owing to Helena Ng, Content Developer with Nelson, who provided support in the development of the manuscript and Shannon Martin, Production Project Manager, also with Nelson. I was particularly fortunate to be able to work with an exceptionally skillful and diligent copy editor, Karen Rolfe. In addition, thanks are due to Natalie Barrington, Photo and Permissions Researcher, and Daniela Glass, Senior Rights Project Manager at Nelson. Finally, I should single out Udhaya Harisudan and Magesh Rajagopalan, Project Managers, SPi Global.

The seventh edition would never have been completed without the amazing medical treatment and support provided to me by the specialists, physicians, and nurses at the Lion's Gate Hospital, North Vancouver, and the British Columbia Cancer Agency in Vancouver. Their dedication and expertise are truly exceptional.

Lastly, but of very great importance, is the unflinching support provided by my wife, Valerie, who had to act as caregiver to a sick author of a book that was completely outside her own area of expertise. I have no doubt that this author was not an easy patient to deal with, given the very lengthy process that moves from writing to ultimate publication in many stages over an extended period.

CHAPTER 1

INTRODUCTION TO CANADIAN CRIMINAL LAW

Learning Objectives

After reading this chapter, you will be able to understand:

- the nature and sources of criminal law in Canada;
- the difference between "true crimes" and "regulatory offences";
- the significance of the exclusive jurisdiction of the federal Parliament to enact criminal law;
- the impact of the *Canadian Charter of Rights and Freedoms* [the *Charter*] on the judicial interpretation and application of the criminal law; and
- the extent to which infringements of the rights of Canadians under the *Charter* may be justified by the "pressing and substantial" concerns that motivated federal and provincial/territorial legislatures to enact the legislation subjected to a *Charter* challenge.

WHAT IS CRIMINAL LAW?

The Definition of Crime in Canada

Before embarking on an analysis of criminal law, it is necessary to define the legal concept of a crime and to explain how crimes are classified within the Canadian criminal justice system. It is essential to recognize the importance of legal definitions and categories because they have enormously practical consequences. For example, the legal definition of a crime is a matter of critical significance because only the Parliament of Canada has the jurisdiction under the ***Constitution Act*, 1867**, 30 & 31 Vict, c. 3, to enact **criminal law** and thereby create crimes; this jurisdiction is known as the **federal criminal law power**. Similarly, the manner in which individual crimes are categorized determines how they are tried and the penalties that may be imposed on conviction.

In Canada, a **crime** consists of two major elements:

1. conduct that is prohibited because it is considered to have an "evil or injurious or undesirable effect upon the public,"[1] and
2. a penalty that may be imposed when the prohibition is violated.

The conduct that is prohibited may include not only actions but also a failure to act when there is a legally imposed duty to take action. The penalty may range from a fine to a sentence of imprisonment.

In Canada, crimes are classified into three categories, as illustrated in Figure 1.1.

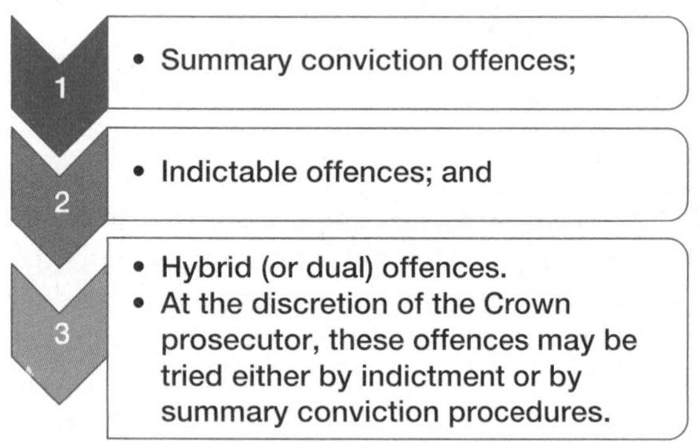

Figure 1-1
The Three Categories of Crimes in Canada

1. The phrase "evil or injurious or undesirable effect upon the public" was coined by Justice Rand in the *Margarine Reference* case (1949), which is discussed later in this chapter.

Summary conviction offences may be tried only before a provincial/territorial court judge or justice of the peace sitting alone, and the maximum penalty is normally a fine of $5000 or a sentence of six months in prison or both. "Summary" refers to the fact that these offences are tried rapidly within the provincial/territorial court and without any complex procedures. Examples of summary conviction offences are carrying a weapon while attending a public meeting; obtaining food, a beverage, or accommodation by fraud; wilfully doing an indecent act in public; being nude in a public place without lawful excuse; causing a disturbance in a public place; disturbing a religious service; and taking a motor vehicle without consent ("joyriding").

Indictable offences are more serious in nature and are punishable by more severe sentences (in some cases, life imprisonment). The indictment is the formal document that sets out the charge(s) against the **accused** person and is signed by the Attorney General or their agent. Unlike summary conviction offences, indictable offences may be tried by more than one court procedure, depending on the seriousness of the offence concerned. Some serious indictable offences, such as murder, may be tried only by a superior court judge sitting with a jury, while some less serious indictable offences may be tried only by a provincial/territorial court judge without a jury. However, in most cases, a person charged with an indictable offence may elect to be tried by a provincial /territorial court judge, a superior court judge sitting alone, or a superior court judge sitting with a jury. There are, therefore, three categories of indictable offences, as seen in Figure 1.2.

In most cases, individuals charged with an indictable offence have the right to a preliminary inquiry before a provincial/territorial court judge, who will

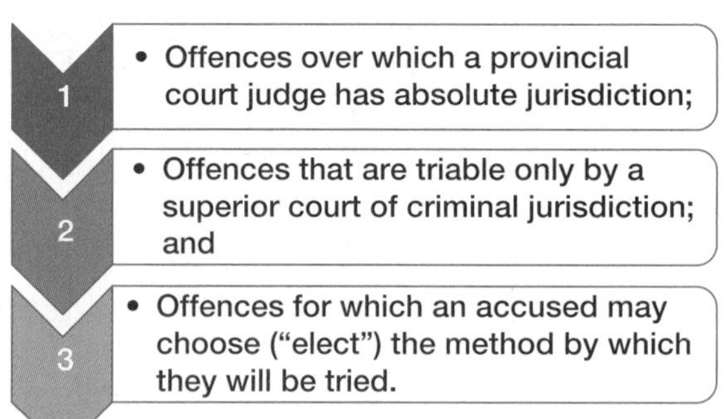

Figure 1-2
The Three Categories of Indictable Offences

decide whether there is "sufficient evidence" to put the accused person on trial. Examples of indictable offences are murder, manslaughter, sexual assault with a weapon, aggravated sexual assault, robbery, theft over $5000, and breaking and entering.

Most offences in Canada's *Criminal Code* are **hybrid (or dual) offences**. There are very few *Criminal Code* offences that may be tried only by summary conviction procedures; however, it is significant that most hybrid (or dual) offences are, in practice, tried by summary conviction procedures. Examples of hybrid (or dual) offences are assault, assaulting a peace officer, sexual assault, unlawful imprisonment, theft under $5000, fraud not exceeding $5000, and failing to comply with a probation order.

True Crimes and Regulatory Offences

A noteworthy distinction that must be drawn before one embarks on a study of criminal law is the distinction between **true crimes** and **regulatory offences**. The courts treat these two types of offence in a significantly different manner and the consequences for a person convicted of one of the two types of offence differ significantly in terms of the severity of the penalties that may be imposed, and the degree of stigma associated with a finding of guilt. Justice Cory of the Supreme Court articulated the nature of the distinction between true crimes and regulatory offences in his judgment in *Wholesale Travel Group Inc.* (1991):

> Acts or actions are criminal when they constitute conduct that is, in itself, so abhorrent to the basic values of society that it ought to be prohibited completely. Murder, sexual assault, fraud, robbery and theft are all so repugnant to society that they are universally recognized as crimes. At the same time, some conduct is prohibited, not because it is inherently wrongful, but because unregulated activity would result in dangerous conditions being imposed upon members of society, especially those who are particularly vulnerable.

The objective of regulatory legislation is to protect the public or broad segments of the public (such as employees, consumers, and motorists, to name but a few) from the potentially adverse effects of otherwise lawful activity. Regulatory legislation involves a shift of emphasis from the protection of individual interests and the deterrence and punishment of acts involving moral fault to the protection of public and societal interests. While criminal offences are usually designed to condemn and punish past, inherently wrongful conduct, regulatory measures are generally directed to the prevention of future harm through the enforcement of minimum standards of conduct and care. As Moldaver J. stated, on behalf of the Supreme Court of Canada in *Wilson v. British Columbia (Superintendent of Motor Vehicles* (2015): "... it has long been recognized that regulatory legislation ... differs from criminal legislation in the way it balances individual liberties against the protection of the public. Under regulatory legislation, the public good often takes on greater weight."

Regulatory offences arise under both federal and provincial/territorial legislation and deal with diverse matters such as the maintenance of the quality of meat sold to the public, the regulation of the packaging of food products, the establishment of rigorous standards concerning the weights and measures used by retailers, the regulation and control of pollution, the control of misleading advertising, and the establishment and maintenance of a regime of traffic regulation. Indeed, as Justice Cory stated in *Wholesale Travel Group Inc.*, "Regulatory measures are the primary mechanisms employed by governments in Canada to implement public policy objectives," and "it is through regulatory legislation that the community seeks to implement its larger objectives and to govern itself and the conduct of its members." He went on to say that:

> ... regulation is absolutely essential for our protection and well being as individuals, and for the effective functioning of society. It is properly present throughout our lives. The more complex the activity, the greater the need for and the greater our reliance upon regulation and its enforcement. ... Of necessity, society relies on government regulation for its safety.

One of the most significant aspects of the distinction between true crimes and regulatory offences is to be found in the differing concepts of fault that underlie the two categories of prohibited conduct. Conviction of a true crime (such as murder or robbery) necessarily involves a judgment that the offender has seriously infringed basic community values and is, therefore, considered to be morally culpable for their actions. In contrast, conviction of a regulatory offence (such as accidentally mislabelling a food item) may involve very little (if any) moral culpability on the part of the offender. Similarly, the penalties that may be imposed following conviction of a true crime are generally far more severe than those that may be imposed when a person has been found guilty of a regulatory offence.

In the *Roy* case (2012), the Supreme Court of Canada examined the essential difference between the *Criminal Code* offence of dangerous operation of a motor vehicle, a *true crime*, and the provincial *regulatory offence* of careless driving (or driving without due care and attention). On behalf of the Court, Justice Cromwell stated that:

> Dangerous driving causing death is a serious criminal offence punishable by up to 14 years in prison. Like all criminal offences, it consists of two components: prohibited conduct—operating a motor vehicle in a dangerous manner resulting in death—and a required degree of fault—a marked departure from the standard of care that a reasonable person would observe in all the circumstances. The fault component is critical, as it ensures that criminal punishment is only imposed on those deserving the stigma of a criminal conviction. …
>
> Giving careful attention to the fault element of the offence is essential if we are to avoid making criminals out of the merely careless. …

Justice Cromwell emphasized that the criminal law does not punish the type of ordinary negligence or carelessness that may render an individual liable in a civil law suit or that may lead to the imposition of a fine for "careless driving" or "driving without due care and attention"—offences that are contained in provincial/territorial motor vehicle legislation. Instead, the offence of dangerous operation of a motor vehicle, a *Criminal Code* offence, requires a much higher degree of negligence in order to sustain a conviction. The requirement is that the Crown prove that the accused's driving represented "a marked departure" from the standard of care expected of a reasonable driver acting prudently. The greater degree of fault, embodied in the "marked departure" standard, justifies the imposition of a harsher penalty and enhanced measure of stigma under the *Criminal Code*.

In brief, true crimes are acts that are generally considered to be inherently wrong by the majority of Canadians (e.g., murder, burglary, and sexual assault). On the other hand, regulatory offences are directed toward the control of activities that are considered by the majority of Canadians to be inherently lawful (selling food, driving a motor vehicle, or placing an advertisement in the local newspaper). Business, trade, and industry need to be regulated for the benefit of society as a whole, and penalties may be imposed for breach of the requirements of the regulatory regime. For example, whether Canadians should drive on the left or right side of the road does not raise a question of fundamental values. To avoid chaos, however, each country has to make a choice as to which side of the road its motorists should use; it would be absurd to permit individual motorists to make that choice for themselves. In other words, although driving is an inherently legitimate activity, there has to be a regulatory regime to protect the interests of all those individuals who use the highways. The penalties associated with regulatory offences are directed not at the underlying activities themselves but rather at breaches of the regulatory regime that ensures the orderly and safe conduct of those activities.

It should be noted, however, that a federal regulatory statute may create a true crime. For example, the *Income Tax Act*, R.S.C. 1985, c. 1 (5th Supp.), is a regulatory statute, but the offence of tax evasion, under section 239(1), is a real crime, carrying a maximum penalty of up to two years' imprisonment and a potentially large fine. Evasion of taxation would rightly be considered an action that is inherently wrong and deserving of punishment.

In Chapter 6, we shall examine regulatory offences in more depth and demonstrate that the prosecution (the Crown) has been granted the benefit of certain advantages that render it easier to obtain a conviction in relation to a regulatory offence than in relation to a true crime. Most significantly, when an accused person is charged with a true crime, the general rule is that the Crown must prove all the elements of the offence beyond a reasonable doubt. However, when the charge in question concerns a regulatory offence, the Crown merely has to prove that the accused person committed the act prohibited by the legislation in question: once the commission of the prohibited act has been established, then the accused person must prove, on the balance of probabilities, that they were not negligent.

Since regulatory offences differ significantly from true crimes, they are frequently characterized as constituting a body of **quasi-criminal law**.[2] This term means that the body of regulatory offences closely resembles criminal law but nevertheless lacks two key characteristics of criminal law—namely, the prohibition of conduct that is regarded as inherently wrong and the potential severity of the sentences that may

2. The prefix **quasi-** means "seeming," "not real," or "halfway."

be imposed. Later in this chapter, we shall explore the implications of the concept of quasi-criminal law for the field of constitutional law in Canada.

CRIMINAL LAW AS A FORM OF PUBLIC LAW

Law may generally be defined as the collection of rules and principles that govern the affairs of a particular society and that are enforced by a formal system of control (courts, police, etc.). It is usual to divide law into two parts: public law and private law.

Public law is concerned with issues that affect the interests of the entire society. Constitutional law deals with the allocation of powers between the various provinces/territories of Canada and the various levels of government (legislature, courts, and executive). It also deals with the relationship between the state and individual citizens. Administrative law defines the powers, and regulates the activities, of government agencies, such as the Immigration and Refugee Board and the Canadian Radio-television and Telecommunications Commission. Criminal law is also considered to be part of public law because the commission of a crime is treated as a wrong against society as a whole and it is the Crown that prosecutes criminal cases on behalf of all Canadians; indeed, all criminal cases are catalogued as *Regina* (the Queen) versus the accused person concerned.

Private law is concerned with the regulation of the relationships that exist among individual members of society. It includes the legal rules and principles that apply to the ownership of property, contracts, torts (injuries inflicted on another individual's person or damage caused to the individual's property), and the duties of spouses and other family members toward one another. The resolution of private disputes may be sought through the commencement of a "civil suit" in the appropriate court.

THE SOURCES OF CRIMINAL LAW IN CANADA

Perhaps the most basic question we can raise in relation to the Canadian criminal law is, "Where does it come from?" The answer is that there are two **primary sources of law** (or main **sources of criminal law**): (1) legislation and (2) judicial decisions that either interpret such legislation or state the "common law."

FEDERAL LEGISLATION

Since Canada is a federal state, legislation may be enacted by both the Parliament of Canada and the provincial or territorial legislatures. However, under the Canadian *Constitution*, there is a distribution of legislative powers between the federal and provincial/territorial levels of government. Which level of government has the power to enact criminal law? It is clear that criminal law is a subject that falls within the exclusive jurisdiction of the Parliament of Canada. Indeed, by virtue of section 91(27) of the *Constitution Act, 1867*, the federal Parliament has exclusive jurisdiction in the field of "criminal law and the procedures relating to criminal matters."

Just how extensive is the scope of the criminal law power under section 91(27) of the *Constitution Act*? As we have seen, two essential characteristics of a crime are a *prohibition* of certain conduct and an accompanying *penalty* for violating that prohibition. Does that mean that the Canadian Parliament can pass legislation on any issue that it chooses and justify it on the basis that, because it contains both a prohibition and a penalty, it must be criminal law? If this were the case, there would be absolutely no limits on the scope of the criminal law power. In fact, the Supreme Court of Canada has stated clearly that there must be a third factor, in addition to a prohibition and a penalty, for legislation to be recognized as a genuine exercise of the criminal law power. What is this third factor?

In the famous *Margarine Reference* case (1949), Justice Rand of the Supreme Court of Canada argued that the additional factor is the requirement that the prohibition and penalty contained in the legislation are directed toward a "public evil" or some behaviour that is having an injurious effect upon the Canadian public:

> A crime is an act which the law, with appropriate penal sanctions, forbids; but as prohibitions are not enacted in a vacuum, we can properly look for some evil or injurious or undesirable effect upon the public against which the law is directed. That effect may be in relation to social, economic or political interests; and the legislature has had in mind to suppress the evil or to safeguard the interest threatened.

Justice Rand asserted that, if the Parliament of Canada chooses to prohibit certain conduct under the criminal law power, then this prohibition must be enacted "with a view to *a public purpose which can support it as being in relation to criminal law.* ..." The public purposes that would be included in this category are "public peace, order, security, health, [and] morality," although Justice Rand acknowledged that this is not an exclusive list.

In *Syncrude Canada Ltd. v. Canada (Attorney General)* (2016), the Federal Court of Appeal considered the significant question of whether the federal criminal law power could be used to punish those who engage in acts that contribute to environmental pollution. Federal regulations, issued under the *Canadian Environmental Protection Act*, 1999, S.C. 1999, c. 33, required that all diesel fuel produced, imported or sold in Canada contain at least 2 percent renewable fuel. Syncrude Canada Ltd. produced diesel fuel at its oil sands project in Alberta and it sought a declaration that the regulations were invalid on, *inter alia*, constitutional grounds. The Federal Court of Appeal, relying on an earlier decision of the Supreme Court of Canada in *Hydro-Québec* (1997), ruled that the regulations were valid because protecting the environment was unequivocally a legitimate exercise of the federal criminal law power.

The Federal Court of Appeal noted that the Supreme Court of Canada had established a three-part test for determining whether there has been a valid exercise of the federal criminal law power: (1) a prohibition, (2) backed by a penalty, (3) for a criminal purpose. In this case, the only issue at play was the third requirement, the "criminal purpose." Referring to the *Margarine Reference Case*, the Court took account of the jurisprudence which indicated that the requirement of a "criminal purpose" turned on whether the law in question was aimed at suppressing or reducing "an evil." More specifically, the "law must address a public concern relating to peace, order, security, morality, health or some other purpose." The Federal Court of Appeal had absolutely no doubt that protecting the environment was a "criminal law purpose." Quoting the Supreme Court of Canada, Rennie J.A. said "pollution is an 'evil' that Parliament can legitimately seek to suppress."

However, the Parliament of Canada may not purport to exercise its criminal law power in those areas of jurisdiction that are assigned exclusively to the provinces unless the legislation really does meet the test set out in the *Margarine Reference* case: namely, there must be a prohibition and a penalty that are designed to combat a "public evil" or some other behaviour that is having an injurious effect upon the Canadian public. For example, the Supreme Court of Canada struck down most of the provisions of the *Assisted Human Reproduction Act*, S.C. 2004, c. 2 because they did not constitute "in pith and substance" criminal law. This legislation was enacted to address various concerns about certain undesirable practices that had arisen with the development of new medical technologies designed to assist the conception and birth of children (these included *in vitro* fertilization, artificial insemination, egg or embryo donation, and drug therapies). However, the Act was challenged on the grounds that most of its provisions did not represent a valid exercise of Parliament's criminal law power. Indeed, it was argued that, insofar as these provisions were really concerned with the comprehensive regulation of medical practice and research in relation to assisted reproduction, they actually constituted *health*—and not criminal—legislation. Health falls within the exclusive legislative jurisdiction of the provinces and, therefore, it was contended that the "impugned" provisions of the Act were invalid. In *Reference re Assisted Human Reproduction Act* (2010), the Supreme Court of Canada agreed with this argument and declared *most* of the sections of the Act to be invalid since Parliament did not have the authority to enact health legislation. Justice Cromwell, who cast the deciding vote in a 5-4 split decision stated that:

> [T]he essence of the impugned provisions of the *Assisted Human Reproduction Act, S.C. 2004, c. 2*, is regulation of virtually every aspect of research and clinical practice in relation to assisted human reproduction. ...
>
> [T]he "matter" of the challenged provisions, viewed as a whole, is best classified as being in relation to three areas of exclusive provincial legislative competence: the establishment, maintenance and management of hospitals; property and civil rights in the province; and matters of a merely local or private nature in the province ... the "matter" of the challenged provisions cannot be characterized as serving any criminal law purpose recognized by the Court's jurisprudence.

However, the Supreme Court upheld a *few* of the provisions of the *Assisted Human Reproduction Act* because they did constitute a valid exercise of the criminal law power. These provisions were concerned with preventing the use of a donor's reproductive material or an *in vitro* embryo from being used for purposes to which the donor had not given consent. They also prohibited the use of sperm or human eggs from a donor under the age of 18 and required that any consent given must be free and informed. Finally, they prevented the commercialization of the reproductive functions of women and men (e.g., engaging in surrogacy for profit). Justice Cromwell concluded that these provisions "prohibit negative practices associated with assisted reproduction and that they fall within the traditional ambit of the federal criminal law power."

What important pieces of legislation (or statutes) has the Canadian Parliament enacted in the field of criminal law? Undoubtedly, the most significant federal statute, dealing with both the substantive criminal law and the procedural law relating to criminal matters, is the ***Criminal Code***, R.S.C. 1985, c. C-46 (first enacted in 1892). **Substantive criminal law** refers to legislation that defines the nature of various criminal offences (such as murder, manslaughter, and theft) and specifies the various legal elements that must be present before a conviction can be entered against an accused person. Similarly, in this context, the term refers to legislation that defines the nature and scope of various defences (such as provocation, duress, and self-defence).

The term **criminal procedure** refers to legislation that specifies the procedures to be followed in the prosecution of a criminal case and defines the nature and scope of the powers of criminal justice officials. For example, as we have already noted, the procedural provisions of the *Criminal Code* classify offences into three categories: indictable offences, offences punishable on summary conviction, and dual (or hybrid) offences. These provisions then specify the manner in which these categories of offences may be tried in court. For example, they specify whether these offences may be tried by a judge sitting alone or by a judge and jury and indicate whether they may be tried before a judge of the superior court or a judge of the provincial (or territorial) court.

The procedural provisions of the *Criminal Code* are also concerned with the powers exercised by criminal justice officials. For example, the *Code* clearly specifies the nature and scope of the powers of the police in relation to the arrest and detention of suspects. Similarly, it also specifies the powers of the courts in relation to matters such as sentencing. In addition to the *Criminal Code*, there are a number of other federal statutes that undoubtedly create "criminal law." These include the *Controlled Drugs and Substances Act*, S.C. 1996, c. 19, the *Crimes against Humanity and War Crimes Act*, S.C. 2000, c. 24, and the *Youth Criminal Justice Act*, S.C. 2002, c. 1.

It should be noted that two other significant federal statutes have an indirect impact upon the criminal law. These are the *Canada Evidence Act*, R.S.C. 1985, c. C-5, and the *Constitution Act, 1982*, as enacted by the *Canada Act 1982* (U.K.), c. 11. The *Canada Evidence Act*, as its name would suggest, is concerned with establishing various rules concerning the introduction of evidence before criminal courts. For example, the Act indicates when a wife or husband may be compelled to give evidence against their spouse and indicates in what circumstances the evidence of a child under 14 years of age may be admissible in a criminal trial. The *Constitution Act, 1982* is of great significance to both the substantive criminal law and the law of criminal procedure, since Part I of the Act contains the *Canadian Charter of Rights and Freedoms*. The *Charter* is of immense importance because, as we shall shortly see, it permits courts to strike down, and declare invalid, any legislative provisions that infringe upon the fundamental rights and freedoms of Canadians.

Quasi-Criminal Law: Regulatory Offences and the Constitution

In the preceding section, it was established that the *Constitution Act, 1867* granted the federal Parliament exclusive jurisdiction in the field of criminal law and the procedures relating to criminal matters. At this point, readers no doubt feel that they have a clear grasp of the principle involved. Unfortunately, the situation is rendered considerably more complex by the existence of the body of regulatory offences that we have described as "quasi-criminal law." Under the *Constitution Act, 1867*, the provincial/territorial legislatures have been granted the power to enact laws in relation to a number of specific matters. For example, section 92 of the Act indicates, ***inter alia***, that "property and civil rights in the province" and "generally all matters of a merely local or private nature in the province" fall within the exclusive jurisdiction of the provincial/territorial legislatures. By virtue of judicial interpretation of the various provisions of section 92, it is clear that a number of other critical matters fall within the legislative jurisdiction of the provinces/territories, such as municipal institutions, health, education, highways, liquor control, and hunting and fishing.

Significantly, section 92(15) of the *Constitution Act, 1867* provides that the provincial/territorial legislatures may enforce their laws by "the imposition of punishment by fine, penalty or imprisonment." At this point, the reader will immediately exclaim that the imposition of fines, penalties, or imprisonment looks suspiciously like the apparatus of criminal law. One is compelled to ask whether this means that the *Constitution Act, 1867* is contradicting itself, since criminal law is a matter reserved to the exclusive jurisdiction of the federal Parliament. However, the answer is in the negative because such provincial/territorial legislation is not considered "*real*" criminal law. Instead, lawyers have termed it "*quasi-criminal law*." Since this type of provincial/territorial legislation is considered "quasi" rather than "real" criminal law, it is possible to argue that it does not impinge upon the federal Parliament's exclusive jurisdiction in the field of (real) criminal law.

Cynics will, no doubt, point to the semantic acrobatics involved in the categorization of the provincial/territorial offences as quasi-criminal laws. However, the designation of quasi-criminal law can be very well justified on a pragmatic basis. As mentioned earlier in this chapter, regulatory offences are generally far less serious in nature than the "true crimes" that may be committed in violation of the *Criminal Code* or other federal legislation, such as the *Controlled Drugs and Substances Act*.

Provincial/territorial legislatures may delegate authority to municipalities to enact municipal ordinances or **bylaws**. This municipal "legislation" may also be enforced by the "big stick" of fines or other penalties. Municipal bylaws or ordinances may be considered to fall within the category of quasi-criminal law.

It should be added that regulatory offences may also be found in a broad range of federal statutes (e.g., the *Canada Consumer Product Safety Act*, S.C. 2010, c. 21; *Competition Act*, R.S.C. 1985, c. C-34; the *Food and Drugs Act*, R.S.C. 1985, c. F-27; the *Fisheries Act*, R.S.C. 1985, c. F-14; the *Migratory Birds Convention Act*, S.C. 1994, c. 22; the *Motor Vehicle Safety Act*, S.C. 1993, c. 16; the *Nuclear Safety and Control Act*, S.C. 1997, c. 9; the *Plant Protection Act*, S.C. 1990, c. 22; *Safe Food for Canadians Act*, S.C. 2012, c. 24; the *Species at Risk Act*, S.C. 2002, c. 29; the *Tobacco and Vaping Products Act*, SC 1997, c. 13; and the *Trade-Marks Act*, R.S.C. 1985, c. T-13).

Taken together with quasi-criminal offences generated under provincial/territorial and municipal legislation, these federal offences contribute to a vast pool of regulatory law that has become increasingly complex as modern society has developed. As Justice Cory remarked in *Wholesale Travel Group Inc.* (1991), "There is every reason to believe that the number of public welfare [or regulatory] offences at both levels of government has continued to increase." Indeed, the Law Commission of Ontario noted that in 2009 more than two million charges involving regulatory offences were laid, just in Ontario, under the *Provincial Offences Act*, R.S.O. 1990, c. P.33.

This vast body of regulatory criminal law does not make good bedtime reading for the average citizen. Indeed, even the average lawyer is acquainted with only a fraction of the regulatory offences that currently exist. Nevertheless, as we shall see in Chapter 9, it is a firm principle of criminal law that "ignorance of the law is no excuse."

Problems of Jurisdiction in the Enactment of Legislation

Before leaving the complex area of quasi-criminal law, it is important to remember that the provincial/territorial legislatures are restricted to the enactment of legislation genuinely falling within the jurisdiction assigned to them under the *Constitution Act, 1867*. More specifically, it is clear that provincial/territorial legislatures may not encroach upon the exclusive federal jurisdiction to legislate "real" criminal law. Unfortunately, it is often difficult for the courts to determine whether provincial/territorial legislation has strayed beyond the boundaries of the jurisdiction assigned to the provinces/territories under the *Constitution Act* and whether such legislation is invalid because it has infringed upon the federal Parliament's exclusive criminal law domain. The formidable challenge posed by this task can best be demonstrated by some illustrative cases.

Municipalities are enabled to pass bylaws by provincial/territorial legislation and they may not enact bylaws that usurp the federal criminal law power. For example, in *Smith v. St. Albert (City)* (2012), a judge of the Alberta Court of Queen's Bench declared two City bylaws to be invalid because they constituted "in pith and substance" criminal legislation and, therefore, fell within the exclusive jurisdiction of the Parliament of Canada. The bylaws were enacted to discourage certain stores from trading in drug paraphernalia (such as "any device intended to facilitate smoking activity"). The Judge noted that the "practical effect of the bylaw is to preclude the licensing or successful operation of what have become colloquially known as bong or head shops."[3] In the words of T.D. Clackson J.:

> In my view the amending bylaw has the look and feel of morality legislation. What was plainly in the mind of the City was illegal narcotics. The amending bylaw has the look and feel of a statement that "this kind of thing isn't going to happen in my City" and it is plainly designed to address the perceived enforcement difficulties associated with the *Criminal Code* provisions relating to items which might be considered drug paraphernalia.

By way of contrast, in *Goodwin v. British Columbia (Superintendent of Motor Vehicles)* (2015), the Supreme Court of Canada upheld the constitutionality of British Columbia's Automatic Roadside Prohibition (ARP) scheme, which it introduced in 2010. This program, incorporated in the *Motor Vehicle Act*, R.S.B.C. 1996, c. 318, represented an extension of the Province's administrative scheme to take impaired drivers off the road by means of on-the-spot licence suspensions, penalties, and remedial courses. Using an approved screening device, police officers were empowered to take and analyze breath samples taken from drivers at the roadside. Depending on the results of the breath tests, drivers' licences could be suspended for 90 days or they could be handed a shorter suspension of between 3 and 30 days.

Goodwin argued that the program of automatic roadside suspensions was beyond the power of the Province to enact because it fell within the exclusive criminal law jurisdiction of the federal Parliament. However, on behalf of the Supreme Court of Canada, Karakatsanis J. rejected this argument and ruled that the scheme fell within the scope of provincial legislation. He agreed that the "pith and substance of the ARP scheme is the licensing of drivers, the enhancement of traffic safety and the deterrence of persons from driving while impaired by alcohol." More specifically, the ARP program is a valid exercise of the Province's jurisdiction to legislate in the area of "property and civil rights" under section 92(13) of the *Constitution Act, 1867*. The fact that the *Criminal Code* also contains provisions that criminalize drunk driving or being in care of control of a vehicle while intoxicated by alcohol and/or another drug does not prevent the provinces and territories from enacting preventive legislation. In this respect, Karakatsanis J. stated that:

> Provinces thus have an important role in ensuring highway safety, which includes regulating who is able to drive and removing dangerous drivers from the roads. Provincial drunk-driving programs and the criminal law will often be interrelated. Some provincial schemes have relied incidentally on criminal convictions. ... A number of provincial courts of appeal have also upheld schemes that are not dependent on criminal convictions but rely incidentally on *Criminal Code* provisions. ... This jurisprudence makes clear that a provincial statute will not invade the federal power over criminal law merely because its purpose is to target conduct that is also captured by the *Criminal Code*.

Deciding whether provincial/territorial legislation should be struck down on the basis that it infringes on the federal criminal law power clearly involves a considerable degree of judicial discretion, and the outcome may be almost impossible to predict with any degree of certainty. Indeed, there may well be some justification for the view that criminal law, like beauty, lies in the eye of the beholder. In general, the courts are reluctant to strike down laws passed by elected members of a legislature and will exercise a certain degree of judicial restraint when called upon to determine whether specific laws or parts of laws fall outside provincial jurisdiction. If the courts find that the "impugned" legislation has both a federal (criminal law) aspect and a provincial aspect, it may apply the "double aspect doctrine of judicial restraint" and affirm the validity of the provincial legislation.

In *Keshane* (2012), the central question was whether part of a bylaw passed by the City of Edmonton was valid (the city's authority to pass a bylaw was derived from an act of the provincial legislature, which could delegate such authority only within the scope of the powers granted to the province under the *Constitution Act, 1867*). The bylaw provision in question prohibited fighting in a public place and was challenged on the basis that, since the fighting ban was in reality a matter of criminal law, it was an issue that fell

3. A bong is a device (usually a pipe with a filter) generally used for smoking drugs.

Illustrations by Greg Holoboff

B.C. legislation establishing a scheme of automatic roadside suspensions for drivers whose breath samples indicate certain levels of alcohol in their blood streams is valid and does not infringe the exclusive criminal law power of the federal Parliament.

exclusively within federal jurisdiction: therefore, it was argued that this part of the bylaw was invalid because it fell outside the city's authority to enact. However, the Alberta Court of Appeal upheld the validity of the fighting prohibition in the bylaw. The Court stated that:

> Where the dominant feature of a provincial law relates to a federal head of power, the provincial law will be declared invalid as being *ultra vires*, or beyond the jurisdiction of the province, and *vice versa*.
>
> If no dominant purpose can be ascertained, i.e., the provincial and federal aspects of the impugned provision are of "roughly equal importance," at least where there is no actual conflict with other validly enacted legislation ... the "double aspect doctrine" of judicial restraint applies to uphold the validity of the provision.

The Court took the view that the aim of the fighting ban was to "regulate the conduct and activities of people in public places so as to promote the safe, enjoyable, and reasonable use of such property for the benefit of all citizens of the City." This objective falls with the legislative authority of the province (and the city) since it involved property and civil rights under section 92(13) of the *Constitution Act,1867* and/or should be considered a matter of a merely local nature under section 92(16). The Court readily agreed that there was also a federal (criminal law) aspect to the fighting ban because it engaged the public interest in preserving public peace and order and overlapped with various offences in the *Criminal Code*. However, the Court held that neither the provincial nor the federal aspect of the fighting ban was "dominant": therefore, it applied the dual aspect doctrine of judicial restraint and upheld the validity of the fighting ban in the bylaw.

Judicial Decisions as a Source of Criminal Law

In addition to legislation, such as the *Criminal Code*, a major source of criminal law is the numerous judicial decisions that either interpret criminal legislation or expound the "common law." A significant proportion of this book is concerned with the interpretation of the provisions of the *Criminal Code* by Canadian courts. However, the common law still plays an important role in Canadian criminal jurisprudence. Essentially, **common law** refers to that body of judge-made law that evolved in areas that were not covered by legislation.

Historically, a considerable proportion of English criminal law was developed by judges, who were required to deal with a variety of situations that were not governed by any legislation. Indeed, until relatively recently, much of the English law concerning theft and fraud was developed by judges in this way. One common law offence that is of particular relevance to present-day criminal law in Canada is **contempt of court**. However, the common law not only expanded the number of offences in the criminal law but also developed special defences that were not covered by any legislation. For example, the Canadian courts have single-handedly developed the law relating to the defence of necessity (a defence that does not appear in the *Criminal Code*); hence, necessity is known as a common law defence. They have also developed a common law defence of duress that has largely replaced the statutory version of this defence, defined in section 17 of the *Criminal Code* (see the discussion in Chapter 11).

It should be noted that, since 1954, *with the single exception of the offence of contempt of court*, it has not been possible for a Canadian to be convicted of a common law offence (see section 9 of the *Criminal Code*). However, section 8(3) of the *Criminal Code* preserves any common law "justification," "excuse," or "defence" to a criminal charge "except in so far as they are altered by or are inconsistent with this Act or any other Act of the Parliament of Canada." This provision is particularly significant since it means that common law defences, such as necessity and duress, are still applicable in a Canadian criminal trial. In short, although Canadian judges cannot create any new offences at common law, they may still apply the common law principles relating to certain defences, provided, of course, that these principles are not inconsistent with legislation enacted by the Canadian Parliament.

THE IMPACT OF THE *CANADIAN CHARTER OF RIGHTS AND FREEDOMS* ON THE CRIMINAL LAW IN CANADA

The enactment of the *Canadian Charter of Rights and Freedoms* as part of the *Constitution Act, 1982* heralded a dramatic new era in the relationship between the members of Canada's judiciary, on the one hand, and the elected representatives of Canada's federal Parliament and provincial/territorial legislatures, on the other. As an entrenched bill of rights, the *Charter* empowers judges, in certain circumstances, to declare any piece of legislation to be invalid—and of no force or effect—if the latter infringes upon an individual's protected rights. As (then) Chief Justice Dickson pointed out, in the case of *Morgentaler, Smolig and Scott* (1988):

> Although it is still fair to say that courts are not the appropriate forum for articulating complex and controversial programs of public policy, Canadian courts are now charged with the crucial obligation of ensuring that the legislative initiatives pursued by our Parliament and legislatures conform to the democratic values expressed in the *Canadian Charter of Rights and Freedoms*.

Canadian judges have demonstrated their willingness to use this far-reaching power where they believe that it is absolutely necessary to do so. A dramatic example of the judicial power under the *Charter* to strike down provisions of the *Criminal Code* is the case of *Canada (Attorney General) v. Bedford* (2013). In this case, three current or former sex workers sought a declaration that three *Criminal Code* provisions[4] relating to the sex trade were invalid in light of section 7 of the *Charter*, which guarantees the "right to life, liberty and security of the person and the right not to be deprived thereof except in accordance with the principles of fundamental justice." In declaring these *Criminal Code* provisions to be invalid, (then) Chief Justice Beverley McLachlin argued that they put the physical security of sex trade workers at risk by denying them the opportunity to employ protective measures, such as hiring security guards or implementing measures to screen clients. In her words, "the impugned laws deprive people engaged in a risky, but legal, activity of the means to protect themselves against [the] risks of disease, violence and death" at the hands of "pimps and johns." Significantly, the Supreme Court suspended the implementation of its ruling for one year in order to grant the Parliament of Canada sufficient time to enact new legislation which would regulate the sale and purchase of sexual services in a manner that does not place the physical security of sex workers at risk. As the Chief Justice noted, striking down the impugned

4. Section 210 (keeping or being in a bawdy-house), insofar as that section related to prostitution; section 212(1)(j) (living on the avails of prostitution); and section 213(1)(c) (communicating in public for the purposes of prostitution).

prostitution-related provisions of the *Criminal Code* did not mean that "Parliament is precluded from imposing limits on where and how prostitution may be conducted." Parliament responded by enacting the *Protection of Communities and Exploited Persons Act* (S.C. 2014, c. 25), which amended the *Criminal Code* so as to criminalize the *purchase*, but not the *sale*, of sexual services a crime.[5]

Another illustration of the importance of the judicial power to strike down legislation that infringes the *Charter* is the decision to rule that a mandatory minimum sentence imposed by Parliament is invalid because it infringes section 12 of the *Charter*, which protects citizens from "cruel and unusual punishment." For example, in *Lloyd* (2016), the Supreme Court of Canada stuck down subsection 5(3)(a)(i)(D) of the *Controlled Drugs and Substances Act*, S.C. 1996, c. 19, which provided a mandatory minimum sentence of one year of imprisonment for trafficking or possession for the purpose of trafficking of certain drugs, if the offender had been convicted of any drug offence (except possession) within the past 10 years. (Then) Chief Justice McLachlin stated that the courts will consider a mandatory minimum sentence to

5. See revisions to sections 213 of the *Criminal Code* and new sections 286.1 to 286.5.

Supervised Injection Sites and Section 7 of the *Canadian Charter of Rights and Freedoms*.

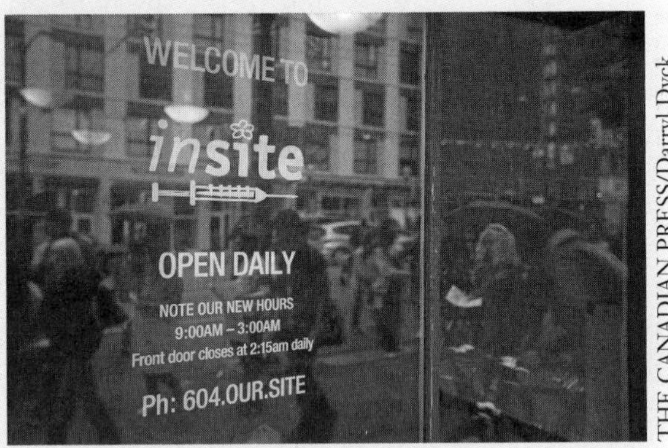

THE CANADIAN PRESS/Darryl Dyck

• • • • • •

The *Charter* grants the courts very wide powers that are not limited to declaring certain elements of legislation invalid. In fact, there is a variety of remedies that may be granted when a *Charter* right has been violated. Indeed, section 24(1) of the *Charter* empowers courts to provide such remedy as they consider "appropriate and just in the circumstances." For example, the courts may grant a declaration that a *Charter* right has been infringed and order that a minister or a government department carry out a certain action. This situation occurred in *PHS Community Services Society v. Canada (Attorney General)*, decided by the Supreme Court of Canada in 2011. The case involved the rights of health care workers to operate, and intravenous drug users to access, a safe injection facility in Vancouver (a facility known as "Insite"). In the words of (then) Chief Justice McLachlin,

> Local, provincial and federal authorities came together to create a legal framework for a safe injection facility in which clients could inject drugs under medical supervision without fear of arrest and prosecution. Insite was widely hailed as an effective response to the catastrophic spread of infectious diseases such as HIV/AIDS and hepatitis C, and the high rate of deaths from drug overdoses in the DTES.

Between 2003 and 2008, Insite had been able to operate legally because it had received an exemption from the provisions of the *Controlled Drugs and Substances Act*, S.C. 1996, c. 19. Section 56 of this Act grants the federal Minister of Health the authority to exempt any person or class of persons from the application of all or any of the provisions of the Act on the basis of a "medical purpose." An exemption in the case of Insite was necessary because, otherwise, the staff and clients could be charged with possession of proscribed drugs.

In 2008, the federal Health Minister failed to extend Insite's exemption and an action was brought seeking, in part, a declaration that the Minister's actions constituted a violation of the rights of the Insite staff and their clients under section 7 of the *Charter*. The Supreme Court of Canada ruled that the Minister's actions did indeed constitute a violation of the section 7 rights of the Insite staff and their clients and the Court ordered the Minister to issue an exemption under section 56 of the *Controlled Drugs and Substances Act*. In summarizing the conclusions of the Court, Chief Justice McLachlin stated that, if the Minister's decision not to extend the exemption had been upheld, drug users would have been prevented from accessing the health services provided by Insite and the absence of these services would have threatened the health and even the lives of Insite's vulnerable clients. In these circumstances, the section 7 *Charter* interests of the Insite clients were engaged and their rights were undoubtedly infringed. In these circumstances, it was the view of the Supreme Court that the Minister's decision was:

> ... arbitrary, undermining the very purposes of the *CDSA*, which include public health and safety. It is also grossly disproportionate: the potential denial of health services and the correlative increase in the risk of death and disease to injection drug users outweigh any benefit that might be derived from maintaining an absolute prohibition on possession of illegal drugs on Insite's premises.

The year 2015 saw the election of a new federal government, which was more sympathetic to the need to support the creation of "supervised consumption sites." Furthermore, by 2016, there was a rapid increase in the number of fatal opioid overdoses in Canada: for example, in that year, there were 726 such deaths just in the province of Ontario. The ready availability of street drugs, contaminated by synthetic opioids such as fentanyl and carfentanil, has created an opioid crisis in Canada. In 2017, there were 1125 overdose deaths in British Columbia, the province most severely affected. Against the background of this crisis, supervised consumption sites have now been established or are in development in four provinces as a means of preventing deaths from opioid overdoses, particularly those involving contaminated street drugs. The decision of the Supreme Court of Canada in *PHS Community Services Society v. Canada (Attorney General)* vividly demonstrates the broad powers conferred on the courts by the *Charter* and the use that can be made of those powers to safeguard the lives and health of Canadians.

Do you think that the majority of Canadians favour the view taken by the Minster of Health and the government of Canada in 2008, or the view that harm-reduction strategies with respect to illegal drug use constitute an essential element in protecting public health and safety? Should judges be in a position to override the policy choices of an elected government? What role should scientific evidence play in judicial decision making with respect to the *Canadian Charter of Rights and Freedoms*? What should judges do when the scientific evidence is conflicting?*

* Beyrer, C. (2011). Safe injection facilities save lives. *The Lancet*, 377(9775), 1385–1386.

constitute "cruel and unusual punishment" if it is "grossly disproportionate to the offence and its circumstances."[6]

However, it is important to recognize that the *Charter* does not require that the courts strike down every legislative provision that is considered to be in violation of an accused person's constitutional rights. Indeed, as we have already seen, section 1 of the *Charter* states that:

> The *Canadian Charter of Rights and Freedoms* guarantees the rights and freedoms set out in it subject only to such reasonable limits prescribed by law as can be demonstrably justified in a free and democratic society. [emphasis added]

As Chief Justice McLachlin said in delivering the judgment of the Supreme Court of Canada in *Canada (Attorney General) v. JTI-Macdonald Corp.* (2007), "Most modern constitutions recognize that rights are not absolute and can be limited if this is necessary to achieve an important objective and if the limit is appropriately tailored, or proportionate."

Section 1, in effect, requires the courts to engage in an elaborate balancing act in which they must decide whether the infringement of an individual's rights can be justified in the name of some "higher good." In the *Oakes* case (1986), the Supreme Court of Canada devised a specific test for the purpose of identifying the factors that should be considered when the courts attempt to decide whether the violation of a *Charter* right is justifiable as a "reasonable limit" in a "free and democratic society." This test has since become known as the ***Oakes* test**.

In delivering the judgment of the majority of the justices of the Supreme Court of Canada in the *Oakes* case (1986), Chief Justice Dickson prefaced his remarks concerning section 1 of the *Charter* by emphasizing that the burden of establishing that an infringement of a *Charter* right is justified as a reasonable limit is on the "party seeking to uphold the limitation": in a criminal case, this will nearly always be the Crown. In other words, there will have to be very strong grounds for overriding individual rights guaranteed by the *Charter*. However, the Chief Justice recognized that rights and freedoms

6. See also *John* (2018) and *Swaby* (2018), which declared the mandatory minimum sentences then applicable for possession of child pornography, under subsections 163.1(4)(a) & (b) respectively, of the *Criminal Code*, to be invalid and of no force and effect because they contravened section 12 of the *Charter*.

guaranteed by the *Charter* "are not absolute" and that "it may become necessary to limit rights and freedoms in circumstances where their exercise would be inimical to the realization of collective goals of fundamental importance."

What issues should a court address when attempting to decide whether a *Charter* violation is justified under section 1? In the *Oakes* case, Chief Justice Dickson stated that this process should be divided into two separate questions:

> To establish that a limit is reasonable and demonstrably justified in a free and democratic society, two central criteria must be satisfied. First, the objective, which the measures responsible for a limit on a *Charter* right or freedom are designed to serve, must be "of sufficient importance to warrant overriding a constitutionally protected right or freedom." ... It is necessary, at a minimum, that an objective relate to concerns which are pressing and substantial in a free and democratic society before it can be characterized as sufficiently important.
>
> Secondly, once a sufficiently significant objective is recognized, then the party invoking s. 1 must show that the means chosen are reasonable and demonstrably justified. This involves "a form of proportionality test." ... Although the nature of the proportionality test will vary depending on the circumstances, in each case courts will be required to balance the interests of society with those of individuals and groups. There are, in my view, three important components of a proportionality test. First, the measures adopted must be carefully designed to achieve the objective in question. They must not be arbitrary, unfair or based on irrational considerations. In short, they must be rationally connected to the objective. Secondly, the means, even if rationally connected to the objective in the first sense, should impair "as little as possible" the right or freedom in question. ... Thirdly, there must be a proportionality between the *effects* of the measures which are responsible for limiting the *Charter* right or freedom, and the objective which has been identified as of "sufficient importance."
>
> With respect to the third component, it is clear that the general effect of any measure impugned under s. 1 will be the infringement of a right or freedom guaranteed by the *Charter*; that is the reason why resort to s. 1 is necessary. ... Even if an objective is of sufficient importance, and the first two elements of the proportionality test are satisfied, it is still possible that, because of the deleterious effects of a measure on individuals or groups, the measure will not be justified by the purposes it intends to serve. The more severe the deleterious effects of a measure, the more important the objective must be if the measure is to be reasonable and demonstrably justified in a free and democratic society.

In the *Oakes* case itself, the Supreme Court of Canada had been faced with the question of whether or not to rule that section 8 of the (now repealed) *Narcotic Control Act*, R.S.C. 1985, c. N-1 was invalid in light of the *Charter*. Section 8 placed a peculiar burden upon the shoulders of an accused person charged with trafficking in narcotics (contrary to section 4(1) of the Act): specifically, the provision stated that once the Crown had proved that the accused was in possession of a narcotic, then the **burden of proof** automatically fell on the accused to establish that they were *not* in possession for the purpose of trafficking.

The Supreme Court briskly found that section 8 infringed an accused person's right—enshrined in section 11(d) of the *Charter*—"to be presumed innocent until proven guilty." Undoubtedly, section 8 of the *Narcotic Control Act* forced accused persons into the position of having to prove their innocence and, in so doing, constituted a clear breach of section 11(d) of the *Charter*. However, the critical issue in *Oakes* was whether section 8 of the *Narcotic Control Act* could be "saved," under the terms of section 1 of the *Charter*, as a "reasonable limit" on the presumption of innocence. Ultimately, the Supreme Court took the view that section 8 did not constitute a reasonable limit that could be "demonstrably justified in a free and democratic society" and declared it to be invalid and "of no force and effect."

In applying what is now known as the *Oakes* test, Chief Justice Dickson first inquired whether Parliament's objective in enacting section 8 of the *Narcotic Control Act* was sufficiently important to justify overriding a *Charter* right. The chief justice noted that Parliament's objective was manifestly that of "curbing drug trafficking" by rendering it easier for the Crown to obtain convictions of those who engaged in such harmful conduct. There was absolutely no doubt that Parliament's objective of reducing the extent of drug trafficking in Canada could be characterized as being "pressing and substantial" in nature, and Chief Justice Dickson was clearly convinced that there was a need to protect society "from the grave ills associated with drug trafficking."

Having determined that Parliament's objective in enacting section 8 of the Narcotic Control Act was sufficiently important to warrant overriding a Charter right, Chief Justice Dickson turned to the second part of the test that he articulated in the *Oakes* case. More specifically, were the means used by Parliament (placing the onus of proof on the shoulders of an accused person found in possession of narcotics to establish that they were not in such possession for the purpose of trafficking) proportional to Parliament's objective? As we noted, Chief Justice Dickson referred to three different components of the proportionality test. However, in the *Oakes* case itself, he stated that it was necessary to refer only to the first of these components; namely, was there a rational connection between section 8 and Parliament's objective of reducing drug trafficking? Chief Justice Dickson concluded that there was no such rational connection. Possession of a minute amount of narcotics does not automatically warrant drawing the inference that the accused intended to traffic in such drugs. Indeed, he said that it "would be irrational to infer that a person had an intent to traffic on the basis of their possession of a very small quantity of narcotics." Although section 8 might ensure that more accused persons will be convicted of drug trafficking, a conviction of a person found in possession of only a minimal amount of drugs does nothing to reduce the actual incidence of trafficking in narcotics because such an individual is clearly not involved in such activity in the first place! As the chief justice remarked, "The presumption required under s. 8 of the Narcotic Control Act is overinclusive and could lead to results in certain cases which would defy both rationality and fairness."

It should be noted that the nature of the third step in the proportionality test articulated in Oakes was subsequently clarified by the Supreme Court of Canada in the *Dagenais* case (1994), in which Chief Justice Lamer suggested that it is important for the courts to examine both the salutary and deleterious effects of an impugned legislative provision on both individuals and groups in Canadian society. He therefore stipulated that the third step in the Oakes test should be rephrased in the following manner: "[T]here must be a proportionality between the deleterious effects of the measures which are responsible for limiting the rights or freedoms in question and the objective, and there must be a proportionality between the deleterious and the salutary effects of the measures."

In *R. v. N.S.* (2012), the Supreme Court emphasized that the weighing of salutary and deleterious effects under the *Oake*s test may involve attempting to reconcile a conflict between opposing *Charter* rights. In this case, the issue concerned the right of a Muslim witness who, for religious reasons, wished to testify with her face covered by a niqab (or veil). The Court noted that there was a potential conflict between the witness's *Charter* right to religious freedom and the accused person's *Charter* right to a fair trial. Chief Justice McLachlin emphasized that resolution of this potential conflict between *Charter* rights must be undertaken on a case-by-case basis, carefully balancing the salutary and deleterious effects of prohibiting or permitting the wearing of the niqab on the rights of both the witness and the accused person:

> A secular response that requires witnesses to park their religion at the courtroom door is inconsistent with the jurisprudence and Canadian tradition, and limits freedom of religion where no limit can be justified. On the other hand, a response that says a witness can always testify with her face covered may render a trial unfair and lead to wrongful conviction. What is required is an approach that balances the vital rights protecting freedom of religion and trial fairness when they conflict. The long-standing practice in Canadian courts is to respect and accommodate the religious convictions of witnesses, unless they pose a significant or serious risk to a fair trial. The *Canadian Charter of Rights and Freedoms*, which protects both freedom of religion and trial fairness, demands no less.

The Supreme Court, therefore, resolved any potential conflict between the right to religious freedom and the right to a fair trial by articulating a test that would require the removal of the niqab only when it is necessary to do so because there are no other viable alternatives, and only when the salutary effects outweigh the deleterious effects (particularly with respect to the impact such a requirement might have on the right to freedom of religion):

> [A] witness who for sincere religious reasons wishes to wear the niqab while testifying in a criminal proceeding will be required to remove it if:
>
> (a) requiring the witness to remove the niqab is necessary to prevent a serious risk to the fairness of the trial, because reasonably available alternative measures will not prevent the risk; and
>
> (b) the salutary effects of requiring her to remove the niqab, including the effects on trial fairness, outweigh the deleterious effects of doing so, including the effects on freedom of religion.

It is possible that a court might find that a particular legislative provision—adopted by Parliament to achieve a "pressing and substantial" objective—creates relatively few deleterious effects. However, this should not mean that the provision automatically meets the requirements of the third component of the proportionality test. Indeed, it may well be the case that the legislative provision in question, although it does not have any significantly harmful effects, does not produce any significantly salutary effects either! If a court should come to this conclusion, then it should rule that the legislative provision has failed the third component of the proportionality test; after all, any infringement of *Charter* rights is a serious matter and certainly cannot be justified if it does not have any significantly positive effects. Section 1 of the *Charter* should not be used to "save" legislation from invalidation unless the positive benefits of the legislation substantially outweigh any of its potentially negative impacts upon both individual Canadians and Canadian society as a whole.

The *Oakes* test has been routinely applied by Canadian courts whenever they have been confronted with the arduous, but nevertheless delicate, task of balancing the individual rights of Canadians against the collective rights of society under section 1 of the *Charter*. Therefore, in applying the *Oakes* test, the courts are required to pay very close attention to the broader social context within which a particular case may be located. As Justice Bastarache stated, in delivering the majority opinion of the Supreme Court of Canada in *Thomson Newspapers v. Canada (Attorney General)* (1998),

> The analysis under s. 1 of the *Charter* must be undertaken with a close attention to context. This is inevitable as the test devised in *R. v. Oakes* ... requires a court to establish the objective of the impugned provision, which can only be accomplished by canvassing the nature of the social problem which it addresses. Similarly, the proportionality of the means used to fulfil the pressing and substantial objective can only be evaluated through a close attention to detail and factual setting. In essence, context is the indispensable handmaiden to the proper characterization of the objective of the impugned provision, to determining whether that objective is justified, and to weighing whether the means used are sufficiently closely related to the valid objective so as to justify an infringement of a *Charter* right.

Before leaving this discussion of the impact of the *Charter* on the fabric of the criminal law in Canada, it should be emphasized that there may well be a tendency to exaggerate the extent to which the courts may use their *Charter* powers to override the will of democratically elected legislators. Indeed, it is highly significant that the Supreme Court of Canada stated in the *Mills* case (1999) that, in the context of the application of the *Charter*, it is more useful to view

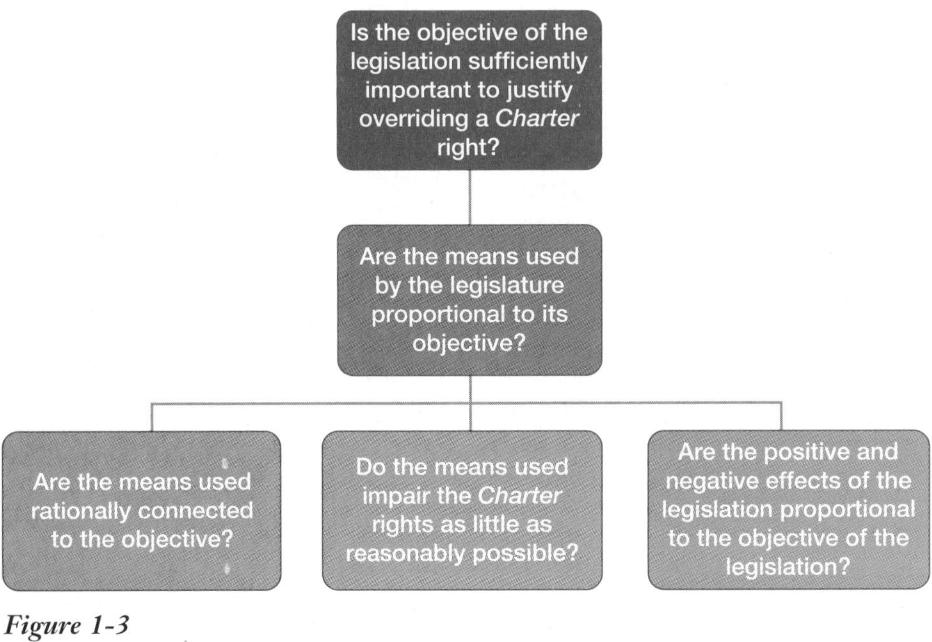

Figure 1-3
The Oakes *Test*

the relationship between Parliament and the courts as being one of *constructive "dialogue."* For example, Justices McLachlin and Iacobucci emphasized the view that the courts must always presume that Parliament intends to enact legislation that meets the requirements of the *Charter* and, therefore, must do all they can to give effect to that intention. What the Supreme Court appears to be suggesting is that the invalidation of legislation enacted by democratically elected representatives is a step that should be undertaken only very reluctantly on the part of the courts. Furthermore, even when legislation is struck down as being of no force or effect, it is always possible for Parliament or the provincial or territorial legislature to enact new statutory provisions that respond to the *Charter* concerns expressed by the courts. The *Mills* case (1999) suggests that, ultimately, these new provisions will be upheld if the legislators have "listened" to what has been said by the judges in their ongoing dialogue with Parliament and the provincial/territorial legislatures. In essence, according to the Supreme Court in the *Mills* case, the appropriate role of the courts is to assist legislators to implement the will of the people in a manner that is consistent with the Canadian values expressed in the *Charter*. In this view, legislators and courts are working in a partnership and it would be wrong to suggest that the *Charter* is being used to frustrate decisions made in a democratic manner.

In *Mills*, the Supreme Court rejected a *Charter* challenge to provisions of the *Criminal Code* that were enacted in 1997 with the objective of restricting the use that may be made by lawyers for the accused of the confidential therapeutic records of complainants in trials involving charges of sexual assault. Such records may have been made by psychiatrists, psychologists, or counsellors when a victim of sexual assault has sought assistance and may give intimate information that the victim has every reason to believe will be kept in confidence. In Mills, **counsel** for the defence had claimed that, by restricting access to such records and by limiting the circumstances in which they could be used in evidence, the new provisions of the *Criminal Code* seriously infringed the accused's right to make "full answer and defence"—a right that is enshrined in sections 7 and 11(d) of the *Charter*. However, the Supreme Court firmly rejected this argument and declined to invalidate provisions that represented the will of elected members of Parliament to protect the victims of sexual assault from unconscionable attacks by defence counsel. Justices McLachlin and Iacobucci advanced the view that "constitutionalism can facilitate democracy rather than undermine it" and that "one way in which it does this is by ensuring that fundamental human rights and individual freedoms are given due regard and protection." It is noteworthy that the two justices admitted that "Courts do not hold a monopoly on the protection and promotion of rights and freedoms; Parliament also plays a role in this regard and is often able to act as a significant ally for vulnerable groups." In their view, this principle is of particular importance in the context of sexual violence and they conclude that:

> If constitutional democracy is meant to ensure that due regard is given to the voices of those vulnerable to being overlooked by the majority, then this court has an obligation to consider respectfully Parliament's attempt to respond to such voices.

In addition to the notion that the courts should engage in a "constructive dialogue" with Parliament, it is important to bear in mind that, when judges interpret legislation such as the *Criminal Code*, they will *presume* that Parliament intended to conform to the basic values enshrined in the *Charter*. The implications of this approach were clearly articulated by Justices Iacobucci and Arbour in *Application under s. 83.28 of the Criminal Code (Re)*, decided by the Supreme Court of Canada in 2004. In their judgment, they referred to "the presumption that legislation is enacted to comply with constitutional norms, including the rights and freedoms enshrined in the *Charter*" and added:

> This presumption acknowledges the centrality of constitutional values in the legislative process, and more broadly, in the political and legal culture of Canada. Accordingly, where two readings of a provision are equally plausible, the interpretation which accords with *Charter* values should be adopted ...

It is clear that the Supreme Court of Canada is far from being overzealous in its application of the *Canadian Charter of Rights and Freedoms* to legislation enacted by the Parliament of Canada under the authority of its criminal law power. The fear expressed by some politicians and commentators that the democratic will of Canadians may be thwarted by unelected judges using the *Charter* to strike down criminal legislation is not based on a sound analysis of the manner in which the Supreme Court of Canada has actually interpreted and applied the *Charter*. Although the Court has indeed declared certain legislation to be invalid, it has generally expressed its reluctance to do so. Following the *Mills* case, it would appear that the Supreme Court of Canada will view its role as being that of assisting Parliament and the various provincial and territorial legislatures to implement the will of Canadians in legislation that is consistent with the basic principles expressed in the *Charter*.

Finally, it is important to recognize that declaring a statutory provision invalid in light of the *Charter* is considered a measure of last resort. For example, a court may decide that the provision may be found valid if one or more offending phrases are "*severed*," or removed, from it. Furthermore, a court may rule that the constitutional validity of a statutory provision may be affirmed by "*reading in*" (adding) words that would safeguard the individual's *Charter* rights or by giving it a very narrow interpretation so that it does not violate the *Charter* ("*reading down*"). As Chief Justice McLachlin stated, in delivering the judgment of the Supreme Court of Canada in *Ferguson* (2008),

> Section 52(1) [of the *Constitution Act, 1982*] grants courts the jurisdiction to declare laws of no force and effect only "to the extent of the inconsistency" with the Constitution. It follows that if the constitutional defect of a law can be remedied without striking down the law as a whole, then a court must consider alternatives to striking down. Examples of alternative remedies under s. 52 include severance, reading in and reading down.

However, the courts cannot "read in" or "read down" words in a statutory provision if to do so would clearly contravene the intention of the Parliament of Canada or of the relevant provincial or territorial legislature. Chief Justice McLachlin also addressed this issue in *Ferguson*:

> [I]t has long been recognized that in applying alternative remedies such as severance and reading in, courts are at risk of making inappropriate intrusions into the legislative sphere. An alternative to striking down that initially appears to be less intrusive on the legislative role may in fact represent an inappropriate intrusion on the legislature's role. This Court has thus emphasized that in considering alternatives to striking down, courts must carefully consider whether the alternative being considered represents a lesser intrusion on Parliament's legislative role than striking down. Courts must thus be guided by respect for the role of Parliament, as well as respect for the purposes of the *Charter*.

A recent example of the willingness of the Supreme Court of Canada to remove ("sever") words that infringe a *Charter* right while upholding the constitutionality of what remains of the statutory provision in question is *Saskatchewan (Human Rights Commission) v. Whatcott* (2013). This case involved a challenge to the constitutionality of section 14(1)(b) of the *Saskatchewan Human Rights Code*, S.S. 1979, c. S-24.1, which prohibited publications that promoted hatred of individuals on the basis of a "prohibited ground," such as sexual orientation. Section 14(1)(b) stated:

> No person shall publish or display, or cause or permit to be published or displayed, on any lands or premises or in a newspaper, through a television or radio broadcasting station or any other broadcasting device, or in any printed matter or publication or by means of any other medium that the person owns, controls, distributes or sells, any representation, including any notice, sign, symbol, emblem, article, statement or other representation …
>
> (b) that exposes or tends to expose to hatred, ridicules, belittles or otherwise affronts the dignity of any person or class of persons on the basis of a prohibited ground.

The Supreme Court ruled that section 14(1)(b) infringed both the right to freedom of expression (section 2(b) of the *Charter*) and the right to freedom of conscience and religion (section 2(a) of the *Charter*). However, the Court ruled that, since it was designed to prohibit hate speech, section 14(1)(b) was saved by section 1 of the *Charter*. Indeed, it was a reasonable limit on *Charter* rights that was demonstrably justified in a free and democratic society. However, in order to uphold the constitutionality of section 14(1)(b), the Court held that the words "ridicules, belittles or otherwise affronts the dignity of" had to be severed, or removed, from the provision. The Court reasoned that there has to be a very strong justification for the Saskatchewan legislature to impinge on the fundamental rights to freedom of speech and freedom of conscience and religion. Such justification lies in the fact that hate speech legislation targets only those who promote the very powerful feelings associated with the word "hatred." According to the Supreme Court, only such terms as "vilification" and "detestation" reflect "the ardent and extreme nature of feelings constituting 'hatred.'" Statements that do not promote such strong feelings should not be prohibited by legislation. The Supreme Court held that the words "ridicules, belittles or otherwise affronts the dignity of" had to be severed from section 14(1)(b) because they "are not synonymous with 'hatred' or 'contempt.'" Indeed, human "expression that 'ridicules, belittles or otherwise affronts the dignity

PRESUMPTION OF CONSTITUTIONALITY:	SEVERANCE:	READING DOWN:	READING IN:	APPLYING SECTION 1:
A presumption that the legislature intended to enact legislation that conforms with *Charter* requirements	Cutting out offending words and leaving the remainder of the legislation in compliance with the *Charter*	Interpreting legislation in a strict, narrow manner so that it does not violate the *Charter*	Adding words to the legislation that renders it in compliance with the *Charter*	An infringement of a *Charter* right may be justified as a reasonable limit in a free and democratic society

Figure 1-4

Methods of Avoiding Declaring a Statutory Provision Invalid under the Canadian Charter of Rights and Freedoms

of' [protected groups] does not rise to the level of ardent and extreme feelings" that justify an infringement of fundamental *Charter* rights:

> Rather, they refer to expression which is derogatory and insensitive, such as representations criticizing or making fun of protected groups on the basis of their commonly shared characteristics and practices, or on stereotypes.

By severing the unconstitutional words from section 14(1)(b) of the *Saskatchewan Human Rights Code*, the Supreme Court of Canada was able to declare the remainder of the provision to be valid.

Study Questions

1. In what ways does criminal law differ from private law?
2. What are the main branches of public law?
3. Do you think that the Parliament of Canada may use its criminal law power under the *Constitution Act, 1867* to prohibit any conduct that it considers harmful to Canadians?
4. May a provincial legislature prohibit any conduct it considers harmful and impose a fine if the prohibition is violated?
5. Why are judicial decisions considered one of the sources of criminal law in Canada?
6. Do you think that the so-called *Oakes* test is an appropriate mechanism for determining whether a particular legislative provision should be considered valid even though it infringes one or more of the rights guaranteed by the *Canadian Charter of Rights and Freedoms?*
7. Did the Parliament of Canada respond appropriately to the decision of the Supreme Court of Canada's decision in the *Bedford* case, when legislators decided to adopt the so-called "Nordic Model" and criminalize those who *purchase* sexual services, but not those sex workers who *sell* such services? Could this approach drive the purchasers of sexual services underground, thereby exposing sex workers to the very same dangers identified by Chief Justice McLachlin in her judgment on behalf of the Court?
8. How do the courts distinguish between true crimes and regulatory offences?
9. Why are Canadian courts reluctant to invalidate legislation enacted by Parliament and provincial/territorial legislatures? What mechanisms do they use to avoid invalidating legislation unnecessarily?
10. What is meant by the suggestion that interpretation of the *Canadian Charter of Rights and Freedoms* should be viewed as a "constructive dialogue" between the courts and the Parliament of Canada and provincial/territorial legislatures?

CHAPTER

2

THE *ACTUS REUS* ELEMENTS OF A CRIMINAL OFFENCE

Learning Objectives

After reading this chapter, you will be able to understand:

- how to study the basic elements of a crime in terms of *actus reus* and *mens rea*;
- how to analyze the *actus reus* elements of a crime in terms of conduct, circumstances, and consequences;
- the circumstances in which a failure to act (an omission) may constitute a critical component of the *actus reus* of an offence;
- the requirement that the *actus reus* and *mens rea* elements of an offence must coincide in order to convict an accused person; and
- the fundamental requirement that the conduct (act or omission) component of the *actus reus* must be *voluntary*—the exercise of a conscious choice on the part of the accused person.

INTRODUCTION

In the decision of the Supreme Court of Canada in the case of *Mabior* (2012), Chief Justice McLachlin restated a very basic principle that underlies the fabric of Canadian criminal law:

> A criminal conviction and imprisonment, with the attendant stigma that attaches, is the most serious sanction the law can impose on a person, and is generally reserved for conduct that is highly culpable—conduct that is viewed as harmful to society, reprehensible and unacceptable. It requires both a culpable act—***actus reus***—and a guilty mind—***mens rea***—the parameters of which should be clearly delineated by the law.

Following this principle, we can say that, in general, an accused person may not be convicted of a criminal offence unless the prosecution can prove *beyond a reasonable doubt*

- that a particular event or state of affairs was "caused" by the accused's conduct (*actus reus*); and
- that this conduct was accompanied by a certain state of mind (*mens rea*).

With their ingrained love of mystification, lawyers have traditionally referred to a famous Latin maxim to summarize this critical legal principle: "*Actus non facit reum nisi mens sit rea*." Translated literally, this means that an act does not render a person guilty of a criminal offence unless their mind is also guilty. In legal parlance, the concept of *mens rea* refers to the mental elements of an offence, while the term *actus reus* refers to all the other elements of the offence that must be proved by the Crown beyond a reasonable doubt.

As Justice Cory pointed out in delivering the judgment of the majority of the justices of the Supreme Court of Canada in the case of *Daviault* (1994):

> Originally a crime was considered to be the commission of a physical act which was specifically prohibited by law. It was the act itself which was the sole element of the crime. If it was established that the act was committed by the accused then a finding of guilt would ensue. However, as early as the 12th century, in large part through the influence of canon law, it was established that there must also be a mental element combined with the prohibited act to constitute a crime. That is to say that the accused must have *meant* or intended to commit the prohibited act. The physical act and the mental element which together constitute a crime came to be known as the *actus reus* denoting the act, and the *mens rea* for the mental element. Like so many maxims they are imprecise and in many instances misleading.

In practice, the courts do not draw a sharp line between the physical and mental elements of an offence. Indeed, Canadian courts increasingly accept the view that the actus reus of a criminal offence includes the element of voluntariness (discussed later in this chapter). As Justice McLachlin said in delivering the judgment of the majority of the justices of the Supreme Court of Canada in the case of *Théroux* (1993), "The term mens rea, properly understood, does not encompass all of the mental elements of crime. The actus reus has its own mental element; the act must be the voluntary act of the accused for the actus reus to exist."

Leaving aside the issue of voluntariness for the moment, why is it important to focus on the *actus reus* elements of criminal offences? In response to this question, Alan Gold, for example, has suggested that it is necessary to undertake this task because the *actus reus* elements "identify a human oriented act that merits designation as a crime by society and merits society's undertaking to locate and deal with those human actors responsible."[1] In other words, it is the existence of the *actus reus* elements of an offence that justifies the intervention of the criminal justice system. It is not enough that an individual may be considered dangerous and that they *might* commit a crime in the future. On the contrary, before an accused person may be held criminally responsible, the Crown must establish that they have engaged in *conduct that is defined as criminal in the sense that all the necessary* actus reus *elements can be proved beyond a reasonable doubt*.

One important legal principle that inevitably flows from the maxim *Actus non facit reum nisi mens sit rea* is that, even in situations where the accused person has the necessary *mens rea* for a particular offence, they nevertheless may not be convicted of that offence unless the *mens rea* coincides with the commission of the *actus reus* of the offence. For example, let us suppose that Casanova becomes disillusioned with his marriage to Henriette and commences an affair with Bettina. Casanova then decides to leave his wife and persuades Bettina (who is unaware of Henriette's existence) to marry him. Casanova and Bettina subsequently participate in a marriage ceremony. Casanova derives some perverse pleasure from his belief that the marriage to Bettina is bigamous. However, Casanova subsequently receives a telephone

1. Gold, A.D. 1994. Lessons about *Mens Rea*: Three Recent Cases. *Criminal Law Quarterly*, *36*: 157–167, at 157.

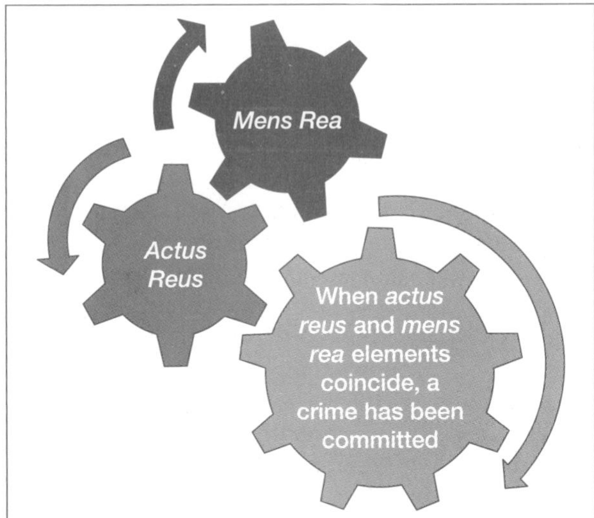

Figure 2-1

Actus Reus *and* Mens Rea

call and is informed that Henriette was struck by a car and expired 20 minutes before the marriage ceremony with Bettina. It is clear that Casanova had the necessary *mens rea* for the offence of bigamy (section 290 of the *Criminal Code*). However, he cannot be convicted of the offence of **bigamy** because he did not commit the *actus reus* of the offence. Section 290(1)(a)(i) indicates that the offence of bigamy is committed where, *inter alia*, an accused person "*being married*, goes through a form of marriage with another person." Although Casanova fully *intended* to enter into a bigamous union with Bettina, he was (as a consequence of the fatal mishap that befell Henriette) no longer a married person at the time of the wedding ceremony.

This tale represents a clear illustration of an underlying principle of criminal law—namely, that the state should punish citizens for *overt actions* rather than for their "wicked" **intentions**. Canadian criminal law generally requires that, before an individual may be convicted of an offence, the Crown must prove both an element of conduct and an accompanying mental element. As Herbert Packer said in *The Limits of Criminal Sanction*, "The limitation of criminal punishment to conduct constitutes the first and most important line of defense against erosion of the idea of culpability, for it keeps the criminal law from becoming purely the servant of the utilitarian ideal of prevention."[2]

2. Packer, H.L. 1968. *The Limits of the Criminal Sanction*. Stanford, CA: Stanford University Press, at 76.

THE *ACTUS REUS* AS A COMBINATION OF CONDUCT, CIRCUMSTANCES, AND CONSEQUENCES

In general, it is possible to identify three separate elements of the *actus reus* of a criminal offence:

1. **conduct** (a *voluntary* act or omission constituting the central feature of the crime);
2. the surrounding and "material" **circumstances**; and
3. the **consequences** of the voluntary conduct.

As an illustration of the application of this analytical framework, we may turn to the offence of assault causing bodily harm. To define the elements of the *actus reus* of this offence, it is necessary to refer to three different sections of the *Criminal Code*. First, section 265 defines the nature of an **assault**: in particular, section 265(1)(a) states:

> A person commits an assault when
>
> (a) without the consent of another person, he applies force intentionally to that other person, directly or indirectly.

Second, we must turn to section 267 of the *Code* to find the provision that establishes the offence of assault causing bodily harm. This section proclaims:

> Every one who, in committing an assault,
>
> (a) carries, uses or threatens to use a weapon or an imitation thereof, or
>
> (b) *causes bodily harm to the complainant*, is guilty of an indictable offence. [emphasis added]

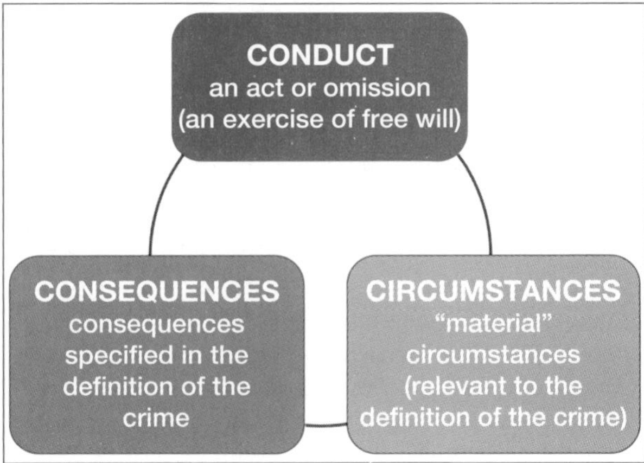

Figure 2-2

The Three Components of the Actus Reus

The third, and final, piece of the definitional jigsaw puzzle is to be found in section 2 of the *Code*, which stipulates that "[B]odily harm" means any hurt or injury to a person that interferes with the health or comfort of the person and that is more than merely transient or trifling in nature."

How can we analyze the offence of assault causing bodily harm in terms of the three elements of conduct, circumstances, and consequences? The element of *conduct* is represented by the application of force to the person of the victim. The most critical of the material *circumstances* is that such force was applied without the consent of the victim. Finally, the *consequence*, which must be proved, is that the victim sustained actual bodily harm. As to this final requirement, it may be noted that in the case of *Robinson* (2001), the Ontario Court of Appeal agreed with the trial judge's ruling that the accused had caused bodily harm when he rubbed his beard against the victim's chin with such an excessive degree of vigour that the skin was rubbed off, leaving an oozing sore. Such an injury clearly interfered with the health or comfort of the victim and could not be considered as being merely transient or trifling in nature. In *Moquin* (2010), the victim was assaulted five times by the accused and suffered bruising that lasted from several days to over two weeks, as well as a sore throat and sore hand. The sore hand made it necessary for her to seek assistance to open doors for a few days. The trial judge acquitted Moquin of assault causing bodily harm and convicted him instead of common assault. The judge believed that the definition of bodily harm required that there be an actual impairment of the victim's physical functioning and concluded that, since bruising to the arm did not prevent her from using her arm and the soreness in her throat did not prevent her from swallowing, the victim's injuries did not meet the criteria specified in section 2 of the *Criminal Code* ("interferes with the health or comfort of the person and that is more than merely transient or trifling in nature"). The trial judge, therefore, entered a conviction only for common assault. The Crown appealed to the Manitoba Court of Appeal, which overturned the verdict at trial and entered a conviction for assault causing bodily harm. On behalf of the Court of Appeal, Justice Beard articulated the reasons for finding that there had, indeed, been bodily harm:

> Although a functional impairment may accompany bodily harm, it is not a necessary component of bodily harm as it is defined in s. 2 of the *Code*, and it is not a requirement in any of the cases that have interpreted and applied that section. Interference with comfort—that is, discomfort—is sufficient to constitute bodily harm, if it is more than trifling and transient. Pain causing discomfort, if it is more than trifling and transient, is sufficient, even if it does not impair a person's ability to function.

The courts have also held that the Crown is not required to introduce specific evidence to prove that the harm inflicted on the victim caused discomfort that was more than merely transient or trifling in nature. In many cases, this element of the *actus reus* will be obvious. For example, in *Bulldog* (2015), three inmates attacked the victim in a prison exercise yard. Correctional officers noted that the victim was bleeding from the head and neck. He was taken to hospital, where the records indicated that he had cuts and swelling to his face. The accused were convicted of assault causing bodily harm and appealed to the Alberta Court of Appeal, which dismissed their appeals. One of the grounds of appeal was that there had been no evidence that specifically addressed how long the injuries lasted and the degree of discomfort experienced by the victim. The Court of Appeal rejected this contention by stating that, given the nature of the wounds seen by the correctional officers and the notes made by the hospital, the trial judge was entitled to draw the conclusion that the injuries were neither transient nor trifling in nature: "[The victim's] sustained visible wounds clearly constitute "bodily harm," which required treatment at the hospital and post-treatment monitoring and would also obviously have caused discomfort. It would have defied good sense for the trial judge to have concluded otherwise."

Does the term "bodily harm" include *psychological* harm? In the case of *McCraw* (1991)—a case involving threats of sexual assault—the Supreme Court of Canada answered this question in the affirmative: "there can be no doubt that psychological harm may often be more pervasive and permanent in its effect than any physical harm." In the *Moquin* case (2010), discussed above, the Manitoba Court of Appeal ruled that the Crown does not have to prove that the assaults by the accused were the sole cause of any psychological distress suffered by the victim: indeed, it is sufficient to prove that the assaults were a "*significant, contributing cause*" to such distress. The fact that there were other psychologically distressing elements in the victim's life did not automatically absolve Moquin of his criminal responsibility.

This method of analyzing the basic elements of the *actus reus* may also be profitably applied to the offence of sexual assault. Section 271 of the *Criminal Code* indicates that "[e]very one who commits a sexual assault is guilty of" either an indictable or summary conviction offence. The section does not, however, define what a sexual assault is. To formulate such a definition, it is necessary to look first at section 265, which defines assault in general:

> (1) A person commits an assault when
>
> (a) without the consent of another person, he applies force intentionally to that other person, directly or indirectly;
>
> (b) he attempts or threatens, by an act or gesture, to apply force to another person, if he has, or causes that other person to believe upon reasonable grounds that he has, present ability to effect his purpose; or
>
> (c) while openly wearing or carrying a weapon or an imitation thereof, he accosts or impedes another person or begs.
>
> (2) This section applies to all forms of assault, including sexual assault.

Since Parliament has not defined the word "sexual" in the context of the offence of "sexual assault," this task has been left to the courts.

How can the basic elements of sexual assault be identified in terms of the requirements of conduct, circumstances, and consequences? In essence, the element of *conduct* generally consists of the intentional application of force (or the threat of the application of force) to the person of the victim. The *consequences* that must be established are either that the accused actually applied force to the victim or that the accused caused the victim to believe on reasonable grounds that the accused had "the present ability" to apply such force [subsection 265(1)(b)]. The relevant *circumstances* that must be proved are that the application of force or the threat of such force took place without the consent of the victim and that the assault is of a "sexual nature."

The requirement that the assault be of a "sexual nature" was considered by the Supreme Court of Canada in *Chase* (1987). In this case, Chase took hold of a 15-year-old girl around her shoulders and arms and grabbed her breasts. When the girl struggled, Chase said, "Come on, dear, don't hit me. I know you want it." According to the victim, he also tried to grab her "private" but she prevented him from doing so. Chase was convicted of sexual assault, but he appealed to the New Brunswick Court of Appeal, which substituted a verdict of guilty of common assault. The Court of Appeal held that, for an accused person to be convicted of *sexual* assault, there must be contact with the genitals. The Crown appealed against this decision on the basis that the Court of Appeal's definition of sexual assault was too narrow. The Supreme Court of Canada agreed with the Crown and restored Chase's conviction for sexual assault. In delivering the judgment of the Supreme Court, Justice McIntyre asserted that:

> Sexual assault is an assault within any one of the definitions of that concept in s. [265(1)] of the *Criminal Code* which is committed in circumstances of a sexual nature, such that the sexual integrity of the victim is violated. The test to be applied in determining whether the impugned conduct has the requisite sexual nature is an objective one: "Viewed in the light of all the circumstances, is the sexual or carnal context of the assault visible to a reasonable observer." ... The part of the body touched, the nature of the contact, the situation in which it occurred, the words and gestures accompanying the act, and all other circumstances surrounding the conduct, including threats which may or may not be accompanied by force, will be relevant.

In this particular case, the Supreme Court found no difficulty in deciding that a reasonable observer, in light of all the circumstances, would have concluded that Chase's grabbing of the victim's breasts was of a sexual nature.

In *Semchuk* (2012), somewhat different circumstances nevertheless led to the same outcome. The accused was an elementary school teacher who also acted as a track and field coach. He was charged with the sexual assault of a Grade 3 student who participated in a "run for fun" program. After completing a lunchtime run, the complainant was "doubled over and struggling for breath." According to the evidence, Mr. Semchuk stood behind her and rubbed her ribcage, arms, shoulders, and chest in continuous progression, telling her to breathe deeply and attempting to move her to a standing position. She testified that his hands came around to her front and he rubbed her breasts with both hands.

Semchuk denied the allegation of sexual assault. He claimed that he had no memory of the incident in question and that he had, on occasion, provided purely medical assistance to students who had difficulty breathing. The trial judge found that by rubbing the complainant's breasts, Semchuk had violated her sexual integrity and convicted him of sexual assault. The provision of medical assistance would not encompass rubbing a student's breasts.

The B.C. Court of Appeal affirmed the conviction. In delivering the judgment of the Court of Appeal, Justice Bennett clarified the *actus reus* requirements of the offence of sexual assault:

> The *actus reus* of the offence has three elements: i) touching, ii) the sexual nature of the contact, and iii) the absence of consent. ... Only the sexual nature of the contact is at issue on this appeal. The sexual nature of the offence is an objective determination. An accused does not have to intend that any touching be of a sexual nature. The *mens rea* requirement is established by proof that the accused intended to touch the complainant and knowledge of a lack of consent on the part of the complainant. ... Consent is not in issue in this case given the age of S.F. ...
>
> The trial judge accepted that Mr. Semchuk rubbed the breasts of S.F. A reasonable observer would likely conclude that a teacher simply assisting a distressed child is not sexual in nature. That is not the finding of fact in this case. The finding of fact is that he rubbed her breasts. This takes the circumstances beyond simply assisting a child and indicates that he touched her in a manner which interfered with her sexual integrity. This conclusion is amply supported by the evidence.

The *Semchuk* case clearly demonstrates that it is possible for a court to hold that an assault was sexual in nature even if the accused person establishes that their intent was *not* to obtain sexual gratification. The subjective intent of the accused person is only one among a number of factors that must be considered in making the determination that the assault was sexual in nature. The application of the objective test was applied in a particularly strict manner in the case of *V. (K.B.)* (1993), in which the accused had, on several occasions, violently grabbed his three-year-old son's genitals in order to deter him from grasping the genital region of adults. The accused was charged with *sexual* assault even though he claimed that his actions were motivated solely by considerations of discipline. Despite this argument, the accused was convicted at trial and his conviction was ultimately upheld by the Supreme Court of Canada. The majority of the justices ruled that a reasonable observer would have concluded that the "sexual integrity" of the victim had been violated even if the father had not engaged in this conduct for any sexual purpose. As Justice Iacobucci said:

> Among other things, [the father], on three occasions, violently clutched the little boy's scrotum and there was evidence of bruising and severe pain. In my view, it was clearly open to the trial judge to conclude from all the circumstances that the assault was one of a sexual nature and that the assault was such that the sexual integrity of the ... son was violated.

Applying an objective test to determine whether an assault was sexual in nature does allow courts to take a common sense approach and to avoid the possibility that an accused person may escape conviction by raising a reasonable doubt with respect to their motivation. For example, in the case of *Larue* (2003), the **complainant** was naked from the waist down and the accused was on top of her with a knife. In the circumstances, the Supreme Court of Canada held that any reasonable observer would, on this evidence alone, conclude that the assault was sexual in nature and it was not necessary to speculate as to whether the accused person did, in fact, have a sexual motive.

In the *Ewanchuk* case (1999), the Supreme Court of Canada made an important point about the circumstances that the Crown has to prove as a critical component of the *actus reus* of sexual assault. Specifically, the Court noted that, whereas the issue of whether an assault is "sexual" in nature is decided on an objective basis, the decision as to whether there was a lack of consent to sexual touching must be decided on a purely subjective basis. Of course, in determining whether there was a lack of consent, the court is concerned with the *subjective intent of the complainant* rather than that of the accused. As Justice Major noted:

> The sexual nature of the assault is determined objectively; the Crown need not prove that the accused had any *mens rea* with respect to the sexual nature of his or her behaviour. ...
>
> The absence of consent, however, is subjective and determined by reference to the complainant's subjective internal state of mind towards the touching, at the time it occurred.

EXCEPTIONS TO THE GENERAL RULE REQUIRING CONDUCT, CIRCUMSTANCES, AND CONSEQUENCES

OFFENCES WHERE CONSEQUENCES ARE NOT A REQUIRED ELEMENT OF THE *ACTUS REUS*

Although the three elements of conduct, circumstances, and consequences are usually present in the *actus reus* of a criminal offence, there are nevertheless certain exceptions to the general rule. For example, there is a significant number of offences in relation to which the Crown is not required to prove that the accused's conduct caused any particular consequences. Illustrative of such offences is the crime of perjury. Section 131(1) of the *Code* states that "[E]very one commits perjury who, with intent to mislead, makes before a person who is authorized by law to permit it to be made before him a false statement under oath or solemn affirmation, by affidavit, solemn declaration or deposition or orally, knowing that the statement is false."

It is clear that the offence is complete just as soon as the accused has intentionally uttered the false statement; it is not necessary for the Crown to prove that anyone either believed or was influenced by the false statement. As Justice Lyon stated, in delivering the judgment of the Manitoba Court of Appeal in *Evans* (1995), "[I]t is not necessary that the false statement actually misled the court, but only that the accused intended to mislead the court." In other words, the *actus reus* of perjury lacks the element of consequences since the accused may be convicted of the offence regardless of whether their false statement influenced anyone.

However, as one might expect, the element of consequences does constitute an essential feature of the *actus reus* of most criminal offences.

For example, in the case of *Bear* (2013), the accused was HIV-positive and had a cut lip. He deliberately spat in the face of a police officer, threatening to expose him to HIV. Bear was charged with aggravated assault under section 268 of the *Criminal Code*. However, in order to prove this charge, the Crown had to prove that Bear's conduct "endangered the life" of the police officer. The trial judge found that there was "no realistic possibility" that HIV could be transmitted by means of spitting and found Bear not guilty of aggravated assault. Clearly, the Crown had failed to prove the *consequence* of endangerment of life. However, the Manitoba Court of Appeal nevertheless convicted Bear of *attempted* aggravated assault because he had the *intent* to transmit the virus, even if it was not in fact possible for him to do so by the simple act of spitting in the officer's face.

OFFENCES WHERE CONDUCT IS NOT A REQUIRED ELEMENT OF THE *ACTUS REUS*

Although *conduct* constitutes a vital element of the *actus reus* of the great majority of criminal offences, there is an exceptional group of offences that do not require the proof of any conduct on the part of the **defendant**. To obtain a conviction in relation to such an offence, the Crown is merely required to prove that *the accused was discovered in a particular "condition" or "state."* Examples of such offences are being in possession of housebreaking instruments; being an occupant of a motor vehicle knowing that it was taken without the consent of the owner; and being in "care or control" of a motor vehicle while impaired or "above 80."

Being in Possession of Housebreaking Instruments

Section 351(1) of the *Code* provides:

> Every person who, without lawful excuse, has in their possession any instrument suitable for the purpose of breaking into any place, motor vehicle, vault or safe knowing that the instrument has been used or is intended to be used for that purpose,
>
> (a) is guilty of an indictable offence and liable to imprisonment for a term not exceeding ten years; or
>
> (b) is guilty of an offence punishable on summary conviction.

A classic example of an individual who would be "caught" by this section is someone who is discovered lurking around a house at 2:00 a.m. with a large crowbar in their hand. However, a legitimate tradesperson with a set of professional tools would not be caught under this provision if they were arriving at the house in order to carry out repairs at the request of the owner. Clearly, the tradesperson would have a "lawful excuse" for being in possession of the tools concerned, whereas the "lurking individual" would manifestly not have any such justification.

An instructive application of section 351 occurred in *K. (S.)* (1995).[3] In this case, the accused was charged with possession of instruments suitable for breaking into a motor vehicle. He had been discovered with a knapsack, out of the top of which was sticking an "ignition punch." The arresting police officer searched the knapsack and found "vice grips, gloves, seven assorted screws of different sizes, and a

3. *K. (S.)* was decided under a previous version of s. 351, which was amended in 2018 by s. 37 of *An Act to amend the Criminal Code and the Department of Justice Act and to make consequential amendments to another Act*, SC 2018, c 29. The amended s. 351 now requires that the accused knew that "the instrument has been used or is intended to be used" for housebreaking, etc.

slot-head screwdriver." The accused was convicted at his trial and his appeal to the British Columbia Court of Appeal was dismissed. In delivering the judgment of the Court of Appeal, Justice Prowse noted that although the instruments found in the possession of the accused "can be used for legitimate automotive purposes, they are also well known to police for their use in the breaking into, and theft of, automobiles" and that this "is particularly true of the ignition punch." There was no doubt, therefore, that the tools discovered in the knapsack were suitable for breaking into motor vehicles, and it was perfectly clear that the accused had no legitimate reason for possessing them. However, the accused asserted that the Crown must prove that he had "targeted" a particular motor vehicle before it could be established that it was reasonable to draw the inference that the tools were intended to be used for the purpose of break-ins. In dismissing this argument, Justice Prowse stated:

> While a nexus in time and place between an accused's possession of the instruments and a particular automobile would be a significant factor in determining whether it was appropriate to draw an inference that the accused intended to use the instruments for the prohibited purpose, the absence of such a nexus would not be fatal to a conviction if the other surrounding circumstances were sufficiently compelling to permit the inference to be drawn.

In other words, accused persons can be convicted of possession under section 351 even if they have not given any thought to the question of which particular house, car, and so forth will be the target of their break-in activities. All that the Crown must establish is that the instruments in the accused's possession are suitable for the purpose of breaking into houses or cars in general and that the accused knew that the instruments had been used or were intended to be used for that purpose. Evidently, the offence of unlawful possession of housebreaking instruments does not involve any act on the part of the accused; instead, they must merely "be found" in possession of the illicit instruments. Of course, the rationale supporting this offence is one of crime prevention. It is better to intervene and arrest aspiring burglars before they actually use the housebreaking instruments to enter someone's house or business premises and commit theft or other crimes therein.

In *Asouth* (2017), Justice Howard, of the Ontario Superior Court of Justice, convicted the accused of the offence under section 351(1), following some break-ins to some motor vehicles. What is interesting about this case is the "instruments" that were the subject of the conviction: Asouth was convicted of "possessing certain instruments, namely, gloves, suitable for the purpose of breaking into a motor vehicle, contrary to s. 351(1) of the *Code*." The trial judge's reasoning was as follows:

> In my view, there was no other reasonable explanation for Mr. Asouth to be wearing the gloves except to ensure that he did not leave fingerprints. Even on the evidence of Mr. Asouth, Ali and Hassan handed him the gloves at the same time that they gave him the backpack to store the proceeds of his crime; on Mr. Asouth's own evidence, he was being given the "tools of the trade" that he would assist him in break into vehicles.

Being the Occupant of a Motor Vehicle Knowing That It Was Taken without the Owner's Consent

Section 335(1) of the *Criminal Code* makes it a summary conviction offence to be "the occupant of a motor vehicle knowing that it was taken without the consent of the owner." It is not necessary that the Crown establish that a person accused of this offence was involved in the *taking* of the vehicle without the owner's consent: indeed, all that has to be proved is that they were *found in the vehicle* with the necessary guilty knowledge. Significantly, section 335(1.1) does provide the accused with a defence—namely, the accused will be acquitted if it can be shown that "on becoming aware that [the vehicle] was taken without the consent of the owner, [they] attempted to leave the motor vehicle, to the extent that it was feasible to do so, or actually left the motor vehicle."

In the case of *H. (P.)* (2000), it is noteworthy that the Ontario Court of Appeal soundly rejected the view that section 335(1) imposed liability upon individuals for "morally blameless conduct" and, therefore, refused to find that it violated sections 7 and 11(d) of the *Charter*. Indeed, the court clearly stated that, "[B]y its terms, s. 335 plainly requires the Crown to establish beyond a reasonable doubt that the occupant of the motor vehicle knows that the vehicle was taken without the consent of the owner" and this does not constitute a "morally blameless state of mind." In *T.D. (YO)* (2002), the accused young person entered a vehicle as a passenger, not knowing at the time that it had been stolen. Within seconds, the accused heard police sirens and the car sped away, hitting a police car as it exited the scene.

The accused and the driver jumped out of the car while it was still moving. The accused was charged under section 335(1) and convicted at trial. The B.C. Court of Appeal overturned the conviction and entered an **acquittal** because the accused only had between two and six seconds to become aware of the fact that the vehicle was stolen and to exit it before it was driven away at high speed.

Being in Care or Control of a Motor Vehicle While Impaired or "Above 80"

Perhaps the best-known example of an offence that does not require proof of any conduct on the part of the accused is having the **care or control** of a motor vehicle either while one's ability to drive a motor vehicle has been impaired by "alcohol or a drug" or while one's blood alcohol level is above that of 80 milligrams of alcohol in 100 millilitres of blood (section 253(1) of the *Criminal Code*).[4]

Once again, this offence does not require that the Crown prove that the accused was engaged in any act, such as driving; instead, it must merely be established that the *accused was found to be in the condition of having care or control of a vehicle while their ability to drive was impaired or while their blood alcohol level* was above the prescribed level (often referred to as being "above 80"). Again, the objective of Parliament is *preventive*: this offence allows police officers to intervene in a potentially dangerous situation and to eliminate the possibility that an intoxicated individual will set their vehicle in motion and cause harm to themselves and/or others.

The first element of the *actus reus* that the Crown must prove under section 253 is that the accused was "impaired" or "above 80." The latter condition must be proved by submitting the results of tests conducted on samples of the accused's breath or blood. In terms of "impairment," the Crown must prove that the accused person's ability to drive was impaired by alcohol and/or another drug, such as cannabis. In *Stellato* (1993), Justice Labrosse, speaking on behalf of the Alberta Court of Appeal, held that "impairment is an issue of fact which the trial judge must decide on the evidence," and that:

> ... before convicting an accused of impaired driving, the trial judge must be satisfied that the accused's ability to operate a motor vehicle was impaired by alcohol or a drug. If the evidence of impairment is so frail as to leave the trial judge with a reasonable doubt as to impairment, the accused must be acquitted. If the evidence establishes *any degree of impairment ranging from slight to great*, the offence has been made out. [emphasis added]

The Supreme Court of Canada later indicated its total agreement with Justice Labrosse's ruling on this issue [see *Stellato* (1994)].

However, it is important to emphasize that the critical issue under section 253 is not whether the accused's *general abilities* are impaired by alcohol or other drugs but rather whether their *ability to drive* is impaired. As Justice Conrad said, in delivering the majority judgment of the Alberta Court of Appeal in *Andrews* (1996),

> The courts must not fail to recognize the fine but crucial distinction between "slight impairment" generally, and "slight impairment of one's ability to operate a motor vehicle." Every time a person has a drink, his or her ability to drive is not necessarily impaired. It may well be that one drink would impair one's ability to do brain surgery, or one's ability to thread a needle. *The question is not whether the individual's functional ability is impaired to any degree. The question is whether the person's ability to drive is impaired to any degree by alcohol or a drug.* [emphasis added]

Similarly, in *Tran* (2001), the Ontario Court of Appeal ruled that it is not enough for the trial judge to find that alcohol or another drug merely had "some effect" on the accused person's driving: rather, there must be a finding that the accused person's "ability to drive his motor vehicle at the time of the accident was impaired."

It should be noted that the possession of recreational cannabis was legalized by the *Cannabis Act*, S.C. 2018, c. 16. The possibility that drivers may operate or be *in care or control* of a vehicle, while under the influence of cannabis or other drugs and/or alcohol, led the Parliament of Canada to make extensive amendments to the *Criminal Code*,[5] permitting the Attorney General of Canada to issue regulations which set prescribed limits for the amount of a drug

4. In 2008, the *Criminal Code* was amended and s. 253(2) was added. It reads: "For greater certainty, the reference to impairment by alcohol or drug ... includes impairment by a combination of alcohol and a drug." With the legalization of recreational cannabis in Canada, since 2018, extensive amendments to the *Criminal Code* and regulation issued under the authority of the *Code* have addressed the need to develop effective testing for such drugs as cannabis and the issue of regulations determining, for example, the concurrent levels of alcohol and cannabis that indicate impairment.

5. *An Act to amend the Criminal Code (offences relating to conveyances) and to make consequential amendments to other Acts*, S.C. 2018, c. 21.

and/or alcohol that is found in an individual's blood[6] and which approve the tests and devices that may be used by peace officers to assess impairment.[7] The changes to the *Criminal Code* provide that, in certain circumstances, an accused person may be convicted up to two hours *after they have ceased to be "in care or control"* unless "after ceasing" to be "in care or control," "they had no reasonable expectation that they would be required to provide a sample of a bodily substance."[8]

The next element of the *actus reus* that must be established under section 253 of the *Code*, assuming that the accused was not driving the vehicle concerned, is that they were "in care or control" of the vehicle. It is important to recognize that the courts have interpreted the concept of being in care or control of a motor vehicle in an expansive manner.

The leading case that defines "care or control" is the decision of the Supreme Court of Canada in *Boudreault* (2012). In this case, Boudreault had been drinking at a bar and recognized that he was too intoxicated to drive home in his truck. He asked a friend to call a taxi to take him home. In fact, she called for a taxi to take Boudreault home and for a second operator to drive Boudreault's truck to his residence. After 20 to 25 minutes, no taxi had appeared, so the friend made a second call. At this point, she told Boudreault to wait outside. She told him that the taxi was on its way and that he should warm up his truck and stay inside it. The weather was bitterly cold and there was a strong wind. Boudreault entered the truck, started the engine, and turned on the heater. The truck was located "in a private driveway, on level terrain, its automatic transmission set to 'park.'" The taxi arrived 20 minutes later and, by this time, Boudreault was fast asleep in the driver's seat. Instead of taking Boudreault home, the taxi driver summoned the police. Boudreault was undoubtedly impaired (his blood alcohol readings were over three times the legal limit), and he was charged with having care or control of a motor vehicle while his ability was impaired by alcohol and with more than 80 milligrams of alcohol in 100 millilitres of his blood. The trial judge acquitted Boudreault, but the Quebec Court of Appeal set aside the acquittals and entered convictions. Boudreault appealed to the Supreme Court of Canada, which restored the acquittals.

On behalf of the majority of the Supreme Court, Justice Fish acknowledged that there was no doubt that Boudreault had been impaired. However, the real question in the case was whether he was in "care or control" of his truck. Justice Fish articulated the legal test that must be applied in order to answer this question:

> "[C]are or control," within the meaning of s. 253(1) of the *Criminal Code*, signifies (1) an intentional course of conduct associated with a motor vehicle; (2) by a person whose ability to drive is impaired, or whose blood alcohol level exceeds the legal limit; (3) in circumstances that create a *realistic risk*, as opposed to a *remote possibility*, of danger to persons or property.

In Boudreault's case, the critical element was whether there was a "realistic risk" of danger. The trial judge, who had heard the evidence at first hand, found that Boudreault would not have put his vehicle in motion and, hence, there was no realistic risk of danger to persons or property. Since this was a finding of fact (and not a question of law), the Supreme Court ruled that the Crown had no right to appeal the acquittals.

Justice Fish noted that the circumstances in Boudreault's case were somewhat unusual, since they would normally prompt a court to rule that there was "care or control" of the vehicle:

> I recognize, as the trial judge did, that a conviction will normally ensue where the accused, as in this case, was found inebriated behind the wheel of a motor vehicle with nothing to stop the accused from setting it in motion, either intentionally or accidentally.
>
> Impaired judgment is no stranger to impaired driving, where both are induced by the consumption of alcohol or drugs. Absent evidence to the contrary, a present ability to drive while impaired, or with an excessive blood alcohol ratio, creates an inherent risk of danger. In practice, to avoid conviction, the accused will therefore face a tactical necessity of adducing evidence tending to prove that the *inherent* risk is not a *realistic* risk in the particular circumstances of the case.

The game changer in Boudreault's case was the fairly elaborate plan that he had devised to ensure that he would be driven home safely by a taxi driver. The plan was substantiated by his friend, and he had a very sound reason for starting the engine—without

6. *Blood Drug Concentration Regulations*, SOR/2018-148. These regulations apply when the accused is charged with impaired *operation* of a vehicle, under subsection 320.14(1) of the *Criminal Code*. The discussion in the text above, however, is limited to the issue of "care or control."

7. See. s. 254.01 of the *Criminal Code* and *Evaluation of Impaired Operation (Drugs and Alcohol) Regulations*, SOR/2008-196.

8. See subsections 253(3) & (4) of the *Criminal Code*, enacted by S.C. 2018, c. 21.

the benefit of a heater, he would have been exposed to a chilling temperature (minus 15 degrees Celsius). The trial judge clearly found that Boudreault had no intention of driving his vehicle, and the Crown had not raised the possibility that Boudreault might have set his truck in motion *accidentally*. As Justice Fish observed with respect to Boudreault's "alternate plan" to ensure his safe transportation home:

> The impact of an "alternate plan" of this sort on the court's assessment of the risk of danger depends on two considerations: first, whether the plan itself was objectively concrete and reliable; second, whether it was in fact implemented by the accused. A plan may seem watertight, but the accused's level of impairment, demeanour or actions may demonstrate that there was nevertheless a realistic risk that the plan would be abandoned before its implementation. Where judgment is impaired by alcohol, it cannot be lightly assumed that the actions of the accused when behind the wheel will accord with his or her intentions either then or afterward. …

As Justice Fish recognized, *the presence or absence of a realistic risk of danger to persons or property* is a question of fact that has to be determined in the particular circumstances of each individual case that comes before the courts. In Boudreault's case, the trial judge's finding of fact was that there was no realistic risk that the accused would attempt to drive himself home.

It is helpful to compare the result in *Boudreault* with the outcome of other cases decided before it. For example, in *Coleman* (2012), the Saskatchewan Court of Appeal focused on the risk posed to public safety when an impaired driver pulled off the road to have a nap because he felt sleepy. While the keys were in the ignition, the engine of the vehicle was not running. Although it was argued that the criminal law should not penalize drivers who recognize that they are impaired and pull off the road, Justice Richardson, on behalf of the Court of Appeal, rejected that assertion and ruled that Coleman had been properly convicted at his trial:

> An impaired person behind the wheel of a parked vehicle might pose a less acute danger to the public than an impaired person behind the wheel of a moving vehicle. But that does not mean the latter situation is risk free. Parliament has attempted to address both issues by aiming criminal sanctions not just at those individuals who drive while impaired, but also at those who assume care and control of a vehicle while impaired. … Section 253(1) of the *Criminal Code* is directed at the very root of the impaired driving problem. Its object is to stop intoxicated or otherwise impaired individuals from endangering themselves and the public by having care or control of a motor vehicle.

Coleman had not indicated that he would stay off the road until he sobered up. Indeed, he had stated only that he planned to take a "five-minute nap" before proceeding on his journey. This situation created a real risk to the public because he was "behind the wheel of his car and he was of a mind to deliberately put it in motion even though he was impaired."

On the other hand, in the case of *Toews* (1985), the Supreme Court of Canada ruled that the accused could not be considered to be in care or control of a vehicle where he was merely using his truck as a bedroom. The police had found Toews's truck on private property at 5:15 a.m. He was lying on the front seat, wrapped up in a sleeping bag. The key was in the ignition, but the engine was not running. Speaking for the Court, Justice McIntyre stated that:

> *[A]cts of care or control, short of driving, are acts which involve some use of the car or its fittings and equipment, or some course of conduct associated with the vehicle which would involve a risk of putting the vehicle in motion so that it could become dangerous.* Each case will depend on its own facts and the circumstances in which acts of care

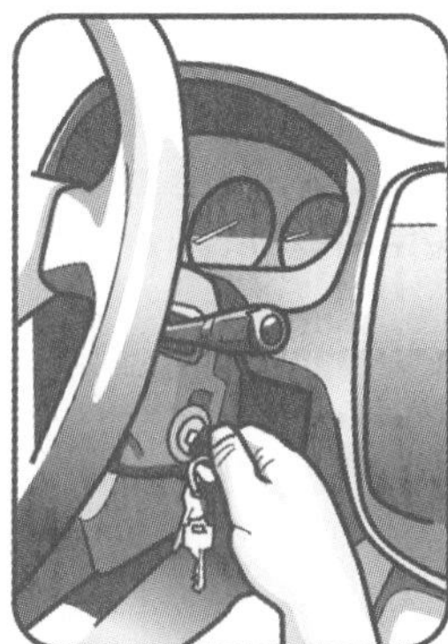

Illustrations by Greg Holoboff

"Care or control": The Coleman *case (2012)—a realistic risk that the car would be set in motion.*

> or control may be found will vary widely. ... In the case at bar the car was on private property and the respondent was not in occupation of the driver's seat. He was unconscious and clearly not in *de facto* control. The fact of his use of a sleeping bag would support his statement that he was merely using the vehicle as a place to sleep. ... It has not been shown then that the respondent performed any acts of care or control and he has therefore not performed the *actus reus*. [emphasis added]

It appears that the critical facts in this case were that Toews's vehicle was on private property and that he was lying on the front seat wrapped up in a sleeping bag. Although the key was in the ignition, it was there for the purpose of playing the stereo system and not for starting the motor. Furthermore, Toews had been driven to the party by a friend and was waiting for that friend in his truck. The verdict might have been very different if Toews had driven himself to the party and parked his truck in the street, returning some time later and placing the key in the ignition: in these circumstances, the Court might well have concluded that the accused was in a position to set the vehicle in motion, thereby constituting a real risk of danger to the public.

Although it may seem somewhat strange to convict someone of an offence in the absence of any conduct on their part, it cannot generally be called unjust since the condition or state in which the accused is found is invariably *preceded* by voluntary conduct that is accompanied by *mens rea* (guilty mind). Would-be housebreakers deliberately arm themselves with the tools of their trade, and they do so with the manifest

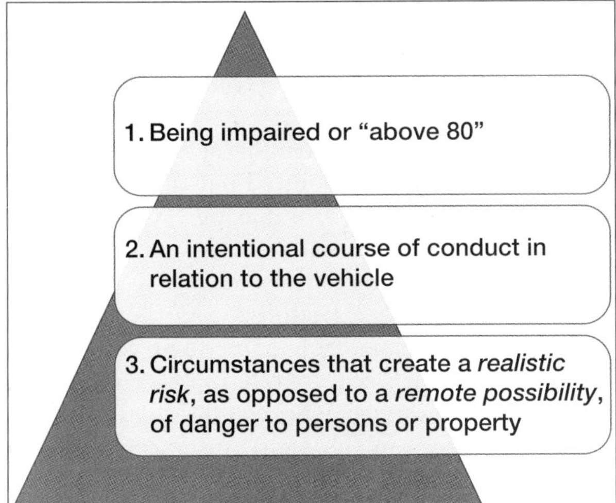

1. Being impaired or "above 80"
2. An intentional course of conduct in relation to the vehicle
3. Circumstances that create a *realistic risk*, as opposed to a *remote possibility*, of danger to persons or property

Figure 2-3

The Actus Reus *Elements of the Offence of Being in Care or Control of a Vehicle While Impaired or Above 80*

purpose of engaging in nefarious criminal activities. Similarly, impaired drivers drink voluntarily, with the knowledge that drinking may impair their ability to drive, before they ever enter a motor vehicle. As Chief Justice Lamer, of the Supreme Court of Canada, said in the *Penno* case (1990):

> Such persons can reasonably be held responsible when they voluntarily consume intoxicating substances and risk putting the public safety in danger by assuming care or control of a motor vehicle, whether they intended to assume care or control or whether intoxication did not allow them to realize what they were doing. By voluntarily taking the first drink, an individual can reasonably be held to have assumed the risk that intoxication would make him or her do what he or she otherwise would not normally do with a clear mind.

In the cases of both the housebreaker and the impaired driver, it is clear that voluntary (and culpable) conduct precedes the discovery of the accused in the prohibited state or condition. On the other hand, where the accused's condition or state has not been voluntarily induced, then it would be unreasonable to convict them of such an offence. For example, in *Butler* (1939), it was suggested in the Alberta Court of Appeal that a highly intoxicated person who, without their knowledge or consent is placed in a motor vehicle by their "friends," may not be convicted of having care or control of a vehicle while impaired. Clearly, in this situation, the accused would not have entered the vehicle voluntarily and, since they would not have foreseen that their friends would place their insensible body in the vehicle, it would be patently unjust to convict them of an offence. In such circumstances, there would be no *actus reus*, because there was no voluntary action on the part of the accused.

Nevertheless, it is significant that it has been suggested that there are certain elements of the offence of "being in care or control" of a motor vehicle while "impaired" or "above 80" that may subject an accused person to the very real threat of unjust treatment. Those who consider the offence created by section 253 to be problematic, in terms of its basic fairness, point to section 258(1)(a) of the *Code*, which must be read in conjunction with section 253. Section 258(1)(a) states:

> Where it is proved that the accused occupied the seat or position ordinarily occupied by a person who operates a motor vehicle ... the accused shall be deemed to have had the care or control of the vehicle ... *unless the accused establishes that the accused did not occupy that seat or position for the purpose of setting the vehicle* ... in motion. [emphasis added]

This section requires trial courts to make the finding that accused persons discovered sitting in the driver's seat of a motor vehicle were in care or control of that vehicle for the purposes of section 253 of the *Code* unless they can establish that they did not occupy the driver's seat for the purpose of setting the vehicle in motion. Obviously, this places an extremely valuable weapon in the arsenal of the prosecution, because the Crown does not have to prove the *actus reus* element of being in care or control once it can demonstrate that the accused was sitting in the driver's seat: they will automatically be *deemed* to have been in care or control. Where the Crown relies on the "presumption of care or control" articulated in section 258(1)(a), the onus shifts to the accused to prove that, although sitting in the driver's seat, they did not have any intention of driving the vehicle in question.

The operation of section 258(1)(a) is well illustrated by the case of Hatfield (1997), in which the accused was sleeping on the fully reclined driver's seat of his car, which had been parked in an industrial parking lot. He was discovered by the police in this position and was charged with being in care or control of a motor vehicle while impaired or "above 80." Hatfield's defence was that he had been drinking at a restaurant, had driven a short distance, and immediately decided that he was not fit to drive; therefore, he proceeded to the parking lot in order to "sleep it off." The Ontario Court of Appeal was required to determine whether the presumption encapsulated in section 258(1)(a) applied to the particular circumstances of Hatfield's case: it answered this question in the affirmative and upheld Hatfield's conviction of being in care or control while impaired. Speaking for the court, Justice Goudge emphasized that it was irrelevant that the driver's seat was in a fully reclined position at the time of the police intervention. It was indisputable that Hatfield was occupying the seat ordinarily occupied by the operator of the motor vehicle. Therefore, the "plain language of the section" dictated that the presumption of care or control should be triggered in the Crown's favour: "Where all that is necessary is for the occupant to bring the driver's seat up to its vertical position, the presumption must apply unless rebutted." The next issue that arose was whether Hatfield could successfully rebut the presumption by claiming that, at the time the police officers found him in the parking lot, his intention was merely to sleep—not to put the vehicle in motion. The Court of Appeal strongly rejected Hatfield's argument: "The appellant occupied the driver's seat in order to drive the vehicle away from the restaurant where he had been drinking. He intended to continue driving when he decided that he was no longer impaired."

Does section 258(1)(a) infringe section 11(d) of the *Charter*, which enshrines the presumption of innocence? Under this provision of the *Charter*, if legislation stipulates that an accused person can be convicted of an offence even though there is a reasonable doubt as to their guilt or innocence, the legislation will be held to be in violation of section 11(d). The question then becomes one of whether it can be saved under section 1 of the *Charter* as a "reasonable limit" on a *Charter* right. When Parliament uses phrases such as "unless the accused establishes," the courts usually interpret this as meaning that the accused must prove the issue (e.g., the absence of an intent to drive a vehicle) "on the balance of probabilities." In this light, it is clear that, under the terms of section 258(1)(a), accused persons can escape conviction under section 253 only by proving that it is more probable than not that they occupied the driver's seat *without entertaining any intention to drive the vehicle in question*. It is not enough for them to raise a reasonable doubt as to their intentions in this respect.

On the face of it, therefore, it would appear that section 258(1)(a) infringes section 11(d) of the *Charter* because an accused person may be convicted of the offence of being in care or control under section 253 even if, at the end of the trial, there is a reasonable doubt as to whether they occupied the driver's seat with the intention of setting the vehicle in motion. In the case of *Whyte* (1988), the Supreme Court of Canada held that section 258(1)(a) did indeed infringe section 11(d) of the *Charter*. However, the Court refused to declare section 258(1)(a) invalid because it considered it to be a reasonable limit under section 1 of the *Charter*.

In delivering the judgment of the Supreme Court, Chief Justice Dickson pointed out that it does not follow, as a matter of inexorable logic, that everyone who is found sitting in the driver's seat of a vehicle has care or control of that vehicle for the purposes of the offences under section 253 of the *Code*. For example, a taxi driver may enter their vehicle and occupy the driver's seat merely in order to use the radio to report an accident; clearly, the taxi driver has no intention, in these circumstances, of doing anything to the vehicle that might set it in motion. As Chief Justice Dickson stated:

> A person can be seated in the driver's seat without an intention to assume care or control of the vehicle within the meaning of [s. 253] ... reasonable explanations for sitting in the driver's seat can readily be

> imagined. It cannot be said that proof of occupancy of the driver's seat leads inexorably to the conclusion that the essential element of care or control exists.

The Chief Justice went on to say:

> [Section 258(1)(a)] requires the trier of fact to accept as proven that an accused had care or control of a vehicle, an essential element of the offence, *in spite of a reasonable doubt about the existence of that element.* The section therefore breaches the presumption of innocence guaranteed by s. 11(d) of the *Charter*. [emphasis added]

In ruling that section 258(1)(a) was "saved" by section 1 of the *Charter*, the Supreme Court noted that it would be impractical to require the Crown to prove that the accused intended to drive the vehicle of which they were found to be in care or control. If proof of such an intention were required to convict an accused person under section 253 of the *Code*, it might be possible for extremely intoxicated persons to claim that they were "too drunk" to form the intent to drive, even though their advanced state of intoxication rendered them a serious danger to the public. According to Chief Justice Dickson, the "presumption of care or control" contained in section 258(1)(a) represents a reasonable compromise in attempting to deal with the manifest dangers posed by drunk drivers. On the one hand, the Crown does not have to shoulder the impossible burden of proving that the accused intended to drive their vehicle; indeed, the Crown has to establish only that the accused became intoxicated voluntarily. On the other hand, an accused person will not be convicted *automatically* merely because they were found sitting in the driver's seat while impaired or "over 80." Section 258(1)(a) does permit such a person to escape conviction by showing that there was some reason (other than driving) for entering the vehicle and occupying the driver's seat. The Supreme Court, therefore, found section 258(1)(a) to be a "restrained parliamentary response to a pressing social problem" and, accordingly, ruled that it was a "reasonable limitation" on the presumption of innocence.

Having examined the difficult exceptions to the general rule that the *actus reus* of an offence consists of conduct, circumstances, and consequences, we now turn our attention to the problems that arise when the Crown claims that the accused's conduct consisted of a "failure to act."

In 2018, Parliament enacted An Act to amend the Criminal Code (offences relating to conveyances) and to make consequential amendments to other Acts, S.C. 2018, c. 21.

This legislation has made major changes to the law relating to the use of alcohol and/or drugs in connection with driving. The legislation was enacted after this section of the chapter was written. Therefore, the section numbers have been changed since this part of the 2018 Act was brought into force in June, 2018.

Under the new legislation, s. 320.14 (1) (a) states that an person commits an offence who "operates a conveyance while the person's ability to operate it is impaired to any degree by alcohol or a drug or by a combination of alcohol and a drug". S. 320.11 defines "operate" as "in respect of a motor vehicle, to drive it or to have care of control of it."

S. 320.35 states that in respect of an offence under s. 320.14, "if it is proved that the accused occupied the seat or position ordinarily occupied by a person who operates a conveyance, the accused is presumed to have been operating the conveyance unless they establish that they did not occupy that seat or position for the purpose of setting the conveyance in motion."

CAN A FAILURE TO *ACT* CONSTITUTE A CRIMINAL OFFENCE?

THE GENERAL PRINCIPLE: NO LIABILITY FOR OMISSIONS UNLESS THERE IS A PREEXISTING DUTY TO ACT

In the preceding discussion of the essential elements of the *actus reus*, it was pointed out that some conduct on the part of the accused is, generally, a prerequisite for conviction of a criminal offence. In what circumstances may a mere failure to act—an **omission**—render an accused person liable to conviction of a criminal offence?

Let us suppose that Murdstone is walking past a lake. As he walks along, he hears pitiful screams emanating from Kit, a four-year-old boy who is drowning in the lake. Murdstone, who is quite capable of rescuing Kit from the relatively shallow water, callously ignores the pleas for help and walks directly to his place of business. Can Murdstone be convicted of the offence of manslaughter for failing to rescue Kit? The simple answer to this blunt question is no (except, perhaps, in Quebec, where there is a statutory duty to rescue those in danger where this may be done without undue risk to the rescuer). The principle of law applicable to this situation is that *an accused person may not be convicted on the basis of a mere omission unless they are under a prior (legal) duty to act.* For example, if Kit had been Murdstone's son, the outcome would have been very different because a parent is under a legal duty to preserve the life of their child when it is reasonably possible for them to do so (see section 215(1)(a) of the *Code*, which places a parent or guardian under a duty to provide the "necessaries of life" to a child under the age of 16 years).

A valuable illustration of the application by the courts of the general principle just outlined is furnished by the case of *Browne* (1997). Here, Browne (aged 22) and his female friend Greiner (aged 19) were dealers in crack cocaine. The trial judge noted that they were "at the very least close friends, probably boyfriend–girlfriend," although they did not live with each other. Both Browne and Greiner had been searched by the police in a drug "crackdown" and subsequently released. However, in order to avoid detection, Greiner had swallowed a plastic bag containing crack cocaine. Tragically, she could not subsequently throw up the bag and the drug entered her system, causing a highly toxic reaction. By the time Greiner reached the hospital, she was dead. Browne was charged with criminal negligence causing death on the basis that he had "failed to render assistance to Audrey Greiner by failing to take her immediately to the hospital." The Ontario Court of Appeal noted that the relationship between Greiner and Browne did *not* fall into any of the categories of relationship (such as husband–wife, parent–child, or caregiver–dependent) that impose an automatic legal duty to provide care and assistance. Therefore, Browne was under no duty to take care of Greiner: the existence of a "boyfriend–girlfriend" relationship does not ***per se*** render either of the parties criminally liable for a failure to act.

VOLUNTARILY ASSUMING A LEGAL DUTY UNDER SECTION 217 OF THE *CRIMINAL CODE*

Even though individual citizens in Canada are under no general legal duty to act, it is possible that they may voluntarily assume responsibility for undertaking a particular service and, in certain circumstances, they will be required to fulfill that commitment if a failure to do so would be dangerous. This legal principle is enshrined in section 217 of the *Criminal Code*, which states, "Every one who undertakes to do an act is under a legal duty to do it if an omission to do the act is or may be dangerous to life." The courts have emphasized that section 217 applies only where the accused makes a serious, conscious undertaking to carry out a certain task and where reliance by another person on this undertaking would be considered reasonable in all of the circumstances. Take, for example, the case of *Browne* (1997). The trial judge had found that Browne had given an undertaking to Greiner to render assistance to her and to take her to the hospital as rapidly as possible. This undertaking, which the trial judge ruled fell within the scope of section 217, was made when Browne "took charge" of Greiner, "after he knew that she had ingested crack." The accused was convicted of criminal negligence causing death because, according to the trial judge, his failure to call 911 instead of taking her to the hospital in a taxi constituted "wanton and reckless disregard" for Greiner's life. However, the Ontario Court of Appeal unanimously set aside the conviction and acquitted Browne. Justice Abella pointed out that the word "undertaking" in section 217 must be interpreted in light of the fact that an accused person, such as Browne, could be liable to a maximum sentence of life imprisonment if there is a conviction for criminal negligence causing death that is based on a failure to perform such an undertaking:

> The threshold definition must be sufficiently high to justify such serious penal consequences. The mere expression of words indicating a willingness to do an act cannot trigger the legal duty. There must be something in the nature of the commitment, generally, though not necessarily, upon which reliance can reasonably be said to have been placed.

Essentially, the trial judge had found that, because Browne and Greiner were partners in drug dealing, Browne had made an implicit undertaking that he would take Greiner to hospital if she were ever to swallow cocaine. However, the Court of Appeal took the view that there was absolutely no undertaking "in the nature of a binding commitment." As Justice Abella stated, Browne's words to Greiner when he knew she was in a life-threatening situation—"I'll take you to the hospital"—"hardly constitute a legal undertaking creating a legal duty under s. 217" and, in the absence of such an undertaking, "there can be no finding of a legal duty."

Of course, one can readily think of situations in which courts would almost certainly find that a binding commitment has been made. For example, a mountain guide is not forced to take a group of climbers into dangerous terrain that is unknown to them. However, once the expedition is underway, the guide cannot suddenly flee the scene if it would create a situation that would be dangerous to the climbers' lives. Under these circumstances, the guide would be considered to have made a solemn undertaking that clearly falls

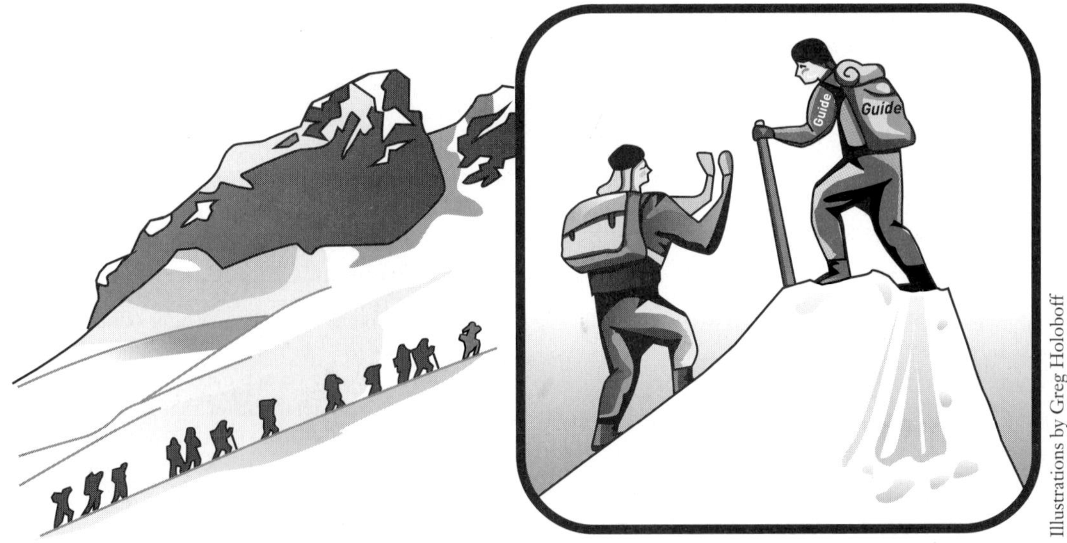

Section 217: "Every one who undertakes to do an act is under a legal duty to do it if an omission to do the act is or may be dangerous to life."

within the purview of section 217. If, as a direct consequence of the guide's abandonment of their duty, one of the climbers fell down a precipice and died, then the guide would be liable to conviction for criminal negligence causing death or manslaughter.

SPECIFIC LEGAL DUTIES IMPOSED BY THE *CRIMINAL CODE*

A number of statutory provisions impose a legal duty to act in a variety of situations in Canada; for example, section 129(b) (duty to assist a police officer); section 215 (duty to provide the necessaries of life to children, spouses, common law partners, and individuals who are in a position of dependence on others); section 217.1 (the duty of a person who undertakes, or has the authority, to direct how another person performs their work activities to "take reasonable steps to prevent bodily harm from occurring either to that person or to a third party as a consequence of performing tasks related to that work");[9] and section 263 (duty to safeguard an opening in ice or an excavation on land so that people do not fall in).

THE DUTY TO PROVIDE THE NECESSARIES OF LIFE TO DEPENDENT PERSONS

Section 215 is a very significant provision that imposes a duty to act on persons who are, in one way or another, responsible for the welfare of others. Section 215 states that:

> (1) Every one is under a legal duty
>
> (a) as a parent, foster parent, guardian or head of a family, to provide necessaries of life for a child under the age of sixteen years;
>
> (b) to provide necessaries of life to their spouse or common-law partner; and
>
> (c) to provide necessaries of life to a person under his charge if that person
>
> (i) is unable, by reason of detention, age, illness, mental disorder or other cause, to withdraw himself from that charge, and
>
> (ii) is unable to provide himself with necessaries of life.[10]
>
> (2) Every person commits an offence who, being under a legal duty within the meaning of subsection (1), fails without lawful excuse to perform that duty, if
>
> (a) with respect to a duty imposed by paragraph (1)(a) or (b),

9. This duty would be imposed on the manager of a construction site, by way of illustration.

10. In *Peterson* (2005), a son was convicted of having failed to provide the necessaries of life to his father, who was too sick to look after himself.

(i) the person to whom the duty is owed is in destitute or necessitous circumstances, or,

(ii) the failure to perform the duty endangers the life of the person to whom the duty is owed, or causes or is likely to cause the health of that person to be endangered permanently; or

(b) with respect to a duty imposed by paragraph (1)(c), the failure to perform the duty endangers the life of the person to whom the duty is owed or causes or is likely to cause the health of that person to be injured permanently.

By "necessaries of life," Parliament meant to include not only food and drink but also medical care and any other goods or services that preserve life. For example, a parent is under a duty to rescue a child from perishing in a fire or drowning in a swimming pool if it is reasonably possible for them to do so in all the particular circumstances of the case.

An important question that arises under section 215 is whether the accused was aware of the fact that a person to whom they owed a duty to provide the necessaries of life was actually in need of the accused's assistance. For example, parents may not be convicted of an offence under section 215 for failing to provide medical services to a child if they had no reason to know that their child was suffering from a medical problem. However, does this mean that a parent who has an *unreasonable* belief that a child is not sick is entitled to an acquittal on this basis?

An example of an unreasonable belief arises in the situation where a parent knows that a child needs a certain medical treatment to maintain life (e.g., insulin injections for a child with diabetes) but withdraws all treatment because an "angel" told the parent that the child was cured. Although the parent in this example may be totally sincere about their religious belief, there is no doubt that most people would regard the withdrawal of treatment from a sick child in these circumstances as unreasonable. Parents do have the absolute right to refuse treatment for themselves, but there is no right to withhold treatment from their children who are too young to make such important decisions for themselves. If the test of criminal responsibility under section 215 is purely *subjective* (based on what the particular accused believed, regardless of the reasonableness of that belief), the accused must be acquitted. However, if the test is *objective* in nature (based on what the *reasonable* parent would have appreciated in the circumstances), the accused must be convicted. What test should be applied by the courts?

In the case of *Naglik* (1993), the Supreme Court of Canada held that the standard to be applied under section 215 of the *Code* is an *objective* one. *Naglik* involved a situation in which the accused and her common law husband had been charged with aggravated assault and failing to provide the necessaries of life to their son, aged 11 weeks. The charge of failing to provide necessaries related to a failure to take the infant for urgent medical treatment. Chief Justice Lamer stated that:

> Section 215 is aimed at establishing a uniform minimum level of care to be provided for those to whom it applies, and this can only be achieved if those under the duty are held to a societal, rather than a personal, standard of conduct. While the section does not purport to prescribe parenting or caregiving techniques, it does serve to set the floor for the provision of necessaries, at the level indicated by, for example, the circumstances described in subs. (2)(a)(ii). The effects of a negligent failure to perform the duty will be as serious as an intentional refusal to perform the duty. …
>
> [S.] 215(2)(a)(ii) punishes a marked departure from the conduct of a reasonably prudent parent in circumstances where it is objectively foreseeable that the failure to provide the necessaries of life would lead to a danger to the life, or a risk of permanent endangerment to the health, of the child.

In *Stephan* (2018), the Supreme Court of Canada reaffirmed the importance of emphasizing the need to establish a marked departure from the standard of care expected of reasonable parents facing the same circumstances as the accused. The Supreme Court ordered a new trial on a charge of failing to provide the necessaries of life to a child (in this case, an alleged failure to provide conventional medical treatment) because the trial judge did not adequately explain the principle of a marked departure to the jury members.

An illuminating application of section 215 occurred in the case of *Barry* (2004). Ms. Barry was charged with failing to provide the necessaries of life to her infant daughter, who was less than one month old. The basis of the charge was Barry's failure to seek prompt medical attention for her baby, who had fractures in both of her arms. Before leaving hospital following the baby's birth, Barry was warned by a childcare worker that Barry's boyfriend, Shawn Sheppard, had been charged with assaulting a child. Barry made an agreement with the childcare worker to the effect that Sheppard would not be present in her home with the children unless she or her grandmother were present and would not be permitted there overnight. This agreement was not honoured by Barry. The Crown alleged that Barry's failure to perform her duty to provide the necessaries of life to her baby met the criteria specified in section 215(2)(a)(ii)—namely, that "the failure to perform the duty endangers the life of the person to whom the duty is owed or causes or is likely to cause the health of that person to be endangered permanently." In delivering the judgment of the Newfoundland and Labrador Court of Appeal, Justice Welsh stated that there had been ample evidence presented at the trial upon which it could be concluded that it was objectively foreseeable that the accused's failure, in her particular circumstances, to obtain punctual medical attention for her daughter was likely to place her at risk of "permanent harm to her health":

> The uncontradicted evidence of the physicians is that the injury would have been painful. If Ms. Barry was present when the injury occurred, acting as a reasonably prudent parent, she would have sought medical assistance without delay. If she was not present, a reasonably prudent parent in her position would have soon recognized the likelihood the baby had been injured, given the baby's crying, the lack of mobility in the arm, the clammy condition of her skin, and the presence of Shawn Sheppard whom child care workers had advised her could not be left alone with the baby. In the circumstances, a heightened level of awareness and vigilance was appropriate and, indeed, required.

Given the particular situation in which Barry found herself, Justice Welsh concluded that her conduct constituted "a marked departure from the standard of a reasonably prudent parent in the circumstances."

On the other hand, in the case of *P. (K.)* (2007), the Ontario Court of Appeal ruled that the Crown had not proved that an infant boy's health had been "permanently endangered" when his mother had delayed seeking medical treatment for injuries to her son's leg. The Court reached that conclusion because the delay had lasted for only one weekend.

It is important to recognize that section 215(2) of the *Criminal Code* makes a specific defence available to those individuals who have been charged with failing to provide the necessaries of life: namely, the defence of "lawful excuse." Prior to 2018, subsection 215(2) stated that the burden of proving the defence lay on the shoulders of the accused. However, this requirement was removed by an amendment to the *Criminal Code*.[11] Now the Crown has to prove beyond a reasonable doubt that the accused did not have a lawful excuse for their failure to provide the necessaries of life.

As far as the substance of the "lawful excuse" defence is concerned, one can well imagine circumstances in which parents, for example, might not be aware that their child is in necessitous circumstances: if such parents have acted reasonably, then the absence of any knowledge of the danger threatening their child would constitute a "lawful excuse." Similarly, an individual who sees their spouse drowning in a swollen, fast-running, deep river would be considered to have a "lawful excuse" not to jump in to the rescue if they are unable to swim (of course, one would expect the individual concerned at least to seek help from other parties, and there would generally be no "lawful excuse" for failing to do so).

The *Criminal Code* also makes provision for the offence of abandoning a child under the age of 10. Section 218 provides:

> Every one who unlawfully abandons or exposes a child who is under the age of ten years, so that its life is or is likely to be endangered or its health is or is likely to be permanently injured,
>
> (a) is guilty of an indictable offence and liable to imprisonment for a term not exceeding five years; or
>
> (b) is guilty of an offence punishable on summary conviction and liable to imprisonment for a term not exceeding eighteen months.

Like section 215, the offence under section 218 is based on the failure to perform a legal duty that has been imposed on the accused person. Unlike section 215, however, the offence of abandoning a child under 10 requires proof of subjective *mens rea*. This requirement was affirmed by the Supreme Court of Canada in *H. (A.D.)* (2013). In this strange case, the accused gave birth to a baby boy in the toilet of a Walmart store. She had not previously been aware that she was pregnant. The baby was blue and did not show any signs of life. The accused left the washroom but later learned that the baby was alive. She then readily admitted to being the mother. She was charged with abandoning her child contrary to section 218. At her trial, the accused declared that "she believed the baby was dead, was scared and confused, and did not intend to abandon the baby." An expert in the field of childbirth testified that, in rapid births such as this one, the baby can emerge in a shock-like state and appear to be dead for 5 to 10 minutes. The trial judge acquitted the accused of the charge of

11. *An Act to amend the Criminal Code and the Department of Justice Act and to make consequential amendments to another Act*, S.C. 2018, c. 29, s. 18.

abandonment and the Saskatchewan Court of Appeal upheld the acquittal. The Supreme Court of Canada also affirmed the acquittal and agreed with the lower courts that the *mens rea* for the offence was subjective rather than objective in nature.

An objective test would require only that a reasonable person, placed in the same circumstances as the accused, would have foreseen that their conduct was likely to endanger the life or health of their child and that the accused's conduct constituted a marked departure from what a reasonable person would have done. On the other hand, a subjective test would focus on what the accused actually knew and the question would be whether she realized that abandoning the child would put the child's life or health at risk. In this particular case, the accused person asserted that she believed the child was dead when she left him in the washroom: if she held this belief, then she would not know that abandoning the child would put his life or health at risk. The Supreme Court interpreted section 218 as requiring proof of subjective *mens rea* and, therefore, agreed with the accused's acquittal. Justice Cromwell stated, on behalf of the Supreme Court:

> There is no doubt that the purpose of the abandonment offence is the protection of children from risk even when no harm occurs. ...
>
> It follows that the scope of potential liability under s. 218 of the *Code* is very broad, encompassing a wide range of persons and conduct. Liability is not restricted to those who are related to the child, or who have any duties in relation to the child or even to those who are in charge of the child at the time. In addition, a very wide range of conduct falls within the words "abandon" and "expose." These are broad words that are not exhaustively defined under the *Code*.

It was Justice Cromwell's view that, since the scope of potential criminal liability under section 218 was so broad, it was necessary for the courts to require subjective *mens rea* in order to ensure that the long arm of the law did not stretch too far and punish people who were not genuinely at fault in the sense of having made a deliberate choice to do something they knew to be wrong.

CRIMINAL NEGLIGENCE, MANSLAUGHTER, AND FAILURE TO ACT

If a failure to perform a legal duty results in death or bodily harm to the person to whom the duty is owed, the accused may be liable to conviction for the more serious offences of *causing death by criminal negligence* (section 220 of the *Code*) or *causing bodily harm by criminal negligence* (section 221 of the *Code*). According to section 219(1)(b) of the *Code*, if an accused person fails to perform a legally imposed duty and, by this failure, "shows wanton or reckless disregard for the lives or safety of other persons," they are guilty of **criminal negligence** causing bodily harm or death (as the case may be). It is also important to bear in mind that the offence of **manslaughter** may be committed where the accused causes the death of their victim as a consequence of criminal negligence on the part of the accused (see sections 222(5)(b) and 234 of the *Code*). The elements that the Crown must prove to obtain a conviction for the offences of both criminal negligence causing death and manslaughter (by means of criminal negligence) are identical in each case. Which charge the Crown ultimately chooses to pursue is primarily a matter of prosecutorial tactics.

One possible explanation for the existence of these twin charges is that, historically, Canadian juries were reluctant to convict motorists charged with manslaughter as a consequence of criminally negligent driving conduct. Therefore, it has been suggested that juries were more willing to convict the accused for engaging in such conduct where the charge was that of criminal negligence causing death, which was generally perceived to bear a lesser degree of stigma than the crime of manslaughter (even though conviction of this charge carries exactly the same maximum penalty of life imprisonment). Apparently for this reason, the offence of criminal negligence causing death was added to the provisions of the *Criminal Code*. However, it seems that even this change did not bring about a satisfactory rate of conviction of motorists who caused death on the roads and, in 1985, Parliament created the offences of dangerous driving causing death [s. 320.13(3)] and impaired driving causing death [s. 320.14(3)]. Both the offences of dangerous driving causing death and impaired driving causing death while impaired or "above 80" [s. 320.21] impose a maximum penalty of life imprisonment.[12]

12. These offences and punishments were significantly amended (and renumbered) by *An Act to amend the Criminal Code (offences relating to conveyances) and to make consequential amendments to other Acts*, S.C. 2018, c. 21.

If an individual starts a fire accidentally and fails to take remedial measures, they may be convicted of arson.

Is There a Duty to Act When a Person Creates a Dangerous Situation by Accident?

Should the criminal law impose a duty to act upon an individual who creates a dangerous situation by accident? Needless to say, the nature of the duty would be to take steps to combat the dangerous situation created by the accused's own act. Apparently, there is no authoritative Canadian precedent on this point; however, this issue was considered by the House of Lords in the English case of *Miller* (1983), in which the accused had been drinking and had subsequently stretched himself out on his mattress and lit a cigarette. He fell asleep while smoking and awoke to find the mattress on fire. However, instead of dealing with the fire, he just went into another room and went to sleep. He was charged with arson. It was clear that the fire had started through the **negligence**, rather than the deliberate conduct, of the accused. The House of Lords ruled that Miller had created a dangerous situation by accidentally starting a fire and had then failed to take any steps to mitigate the damage that could be caused by that fire. There were measures that he could have taken that were clearly within his capabilities to carry out; for example, trying to extinguish the fire with water or even just alerting the fire department. Since Miller realized that the fire was likely to cause damage to property, he had the *mens rea* for the crime of arson and he was, therefore, convicted of that offence.

The *Miller* case opens the door to a potentially significant expansion of criminal liability in relation to omissions. To date, the principle that one may be held criminally responsible for failing to act when one has created a dangerous situation has not been embraced by any appellate court in Canada. However, it was applied by Judge Bourassa, of the Territorial Court of the Northwest Territories, in the case of *Tesar* (1992). The accused was charged under section 140(1)(b) of the *Criminal Code*, which provides:

> Every one commits public mischief who, with intent to mislead, causes a peace officer to enter on or continue an investigation by … doing anything intended to cause some other person to be suspected of having committed an offence that the other person has not committed, or to divert suspicion from himself.

On March 6, 1991, Tesar had informed the police that someone had forged her signature to gain credit for the purchase of groceries and named a particular suspect—a woman called Arsenault. However, on March 13, Tesar's sister telephoned her to let her know that it was she (the sister) who had actually forged Tesar's signature. Tesar did not provide the police with the information about her sister's confession, and Arsenault was arrested at her home on March 19 and released the following day. However, Arsenault later confronted Tesar's sister, who admitted that she had forged the signature, and this information was relayed to the RCMP. Two days before Arsenault's arrest, Tesar had been in contact with the investigating officer and had failed to provide him with the information that her sister had confessed—even though that information would have entirely absolved Arsenault of any responsibility for the forgery.

The issue before Judge Bourassa was whether Tesar could be convicted of public mischief because she failed to provide the information about her sister's confession to the police. Judge Bourassa referred to the judgment of Lord Diplock in the *Miller* case (1983) and found that Tesar had created a dangerous situation by contacting the police and casting suspicion on Arsenault. After Tesar became aware that her accusation was unjustified, she developed the *mens rea* for the offence of public mischief. Here, Tesar had the power to prevent the police from pursuing an innocent woman but she deliberately refrained from doing so. The situation was parallel to what occurred in the *Miller* case, and Tesar was convicted of public mischief. In the circumstances, her failure to take remedial steps after having created a dangerous situation constituted the *actus reus* of the offence. In the words of Judge Bourassa:

> Again, going back to March 13th, which in my view is the pivotal turning point in the case. Bryony Tesar knew her sister had forged her signature. She did absolutely nothing about it. She was in contact with the Police before an innocent person was arrested, and did not inform them of the facts.
>
> In my view, the mental element crystallized on the 13th, and it operated in conjunction with the danger that she created. I have both the mental elements and the factual elements necessary for criminal liability.

SHOULD THERE BE A DUTY TO RESCUE?

There has been a good deal of heated controversy concerning the approach of the criminal law in the area of omissions. More specifically, it has been contended that every citizen should be under a duty to rescue a fellow citizen whose life or safety is in peril, provided, of course, that it is reasonably safe and practical to undertake such a rescue. Proponents of this viewpoint would urge that criminal liability should be imposed on such a person as Murdstone, who, in the example outlined previously, declined to assist a drowning child.

Indeed, the Law Reform Commission of Canada recommended that the *Criminal Code* impose a general duty on all citizens to render aid in an emergency. The Commission pointed to the single exception to the general legal rule in Canada as a concrete demonstration that the proposal is certainly within the realm of practicality. This exception is contained in legislation passed by Quebec. Section 2 of the Quebec *Charter of Human Rights and Freedoms*, CQLR c. C-12, provides:

> Every human being whose life is in peril has a right to assistance. Every person must come to the aid of anyone whose life is in peril, either personally or calling for aid, by giving him the necessary and immediate physical assistance, unless it involves danger to himself or a third person, or he has another valid reason.

The Quebec provision does not create a criminal offence *per se*; in other words, there is no offence of failing to rescue a person in danger. However, the provision may nevertheless play a significant role in leading to the conviction of an accused person under the *Criminal Code* because the *Code* imposes criminal liability, in certain circumstances, for failure to perform a duty imposed by law. The Quebec provision imposes just such a duty. For example, a failure to provide assistance to a victim who subsequently dies, in circumstances indicating a wanton and reckless disregard for the life or safety of the victim, could possibly result in a conviction of manslaughter by criminal negligence or criminal negligence causing death.[13]

However, the present approach of Canadian criminal law is, as we have seen, to impose criminal liability for a failure to act only when such an omission occurs in the context of a prior legal duty to act. Among the arguments in support of the *status quo* is the contention that it would be difficult to enforce a "duty to rescue." Just how far are individual citizens expected to go in attempting to save their fellows from danger? This question is almost impossible to answer in the abstract, and it has always been felt that the criminal law should set clear standards of liability so that

13. In *Maltais v. Simard* (2006), the Quebec Court of Appeal rejected the argument that other people had a duty, under s. 2 of the *Charter*, to intervene and prevent a heavily intoxicated Maltais from diving into shallow water.

every citizen knows, ahead of time, exactly what they must do to avoid criminal liability. Furthermore, it is suggested that the criminal law should abstain from trying to force people to live up to a higher standard of morality; this should be a job for organized religion or the schools rather than the blunt instrument of the criminal sanction.

When a Failure to Act May Render an Accused Person Liable as a Party to an Offence Committed by Another Person

To this point, we have been discussing the circumstances in which an accused person may be convicted of an offence in which the *actus reus* element of conduct may consist of a failure to act on their part. However, there are some situations in which a failure to act may lead to an accused person becoming a party to an offence that is *actually committed by someone else*. This might occur where the accused fails to perform a legal duty and this failure to act is considered to amount to aiding and/or abetting (assisting or encouraging) an offence committed by another party. Paragraphs (b) and (c) of section 21(1) of the *Code* provide that an accused person is a "party to an offence" if that person "does or omits to do anything for the purpose of aiding any person to commit it" or "abets any person in committing it."

For example, in the case of *Nixon* (1990), the accused was the officer in charge of the lock-up, or jail, where a prisoner was assaulted. The accused was charged with aggravated assault, but the trial judge was not satisfied that he had actually committed the assault himself. However, the B.C. Court of Appeal ruled that the trial judge was correct in convicting the accused on the basis that he aided or abetted the officers who did commit the assault. The accused was unquestionably under a duty to protect the prisoner under both British Columbia's *Police Act* and the *Criminal Code* as well as the common law. Nixon's failure to protect the prisoner, when he was under a clear legal duty to do so, therefore constituted aiding or abetting of the assault committed by his fellow officers (assuming that this failure to act was prompted by the *intention* to assist or encourage the other officers in their criminal activities). As Justice Legg stated, in delivering the judgment of the Court of Appeal:

> A person becomes a party under s. 21(1)(b) if he fails to act for the purpose of aiding in the commission of the offence. Where there is a duty to act, and the accused does not act, it is open to the court to infer that the purpose of the failure to act was to aid in the commission of the offence.
>
> Similarly, under s. 21(1)(c), a person who "abets" the offence becomes a party. The cases show that in some circumstances a failure on the part of the accused to act to prevent the offence may constitute positive encouragement. One situation in which this will be the case is where the accused had a duty to prevent the offence and failed to act. Thus, s. 21(1)(c) also punishes omissions in the sense that it punishes the encouragement of an offence that is provided by the omission.

The Court of Appeal agreed with the trial judge that Nixon had encouraged the perpetration of the assault on the prisoner by virtue of the fact that he was present at the scene of the vicious crime and failed to intervene to protect the prisoner. He had a general duty as a police officer to enforce the law and a specific legal duty, as the officer in charge of the lock-up, to protect the prisoner. The trial judge also found that Nixon had the necessary *mens rea* for aiding and/or abetting the assault on the prisoner: by failing to intervene when he was under a duty to do so, he evidenced an intention to facilitate and/or encourage the crime.

The Need for the *Actus Reus* and *Mens Rea* to Coincide

The phrase *actus non facit reum nisi mens sit rea* necessarily implies that, before an accused person may be convicted of a crime, the Crown must prove that there was a moment when both the *actus reus* and *mens rea* elements of the offence coincided. In other words, there is a requirement of simultaneity between the *actus reus* and *mens rea* elements of an offence.

The requirement of simultaneity clearly makes excellent sense when applied to the great majority of situations in which it is alleged that the accused has committed a crime. However, there are certain circumstances in which the application of this principle becomes problematic. In a case of homicide, for example, it may well happen that the victim dies as a consequence of a series of violent acts committed by the accused over an extended period. In such circumstances, the Crown may not be able to prove that the accused had the necessary *mens rea* for murder or manslaughter at the exact moment that the fatal blow was delivered, even though it is clear that the accused did have such *mens rea* at some stage during the series of acts that resulted in the victim's death. Does this mean that the accused must be acquitted of murder or manslaughter because the Crown cannot prove the simultaneity of *actus reus* and *mens rea*? In the case of *Cooper* (1993), the Supreme Court of Canada answered this question in the negative.

Cooper was charged with murder after fatally strangling a young woman. He stated that he became angry with the victim, hit her, grabbed her by the throat, and shook her. He claimed that he could not remember anything else until he woke up and discovered the victim's body next to him. Expert evidence established that the victim had died of manual strangulation and that death had occurred between 30 seconds and two minutes after pressure was applied to her neck. Under section 229(a) of the *Criminal Code*, culpable homicide is murder where the accused either intends to kill the victim or "means to cause" the victim "bodily harm that he knows is likely to cause his death, and is reckless whether death ensues or not." Cooper asserted that he did not have the necessary *mens rea* for murder at the time that the victim was actually killed because he had "blacked out" before her death occurred. Nevertheless, he was convicted at trial and the Supreme Court of Canada ultimately ruled that his conviction was justified.

Justice Cory pointed out that where an accused person has committed a series of acts that result in the death of the victim, these acts should be considered as being "all part of the *same transaction*," and that, if the necessary *mens rea* for murder coincides *at any time* with one or more of these separate acts, the accused may be convicted. For example, let us suppose that an individual repeatedly beats a victim about the head with a baseball bat. It is clear that this individual could be convicted of murder if, at any time, the necessary *mens rea* for murder coincided with one or more of the blows administered by the accused.

In *Cooper*, the Crown took the view that the accused did, at some point, have the intention to inflict bodily harm that he knew was likely to cause death and was reckless whether death ensued or not [s. 229(a)(ii)]. After all, the accused must have been aware that "breathing is essential to life" and that strangulation was likely to cause the victim's death. Justice Cory held that the jury had acted reasonably in concluding that the necessary *mens rea* did exist at some stage, even though it might not have lasted during the whole episode of strangulation. In his view:

> I do not think that it is always necessary that the requisite *mens rea* (the guilty mind, intent or awareness) should continue throughout the commission of the wrongful act.
>
> There is no question that in order to obtain a conviction the Crown must demonstrate that the accused intended to cause bodily harm that he knew was ultimately so dangerous and serious that it was likely to result in the death of a victim. But that intent need not persist through the entire act of strangulation. …
>
> Here the death occurred between 30 seconds and two minutes after he grabbed her by the neck. It could be reasonably inferred by the jury, that when the accused grabbed the victim by the neck and shook her that there was, at that moment, the necessary coincidence of the wrongful act of strangulation and the requisite intent to do bodily harm that the accused knew was likely to cause death. … *It was sufficient that the intent and the act of strangulation coincided at some point. It was not necessary that the requisite intent continue throughout the entire two minutes required to cause the death of the victim.* [emphasis added]

The notion of a continuing *actus reus* was also utilized by the Ontario Court of Appeal in the highly disturbing case of *Bottineau* (2011). Elva Bottineau and Norman Kidman, who were common law partners, were convicted at trial of the second-degree murder of their five-year-old grandson, Jeffrey Baldwin, and the forcible confinement of his six-year-old sister, Judy. The Court of Appeal upheld the convictions. The judgment of the Court began with the following statement:

> The circumstances underlying this appeal are abhorrent beyond description. Cruelly, and without remorse, the appellants starved their five-year-old grandson, Jeffrey Baldwin, to death and gravely mistreated his older sister, Judy. As the trial judge correctly observed, "this case involves the relentless pursuit of a course of unyielding inhumanity and degradation."

Jeffrey and Judy had been "confined in a barren, unheated, filthy room for upwards of 12 hours a day." Jeffrey had been given only meagre amounts of food and he slowly starved to death: indeed, he "weighed 9.68 kilograms when he died, less than half the average weight of a boy his age, and less than he weighed when he was fifteen months old and the appellants assumed responsibility for his care." Although it would have been obvious that Jeffrey's health was seriously compromised, Bottineau and Kidman did not seek any medical assistance. There was no doubt that the sustained course of abuse and neglect of the small boy caused his death; therefore, the *actus reus* elements of the offence of murder were proved beyond a reasonable doubt. The critical question was whether the *mens rea* of murder had been established and, if so, whether there was a time when the *actus reus* and *mens rea* elements coincided.

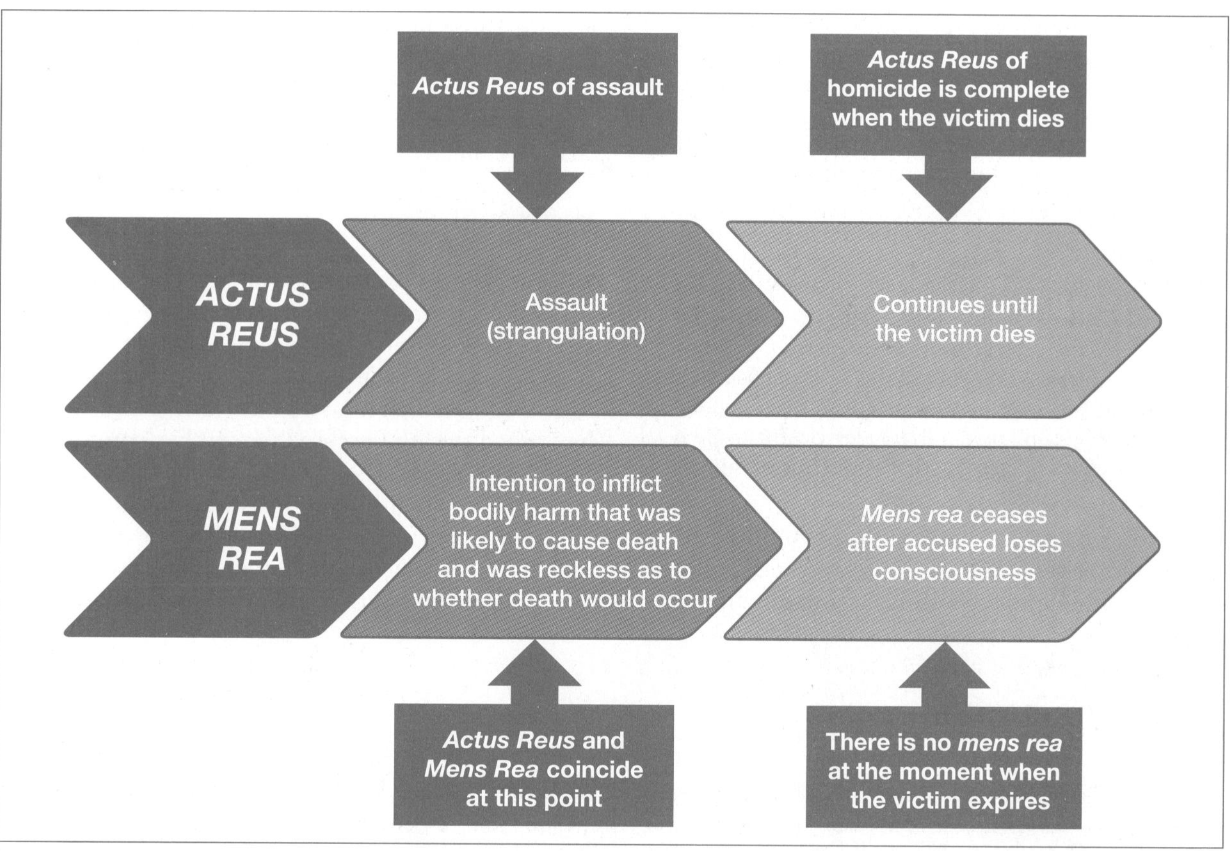

Figure 2-4

Simultaneity of Actus Reus *and* Mens Rea *Elements in* Cooper *(1993)*

The relevant *mens rea* in this case was to be found in section 229(a)(ii) of the *Criminal Code*: culpable homicide is murder when the person who causes the death of a human being "means to cause him bodily harm that he knows is likely to cause death and is reckless whether death ensues or not."

The trial judge, with whom the Court of Appeal agreed, took the view that since Bottineau and Kidman were Jeffrey's sole caregivers, their failure to provide the basic necessities of life and the failure to obtain medical treatment when Jeffrey's life was in obvious danger undoubtedly caused his death. Their actions could be construed as failures to act (omissions) or as actions (deliberately withholding food and medical care). In any event, their omissions and actions persisted over a long period and, in this sense, constituted the ongoing *actus reus* of culpable homicide. The Court of Appeal also agreed with the trial judge's finding that Bottineau and Kidman must undoubtedly have known that their exceedingly abusive and neglectful conduct would result in bodily harm that was likely to cause Jeffrey's death. Persisting in a course of conduct that would inevitably cause bodily harm was indicative of an intent to bring about that result, and since Bottineau and Kidman must have subjectively foreseen the likelihood that Jeffrey would die and were reckless (not caring) with respect to that consequence, the *mens rea* requirements set out in section 229(a)(ii) had been fully established. The Crown did not have to prove the precise moment(s) when the concurrence of the *actus reus* and *mens rea* elements took place: it was sufficient that it must have occurred at some point during the ongoing history of egregious misconduct by Bottineau and Kidman.

The judgment of the Court of Appeal clearly sets out the reasons that there was, indeed, concurrence between the *actus reus* and *mens rea* elements in the *Bottineau* case:

> On the facts as found by the trial judge, the appellants' conduct consisted of the egregious, multi-faceted, long-term mistreatment of Jeffrey combined with the failure to seek medical assistance for Jeffrey in the final

weeks and months of his life when his dire medical condition was obvious. A reasonable trier of fact could readily conclude that Jeffrey's death was the obvious and inevitable consequence of his mistreatment. A reasonable trier of fact could equally infer that at some point during the mistreatment of Jeffrey the appellants appreciated that their continued abuse and neglect of Jeffrey would probably lead to his death.

Whether the appellants' conduct is described as a series of omissions, a series of actions, or a blend of the two, their conduct was of a nature that readily permitted the inference that the appellants knew their conduct would probably bring about Jeffrey's death and yet they chose to persist in that conduct. The facts as found by the trial judge clearly justified the inferences he drew with respect to each appellant's state of mind.

Another problem arises with the application of the principle of simultaneity of *actus reus* and *mens rea* when the accused commits an initially innocent act but subsequently forms the *mens rea* necessary for conviction of a criminal offence. The courts have taken the view that if the *actus reus* committed by the accused was fully completed before the moment that the necessary *mens rea* was formed in the accused's mind, then there is no criminal offence. However, the courts have also held that *mens rea* can be "superimposed" on an initially innocent act so as to justify convicting the accused of a crime. Take the situation where an accused person repeats a false statement on an ongoing basis. Initially, the person wrongly believes the statement to be true but later discovers that it is, after all, false. Here, it could be argued that the accused person has committed a "continuing *actus reus*" (i.e., repeating the false statement) and that, although the statement was initially made innocently, they subsequently developed the necessary *mens rea* when they discovered that it was false. Here, the courts would rule that the *actus reus*

Murder by Reckless Neglect: The Tragic Case of Jeffrey Baldwin

Ashley L. Duffus/A Great Capture

• • • • • •

In this chapter, the *Bottineau* case (2011) is discussed with respect to the requirement that the *actus reus* and *mens rea* elements of a crime must occur simultaneously. However, one very significant aspect of the case is the manner in which the two accused persons were convicted of murder on the basis of their *failure* to act. Their sustained pattern of neglect resulted in the death of their five-year-old grandson, Jeffrey Baldwin. Therefore, this was a case of "reckless murder by neglect."

Elva Bottineau and Norman Kidman were convicted of second-degree murder. They were sentenced to life imprisonment with no possibility of parole for 22 and 20 years, respectively. In March 2011, the Ontario Court of Appeal rejected their appeals against both their convictions and sentences.

The circumstances of Jeffrey's brief life and tragic death were appalling. According to the Court of Appeal, Jeffrey and his sister were "treated like unloved and unwanted animals." They were locked up for more than 12 hours every day in a bare and unheated room that resembled a "dungeon" rather than a bedroom. Neither of the poor children were trained in the use of the toilet and, as a consequence, their room stank of a mixture of urine and feces. Once a day, the siblings were allowed out of their room and sat down on a mat in the kitchen. They were given totally inadequate rations of food which they were required to eat from a bowl placed on the floor.

Jeffrey died just before his sixth birthday. A continuous process of starvation was the catalyst for terminal septicemia, which was ruled the official cause of his death. He weighed less than half the average weight for a young boy of his age. In fact, he weighed even less than when his grandparents had assumed care and control of him some four-and-a-half years previously. Although Jeffrey and his sister were systematically starved, their grandparents were nevertheless pocketing $500 per month for the upkeep of each grandchild.

On the morning when Bottineau dialed 911 to report that Jeffrey was not breathing, first responders arrived to find Jeffrey lying on the kitchen counter "like a bag of groceries." He was taken to hospital, where he was pronounced deceased, but it is likely that he had already died before the 911 call was made. Jeffrey's body bore signs of physical violence as well as profound neglect. There was extensive bruising between his eyes and under the surface of his scalp. Indicative of the astonishing degree of neglect was one of the findings of the post-mortem examination: namely, "Caked-on collections of bacteria over most of Jeffrey's skin." This bacterial growth was described as "extraordinary." There is no doubt that Jeffrey was in acute medical distress for a considerable period before he died. However, he had not been taken to see a physician for almost four-and-a-half years before he died.

The precise cause of death was described by expert witnesses. The Court of Appeal summarized the opinion of one of these witnesses in this manner:

> Dr. Wilson, the senior pathologist at the Hospital for Sick Children, opined that Jeffrey died of acute bacterial bronchial pneumonia occurring as a complication of prolonged starvation. Dr. Wilson testified that the malnutrition occurred over a prolonged period beginning when Jeffrey was about 18 months old. In his view, it was reasonable to conclude that the pneumonia was directly connected to the caked collection of bacteria covering Jeffrey's skin. That bacteria would have entered the respiratory system, eventually leading to the bacterial bronchial pneumonia. Dr. Wilson had never seen the degree of bacterial growth on the skin of a child that he observed on Jeffrey.
>
> Dr. Wilson testified that Jeffrey's chronic malnutrition significantly lowered his resistance to disease, including bacterial pneumonia. Jeffrey's state of hygiene also contributed to the infection and its rapid development into septicaemia. Dr. Wilson believed that the pneumonia would have taken about two days to develop and that death would have followed within hours of the septic shock.

A vital question in a murder case is whether the accused had the necessary *mens rea*. Under section 229(a) of the *Criminal Code*, there are two forms of *mens rea* that will support a conviction of murder: namely, where the accused person

> (i) means to cause his [the victim's] death, or
> (ii) means to cause him bodily harm that he knows is likely to cause his death, and is reckless whether death ensues or not.

In the *Bottineau* case, it would have been difficult for the Crown to prove beyond a reasonable doubt that the accused actually *intended* to kill Jeffrey. Therefore, the Crown relied on the alternative form of *mens rea*—that Bottineau and Kidman meant to cause Jeffrey bodily harm that they knew was likely to cause his death and were reckless as to whether or not death would ensue.

The shockingly debilitated condition of Jeffrey must have made it obvious that he was likely to die without medical attention. Furthermore, Bottineau and Kidman, through their sustained starvation of Jeffrey, must be taken to have intended to cause such a potentially fatal degree of bodily harm because that was the *inevitable consequence* of their appalling lack of care. Finally, it must have been clear to the jury that the accused were reckless—*they just did not care*—whether Jeffrey lived or died.

It is unusual that a pattern of neglect leads to a conviction of murder. However, the appalling level of abuse and neglect in *Bottineau* was so extreme that the accused undoubtedly realized at some point during their so-called "care" of Jeffrey that what they were doing and/or failing to do was likely to cause his death and they were reckless as to that dire outcome—they clearly did not care whether or not he died. There is no doubt that Canadian courts have interpreted the requirement, that the *actus reus* and *mens rea* elements of an offence must occur simultaneously in order to justify a conviction, in a distinctly flexible manner. This meant, in the *Bottineau* case, that the Crown did not have to prove the exact moment(s) when the willful pattern of abuse and neglect coincided with the subjective realization on the part of the accused that it would likely cause Jeffrey's death and the concomitant lack of caring about this devastating outcome. There was clearly no reasonable doubt in the minds of the jurors that the necessary *actus reus* and *mens rea* elements of second-degree murder did occur simultaneously, at least on one occasion—and perhaps on multiple occasions—with respect to each of the accused.

Do you think that the mental elements necessary for conviction of murder, which are set out in section 229(a) of the *Criminal Cde*, are too broad, too narrow, or just right? Was it appropriate to convict Bottineau and Kidman of murder or should they have been convicted of manslaughter (which does not carry a *mandatory* life sentence)? Is murder by reckless neglect more or less heinous than (or equally wicked as) a deliberate act of homicide (such as stabbing or bludgeoning a victim to death)?

and *mens rea* elements of the offence did coincide, at some point, and that, therefore, a crime has been committed.

The notion of a continuing *actus reus* that started innocently but was later rendered criminal when the accused person acquired the necessary *mens rea* was applied by the Supreme Court of Canada in *Detering* (1982). In this case, Detering was charged with fraud, contrary to section 380 of the *Criminal Code*. An employee of the Ontario Ministry of Consumer and Commercial Relations had been involved in the monitoring of garage repair businesses. She had taken a "well-used car" to Detering's repair shop. She knew that the transmission had been "slightly tampered with and could be rectified with a few minutes work." She informed Detering that she had transmission trouble. After road-testing the vehicle, Detering informed her that the transmission needed to be rebuilt and that the repair costs would be $189 plus tax. When the ministry employee reclaimed the car, she paid this sum. The bill indicated that the transmission had been rebuilt; however, it was established that this was not true. Detering was convicted, at his trial, and appealed to the Ontario Court of Appeal, which dismissed his appeal but substituted a conviction for *attempt* to commit fraud since the ministry employee had not, in fact, been deceived by Detering's representation. Detering then appealed to the Supreme Court of Canada.

One of the arguments advanced by his counsel was that there was no concurrence between the *actus reus* of the offence (namely, the representation as to the need for the transmission to be rebuilt) and the requisite *mens rea* (namely, the intent to defraud). In effect, Detering claimed that he made the representation as to the need to rebuild the transmission *before* he knew that it was untrue. Therefore, he asserted that the *actus reus* of the offence was completed before the necessary *mens rea* came into existence. However, the Supreme Court of Canada soundly rejected this contention. In delivering the judgment of the Court, Chief Justice Laskin stated that the accused "renewed" or "continued" his original representation, that the transmission required fixing, after he became aware that it was untrue. In this particular case, therefore, there was a concurrence between the *actus reus* (the representation) and the *mens rea* (knowledge that the representation was false).

In light of cases such as *Cooper*, *Bottineau*, and *Detering*, it is clear that the courts may manifest considerable ingenuity in "bending the rules" concerning the requirement of simultaneity in relation to the *actus reus* and *mens rea* elements of criminal offences in order to achieve what they perceive to be a just result.

THE ELEMENT OF VOLUNTARINESS IN THE *ACTUS REUS*

As Justice LeBel stated in the decision of the Supreme Court of Canada in *Bouchard-Lebrun* (2011), it is a "traditional fundamental principle of the common law" that "criminal responsibility can result only from the commission of a voluntary act." He noted that this critical principle is "based on a recognition that it would be unfair in a democratic society to impose the consequences and stigma of criminal responsibility on an accused who did not voluntarily commit an act that constitutes a criminal offence." A voluntary act is one that is "the product of the accused person's free will." Justice LeBel emphasized that the *actus reus* of a crime cannot be established unless "it is the result of a willing mind at liberty to make a definite choice or decision, or in other words, there must be a willpower to do an act whether the accused knew or not that it was prohibited by law." Therefore, an accused person cannot be found criminally responsible for an act that was involuntary. Justice LeBel also pointed out that there are both physical and moral dimensions to the concept of **voluntariness**:

> An individual's will is expressed through conscious control exerted by the individual over his or her body ... The control may be physical, in which case voluntariness relates to the muscle movements of a person exerting physical control over his or her body. The exercise of a person's will may also involve moral control over actions the person wants to take, in which case a voluntary act is a carefully thought out act that is performed freely by an individual with at least a minimum level of intelligence. ... Will is also a product of reason.

In our discussion of the *actus reus* elements of a criminal offence, the focus is on the *physical* dimension of voluntariness. The *moral* dimension will be discussed later, in the context of such defences as not criminally responsible on account of mental disorder, intoxication, necessity, and duress.

With respect to the requirement of physical voluntariness, take the case of (the perhaps inappropriately named) *Lucki* (1955), who negotiated a right-hand turn on an icy street. *Through no fault of his own*, his car skidded on a sheet of ice and came to rest on the wrong side of the street. He was charged with being on the wrong side of the dividing line but was acquitted on the basis that he had arrived at this position through no voluntary act of his own. Similarly, if an extremely intoxicated person is placed by their friends in a motor vehicle in a state of unconsciousness, they would not be convicted of being in "care or control" of the vehicle because the entry into the vehicle was not voluntary.

In *Fontaine* (2017), the accused was aggressively woken up from a deep sleep by his common law partner and he struck her with such force that he caused significant bodily harm. The Saskatchewan Court of Appeal refused to set aside the decision of the trial judge to acquit Fontaine of the charge of assault causing bodily harm because the blow that he struck was the product of a reflex action and, therefore, entirely involuntary. Chief Justice Richards stated that Fontaine's "conduct has all the hallmarks of a reflexive action to a sudden and rather startling stimulus while in a state of sleep." Since Fontaine's conduct was involuntary, the Crown could not prove the basic *actus reus* requirement of the offence.

Similarly, if the accused claims that the alleged conduct that constitutes the basis for a criminal charge was an *accident*, they are also claiming that there was no *actus reus* and, therefore, no offence. In *Primeau* (2018), the accused had been convicted at trial of first-degree murder even though he had claimed that the gunshot that caused the victim's death was an accident. He had asserted that he had been moving backward as the victim came toward him, lost his balance, and struck a couch, which caused the gun to discharge accidentally. The Quebec Court of Appeal set aside the conviction and ordered a new trial because, *inter alia*, the trial judge had not instructed the jury that if there had been a genuine accident, there could not have been the voluntary action which is an essential component of the *actus reus* element of the offence of murder. Voluntary action cannot occur in the absence of a deliberate and conscious choice. As Healy, J.A. said in delivering the judgment of the Court of Appeal:

> Accident negates the element of conscious choice, or voluntariness, in action as much as it negates specific types of choices as defined in various concepts of *mens rea*. Thus a driver who unavoidably strikes a pedestrian who streaks into the road cannot be held criminally responsible for voluntary conduct or fault in the commission of an offence,

When an accused person acted involuntarily because they were in a seriously *impaired state of consciousness* at the time of the alleged offence, it may be possible to raise the defence of automatism. Since the courts have experienced considerable difficulty in drawing a line between the defence of automatism and the defence of not criminally responsible on account of mental disorder, these two defences will be discussed together in Chapter 8.

Study Questions

1. Blimber is a youth worker who is employed by the provincial government. While he was one of the staff members at a custodial institution, some youths complained that he touched them on the arms and legs. Blimber is surprised that there have been such complaints, and he says that he touched the youths only as a means of demonstrating his genuine concern for their welfare. Crown counsel is considering laying charges of sexual assault against Blimber. Do you think such charges would be likely to succeed at a trial? Why or why not?
2. Jarndyce lives with his five-year-old son, Nemo, and his wife, Matilda, in a third-floor apartment. Since she was severely injured in a car accident some time ago, Matilda has used a wheelchair and requires constant attention. One night, Jarndyce goes out to a bar, where he indulges in some drinking with a friend. When he is walking up the street toward his home, he sees both flames and smoke coming out of the apartment building. There are a number of people outside the building, but there is no sign of the fire department. Jarndyce refuses to enter the building because, he says, he is "frightened of fires." A few minutes later, two neighbours emerge from the building and bring out Nemo and Matilda, who have been burned and are suffering from smoke inhalation. They subsequently recover in hospital. However, a neighbour reports Jarndyce's failure to go into the building and the police decide to lay charges against him. What charge(s), if any, could reasonably be laid against Jarndyce?
3. Quilp is the owner of a clothing store. The central heating system breaks down and, since it is the middle of winter, Quilp makes temporary use of an old-fashioned oil heater. As he is leaving the store, he accidentally knocks the heater over and leaking oil is ignited, causing a fire to ignite and spread. Quilp does nothing to extinguish the fire because he suddenly decides that it would be to his financial advantage to let the store burn down and claim the insurance money. He waits near the store to watch the progress of the fire, unaware that Rudge, a burglar, had hidden in the store with the intention of removing the stock in the middle of the night. Rudge is trapped inside the

store because, owing to the intensity of the fire, he is unable to reach the exit. Rudge screams for help, but Quilp ignores his pleas because he has a deep hatred for burglars. Quilp does not even call 911. In fact, a passerby sees the fire and calls the fire department on his cellphone. When the fire fighters arrive on the scene, it is too late to save Rudge, who has died in the conflagration. Quilp is charged with arson (section 433) and manslaughter (section 236). He claims that he did not start the fire intentionally and that he was under no duty to rescue Rudge. What defence(s), if any, are likely to succeed at his trial for arson and manslaughter?

4. Sparkler is driving, within the speed limit, on a country road. He suddenly skids on some ice and his car slides into a ditch. He leaves the car, with the keys still in the ignition, and asks for help at a nearby farmhouse. The farmer calls for a tow truck and gives Sparkler a few whiskeys, since Sparkler looks as though he is in a state of shock. Sparkler returns to the car to wait for the tow truck. However, a police car arrives and Sparkler is asked to take a breath test. Sparkler is subsequently charged with being in care or control of a motor vehicle while impaired by alcohol (contrary to section 320.14(1)). Is he likely to be found guilty of this offence?
5. Codlin has been drinking alcohol at a party. He leaves his friend's house and drives his car in the direction of his home. However, he realizes that he is quite intoxicated and decides to pull off the road and park his car at a shopping mall. He gets out of his car to make a call on his cellphone because the signal is not very strong in this particular location. He calls a taxi to pick him up and take him home. He then reenters the car and sits in the driver's seat. He removes the key from the ignition and puts it in his pocket. A passing police officer notices Codlin sitting in his vehicle and demands that he undergo a breathalyzer test. Codlin's blood alcohol level is 150 milligrams of alcohol per 100 millilitres of blood. Codlin is charged with being in care or control of a motor vehicle while being "over 80" (contrary to section 320.14(1) of the *Criminal Code*). Does Codlin have any defence(s) to this charge?
6. Lucretia is a single mother who is trying to raise her young daughter, Nell, as best she can. Nell has diabetes and Lucretia's physician has told her that Nell will die if she does not have regular injections of insulin. One day, Lucretia believes that she has experienced a vision and that an angel has told her that Nell has been cured and no longer needs her injections. Lucretia stops giving her daughter the insulin and Nell eventually goes into a coma. By the time Nell is taken to hospital, it is too late to save her and she dies. Lucretia claims that she honestly believed that her daughter was cured and that she did not need any treatment. The police are convinced that Lucretia's religious beliefs are sincerely held. Nevertheless, Crown counsel is considering laying criminal charges against Lucretia. What charges, if any, would be likely to succeed at trial?
7. Rigaud is climbing a mountain with his friend Lightwood. They enter into a ferocious fight and Rigaud knocks Lightwood unconscious by hitting him on the head with an ice pick. Rigaud comes to believe that Lightwood is dead and, four hours later, he throws Lightwood over a cliff. The body is later recovered by the police. Forensic experts are prepared to testify that Lightwood was still alive when he was thrown over the cliff and that he would most probably have survived had he not been so gravely wounded by the fall from the top of the cliff. Rigaud's lawyer claims that her client cannot be convicted of a homicide offence, because when he threw his friend off the cliff, he honestly believed the latter was dead. What charge(s), if any, could be brought against Rigaud, and what degree of success would the charge(s) be likely to have at trial?
8. Dombey is walking down a street when he is hailed by his friend Pinch, who is driving a brand-new sports car. Pinch asks Dombey if he would like a ride in the car and Dombey answers in the affirmative. After they set off, Dombey hears the sound of a police siren and Pinch dramatically increases his speed. Pinch tells Dombey that the car is "hot." Unfortunately, two minutes later, Pinch crashes into a tree and Dombey is trapped in the seriously damaged vehicle. The fire department arrives and a firefighter uses the "jaws of life" to free Dombey, who is then taken to hospital. Dombey is later charged with being the occupant of a motor vehicle knowing that it was taken without the owner's consent, contrary to section 335(1) of the *Criminal Code*. What defence, if any, does Dombey have to this charge? If there is one, do you think the defence is likely to be successful at his trial?

CHAPTER 3

CAUSATION IN THE CRIMINAL LAW

Learning Objectives

After reading this chapter, you will be able to understand:

- the fundamental principles of causation that apply in the criminal law;
- the difference between factual and legal causation;
- the requirement of *reasonable foreseeability* as a vital element in the concept of legal causation, which determines whether an accused *should* be held accountable for their conduct;
- the requirement that the defendant's act be a "significant contributing cause" of the *actus reus* of a criminal offence; and
- the special rules of causation that apply to the law of homicide.

CAUSATION IN CRIMINAL LAW

Where an essential element of the *actus reus* of an offence is the occurrence of certain specified consequences, it must be proved that the defendant's conduct actually caused those consequences. For example, in the *Trotta* case (2004), a husband and wife were charged with various offences following the death of their eight-month-old son. The evidence was to the effect that the husband had assaulted the baby and that the wife, who knew of the physical abuse, did nothing to prevent it. The trial judge instructed the jury that:

> [T]he Crown must prove that Marco Trotta caused the death of Paolo Trotta. Perhaps the best way to approach this third ingredient, the ingredient of causation, is to ask yourselves the following question. Would Paolo Trotta have died if Marco had not committed assaultive behaviour toward him? In other words, would Paolo's death have occurred anyway even if Marco had not been assaultive towards him?

The husband was convicted of second-degree murder and the wife of criminal negligence causing death. Their appeals were dismissed by the Ontario Court of Appeal. One of the grounds of the appeal concerned the trial judge's instruction to the jury on the matter of causation. Justice Doherty stated that he interpreted the trial judge's instruction "as an indication to the jury that it must find a *'but for'* causal link between an assault on Paolo by Marco and Paolo's death" and held that this was "a correct instruction in the circumstances of this case." In all cases where consequences are an essential element of the *actus reus*, it is clear that the Crown must prove that *"but for" the actions of the accused, the prohibited consequences would not have occurred.*

In the *Nette* case (2001), the Supreme Court ruled that there are two—quite distinct—issues that must be considered in determining whether or not the accused's conduct caused a certain prohibited consequence: namely, **factual causation** (or **causation in fact**) and **legal causation** (or **causation in law**). In the words of Justice Arbour:

> In determining whether a person can be held responsible for causing a particular result, in this case death, it must be determined whether the person caused that result both in fact and in law. Factual causation, as the term implies, is concerned with an inquiry about how the victim came to his or her death, in a medical, mechanical, or physical sense, and with the contribution of the accused to that result. Where factual causation is established, the remaining issue is legal causation.
>
> Legal causation, which is also referred to as imputable causation, is concerned with the question of whether the accused person should be held responsible in law for the death that occurred. It is informed by legal considerations such as the wording of the section creating the offence and principles of interpretation. These legal considerations, in turn, reflect fundamental principles of criminal justice such as the principle that the morally innocent should not be punished. ... In determining whether legal causation is established, the inquiry is directed at the question of whether the accused person should be held criminally responsible for the consequences that occurred.

As noted above, to establish factual causation, the Crown must prove that, *"but for" the accused's conduct, the prohibited consequences would never have occurred.* This is generally a simple task, which can often be determined by scientific or other expert evidence. However, merely because there is a causal link between the accused person's conduct and the prohibited consequence does not necessarily mean that the accused should be held criminally responsible. For example, a careful motorist may briefly pull out of his lane to see if they may pass the vehicle in front of them. However, they notice that another car is coming toward them from some considerable distance away and they quite properly pull back into their original lane. Let us suppose that the oncoming driver inexplicably panics and brakes sharply. Their vehicle skids on some ice on the roadway and there is a terrible accident, which kills their passenger. Of course, there is a causal link between the motorist pulling out of their lane and the accident that claimed the life of the passenger in the oncoming vehicle: *"but for"* their action in pulling out of their lane, the fatal accident would never have occurred. However, a court would conclude that, in law, the accident was caused by the negligence of the oncoming driver: the prudent motorist who pulled out of their lane cannot be held responsible for the unforeseeable misconduct of another driver. This was essentially the situation that was found to exist in the case of *Ewart* (1990), in which Justice McClung of the Alberta Court of Appeal said:

> I can agree ... that on the evidence the operation of the Ewart vehicle was the traceable origin of Mrs. Rossman's reaction and the ensuing collision. But that does not cast Ewart's attempt to pass as criminal. ... In a court applying criminal sanction it

is doubtful whether any driver can become, by operation of law alone, an insurer against extreme and unforeseeable responses of other users of the road.

Once factual causation has been established, the next issue to be decided is whether there is *legal causation*. In other words, even if there is a link in fact between the accused person's conduct and the prohibited consequence, it must still be decided whether the conduct should be considered sufficiently blameworthy to warrant criminal punishment. In general, the courts consider prohibited consequences to be imputable to the accused person only if they were foreseeable. As we shall discover in the next two chapters, **foreseeability**—or whether or not a consequence was foreseeable—is also a central issue in deciding whether the *mens rea* elements of the offence in question have been proved. In this respect, Justice Arbour stated in the *Nette* case (2001):

> While causation is a distinct issue from *mens rea*, the proper standard of causation expresses an element of fault that is in law sufficient, in addition to the requisite mental element, to base criminal responsibility. The starting point in the chain of causation which seeks to attribute the prohibited consequences to an act of the accused is usually an unlawful act in itself. When that unlawful act is combined with the requisite mental element for the offence charged, causation is generally not an issue. For example, in the case of murder, where an accused intends to kill a person and performs an act which causes or contributes to that person's death, it is rare for an issue to arise as to whether the accused caused the victim's death.

If the consequences of one's actions are foreseeable, it is relatively simple to conclude that there is a causal link between those actions and their consequences. From another point of view, it might also be pointed out that the requirement of foreseeability ensures that an accused person's criminal responsibility for their actions is not unlimited; they can be punished only for prohibited consequences that could be foreseen.

The distinction between *factual and legal causation* was dramatically illustrated by the tragic case of *Trakas* (2008). Trakas planned to sell a motorcycle. An individual came to Trakas's house and took the machine for a test drive, leaving his pickup truck in the driveway. However, another man who had been hidden drove the pickup truck away, and Trakas realized that he had been duped. Trakas decided to follow the pickup truck in his SUV. The wild chase lasted for

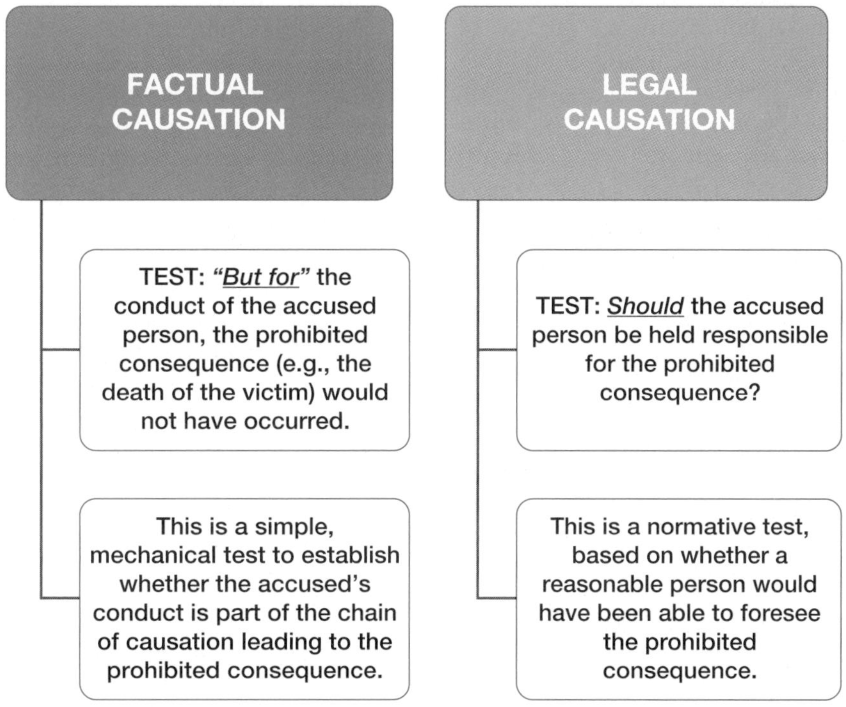

Figure 3-1

Factual and Legal Causation

more than 25 minutes, with the two vehicles reaching speeds ranging between 110 and 180 kilometres an hour. They were also observed running stop signs, tailgating, passing dangerously, making sudden lane changes, and generally driving "erratically." During the pursuit, Trakas repeatedly contacted the police on his cellphone and requested their intervention. A police officer who was intending to deploy a spike belt suddenly entered the roadway on foot and was struck by Trakas's vehicle. The officer was thrown about 88 metres and died from severe injuries.

Trakas was charged with criminal negligence causing death. However, he contended that the officer's decision to suddenly jump into the roadway constituted an intervening act that severed the chain of causation between Trakas's conduct and the police officer's death. There was no doubt that Trakas caused the death of the police officer insofar as *factual causation* was concerned. After all, it was Trakas's vehicle that struck and killed the officer. However, the Crown also had to prove *legal causation* before Trakas could be convicted of the offence with which he had been charged. To do so, the Crown would have to establish that, at the time of the accident, Trakas was driving in a criminally negligent manner, showing wanton and reckless disregard for the lives and safety of other persons. However, Trakas had no reason to believe that a police officer would be on this particular stretch of the highway. In addition, the evidence was that Trakas was not exceeding the speed limit and was driving normally in a lane of traffic when the fatal accident occurred. The jury concluded that the Crown had failed to prove *legal causation* and acquitted Trakas of criminal negligence causing death. However, Trakas was convicted of dangerous driving in light of the evidence of his undoubtedly hazardous driving *prior* to the accident.

The Crown appealed against Trakas's acquittal on the charge of criminal negligence causing death, but the Ontario Court of Appeal rejected the appeal.[1] In delivering the judgment of the Court, Justice Lang noted that the trial judge had correctly instructed the jury about the need for the Crown to prove both factual and legal causation, in accordance with Justice Arbour's judgment in the *Nette* case. Justice Lang stated that:

> First, the trial judge's instructions clearly put before the jury the question of whether the officer's presence on the road was in some way a response to the actions of the respondent in initiating and pursuing the chase or whether it was an independent intervening act. The trial judge specifically instructed the jury to consider whether the collision was "within the scope of the risk created by James Trakas when he was involved in a high-speed pursuit of Mr. Shilon over this great distance." He also put forward the Crown's position that the officer's action in stepping on the road was not an independent intervening cause because he attended at the scene only in response to the dangerous situation created by the respondent. Second, the instruction on legal causation was correctly based on *Nette*. ... Among other instructions, the trial judge instructed the jury that a legally blameworthy cause must be "at least a significant" cause and "more than one that is trifling or minor."

In this case, there was absolutely no doubt that *factual causation* had been established because Trakas had hit the officer with his vehicle and killed the police officer. What was at issue was whether there was an *intervening act* on the part of the police officer that severed the chain of *legal causation* between Trakas's conduct and the officer's demise. Clearly, the jury rejected the contention that Trakas could have foreseen the officer's presence on the road, and, since he was driving normally at the time of the accident, he should not be held legally responsible for the officer's death.

The significance of foreseeability in establishing *legal causation* was also demonstrated in the case of *Shilon* (2006). Shilon was the driver of the pickup truck that Trakas had been pursuing, and he had also been charged with criminal negligence causing death. The *Shilon* case involved the issue of whether the accused should be committed for trial on this charge. The Ontario Court of Appeal ruled that Shilon should indeed be tried for criminal negligence causing death. In delivering the judgment of the Court, Justice Gillese stated:

> Reasonable foreseeability of harm, it seems to me, is relevant in the analysis of legal causation in negligence based offences. On this view, the fact that Trakas actually caused the police officer's death does not preclude an inquiry as to whether the driver of the pickup truck ought also to be held criminally responsible for the death. There is nothing in the wording of the offence that constrains the concept of causation to preclude such an inquiry.
>
> In my view, where conduct is inherently dangerous and carries with it a reasonably foreseeable risk of immediate and substantial harm, the test for legal causation will have been met. On the facts of this case, there is some evidence of both criteria.

1. The Court also rejected Trakas's appeal against his conviction of dangerous driving.

> ... [T]he driver of the pick-up truck drove in a criminally negligent fashion. Not only was the driving inherently dangerous, it clearly carried with it the reasonably foreseeable consequence of immediate and substantial harm. Trakas' actions were reasonably foreseeable—they were a predictable consequence of the actions of the driver of the pick-up truck. Indeed, the preliminary inquiry judge stated that the officer's death was an entirely foreseeable consequence of the conduct of the driver of the pick-up truck.
>
> Accordingly, it was an available inference that the police officer's death occurred in the ambit of the risk created by the actions of the driver of the pick-up truck and that the driver ought reasonably to have foreseen such harm.

Specific Rules Concerning Causation in Homicide Cases

Perhaps because of the severe nature of the crimes concerned, there are a number of special rules concerning the issue of causation in relation to offences such as murder, manslaughter, infanticide, criminal negligence causing death, dangerous driving causing death, and impaired driving causing death.

The Definition of Death for the Purposes of Criminal Law

It almost goes without saying that to convict an accused person of murder, manslaughter, infanticide, criminal negligence causing death, or impaired/dangerous driving causing death, the Crown must prove that the victim was, in fact, *dead* after the accused inflicted injuries on them. In the vast majority of cases, criminal courts have no difficulty deciding when a human being has died. If an individual has ceased breathing and the heart has stopped beating (and normal resuscitation procedures, if appropriate, fail to work), then it is clear that they are dead. However, in today's hospitals, it is possible to use life-support machines that artificially maintain heart and circulatory functions, and the application of this medical technology can potentially create some difficulties for criminal courts that are faced with the problem of pinpointing the moment when a patient can legitimately be considered dead.

Suppose, for example, that Jasper inflicts a severe head injury on Edwin Drood in the course of a robbery. When Drood is taken to hospital, the doctors immediately conclude that, without the use of life-support machinery, he will not be able to breathe or maintain the circulation of blood in his body. After Drood is hooked up to a life-support machine, the attending medical practitioners decide that he has suffered such a massive brain injury that he is "clinically dead." Drood's next of kin is consulted and the life-support machine is switched off by his physician. Could Jasper turn around at his trial and claim that since the life-support machine could have maintained Drood's respiratory and circulatory functions on an indefinite basis, there is no evidence that he killed Drood and that, in fact, it was the physician's act of flicking the switch that really precipitated death? The answer to Jasper's argument would be that if the doctors' diagnosis was that Drood had suffered *total, irreversible brain death*, then he was *dead* from the point of view of modern medical science and switching off the life-support machine was merely a recognition of that tragic reality; hence, Jasper could not claim that Drood was still alive when the artificial life support was withdrawn.

Unfortunately, to date, Parliament has not kept pace with modern medical technology and has not defined death for the purposes of criminal law. However, the Law Reform Commission of Canada recommended, more than 35 years ago, that death should be defined in legislation in a manner that is consistent with modern medical developments. More precisely, the commission advocated the adoption of the following definition: "a person is dead when an irreversible cessation of all that person's brain functions has occurred." In its 1981 report, *Criteria for the Determination of Death*, the commission recommended that the Canadian Parliament amend the *Interpretation Act*, R.S.C. 1985, c. I-21, so as to contain the following provision:

> For all purposes within the jurisdiction of the Parliament of Canada,
>
> (1) a person is dead when an irreversible cessation of all that person's brain functions has occurred.
> (2) the irreversible cessation of brain functions can be determined by the prolonged absence of spontaneous circulatory and respiratory functions.
> (3) when the determination of the prolonged absence of spontaneous circulatory and respiratory functions is made impossible by the use of artificial means of support, the irreversible cessation of brain functions can be determined by any means recognized by the ordinary standards of medical practice.[2]

2. From *Criteria for the Determination of Death*, Law Reform Commission of Canada. Department of Justice Canada, 1981. Reproduced with the permission of the Department of Justice Canada, 2019.

Where an individual is *not* connected to a life-support machine, death will be determined on the basis of whether breathing or blood circulation is still taking place. For example, if Smallweed and Krook both shoot Rigaud within seconds of each other, there may be a question as to whether Rigaud was still alive between the shot by Smallweed and the shot by Krook. If there is evidence of bleeding from both gun shots, then it is clear that Rigaud was still alive at the moment that Krook pulled the trigger.

Various medical protocols have been developed to provide guidance to physicians who are called upon to determine whether an individual who is on life support has suffered total brain death. However, these protocols usually require that the same medical tests be repeated at an interval of 24 hours or so in order to ensure that the patient really has suffered total brain death rather than, for example, a temporary reaction to a drug (such as a barbiturate) that causes a major depression of the nervous system. This means that it takes considerable time before it can be determined beyond question that total brain death has occurred when the patient is being kept artificially alive by life-support machines. Adoption of the Law Reform Commission's definition of death would clearly resolve any uncertainty that currently exists in Canada.

Until 1999, the *Criminal Code* maintained the archaic rule that an accused person could not be convicted of an offence of homicide unless the death of the victim occurred "within one year and one day from the time of the occurrence of the last event by means of which [the accused] caused or contributed to the cause of death." Centuries ago, this old common law rule made some sense insofar as the relatively primitive state of medical science rendered it very difficult for the Crown to prove that there was the necessary causal link if a victim were to linger for a long period. However, today, modern medicine is much better equipped to establish such a link and, for this reason, Parliament repealed section 227 in 1999 [S.C., c. 5, s. 9(1)]. Furthermore, it may be noted that the repeal of section 227 has the effect of forestalling the creation of a situation in which a court may be compelled to acquit an accused person of a homicide offence simply because the victim had been on life-support machines for a period that is greater than one year and a day. Under the current law, this issue now becomes utterly irrelevant.

Acceleration of Death

A most significant legal principle relating to causation is enshrined in section 226 of the *Code*:

> Where a person causes to a human being a bodily injury that results in death, he causes the death of that human being notwithstanding that the effect of the bodily injury is only to accelerate his death from a disease or disorder arising from some other cause.

It is clear that a murderer should not be excused from punishment for a heinous act merely because the victim was, for example, a terminally ill patient who had only a few more days to live. Similarly, it does not matter that an accused person, who is not a medical practitioner, claims that the deceased victim had requested a so-called "mercy killing" because they were suffering from intolerable pain from a terminal illness. Indeed, Section 14 of the *Criminal Code* provides that "No person is entitled to consent to have death inflicted on them, and such consent does not affect the criminal responsibility of any person who inflicts death on the person who gave consent." Active euthanasia (deliberately taking steps to terminate the life of another person) is not permitted under Canadian criminal law: however, it is critical to note that, since 2016, there has been an important exception for medical practitioners who cause the death of their patients if certain statutory criteria have been met: this exception is known as "medically assisted death" (see "Gloria Taylor and the Battle for a Right to a Physician-assisted Suicide" on page 56).

Before any further discussion of the circumstances in which medical practitioners are permitted under the *Criminal Code* to bring about the premature termination of the lives of patients wracked by intolerable pain, it is important to identify two situations that involve the acceleration of death, but which have never been considered criminal in nature. The first situation consists of the administration of strong pain-killing medications that are necessary for the control of pain in terminally ill patients. If physicians inject dying patients with drugs designed to alleviate severe pain and the incidental effect is to hasten death, this is considered to be appropriate **palliative care** and has never been labelled as murder. As Justice Sopinka stated in the case of *Rodriguez*, decided by the Supreme Court of Canada in 1993, "(t)he administration of drugs designed for pain control in dosages which the physician knows will hasten death constitutes active contribution to death by any standard." However, since the physician's *intention was to ease pain* and not to kill the patient, there is no reason to involve the criminal law—even though death has been accelerated.

The second situation that involves the acceleration of death, but which has never been considered criminal, is so-called **passive euthanasia**: this consists of withdrawing medical treatment from a patient even though the inevitable consequence is that death will ensue. Significantly, a physician is required to cease treatment if a *competent* patient requests them to do so because such a patient has the basic right to reject the administration of treatment even if such a refusal will result in their death. For example, in the case of *Nancy B. v. Hôtel-Dieu de Québec* (1992), Nancy B. was a 25-year-old woman who had suffered for two-and-a-half years from an incurable neurological disorder known as Guillain-Barré syndrome. She was paralyzed and depended on a respirator to keep her alive. She knew that her condition could not be reversed and decided that she would rather die than continue her life "literally tied to her hospital bed." She sought a court order directing the hospital and her physician to disconnect the respirator.

Justice Dufour of the Quebec Superior Court determined that Nancy B. was competent to make decisions for herself and that she, therefore, had a right to refuse treatment. The physician was given permission to disconnect the respirator. Nancy B. later died after the physician carried out her request.

Section 241(b) of the *Criminal Code* makes it an offence to aid (or assist) another person to commit suicide. Until 2016, this blanket prohibition included medical practitioners who provided patients living with intolerable pain the means to kill themselves (for example, by providing them with a lethal amount of drugs, such as the barbiturate secobarbital sodium, which they could then take themselves). However, in *Carter v. Canada (Attorney General)* (2015), the Supreme Court of Canada ruled that the prohibition by section 241(b) on *physician-assisted suicide* is unconstitutional. The Supreme Court unanimously decided that sections 241(b) and 14 of the *Criminal Code* prevent a competent adult person, who is suffering intolerable pain, from gaining access to a physician-assisted death. Sections 241(b) and 14, therefore, unjustifiably infringed the right to life, liberty, and security guaranteed by section 7 of the *Charter* and were, therefore, invalid and of no effect. However, the Court addressed only *physician-assisted* suicides and did not set aside the prohibition against assisted suicide in sections 241(b) and 14 for any individuals other than medical practitioners.

Following the Supreme Court's decision in *Carter*, Parliament enacted Bill C-14, the ***Medical Assistance in Dying Act***, which became law on June 17, 2016. This legislation amended section 241 and added sections 241.1 to 241.4 of the *Criminal Code*.[3] These amendments establish a framework for medical practitioners or nurse practitioners to provide "medical assistance in dying" to a patient. This means that, if the statutory criteria are met, medical practitioners and nurse practitioners may engage in both active euthanasia and assisted suicide. (See "Gloria Taylor and the Battle for a Right to a Physician-assisted Suicide" on page 56.)

Liability of the Accused Where There Is More Than One Cause of Death

One principle of causation that is frequently misunderstood concerns the proposition that the defendant's act does not have to be the "sole" cause of the victim's death in order to convict them of culpable homicide. For example, let us suppose that Flintwich strikes and wounds Blandois, who subsequently dies from massive internal hemorrhaging. Medical evidence establishes that Blandois was a hemophiliac and that the wound inflicted by Flintwich would not have caused the death of a person who was not suffering from this medical condition. Flintwich cannot claim that because hemophilia was a significant "cause" of death, he should be excused from liability for culpable homicide. In other words, while Flintwich's wounding of Blandois and the latter's hemophilia both contributed to his demise, Flintwich is still liable to punishment. Depending on his intention at the time of the wounding, Flintwich will be convicted of murder or manslaughter. This example also illustrates the principle that aggressors must "take their victims as they find them." They cannot point to their victims' physical weaknesses as an excuse for their homicidal acts.

The application of this principle was dramatically illustrated in the tragic case of *Smithers* (1977). In this case, the accused was charged with manslaughter. He was a member of a "midget hockey" team. The deceased, Cobby, had been a member of an opposing team that had been playing Smithers' team on the day of

3. S. 14 was also slightly amended.

Gloria Taylor and the Battle for a Right to a Physician-assisted Suicide

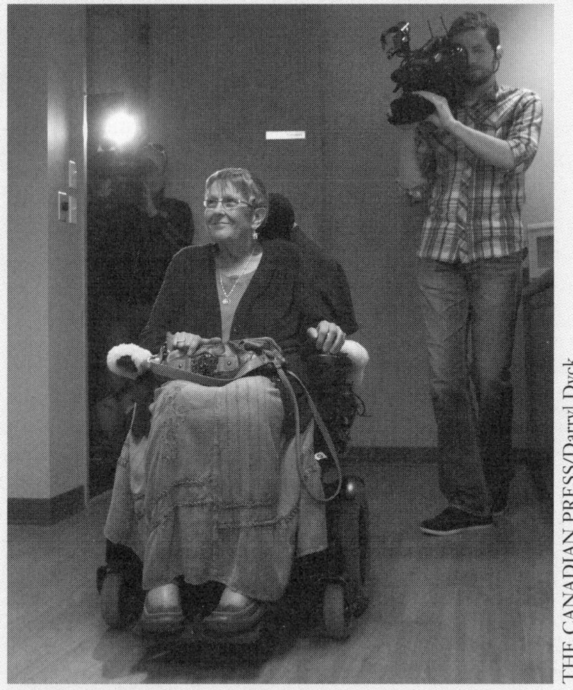

THE CANADIAN PRESS/Darryl Dyck

Assisted suicide occurs when an individual helps another person to commit suicide (by, for example, providing a lethal dose of drugs that the other person takes themselves). When a physician provides this assistance, the act is called **physician-assisted suicide**. Until June 2016, the *Criminal Code* made it a serious crime for *anyone* to encourage another person to commit suicide or to assist someone to commit suicide. Indeed, 241(1) of the *Criminal Code* states that:

> Everyone is guilty of an indictable offence and liable to imprisonment for a term of not more than 14 years who, whether suicide ensues or not,
> (a) counsels a person to die by suicide or abets a person in dying by suicide; or
> (b) aids a person to die by suicide.

Gloria Taylor was the lead plaintiff in an action that was brought in the Supreme Court of British Columbia to seek a declaration that section 241(b) was invalid because it violates the *Charter* insofar as it denied her a physician-assisted suicide.

Gloria Taylor had been diagnosed with amyotrophic lateral sclerosis (ALS)—also known as motor neurone disease or Lou Gehrig's disease. Most people die within three to five years of the appearance of the first symptoms of this progressive and wasting disease. Death is often the result of respiratory failure or pneumonia, and the steady loss of the ability to function independently during the passage to death is frequently a source of extreme physical and emotional distress. Ms. Taylor was seeking the right to have a physician assist her suicide if she came to the point where her symptoms and reduced quality of life were no longer bearable.

In her affidavit for the action in the Supreme Court of B.C., Ms. Taylor stated that:

> I am dying. I do not want to, but I am going to die; that is a fact. I can accept death because I recognize it as a part of life. What I fear is a death that negates, as opposed to concludes, my life. I do not want to die slowly, piece by piece. I do not want to waste away unconscious in a hospital bed. I do not want to die wracked with pain. It is very important to me that my family, and my granddaughter in particular, have final memories that capture me as I really am—not as someone I cannot identify with and have no desire to become.

In *Carter v. Canada (Attorney General)* (2012), the B.C. Supreme Court granted the application by Gloria Taylor and others for a declaration that section 241(b) of the *Criminal Code* was invalid and of no force and effect. Section 241(b) was the part of the prohibition that applies to *aiding or abetting* a person to commit a suicide (the decision had no impact on section 241(a), which prohibited *counselling* a person to commit suicide). As it turned out, Gloria Taylor died in hospital of natural causes on October 4, 2012 (the cause of death was an infection brought on by a perforated colon). However, the Government of Canada appealed the declaration of invalidity to the B.C. Court of Appeal, which by a 2–1 majority set aside the judgment of the trial court and affirmed the constitutionality of the total ban against assisted suicide [*Carter v. Canada (Attorney General* (2013)].

The other plaintiffs in the case successfully appealed to the Supreme Court of Canada. In *Carter v. Canada (Attorney General)* (2015), the Supreme Court of Canada ruled that the prohibition by section 241(b) on *physician-assisted suicide* is unconstitutional. The Supreme Court unanimously decided that sections 241(b) and 14 of the *Criminal Code* prevent a competent adult person who is suffering intolerable pain from gaining access to a physician-assisted death. Sections 241(b) and 14, therefore, unjustifiably infringed the right to life, liberty, and security guaranteed by section 7 of the *Charter* and were, therefore, invalid and of no effect.

The Supreme Court held that the circumstances under which a competent adult person may obtain a medically assisted death are (1) there is a clear consent to the ending of life and (2) "the person has a grievous and irremediable medical condition (including an illness, disease, or disability) that causes enduring suffering that is intolerable to the individual in the circumstances of his or her condition."

The Supreme Court of Canada suspended the declaration of invalidity of section 241(b) for 12 months (until February 2016) to allow Parliament time to amend the Criminal Code. The Court later granted the Government of Canada a further extension of four months (until June 2016). After much debate in both the House of Commons and the Senate, Parliament enacted Bill C-14, the Medical Assistance in Dying Act, which amended the Criminal Code and became law on June 17, 2016.[4] A new section [241(2)] grants an exemption from criminal liability for those medical professionals who provide "medical assistance in dying": "No medical practitioner or nurse practitioner commits an offence under [s. 241(b)] if they provide a person with medical assistance in dying in accordance with [the procedures specified in subsequent provisions in the Criminal Code]."

The new *Criminal Code* provisions [sections 241 to 241.4] define "medical assistance in dying" in a manner that includes both voluntary euthanasia carried out by a medical professional as well as suicide assisted by a medical professional. Section 241.1 states that:

> "medical assistance in dying" means:
> (a) the administering by a medical practitioner or nurse practitioner of a substance to a person, at their request, that causes their death; or
> (b) the prescribing or providing by a medical practitioner or nurse practitioner of a substance to a person, at their request, so that they may self-administer the substance and in doing so cause their own death.

The new *Criminal Code* provisions set out the requirements that must be met before an individual may receive a medically assisted death. Among the most important requirements are the following: the person concerned must be 18, competent to make decisions about their health care, and "have a grievous and irremediable medical condition." [s. 241.2(1)(b) & (c)]. The legislation also mandates that the person must be informed of the alternatives to dealing with their suffering (e.g., palliative care) before they give their consent to a medically assisted death. [s. 241.2(1)(e)].

4. An *Act to amend the Criminal Code and to make related amendments to other Acts (medical assistance in dying)* S.C. 2016, c. 3.

A critical aspect of the new legislation is the definition of "grievous and irremediable medical condition." Section 241.2(2) states that an individual has such a condition only if they meet each of the following requirements:

> (a) they have a serious and incurable illness, disease or disability;
> (b) they are in an advanced state of irreversible decline in capability;
> (c) that illness, disease or disability or that state of decline causes them enduring physical or psychological suffering that is intolerable to them and that cannot be relieved under conditions that they consider acceptable; and
> (d) their natural death has become reasonably foreseeable, taking into account all of their medical circumstances, without a prognosis necessarily having been made as to the specific length of time that they have remaining.

The new *Criminal Code* provisions include various safeguards to ensure, for example, that the individual applying for a medically assisted death is competent to make that decision and that there is a 10-day period during which they may change their mind (see section 241.2).

There are some serious doubts as to whether some aspects of the new Medical Assistance in Dying legislation are constitutional because its criteria are arguably more restrictive than those articulated by the Supreme Court of Canada in the *Carter* case. In particular, the Supreme Court did not limit the right to access medically assisted dying to those individuals whose "natural death has become reasonably foreseeable." It is not clear whether Parliament meant to restrict the administration of medically assisted deaths to individuals who are "terminally ill" since the phrase "reasonably foreseeable," allows for a considerable degree of interpretation.[5] However, it does clearly exclude individuals who may be enduring intolerable suffering but who are not facing death in the foreseeable future. Similarly, the requirement that their death be "reasonably foreseeable" means that individuals with a mental-health condition which is intolerable but not life threatening are potentially excluded from access to a medically assisted death. No doubt, the new legislation will be challenged

5. In *A.B. v. Canada (Attorney General)* (2017), the Ontario Superior Court pointed out that the words "reasonably foreseeable" ... are modified by the phrase "taking into account all of their medical circumstances, without a prognosis necessarily having been made as to the specific length of time that they have remaining." "This language reveals that natural death need not be imminent and that what is a reasonably foreseeable death is a person-specific medical question to be made without necessarily making, but not necessarily precluding, a prognosis of the remaining lifespan."

on constitutional grounds and is likely to bring the issue of medically assisted death back to the Supreme Court of Canada.[6] Finally, it is significant that, on June 5, 2014, the National Assembly of Québec enacted Bill 52, *An Act Respecting End-of-Life Care*. This legislation also permits terminally ill individuals to request assistance from a physician to die. In some respects, the Quebec legislation diverges from the *Criminal Code* provisions and there may be a question of whether there is a conflict between the province's constitutional power to enact health legislation and the power of the federal parliament to enact criminal legislation.[7]

6. See *Lamb v. Canada (Attorney General)* (2017) (B.C. Supreme Court).

7. See *Truchon c. Attorney General of Canada*, 2018 (Quebec Superior Court).

Do you support the legalization of active euthanasia by a physician as provided under the MAID legislation? If so, what criteria do you think should have been prescribed by Parliament and what procedures, in your opinion, should have been required to avoid abuse of the weak and vulnerable? What arguments might be made to support the current law, which totally prohibits assisted suicide by individuals who are not medical practitioners? Should there be a provision in the *Criminal Code* that allows for a reduction in the sentence of individuals who commit a so-called "mercy killing" for a loved one who is not eligible for MAID?

Source: CBC News, "Inside Gloria Taylor's battle for the right to die," October 12, 2012. Online at http://www.cbc.ca/news/canada/inside-gloria-taylor-s-battle-for-the-right-to-die-1.1186092

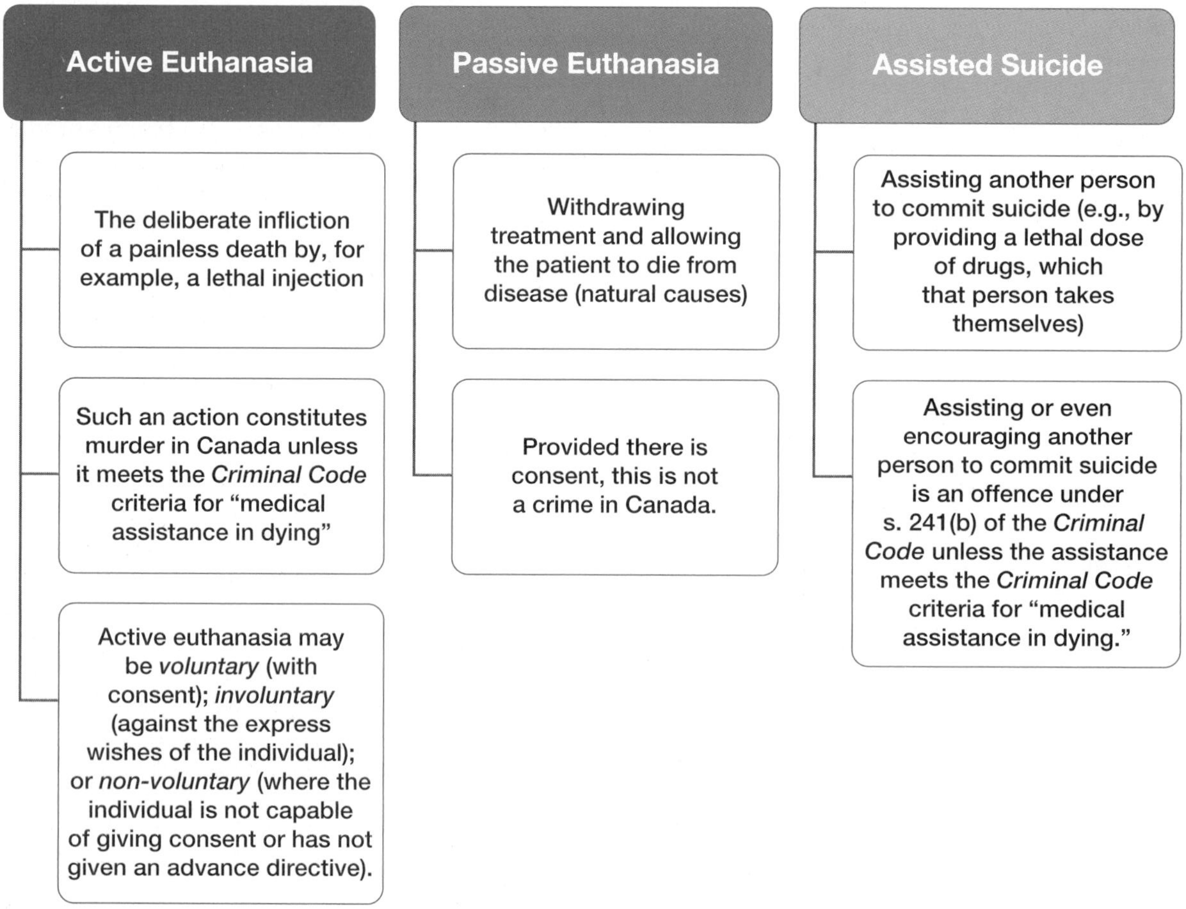

Figure 3-2

Acceleration of Death: Legal Principles and Outcomes

the incident in question. Smithers had been subjected to racial insults by Cobby and others. Smithers and Cobby were later given game misconducts following a "heated and abusive exchange of profanities." Smithers threatened to "get" Cobby, who was very apprehensive as a consequence. When Cobby tried to leave the arena, Smithers pursued him. Cobby hurried toward a waiting car, but Smithers caught up with him and "directed one or two punches" to his head. Smithers' teammates intervened and grabbed him. However, he managed to deliver a hard, fast kick to Cobby's stomach (the latter had been making no effort to defend himself). Seconds after this kick, Cobby collapsed, gasping for air. He stopped breathing and was dead upon his arrival in hospital. It was found that Cobby had died as a result of the "aspiration of foreign materials present from vomiting." Normally, when a human being vomits, the epiglottis comes into operation and covers the windpipe. The folded epiglottis thereby prevents the stomach contents from entering the air passage. For some reason, this mechanism failed in Cobby's case.

Smithers was convicted of manslaughter and ultimately his appeal went to the Supreme Court, where the central issue was that of causation. Smithers' counsel argued that there was insufficient evidence that the accused's kick caused the vomiting. On this issue, Justice Dickson made the observation that:

> [I]t may be shortly said that there was a very substantial body of evidence, both expert and lay, before the jury indicating that the kick was at least a contributing cause, outside the *de minimis* range, and that is all that the Crown was required to establish. It is immaterial that the death was in part caused by a malfunctioning epiglottis to which malfunction the appellant may, or may not, have contributed.

Later in his judgment, Justice Dickson stated that it is a "well-recognized principle that one who assaults another must take his victim as he finds him." Ultimately, Smithers' appeal was dismissed.

Of course, while the accused's conduct does not have to be the "sole" cause of death, it must nevertheless constitute a "significant" cause. In the *Smithers* case, Justice Dickson expressed this principle by stipulating that the accused person's act must be a "contributing cause, outside the *de minimis* range" (i.e., it must be shown to have had more than a minimal impact on the events leading to the victim's death). However, this manner of articulating an important principle may well be confusing to jurors and, subsequently, the Supreme Court of Canada ruled that it would be preferable to instruct juries that the accused person's conduct should constitute a *"significant contributing cause."* As Justice Arbour stated in the *Nette* case (2001):

> The only potential shortcoming with the Smithers test is not in its substance, but in its articulation. Even though it causes little difficulty for lawyers and judges, the use of Latin expressions and the formulation of the test in the negative are not particularly useful means of conveying an abstract idea to a jury. In order to explain the standard as clearly as possible to the jury, it may be preferable to phrase the standard of causation in positive terms using a phrase such as "significant contributing cause" rather than using expressions phrased in the negative such as "not a trivial cause" or "not insignificant." Latin terms such as "*de minimis*" are rarely helpful.

In the *Nette* case, the facts were that the victim, who was a 95-year-old widow living on her own, was discovered dead in her own bedroom. Her house had been robbed and she had been "hog-tied" with electrical wire. The victim's hands had been bound behind her back and her legs had been forced upward behind her back and attached to her hands. An item of clothing had been tied around the victim's head and neck and covered her chin. This "garment formed a moderately tight ligature around her neck, but did not obstruct her nose or mouth." The victim was left alone in this condition and, at some point, she fell off the bed onto the floor. During the period of 24 to 48 hours that followed the robbery, the victim died of asphyxiation. The forensic pathologist, who testified for the Crown, stated that the victim "died as a result of asphyxiation due to an upper airway obstruction." According to this expert, there was no single factor that could be said to have caused death. In his view, there were a number of different factors that contributed to the asphyxiation of the victim—"in particular, her hogtied position, the ligature around her neck, as well as her age and corresponding lack of muscle tone." In addition, the expert agreed that the victim's "congestive heart failure and asthma may possibly have speeded up the process of asphyxiation."

The accused persons argued that this was a case in which there were multiple causes of death and that their own conduct was *not a significant contributing factor* to the victim's death. However, the Supreme Court rejected this line of argument. Indeed, Justice Arbour said:

> [I]t is only in cases involving multiple causes that the jury need be charged on the applicable standard of

causation. In my view, this is not such a case. The fact that the appellant's actions might not have caused death in a different person, or that death might have taken longer to occur in the case of a younger victim, does not transform this case into one involving multiple causes. Clearly, where an accused person hog-ties an elderly woman, places a ligature of clothing around her neck and abandons her, in the knowledge that she lives alone, without notifying anyone of her plight, it is not unexpected that death will result if no one rescues the victim in time.

... There was no evidence that anything other than the actions of the appellant and his accomplice caused Mrs. Loski's death.

Similarly, in the case of *Younger* (2004), the accused was charged with the murder of a two-and-a-half-year-old boy, whom he had kidnapped or unlawfully confined. The child was left in a van in a vacant lot in Winnipeg at a time when the outside temperature was around minus 2 degrees Celsius. Tragically, he died of hypothermia. Younger was convicted of murder at his trial. The Manitoba Court of Appeal dismissed Younger's appeal against his conviction. In delivering the judgment of the Court, Justice Twaddle stated that:

The means by which the death is caused are irrelevant as long as the death is caused in some way by the offender. The abandonment of a scantily clad young child is certainly an act which, in my opinion, can be accepted by a jury as the cause of the child's death.

Causation is a question of fact for the jury to decide subject to this: the offender's conduct need not be the sole cause of death as long as it was a significant contributing cause; a cause that is not trivial or insignificant.

The Special Test of Causation That Applies to First-Degree Murder Under Sections 231(5) and (6) of the *Criminal Code*

Normally, the Crown must prove that a murder was "planned and deliberate" if the accused is to be convicted of **first-degree murder** (see section 231(2) of the *Criminal Code*). However, there are a number of significant exceptions to this general rule (e.g., murder of a peace officer or a prison guard). Among these exceptions is section 231(5) of the *Code*, which stipulates that murder will automatically be treated as first-degree murder where death occurs in the course of the commission (or attempted commission) of certain (very serious) offences, which may best be characterized as crimes of unlawful domination:

Irrespective of whether a murder is planned and deliberate on the part of any person, murder is first degree murder in respect of a person when the death is caused by that person while committing or attempting to commit an offence under one of the following sections:

(a) section 76 (hijacking an aircraft);

(b) section 271 (sexual assault);

(c) section 272 (sexual assault with a weapon, threats to a third party, or causing bodily harm);

(d) section 273 (aggravated sexual assault);

(e) section 279 (kidnapping and forcible confinement);

(f) section 279.1 (hostage taking).

In the case of *Harbottle* (1993), the accused and another man had participated in a sexual assault of a 17-year-old girl and then discussed how they could kill her. The other man eventually strangled the victim with her bra while Harbottle held her legs to prevent her from resisting the deadly attack. The victim died and Harbottle was charged with first-degree murder. The Crown relied on section 231(5) of the *Code* in light of the fact that the victim had died in the course of a sexual assault. The question arose as to whether the *Smithers* test of causation was adequate in the context of a first-degree murder charge. The Supreme Court of Canada ruled that, although the *Smithers* test was adequate for a charge of manslaughter, it was not strict enough for a charge of first-degree murder under section 231(5). However, the Court did not rely on the *Charter* in arriving at this conclusion. Rather, it referred to the seriousness of the consequences of a conviction of first-degree murder and to the specific wording of section 231(5). In delivering the judgment of the Court, Justice Cory noted that:

The consequences of a conviction for first degree murder and the wording of the section are such that the test of causation for [s. 231(5)] must be a strict one. In my view, an accused may only be convicted under the subsection if the Crown establishes that the accused has committed an act or series of acts which are of such a nature that they must be regarded as a substantial and integral cause of the death. ...

The substantial causation test requires that the accused play a very active role—usually a physical

> role—in the killing. Under [s. 231(5)], the actions of the accused must form an essential, substantial and integral part of the killing of the victim.

According to Justice Cory, the evidence in the *Harbottle* case (1993) clearly established that the accused's conduct "was a substantial and an integral cause of the death" of the victim:

> There is every reason to believe that, had it not been for Harbottle's holding of her legs, she would have been able to resist the attempts to strangle her. In those circumstances, it is difficult to believe that Ross could have strangled her in the absence of the assistance of Harbottle.

In the subsequent case of *Nette* (2001), the Supreme Court of Canada ruled that the *Harbottle* case had not changed the factual test of causation in homicide—the *Smithers* test still applies to all cases of homicide (although, as we have seen, the Supreme Court held that the test should be rephrased so as to require that the accused person's conduct constitute a "significant contributing cause"). However, according to Justice Arbour, *Harbottle* (1993) decided that, to reflect the increased sentence and greater degree of stigma associated with first-degree murder, Parliament has imposed an additional "causation" requirement in section 231(5):

> The additional "causation" requirement under s. 231(5) does not refer to factual causation but rather to an increased degree of legal causation. In other words, once the jury has determined that the accused committed murder, which entails a finding that the accused caused the victim's death in both factual and legal terms, it is then necessary to consider whether the moral culpability of the accused, as evidenced by his role in the killing, justifies a verdict of first degree murder. As [Justice] Cory ... states in *Harbottle*, "The gravity of the crime and the severity of the sentence both indicate that a substantial and high degree of blameworthiness, above and beyond that of murder, must be established in order to convict an accused of first degree murder."... Such a high degree of blameworthiness would only be established where the actions of the accused were found to be "an essential, substantial and integral part of the killing of the victim."... The terminology of "substantial cause" is used to indicate a higher degree of legal causation but it is a standard that only comes into play at the stage of deciding whether the accused's degree of blameworthiness warrants the increased penalty and stigma of first degree murder.

Significantly, Justice Arbour pointed out that the wording of section 231(6) is very similar to that of section 231(5) and that, therefore, the "**substantial and integral cause**" test that was articulated in *Harbottle* should also be applied to section 231(6), which deals with murder committed while the accused person is committing or attempting to commit an offence of criminal harassment contrary to section 264 of the *Criminal Code*.[8]

The Problem of Intervening Acts

Some of the most challenging issues of causation in the criminal law relating to homicide undoubtedly arise when there is an **intervening act** or event that occurs between the defendant's original wounding of the victim and the latter's subsequent death. Suppose that Gride stabs Pumblechook with a pocket knife and that, three minutes later, Swiveller arrives on the scene and strangles Pumblechook to death. In terms of the criminal responsibility of Gride, there is a very real issue of causation: namely, did the intervening act of Swiveller sever the chain of causation between the original stab wound inflicted by Gride and Pumblechook's subsequent death? What principles do the courts turn to when confronted by such difficult questions?

We have seen that the *Nette* case (2001) established that an accused person generally cannot be convicted of a homicide offence unless their conduct made a *significant contribution* to the victim's death. In the context of a case involving an intervening act or event, the Crown must show either that the original wound inflicted by the accused person was still a significant contributing cause at the time of the victim's death or that the intervening act, which actually caused the victim's death, was a reasonably foreseeable consequence (or "natural consequence") of the accused person's conduct.

Kitching and Adams (1976) provides an excellent illustration of a case in which it was determined that an intervening act had *not* severed the chain of causation because the original wound and the intervening act were *both* significant contributing causes of death at the time the victim expired. In this case, the defendants were charged with the

8. Parliament later added subsections (6.01), (6.1), and (6.2) to s. 231. These subsections contain similar wording to subsections (5) and (6) and, therefore, it would appear that the *Harbottle* test should also be applied to these new provisions.

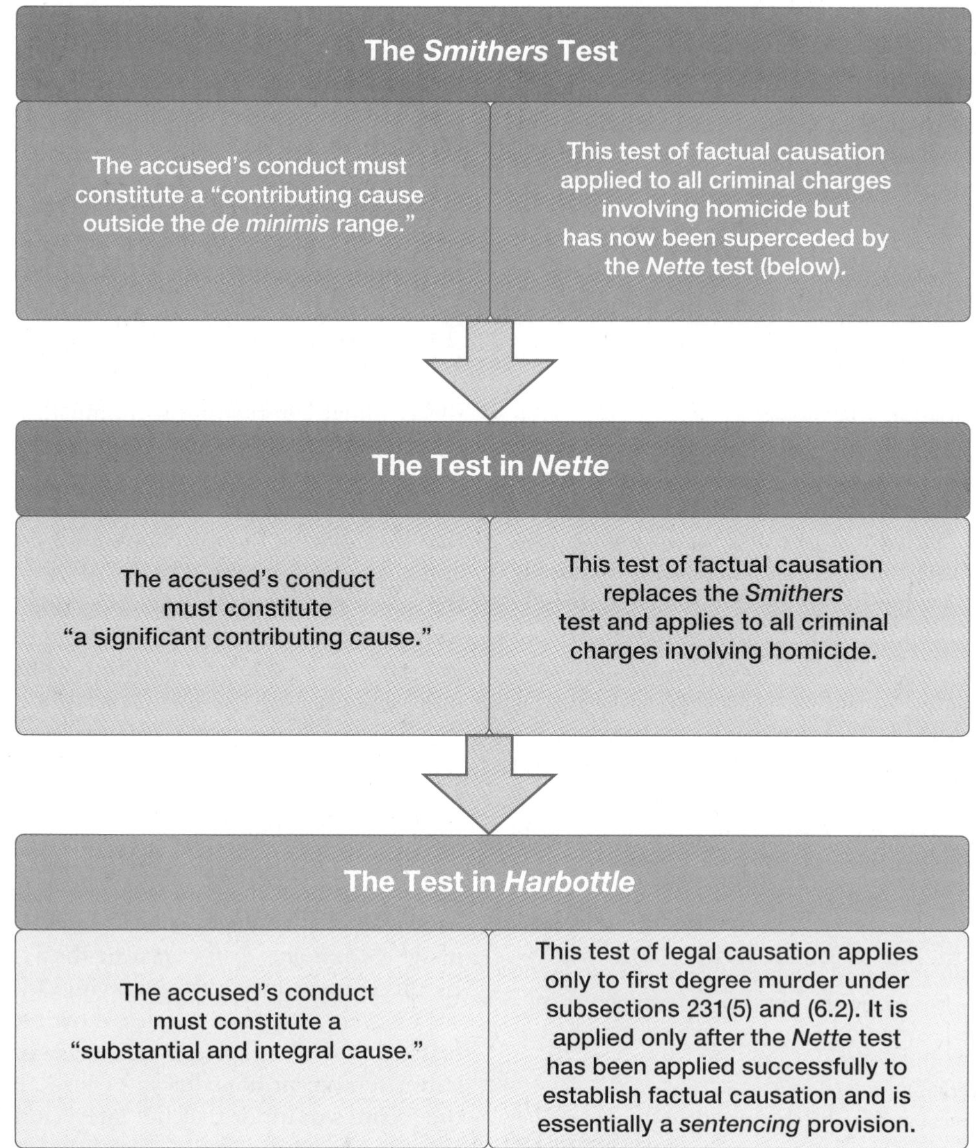

The Smithers Test
The accused's conduct must constitute a "contributing cause outside the de minimis range."
This test of factual causation applied to all criminal charges involving homicide but has now been superceded by the Nette test (below).
The Test in Nette
The accused's conduct must constitute "a significant contributing cause."
This test of factual causation replaces the Smithers test and applies to all criminal charges involving homicide.
The Test in Harbottle
The accused's conduct must constitute a "substantial and integral cause."
This test of legal causation applies only to first degree murder under subsections 231(5) and (6.2). It is applied only after the Nette test has been applied successfully to establish factual causation and is essentially a sentencing provision.

Figure 3-3

Tests of Causation in Homicide Cases

manslaughter of a man called Junor. The defendants inflicted severe brain injuries upon the victim by dropping him on the sidewalk while he was in a state of extreme intoxication. Junor was taken to hospital and attached to a respirator. A neurologist determined that Junor, who was unable to breathe on his own, had suffered complete brain death. However, the respirator continued to maintain the victim's bodily functions until his kidneys could be removed for transplant. After removal of the kidneys, the respirator was switched off. There was some suggestion that the doctors had not followed the correct protocol for establishing total brain death.

At their trial, the defendants were convicted. They then appealed to the Manitoba Court of Appeal. In their appeal, Kitching and Adams contended that it was the removal of the kidneys that actually caused Junor's death and that the conduct of the doctors, in effecting this removal, broke the chain of causation between their conduct and Junor's tragic death. However, this contention was rejected by the Court of Appeal. For example, Justice O'Sullivan said:

> The assumption underlying counsel's conduct in this case is that there can be only one cause of death. I think the law is that the conduct of a defendant in a criminal trial need not be shown to be the sole or "the effective" cause of a crime. It is sufficient if it is a cause. ... I think the authorities are clear that there may be two or more independent operative causes of death.

Whether or not the doctors had acted improperly (and the court was not making any such suggestion in such regard), the critical point must be that their conduct was, in the circumstances, entirely irrelevant to the issue of the criminal responsibility of Kitching and Adams. Even if the doctors' conduct in removing the kidneys of Junor could be said to have contributed to his death, the chain of causation that ran between Kitchen and Adams's dropping of Junor on the sidewalk and his ultimate demise had *not* been severed if their actions still constituted "an operative cause" of Junor's death.

As Justice O'Sullivan pointed out, "On that question, the evidence was overwhelming. Whether or not the kidneys had been removed, the deceased could not have lasted more than a short period of time even with artificial assistance."

In *Maybin* (2012), the Supreme Court of Canada was presented with a case in which the intervening act was another wound inflicted by a third party. The two Maybin brothers had been playing a game of pool, which was interrupted when the victim moved one or two of the balls on the table. One of the brothers repeatedly punched the victim in the head while the other assisted him in doing so. The victim fell into a state of unconsciousness, face down on the pool table. A bouncer at the bar witnessed the attack and asked who started the fight. One of the customers pointed to the victim and the bouncer went up to the pool table, punched the victim in the back of the head, removed him from the bar, and dumped him on the sidewalk. The victim expired as a consequence of head injuries and the Maybin brothers were charged with manslaughter. The trial judge could not decide whether it was the blows administered by the brothers or the blow inflicted by the bouncer that had caused the victim's death and acquitted the Maybin brothers. The Crown appealed the acquittals to the B.C. Court of Appeal, which ordered a new trial for the Maybins. The Court was satisfied that *factual causation* had been proved with respect to the Maybin brothers: "*but for*" their attack on the victim, he would not have been killed. As for *legal causation*, the Court of Appeal suggested that it was open to the trial judge to find that even if it was the blow delivered by the bouncer that actually caused the death, the violent intervention of the bouncer was nevertheless reasonably foreseeable by the Maybin brothers.

The Supreme Court of Canada rejected the subsequent appeal by the Maybin brothers. The Court agreed that the intervention of the bouncer was reasonably foreseeable on the part of the Maybin brothers: in this sense, their initial assault on the victim must be considered a "significant, contributing cause" to his death. The Maybin brothers had initiated a one-sided brawl in a busy bar with many patrons present and consuming alcohol. It was late in the evening, and the Maybin brothers clearly knew that, at that time, there were security personnel in the near vicinity. It was reasonably foreseeable that any fight might escalate to the point where intervention by the security personnel would be required to prevent other patrons from entering the fray or to take control of the situation—by force, if necessary. In this case, the bouncer testified that he hit the victim to gain control of the situation, since he had been told that the victim was the instigator of the fight. Some type of intervening act by the bouncer was, therefore, eminently foreseeable even though the precise nature of that intervention could not be contemplated at the time of the brothers' assault on the victim. On behalf of the Supreme Court of Canada, Justice Karakatsanis concluded that:

> Courts have used a number of analytical approaches to determine when an intervening act absolves the accused of legal responsibility for manslaughter. These approaches grapple with the issue of the moral connection between the accused's acts and the death; they acknowledge that an intervening act that is reasonably foreseeable to the accused may well not break the chain of causation, and that an independent and intentional act by a third party may in some cases make it unfair to hold the accused responsible. In my view, these approaches may be useful tools depending upon the factual context. However, the analysis must focus on first principles and recognize that these tools do not alter the standard of causation or substitute new tests. The dangerous and unlawful acts of the accused must be a significant contributing cause of the victim's death.

Justice Karakatsanis agreed with the Court of Appeal that, in light of the trial judge's findings of fact, it was logical for him to conclude that the general nature of the bouncer's intervention and the likelihood that this might inflict harm on the victim were reasonably foreseeable outcomes of the Maybins' attack on the victim. Furthermore, the bouncer's intervention was a direct response to the assaultive behaviour of the Maybins. In these circumstances, the trial judge was perfectly entitled to conclude that the Maybins' attack on the victim was a "significant contributing cause" of the victim's death—even if the bouncer's blow to the head and dumping of the victim on the sidewalk were also significant contributing causes of his death. In brief, the trial judge could reasonably conclude that the bouncer's actions had *not* severed the chain of causation between the Maybins' assault on the victim and his ultimate demise. In this sense, the Maybins had indeed caused the victim's death, no matter what injuries the bouncer may have inflicted on the victim in the course of his intervention.

Of course, there may be situations in which an intervening act does operate to sever the causal chain between the conduct of the accused in wounding the victim and the ultimate death of that victim. The Supreme Court of Canada dealt with just such a situation in *Sarrazin* (2011), although, in this case, the intervening act that caused death was the victim's own conduct in taking a dangerous drug. Sarrazin and Jean shot Apaid Noël, a member of a rival gang, in the forearm and abdomen. The wound to the abdomen was life threatening, with particularly grave damage to the liver. Highly skillful surgical intervention and expert medical care saved Noël's life and, about a month later, he was released from hospital. However, only five days later, Noël suddenly collapsed and died from a blood clot in the lung. An autopsy revealed that there were trace elements of cocaine in Noël's blood and that the cocaine had been ingested between 30 and 45 minutes before his death. Expert evidence was given to the effect that the fatal blood clot was probably related to the gunshot wound to the abdomen, but, "given that cocaine could cause hypercoagulability (propensity to develop blood clots), the pathologist called by the Crown refused at trial to rule out the possibility that the clot was *entirely* the result of the victim's consumption of cocaine." Sarrazin and Jean argued that it was the cocaine ingested by Noël—and not the abdominal wound—that caused the blood clot that killed him. If this were true, then they would be guilty of *attempted* murder rather than of murder itself. However, the trial judge did not leave the jury with the option of convicting Sarrazin and Jean of attempted murder and they were ultimately convicted of second-degree murder. The Ontario Court of Appeal ordered a new trial for the two accused because the trial judge had made a mistake by refusing to allow the jury to consider the option of a verdict of attempted murder. If the accused could raise a reasonable doubt as to whether they caused the death of Noël, they were entitled to be acquitted of murder: if the blood clot was caused entirely by the consumption of cocaine, then the chain of causation would clearly have been broken between the infliction of the abdominal wound and Noël's ultimate demise.

The Supreme Court of Canada affirmed the ruling of the Court of Appeal. On behalf of the majority of the justices, Justice Binnie said:

> The need to prove causation is common to both murder and manslaughter. The Crown must establish beyond a reasonable doubt that the shooting significantly contributed to Noël's death. ... If the evidence of the Crown pathologist left the members of the jury with a doubt on that account, then at most the respondents could be convicted of an *attempt* to murder—an attempt foiled by the skill of the surgeon, Dr. Freeman. ... As Arbour J. had pointed out in *Nette*, where "causation was not proven, a proper verdict might be attempted murder."

Similar considerations apply when the victim dies as a result of some external event or act of nature that would not have killed the victim if the accused had not wounded the victim and left them exposed to the elements. In these circumstances, the liability of the accused will depend upon *whether the victim's death from the external event or act of nature can be viewed as a "natural consequence" of the accused person's conduct*. In other words, the question is, would a reasonable person have foreseen the likelihood of the victim's death from the external event or act of nature? For example, in the *Younger* case (2004), the accused had left a two-and-a-half-year-old boy in a van in a parking lot in Winnipeg at a time when the outside temperature was around minus 2 degrees Celsius. The boy died of hypothermia. Younger was convicted of murder and his appeal was rejected by the Manitoba Court of Appeal. In delivering the judgment of the Court, Justice Twaddle ruled that the verdict of the jury at Younger's trial was not unreasonable: "The jury was entitled to infer that someone living in Winnipeg in the winter months would know that continued exposure to a sub-zero Celsius temperature for even an hour or so would likely cause the death of a scantily clad young child."

Illustration by Greg Holoboff

Can the victim's death from an intervening event or act of nature be viewed as a "natural consequence" of the accused person's conduct?

On the other hand, in *Nodrick* (2012), the accused took the "frail, diabetic 65-year-old" victim to a remote field and left him there, having removed all his clothes with the exception of his underwear and shoes. Nodrick then attempted to withdraw money from an ATM at a local gas station, having previously extracted the victim's PIN from him at the field. Although there were a farmhouse, various residences, and a golf course very close to the field, the victim wandered around aimlessly and did not find his way out. After two to seven days in the field, he died of hypothermia "following exposure to the elements." At the time, the weather conditions had been relatively clement, with temperatures ranging from highs of 15.9 to 29.4 to lows of 6.7 to 17.2 degrees Celsius. Furthermore, the victim was able to move freely, and there was no evidence to suggest that he was unable to leave the field where he had been left. There was no doubt that there was *factual causation*—after all, if Nodrick had not taken the victim to the field, the victim would not have died from exposure. The central issue, therefore, was whether there was *legal causation*. Would a reasonable person, standing in Nodrick's shoes, have foreseen the likelihood of the victim's death in the circumstances that prevailed at that time? At his trial, the jury acquitted Nodrick of second-degree murder. The Crown appealed against this verdict, but the Manitoba Court of Appeal upheld the acquittal. In delivering the judgment of the Court of Appeal, Justice Chartier ruled that:

> In my view, it seems apparent ... that the jury acquitted the accused not because it had a doubt that the accused's actions were a significant contributing cause of the death, but rather because it had a doubt on the question of whether any reasonable person in the circumstances would think that leaving this victim in the way he was left, on a warm, sunny day, near a farmhouse and golf course, would likely have put him at risk of some harm or injury that was more than brief or minor in nature. In light of the evidence before the jury, it was a finding that was most certainly open to it.

The Impact of Improper Medical Treatment upon the Chain of Causation

A fascinating area of the law concerns the question of whether **improper medical treatment** administered to the victim may be considered to have broken the chain of causation between the accused's original wounding of the victim and the latter's death. Two leading cases in this area are English, but the principles expressed in them have certainly been approved by Canadian courts. In *Jordan* (1956), the accused had been convicted of the murder of a man called Beaumont and had been sentenced to death. Jordan had stabbed Beaumont in the abdomen in the course of a disturbance at a café. However, upon his appeal to the English Court of Criminal Appeal, new medical evidence was introduced. The evidence tended to establish that Beaumont had been subjected to improper medical treatment. First, he had been administered an antibiotic drug to which he proved to be intolerant. After severe diarrhea developed, the administration of the drug was discontinued. However, the next day, a different physician recommenced therapy with the same drug. Second, in the words of the court:

> Other steps were taken which were also regarded by the doctors as wrong—namely, the intravenous introduction of wholly abnormal quantities of liquid far exceeding the output. As a result the lungs became water-logged and pulmonary oedema was discovered. Mr. Blackburn said that he was not surprised to see that condition after the introduction of so much liquid, and that pulmonary oedema leads to broncho-pneumonia as an inevitable sequel, and it was from broncho-pneumonia that Beaumont died.

Another critical element of the medical evidence was the assertion that although the original stab wound had penetrated the intestine of the victim, it had "mainly healed at the time of death." In these circumstances, the court quashed Jordan's conviction. Clearly, the improper (and grossly negligent) treatment had *broken the chain of causation between the original wounding and Beaumont's sad death*. Indeed, since the wound was mainly healed, it could not be said that it was an operative cause of death at the time that Beaumont expired. In effect, it was the physicians who effectively killed Beaumont, not the accused.

In stark contrast to *Jordan* is the English case of *Smith* (1959), in which the accused was convicted by a general court-martial of the murder of Private Creed (a soldier in a "rival" regiment). Smith had stabbed Creed with a bayonet in the course of a confrontation between men of two British regiments stationed in Germany. Creed was dropped twice on his way to the first aid station, where the attending medical officer was so busy dealing with other victims of the disturbance that he did not have time to appreciate the seriousness of Creed's medical condition. He was given artificial respiration (which was an inappropriate treatment given the fact that his lung had been punctured) and a transfusion of saline solution, since no facilities for a blood transfusion were available. The unfortunate Private Creed died approximately two hours after the stabbing had occurred. Medical evidence for the defence contended that had Creed not received such inappropriate treatment and had he been given a blood transfusion, the chances for his recovery would have been "as high as 75 percent."

Defence counsel relied on the *Jordan* case in pressing the Courts-Martial Appeal Court to quash Smith's conviction. Nevertheless, the conviction was upheld. Lord Chief Justice Parker stated that:

> It seems to the court that if at the time of death the original wound is still an operating cause and a substantial cause, then the death can properly be said to be the result of the wound, albeit that some other cause of death is also operating. Only if it can be said that the original wounding is merely the setting in which another cause operates can it be said that the death does not result from the wound. Putting it another way, only if the second cause is so overwhelming as to make the original wound merely part of the history can it be said that the death does not flow from the wound.

Since Private Creed died so quickly after the original stab wounds, it was clear that Smith's conduct was "an operating and substantial cause" of death at the time Creed expired. In the *Jordan* case, the victim died a number of days after the original wounding and, furthermore, the stab wounds had mainly healed when the improper treatments were administered. In this sense, the original wound was "merely part of the history" that led to the victim being in the hospital. In the *Smith* case, Lord Chief Justice Parker concluded the judgment of the Court by saying:

> A man is stabbed in the back, his lung is pierced and haemorrhage results; two hours later he dies of haemorrhage from that wound; in the interval there is no time for a careful examination and the treatment given turns out in the light of subsequent knowledge to have been inappropriate and, indeed, harmful. In those circumstances no reasonable jury or court could, properly directed, in our view possibly come to any other conclusion than that the death resulted from the original wound.

The *Smith* case was decided in England, but the legal principle applied is also enshrined in section 225 of the Canadian *Criminal Code*:

> Where a person causes to a human being a bodily injury that is of itself of a dangerous nature and from which death results, he causes the death of that human being notwithstanding that the immediate cause of death is proper or improper treatment that is applied in good faith.

It will be noted that section 225 refers only to treatment "that is applied in good faith." Presumably,

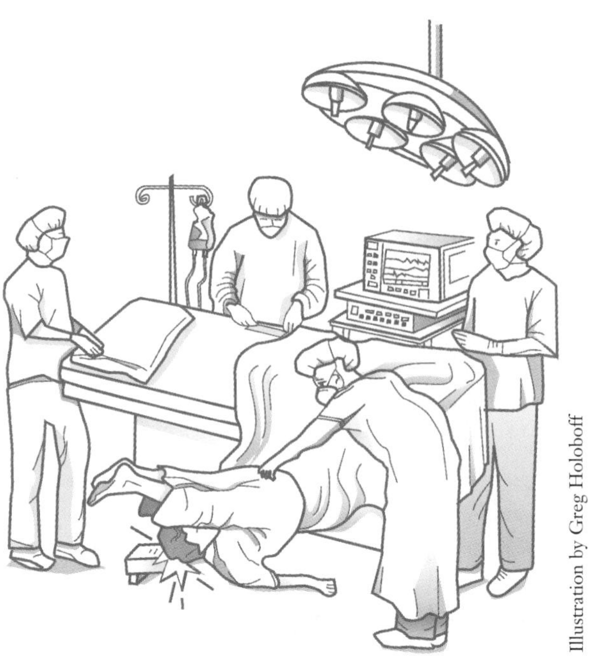

Illustration by Greg Holoboff

A seriously wounded patient crashes to the floor. Is the chain of causation broken?

improper medical treatment that is administered, for example, by a grossly intoxicated surgeon would not be considered to have been applied in good faith; therefore, in such a case, the accused might well argue that the chain of causation has been broken by the improper treatment and that, owing to its specific wording, section 225 is not applicable.

Refusal of Treatment by the Victim of an Assault

Another provision of the *Criminal Code* that raises important issues concerning causation in homicide cases is section 224: "Where a person, by an act or omission, does anything that results in the death of a human being, he causes the death of that human being notwithstanding that death from that cause might have been prevented by resorting to proper means."

One potential application of this section of the *Code* is to the situation where the victim of an assault refuses to take medical treatment. For example, in the old English case of *Holland* (1841), the accused was charged with the murder of a man called Garland. He had severely cut Garland across one of his fingers with an iron instrument during the course of an ambush. Despite medical advice concerning the very real dangers of infection, Garland refused to have his finger amputated. Two weeks later, Garland contracted lockjaw (tetanus) from the wound and, although the finger was then amputated, it was too late to save his life. Holland was, nevertheless, convicted of murder. Justice Maule said:

> [I]t made no difference whether the wound was in its own nature instantly mortal, or whether it became the cause of death by reason of the deceased not having adopted the best mode of treatment, the real question is, whether in the end the wound inflicted by the prisoner was the cause of death?

It might well be contended that the victim did not behave unreasonably in this case, since the standards of surgical amputation in 1841 might well have given cause for second thoughts even to the bravest of people. Today, it is likely that the victim in the *Holland* case would be well advised to have an anti-tetanus injection to prevent a catastrophic infection of his wound. One wonders if a modern court would convict an accused person of murder if the victim of a finger injury chooses to ignore this medical counsel and subsequently succumbs to a tetanus infection? After all, if the defendant can show that a simple injection could have prevented death from a relatively minor wound, should they be convicted of manslaughter if the victim resolutely refused a treatment that would have been highly effective and would have been both safe and relatively painless? Unfortunately, section 224 would appear to require that the accused be convicted in spite of these considerations because it does not require that the original wound be "serious in nature."

Traditionally, criminal law has taken the view that violent persons must take their victims as they find them. It is no defence for an accused person to claim that the victim had a "thin skull" or an exceedingly weak heart. Equally, it is no defence to claim the victim brought about their own death by refusing treatment. Quite simply, the problem is that it is difficult to decide whether a victim's refusal of treatment is *reasonable or unreasonable.* There may be many other reasons why an accused person might refuse treatment. For example, what is the situation where a victim refuses a potentially life-saving treatment because it offends their religious beliefs? Who is to say whether another person's sincerely held religious beliefs are reasonable or unreasonable?

In the case of *Tower* (2008), the accused had struck his neighbour, Grismajer, across the back with some long-handled pruning shears. Grismajer suffered serious injuries, including fractured ribs and a ruptured spleen. Unfortunately, he stubbornly refused all offers of medical treatment and died in police custody two days later. Tower was charged with manslaughter and, at his trial, one of his defences was that the victim's refusal to accept treatment constituted an intervening act that broke the chain of causation. Tower was nevertheless convicted of manslaughter and his appeal against conviction was dismissed by the Nova Scotia Court of Appeal. Justice Cromwell, of the Court of Appeal, noted that "the common law of causation in criminal law has generally held that failing to obtain medical treatment, or receiving inadequate treatment, could not break the chain of causation between an injury and death," and he pointed out that section 224 of the *Criminal Code* "may well reinforce this view." Justice Cromwell also emphasized that, "even with the appropriate care," the victim had suffered "a very serious injury" at Tower's hands and would have required major surgery "with all its inherent risks."

Given the undoubted severity of the injuries inflicted by Tower, few would dispute the justice of his conviction of manslaughter. However, it might well be argued that the *Criminal Code* should be amended so that section 224 applies only to those cases *where the initial injury is serious in nature*. This would mean that Tower would not be able to contend that the chain of causation was broken by his victim's failure to accept treatment, because the wound undoubtedly amounted to a life-threatening injury. On the other hand, Holland (if tried today) would be acquitted under such an amended provision, because the initial injury to the victim's finger was relatively minor and the latter's refusal to take an injection could be considered to have broken the chain of causation. In the *Holland* case, a relatively minor injury led to an infection that killed the victim. In today's setting, he could have avoided this infection very easily by accepting a simple, effective, and (almost) painless injection. To date, no such amendment to the *Criminal Code* has been proposed and, for the present, the courts must continue to convict defendants such as Holland.

Causing Death by Acting on the Victim's Mind

Sections 222(5)(c) and (d) and 228 of the *Criminal Code* establish a number of important principles concerning the causation of death by acting on the victim's mind. Section 222(5)(c) states that a person commits culpable homicide when they cause the death of another person "by causing that human being, by threats of fear or violence or by deception, to do anything that causes his death." This section was applied in the case of *Charbonneau* (2016). The victim, Meunier, was selling drugs in the "territory" of another drug dealer, Charbonneau. He was pepper-sprayed and chased by the "resident" drug dealer and his followers. Seeing no other means of escape, Meunier jumped into a nearby river, in which he sadly drowned. Charbonneau (who considered that Meunier was an interloper on his drug-dealing "territory") and one other accused were convicted of manslaughter. The Quebec Court of Appeal affirmed their convictions. In doing so, Gagnon J.A. stated that:

> ... through their objectively dangerous behaviour, the appellants created the fear in Meunier that he would be the victim of violence. The armed assault, their repeated threats, and the chase made the risk that Meunier would suffer bodily harm that was neither trivial nor transient reasonably foreseeable. Furthermore, the fear created by the remarks and actions of the appellants caused Meunier to throw himself into the water to escape from them, a decision that ultimately cost him his life.

The Court of Appeal noted that Section 222(5)(c) requires a form of "double causation" insofar as the accused has to cause the victim to take action that causes their own death. The Court also rejected a *Charter* challenge to section 222(5)(c), stating that it did not infringe the fundamental principles of justice protected by section 7 of the *Charter*. Gagnon J.A. ruled that the section "is neither too vague nor imprecise, that its scope is not overbroad, and that it does not violate the principles of fundamental justice."

Significantly, section 228 of the *Criminal Code* indicates that there are strict limitations upon the criminal law's power to punish individuals for homicides caused by an "influence on the mind." This section provides that:

> No person commits culpable homicide where he causes the death of a human being

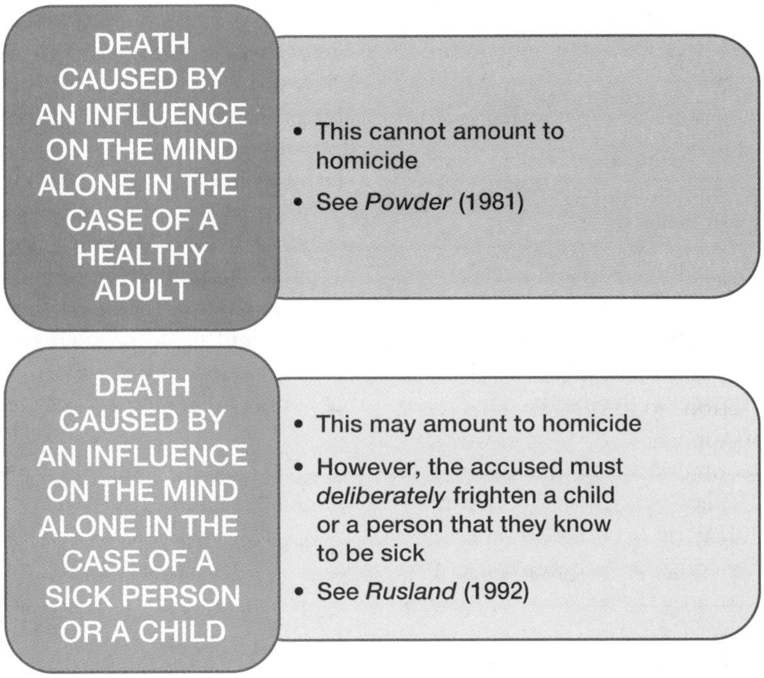

DEATH CAUSED BY AN INFLUENCE ON THE MIND ALONE IN THE CASE OF A HEALTHY ADULT	• This cannot amount to homicide • See *Powder* (1981)
DEATH CAUSED BY AN INFLUENCE ON THE MIND ALONE IN THE CASE OF A SICK PERSON OR A CHILD	• This may amount to homicide • However, the accused must *deliberately* frighten a child or a person that they know to be sick • See *Rusland* (1992)

Figure 3-4

Homicide by an Influence on the Mind [Sections 222(5)(d) and 228]

> (a) by any influence on the mind alone, or
>
> (b) by any disorder or disease resulting from influence on the mind alone, but this section does not apply where a person causes the death of a child or sick person by wilfully frightening him.

Essentially, this provision states that an accused person cannot be convicted of homicide if they cause death solely by psychological means—except where they deliberately frighten a child or sick victim. Section 222(5)(d) explicitly recognizes the exception to the general rule, since it provides that culpable homicide is committed when an accused person causes the death of another "by wilfully frightening that human being, in the case of a child or sick person."

Section 228 was relied upon by the Alberta Court of Appeal when it quashed a verdict of manslaughter in the case of *Powder* (1981). It appears that the accused was involved in a break-in when he was confronted by the deceased. There was a struggle and the deceased died as a result of acute heart failure that had been caused by the "fear and emotional stress" generated by the break-in and subsequent conflict. There was no evidence that the *physical* strain involved in the struggle or any blow struck by the accused contributed in any way to the victim's death. The deceased had a pre existing heart condition that was precipitated by the fear and emotional stress that engulfed him. In other words, the deceased had died as a consequence of an "influence on his mind alone"; therefore, section 228 was applicable and the accused could not be convicted of homicide.

The *Powder* case should be compared with that of *Rusland* (1992). Here, the accused had physically assaulted a 66-year-old man who had suffered a heart attack a few months prior to the assault and was waiting for bypass surgery. The victim died as a consequence of the fracas. The trial judge acquitted Rusland and purported to follow the *Powder* (1981) decision insofar as he concluded that "the death of the deceased, by reason of his medical history, was not culpable homicide, being caused by stress only in an emotional situation." However, the Crown's appeal against this acquittal was allowed by the Ontario Court of Appeal, which ordered a new trial. The Court of Appeal pointed out that there was evidence that Rusland *actually knew about the dangerous health condition* suffered by the victim:

> Despite that knowledge, there is evidence that [Rusland] placed his hands on the deceased's shoulders and pushed or chucked [*sic*] the deceased who had come to intervene after the respondent had struck his own mother in the face."

If the new trial established that Rusland knew about the victim's perilous state of health and *wilfully frightened him*, section 228 would not save him from a conviction of manslaughter—even though the deceased died as a consequence of an "influence on the mind alone."

What is the difference between the *Powder* and *Rusland* cases? In the *Powder* case, the accused did not know of his victim's heart disease and thus a reasonable person in the same circumstances could not have known that wilfully (deliberately) frightening the victim would likely cause him to suffer serious bodily harm. In *Rusland*, there was evidence to suggest that the accused knew about the deceased's cardiac condition and deliberately frightened him by pushing him around: a reasonable person standing in Rusland's shoes would have foreseen that this conduct would cause serious bodily harm to the victim (the *mens rea* for "unlawful act" manslaughter—see Chapter 5).

Study Questions

1. Krook's driving licence has been suspended following a conviction for impaired driving. However, Krook, who has an extensive criminal record, continues to drive a pickup truck even though he has been banned from operating a motor vehicle and has no insurance. While driving in a mainly rural area, Krook is recognized by Boffin, a police officer who is patrolling in a cruiser. Boffin turns on his flashing lights and uses a loudspeaker to order Krook to pull over and stop. Krook deliberately ignores Boffin's command and flees the scene at very high speed. Boffin pursues Krook and turns on his siren. Krook and Boffin reach speeds of 160 kilometres an hour, drive through a red light, and ignore at least one stop sign. Sadly, Boffin's vehicle strikes and kills Pip, a young child who is crossing the road in a small rural town. Krook is charged with the offence of causing death by dangerous operation of a motor vehicle (contrary to subsections 320.13 (1) and 320.21 of the *Criminal Code*). Krook's lawyer contends that his client cannot be convicted of this offence since Krook was not operating the vehicle that actually struck and killed Pip. What arguments could the Crown advance to obtain a conviction?

2. Grimwig attacks Dora with a knife and gravely injures her. He steals her handbag and runs away. Dora is taken to hospital, where she is told that she must have a blood transfusion. She refuses this treatment on religious grounds. Dora dies a day later and Grimwig is charged with murder. A doctor says Dora would have had a 95 percent chance of survival if she had taken the transfusion. Is Grimwig guilty of murder?

3. Sikes is late for a critical business appointment and is desperately searching for a taxi to get him there quickly. He notices that Durdles is just about to enter a taxi, so he violently pushes Durdles away and jumps into the back seat of the vehicle. Tragically, Durdles falls and his head hits the sidewalk. Durdles later dies from his head injuries. The neurological specialist is prepared to testify that Durdles had an "eggshell-thin" skull and that, although the fall would not have killed an ordinary person, the combination of the fall and the structural weakness of the skull was the sole cause of death in this particular case. Sikes is charged with manslaughter. His counsel argues that Sikes did not cause Durdles's death; in fact, she argues, it was caused by what amounts to an "act of God." Does Sikes have a valid defence?

4. Magwitch shoots Compeyson in the abdomen and the latter is immediately taken to hospital. An emergency operation is undertaken and the bullet is removed from Compeyson's body. At first, Compeyson appears to be making excellent progress, but after about a week, he develops some internal bleeding. Compeyson is operated on by Dr. Death, who has taken a large dose of amphetamines. Dr. Death fails to stop the bleeding and Compeyson

dies the next day. An independent medical specialist states that "any competent surgeon" would have saved Compeyson's life. Would Magwitch be considered criminally responsible for Compeyson's death?

5. Duncan attacks Macbeth, who is strolling through a wheat field. Duncan knocks Macbeth unconscious and then leaves him lying on the ground. An hour later, a combine harvester passes over the spot where Macbeth is lying and he is killed. Is Duncan criminally responsible for Macbeth's death?
6. Clara knows that her husband, Sampson, has a very serious heart condition. Indeed, his physician has made it clear to Clara that excessive exertion and/or fright could kill Sampson. One night, Clara turns off all the electrical power in their house and puts on a terrifying mask. She then goes into the room where Sampson is resting on his bed and jumps on him. Sampson believes that Clara is an intruder who is trying to kill him. Suddenly, he loses consciousness and expires then and there. A medical expert concludes that Sampson died of a catastrophic heart attack that had probably been caused by fright. Clara says that she was indulging only in some fun and that she and Sampson frequently played such games with each other. If Clara were to be charged with murder or manslaughter, would she have a defence?
7. Lillyvick, Slackbridge, and Nubbles are drinking heavily in a bar. They enter into a heated argument with Orlick, who is also very intoxicated. Lillyvick, Slackbridge, and Nubbles attack Orlick, who falls to the ground. Each of Orlick's assailants kicks Orlick in the head and upper body. Orlick lapses into a state of unconsciousness. Orlick is taken to the hospital, where he is diagnosed as suffering from a brain injury, and it is decided that he requires immediate surgery to stop the bleeding within his skull. While Orlick is being transported to the operating room, he falls off the trolley and suffers a further injury to his head. This accident occurs because the hospital staff did not follow the recognized procedures for securing an unconscious patient and did not maintain a proper lookout while transporting him. Orlick undergoes surgery and, after two days, he appears to have a chance of recovery. However, he then succumbs to a virulent bacterial infection and dies within a week of the original assault in the bar. There is evidence that the infection was almost certainly caused by negligent sterilization procedures in the operating room. A neurologist will testify that the assault on Orlick in the bar caused serious injury to the brain and that it is impossible to determine whether he would have recovered from this injury if he had not been the object of poor treatment in the hospital. The neurologist also states that the head trauma suffered by Orlick when he fell off the trolley probably aggravated his preexisting injury. Lillyvick, Slackbridge, and Nubbles are charged with manslaughter, but they contend that, in light of what transpired in the hospital, they did not cause Orlick's death. Is it likely that they would be acquitted of manslaughter?
8. Arthur Clennam is dying from an intensely painful form of cancer. His physician, Rachael, thinks that he will certainly die within 48 hours. Arthur begs for more effective pain-killing medications, but he has developed such a high tolerance to the drugs that they no longer provide much relief, even at the maximum doses that are permitted. Arthur's family begs Rachael to "do something" to put Arthur out of his pain. Rachael realizes that there is no time to follow the procedures of the Medical Assistance in Dying legislation so she injects a very large dose of morphine, which brings about a painless death in two hours. A pharmacologist, Sairey Gamp, is prepared to testify that the final dose of morphine that Rachael administered would undoubtedly be fatal for any patient. Rachael said that her sole intention was to reduce Arthur's pain and that the large dose of morphine was necessary since Arthur had developed such a high level of tolerance to the drug. Is Rachael guilty of a criminal offence?
9. Do you think that the Medical Assistance in Dying legislation is constitutional in light of the reasons given in the decision of the Supreme Court of Canada in *Carter v. Canada (Attorney General)* (2015)? What provisions might be vulnerable to a *Charter* challenge?
10. In 2001, the Netherlands legalized—and strictly regulated—euthanasia and assisted suicide, provided they are carried out by medical practitioners. Belgium and Luxembourg later enacted similar legislation. Using the Internet and library-based methods of research, examine the experience with euthanasia and assisted suicide in the Netherlands, Belgium, and Luxembourg. You might also wish to examine the experience of the American states of Montana, Oregon, Vermont, and Washington, which have legalized physician-assisted suicide in certain circumstances. How does the legislation in these

jurisdictions compare to the Canadian Medical Assistance in Dying legislation?

11. Bumble follows his enemy, Gargery, to a deserted beach. Bumble hits Gargery repeatedly on the head with a baseball bat. Gargery is quickly rendered unconscious and Bumble leaves him crumpled up on the sand, knowing that there is a tide that will cause the seawater to advance up the beach where Gargery is lying unconscious. Subsequently, the tide comes in and Gargery is drowned. A postmortem reveals that Gargery died from drowning and that, since no major brain damage could be identified, he would most probably have recovered from his head wounds. Bumble is charged with manslaughter. His defence is that he did not cause Gargery's death: as the medical evidence demonstrates, Gargery died as a result of drowning and not as a consequence of his head wounds. Do you think that Bumble's defence would be successful at trial?

THE MENTAL ELEMENT IN THE CRIMINAL LAW:

Subjective Liability

CHAPTER 4

Learning Objectives

After reading this chapter, you will be able to understand:

- the meaning of *mens rea*: namely, all the mental elements (other than voluntariness) that the Crown must prove to obtain a conviction of a criminal offence;
- the difference between subjective and objective *mens rea*;
- the basic forms of subjective *mens rea*: namely, intention, knowledge, recklessness, and wilful blindness;
- the fact that many crimes require proof of additional mental elements beyond the basic forms of subjective *mens rea*: for example, "fraudulently" (in relation to theft, under section 322), "fraudulent" (in relation to the offence of fraud under section 380), and "planned and deliberate" (in relation to the distinction between first- and second-degree murder, under section 231; and
- the principle that the *Canadian Charter of Rights and Freedoms* may prescribe that the courts impose a minimum requirement of subjective *mens rea* for exceptionally serious crimes, such as murder.

MENS REA: AN INTRODUCTION

In Chapter 2, we saw how the terms *actus reus* and *mens rea* were derived from the Latin maxim "*actus non facit reum nisi mens sit rea*," or "an act does not render a person guilty of a criminal offence unless their mind is also guilty." Chapters 4 and 5 turn the spotlight on the principles that apply when a court is required to determine whether an accused person's "mind is guilty." In short, these two chapters will identify the various *mens rea* elements of a criminal offence that must be established before individuals may be held criminally responsible for their conduct.

In Chapter 2, it was also pointed out that it would be a mistake to assume that there is a clear-cut distinction between the physical and mental elements of a criminal offence. Indeed, since an accused person's act must be *voluntary* for a court to find that the *actus reus* elements are present, the *actus reus* essentially contains its own mental element. So, what is meant by the term *mens rea*? Simply put, ***mens rea*** refers to all of the mental elements (other than voluntariness) that the Crown must prove to obtain a conviction of a criminal offence. These mental elements inevitably vary from crime to crime. The *mens rea* for murder is obviously very different from the *mens rea* required for theft or arson. To ascertain the necessary *mens rea* elements that must be established by the Crown, it is therefore vital to analyze the mental element(s) that are required in relation to each component of the *actus reus* of the specific offence concerned (that is, conduct, circumstances, and consequences). For example, the Crown may be required to prove that the accused acted intentionally, with full knowledge of the relevant circumstances and of the probable consequences of their actions.

The *mens rea* elements of an offence are of paramount importance in criminal law because they operate to ensure that only those who are *morally blameworthy* are convicted of "true crimes" under the *Criminal Code*. As Justice McLachlin of the Supreme Court of Canada said in the case of *Théroux* (1993), "*Mens rea* ... refers to the guilty mind, the wrongful intention, of the accused. Its function in the criminal law is to prevent the conviction of the morally innocent—those who do not understand or intend the consequences of their acts."

Similarly, Justice Lamer of the Supreme Court of Canada said in the *Reference Re Section 94(2) of the Motor Vehicle Act* case (1985):

> It has from time immemorial been part of our system of laws that the innocent not be punished. This principle has long been recognized as an essential element of a system of justice which is founded upon a belief in the dignity and worth of the human person and on the rule of law.

Significantly, Justice Lamer went on to assert that this principle is one of the "fundamental principles of justice" enshrined in section 7 of the *Charter*.

In essence, the *mens rea* requirements of criminal law operate to excuse from criminal liability all those accused persons who cannot be considered to be blameworthy for their conduct. For example, accused persons who act under a fundamental mistake of fact as to an essential element of the *actus reus* of an offence must be acquitted of a true crime because they would lack the necessary *mens rea* for that offence. Consider the situation in which an accused person takes another individual's cellphone, mistakenly believing that it belongs to the accused. There would be no question of convicting the accused of theft because they would lack knowledge of an essential element of the *actus reus* of that crime—namely, that the cellphone was the property of another person. On the facts as the accused honestly believed them to be, they were not committing any crime and, therefore, lacked one of the necessary elements of the *mens rea* for theft.

An accused person may also lack the necessary *mens rea* elements for conviction of an offence where they do not understand or intend the consequences of their actions. Indeed, this proposition was underscored by Justice McLachlin of the Supreme Court of Canada in the case of *Théroux* (1993):

> Typically, *mens rea* is concerned with the consequences of the prohibited *actus reus*. Thus in the crimes of homicide, we speak of the consequence of the voluntary act—intention to cause death, or reckless and wilfully blind persistence in conduct which one knows is likely to cause death. In other offences, such as dangerous driving, the *mens rea* may relate to the failure to consider the consequences of inadvertence.

Clearly, an accused person who does not foresee the consequences of their actions cannot be convicted of murder because it is an essential element of the *mens rea* of murder that the accused person must foresee the likelihood that death will ensue. Similarly, section 16 of the *Criminal Code* provides that those individuals who are so mentally disordered that they do not appreciate what they are doing should be found not criminally responsible: these individuals would not understand the consequences of their actions and are, therefore, lacking in *mens rea*. Likewise, section 13 of the *Criminal Code* stipulates that children who are under the age of 12 cannot be held criminally responsible for their actions. Parliament enacted this provision in recognition of the view that young children are not capable of fully understanding the consequences of their conduct and, in this sense, they do not have the necessary *mens rea* for conviction of a criminal offence.

SUBJECTIVE AND OBJECTIVE *MENS REA*

Although it is clear that an individual who lacks the necessary *mens rea* for an offence cannot be held criminally responsible because they are morally innocent, it is important to recognize that there are two distinct types of *mens rea* requirements in Canadian criminal law. Supreme Court of Canada Justice McLachlin stated in the case of *Creighton* (1993):

> The *mens rea* of a criminal offence may be either subjective or objective, subject to the principle of fundamental justice that the moral fault of the offence must be proportionate to its gravity and penalty. Subjective *mens rea* requires that the accused have intended the consequences of his or her acts, or that, knowing of the probable consequences of those acts, the accused have proceeded recklessly in the face of the risk. The requisite intention or knowledge may be inferred directly from the act and its circumstances. Even in the latter case, however, it is concerned with "what was actually going on in the mind of this particular accused at the time in question." ...
>
> Objective *mens rea*, on the other hand, is not concerned with what the accused intended or knew. Rather the mental fault lies in failure to direct the mind to a risk which the reasonable person would have appreciated. Objective *mens rea* is not concerned with what was actually in the accused's mind, but with what should have been there, had the accused proceeded reasonably.

It is necessary to emphasize that Canadian courts do not apply the rigidly objective test that is implied by Chief Justice McLachlin in the passage in her judgment. As we shall see in Chapter 5, Canadian courts apply a *modified* objective test to crimes that encompass objective *mens rea*. This test takes into account the subjective knowledge that the accused had of the material circumstances and then asks whether a reasonable person acting prudently would have appreciated the risk created by the accused person's conduct. Under the modified objective test, it is still irrelevant whether the accused person subjectively appreciated the risk that their conduct created: however, in asking whether a reasonable person would have appreciated the risk and acted differently, the reasonable person is assumed to have the same knowledge of the circumstances as the accused person had. Therefore, it is important that the courts inquire as to the accused person's subjective knowledge of the material circumstances surrounding the alleged crime even though that crime is one that imposes objective liability. As Charron J. stated in *Beatty* (2008):

> Objective *mens rea* is based on the premise that a reasonable person in the accused's position would have been aware of the risks arising from the conduct. The fault lies in the absence of the requisite mental state of care. ... However, where the accused raises a reasonable doubt whether a reasonable person in his or her position would have been aware of the risks arising from the conduct, the premise for finding objective fault is no longer sound and there must be an acquittal.

Subjective *mens rea* is based on the notion that accused persons may not be convicted of a criminal offence unless they (1) *deliberately intended* to bring about the consequences prohibited by law or (2) *subjectively realized* that their conduct might produce such prohibited consequences and proceeded with this conduct regardless of their actual knowledge of this risk. Subjective *mens rea*, therefore, requires that the Crown prove that the accused *deliberately chose* to do something wrong.

Objective *mens rea*, in contrast, does not require proof that accused persons deliberately intended to bring about a prohibited consequence or even that they subjectively appreciated the risk that their conduct might produce such a result. Objective *mens rea* is predicated on the principle that reasonable persons, in the same circumstances and with the same knowledge of those circumstances as the accused, would have appreciated that their conduct was creating a risk of producing prohibited consequences and would have taken action to avoid doing so. Here the fault of the accused does not lie in deliberately choosing to do something wrong; instead, the fault is to be found in the fact that the accused had the *capacity* to live up to the standard of care expected of a reasonable person and failed to do so. As Justice McLachlin said, in the passage quoted above from the *Creighton* case (1993), "[T]he mental fault lies in failure to direct the mind to a risk which the reasonable person would have appreciated."

It is important to acknowledge that those accused persons who have subjective *mens rea* will generally be treated as being more culpable than those who are convicted on the basis of objective *mens rea:* after all, the former have deliberately chosen to do something wrong, whereas the latter were not even aware of the risk that their conduct was creating (although a reasonable person would have been). The Supreme Court has, therefore, ruled that, to ensure that the degree of punishment imposed on offenders is commensurate with the extent of their fault, the most serious punishments should be reserved for those who are proved to have possessed subjective *mens rea*. As we shall see, the most important example of the application of this principle is in relation to the offence of murder. The Supreme Court of Canada has ruled that since murder carries the most severe penalty in the *Criminal Code* as well as the greatest degree of associated stigma, accused persons may not be convicted of this offence unless they subjectively foresaw the risk that their conduct would bring about someone's death (see the *Martineau* case (1990), discussed later in this chapter).

The Supreme Court of Canada has also repeatedly stated that there is a presumption that the Parliament of Canada intends to require proof of subjective *mens rea* when its legislation creates criminal offences: this means that Parliament has to indicate its intention very clearly before a court will interpret such legislation as imposing objective *mens rea*. As Justice Cromwell said in *R. v. D.L.W.* (2016):

> ... the mental element of many crimes is not specified in the *Code*. Yet, absent a contrary indication, Parliament is presumed to intend that true crimes have a subjective fault component. This is presumed because Parliament is taken to know that under the common law the act is not guilty unless the mind is guilty (*actus non facit reum nisi mens sit rea*). ... Of course, Parliament can provide otherwise, but where it does not, the common law principle is applied.

Justice Cromwell also indicated in *A.D.H.* (2013) that the presumption that Parliament intends to require subjectivity in the absence of a contrary indication is based on a fundamental principle of criminal law: namely, "that the morally innocent should not be punished."

Finally, it is important to bear in mind that there are certain criminal offences that consist of both subjective and objective *mens rea* elements. The appropriate *mens rea* must be identified in relation to each of the components of the *actus reus* of the offence: namely, the conduct, circumstances, and consequences. As Justice Cromwell noted in *A.D.H.* (2013):

> [C]are must ... be taken to distinguish between the act, its circumstances and its consequences in assessing the requisite *mens rea* for the offence.
>
> ... As a general rule, a mental element, whether subjective or objective, will accompany each physical element of a crime, be it the act, its circumstances or its consequences ...
>
> Furthermore, it is worth recalling that a particular offence may well have some mental elements that are assessed subjectively and others that are assessed objectively ...
>
> [O]ne must be careful not to speak of a crime as requiring simply subjective or objective *mens rea*. Such conclusions "tel[l] only part of the story," and a "more precise approach" requires identifying each mental element in relation to its coordinate physical element.

Particular Forms of Subjective *Mens Rea*

The basic forms of subjective *mens rea* that the Crown may be required to prove are *intention*, *knowledge*, *recklessness*, and *wilful blindness*. However, as we shall see later, over and above these basic forms of *mens rea*, there are certain situations in which the Crown must also prove some special mental element that is required by the definition of the particular offence in question (such as "fraud" in the case of a charge of theft under section 322).

The Concepts of Intention and Knowledge

Many of the definitions of criminal offences contained in the *Criminal Code* explicitly require the proof of *mens rea* in the form of an *"intended" consequence or actual "knowledge" of particular circumstances.*

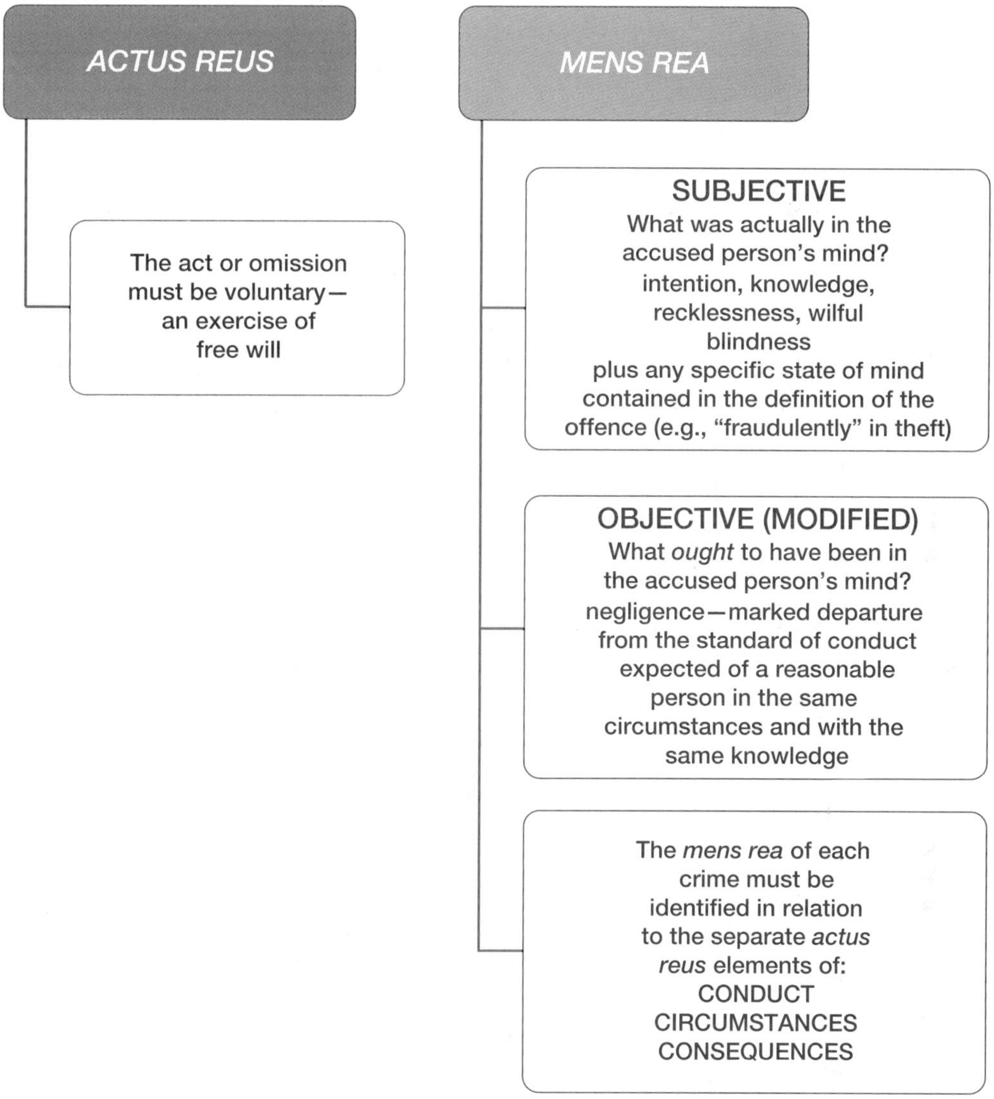

ACTUS REUS

The act or omission must be voluntary—an exercise of free will

MENS REA

SUBJECTIVE
What was actually in the accused person's mind?
intention, knowledge, recklessness, wilful blindness
plus any specific state of mind contained in the definition of the offence (e.g., "fraudulently" in theft)

OBJECTIVE (MODIFIED)
What *ought* to have been in the accused person's mind?
negligence—marked departure from the standard of conduct expected of a reasonable person in the same circumstances and with the same knowledge

The *mens rea* of each crime must be identified in relation to the separate *actus reus* elements of:
CONDUCT
CIRCUMSTANCES
CONSEQUENCES

Figure 4-1
The Mental Element in Criminal Law

For example, subsection 265(1)(a) of the *Criminal Code* provides that:

> A person commits an assault when
>
> (a) without the consent of another person, he applies force *intentionally* to that other person, directly or indirectly. [emphasis added]

Similarly, section 155(1) provides: "Every one commits incest who, *knowing* that another person is by blood relationship his or her parent, child, brother, sister, grandparent or grandchild, as the case may be, has sexual intercourse with that person" [emphasis added].

In other circumstances, the requirement that the accused intended to bring about a certain consequence, or that they engaged in conduct with knowledge of particular circumstances, may not be expressly stated in the *Code*: nevertheless, the courts may well hold that such a requirement is "implied" by the language used by Parliament. For example, in the case of *Lecompte* (2000), the accused had been charged (under section 66 of the *Criminal Code*) with being a member of an unlawful assembly. Section 63 of the *Code* states that:

> An unlawful assembly is an assembly of three or more persons who, with intent to carry out any common

> purpose, assemble in such a manner or so conduct themselves when they are assembled as to cause persons in the neighbourhood of the assembly to fear, on reasonable grounds, that they
>
> (a) will disturb the peace tumultuously; or
>
> (b) will by that assembly needlessly and without reasonable cause provoke other persons to disturb the peace tumultuously.

Section 63 does not state *explicitly* that an accused person must have knowledge of the likelihood that the assembly of which they are a member will disturb the peace or provoke other individuals to disturb the peace tumultuously. Nevertheless, the Quebec Court of Appeal ruled that such knowledge is an implied element of the *mens rea* requirements for this offence. As Justice Beauregard stated:

> I am of the view that, even before the *Charter*, s. 66 had to be interpreted so as not to render culpable a member of an assembly who did not have knowledge of a fact which gave rise to the fear that the peace would be disturbed tumultuously. The criminal law has never intended to punish a person who is unaware of a relevant fact situation.

Sometimes the *Criminal Code* employs other terms to indicate a requirement of intent. For example, section 139(1) states: "Every one who wilfully attempts in any manner to obstruct, pervert or defeat the course of justice in a judicial proceeding," in the specified circumstances, is guilty of an offence. Similarly, section 229 of the *Code* provides that:

> Culpable homicide is murder
>
> (a) where the person who causes the death of a human being
>
> (i) *means to* cause his death, or
>
> (ii) *means to* cause him bodily harm that he knows is likely to cause his death, and is reckless whether death ensues or not. [emphasis added]

Not surprisingly, Canadian courts have ruled that such terms as "wilfully" and "means to" are merely synonymous with the requirement of "intent."

One final point should be made about the *mens rea* requirement of "knowledge." Where the Crown is required to prove *knowledge* of a particular circumstance or set of circumstances, it must also prove that this particular circumstance or set of circumstances did, in fact, exist. As Supreme Court of Canada Justices Cory and Iacobucci stated in the *Dynar* case (1997), *it is not possible to know something that is false*. Put another way, "knowledge implies truth." In *Dynar*, the Supreme Court ruled that an individual may not be convicted of the crime of laundering money "knowing" that the funds in question are the "proceeds of crime" if the funds have not, in fact, been obtained or derived as a consequence of criminal activity. This reasoning applies even if the accused mistakenly *believed* that the money in question constituted the proceeds of crime. It is significant that, in 1997, after the *Dynar* case went to trial, section 462.31 of the *Criminal Code* was amended so that the relevant offence is now one of laundering money "*knowing or believing* that all or a part of that property or of those proceeds was obtained or derived directly or indirectly" from the commission of a crime.

Special Mental Elements That Must Be Proved in Addition to Intention and Knowledge

Canadian courts have ruled that certain terms in the *Criminal Code* have special technical meanings. When such technical terms are employed in the *Code*, the Crown is required to prove a particular mental state in addition to intention or knowledge. Conspicuous examples of such special technical terms are **"fraudulently"** (in relation to theft, under section 322), "fraudulent" (in relation to the offence of fraud under section 380), and **"planned and deliberate"** (in relation to the distinction between first- and second-degree murder under section 231).

The Meaning of "Fraudulently" in Section 322 of the Code (Theft)

An important example of a special mental element that must be established as part of the *mens rea* of an offence is the requirement that the accused person act "fraudulently" in the context of a charge of theft under section 322 of the *Criminal Code*. The implications of this requirement are well illustrated by the application of the legal principle that an accused person may not be convicted of theft if they have engaged in conduct that the court considers to have been merely a "prank" or a "well-intentioned blunder." It has been ruled, in such circumstances, that the accused person did not act *fraudulently* and, therefore, lacked the necessary *mens rea* for conviction of theft. Section 322 of the *Criminal Code* provides that:

> Every one commits theft who fraudulently and without colour of right takes, or fraudulently and

> without colour of right converts to his use or to the use of another person, anything whether animate or inanimate, with intent,
>
> (a) to deprive, temporarily or absolutely, the owner of it, or a person who has a special property or interest in it, of the thing or of his property or interest in it.

In the case of *Wilkins* (1965), the accused was charged with the theft of a police officer's motorcycle. Nichol, the police officer, was engaged in the act of writing out a parking ticket to place on the windshield of a car owned by Wilkins's friend. At this point, Wilkins told Nichol that he would ride the officer's vehicle around the parking lot if Nichol did not cease ticketing the friend's car. The officer did not hear what was being said to him and Wilkins drove the motorcycle down the street, where he was intercepted by a police cruiser. He was subsequently charged with theft. Wilkins stated, most forcefully, that he had no intention of stealing the motorcycle and was merely playing a joke on Nichol. The accused was ultimately acquitted by the Ontario Court of Appeal. In ordering the accused's acquittal, Justice Roach stated that:

> In the instant case the facts could not possibly justify a conviction of theft. The accused did not intend to steal the vehicle, that is, to convert the property in it to his own use but only to drive it ... his intention was merely to play a joke on Nichol and the Judge so found. The intention to perpetrate this joke, stupid though it was, is incompatible with the evil intent which is inherent in the crime of theft.

However, the courts have emphasized that the so-called "prank" defence is one that has a very narrow scope. For example, in the case of *Neve* (1999), the accused was convicted of robbery (an offence that generally requires the Crown to prove *both* an *assault* and a *theft*). Neve believed that the complainant in this case had beaten one of her pregnant friends, causing a miscarriage. Neve and an associate took the complainant to a field located near a major highway just outside Edmonton. Neve and the associate tore off the complainant's clothes with a knife and left her standing naked in the field, in a temperature of about 5 degrees Celsius. The police found one item of the complainant's clothing at the scene of the incident but, owing to the extreme darkness, did not find any of her other clothes in the immediate vicinity. Neve claimed that her sole objective had been to humiliate the complainant to "get even" for what Neve believed the latter had done to a friend. She emphatically denied that she had taken any of the complainant's clothes for the purpose of sale and so forth. Indeed, the defence suggested that the missing items of clothing had been thrown out of Neve's car when she was leaving the field.

To establish that a theft (and, hence, a robbery) had occurred, the Crown was required, under section 322(1), to prove that Neve had acted "fraudulently." However, Neve said that she had not acted dishonestly. Her counsel contended that dishonesty necessarily involves "swindling or trickery" and that, in this case, Neve's actions had taken place without any "deceit, falsehood, or trickery." Indeed, when the complainant had refused to disrobe herself, then Neve and her friend had "simply removed the complainant's clothes in a straightforward and open manner." Both the trial court and the Alberta Court of Appeal soundly rejected this line of argument and Neve's robbery conviction was ultimately upheld. The Court of Appeal noted that it is irrelevant that the complainant's clothes had been removed in an "open manner":

> The reality is that many thefts and robberies are committed openly, without deception or trickery. The fact that an offender openly and blatantly takes property from a victim makes little difference to the victim. The result is the same; the victim's property has been wrongly taken.
>
> [F]or property to be taken "fraudulently," it is enough that the taking be done intentionally, under no mistake, and with knowledge that the thing taken is the property of another person. This will suffice to characterize the taking as fraudulent.

Defence counsel also advanced the argument that Neve had been engaging in a "prank" and, therefore, could not be considered to have acted "fraudulently." Although the Court of Appeal apparently recognized that certain types of pranks may not amount to theft, it emphatically took the view that, in Neve's case, there was absolutely no basis for characterizing her violent act as a "prank":

> A prank is a practical joke. What happened here does not fit that description. It was a taking for the purpose of depriving the victim, albeit not for the benefit of the taker. It was not a joke and motive does not change the character of the act if the property was taken for the purpose of depriving the owner. Accordingly, the defence thesis that Neve did not take the complainant's clothing "fraudulently" must fail.

Incidentally, it is important to remember that section 322(1)(a) of the *Code* provides that, in relation to a charge of theft, the Crown must prove that the accused intended to deprive the victim of their property "*temporarily or absolutely*." Therefore, it is of no importance that Neve intended to keep the complainant's clothes for only a short period; as the Court of Appeal noted, "the obvious intent was to deprive the complainant of [her clothes] for a period of time, however brief."

In this context, it is noteworthy that the Supreme Court of Canada has emphasized that an accused person can be considered to have acted "fraudulently" even if they claim that there was never any intention to cause loss to the victim. For example, in *Skalbania* (1997), the accused had been charged with theft of $100 000. The Crown relied on section 332 of the *Criminal Code*, which specifies that the crime of theft has been committed if the accused, having received money for a specific purpose, "fraudulently" applies that money to some other, unauthorized purpose. Skalbania had approached a man called Gooch and encouraged him to participate in a real estate deal that the accused was seeking to make with a third party. Gooch gave Skalbania a cheque for $100 000, with an explicit direction that it was to be kept in a trust account pending the outcome of the business negotiations. Skalbania instructed his bookkeeper to transfer the $100 000 from his company's trust account to the company's current account, and all of the money was spent on matters entirely unrelated to the business deal in which Gooch was planning to participate. The business deal never came off, and, more than two months later, Skalbania repaid Gooch his $100 000 together with "a sum by way of compensation for delay and inconvenience."

Had Skalbania committed theft when he deliberately misappropriated money that had been given to him for one specific purpose—namely, the proposed joint business venture between Skalbania and Gooch? It was clear that Skalbania had used the funds in the trust account for unauthorized purposes, but had he acted "fraudulently"? The accused claimed that he always intended to reimburse Gooch in full, should the business deal fall through, and that he had demonstrated his good faith by returning the money with interest. The Supreme Court of Canada held that Skalbania had, in fact, acted "fraudulently," even though the accused was adamant that he had not intended to *steal* Gooch's money. As Justice McLachlin said, in delivering the judgment of the Court:

> [A]n intentional misappropriation, without mistake, suffices to establish the *mens rea* under s. 332(1). … The word "fraudulently," as used in this section, connotes no more than this. *The dishonesty inherent in the offence lies in the intentional and unmistaken application of funds to an improper purpose.* …
>
> In short, the trial judge found: that the appellant knew that the money belonged to Mr. Gooch; that the appellant knew the purpose to which the money was supposed to be applied; and that the appellant knowingly, without mistake, applied the money to different purposes. [emphasis added]

However, in the case of *He* (2008), the accused was charged with the theft of electricity, contrary to section 326 of the *Criminal Code.* She was found to be the temporary caretaker of a marijuana grow-op in the basement of a residence. A hydroelectric-bypass was found in the adjoining garage: this device permitted the illegal extraction of free electricity. A wire that passed through a hole in the wall of the garage was visible, but there was no evidence that the accused understood the purpose of this device. Section 326 provides that theft is committed when a person takes electricity "fraudulently, maliciously, or without colour of right." The question in this case was whether the accused acted "fraudulently." She was merely the caretaker of the grow-op and, therefore, it could not be assumed that she knew that electricity was being stolen. To prove the fraud that is a necessary component of the crime of theft, the Crown would have to establish that the accused intentionally and deliberately participated in the scheme to take electricity without paying for it.

Although He was convicted at her trial of the theft of electricity, the B.C. Court of Appeal set aside the conviction and entered an acquittal on this charge because it had not been proved that she had the necessary *mens rea* for theft. In delivering the judgment of the Court of Appeal, Justice Bauman stated that:

> With respect, I think it difficult to infer, from the appellant's knowledge and control of the grow-op, the *mens rea* necessary to support the finding of fraud in the offence created by s. 326(1)(a) of the *Code*. Nor is the appearance of the bypass in the garage, as depicted in the photographic exhibit, so obviously a device for stealing electricity that any non-expert would have appreciated what it was. The opening in the wall does not provide a reasonable

> basis for the judge's finding that the appellant was aware of the bypass.
>
> "Fraudulently" in section 326 connotes an intentional and deliberate taking of service that was not the accused's to obtain. ...

Justice Bauman emphasized that the fact that He knew about, and had control of, the grow-op did not necessarily mean that the Crown could prove beyond a reasonable doubt that she intentionally and deliberately stole the electricity that was necessary to power the grow-op.

The Meaning of "Fraudulent" in Section 380

As Justice Cory pointed out, on behalf of the majority of the Supreme Court of Canada in *Cuerrier* (1998), "[T]he essential elements of fraud are *dishonesty ... and deprivation or risk of deprivation.*" Therefore, in their interpretation of the term "fraudulent" in the specific context of section 380(1) of the *Criminal Code*, the courts have insisted that the Crown prove that the accused acted *dishonestly*. This element of dishonesty is required in addition to proof that the accused acted intentionally or with knowledge of the particular circumstances. The judicial interpretation of the concept of **fraud** has clearly emerged in relation to charges laid under section 380 of the *Criminal Code*. Section 380(1) states: "Every one who, by *deceit, falsehood or other fraudulent means*, whether or not it is a false pretence within the meaning of this Act, defrauds the public or any person, whether ascertained or not, of any property, money or valuable security or any service ... [is guilty of an offence]" [emphasis added].

It is clear that fraud is not confined to the obtaining of property and so forth by deceit or falsehood—forms of behaviour that essentially involve lying, or deceitfully withholding significant information, on the part of the defendant. After all, section 380(1) specifically refers to "other fraudulent means," which means that the concept of fraud in the *Code* extends far beyond situations where the defendant deliberately tells a lie or omits to mention critical facts that might fundamentally influence the other party's decision making. In the case of *Olan, Hudson and Hartnett* (1978), the Supreme Court of Canada ruled that "the words 'other fraudulent means' in s. [380(1)] include means which are not in the nature of a falsehood or a deceit; they encompass all other means which can properly be stigmatized as dishonest."

The facts in the *Olan* case are undoubtedly complex. However, a somewhat simplified version will suffice for our purposes. The accused were charged with defrauding a dry-cleaning company, Langley's Limited, of money and valuable securities worth some $1 million. Beauport Holdings Limited, a company controlled by one of the accused, took over Langley's Limited by purchasing a controlling block of its shares; however, it needed a substantial bank loan to do so. Representatives of Beauport Holdings Limited were then placed in control of the board of directors of Langley's Limited. The new directors caused Langley's Limited to divest itself of its holdings in "blue chip" securities (that is, valuable and secure investments) and to purchase shares in another company, Beauport Financial Corporation Limited, which was controlled by two of the accused. Some $790 000, which was acquired by Beauport Financial as a result of the share purchase, was then loaned to Beauport Holdings. This money was used to pay off part of the bank loan that Beauport Holdings had used to purchase the controlling block of Langley's shares. In essence, Langley's had exchanged its secure and valuable investment portfolio for shares in Beauport Financial, whose principal asset was the debt owed to it by Beauport Holdings. In the previous year, Beauport Holdings sustained a net operating loss and its current liabilities exceeded its assets by more than $1 million. Clearly, the value and security of the shares in Beauport Financial were somewhat shaky at best. On these facts, it was contended by the Crown that the sale of Langley's shares had been carried out for the personal interests of the new directors rather than for the ***bona fide*** business interests of Langley's Limited.

It was clear that the accused had not been deceitful or uttered any falsehood. Indeed, the accused vigorously claimed that their activities had all been "above board." However, the question arose as to whether their conduct nevertheless constituted fraud within the meaning of section 380 of the *Code*. The Court emphasized that the prosecution was not required to prove any deception on the part of the accused. Indeed, Justice Dickson, in delivering the judgment of the Court, stated that the words "other fraudulent means" in section 380(1) "encompass all other meanings which can properly be stigmatized as dishonest." In the view of the Supreme Court of Canada, the prosecution must establish two separate elements to prove fraud; namely, *dishonesty* (the *mens rea*) and *deprivation* (the *actus reus*). Insofar as this particular case was concerned, Justice Dickson said that:

> Using the assets of the corporation for personal purposes rather than *bona fide* for the benefit of the corporation can constitute dishonesty in a case of alleged fraud by directors of a corporation. …
>
> The element of deprivation is satisfied on proof of detriment, prejudice, or risk of prejudice to the economic interest of the victim. *It is not essential that there be actual economic loss as the outcome of the fraud.* [emphasis added]

The Supreme Court of Canada ruled that although the accused may well have intended to have Beauport Holdings repay the loan to Beauport Financial, this would not prevent them from being found fraudulent if their conduct was otherwise shown to involve dishonest deprivation for their own personal ends. There was no doubt that the financial interests of the shareholders of Langley's Limited had been put at risk when the valuable and secure shares were sold and the money reinvested in shares in a company that had more liabilities than assets. The Supreme Court ordered a new trial for Olan and the other accused, and this trial would need to be conducted in accordance with the principles enunciated by Justice Dickson.

The *Olan* case clearly defined fraud as dishonest deprivation. However, Justice Dickson did not provide any detailed guidance as to the necessary *mens rea* that the Crown must prove in a case of fraud. He merely agreed with the trial judge that it must be established that the accused's "conduct must be deliberately dishonest." It was left to the case of *Théroux* (1993) for the Supreme Court of Canada to clarify the *mens rea* requirements of fraud. Indeed, in *Théroux*, Justice McLachlin stated that to establish the *mens rea* elements of fraud, the Crown has to prove only "that the accused knowingly undertook the acts which constitute the falsehood, deceit or other fraudulent means, and that the accused was aware that deprivation could result from such conduct." Most significantly, the Supreme Court ruled that where fraud is charged under section 380 of the *Code*, it is not necessary for the Crown to prove that the accused subjectively appreciated that their conduct was dishonest. If the *mens rea* elements defined by Justice McLachlin are proved, then it does not matter if the accused believes that they were acting in a perfectly legitimate manner.

In *Théroux*, the accused was a businessman who was involved with a company that was constructing two residential housing projects. Théroux falsely represented to potential buyers that their deposits would be insured by the Fédération de construction du Québec. The construction company became insolvent and the projects were not finished. As a consequence, most of the potential buyers lost the entire amount of their deposits. At the accused's trial for fraud, the trial judge found that Théroux honestly believed that the housing projects would succeed and that the buyers would not lose their deposits. However, the trial judge stated that this was not a defence to a charge of fraud and convicted Théroux. The accused's appeals to both the Quebec Court of Appeal and the Supreme Court of Canada were dismissed.

According to Justice McLachlin, the accused's belief that the projects would succeed and that the buyers would not lose any money was irrelevant. In defining the offence of fraud under section 380, she stated that:

> The prohibited act is deceit, falsehood, or some other dishonest act. The prohibited consequence is depriving another of what is or should be his, which may, as we have seen, consist in merely placing another's property at risk. The *mens rea* would then consist in the subjective awareness that one was undertaking a prohibited act (the deceit, falsehood or other dishonest act) which could cause deprivation in the sense of depriving another of property or putting that property at risk. If this is shown, the crime is complete. The fact that the accused may have hoped the deprivation would not take place, or may have felt there was nothing wrong with what he or she was doing, provides no defence. … The personal feeling of the accused about the morality or honesty of the act or its consequences is no more relevant to the analysis than is the accused's awareness that the particular acts constitute a criminal offence.

Justice McLachlin noted that the *actus reus* of the offence is made out when the accused engages in conduct which the reasonable person would consider "dishonest." Once the Crown has proved this element beyond a reasonable doubt, then the necessary *mens rea* will be proved if the accused "knowingly undertook the acts in question, aware that deprivation, or risk of deprivation, could follow as a likely consequence."

As far as the facts in *Théroux* were concerned, it was clear that the accused had committed the *actus reus* of fraud. He had deliberately told falsehoods to the potential buyers, and those lies caused deprivation in two respects: first, the depositors failed to obtain the insurance they were promised; and second, their money was placed at risk (a risk that ultimately did materialize since the majority of them lost the entire amount of their deposits). The critical question, therefore, was whether the *mens rea* elements of fraud had been proved. Justice McLachlin answered this question affirmatively:

> [Théroux] told the depositors they had insurance protection when he knew that they did not have that protection. He knew this to be false. He knew that by this act he was depriving the depositors of something they thought they had, insurance protection. It may also be inferred from his possession of this knowledge that [he] knew that he was placing the depositors' money at risk. That established, his *mens rea* is proved. The fact that he sincerely believed that in the end the houses would be built and that the risk would not materialize cannot save him.

In *Riesberry* (2015), the accused was a horse trainer caught injecting and attempting to inject horses with performance-enhancing drugs before a race. Riesberry was charged, *inter alia*, with defrauding the public of money wagered on the outcome of a horse race [section 380(1)]. Although he was acquitted at trial of this charge, the Ontario Court of Appeal substituted a conviction and this decision was affirmed by the Supreme Court of Canada. Justice Cromwell, in delivering the judgment of the Supreme Court, noted that Riesberry actually knew that his conduct was dishonest because his conduct in injecting the horses was not designed to accomplish any genuine medical purpose, but instead it was intended to enhance the horses' performance in their races. However, knowledge that he was acting dishonestly is not a necessary element of the *mens rea* for fraud. Justice Cromwell pointed out that the necessary *mens rea* was proved by the trial judge's finding that Riesberry "intended to create an unfair advantage for his horses in their races." Therefore, "Mr. Riesberry knew that his dishonest conduct put bettors at risk of deprivation." Clearly Riesberry was well aware that he was "cheating."

However, it is important to acknowledge that an accused person will not be convicted of fraud if they honestly believe that their conduct will not put other people's financial interests at risk. In *Lauer* (2011), the accused, who was a chartered accountant, was hired to manage a corporation. He was given some shares and became a director. The corporation was struggling and could not pay Lauer's management fees, so the board of directors agreed to convert the large amount of money owing to Lauer into shares in the corporation and, as a result, Lauer became the majority shareholder. The action by the board was later set aside by a civil court because the meeting at which the decision was made did not meet the legal requirements of adequate notice and a proper *quorum*. Lauer was later charged with fraud because of the restructuring of the shares. He was convicted at trial, but the Prince Edward Island Court of Appeal ruled that the conviction was unreasonable and, therefore, entered an acquittal. The Crown had not proved the *mens rea* of fraud: indeed, Lauer believed that the fees he had billed to the corporation were legitimate and that converting the debt into shares would actually *enhance* the company's financial position rather than putting it at risk. In the words of Justice Murphy, who delivered the judgment of the Court:

> [T]he intention for fraud is comprised of two components: a) subjective knowledge of the prohibited act, and b) subjective knowledge that the prohibited act could result in deprivation or a risk of it.
>
> The Crown did not establish that the appellant had subjective knowledge that the share exchange would result in a manipulation of Vitrak's share structure and a deprivation for other shareholders. In fact, the evidence at trial disclosed that the appellant believed the expenses he claimed against the company were legitimate; believed that the rate at which the shares were converted was equitable; believed that the exchange was properly approved by both the Board and shareholders; and that it was a gain for the shareholders which would place the company in a better financial position.

Lauer had testified at his trial that he believed he was acting in good faith and in the best interests of the corporation. There was no evidence advanced at his trial that would suggest Lauer knew that his actions had the potential to cause deprivation to the shareholders, nor was he reckless as to this possibility. Therefore, he lacked the *mens rea* for fraud.[1]

---

1. It is significant that the Court also found that the Crown had not proved the *actus reus* of fraud because there was no evidence to suggest that there was any actual deprivation, in the sense of a risk to the financial interests of the shareholders of the corporation.

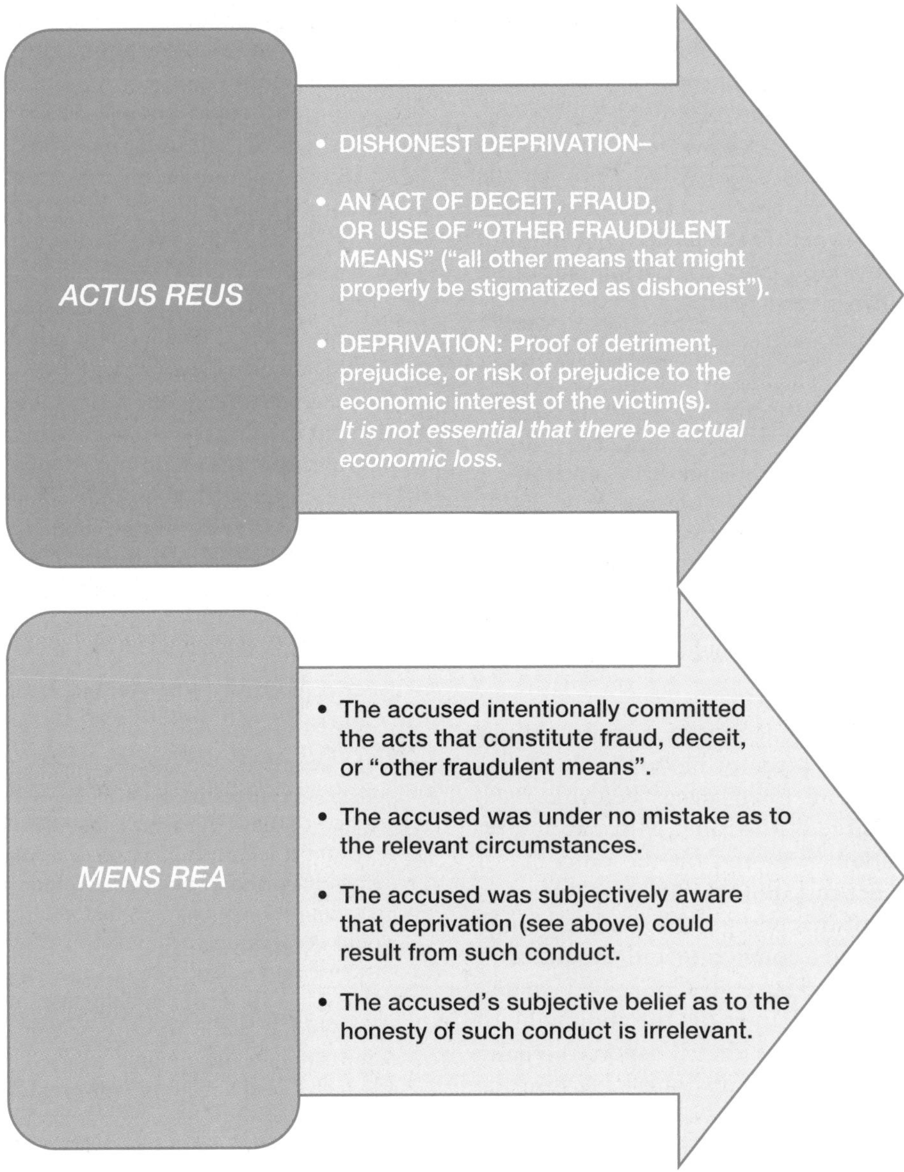

ACTUS REUS
• DISHONEST DEPRIVATION–
• AN ACT OF DECEIT, FRAUD, OR USE OF "OTHER FRAUDULENT MEANS" ("all other means that might properly be stigmatized as dishonest").
• DEPRIVATION: Proof of detriment, prejudice, or risk of prejudice to the economic interest of the victim(s). It is not essential that there be actual economic loss.
MENS REA
• The accused intentionally committed the acts that constitute fraud, deceit, or "other fraudulent means".
• The accused was under no mistake as to the relevant circumstances.
• The accused was subjectively aware that deprivation (see above) could result from such conduct.
• The accused's subjective belief as to the honesty of such conduct is irrelevant.

Figure 4.2

The Elements of Fraud under Section 380 of the Criminal Code

The Meaning of "Planned and Deliberate" in Section 231(2) (First-Degree Murder)

A final example of a special mental element that the Crown must establish to achieve a conviction is contained in section 231(2) of the *Criminal Code*. This provision states that "murder is first degree murder when it is planned and deliberate." To convict an accused person of the crime of murder, the Crown is normally required to prove that the accused intended to kill their victim or meant to cause bodily harm that is likely to cause death and is reckless whether death ensues or not [section 229(a) of the *Code*]. Once the Crown has established that the accused acted intentionally, the issue then arises as to whether they should be found guilty of first- or second-degree murder. Section 235 of the *Code* provides that, in either case, the accused will be sentenced to life imprisonment. However, Parliament has drawn a clear distinction between first- and second-degree murder in relation to the time that individuals must serve before they may be eligible for parole. Section 745(a) provides that persons convicted of first-degree murder will automatically be ineligible for parole until they have served 25 years of their sentence. However, when an individual is convicted of second-degree murder, there is more flexibility in the sentence.[2] The period of ineligibility for parole may range from a minimum of 10 years to a maximum of 25 years: the trial judge makes this decision, after seeking advice from the jury [sections 745(c), 745.2, and 745.4 of the *Criminal Code*].

Under the current *Criminal Code* provisions, individuals who have been convicted of murder and whose parole ineligibility exceeds 15 years may seek a review of their ineligibility period after they have served 15 years of their life sentence—the so-called "faint hope clause" (section 745.6). However, this procedure does not apply to individuals convicted of multiple murders and is *available only to offenders who committed murders before December 2, 2011* [subsections 745.6 (1) and (2)]. The application must be made to the Chief Justice of the province or territory in which the offender was convicted of murder. The Chief Justice must decide whether "the applicant has shown, on a balance of probabilities, that there is a substantial likelihood that the application will succeed" [section 745.61(1)]. If the applicant clears this hurdle, the period of parole ineligibility will be reviewed by a jury, sitting with a superior court judge. The jury may decide not to reduce the period of ineligibility for parole, may terminate the period altogether, or may reduce it by a specified number of years (section 745.63).[3]

To establish first-degree murder, the Crown must normally prove not only that the accused intended to kill their victim but also that they did so in a "planned and deliberate manner."[4] What do these words mean? In the case of *Banwait* (2011), the Supreme Court of Canada approved the following instruction given by the trial judge to the jury:

> A planned murder is one that is committed as a result of a scheme or plan that has been *previously formulated or designed.* It is the implementation of that scheme or design. A "murder" committed on a sudden impulse and without prior consideration, even with an intention to kill is not a planned murder.
>
> "Deliberate" is not a word that we often use when speaking to other people. It means "considered, not impulsive," "carefully thought out, not hasty or rash," "slow in deciding, "cautious."
>
> A deliberate act is one that the actor has taken time to weigh the advantages and disadvantages of. The deliberation must take place before the act of murder. ... A murder committed on a sudden impulse and without prior consideration, even with an intention to kill is not a deliberate murder.

An instructive example of the judicial interpretation of the words "planned and deliberate" is furnished by the case of *Smith* (1980), in which the accused was charged with first-degree murder following the death of a man named Skwarchuk. Smith and Skwarchuk had been on a hunting trip together. After stopping at an abandoned farmhouse, a vigorous argument erupted, and Smith shot Skwarchuk in the left elbow. Skwarchuk ran away from Smith. Skwarchuk's arm was hanging down and blood was squirting on the ground. However, Smith reloaded his shotgun and shot Skwarchuk, at least twice, from long range. It appeared that some pellets from Smith's gun hit Skwarchuk in the back. Skwarchuk continued to run, but Smith shot Skwarchuk again and the latter fell down. Smith then approached Skwarchuk, who was sitting on the ground, and shot him in the back of the head. At this point, Skwarchuk died. Smith was subsequently arrested by the police and charged. At his trial, he was convicted of first-degree murder; however, on appeal, the Saskatchewan Court of

2. Unless the accused person has previously been convicted of another murder, in which case the period of ineligibility for parole is 25 years [s. 745(b)]. In the case of multiple murders, the trial judge may order that the periods of ineligibility for parole be served consecutively (s. 745.51).

3. The criteria for making this decision are set out in s. 745.63(1) of the *Criminal Code*.

4. Section 231 also specifies certain circumstances in which an accused person may be found guilty of first-degree murder, *even though the homicide was not "planned and deliberate"*: namely, murder of a police officer, sheriff, prison warden, prison guard, and so forth, if the killing occurs while the victim is acting in the course of their duties; and murder committed in the course of hijacking, sexual assault, kidnapping or hostage taking, criminal harassment, terrorist activity, using explosives in connection with the activities of a criminal organization, or intimidation.

Appeal substituted a conviction for second-degree murder. The Court of Appeal was not satisfied that the killing was both "planned and deliberate." Chief Justice Culliton stated that:

> There must be some evidence the killing was the result of a scheme or design previously formulated or designed by the accused and the killing was the implementation of that scheme or design. It is obvious a murder committed on a sudden impulse and without prior consideration, even though the intent to kill is clearly proven, would not constitute a planned murder.
>
> In the present case, there is not the slightest evidence the appellant (Smith) had given any consideration to the murder of Skwarchuk until after he and Skwarchuk had left the house. …
>
> I am satisfied that there was no evidence whatever to support the conclusion that the actions of the appellant, cruel and sadistic as they were, in killing Skwarchuk was the implementation of a previously determined design or scheme. I think it is obvious his actions were the result of a sudden impulse. It would be pure speculation to try and determine what triggered that impulse.

The decision in *Smith* should be contrasted with the case of *Fraser* (2015), which established that a murder can be both planned and deliberate even if the accused makes the decision to kill in a relatively short period. Fraser was convicted of one count of second-degree murder and one count of first-degree murder. Fraser and Yaretz had been jointly involved in a marijuana grow operation and Fraser was angry with Yaretz for a number of reasons, including the fact that Yaretz had not returned Fraser's truck. The Crown asserted that Yaretz and another man, Marks, came to the property to collect some of Yaretz's belongings, at which time Fraser shot Yaretz over the truck, and stabbed and shot Marks because he was a witness to the shooting. According to the Crown, Fraser shot Yaretz in the doorway of Fraser's house. He then stabbed and shot Marks in the van as he tried to escape. Fraser was convicted of the second-degree murder of Yaretz and the first-degree murder of Marks. The B.C. Court of Appeal rejected Fraser's appeal, noting that the trial jury was perfectly entitled to conclude that he both planned and deliberated the murder of Marks after he had killed Yaretz. The Court of Appeal ruled that it was reasonable for the jury to conclude that, in the interval between the shooting of Yaretz and the fatal attack on Marks, Fraser "planned and deliberated" the murder of Marks. As Madam Justice MacKenzie indicated, the time necessary for planning and deliberation can be brief:

> This is not a case where any significant time was required to form a plan to murder. In this scenario, [Fraser] was already holding the gun he had just fired. The jury could reasonably infer [Fraser] planned in this brief period of time to chase down Marks, incapacitate him by stabbing him, pull him out of the van and shoot him to ensure his death. Likewise, the jury could infer [Fraser] deliberated on the killing of Marks in that interval of time. That is, having rapidly considered his options, he chose, in the interests of self-preservation, to eliminate a witness rather than to allow Marks to escape and incriminate him.

However, each case will depend on its specific facts. In *Robinson* (2017), the accused, who had been drinking heavily, had an argument with the victim and fetched an aluminum pipe with which to "shoo" the victim out of his house. As the victim was leaving, Robinson noticed that the victim was taking some of Robinson's property with him and he became enraged. He hit the victim twice on the head, with fatal consequences. The evidence indicated that he was "very upset and started to cry." Robinson was convicted at trial of first-degree murder. However, the Ontario Court of Appeal set aside this conviction and ordered a new trial for second-degree murder because there was no evidence that the killing was planned and deliberate. Justice Doherty commented that:

> A finding that the [Robinson] decided seconds or a few minutes before inflicting the harm, to intentionally inflict bodily harm knowing that death was likely to ensue, is not the same as concluding that the appellant planned and deliberated upon the attack before commencing that attack. …, there has to be evidence from which a jury could reasonably infer that [Robinson's] attack on Mr. Fair was the product "of a calculated scheme", arrived at after weighing "the nature and consequences" of that scheme. In addition to evidence of planning, there had to be evidence that having made the plan, [Robinson] "deliberated", that is weighed the pros and cons of putting the plan into action.

Only a couple of minutes passed between the time when Robinson returned with the pipe and his assault on the victim. Furthermore, Robinson's distraught reaction militated against a finding that he had planned the killing and acted in a deliberate, as opposed to an impulsive, manner.

The courts have often recognized that a critical factor to consider in determining whether the accused acted in a "planned and deliberate" manner is whether the accused acted in a state of intoxication. As we shall see in Chapter 10, if intoxication prevents the accused person from forming the specific intent to kill, it serves as a **partial defence** and reduces the severity of the charge from murder to manslaughter. However, it may well be that the accused's state of intoxication was not so serious as to prevent them from forming the **specific intent** to kill. Nevertheless, their state of intoxication may still be particularly relevant to the issue of whether the accused acted in a planned and deliberate manner when they killed the victim. Indeed, intoxication may well prevent the accused person from formulating a plan or from acting in a deliberate manner.

In the case of *Wallen* (1990), the Supreme Court of Canada ruled that a trial judge must always direct the jury to consider the issue of intoxication and its effect on whether the accused acted in a planned and deliberate manner quite separately from the issue of intoxication and its effect on whether the accused formed the intent to kill. After all, a lesser degree of intoxication may be sufficient to negative the mental state of planning and deliberation that is necessary to prevent the accused from forming the necessary intent for murder. Furthermore, in *Turningrobe* (2008), the Supreme Court ordered a new trial for the accused because the trial judge had instructed the jury in such a manner that they may well have concluded that the central issue for them to decide was whether alcohol had affected Turningrobe's *capacity* to act in a planned and deliberate manner. The central issue, however, was whether, in all the circumstances—including her heavy drinking—she did, in fact, carry out the killing of the victim in a planned and deliberate manner. Merely possessing the *capacity* to formulate a plan or to act deliberately does not mean that one actually did so at the time that the victim was killed.

Similarly, the Supreme Court of Canada has clearly acknowledged that mental illness may also have the effect of negating the element of *planning and deliberation* required for conviction of first-degree murder. As Chief Justice Lamer stated in the *Jacquard* case (1997):

> It is true that some factor, such as a mental disorder, that is insufficient to negative the charge that the accused *intended* to kill, may nevertheless be sufficient to negative the elements of *planning and deliberation*. This is because one can intend to kill and yet be impulsive rather than considered in doing so. It requires less mental capacity simply to intend than it does to plan and deliberate.

Of course, it must be emphasized that if an accused person suffered from a particularly severe form of *mental disorder* at the time the alleged offence was committed, then it is possible that the accused might be able to prove that they should be found "not criminally responsible on account of mental disorder" (NCRMD) under the terms of section 16 of the *Criminal Code* (a special defence that is discussed in Chapter 8). However, an accused person who is not successful in raising this defence and is convicted of murder may still point to the mental disorder at the time of the killing and claim that it prevented them from acting *with planning and deliberation*. If the accused manages to raise a reasonable doubt on this issue, then there must be a conviction of *second-degree*, rather than first-degree, murder.

The *Allard* case (1990) demonstrates the various stages that must be followed when the issue of mental disorder is raised in relation to a charge of first-degree murder. The accused was charged with this offence after she administered a vitamin capsule, laced with a fatal dose of strychnine, to her husband. The accused's defence was that she was not criminally responsible on account of mental disorder and that, in any event, she did not kill her husband intentionally or in a planned and deliberate manner. The trial judge instructed the jury that if the accused failed to prove that she was not criminally responsible under section 16 of the *Code*, they must "disregard [the mental disorder] defence completely." Allard was subsequently convicted of first-degree murder. However, the Quebec Court of Appeal allowed her appeal and ordered a new trial. The court found that the original trial judge should have pointed out to the jury that even if the accused had not proved that she was not criminally responsible under the terms of section 16 of the *Code*, she might be able to raise a reasonable doubt as to whether her mental disorder prevented her from forming the intent to kill; if she did raise such a doubt, she would have to be acquitted and convicted of manslaughter instead. However, if the jury were satisfied beyond a reasonable doubt that the accused did form the intent to kill her husband, it would still have to consider the totally separate question of whether her mental disorder prevented her from acting in a planned and deliberate manner; if she could raise a reasonable doubt on this score, she would be acquitted of first-degree murder and convicted of second-degree murder.

The Distinction between Direct and Indirect Intention

For the purpose of legal analysis, it is possible to draw a distinction between *direct* and *indirect intention*. The term **direct intention** refers to intention in the popular sense of an individual acting with the desire, purpose, aim, objective, or design to achieve a certain consequence. In this sense, this term clearly reflects the average citizen's comprehension of the word "intention."

What is meant by **indirect intention**? Let us suppose that Marley does not desire that his conduct produce a certain consequence, B, but nevertheless knows that consequence B is a necessary step on the way to accomplishing the objective that he really does wish to achieve (consequence A). Can we say that Marley "intends" the undesired consequence B? The answer is yes. Imagine that Cratchitt wishes to wound Scrooge by hurling a rock at him. Scrooge unfortunately happens to be visiting Fred's house. Cratchitt is a close friend of Fred's and would certainly not intend to cause him any grief. Nevertheless, the only way in which Cratchitt can accomplish his objective of wounding Scrooge is by hurling the rock through the closed window. There is no doubt that Cratchitt does not desire to break the window, but, on the other hand, he realizes that he must do so in order to attain his objective of wounding Scrooge. Let us suppose that Cratchitt throws the rock at Scrooge, knowing the window is closed. There is no difficulty in determining that Cratchitt intends to wound Scrooge. However, does he "intend" to break Fred's window? For the purpose of the criminal law, Cratchitt will be held to have *indirectly* intended to break the window and is liable to conviction of mischief [wilful damage of property, contrary to section 430(1)(a) of the *Criminal Code*]. Putting it in legal terms, Cratchitt is deemed to have intended to break the window because he knew this *undesired* consequence was a condition precedent to the realization of his *desired* objective of wounding Scrooge.

There is another situation in which the concept of indirect intention becomes of critical importance. Consider the following hypothetical example. Murdstone joins a gang of terrorists and is ordered to destroy a shipment of arms destined for the military. To this end, he buries a land mine under the road. The land mine is designed to detonate by remote control, and Murdstone's plan is to explode the bomb as the truck carrying the shipment passes over it. Murdstone does not wish to kill the driver of the truck, but he necessarily knows that the explosion is "virtually certain" to cause the driver's death. It is just possible that the driver may escape alive, but Murdstone knows that this is highly unlikely. When the truck passes over the land mine, Murdstone detonates it and, in the ensuing explosion, the driver (Noggs) is killed instantaneously. Did Murdstone "intend" to kill Noggs, even though he did not wish to cause this consequence? The answer must be in the affirmative. Murdstone realized that the death of the driver of the truck was *virtually certain* to happen, even though he hoped that the driver would not be killed and thought there was a remote possibility that the driver might miraculously escape death. In these circumstances, Murdstone would be deemed to have *indirectly* intended the death of Noggs and, therefore, would be guilty of murder.

The concept of indirect intention was applied in the unusual case of *Guess* (2000). The accused was charged under section 139(2) of the *Criminal Code*, with attempting to obstruct, pervert, or defeat the course of justice by engaging in a "personal relationship" with a defendant (Gill) who was being tried on a charge of homicide. The charge arose from the fact that Guess was a juror in the trial of Gill. Although Guess's main objective was to engage in a romantic relationship with Gill, she nevertheless knew that an inevitable consequence of this relationship would be to obstruct or pervert the trial process. Guess was convicted at her trial and her subsequent appeal was dismissed by the B.C. Court of Appeal. In the words of Justice Hall of the Court of Appeal:

> That the appellant [Guess] well knew what she was doing in carrying on an affair with an accused was not in accord with her duties as a juror is clear from the evidence. She was secretive about the matter and in discussions with her sister and friends she acknowledged that what was occurring was wrong. She observed that she felt "conflicted." That, of course, precisely identifies the difficulty—she was in a position of impossible conflict. Would this conduct have a tendency to pervert or obstruct the course of justice? The answer to this question is obviously in the affirmative. The juror would be privy knowingly or unknowingly to information not possessed by other jurors and because of the emotional ties between her and the accused would

be hampered in properly performing the impartial functions of a judicial officer. In the context of this offence, the term "wilfully" may be taken to connote the concept that the offence could not be made out of the basis of accidental or unknowing conduct. But as the conversations of the appellant that were placed before the jury indicated, she was keenly aware that she was doing what she ought not to do during the course of the trial when she was serving as a juror. These words of Martin J.A. in the case of *R. v. Buzzanga and Durocher* … are apposite here: … as a general rule, a person who foresees that a consequence is certain or substantially certain to result from an act which he does in order to achieve some other purpose, intends that consequence. The actor's foresight of the certainty or moral certainty of the consequence resulting from his conduct compels a conclusion that if he, none the less, acted so as to produce it, then he decided to bring it about (albeit regretfully), in order to achieve his ultimate purpose. His intention encompasses the means as well as to [*sic*] his ultimate objective.

Intention and Motive Distinguished

It is important to draw a clear distinction between intention and motive. Indeed, in the *Lewis* case (1979), Justice Dickson, of the Supreme Court of Canada, stated that:

> In ordinary parlance, the words "intent" and "motive" are frequently used interchangeably, but in the criminal law they are distinct. In most criminal trials, the mental element, the *mens rea* with which the Court is concerned, relates to "intent," i.e., the exercise of a free will to use particular means to produce a particular result, rather than with "motive," i.e., that which precedes and induces the exercise of the will. The mental element of a crime ordinarily involves no reference to motive. …

In the decision of the Supreme Court of Canada in the *United States v. Dynar* case (1997), Justices Cory and Iacobucci articulated a clear rationale for drawing this distinction between intention and motive:

> Society imposes criminal sanctions in order to punish and deter undesirable conduct. It does not matter to society, in its efforts to secure social peace and order, what an accused's motive was, but only what the accused intended to do. It is no consolation to one whose car has been stolen that the thief stole the car intending to sell it to purchase food for a food bank.

As Justice McLachlin, of the Supreme Court of Canada, said in the case of *Théroux* (1993), an accused person's personal system of values is not a relevant consideration in determining whether they have the necessary *mens rea* for conviction of an offence:

> A person is not saved from conviction because he or she believes that there is nothing wrong with what he or she is doing. The question is whether the accused subjectively appreciated that certain consequences would follow from his or her acts, not whether the accused believed the acts or their consequences to be moral. Just as the pathological killer would not be acquitted on the mere ground that he failed to see his act as morally reprehensible, so the defrauder will not be acquitted because he believed that what he was doing was honest.

As we noted in Chapter 3, with the exception of medical practitioners who perform a role in medically assisted dying and who follow all of the requirements specified in the *Criminal Code*, any individual who kills someone—even with their consent—in order to terminate the painful existence caused by a debilitating disease will nevertheless be convicted of murder on the basis that they *intended* to cause death—despite the fact that their **motive** was solely to bring about an end to extreme suffering. In short, if defendants cause the *actus reus* of a crime with the necessary *mens rea*, it is entirely irrelevant that they claim to be acting out of what some may consider to be the laudable motive of carrying out a so-called "mercy killing." The *mens rea* for murder is, normally, an intention to kill or an intention to inflict bodily harm that is likely to cause death coupled with recklessness as to whether or not death ensues. The individual who deliberately causes the death of another as part of a "mercy killing" has committed the *actus reus* of murder together with the requisite *mens rea*. Their motive is absolutely irrelevant because it is not part of the definition of the crime of murder. In this particular case, if the individual was convicted of first-degree murder, the sentencing judge could not take the motive into account because there is a fixed sentence (life sentence with a minimum non-eligibility-for-parole period of 25 years). However, for most other offences, trial judges have considerable discretion in setting the appropriate sentence, and it is highly likely that noble (albeit misguided) motives will result in a more lenient sentence being imposed. Conversely, as Justice L'Heureux-Dubé stated in the Supreme Court of Canada's decision in *Hinchey* (1996), a corrupt or evil motive will lead to a more severe sentence.

Motive is generally irrelevant to the definition of a crime.

The *Latimer* case (2001) illustrates the immense difficulty that may arise when an accused person's motives may not be taken into account because of a mandatory sentence prescribed in the *Criminal Code*. Robert Latimer asphyxiated his severely disabled 12-year-old daughter with carbon monoxide and claimed that he had killed her out of compassion—his motive had been to end (what he perceived to be) his daughter's intolerable suffering. Since it was clear that Latimer carried this act out *intentionally*, he was convicted of second-degree murder. Both the trial judge and jury appeared to accept that Latimer was telling the truth when he stated that he had engaged in a so-called mercy killing. However, section 745 of the *Code* imposes a mandatory sentence for second-degree murder. That sentence is one of life imprisonment, with no eligibility for parole for a period of between 10 and 25 years (this period is to be set by the trial judge, who is required to consult with the jury on the issue). When consulted in relation to the appropriate period of ineligibility for parole, the jury in the *Latimer* case recommended that the accused be eligible for parole after only one year in custody (a sentence that is not permitted, in light of the *mandatory minimum* period of 10 years that is imposed by section 745). In a highly unusual move, the trial judge ruled that in light of the fact that Latimer acted out of compassionate (albeit profoundly misguided) motives, it would constitute cruel and unusual punishment under section 12 of the *Charter* to sentence him to life imprisonment with no eligibility for parole for 10 years. Consequently, Justice Noble granted Latimer a **constitutional exemption** from the provisions of section 745 and sentenced him to one year in prison and one year on probation. However, the Crown appealed this sentence and the Saskatchewan Court of Appeal set it aside, substituting a sentence of life imprisonment with no eligibility for parole for 10 years. The Court of Appeal rejected the notion that Latimer was entitled to a constitutional exemption and stated that it is up to Parliament to deal with the question of whether there should be special sentencing provisions to deal with the issue of so-called mercy killing.

The Supreme Court of Canada later affirmed the decision of the Court of Appeal. In the words of the Court:

> On the one hand, we must give due consideration to Mr. Latimer's initial attempts to conceal his actions, his lack of remorse, his position of trust, the significant degree of planning and

premeditation, and Tracy's extreme vulnerability. On the other hand, we are mindful of Mr. Latimer's good character and standing in the community, his tortured anxiety about Tracy's well-being, and his laudable perseverance as a caring and involved parent. Considered together we cannot find that the personal characteristics and particular circumstances of this case displace the serious gravity of this offence.

The Court concluded that "the minimum mandatory sentence is not grossly disproportionate in this case" and that "we cannot find that any aspect of the particular circumstances of the case or the offender diminishes the degree of criminal responsibility borne by Mr. Latimer." However, the Supreme Court of Canada did emphasize the fact that the Government of Canada has the power to grant clemency in cases such as that of *Latimer*. This power is known as the "royal prerogative of mercy" and is found in sections 748 and 749 of the *Criminal Code*. Significantly, the Supreme Court emphasized that "the prerogative is a matter for the executive, not the courts."

The question of whether those who commit murder from compassionate motives should be treated more leniently than other individuals who perpetrate this crime is highly controversial and has deeply divided Canadians. Some would argue that the justice system is functioning in a profoundly unjust manner if "mercy killers," such as Latimer, are treated in the same manner as those who kill for motives of which we profoundly disapprove. On the other hand, some would contend that the life of Latimer's daughter was taken *without her consent* and that she was killed because she was severely disabled; therefore, it may be argued, if we grant more lenient sentences to those who kill in such circumstances, we are effectively devaluing the lives of all persons with a disability. Of course, now that medically assisted dying may be performed legally under the *Criminal Code*, it is likely that there will be less public sympathy for individuals who are not medical professionals, but nevertheless engage in so-called mercy killing.

Although the accused's motive is not one of the mental elements that must be established by the Crown to establish criminal responsibility, it may nevertheless be very relevant to the trial process. More specifically, the presence or absence of motive(s) may well be a critical issue in determining the innocence or guilt of the accused person. As Justice Saunders said, in the decision of the B.C. Court of Appeal in *Zoraik* (2012), "Motive is not an essential element of an offence, nor does its absence provide a defence. It is simply a circumstance that may support, or not, the identity of the accused as the offender."

As Justice Dickson asserted, in delivering the Supreme Court's judgment in the case of *Lewis* (1979), the prosecution can always introduce evidence that an accused person had a motive for committing the offence, because if it can prove the existence of such a motive, it is more likely that the accused did commit the offence. As Justice Dickson pointed out, "[M]en (sic) do not usually act without a motive." Conversely, if the accused can establish that they had no motive for committing the crime, then this is an important fact in their favour when the **trier of fact** comes to consider the question of innocence or guilt. For example, in the *Stone* case (1999), Justice Bastarache, on behalf of the majority of the Supreme Court of Canada, emphasized that the credibility of a defence of *automatism* (see Chapter 8) is considerably enhanced if there is no apparent motive for the alleged crime: "[T]he plausibility of a claim of automatism will be reduced if the accused had a motive to commit the crime in question. ... On the other hand, if the involuntary act is random and lacks motive, the plausibility of the claim of automatism will be increased."

Similarly, in *Jeffers* (2012), the accused had been charged with counselling murder. The Ontario Court of Appeal set aside his conviction at trial and entered an acquittal, largely because Jeffers had no motive for counselling the death of the alleged victim. Justice Laskin stated that:

> [A]s evidence motive is always relevant to the issue of intention and this case is no different. ... The existence of a motive makes it more likely that a person committed the crime. Persons do not usually act without a motive. Mr. Jeffers had no motive to want Councillor Thompson murdered. The councillor had helped him in the past and had never done him any harm. Mr. Jeffers' lack of motive to want Councillor Thompson killed is a strong piece of circumstantial evidence that he never intended to encourage his murder.

Although motive is generally not one of the elements in the *mens rea* of an offence, the definition of some crimes in the *Criminal Code* may actually include a specific requirement that the accused person commit the prohibited act with a particular motive. Conviction of these crimes, therefore, requires that the Crown prove that the accused intentionally committed a certain act with a specific motive in mind. Here, motive becomes an essential constituent of the *mens rea* of the offence in question. For example, one of the elements in the definition of "terrorist activity" with respect to offences defined in Part II.1 of the *Criminal Code* is that an act or omission is committed "in whole or part for a political, religious or ideological purpose, objective or cause" [section 83.01(1)(b)(i)(A)].[5]

The Concept of Transferred Intent

Let us suppose that Guppy throws a rock with the intention of hitting Skimpole. However, the rock misses its mark and instead hits and wounds Arabella. It is clear that Guppy "intended" to hit Skimpole. However, can he be convicted of an assault causing bodily harm to Arabella? The answer is that Guppy could, indeed, be convicted under section 267 of the *Code* because of the operation of the ancient common law principle of **transferred intent**. As the Ontario Court of Appeal stated in *Gordon* (2009):

> The common law doctrine of transferred intent takes the *mens rea* of an offence in relation to an intended victim and transfers it to the *actus reus* of the same offence committed upon another victim. Considered separately, each prospective crime lacks an essential part. The *mens rea* (intended victim) lacks an *actus reus*. And the *actus reus* (actual victim) lacks *mens rea*. In combination, however, they amount to a whole crime through the application of a legal fiction.

In essence, the principle of transferred intent provides that Guppy's intention to hit Skimpole can be *transferred* to the assault actually committed against Arabella. Guppy intended to commit the *actus reus* of an assault (albeit the victim was supposed to be Skimpole) and actually committed the *actus reus* of assault when he hit Arabella. Therefore, it seems to be both just and reasonable to convict him of assault causing bodily harm.

A specific example of the general principle of transferred intent may be found in section 229(b) of the *Criminal Code*:

> Where a person, meaning to cause death to a human being or meaning to cause him bodily harm that he knows is likely to cause death, and being reckless whether death ensues or not, by accident or mistake causes death to another human being, notwithstanding that he does not mean to cause death or bodily harm to that human being ... [is guilty of murder].

A rather bizarre set of circumstances led to the application of this section by the Supreme Court of Canada in *Droste* (1984). In this case, the defendant was charged with first-degree murder. The Crown introduced evidence to the effect that Droste had told his co-workers that he intended to kill his wife. It appeared that he was sexually involved with another woman and that he wished to recover the proceeds of an insurance policy that had recently been placed on Mrs. Droste's life. He told one of his co-workers that he planned to crash his car, set it on fire, and leave his spouse to perish in the conflagration. On the day of the incident in question, Droste was seen to be applying gasoline to the inside of his car. He later entered the car with his wife and their two small children and left for a birthday party. On the way, a fire broke out. His wife stated that Mr. Droste then tried to hit her on the head with a screwdriver and yelled at her to release her grip on the steering wheel. Tragically, the car struck the abutment of a bridge. The parents managed to extricate themselves from the blazing wreck, but they were unable to save the children, who were asphyxiated by the smoke. There was no evidence whatsoever that Mr. Droste harboured any ill will toward his children.

The trial judge instructed the jury that if they were satisfied beyond a reasonable doubt that Droste's intention to kill his wife was planned and deliberate and that in the course of carrying out that intention he caused the death of his children by accident or mistake, the resulting homicide constituted first-degree murder. The jury convicted, and both the Ontario Court of Appeal and the Supreme Court ultimately upheld the conviction. Justice Dickson noted, in the Supreme Court, that "The jury found that Mr. Droste, meaning to cause the death of a human being (Mrs. Droste), by accident caused the death of another human being (each of the children). He is therefore guilty of murder pursuant to [s. 229(b)]."

Similarly, in *Fry* (2011), the accused, using a blowtorch and a large amount of gasoline, deliberately set fire to the house of his intended victim. His motive was revenge on the victim, who had given the police a statement implicating the accused. There was an explosion that killed five other people in the house. The actual target of the attack survived, although he was badly burned. The B.C. Court of Appeal upheld Fry's convictions on five counts of first-degree

5. In the case of *Khawaja* (2012), the Supreme Court of Canada ruled that this so-called motive clause does not violate either s. 7 or s. 2 of the *Charter*.

murder and one of attempted murder. The Court of Appeal ruled that the trial judge had correctly instructed the jury on the application of the doctrine of transferred intent in section 229(b) to the murder charges. Justice Rowles stated, on behalf of the Court, that:

> The judge instructed the jury that if they were satisfied beyond a reasonable doubt that the appellant intended to cause Bolingo's death or intended to cause him bodily harm knowing that it was likely to cause his death and was reckless whether death ensued or not, but by accident or mistake caused the deaths of the victims named in counts one to five, he was guilty of the murder of those victims. The judge also made plain that if the jury were satisfied beyond a reasonable doubt that the appellant planned and deliberated the murder of Bolingo, he was guilty of the first degree murder of the victims in all of those counts. The instructions given were correct in law.

However, in the case of *Fontaine* (2002), the Manitoba Court of Appeal held that the doctrine of transferred intent embodied in section 229(b) does not apply to the situation where the accused attempts to commit suicide and accidentally kills another person. In this case, the accused had attempted to commit suicide by driving his vehicle into a parked semitrailer. Instead, he caused the death of one of the passengers in his car. In the view of the Court of Appeal, there was a marked difference between the intent to commit suicide and the intent to kill another person:

> First degree murder is perhaps the most stigmatizing offence known to law. It carries with it the most draconian minimum sentence of life imprisonment with no parole for 25 years. It is normally associated with the act of one who plans and deliberates to take the life of another person. Society as a whole condemns this crime.
>
> Suicide on the other hand is normally seen as an act of desperation, often impulsive, and the act of a person who is ill and in need of treatment. By removing the crime of attempted suicide from the *Criminal Code*, Parliament recognized society's desire to see individuals who attempt suicide treated instead of criminalized.

The principles underlying transferred intent apply to crimes that require a result as part of the *actus reus*; for example, death of a human being in cases of unlawful homicide. But inchoate crimes in general, and attempted murder in particular, do *not* require a result or harm as part of their *actus reus*. The *actus reus* is complete upon the first act beyond preparation.

As noted by the Manitoba Court of Appeal in *Vandergraaf* (1994), a critical component of the doctrine of transferred intent is the requirement that the accused's intent may be transferred only where the *actus reus* and *mens rea* of the same offence coincide. In this case, the accused had intended to throw a small jar of peanut butter onto the ice at a hockey arena. As was the case for many other fans, he was upset that the team he supported had lost a game in overtime. Sadly, his aim was erratic, and the jar hit a woman who was standing in the front row at ice-level, causing an injury to her. The accused was charged with assault with a weapon (section 267). The trial judge convicted the accused because he had the "intention to apply force in a general sense." However, the Manitoba Court of Appeal allowed Vandergraaf's appeal and entered an acquittal. As Justice Philp said, "[W]ithout proof of an intention to apply force to the complainant, or to another person, there cannot be a conviction of assault." Vandergraaf never intended to apply force to a human being and he, therefore, lacked the *mens rea* for assault even though he accidentally committed the *actus reus* of this offence. Therefore, the doctrine of transferred intent could not apply.

The limitations on the doctrine of transferred intent may be illustrated by considering the following hypothetical examples:

1. Let us suppose that Sinbad, the knife thrower at the local circus, has a burning desire to kill Hercules (the circus strong man). One evening, as dusk falls, he sees what he thinks is the silhouette of Hercules against the evening sky. He throws a knife at the figure and his aim is true. However, when Sinbad goes to inspect the corpse, he discovers that he has killed Leo (the lion tamer) by mistake. In these circumstances, it is clear that Sinbad is guilty of murder. After all, he killed the person at whom he was aiming his knife, and it is irrelevant that he was mistaken as to the person's identity.
2. Sinbad is walking in the local park when he sees Hercules coming toward him. He decides to seize his chance to kill Hercules and takes aim with one of his knives. Just as he is throwing the knife, he trips and the knife deviates from its course, killing Chuckles, the clown, who was walking unseen in the long grass. Once again, it is clear that Sinbad is guilty of murder under section 229(b). He intended to kill one human being and actually killed another.

3. Sinbad is still desperate to kill Hercules. He sees him walking side by side with Jumbo, the circus elephant, in a parade. Once again, he decides to strike while the iron is hot and aims his knife at Hercules. However, the knife misses its mark and instead kills Jumbo. Unlike examples 1 and 2, the doctrine of transferred intent may not be applied since the *actus reus* and *mens rea* of the same crime do not coincide. Although Sinbad committed the *actus reus* of killing an animal, contrary to section 445 of the *Code*, he did not intend to commit this offence and his intention to commit murder (in relation to Hercules) cannot be transferred from one type of offence to another. In brief, intention can be transferred only within the limits of the same offence.
4. A dispirited Sinbad decides to kill Bruin, the circus bear. He takes aim with his knife and throws it toward the bear. However, at the last minute the knife deviates from its course and kills Hercules. Sinbad's intent to kill an animal (contrary to section 445 of the *Code*) cannot be transferred so as to convict him of murder—even though he has committed the *actus reus* of homicide by killing Hercules. Of course, it is probable that Sinbad would be convicted of causing death by criminal negligence, contrary to section 220 of the *Code*. It is also probable that Sinbad could be convicted of an attempt to kill an animal, just as he could have been convicted of attempted murder in example 3. However, liability for these attempted offences would clearly not be based upon the doctrine of transferred intent, but rather on general principles of criminal law.

The doctrine of transferred intent has been criticized because it might lead to a situation in which an individual is punished for what is, at best, an *accident*. The Ontario Court of Appeal expressed some sympathy for this view in *Irwin* (1998). In this case, the accused was fighting a man called Graham on the outdoor patio of a restaurant. As the two men grappled with each other, they fell over the victim, causing him serious injuries. The Crown laid a charge of assault causing bodily harm and relied on the principle of transferred intent. The accused was convicted and appealed to the Ontario Court of Appeal. This court took the view that the doctrine of transferred intent, in the specific context of an *assault* charge, "raises difficult problems." Justice Doherty stated that "these problems could have been avoided had the appellant been charged with unlawfully causing bodily harm to [the victim]" (see section 269 of the *Criminal Code*). The court amended the indictment so as to charge Irwin with unlawfully causing bodily harm and then affirmed his conviction. What the Court of Appeal did in *Irwin* is to signal to Crown counsel that, wherever possible, they should try to avoid using the theory of transferred intent in cases of this type. The offence of unlawfully causing bodily harm was an appropriate charge to lay in the *Irwin* case because the accused's unlawful behaviour had caused injury to the victim and it was necessary for the Crown only to prove that any reasonable person engaged in fighting in a public place would have foreseen the risk that someone in the vicinity of the fight might be physically injured. This approach neatly avoids the need to rely on the doctrine of transferred intent.

RECKLESSNESS AS A FORM OF SUBJECTIVE *MENS REA*

Definition of Recklessness

One form of subjective *mens rea* that may be sufficient for conviction of a criminal offence is **recklessness**. As the Supreme Court of Canada stated, in *H. (A.D.)* (2013), recklessness means "that the accused persisted in a course of conduct knowing of the risk which it created."

For many offences in the *Criminal Code*, Parliament has specifically legislated that recklessness is a form of *mens rea* sufficient for conviction of the accused person. However, there are also many *Criminal Code* offences for which Parliament has not specifically defined the necessary *mens rea* elements. In general, the courts have ruled that if an offence of this type requires proof of subjective *mens rea*, then recklessness will be one form of *mens rea* that will be sufficient for conviction. For example, in *H. (A.D.)* (2013), the Supreme Court of Canada was required to define the *mens rea* elements of the offence of unlawfully abandoning a child under 10 years. Section 218 of the *Criminal Code* provides that "Every one who unlawfully abandons or exposes a child who is under the age of ten years, so that its life is or is likely to be endangered or its health is or is likely to be permanently injured … [is guilty of an indictable or summary conviction offence]."

Parliament did not clearly indicate the *mens rea* elements that need to be established for this offence. Therefore, the Supreme Court made the decision that this offence required proof of subjective *mens rea* and went on to rule that this would include intention, knowledge, recklessness, and wilful blindness:

> [A] subjective standard means, in the context of an offence under s. 218 of the *Code*, that the fault element requires proof at least of recklessness, in other words that the accused persisted in a course of conduct knowing of the risk which it created. Subjective fault, of course, may also refer to other states of mind. It includes *intention* to bring about certain consequences; actual *knowledge* that the consequences will occur; or *wilful blindness*—that is, knowledge of the need to inquire as to the consequences and deliberate failure to do so. ... It is because the definition of the offence incorporates the notion of risk to life or health that a subjective fault element would require the Crown to show at least recklessness, that is, that the accused actually knew of the risk to the child's life or health.

Before discussing some other offences that include recklessness as a sufficient form of *mens rea*, it is necessary to more fully define the concept.

People are reckless, with respect to a *consequence* of their actions, when they foresee that it may occur but do not desire it or foresee it as certain. For example, suppose that Merdle fires a gun into a crowded lecture hall in order to "scare people." Merdle does not wish to kill anyone, but he necessarily realizes that someone may be killed. He decides to proceed with his irresponsible conduct regardless of this risk. In these circumstances, we would clearly say that Merdle is reckless as to the consequence that someone may be killed by his actions. People are reckless with respect to a *circumstance* when they realize that it may exist but neither know, nor desire, that it does exist. For example, suppose that Verisopht points a revolver at Slackbridge. Verisopht does not know whether the gun is loaded. He hopes that the gun is not loaded but decides to pull the trigger regardless. We would have little difficulty in branding Verisopht as reckless. It will be noted that, in both the above examples, the accused undoubtedly foresee the risk that their conduct creates. They then decide to proceed with their course of conduct regardless of their appreciation of the inherent risk of so doing.

Recklessness contains both a subjective and an objective element. The subjective element consists of subjective foresight of the risk(s) created by the conduct of the accused person. The objective element consists of an unreasonable assumption of that risk—in the sense that a reasonable person acting prudently would not have assumed the risk that the accused foresaw. Clearly, it would be absurd to penalize everyone who foresees that their conduct creates a risk; therefore, the objective element of recklessness is a vital component of this particular form of *mens rea*. The subjective element of recklessness requires that the accused person actually foresees the risk created by their conduct, and, for this reason, recklessness is sometimes referred to as advertent negligence: a reckless person "adverts," or directs their mind, to the risk in question. As Justice Moldaver stated, on behalf of the Supreme Court of Canada in *Tatton* (2015), "Recklessness describes the act of one who sees the risk and acts without regard for the consequences. ... It always involves a subjective inquiry."

The objective element of recklessness is based on the recognition that the criminal law should punish only individuals who assume *unreasonable* risks. If a reasonable person, acting prudently and facing the same circumstances as the accused, would have assumed the risk in question, then the accused person's conduct may not be branded as reckless. For example, a surgeon may assume a high degree of risk in carrying out a particular surgical procedure if this is the only way in which they may save the life of a patient. If the procedure has a 60 percent chance of failure, the surgeon may still be justified in proceeding with the surgery if the only alternative (a failure to intervene) is certain death. Conversely, a surgeon would not be justified in carrying out a high-risk procedure if there are alternative procedures that are less perilous and offer the patient equal, if not better, chances for recovery.

By way of summary, therefore, it can be stated that reckless people subjectively appreciate the risk that their conduct creates; however, criminal responsibility is imposed only if reasonable persons would not have assumed such a risk in the same circumstances. Since reckless people fully appreciate that their conduct creates a substantial risk and proceed regardless, we may say that they deliberately choose to do something wrong. Liability for recklessness, therefore, is clearly based upon the moral blameworthiness of the individual defendant.

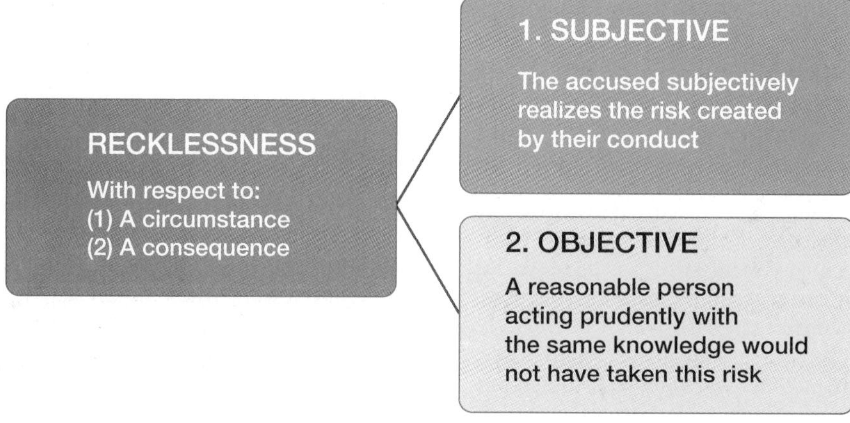

Figure 4-3
Recklessness as a Form of Subjective Mens Rea

Examples of *Criminal Code* Offences Requiring Proof of Recklessness

Although the courts have themselves expanded the concept of *mens rea* to include recklessness in relation to a number of criminal offences, the *Criminal Code* expressly states that recklessness is a sufficient form of *mens rea* for conviction in relation, for example, to the three following categories of offences.

1. Murder

Section 229 of the *Criminal Code* provides that:

> Culpable homicide is murder
>
> (a) Where the person who causes the death of a human being
>
> (i) means to cause his death, or
>
> (ii) means to cause him bodily harm that he knows is likely to cause his death, and is reckless whether death ensues or not.

Section 229(a)(ii) deals with the situation where the accused person has killed someone, and the Crown can prove that they intentionally inflicted bodily harm that they subjectively realized would be likely to cause death. If the Crown can also establish that the accused continued with the assault on the victim, regardless of their knowledge of that deadly risk, there will be a conviction of **murder**. This would be a classic example of recklessness as a form of subjective *mens rea*, because the accused clearly chooses to inflict a degree of injury that they subjectively realize is likely to cause the death of the victim. As Chief Justice Finch, of the Court of Appeal of the Yukon Territory, remarked in *Rodrigue* (2007):

> [W]ithin the meaning of s. 229(a)(ii), reckless refers to the foreseeability of a likely, as opposed to simply a possible, consequence flowing from the bodily harm that he is occasioning the victim. ... In other words, within the legal definition of the mental element for murder, reckless is synonymous with a substantially subjective state of mind, and not with imprudence or carelessness.

Although recklessness coupled with an intent to inflict deadly harm is a sufficient basis for establishing murder under section 229(a)(ii), it is important to recognize that the Crown nevertheless has to establish an onerous *mens rea* requirement in order to obtain a conviction. As Justice Cory of the Supreme Court of Canada emphasized, in the *Cooper* case (1993), "it is not sufficient that the accused foresee simply a danger of death; the accused must foresee a *likelihood* of death flowing from the bodily harm that he is occasioning the victim" [emphasis added]. Furthermore, as the Ontario Court of Appeal emphasized in *Zoldi* (2018), simple recklessness is not *per se* sufficient for conviction under section 229(a)(ii): "The recklessness component within s. 229(a)(ii) requires proof of knowledge that death will *likely* result and a deliberate disregard for this consequence by going ahead anyway."

In all cases involving section 229(a)(ii), juries must be instructed that *subjective foresight* of the likelihood of death is critical to a guilty verdict.

2. Damage to Property, Etc.

Section 429(1) of the *Criminal Code* provides that:

> Every one who causes the occurrence of an event by doing an act or by omitting to do an act that is his duty to do, knowing that the act or omission will probably cause the occurrence of the event and being reckless whether the event occurs or not, shall be deemed, for the purposes of this Part, wilfully to have caused the occurrence of the event.

Parliament has unequivocally chosen to treat reckless defendants in exactly the same manner as those who have acted wilfully (or intentionally) in relation to the various property offences set out in Part XI of the *Code*. These offences include mischief in the sense of damage to property, data, religious property, and so forth (section 430); "kills, maims, wounds, poisons or injures dogs, birds or animals that are kept for a lawful purpose" [subsection 445(1)(a)]; causing unnecessary suffering to animals or birds [subsection 445.1(1)(a)]; and wilful neglect causing damage or injury to animals or birds for which one has a legal responsibility (section 446).

3. Arson

Sections 433, 434, and 434.1 of the *Criminal Code* impose criminal liability for both intentional and reckless damage to property that is caused by fire or explosion. Section 433 states that:

> Every person who intentionally or recklessly causes damage by fire or explosion to property, whether or not that person owns the property, is guilty of an indictable offence and liable to imprisonment for life where
>
> (a) the person knows that or is reckless with respect to whether the property is inhabited or occupied; or
>
> (b) the fire or explosion causes bodily harm to another person.

Section 434 states:

> Every person who intentionally or recklessly causes damage by fire or explosion to property that is not wholly owned by that person is guilty of an indictable offence and liable to imprisonment for a term not exceeding fourteen years.

Section 434.1 states:

> Every person who intentionally or recklessly causes damage by fire or explosion to property that is owned, in whole or in part, by that person is guilty of an indictable offence and liable to imprisonment for a term not exceeding fourteen years, where the fire or explosion seriously threatens the health, safety or property of another person.

Section 433 is the most serious offence, carrying a maximum sentence of life imprisonment, because of the danger to human life and limb caused by the arson. Section 433(a), for example, applies where the accused intentionally or recklessly causes damage by fire and "the person knows that or is reckless with respect to whether the property is inhabited or occupied." Interestingly, in *Ludwig* (2018), the Ontario Court of Appeal ruled that this provision did not apply when an accused owned the property and was the sole occupant at the time. He had apparently set a fire in an attempt at suicide and was the only person who ran the risk of death or bodily harm. Justice Doherty stated that:

> Section 433(a) targets arsonists who endanger others by setting fires in places in which others live, or in places occupied by others. Knowledge or recklessness in the presence, or perhaps the potential presence, of others in those locations is what warrants characterizing the accused's actions as the most serious kind of arson.

Brain (2003) involved a charge under the less serious offence under section 434. The accused in this case was charged with "intentionally or recklessly" causing "damage by fire or explosion to property that is not wholly owned by that person." He had set fire to a storage hut and denied that he had done so intentionally. However, he admitted that he had been smoking cigarettes in the hut and that the fire might have started as a consequence of his having accidentally discarded or flipped a cigarette butt into a cardboard container. The trial judge convicted Brain on the basis that Brain had started the fire "recklessly." The judge held that:

> [T]he defendant must have known that his conduct, the reckless flipping of a live cigarette [butt] into flammable material, would cause the event, namely a fire, and that he was reckless as to whether or not the fire occurred. In other words, he just did not care one way or the other, and that moves the conduct into the realm of the criminal.

The British Columbia Court of Appeal unanimously rejected an appeal by Brain against his conviction.

It is important to bear in mind that, under section 434, the Crown has to prove that the accused was intentional or reckless with respect to the issue of *damage to property*. In *Tatton* (2015), the accused had started a fire that destroyed the contents of the home occupied by his ex-girlfriend. While intoxicated, he left a pan containing oil on the burner of the stove, with the heat set to high. Tatton then walked out of the house and went to a Tim Horton's outlet to purchase a coffee. He did not return for 20 minutes. When he did so, the house was on fire. He was charged with arson under section 434 and was acquitted at trial. He had claimed the fire was an accident and the trial judge ruled that Tatton could rely on his intoxication as a defence. The acquittal was upheld by the Ontario Court of Appeal, but the Supreme Court of Canada set aside the acquittal and ordered a new trial. The Supreme Court ruled as a matter of law that self-induced intoxication is not a defence to arson—unless Tatton could prove that he was in a state "akin to automatism" (i.e., that he was in such an extreme state of incapacitation that he was acting involuntarily). In delivering the judgment of the Supreme Court, Justice Moldaver made some critical points about the *mens rea* for arson under section 434, with particular reference to recklessness:

> Deciding how the fire started is only one of the factors a trier of fact may wish to consider. The end game involves looking at all of the surrounding circumstances to determine whether it can be inferred that the accused intended to cause damage to someone else's property or was reckless whether damage ensued or not. The mere fact that the fire was set intentionally or recklessly may not be enough to establish that the accused intentionally or recklessly caused damage to the property. Context is important and will play a key role in determining whether such an inference can be drawn. …
>
> In summary, the determinative question is not how the fire was started, although the answer to that question may provide important context. An accused's guilt under s. 434 hinges on whether he or she intentionally or recklessly caused damage to the property in question.

Justice Moldaver gave two examples to illustrate the importance of context. In one example, an individual burns leaves in a controlled fire in a fire pit and a gust of wind blows some burning leaves onto a neighbour's shed located 20 metres away, causing it to catch fire. Although the individual deliberately set the fire, there would certainly be a serious question as to whether they intentionally or recklessly caused damage to the shed. The second example involved an individual who deliberately set fire to a towel, dropped it on a carpet and walked away without making any effort to extinguish it. In these circumstances, it would undoubtedly be a reasonable inference to draw that this individual intentionally or recklessly caused damage to the carpet.

WILFUL BLINDNESS AS A FORM OF SUBJECTIVE *MENS REA*

Canadian courts have expanded the *mens rea* requirement of certain offences to include **wilful blindness**. This form of *mens rea* exists when accused persons are virtually certain that particular circumstances exist (e.g., that goods are stolen) but deliberately "shut their eyes" to these circumstances. In *Briscoe* (2010), the Supreme Court of Canada held that wilful blindness is best described as "*deliberate ignorance*" and emphasized that it should be treated as a state of mind that is equivalent to actual knowledge. The Supreme Court also emphasized that wilful blindness is a form of *subjective mens rea*: "wilful blindness … involves no departure from the subjective inquiry into the accused's state of mind which must be undertaken to establish an aider or abettor's knowledge."

It certainly seems reasonable that accused persons who suspect that they are involved in criminal activities but deliberately refrain from "asking the final question" that will reveal all should be treated as though they actually knew the circumstances that rendered conduct criminal. If the law did not adopt this policy, unscrupulous defendants would be permitted to cheat justice with impunity. In *Brown* (2018a), the Ontario Court of Appeal neatly summarized the manner in which the courts have addressed this aspect of the concept:

> Wilful blindness is not simply a failure to inquire, but "deliberate ignorance" involving "an actual process of suppressing a suspicion" … To be wilfully blind an accused "must shut his eyes because he [knows] or strongly suspects that looking [will] fix him with knowledge" …

Although wilful blindness may appear to be a close relative of recklessness, it is imperative to distinguish between the two concepts. Indeed, in the case of *Sansregret* (1985), Justice McIntyre, on behalf of the Supreme Court of Canada, asserted:

> Wilful blindness is distinct from recklessness because, while recklessness involves knowledge of a danger or risk and persistence in a course of conduct which creates a risk that the prohibited result will occur, wilful blindness arises where a person who has become aware of the need for some inquiry declines to make the inquiry because he does not wish to know the truth. He would prefer to remain ignorant. The culpability in recklessness is justified by consciousness of the risk and by proceeding in the face of it, while in wilful blindness it is justified by the accused's fault in deliberately failing to inquire when he knows there is reason for inquiry.

It is significant that Canadian courts have routinely expanded the scope of subjective *mens rea* to include wilful blindness, even when Parliament has not referred to it in its definition of an offence in the *Criminal Code*. The reason for this approach lies in the judicial view that wilful blindness is the *equivalent* of, or can *substitute* for, actual knowledge. As the Supreme Court of Canada noted in *Briscoe* (2010):

> Wilful blindness does not define the *mens rea* required for particular offences. Rather, it can substitute for actual knowledge whenever knowledge is a component of the *mens rea*. The doctrine of wilful blindness imputes knowledge to an accused whose suspicion is aroused to the point where he or she sees the need for further inquiries, but *deliberately chooses* not to make those inquiries. ... "[A] finding of wilful blindness involves an affirmative answer to the question: Did the accused shut his eyes because he knew or strongly suspected that looking would fix him with knowledge?"

The significance of the conceptualization of wilful blindness as a substitute for actual knowledge is well illustrated by the decision of Alberta Court of Appeal in *Vinokurov* (2001). In this case, the accused was the manager of a pawnshop and had received stolen goods from a customer. He was charged with several counts of possession of stolen property. Section 354(1) of the *Criminal Code* states:

> Every one commits an offence who has in his possession any property or thing or any proceeds of any property or thing knowing that all or part of the property or thing or of the proceeds was obtained by or derived directly or indirectly from
>
> (a) the commission in Canada of an offence punishable by indictment; or
>
> (b) an act or omission anywhere that, if it had occurred in Canada, would have constituted an offence punishable by indictment.

Section 354(1) clearly requires that the accused person *know* that the property was stolen. The Alberta Court of Appeal ruled that wilful blindness is equivalent to actual knowledge and that it is, therefore, sufficient *mens rea* for conviction of the offence. In this respect, it is most significant that, on the other hand, the Court also ruled that recklessness would not be sufficient. As Justice Berger stated, "[W]ilful blindness is imputed knowledge while recklessness is 'something less than that.'" Vinokurov's convictions were set aside and a new trial was ordered because the trial judge had erroneously taken the view that recklessness was sufficient *mens rea* for conviction of the offence of possessing stolen property.

Examples of Wilful Blindness

The leading case dealing with wilful blindness is the decision of the Supreme Court of Canada in *Briscoe* (2010). The facts of this case are undoubtedly horrific. Briscoe was charged with the kidnapping, aggravated sexual assault, and first-degree murder of a 13-year-old girl, Nina Courtepatte. Around midnight, Laboucan, a 19-year-old man, along with three youths, lured the victim and her young friend into a car driven by Briscoe. The bait was that they would be taken to a party, but instead of being transported to a location suitable for a party, Briscoe drove them to a deserted golf course west of Edmonton. Tragically, the victim and her friend did not know that, earlier in the day, Laboucan had told Briscoe and the three youths in his group that "he would like to find someone to kill." The proposal was warmly endorsed by Laboucan's group and they selected Ms. Courtepatte for this purpose.

What happened after Briscoe had driven the victim and her friend to the golf course was summarized by Justice Charron, on behalf of the Supreme Court of Canada:

> Mr. Briscoe drove the group to a secluded golf course. Everyone got out of the car. Mr. Briscoe opened the trunk and, at Mr. Laboucan's request, handed him some pliers. One of the youths, S.B., hid a wrench up her sleeve. A sledgehammer or mallet was also taken. Except for Mr. Briscoe, everyone started to walk down a path on the golf course. For the benefit of the unsuspecting Ms. Courtepatte and her friend Ms. K.B., Mr. Laboucan and some of the others pretended to be looking for the party.
>
> At some point during the walk, Ms. S.B. struck Ms. Courtepatte from behind with the wrench. She cried out and ran to Mr. Laboucan. He whispered something that terrified her and she broke away,

> pleading with him not to make good on his threat. Around this time, Mr. Briscoe rejoined the group. For a moment, he held on to Ms. Courtepatte and angrily told her to be quiet or shut up. Mr. Laboucan then raped her. One of the youths, Mr. M.W., did the same. They then hit her in the head multiple times with the sledgehammer or mallet, and Mr. Laboucan choked her from behind with a wrench. Mr. Laboucan also directed another youth, Ms. D.T., to stab Ms. Courtepatte's throat with a throwing knife. She did. Mr. Briscoe stood by and watched the rape and murder. Ms. K.B. witnessed some of the gruesome events, but was physically unharmed. Ms. Courtepatte's badly beaten body was left behind on the golf course where it was discovered a day later.

The charges against Briscoe were based on the premise that he had aided and/or abetted the horrific crimes committed against Ms. Courtepatte and was, therefore, a party to these crimes by virtue of sections 21(1)(b) and (c) of the *Criminal Code*. To convict Briscoe, the Crown would have to prove that he intended to assist and/or encourage Laboucan and the others to commit the crimes and that he did so with sufficient knowledge of what they planned to do to the victim. The trial judge found that Briscoe had certainly committed the *actus reus* of assisting Laboucan and the others to commit the crime. Briscoe had driven the victim and Laboucan's group to a secluded location, had—at Laboucan's request—opened the trunk of the car, from which various weapons were taken, and had held on to the victim and angrily ordered her to remain quiet immediately before she was brutally assaulted, raped, and killed. The central issue, therefore, was whether the Crown could prove the necessary *mens rea* to convict Briscoe as a party to the crimes. The trial judge found that Briscoe did not have actual knowledge of what Laboucan and his group were planning to do and, therefore, Briscoe lacked the requisite *mens rea* for aiding and/or abetting. Briscoe was acquitted of all charges. The Alberta Court of Appeal allowed an appeal by the Crown and ordered a new trial for Briscoe because the trial judge had failed to consider whether or not Briscoe had been "wilfully blind" as to the intentions of Laboucan and his group. The Supreme Court of Canada rejected an appeal by Briscoe and upheld the decision of the Court of Appeal.

The Supreme Court reviewed statements made to the police by Briscoe after his arrest and ruled that they called out for an analysis of wilful blindness. Briscoe admitted that he had heard Laboucan talk about his plan to murder someone. He also conceded that when he drove the victim to the golf course, he knew something was going to happen, although he did not know exactly what would take place. Finally, he stated that when he rejoined the group on the golf course and stood by, watching the callous rape and vicious killing of Ms. Courtepatte, he "did not want to know what was happening." On behalf of the Supreme Court, Justice Charron concluded that:

> [W] ilful blindness is not simply a failure to inquire but ... "deliberate ignorance."
>
> In this case, I agree ... that the trial judge erred in law by failing to consider wilful blindness. As he noted, even Mr. Briscoe's own statements to the police suggest that he had a "strong, well-founded suspicion that someone would be killed at the golf course" ... and that he may have been wilfully blind to the kidnapping and prospect of sexual assault. His statements also show that he deliberately chose not to inquire about what the members of the group intended to do because he did not want to know. As he put it, "whatever you guys wanna do just do it. Don't do it around me I don' want to see nothing I don't know what the fuck you're gonna do." The trial judge relied heavily upon the statements in his reasons but did not refer to the doctrine of wilful blindness. Of course, whether Mr. Briscoe had the requisite *mens rea* for the three offences was a question for the trier of fact, and Mr. Briscoe is entitled to the benefit of any reasonable doubt on this issue. However, from a legal standpoint, it is my respectful view that the evidence cried out for an analysis on wilful blindness.

In April 2012, Briscoe was convicted at his retrial of the first-degree murder, kidnapping, and sexual assault of Nina Courtepatte and was sentenced to life imprisonment with no possibility of parole for 25 years.

The doctrine of wilful blindness was also applied by the Quebec Court of Appeal in *Cedeno* (2010). Nancy Cedeno was charged with a number of counts of conspiracy to import cocaine in association with a criminal organization. At the relevant time, she was a customs officer for the Canada Border Services Agency, working at the Pierre Elliott Trudeau International Airport in Montreal. She provided an associate with both prestamped customs declaration forms and the daily codes that would enable a person carrying these forms to avoid inspection of their luggage when they arrived on international flights. Although the trial judge found that there had indeed

Wilful Blindness Is Equivalent to Actual Knowledge: The Case of Michael Briscoe (2010)

• • • • • • •

The decision of the Supreme Court of Canada in *Briscoe* (2010), discussed in this chapter, constitutes the leading authority on wilful blindness as a form of subjective *mens rea*. The facts of the *Briscoe* case are undeniably shocking (the details are provided in the section on wilful blindness). It will be recalled that Briscoe was charged with the kidnapping, aggravated sexual assault, and first-degree murder of a 13-year-old girl, Nina Courtepatte, who was lured to an Edmonton golf course, where she was raped and brutally killed by Laboucan and other members of his group. Briscoe did not actually commit these offences himself, but it was alleged by the Crown that he aided or abetted them and, therefore, under section 21(2) of the *Criminal Code*, he should be convicted as a party to them.

Briscoe was acquitted at his original trial because the trial judge ruled that the Crown had not proved that Briscoe had *actual knowledge* of what Laboucan and the others were planning to do. Ultimately, the Supreme Court of Canada agreed with the Alberta Court of Appeal that there should be a new trial of Briscoe in which the trial judge should consider whether or not Briscoe was "wilfully blind" as to the intentions of Laboucan and his group when he drove them to the scene of the crimes and provided other forms of assistance. The Supreme Court emphasized that wilful blindness is equivalent to actual knowledge and, therefore, is a highly culpable form of *mens rea*—indeed, more culpable than recklessness.

At the new trial, in April 2012, Briscoe was convicted of the first-degree murder, kidnapping, and sexual assault of Nina Courtepatte and was sentenced to life imprisonment with no possibility of parole for 25 years. Contrary to the findings of the trial judge at Briscoe's first trial, Justice Yamauchi found that Briscoe *actually knew* what Laboucan and his group of followers were planning to do and intentionally assisted them in carrying out their plans. This perhaps indicates that there is a very fine line between actual knowledge and wilful blindness and that this close similarity in terms of the accused person's mental state is why the Supreme Court of Canada ruled that they should be treated as equivalent forms of *mens rea*.

Justice Yamauchi found that Briscoe had been present when Laboucan had committed an earlier murder that was eerily similar to the killing of Nina Courtepatte:

> Briscoe had previously observed Laboucan identify a woman, lure that woman into a car which travelled to an isolated and rural location, where she was beaten to death with blows to the head. The body was then abandoned at that rural location.
>
> Briscoe also knew that Laboucan was in possession of a severed human finger. The conclusion that flows from these facts is that Laboucan was sufficiently violent to injure severely, if not kill, another person or, at the very least, participate in such an activity.

The trial judge then ruled that Briscoe had heard Laboucan say that he "wanted to kill someone" just before the kidnapping, rape, and murder of Nina Courtepatte and that, given his knowledge of Laboucan's homicidal past, Briscoe would take such expressions of intent seriously:

> Briscoe had good reason to believe that when Laboucan said he wanted to kill someone, Laboucan could carry through with that intention. ... On April 2, 2005, Laboucan announced that he wanted to kill someone. Briscoe reported that he heard those statements. He heard it at Humpty's Restaurant. He heard it at Boston Pizza. He heard it when Schoenberg was in the car. Briscoe testified he heard Laboucan say "five or six times" during the day before the group travelled to the Golf Resort that, "I feel like killing somebody."

Justice Yamauchi also found that Briscoe's statement to the RCMP that he "never expected anyone to be killed" was "extremely implausible" because he knew firsthand that Laboucan was a murderer. In addition, "Briscoe knew Laboucan planned to find someone, and that person could very well be his next victim." Justice Yamauchi went on to say that:

> This Court concludes that Briscoe knew that Laboucan's plan was to murder someone. Briscoe may not have known all the details, but he knew that fact. By the time Briscoe told that to Cst. Waldorf, he knew that on at least one previous occasion, Laboucan had carried through on that plan.

Justice Yamauchi was satisfied beyond a reasonable doubt that Briscoe had knowingly provided the tools that were used in the attack on Nina Courtepatte by handing them to Laboucan who then handed the wrench and the pliers to Bird.

The trial judge summed up his findings with respect to Briscoe's knowledge of Laboucan's plans and what he intended to do once the victim was taken to the golf course:

> In summary, Briscoe:
>
> 1. knew Laboucan previously had killed or assisted in the killing of another person,
> 2. knew Laboucan said he wanted to kill someone,
> 3. knew there was no rave or party,
> 4. knew where Laboucan wanted to take his victim, viz., the Golf Resort, and the route to that area,
> 5. knew the Golf Resort was in an isolated area, and
> 6. had some idea of why Laboucan wanted tools, and that the tools were not for a break and enter.
>
> Briscoe need not have known exactly how Laboucan would commit the offences. ... He did not need to know the exact victim.

Most significantly, in terms of the requirements for a conviction of Briscoe as an aider/abetter under section 21(2) of the *Criminal Code*, Justice Yamauchi found that Briscoe *intended to assist* Laboucan in the commission of the kidnapping and unlawful confinement of Nina Courtepatte, the sexual assault on her, and her murder. As far as the first-degree murder charge was concerned, Justice Yamauchi stated that:

> Briscoe might not have been part of Laboucan's actual planning and deliberation of Courtepatte's murder. However, he knew Laboucan's plan and intended to assist Laboucan in fulfilling it. Part of the plan involved Courtepatte's kidnapping and unlawful confinement. These are offences involving the illegal domination over Courtepatte and enhances Briscoe's moral blameworthiness:
>
> Briscoe is therefore guilty of first degree murder of Courtepatte. He assisted Laboucan by delivering Courtepatte to where she was ultimately killed. He knew that a murder was something that Laboucan had planned.
>
> The second basis on which this Court concludes that Briscoe assisted Laboucan in Courtepatte's murder is that he provided Laboucan with the murder weapons (the tools) from the car trunk.
>
> This Court concludes, beyond a reasonable doubt, that Briscoe provided Laboucan with those tools with knowledge that Laboucan planned to use those tools to kill. That aided Laboucan in the commission of the murder, making Briscoe also guilty of murder on that basis, as well.

Why do you think two separate trial judges came to such remarkably different decisions with respect to Briscoe's knowledge of Laboucan's plans? Does the concept of "wilful blindness" allow judges (and jury members) to draw the inference that the accused *"must have known"* the critical facts and, therefore, convict them even though the Crown has not proved actual knowledge beyond a reasonable doubt? Would drawing such an inference meet the requirement that the accused should manifest at least "deliberate ignorance" (the term the Supreme Court believed was a more helpful description of the state of wilful blindness)? In other words, is "deliberate ignorance" a specific state of mind that must be proved, as opposed to a judge or jury merely making the *assumption* the accused *"must have had"* knowledge because the circumstances are highly suggestive of actual knowledge? Why did the Supreme Court of Canada draw such a sharp distinction between recklessness and wilful blindness?

been a conspiracy to import cocaine and to possess it for the purpose of trafficking, he nevertheless ruled that there was no evidence to establish that Cedeno knew its purpose. The trial judge refused to apply the doctrine of wilful blindness to prove that Cedeno knew the objective of the conspiracy and acquitted her of the conspiracy charges. The Court of Appeal allowed the Crown's appeal and ordered a new trial on the conspiracy charges. The Court ruled that the trial judge had made an error when he had ruled that wilful blindness cannot substitute for knowledge in the context of a conspiracy charge. Whenever knowledge is an element of the *mens rea* for an offence, wilful blindness may be substituted for it. In the words of the judgment of the Court of Appeal:

> [I]t is true that many of the respondent's statements both upon her first arrest on May 8, 2006, and at trial support the conclusion that she was closing her eyes to the purpose of the conspiracy because she knew or strongly suspected that if she were to open them, she would discover that the conspiracy was indeed to import narcotics.

The courts have repeatedly stressed that wilful blindness exists only when accused persons have every reason to suspect the existence of circumstances that would render their actions criminal but deliberately shut their eyes because they think it will serve their purposes to plead ignorance to the authorities. It is not enough for the Crown to contend that the accused was negligent in the sense of failing to make the inquiries that a reasonable person would have made in the circumstances. Merely neglecting to make inquiries (even those that a "reasonable person" might make) does not *per se* constitute wilful blindness—a considerably more culpable state of mind must be proved by the Crown.

SUBJECTIVE *MENS REA* AS A *CHARTER* REQUIREMENT: THE CASE OF MURDER

Impact of the *Charter* on the Doctrine of *Mens Rea*

We have seen that the *mens rea* elements of a criminal offence may be based on subjective or objective liability. However, Parliament does not have a totally free hand in making this decision. Indeed, the Supreme Court of Canada has ruled that the *Charter* demands that there be a minimum requirement of subjective *mens rea* for a very small number of serious offences, such as murder.

In the case of *Martineau* (1990), the Supreme Court of Canada decided that although Parliament may impose objective liability in relation to certain *Criminal Code* offences, such as dangerous driving or manslaughter, the crime of murder is so serious that the *Charter* requires that the Crown prove that the accused either deliberately intended to kill or, at the very least, subjectively foresaw the risk that their conduct was likely to cause death. To convict an accused person in the absence of these subjective elements would amount to depriving them of "the right to life, liberty and security of the person" in a manner that contravenes the "fundamental principles of justice" enshrined in section 7 of the *Canadian Charter of Rights and Freedoms*. As Chief Justice Lamer stated:

> In my view, in a free and democratic society that values the autonomy and free will of the individual, the stigma and punishment attaching to the most serious of crimes, murder, should be reserved for those who choose to intentionally cause death or who choose to inflict bodily harm that they know is likely to cause death. The essential role of requiring subjective foresight of death in the context of murder is to maintain a proportionality between the stigma and punishment attached to a murder conviction and the moral blameworthiness of the offender. Murder has long been recognized as the "worst" and most heinous of peace-time crimes. It is, therefore, essential that to satisfy the principles of fundamental justice, the stigma and punishment attaching to a murder conviction must be reserved for those who either intend to cause death or to cause bodily harm that they know will likely cause death.

In *Vaillancourt* (1987), *Martineau* (1990), and *Sit* (1991), the Supreme Court of Canada declared the various parts of section 230 of the *Criminal Code* invalid under the *Charter*. Section 230 had made it possible to convict accused persons of murder even though they did not subjectively foresee even the possibility that their conduct would cause death. Since this section is now invalid, it will not be discussed further. However, the constitutional requirement—that *subjective foresight of the likelihood of death must be proved before an individual may be convicted of murder*—is clearly of vital significance to the development of Canadian criminal law. What remains to be seen is the extent, if any, to which the Supreme Court may be willing to expand the category of offences for which proof of subjective *mens rea* is a *Charter* requirement.

The *Charter* Requirement of Subjective *Mens Rea* and Section 229(c) of the *Criminal Code*

Section 229 of the *Criminal Code* defines the circumstances in which culpable homicide will be categorized as murder. Section 229(a) states that:

> Culpable homicide is murder
>
> (a) where the person who causes the death of a human being
>
> (i) means to cause his death, or
>
> (ii) means to cause him bodily harm that he knows is likely to cause his death, and is reckless whether death ensues or not.

The vast majority of murder charges fall within the scope of section 229(a) of the *Code*, and it is clear that both of the *mens rea* requirements under subsections (i) and (ii) are based on the accused's *subjective foresight of the likelihood of death*. Therefore, section 229(a) clearly meets the constitutional standard prescribed by the Supreme Court in the *Martineau* case (1990). However, section 229(c) of the *Code* expands the scope of the crime of murder to cover another set of circumstances, and in so doing, it raises doubts concerning its constitutional validity. Section 229(c) states that murder has been committed:

> (c) where a person, for an unlawful object, does anything that he knows or ought to know is likely to cause death, and thereby causes death to a human being, notwithstanding that he desires to effect his object without causing death or bodily harm to any human being.

In essence, section 229(c) states that an accused person may be convicted of murder if they caused the death of the victim in pursuit of an "unlawful object" and that they did so either:

1. with actual knowledge that they were doing something that was "likely" to cause death to someone, or
2. in circumstances in which they "ought" to have known that the death of someone was a "likely" consequence of their conduct.

The use of the words "ought to know" clearly indicates that Parliament intended to impose an *objective* test of criminal responsibility in those situations where the Crown is unable to prove that the accused person had actual knowledge that death was a likely consequence of their conduct. In other words, the court is directed to consider what *reasonable* persons would have contemplated had they been confronted by exactly the same set of circumstances as the accused. This means that an accused person may be convicted of murder, under the provisions of section 229(c), even if they did not *subjectively* foresee the likelihood of death ensuing from their conduct: all that the Crown needs to prove is that a *reasonable person would have done so.* In this sense, the use of the words "ought to know" undoubtedly infringes the *Charter* requirement that an individual may be convicted of the extraordinarily serious crime of murder only where the Crown can prove subjective foresight of death.

In *Martineau* (1990), Chief Justice Lamer expressed the view that the requirement of subjective foresight as a precondition for conviction of murder "casts serious if not fatal doubt on the constitutionality of part of [section 229(c)] of the *Code*, specifically the words 'ought to know is likely to cause death.'" He went on to state that:

> In my view, subjective foresight of death must be proven beyond a reasonable doubt before a conviction of murder can be sustained and, as a result, it is obvious the part of [s. 229(c)] of the *Code* allowing for a conviction upon proof that the accused ought to have known that death was likely to result violates ss. 7 and 11(d) of the *Charter*.

The chief justice also contended that the words "ought to know" in section 229(c) could not be saved by section 1 of the *Charter* as a "reasonable limit in a free and democratic society."

Chief Justice Lamer's views on section 229(c) were not necessary to the decision in *Martineau*, which was actually concerned with the constitutionality of section 230 of the *Criminal Code* and were not technically binding on other courts. However, it is now generally accepted that section 229(c) applies only where an accused person engages in a dangerous act that they subjectively foresee is likely to cause death, and does so for a *separate, unlawful object.*

In *Shand* (2011), the Ontario Court of Appeal dealt directly with the constitutionality of section 229(c) in light of the *Charter* and took the view that Chief Justice Lamer's statement about it in *Martineau* had definitively settled the issue. Shand had been a party to a home invasion whose objective was to steal marijuana from someone known to be a dealer. When the occupants of the house were gathered in a basement bedroom, Shand took out a handgun to subdue them. The most favourable interpretation of the evidence with respect to Shand was that the gun discharged accidentally and killed one of the male occupants. Shand was convicted of second-degree murder and appealed his conviction to the Ontario Court of Appeal. However, his appeal was dismissed.

Shand challenged the constitutionality of section 229(c) on the basis that section 7 of the *Charter* requires that, as a minimum *mens rea* for conviction of murder, the Crown must prove that the accused person intended to cause serious bodily harm to the victim. The Court of Appeal rejected this assertion and ruled that the Supreme Court of Canada had already decided, in the *Martineau* case, that section 229(c) is constitutional because, if courts exclude the words "or ought to know" as being invalid, it meets the *Charter* requirement that there must be proof of "subjective foresight of the likelihood of death." In delivering the judgment of the Court of Appeal, Justice Rouleau referred to the words of Chief Justice Lamer in *Martineau*:

> I can only conclude that Lamer C.J.C. considered the remainder of s. 229(c), after removal of the "ought to know" portion, to be constitutional. Subjective

> foresight of death coupled with the unlawful object in s. 229(c) met the constitutional minimum. The specific intent to kill or to cause serious bodily harm was not required.

Justice Rouleau emphasized that:

> [S.] 229(c) requires an intent to further the pursuit of an unlawful object, which is itself an indictable offence requiring full *mens rea*. When the subjective foresight of death is combined with an ulterior intent that is itself sufficiently culpable, together they constitute a proper normative substitute for an intent to kill.

It is important to take into account that section 229(c) sets a high bar for the Crown. The courts have underscored the requirement that the accused subjectively foresaw the *likelihood* that someone would die as a consequence of their pursuit of an unlawful object. In *Roks* (2011), the accused was charged with second-degree murder and conspiracy to commit arson. Roks had been involved in a scheme to burn down a building and make a false insurance claim. Roks's role in the scheme was to select the arsonists and concoct an alibi for the owner of the torched building. The arsonists used an excessive amount of accelerant and caused an explosion that killed one of them and severely injured another. The murder charge was based on section 229(c). Roks was convicted at trial and appealed to the Ontario Court of Appeal, which set aside the murder conviction and substituted a conviction of manslaughter. The Court of Appeal concluded that, in the circumstances of this particular case, it was not reasonable to conclude that Roks subjectively foresaw that it was likely that someone would die as a consequence of the arson scheme.

On behalf of the Court of Appeal, Justice Watt pointed out that there was no statement by Roks that he knew it was likely that someone would die. Justice Watt also stated that it would not be reasonable to draw the inference that Roks had such knowledge: Roks was not present at the scene of the crime; did not know what accelerant would be used; knew that the fire would be set at night, when other people would not be in the vicinity; and had been told that there would be someone with "fire suppression" training when the fire was set. Clearly, the Crown had not proved that Roks had subjective knowledge that death was a *likely* consequence of setting fire to the building.

A critical component of murder under section 229(c) is the requirement that the dangerous act that caused death must have been carried out in pursuit of an "unlawful object." What is meant by "unlawful object" in the specific context of section 229(c)? This aspect of the section was interpreted by the Supreme Court in the case of *Vasil* (1981), in which Justice Lamer stated that "unlawful object" in this particular context means "the object of conduct which, if prosecuted fully, would amount to a serious crime, that is an indictable offence requiring *mens rea*." In the *Vasil* case, the Supreme Court stated that an intent to destroy property (which, if carried out, would constitute an indictable offence under section 430)

Section 229(c): Committing an inherently dangerous act for an unlawful purpose and which causes the death of a human being.

constitutes an "unlawful object" under section 229(c), but an intent to seek revenge would not. Similarly, in *Magno* (2006), the unlawful object of a fatal incident of arson was alleged to be a conspiracy to commit arson for a fraudulent purpose (an indictable offence contrary to section 465 of the *Criminal Code*), the object of the arson being the intention to submit a fraudulent claim to an insurance company.

A particularly dramatic illustration of the application of section 229(c) occurred in the extraordinary case of *Meiler* (1999). The accused was convinced that his estranged wife was "seeing" a man called Roach. He later admitted that he decided to kill Roach and then commit suicide. He took a loaded shotgun, cocked it, and put his finger on the trigger with the intention of killing Roach. It appeared that Skrinjaric intercepted Meiler and jumped on his back. There was a struggle for the gun, which tragically discharged and killed Nick Biuk, who was standing close by. Meiler was charged with second-degree murder. The Crown relied on the provisions of section 229(c) of the *Code* to establish the necessary *mens rea* for murder. The trial judge instructed the members of the jury that Meiler could be convicted of murder under section 229(c) if they found that, for the unlawful object of killing Roach, the accused had carried a loaded gun with his finger on the trigger and that he had known that what he was doing was *likely to cause the death of a human being*. The trial judge also stated that if Meiler's conduct had caused the death of Biuk and if he had the necessary *mens rea* under section 229(c), then it was irrelevant that the gun discharged accidentally. Meiler was convicted of second-degree murder and his subsequent appeal to the Ontario Court of Appeal was dismissed.

In delivering the judgment of the Court of Appeal, Justice O'Connor held that the Crown had established the necessary *mens rea* requirements for conviction of murder under the provisions of section 229(c). Furthermore, the court rejected Meiler's argument that it would be unfair to convict him of murder when he did not foresee the *precise circumstances* in which a human being was likely to be killed (Meiler contended that he had intended to kill Roach, not Biuk, and the immediate cause of death had been the *accidental* discharge of the firearm during Meiler's tussle with Skrinjaric). Justice O'Connor stated that:

> In my view, s. 229(c) does not require that an offender foresee the precise situation or all of the events that result in the death. It is sufficient if the offender has the subjective foresight that the acts done for the unlawful object are likely to cause death and those acts are sufficiently linked to the death to have caused the death within the meaning of the section. …
>
> The moral blameworthiness of an offender who does certain acts for an unlawful object knowing

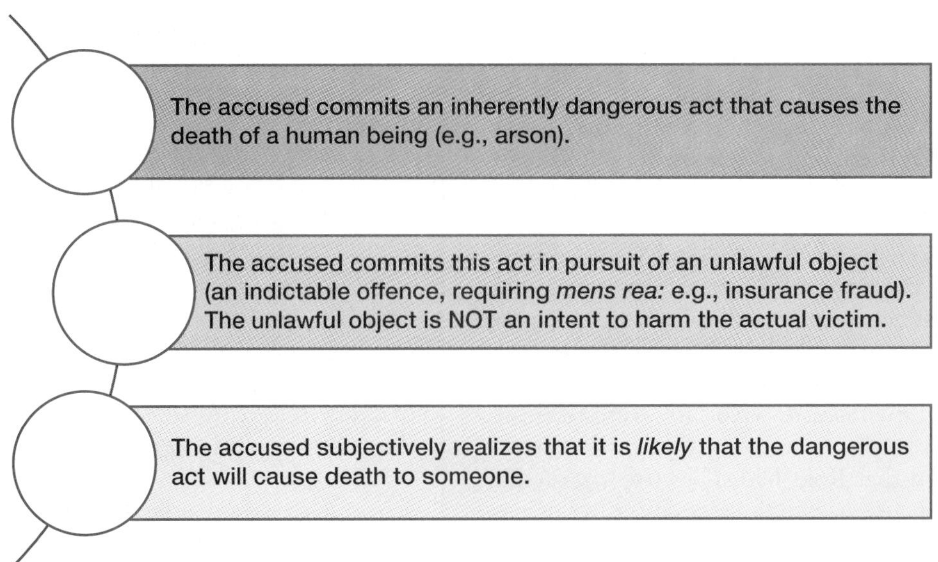

The accused commits an inherently dangerous act that causes the death of a human being (e.g., arson).
The accused commits this act in pursuit of an unlawful object (an indictable offence, requiring *mens rea:* e.g., insurance fraud). The unlawful object is NOT an intent to harm the actual victim.
The accused subjectively realizes that it is *likely* that the dangerous act will cause death to someone.

Figure 4-4

Murder under Section 229(c) of the Criminal Code

> that those acts are likely to cause death to someone other than the subject of the unlawful object is no less serious because the offender does not foresee the very situation or the precise circumstances that ultimately lead to that death.

A somewhat similar application of section 229(c) occurred in *Mckenna* (2018) when, in the course of a home invasion, McKenna pointed a loaded gun at the victim with the purpose of extorting money. According to Mckenna, the victim grabbed the gun, which he claimed discharged accidentally. The New Brunswick Court of Appeal upheld the jury's verdict of second-degree murder. Justice Larlee agreed with the trial judge's instruction to the jury that it did not matter that McKenna would have preferred to obtain the money without harming the victim but, if he knew that pointing a loaded shotgun was likely to cause death, he had the necessary intent for murder under section 229(c). Of course, the unlawful object here was the indictable offence of extortion.

Study Questions

1. Gride is a member of a violent gang that is involved in drug trafficking. Gride's gang is determined to eliminate the members of any other gang that attempts to deal drugs in what it considers its territory. Gride is given information that two members of a rival gang are sitting by the front window of a local restaurant. He drives to the restaurant and fires an automatic weapon at the two rival gang members. The bullets miss their intended targets and, unfortunately, ricochet off the walls of the restaurant. One bullet strikes and kills Dombey, a small boy who is standing outside the restaurant, and another bullet strikes and kills Bowser, a bulldog that is being exercised by a passerby. The Crown wishes to lay a charge of murder in relation to the death of Dombey (contrary to section 235 of the *Criminal Code*) and wilfully killing a dog (contrary to subsection 445(1)(a) of the *Criminal Code*). Do you think that these charges would be likely to succeed at Gride's trial? If you were asked to give advice to Crown counsel, would you recommend laying different charges?
2. Nero sets fire to his pet food store at 2 a.m. on a Sunday in order to collect the insurance money. The store is located near a number of other business premises. There is a major fire, and an alert passerby, seeing the flames, makes a 911 call. Owing to an unfortunate error on the part of the dispatcher, the fire department takes some time to arrive. In the meantime, the fire has spread to another building, a photography studio, owned by Claudius. Both Nero's store and Claudius's studio are reduced to mere burnt-out shells. Worse still, the firefighters discover the charred body of Tiberius, a homeless person who was using Claudius's studio as a place to sleep. There is some evidence that Nero knew that Tiberius was present in Claudius's studio at night. Nero is charged with murder. Is he guilty of this offence?
3. Job Trotter is a young law and security student. On registration day, he goes to a crowded registrar's office and proceeds to a cashier's desk, where he loudly demands "all the cash" and states that he has a gun in his pocket. When the cashier dutifully produces the money, Trotter takes it, but seeing a security guard approaching in the distance, he suddenly scatters the money in the air and shakes the hand of the cashier, saying that, of course, he was "only joking." The police are immediately called to investigate this incident, and they ask Trotter to turn out the contents of his pockets. Among the contents is a screwdriver. Trotter claims that he has a reputation for being a practical joker. What charges could reasonably be laid against Trotter? Which, if any, would be most likely to result in conviction?
4. Bucket works for a government agency. His salary has been frozen for three years and he is becoming frustrated with his financial position. He complains to his immediate superior, who suggests that Bucket should "inflate" his expense accounts to compensate for his inadequate salary. Bucket follows this advice, but an auditor questions him and discovers that Bucket has submitted expense claims that exceed his actual expenditures by some $10 000. Bucket vociferously declares that he thought he was not doing

anything wrong because his superior had encouraged him to follow this course of action and because he had a moral right to rectify the injustice he had suffered as a consequence of the salary freeze maintained by the government. If you were Crown counsel in this case, what charge(s), if any, would you lay against Bucket?

5. Bitzer is sitting at a bar, consuming a considerable quantity of alcohol. He is upset because he has been fired from his job as a security officer. He stands up and shouts, "I'm mad and I'm not going to take it anymore; I think I'm going to kill someone." He rushes out of the bar and makes his way up Main Street. He suddenly goes into a parking lot and decides to steal a car. He is just about to enter a car when he is challenged by Centurion, the night attendant. Without warning, Bitzer swings around and shoots Centurion in the chest. Centurion dies before the ambulance arrives. Bitzer is arrested and charged with first-degree murder. Medical witnesses are agreed that Bitzer was not so drunk as to prevent him from forming the intent to kill Centurion. Is he likely to be convicted of first-degree murder? Would it make any difference to your answer if there is evidence that Bitzer was mentally disordered rather than intoxicated?
6. Snubbin goes into a bar, where he meets Bumble, who claims that he is an artist. Bumble offers Snubbin a beautiful painting of a polar bear and says that he can have it for the sum of $100, provided that Snubbin gives him cash immediately. Snubbin purchases the painting and displays it in his office. Some days later, the police inform Snubbin that the painting was stolen from a famous art gallery and that it is actually worth $20 000. If you were Crown counsel, would you prosecute Snubbin even though he loudly proclaims that he did not know that the painting was stolen?
7. Steerforth is very angry with his friend Nadgett because the latter gave him a cheque that has been rejected by the bank on the basis of "insufficient funds." Steerforth decides to teach Nadgett a lesson by savagely beating him with a crowbar. Nadgett suffers such ghastly head injuries that he subsequently dies. Steerforth says that he realized that Nadgett was "hurting badly," but he claims that he never intended to kill him. Would it be possible to charge Steerforth with first- or second-degree murder?
8. Bill Sykes has recently separated from his spouse, Nancy. Sykes knows very well that Nancy does not want to have any form of communication with him and has told him that, if he does not leave her alone, she will summon the police. Sykes makes no effort to communicate with Nancy, but he frequently parks his car a few hundred yards up the street from Nancy's house and keeps an eye on who is entering and leaving the residence. Nancy sees Sykes's car on a number of occasions and, fearing for her safety, calls the police. Sykes is arrested and subsequently charged with criminal harassment. Sykes indignantly claims that he had absolutely no intention of harassing Nancy and that he believed she was entirely unaware of his presence in the street. Would Sykes have any defence against the charge laid against him?
9. The Artful Dodger decides to play a practical joke on his friend Mr. Bumble. He takes a statue from Mr. Bumble's garden and places it in front of the local police station. The Dodger thinks that what he has done is very amusing, but Mr. Bumble is very angry and is pressing the police to lay a charge of theft. If you were Crown counsel, would you charge the Artful Dodger with theft?
10. Mulberry Hawk steals Sissy Jupe's van from an underground parking lot. While Hawk is trying to exit the parking lot, he is confronted by Betsy Quilp, who is the security guard. Hawk refuses to stop and deliberately drives the van toward Quilp, who is killed in the ensuing collision. There is evidence that, on the previous day, Hawk told an acquaintance that he was intending to steal a van and that he would kill anyone who dared to stand in his way. A physician is also prepared to testify that Hawk had been drinking and that his blood alcohol level was "80 milligrams per 100 millilitres." Should Mulberry Hawk be charged with first-degree murder?
11. Durdles decides to kill Jasper, whom Durdles believes to be having an affair with Durdles's spouse. Durdles takes a loaded rifle and drives to Jasper's house. As Durdles is exiting his vehicle, he trips and the gun discharges. Tragically, the bullet kills Edwin, who happens to be walking along the sidewalk. If you were Crown counsel, would you charge Durdles with second-degree murder? If Durdles is acquitted of a charge of murder, is it likely that he would be convicted instead of manslaughter?

THE MENTAL ELEMENT IN THE CRIMINAL LAW:

Objective Liability

CHAPTER 5

Learning Objectives

After reading this chapter, you will be able to understand:

- the basic legal principle that the prosecution must prove a marked departure from the standard of care expected of the reasonable person acting prudently in order to obtain a conviction for offences imposing objective liability;
- the "modified objective" approach, which requires that the application of the reasonable person test must be based on the subjective knowledge that the accused had of the circumstances in which they found themselves;
- the basic elements of significant offences that impose objective liability: namely, dangerous operation of a motor vehicle, unlawful act manslaughter, criminal negligence causing death or bodily harm, manslaughter by criminal negligence, infanticide, unlawfully causing bodily harm, assault causing bodily harm, and aggravated assault;
- the requirement that, for crimes involving criminal negligence, the prosecution must prove that the accused's conduct amounted to a *marked and substantial* departure from the standard of the reasonable person acting prudently; and
- the nature of crimes that impose an elevated standard of care for those individuals (such as surgeons) who engage in inherently dangerous activities that require a certain level of training and

skill: examples of crimes for which the *Criminal Code* imposes an elevated standard of care are possession of explosives [s. 79], use and storage of firearms [s. 86(1)], and administration of surgical and medical treatment [s. 216].

WHAT IS OBJECTIVE LIABILITY?

Objective liability refers to the imposition of criminal liability on the basis of the standard of the hypothetical "reasonable person" rather than the subjective state of mind of the accused person. When the definition of a criminal offence incorporates objective *mens rea* elements, the Crown has to prove only that the accused person's conduct constituted a *marked departure* from the standard of care expected of the hypothetical reasonable person acting prudently: The Crown is not required to prove that the accused person was subjectively aware of the risk created by their conduct. If a reasonable person, placed in the same circumstances and with the same knowledge of those circumstances as the accused, would have been aware of the risk and would have avoided taking it, then the accused is guilty of the offence. This form of liability is objective in nature because it does not consider what, if anything, actually went on in the accused's mind with respect to the risk that their conduct was creating.

As Justice McLachlin stated, in delivering the judgment of the majority of the justices of the Supreme Court of Canada in the *Creighton* case (1993), the mental fault in objective *mens rea* "lies in failure to direct the mind to a risk which the reasonable person would have appreciated." Therefore, "objective *mens rea* is not concerned with what was actually in the accused's mind, but with what should have been there, had the accused proceeded reasonably."

In Canada, the courts do not apply a completely objective test in the sense that no consideration whatsoever is paid to what was going on inside the head of the accused person at the time of the alleged offence. Indeed, the Supreme Court of Canada has decreed that courts must apply a **modified objective test** in the sense that the accused person's subjective knowledge of the material circumstances is a relevant consideration: when deciding whether a reasonable person would have appreciated the risk created by the accused person's conduct, it must be assumed that the reasonable person has exactly the same knowledge of the material circumstances as the accused person. As Justice Charron stated, in delivering the judgment of the Supreme Court of Canada in *Beatty* (2008):

> [A] reasonably held mistake of fact may provide a complete defence if, based on the accused's reasonable perception of the facts, the conduct measured up to the requisite standard of care. It is therefore important to apply the modified objective test in the context of the events surrounding the incident. If an accused ... has an honest and reasonably held belief in the existence of certain facts, it may be a relevant consideration in assessing the reasonableness of his conduct. For example, a welder, who is engaged to work in a confined space believing on the assurance of the owner of the premises that no combustible or explosive material is stored nearby, should be entitled to have his perception, as to the presence or absence of dangerous materials, before the jury on a charge of manslaughter when his welding torch causes an explosion and a consequent death.

What Is the Minimum *Mens Rea* Requirement for Crimes Imposing Objective Liability?

A person whose conduct falls below the standard of the reasonable person is considered to have acted *negligently*. However, it is only the more serious forms of negligence that will lead to an individual being convicted of a crime under the *Criminal Code*. Mere **carelessness** (that is, conduct that falls even just a relatively small degree below the standard expected of the reasonable person) may render one liable, at **civil law**, to pay compensation, but it will not make one a criminal. As Justice Charron, of the Supreme Court of Canada, said in the case of *Beatty* (2008):

> Unquestionably, conduct which constitutes a departure from the norm expected of a reasonably prudent person forms the basis of both civil and penal negligence. However, it is important not to conflate the civil standard of negligence with the

> test for penal negligence. Unlike civil negligence, which is concerned with the apportionment of loss, penal negligence is aimed at punishing *blameworthy* conduct.

What this means is that, if someone carelessly causes harm to another person or damage to that person's property, fairness demands that the individual who caused that harm or damage should compensate the victim of that carelessness. After all, the party who was careless, rather than the innocent victim, should be made to shoulder the financial loss.

Suppose, for example, that I accidentally break my friend's antique porcelain figurine by knocking it off a table with my elbow. I am reading about the latest scandal involving a movie star and am so absorbed in this activity that I forget where I am. Suddenly, my cellphone chimes and I automatically get up from the table, not realizing that my elbow is next to the figurine. I am deeply shocked to find that I have knocked the figurine onto the floor, smashing it to pieces. I can honestly say that I caused this damage completely inadvertently (i.e., without being at all aware of the risk that my elbow might hit the figurine and cause it to fall on the floor). My friend would understandably say that I have been negligent because a reasonable person would have been more careful in the circumstances. However, what I have done would not be considered a serious case of negligence. This is definitely not a situation where there has been a marked departure from the standard of the reasonable person: indeed, it is the kind of accident that could happen to anyone. Clearly, I should not be convicted of an offence under the *Criminal Code* for such simple carelessness. However, in all fairness, I should feel obligated to compensate my friend for the loss of the figurine, since I was the one who was careless, and if I were to be so ungenerous as to refuse to pay up, my friend might be able to sue me for damages in a civil court.

Again, although mere carelessness may render an individual liable to be sued in a civil court, it is not sufficient to render them liable for conviction of an offence under the *Criminal Code*. On the contrary, it is only where there is a marked departure from the standard of care expected of a reasonable person that the accused can be convicted of a *Criminal Code* offence. In other words, under this **marked departure test**, only the most serious forms of negligent behaviour can lead to a conviction of a true crime. As Justice Charron said in *Beatty* (2008), "[I]t is only when there is a marked departure from the norm that objectively dangerous conduct demonstrates sufficient blameworthiness to support a finding of penal liability."

The Supreme Court of Canada emphasized, in *Roy* (2012), that *the minimum standard of objective liability is the marked departure standard*. This basic principle of Canadian criminal law is extremely important because the Supreme Court of Canada has ruled that section 7 of the *Charter*, which guarantees that no person may be deprived of life, liberty, or security of the person except in accordance with the fundamental principles of justice, encompasses the basic legal norm that an accused person may not be convicted of an offence under the *Criminal Code* unless they are morally blameworthy. Is a person whose behaviour constitutes a marked departure from the standard of the reasonable person morally blameworthy? In the *Creighton* case (1993), Justice McLachlin, speaking on behalf of the majority of the justices of the Supreme Court of Canada, answered this question in the affirmative:

> It is now established that a person may be held criminally responsible for negligent conduct on the objective test, and that this alone does not violate the principle of fundamental justice that the moral fault of the accused must be commensurate with the gravity of the offence and its penalty. ...
>
> Moreover, the constitutionality of crimes of negligence is also subject to the caveat that *acts of ordinary negligence may not suffice to justify imprisonment.* ... The negligence must constitute a "marked departure" from the standard of the reasonable person. *The law does not lightly brand a person as criminal.* [emphasis added]

Justice McLachlin also made the important point that, in general, a person who commits an offence negligently should receive a less severe sentence than a person who acts with subjective awareness of the risk that their conduct creates. This merely reflects the principle that the punishment for an offence should be commensurate with the degree of fault manifested on the part of the offender.

A valuable example of the application of the principle that a high degree of negligence is required before an individual may be convicted of an offence under the *Criminal Code* is furnished by the case of *Finlay* (1993), in which the accused was charged with storing firearms and ammunition in a careless manner, contrary to the provisions of what was then section 86(2) of the *Criminal Code*. Section 86(2) stated that "Every person who, without lawful excuse, uses, carries, handles, ships or stores any firearm or ammunition in a careless manner or without reasonable precautions for the safety of other persons" is guilty of an offence.[1]

On the face of it, section 86(2) undoubtedly imposed objective liability, but it also seemed to require the conviction of an accused person who has merely been *careless* in the storage of firearms and ammunition. However, the Supreme Court of Canada, while holding that section 86(2) did indeed impose objective liability, nevertheless stated that the fault requirement consisted of "conduct that is a marked departure from the standard of a reasonable person in the circumstances." If the Court had ruled that section 86(2) required the conviction of individuals who had merely acted *carelessly*, it would have been obliged to find that it was in violation of section 7 of the *Charter*. However, by interpreting the section as requiring a marked departure from the standard of the reasonable person, the Court was able to find that it met the requirement that a person may not be convicted of a *Criminal Code* offence unless they are morally blameworthy. Indeed, as Chief Justice Lamer noted in his judgment, section 86(2) of the *Code* clearly met the "minimal fault requirement" that is inherent in the principles of fundamental justice enshrined in section 7 of the *Charter*:

> By enacting s. 86(2), Parliament has seen fit to impose on all people owning firearms a specific and rigorous duty of care. It is a basic tenet of the principles of fundamental justice that the state not be permitted to punish and deprive of liberty the morally innocent. Those who have the capacity to live up to a standard of care and fail to do so, in circumstances involving inherently dangerous activities ... cannot be said to have done nothing wrong.

The modified objective test of criminal liability does not consider the peculiar personal characteristics of the accused person (such as background, education, or psychological disposition) except in the relatively rare circumstance where the accused lacks the capacity to understand the nature and quality or the consequences of their acts or to appreciate the risk involved in their conduct. As Justice Cromwell stated, on behalf of the Supreme Court of Canada, in *Roy* (2012), "The modified objective standard means that, while the reasonable person is placed in the accused's circumstances, evidence of the accused's personal attributes (such as age, experience and education) is irrelevant unless it goes to the accused's incapacity to appreciate or to avoid the risk."

In what circumstances may a court find that there is a lack of capacity to appreciate the risk that has been created by the accused person's conduct? For example, a visually impaired person might not have the physical capacity to appreciate a risk that would be obvious to someone who had normal vision, and, in this particular circumstance, a court would be obliged to enter an acquittal because it would be grossly unjust to hold an accused person to a standard of care that is physically impossible for them to meet. Similarly, an individual who has a reading disability and mishandles a bottle of nitroglycerine, without realizing what it contains, would not be held to the standard of the hypothetical "reasonable" person, who would, of course, be able to read the label on the bottle.

Why is it necessary to maintain a single, uniform legal standard of conduct in the application of the test of objective liability? According to Justice McLachlin in *Creighton* (1993):

> The purpose of Parliament in creating an offence of objective foresight, as in manslaughter, is to stipulate a minimum standard which people engaged in the activity in question are expected to meet. If the standard is lowered by reason of the lack of experience, education, or the presence of some other "personal characteristic" of the accused, the minimum standard which the law imposes on those engaging in the activity in question will be eroded. The objective test inevitably is transformed into a subjective test, violating the wise admonition ... that there should be a clear distinction in the law between subjective and objective standards, and negating the legislative goal of a minimum standard of care for all those who choose to engage in criminally dangerous conduct.

According to Justice McLachlin, the reasons why people fail to appreciate the risk inherent in their conduct are "legion":

> They range from simple absent-mindedness to attributes related to age, education and culture. To permit such a subjective assessment would be "coextensive with the judgment of each individual, which would be as variable as the length of the foot of each individual" leaving "so vague a line as to afford no rule at all, the degree of judgment belonging to each individual being infinitely various." ... *Provided the*

1. S. 86 of the *Criminal Code* was amended in 1995. The current provision, which replaced the subsection discussed in the text above, is s. 86(1): "Every person commits an offence who, without lawful excuse, uses, carries, handles, ships, transports or stores a firearm, a prohibited weapon, a restricted weapon, a prohibited device or any ammunition in a careless manner or without reasonable precautions for the safety of other persons."

capacity to appreciate the risk is present, lack of education and psychological predispositions serve as no excuse for criminal conduct, although they may be important factors to consider in sentencing. [emphasis added]

Although the courts will not take account of personal characteristics of the accused when applying the objective test of liability, it is important to bear in mind that the test is not applied in a total vacuum. The court must take account of the nature of the particular activity in which the accused was engaged and the specific knowledge that they had of the relevant circumstances. The question for the court then becomes, "would a reasonable person, having exactly the same knowledge of the relevant circumstances as the accused, realize that their conduct was creating a risk of bringing about consequences that are prohibited by the criminal law?" This, of course, is the modified objective test.

OFFENCES IMPOSING OBJECTIVE LIABILITY

Driving Offences and Objective Liability

There are two general offences that may arise from poor driving behaviour on the part of Canadian motorists: dangerous driving and careless driving.

Dangerous driving (or, more precisely, "dangerous operation of a conveyance") is an offence that now arises under subsection 320.13(1) of the *Criminal Code*, which was, of course, enacted by the Parliament of Canada. In 2018, Parliament enacted *An Act to amend the Criminal Code (offences relating to conveyances) and to make consequential amendments to other Acts*, S.C. 2018, c. 21. Previously, the offence of dangerous operation of a motor vehicle was contained in section 249(1) of the *Criminal Code*.[2] Subsection 320.13(1) states that:

Everyone commits an offence who operates a conveyance in a manner that, having regard to all of the circumstances, is dangerous to the public.[3]

This offence is hybrid in nature, imposing a maximum punishment of 10 years' imprisonment on indictment and two years less a day, on summary conviction.[4] If the dangerous operation causes bodily

2. S. 249(1) stated that:

(1) Every one commits an offence who operates

(a) a motor vehicle in a manner that is dangerous to the public, having regard to all the circumstances, including the nature, condition and use of the place at which the motor vehicle is being operated and the amount of traffic that at the time is or might reasonably be expected to be at that place. …

3. "Conveyance" is defined in s. 320.11 as "a motor vehicle, a vessel, an aircraft or railway equipment." "Operate" is defined as "in respect of a motor vehicle, to drive it or to have care or control of it."

4. S. 320.19(5).

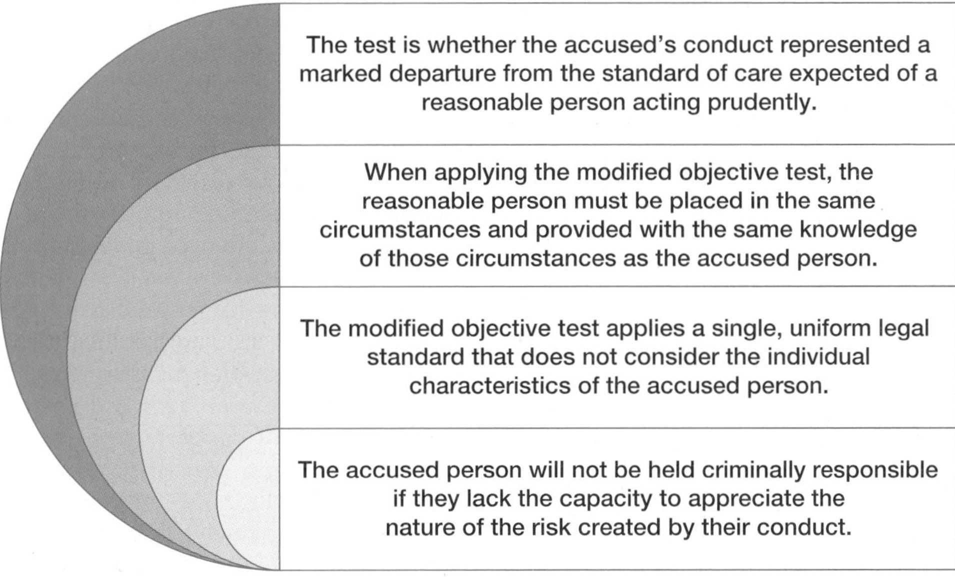

Figure 5-1

The Modified Objective Test of Criminal Responsibility

harm, the offence is also hybrid, but the maximum penalty on indictment is 14 years' imprisonment, and two years less a day on summary conviction.[5] Finally, if the dangerous operation causes death, the charge may be tried only on indictment and the maximum penalty is life imprisonment.[6]

Given the very recent enactment of the new legislation relating to dangerous operation of a "conveyance," including a motor vehicle, the extensive body of case law concerning the "old" section 249(1) should provide clear guidance as to how the courts will interpret and apply the "new" section 320.13(1). The "old" and "new" provisions are very similar so we shall examine the case law concerning section 249(1) and assume that it will continue to apply to the "new" section 320.13(1). We shall also refer to the offence as dangerous driving since the case law generally uses that term.

Careless driving is an offence that arises under the various provincial/territorial statutes that govern the operation of motor vehicles on the highways. For example, in Ontario, section 130 of the *Highway Traffic Act*, R.S.O. 1990, c. H.8 provides that:

> **130**(1) Every person is guilty of the offence of driving carelessly who drives a vehicle or street car on a highway without due care and attention or without reasonable consideration for other persons using the highway.

Similarly, in British Columbia, the offence is known as "driving without due care and attention," contrary to section 144 of the *Motor Vehicle Act*, R.S.B.C. 1996, c. 318.[7]

Both of these driving offences involve the imposition of objective liability in the sense that the Crown does not have to prove that the accused was subjectively aware of the risk that their driving conduct created for other users of the highway. For each offence, the Crown has to establish negligence only in the sense that the accused's driving conduct fell below the standard of the reasonable driver acting prudently in all of the circumstances. The critical distinction between the two driving offences lies in the extent to which the Crown must prove that the accused departed from the standard of the reasonable driver. Conviction of dangerous driving can take place only where the accused's driving conduct constitutes a marked departure from the standard of care expected of the reasonable driver in the particular circumstances facing the accused.

For example, in *Beatty* (2008), the Supreme Court of Canada held that a "momentary lapse of attention" on the part of the driver did not constitute a marked departure from the standard of the reasonable driver, even though it resulted in the deaths of three people. The driver's conduct certainly fell below the standard of care expected of the reasonable driver and would constitute driving without due care and attention; it would also render him liable to pay compensation at civil law. However, it was not sufficiently culpable to attract criminal liability under the *Criminal Code*. As Justice Charron commented, "If every departure from the civil norm is to be criminalized, regardless of the degree, we risk casting the net too widely and branding as criminals persons who are in reality not morally blameworthy."

Before embarking on a more detailed discussion of the offence of dangerous driving, it should be pointed out that it would be possible for motorists to be charged with the general offences of manslaughter, criminal negligence causing bodily harm, or criminal negligence causing death as a consequence of their driving misconduct. However, it seems that it is now less likely that prosecutors will turn to these general charges when the specific offences of dangerous driving, dangerous driving causing death, and dangerous driving causing bodily harm are open to them. Indeed, the new offences under subsections 320.13 (1) to (3) impose severe penalties, particularly when death is caused by dangerous driving, where the maximum penalty is life imprisonment (which is exactly the same penalty as for manslaughter).[8]

What are the *actus reus* and *mens rea* elements of the offence of dangerous operation of a motor vehicle? The *actus reus* of the offence was clearly articulated in the "old" section 249(1)(a) of the *Criminal Code*: namely, driving "in a manner that was dangerous to the public, having regard to all the

5. S. 320.2. There is also provision for a mandatory minimum sentence, ranging from a fine of $1,000 for a first offence to 120 days' imprisonment for a third or subsequent conviction.

6. S. 320.21. There is also the same provision for a mandatory minimum sentence as for s. 320.2.

7. S. 144 (1): A person must not drive a motor vehicle on a highway (a) without due care and attention, (b) without reasonable consideration for other persons using the highway, or (c) at a speed that is excessive relative to the road, traffic, visibility or weather conditions. (2) A person who contravenes subsection (1) (a) or (b) is liable on conviction to a fine of not less than $100 and, subject to this minimum fine, s. 4 of the *Offence Act* applies.

8. S. 236(b).

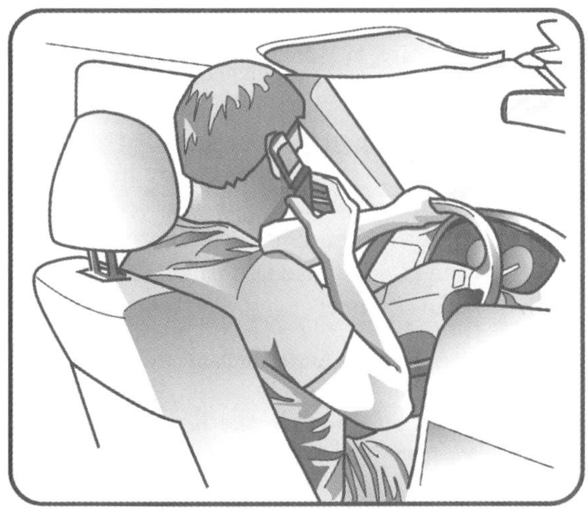

Illustration by Greg Holoboff

The offence of careless driving involves momentary inattention that falls below the standard of the reasonable driver.

circumstances, including the nature, condition and use of the place at which the motor vehicle is being operated and the amount of traffic that at the time is or might reasonably be expected to be at that place." The "new" section 320.13(1) is very similar, but much more succinct: "Everyone commits an offence who operates a conveyance in a manner that, having regard to all of the circumstances, is dangerous to the public."

As Justice Cromwell stated, on behalf of the Supreme Court of Canada, in *Roy* (2012) in relation to section 249(1):

> In considering whether the *actus reus* has been established, the question is whether the driving, viewed objectively, was dangerous to the public in all of the circumstances. The focus of this inquiry must be on the risks created by the accused's manner of driving, not the consequences, such as an accident in which he or she was involved.

The *mens rea* of dangerous driving is objective, although based on the principle of modified objective liability. Justice Cromwell also identified the *mens rea* elements of the offence in *Roy*:

> The focus of the *mens rea* analysis is on whether the dangerous manner of driving was the result of a marked departure from the standard of care which a reasonable person would have exercised in the same circumstances. ... It is helpful to approach the issue by asking two questions. The first is whether, in light of all of the relevant evidence, a reasonable person would have foreseen the risk and taken steps to avoid it if possible. If so, the second question is whether the accused's failure to foresee the risk and take steps to avoid it, if possible, was a *marked departure* from the standard of care expected of a reasonable person in the accused's circumstances.

It is clear that the courts have consistently placed great stress on the *fault element* of dangerous driving to distinguish it from the provincial or territorial offences of careless driving. For example, in *Laverdure* (2018), the Ontario Court of Appeal stated: that "The fault component of dangerous driving focuses on the conduct of the accused and is intended to distinguish driving that is sufficiently egregious in all of the circumstances to warrant criminalization from other less serious forms of bad driving, such as careless driving."

The Supreme Court of Canada has made three keynote decisions with respect to dangerous driving: *Hundal* (1993), *Beatty* (2008), and *Roy* (2012). In *Hundal*, Justice Cory asserted the view of the Court that modified objective liability should be the form of *mens rea* required when dealing with charges of dangerous driving. He noted it would not be practical to require the Crown to prove that the accused subjectively appreciated the risk created by their driving conduct. After all, driving is an "automatic" type of behaviour to which the operator of a motor vehicle assigns very little conscious thought and it would be well-nigh impossible for the Crown to establish that the accused person subjectively appreciated the risk created by their driving conduct at the precise moment(s) when that driving became dangerous in nature. Given the nature of driving behaviour, Justice Cory ruled modified objective liability was particularly appropriate as the basis for criminal punishment. Courts should apply the marked departure standard of responsibility in light of the particular circumstances of the case and the accused person's subjective knowledge of those circumstances:

> Although an objective test must be applied to the offence of dangerous driving, it will always remain open to the accused to raise a reasonable doubt that a reasonable person would have been aware of the risks in the accused's conduct. The test must be applied with some measure of flexibility. That is to say the objective test should not be applied in a vacuum but rather in the context of the events surrounding the incident.

Justice Cory provided some most helpful examples of situations in which the modified objective test would provide a defence to a person accused of dangerous driving. For example, if the accused suffers a totally unexpected heart attack, epileptic incident, or detached retina, they may engage in driving conduct that, from an objective point of view, represents a marked departure from the standard of the reasonable driver: indeed, the accused may, in such circumstances, become involved in a horrendous accident. However, the accused would be acquitted under the modified objective test because even a reasonable person, with the knowledge that the accused had, could not have foreseen that such a disastrous event might happen.[9] On the other hand, if the accused knew that there was a chance, for example, that they were likely to have an epileptic incident, there would be a conviction of dangerous driving because a reasonable person, armed with that knowledge, would have foreseen the risk created by continuing to drive and would have refrained from doing so. As Justice Cory put it:

> If an explanation is offered by the accused, such as a sudden and unexpected onset of illness, then in order to convict, the trier of fact must be satisfied that a reasonable person in similar circumstances ought to have been aware of the risk and of the danger involved in the conduct manifested by the accused.

Justice Cory also stated that the modified objective test satisfied the minimal *mens rea* requirements dictated by the *Charter*. Indeed, he asserted the view that the *mens rea* requirement for dangerous driving articulated in the *Hundal* case was particularly appropriate for such an offence:

> The *mens rea* for the offence of dangerous driving should be assessed objectively but in the context of all the events surrounding the incident. ... As a general rule, personal factors need not be taken into account. This flows from the licensing requirement for driving which assures that all who drive have a reasonable standard of physical health and capability, mental health, and a knowledge of the reasonable standard required of all licensed drivers.
>
> In light of the licensing requirement and the nature of driving offences, a modified objective test satisfies the constitutional minimum fault requirement for [s. 249] of the *Criminal Code* and is eminently well suited to that offence.

In the *Hundal* case itself, the accused had driven his overloaded dump truck into an intersection in downtown Vancouver, where he collided with another vehicle, killing its driver. The evidence was that Hundal had entered the intersection after the relevant traffic light had turned red, while the deceased driver had proceeded into the intersection after receiving a green light. The accused claimed that the traffic light had just turned to amber and that, at this point, it was too late for him to try to stop his vehicle. However, several witnesses stated that the dump truck drove through the red light, and it was estimated that at least one second passed between the end of the amber light and the time when the accused's vehicle proceeded into the intersection. The trial judge, therefore, rejected Hundal's explanation for the accident and convicted him of dangerous driving. The Supreme Court of Canada ultimately upheld the conviction. As Justice Cory noted:

> The trial judge carefully examined the circumstances of the accident. He took into account the busy downtown traffic, the weather conditions, and the mechanical conditions of the accused [*sic*] vehicle. He concluded, in my view very properly, that [Hundal's] manner of driving represented a gross departure from the standard of a reasonably prudent driver. No explanation was offered by the accused that could excuse his conduct. ...

9. In *Beatty* (2008), Justice Charron provided another useful example of how the principle of modified objective liability would provide a defence to an accused person in the appropriate circumstances: "Similarly, a driver who, in the absence of any warning or knowledge of its possible effects, takes a prescribed medication which suddenly and unexpectedly affects the driver in such a way that the manner of driving was dangerous to the public, could still establish a good defence to the charge although it [dangerous driving] had been objectively established."

The authority of the modified objective test articulated in *Hundal* (1993) was strongly reaffirmed by the Supreme Court of Canada in *Beatty* (2008). In this tragic case, Beatty had been charged with three counts of dangerous driving causing death. For no apparent reason, his car had crossed the double solid centre line in the road and crashed into an oncoming vehicle, killing all three of its occupants. Beatty's driving was completely normal prior to the accident. There was no mechanical defect in his vehicle, and there was no evidence of any intoxicants that may have affected his driving. Beatty could not remember what had happened, stating that he had lost consciousness—perhaps, because of heat stroke (it was extremely hot on that day) or because he had fallen asleep. An expert witness indicated that it would have taken only 0.00268 seconds for Beatty's car to cross the centre line and make contact with the victims' car.

The trial judge acquitted Beatty of the charges because she believed that the momentary lapse of attention on Beatty's part did not constitute a marked departure from the standard of care expected of a reasonable person driving prudently. In her view, this was a case involving civil, but not criminal, negligence. The B.C. Court of Appeal allowed the Crown's appeal and ordered a new trial. However, the Supreme Court of Canada restored the acquittals, stating that the Crown had not proved the *mens rea* element of the offence of dangerous driving. Undoubtedly, the Crown had proved the *actus reus* element—suddenly crossing the centre line and crashing into an oncoming vehicle is the very essence of dangerous driving conduct. However, conviction of dangerous driving also requires proof of morally blameworthy behaviour (the *mens rea* element). While Beatty's driving conduct fell below the standard expected of the reasonable driver, a momentary lapse of attention could not be considered to constitute a *marked* departure from that standard of care. It could certainly be regarded as a case of civil negligence, giving rise to a duty to provide compensation, but it was not sufficiently blameworthy to deserve punishment in the criminal justice system. For this reason, the Supreme Court agreed with the decision made by the trial judge.

More specifically, Justice Charron supported the trial judge's view of the evidence presented in court:

> The trial judge appropriately focused her analysis on Mr. Beatty's manner of driving in all the circumstances. She noted that there was no evidence of improper driving before the truck momentarily crossed the centre line and that the "few seconds of clearly negligent driving" was the only evidence about his manner of driving. She appropriately considered the totality of the evidence in finding that "the only reasonable inference" was that "he experienced a loss of awareness" that caused him to drive straight instead of following the curve in the road. In her view, this momentary lapse of attention was insufficient to found criminal culpability. She concluded that there was "insufficient evidence to support a finding of a *marked* departure from the standard of care of a prudent driver."
>
> Based on the totality of the evidence, I see no reason to interfere with the trial judge's assessment of Mr. Beatty's conduct in this case and her conclusion on Mr. Beatty's criminal liability.

In Beatty's case, the application of the modified objective test resulted in his acquittal because a reasonable person, armed with the knowledge of the circumstances that Beatty possessed, would not have foreseen that there might be a momentary loss of consciousness and a loss of control of the vehicle. However, if Beatty had previously experienced fainting attacks or sudden lapses in attention, his defence would have been rejected because a reasonable person who was aware of these medical problems would certainly have avoided driving and sought treatment. Driving while knowingly creating a risk of a serious accident would generally be regarded as a marked departure from the standard of care expected of the reasonable driver.

In *Roy* (2012), the accused was charged with dangerous driving causing death. Roy had been driving his motor home on an unpaved road that was steep, snow-covered, and slippery. The visibility was poor because of thickening fog in the area. Roy reached an intersection with a major highway, stopped, and then turned right onto the highway. Tragically, a tractor-trailer travelling on the highway could not avoid a violent collision with Roy's vehicle and a passenger riding with Roy was killed. Roy had no memory of the accident and, therefore, could provide no explanation for what had happened. The trial judge convicted Roy, stating that his driving was objectively dangerous and that there was no explanation that might have raised a reasonable doubt that a reasonable person would have been aware of the risks in the accused's conduct. Roy's appeal to the B.C. Court of Appeal was dismissed and his case came before the Supreme Court of Canada, which set aside the conviction and entered an acquittal.

The Supreme Court took the view that the trial judge had failed to consider whether the *mens rea* of the offence had been proved. He appeared to have decided that, simply because the driving behaviour was objectively dangerous (with a disastrous outcome), there had been a marked departure from the standard of care expected of a reasonable driver, and since Roy had not been able to provide an explanation that would excuse him, the trial judge entered a conviction. The Supreme Court entered an acquittal because the trial judge had not adequately reviewed the actual manner of Roy's driving to establish whether it was sufficiently culpable to merit conviction of a serious criminal offence. In the words of Justice Cromwell:

> Dangerous driving causing death is a serious criminal offence punishable by up to 14 years in prison. Like all criminal offences, it consists of two components: prohibited conduct—operating a motor vehicle in a dangerous manner resulting in death—and a required degree of fault—a marked departure from the standard of care that a reasonable person would observe in all the circumstances. The fault component is critical, as it ensures that criminal punishment is only imposed on those deserving the stigma of a criminal conviction. While a mere departure from the standard of care justifies imposing civil liability, only a marked departure justifies the fault requirement for this serious criminal offence.
>
> Defining and applying this fault element is important, but also challenging, given the inherently dangerous nature of driving. Even simple carelessness may result in tragic consequences which may tempt judges and juries to unduly extend the reach of the criminal law to those responsible. ... Giving careful attention to the fault element of the offence is essential if we are to avoid making criminals out of the merely careless.

The Supreme Court emphasized that courts should not conclude that a driver's conduct constituted a marked departure from the reasonable standard of care merely because that conduct was objectively dangerous and/or because there were tragic consequences. In the *Roy* case, Justice Cromwell concluded that:

> In my view, the appellant's decision to pull onto the highway is consistent with simple misjudgment of speed and distance in difficult conditions and poor visibility. The record here discloses a single and momentary error in judgment with tragic consequences. It does not support a reasonable inference that the appellant displayed a marked departure from the standard of care expected of a reasonable person in the same circumstances so as to justify conviction for the serious criminal offence of dangerous driving causing death.

"Dangerous Driving Causing Death is a Serious Criminal Offence": The Case of Randy Leigh Roy

Ingram Publishing/Thinkstock

In this chapter, the case of *Roy* (2012) is identified as the leading authority on the "old" offence of dangerous operation of a motor vehicle causing death [s. 249(4)]. It will be recalled that Roy had been travelling on an unpaved highway, which was affected by snow and was slippery. In thickening fog, he made a right turn onto a major highway and was struck by a tractor-trailer. The consequences were catastrophic: Roy's passenger (friend) and his dog were killed, and Roy was severely injured, losing all memory of the accident.

The trial judge convicted Roy of dangerous driving causing death and the B.C. Court of Appeal rejected Roy's appeal. However, the Supreme Court of Canada set aside the conviction and entered an acquittal.

The *Roy* case demonstrates that although the consequences of Roy's misjudgment were devastating, they did not turn what was, at best, a moment of carelessness into a serious criminal act. The judgment of the Supreme Court begins with the statement that "Dangerous driving causing death is a serious criminal offence punishable by up to 14 years in prison" (now, section 320.21 provides for a maximum sentence of life imprisonment) and concludes with the statement that "The record here discloses a single and momentary error in judgment with tragic consequences." The Crown had not proved that there was a marked departure from the standard of care expected of a reasonable driver in the same circumstances as the accused (bad road conditions, snow, and thickening fog). However, it took eight years from the time of the accident for Roy to be vindicated by the Supreme Court of Canada. For six years, he lived with a conviction that turned out to have been unjustified.

In *Roy*, the Supreme Court of Canada undeniably set a high bar for conviction of dangerous driving. The case of *Bélanger* (2013) neatly illustrates when that bar has been reached. Bélanger was driving at night and deliberately crossed a solid double line on the roadway in an attempt to pass a pickup truck in front of him. However, the location where he pulled out was a blind spot and when he saw the headlights of another vehicle coming towards him, it was too late to pull back into the lane behind the truck. The consequence was a head-on collision in which the driver of the oncoming vehicle was killed and Bélanger's passenger was seriously injured. The evidence was that Bélanger knew the road well and was aware that if he had waited for a short while, he would have been able to take advantage of a passing lane that lay just ahead. Bélanger was convicted of two counts of dangerous driving causing bodily harm and death. The Quebec Court of Appeal set aside the convictions, but the Supreme Court of Canada restored the convictions. Wagner, J. stated that "It is common ground that passing on a double line does not on its own suffice to establish the respondent's criminal liability" and that a trial court must consider "all the circumstances of the case." Here, the trial judge had undoubtedly done so. If Bélanger had just crossed the double line as a result of a momentary lapse in attention, he would not have been convicted. However, the trial judge ruled there had been a marked departure from the standard of care expected of a reasonable driver because Bélanger deliberately chose to cross the double line in an attempt to pass another vehicle and had done so even though he knew there was a passing lane coming up ahead. Significantly, there was absolutely no urgent reason for him to take such a perilous risk.

The *Bélanger* case may be usefully compared with a case from Ontario. In *Brown* (2018a), the accused, who was unaccompanied, drove his car on to a sidewalk at 1:28 a.m. In just three seconds, he crashed into a metal pole, a bicycle ring, and a refuse bin, fatally struck the victim, collided with a second bicycle ring and finally ran into a tree. At his trial for dangerous driving causing death, there was no evidence of excessive speeding or any mechanical failure. However, the Crown did introduce evidence that Brown was a suspended G1 driver and that, in any event, the conditions attached to his G1 licence prohibited him from driving both unaccompanied and between midnight and 5 a.m.

The trial judge acquitted Brown because he had experienced a "momentary lapse of attention," and therefore, the Crown had failed to prove that Brown's driving conduct represented a marked departure from the required standard. Brown's licensing status was considered irrelevant in these particular circumstances.

The Ontario Court of Appeal rejected the Crown's appeal against Brown's acquittal. Justice Sharpe stated that Brown's G1 licensing status did not have "any bearing on the risk at issue in this case where the trial judge concluded that there had been a momentary lapse of attention." He went on to say that:

> To hold a G1 driver criminally liable for a conduct that would not be criminal if committed by a properly licensed driver on the basis of restrictions on his or her licence, and without regard to whether such restrictions are relevant to the driver's ability to appreciate the specific risk, would allow for a variable standard inconsistent with "the principles of equality and individual responsibility which should pervade the criminal law" ...

Do you think that the line between careless driving and dangerous driving is sufficiently clear? Should it make a difference to the outcome of a case if the court discovers that it was common for other drivers on the same stretch of road to break the law by speeding? Would changing the channel on a car radio or music system or answering a phone call (if it is not "hands-free") amount to a momentary lapse of attention or a marked departure from the standard of care expected of the reasonable driver? Is the modified objective test an appropriate standard to apply to dangerous driving? Should the test be made more or less objective, or does it already represent a satisfactory balance of objectivity and subjectivity?

Dangerous Driving and Criminal Negligence

Sections 220 and 221 of the *Criminal Code* provide for the offences of *criminal negligence causing death* and *criminal negligence causing bodily harm*, respectively. It is possible for the Crown to advance either of these charges in situations where an accused person's driving behaviour has caused death or bodily harm. This immediately raises the question of how one is to distinguish between the offences of dangerous driving causing death or bodily harm [the "old" sections 249(3) and (4) and the "new" subsections 320.13(2) & (3)] and the offences of criminal negligence causing death or bodily harm (sections 220 and 221). It appears that *both offences require proof of a "marked departure"* from the standard of the reasonable driver and that the *mens rea for both offences is objective in nature*. Therefore, the difference between the two sets of offences lies in *the degree to which the accused's behaviour departs from the standard of the reasonable person*.

Section 219 of the *Criminal Code* defines criminal negligence as an act or omission that "shows wanton or reckless disregard for the lives and safety of other persons." To reflect the extreme nature of the criminal conduct encapsulated in this definition, the courts have stated that criminal negligence requires proof that there was a *marked and substantial departure* from the standard expected of the reasonable person.

For example, in the case of *Laine* (2015), the accused was speeding on a rural road, which he knew well. His front-seat passenger was egging Laine on and was even recording the events. At a curving, hilly section of that road, Laine lost control of his vehicle on a bend. It flipped over and crashed into a hydro pole, killing two of his passengers and seriously injuring a third. At trial, Laine was convicted of two counts of criminal negligence causing death and one count of criminal negligence causing bodily harm. The Ontario Court of Appeal affirmed the convictions. As MacFarland J.A. pointed out:

> This is not a case of an inexperienced driver who made a bad turn while going slightly over the speed limit. His speed was grossly excessive, 140 km/h at the time Ms. Sheppard observed the speedometer, on a narrow two-lane highway. Even after the near-miss at Curve 1, the appellant continued his wanton conduct without regard for the lives of those passengers in his vehicle or indeed others using the road. He was not chastened by the near-miss; instead, he increased his speed.
>
> I see no basis to interfere with the trial judge's conclusion that the appellant's conduct constituted *a marked and substantial departure from the conduct of a reasonably prudent person in the circumstances*. [emphasis added]

An illuminating example of the difference between the offences is the case of *Tayfel* (2009). Here, the accused was a pilot who ignored the applicable *Canadian Aviation Regulations* and miscalculated the amount of fuel remaining in his small commercial aircraft. As a consequence, he was obliged to land on a downtown Winnipeg street when he ran out of fuel. One death and numerous serious injuries occurred among the passengers. Tayfel was charged with criminal negligence causing death and bodily harm and dangerous operation of an aircraft. The trial judge convicted Tayfel of both offences, but the Manitoba Court of Appeal set aside the convictions of criminal negligence and affirmed the conviction of dangerous operation of an aircraft because Tayfel's conduct, while deserving of a conviction of dangerous operation, was not sufficiently culpable to merit conviction of the more serious offences involving criminal negligence. On behalf of the Court of Appeal, Justice Hamilton stated that:

> However flawed his conduct was in addressing the sufficiency of the fuel for the flight, I am of the view that this conduct, when considered in the context of all of the evidence, is not conduct that meets the very high threshold of wanton or reckless disregard for the lives or safety of other persons.

However, the Court of Appeal also took the view that Tayfel's conscious failure to follow the aviation regulations constituted a marked departure from the reasonable person standard and, therefore, merited conviction of the less serious offence of dangerous operation of an aircraft.

Unlawful Act Manslaughter

In a following section, we shall see that individuals may be convicted of manslaughter on the basis that they caused the death of a human being (*actus reus*) by criminal negligence (*mens rea*). However, this is not the only basis upon which individuals may be convicted of manslaughter under the *Criminal Code*. Indeed, there is another form of manslaughter that is known as **unlawful act manslaughter**. What is meant by this term? To explain its meaning, it is first necessary to examine the *Code* provisions that deal with culpable homicide.

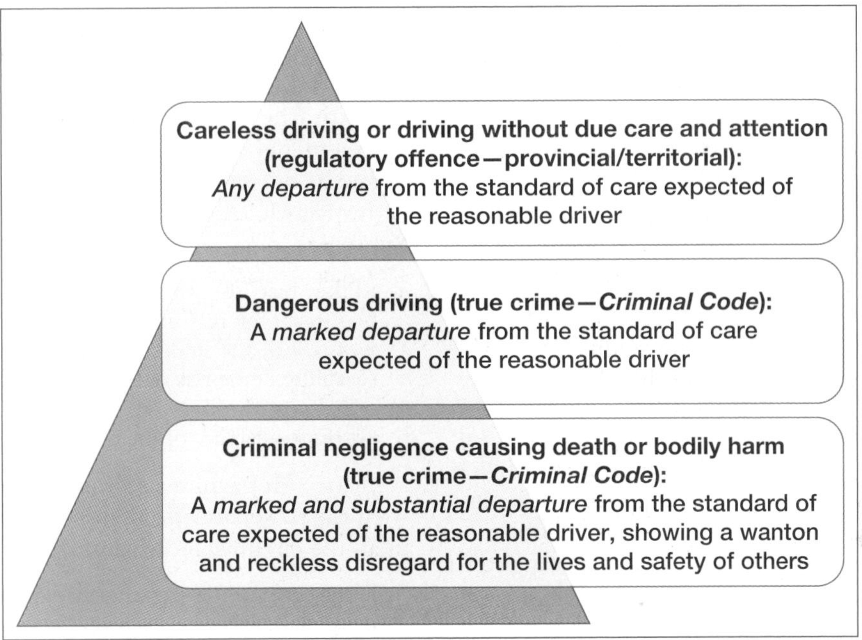

Figure 5-2
The Mens Rea *Requirements for Three Driving Offences*

Section 222(4) of the *Criminal Code* identifies the various forms of culpable homicide: murder, manslaughter, and infanticide. Subsection 222(5) indicates four means by which culpable homicide may be committed:

> A person commits culpable homicide when he causes the death of a human being,
>
> (a) by means of an unlawful act,
>
> (b) by criminal negligence,
>
> (c) by causing that human being, by threats of fear or violence or by deception, to do anything that causes his death, or
>
> (d) by wilfully frightening that human being in the case of a child or sick person.

What are the distinctions between murder, infanticide, and manslaughter? Section 234 of the *Criminal Code* states that "Culpable homicide that is not murder or infanticide is manslaughter." In other words, manslaughter is a *residual* category of culpable homicide because it is defined in terms of what it is not, rather than what it is. If culpable homicide is neither murder nor infanticide, then it must be categorized as manslaughter. Murder (according to section 229) is, in general terms, defined in terms of the accused's intent to kill, while **infanticide** (according to section 233) is committed where a woman kills her "newly-born child"[10] and her mind is "disturbed" because she has not fully recovered from the effects of giving birth or because of "the effect of lactation consequent on the birth." By a process of elimination, one may draw the conclusion that manslaughter must generally be defined as an unintentional form of killing that cannot be excused as an accident or justified in some other manner (such as self-defence). Section 222(5) indicates that, in general, there are two distinct forms of manslaughter: *manslaughter by criminal negligence* and *unlawful act manslaughter*.

As we shall see in the next section, manslaughter by criminal negligence is defined by referring to a combination of sections 222(5)(b) and 234 of the *Code*. However, another form of manslaughter may arise as a consequence of combining sections 222(5)(a) and 234; this is what has become known as "unlawful act" manslaughter. When the accused commits an unlawful act (usually an assault) that results in death, they will be convicted of murder if there is an intent to kill or if there is an intent to inflict bodily harm that the accused knows is

10. S. 2 of the *Criminal Code* states that this term "means a person under the age of one year."

likely to cause death and is reckless as to whether death ensues or not [section 229(a)]. Indeed, as the *Martineau* case (1990) established, an accused person cannot be convicted of murder in Canada unless they subjectively foresee the likelihood of death ensuing from their conduct.

However, let us suppose that an accused person causes the death of a victim as a consequence of an unlawful act (such as an assault) but does not possess the necessary *mens rea* for murder. In these circumstances, it is likely that the accused will be convicted of unlawful act manslaughter. Unfortunately, although section 222(5)(a) states that culpable homicide may be committed "by means of an unlawful act," it does not define the necessary *mens rea* for conviction of unlawful act manslaughter. As noted above, section 234 merely states that any culpable homicide that is neither murder nor infanticide is manslaughter. Since the *Code* provides no guidance in this respect, the Supreme Court of Canada has articulated the test that must be used by the courts when determining if the accused had the necessary *mens rea* for unlawful act manslaughter.

In the *Creighton* case (1993), the Supreme Court of Canada ruled that the *mens rea* for unlawful act manslaughter is the *objective foresight of the risk of bodily harm that is neither trivial nor transitory in nature*. In other words, to convict the accused of unlawful act manslaughter, the Crown must prove that the accused had the necessary *mens rea* for the commission of the unlawful act that resulted in death (e.g., an assault) and that a reasonable person, in the same circumstances as the accused, would have foreseen the risk of non-trivial bodily harm, given the inherently dangerous nature of the unlawful act. In the *Creighton* case itself, the accused had been charged with (unlawful act) manslaughter after he had injected a quantity of cocaine into the arm of the victim. He had not sought to determine the quality or strength of the drug before doing so. After the injection, the victim went into violent convulsions and appeared to stop breathing. The accused would not permit a friend to call 911 for emergency assistance, and the victim was left on her bed for six to seven hours before such assistance was finally called. At this point, she was pronounced dead.

What was the alleged "unlawful act" in *Creighton*? The Crown successfully argued that the accused had been trafficking in narcotics contrary to section 4 of the (now repealed) *Narcotic Control Act*, R.S.C. 1985, c. N-1.[11] Under that act, the word "traffic" included "giving" or "administering" a narcotic. Granted that Creighton had committed an unlawful act resulting in death (the *actus reus* of manslaughter), what *mens rea* elements must the Crown prove in order to obtain a conviction of manslaughter?

Justice McLachlin, speaking for a majority of the Supreme Court, stated that:

> [T]he test for the *mens rea* of unlawful act manslaughter in Canada ... is (in addition to the *mens rea* of the underlying offence) objective foreseeability of the risk of bodily harm which is neither trivial nor transitory, in the context of a dangerous act. Foreseeability of the death is not required.

Justice McLachlin also stated that the "question is what the reasonably prudent person would have done in all the circumstances" and that:

> [T]he *mens rea* for objective foresight of risking harm is normally inferred from the facts. The standard is that of the reasonable person in the circumstances of the accused. If a person has committed a manifestly dangerous act, it is reasonable, absent indications to the contrary, to infer that he or she failed to direct his or her mind to the risk and the need to take care. However, the normal inference may be negated by evidence raising a reasonable doubt as to lack of capacity to appreciate the risk. Thus, if a *prima facie* case for *actus reus* and *mens rea* is made out, it is necessary to ask a further question: did the accused possess the requisite capacity to appreciate the risk flowing from his conduct? If this further question is answered in the affirmative, the necessary moral fault is established and the accused is properly convicted. If not, the accused must be acquitted.

As far as the facts in the *Creighton* case were concerned, Justice McLachlin emphasized that the central issue was "whether the reasonable person in all the circumstances" facing the accused "would have foreseen the risk of bodily harm." To this question, Justice McLachlin believed there was a simple answer: "At the very least, a person administering a dangerous drug like cocaine to another has a duty to inform himself as to the precise risk the injection entails and to refrain from administering it unless reasonably satisfied that there is no risk of harm. That was not the case here."

In *Vogel* (2011), the accused's wife had died as a result of falling down the stairs. The Crown had

11. The equivalent offence is now contained in s. 5 of the *Controlled Drugs and Substances Act*, S.C. 1996, c. 19. "Traffic" is defined in s. 2 of the Act.

argued that Vogel had deliberately pushed her down the stairs and charged him with second-degree murder. He was convicted of manslaughter at trial. One of the possible interpretations of the evidence was that Vogel had just pushed his wife aside at the top of the stairs as opposed to deliberately pushing her down the stairs. When the jury had asked the trial judge about Vogel's potential criminal liability in this scenario, the judge told them that, "I instruct you, as a matter of law, that an intentional application of force without consent constitutes an assault in law and that is an unlawful act" and also that "the strength of the force is immaterial." This statement effectively instructed the jury that even pushing aside the victim would support a verdict of unlawful act manslaughter. However, the scenario envisaged by the jury would not constitute an inherently dangerous act, as required by the *Creighton* case. Therefore, the Ontario Court of Appeal set aside the conviction and ordered a new trial:

> First, it is not necessarily obvious that pushing the deceased out of the way in the hallway, not intending that she fall down the stairs, is an objectively dangerous act. Second, the instruction that "the strength of the force is immaterial" is simply wrong. The trial judge should have instructed the jury that the mental state required for unlawful act manslaughter is "objective foreseeability of the risk of bodily harm which is neither trivial nor transitory, in the context of a dangerous act".

A very straightforward example of unlawful act manslaughter occurred in the distressing case of *Sinclair* (2008). The accused was charged with the manslaughter of his four-year-old daughter. The evidence was that the young girl refused to go to bed. Sinclair picked her up, shook her, and threw her onto the bed. Unfortunately, the child bounced off the bed, hit the wall, and landed on the floor. She suffered a traumatic injury to the brain, from which she later died. Sinclair was convicted by a jury of manslaughter and his subsequent appeal to the Manitoba Court of Appeal was rejected. Chief Justice Scott, in delivering the judgment of the Court, stated that "Here, it cannot be doubted that the accused's conduct caused the child's death, and that the risk of non-trivial bodily harm arising from the accused's actions was objectively foreseeable. All the required elements of unlawful act manslaughter were present."

The Court of Appeal also rejected the argument that Sinclair did not commit an assault on his daughter because, as a parent, he was using force by way of "reasonable correction" under section 43 of the *Criminal Code*.[12] On this issue, Chief Justice Scott ruled that:

> Corporal punishment has always been and still is the prerogative of parents. It is unacceptable, however, if it is administered arbitrarily, motivated by anger, and if it does not serve the purpose of educating the child.
>
> ... The accused "snapped," as he said, and in anger and out of frustration threw his child onto the bed, thus depriving himself of the justification afforded by s. 43.

Not every unlawful act that results in death constitutes unlawful act manslaughter. This proposition is illustrated by the case of *Vaillancourt* (1995), in which the accused and his friend Palardy had gone to pick up a videocassette in Vaillancourt's apartment. Palardy noticed a .32 calibre revolver on the accused's night table and asked Vaillancourt how the firearm worked. The accused opened the magazine of the gun and let the bullets slide out into the palm of his hand. Vaillancourt closed the magazine without checking to see if any bullets remained inside it. He then pulled the trigger, and on four occasions nothing happened. However, by the fifth try, Vaillancourt was pointing the gun at Palardy's head, and when the accused pulled the trigger, a bullet, which had remained inside the magazine, was discharged and killed Palardy. Vaillancourt was charged with unlawful act manslaughter.

There was no doubt that Vaillancourt had engaged in an "unlawful act" because the *Criminal Code* (section 87) renders it an offence to point a firearm (*whether loaded or unloaded*) at another person if this is done "without lawful excuse." However, the critical issue in the case was whether Vaillancourt had the necessary *mens rea* for manslaughter. The evidence was to the effect that the accused honestly believed that the magazine had been fully emptied because it had an extractor, which was supposed to expel all the bullets when it was opened. There was no evidence of any animosity between Vaillancourt and Palardy, and the latter showed no fear at the time of the shooting because he also believed that the gun was unloaded. Indeed, as the trial judge noted, Vaillancourt was,

12. S. 43 states: "Every schoolteacher, parent or person standing in the place of a parent is justified in using force by way of correction toward a pupil or child, as the case may be, who is under his care, if the force does not exceed what is reasonable under the circumstances."

at Palardy's request, "simply demonstrating the operation of the gun." The trial judge emphasized that the accused had "taken the precaution of emptying the magazine, that he was familiar with the gun and that he had every reason to believe that all of the bullets had fallen out of it." The trial judge, therefore, acquitted the accused because there was *no evidence that a reasonable person, on the facts as the accused perceived them to be, would have foreseen the risk of non-trivial bodily harm* to Palardy. After all, in most circumstances, an unloaded firearm does not *per se* pose a threat of bodily harm, and Vaillancourt *honestly* (and *reasonably*) believed that the gun did not contain any bullets. Put another way, the pointing of an unloaded firearm is not a "manifestly dangerous act" (a requirement identified by Justice McLachlin in the *Creighton* case (1993) as being an essential element in unlawful act manslaughter), and Vaillancourt believed that he was merely demonstrating the operation of an unloaded revolver at the time of the fatal tragedy. The Quebec Court of Appeal upheld the acquittal of Vaillancourt. As Justice Brossard noted, on behalf of the court, "in so far as the **respondent** is concerned, he pointed an unloaded gun, in the quite amicable context of demonstrating the handling of the gun, and without any malevolent intention of any nature whatsoever."

The unlawful act may be a failure to perform a legally required duty. For example, in *Plein* (2018), the accused, who was under a duty, imposed by subsection 215(1)(c) of the *Criminal Code*, to provide the necessaries of life to his blind and cognitively impaired mother, allowed her to die a terrible death from starvation. His conviction of unlawful act manslaughter was upheld by the Ontario Court of Appeal.

The Offences of Unlawfully Causing Bodily Harm and Assault Causing Bodily Harm

The offences of **unlawfully causing bodily harm** (section 269 of the *Code*) and *assault causing bodily harm* (section 267) also provide two significant examples of the imposition of objective *mens rea*. In the *DeSousa* case (1992), the Supreme Court of Canada held that the *mens rea* for unlawfully causing bodily harm is *objective foresight of bodily harm*. If an accused person commits an "unlawful act" (an offence under federal or provincial/territorial legislation) that is *objectively dangerous*, then, if bodily harm is the consequence of that unlawful act, they will be convicted of unlawfully causing bodily harm. Put another way, if a reasonable person would have foreseen the risk of *non-trivial bodily harm*, then it is irrelevant whether this particular accused subjectively foresaw such a consequence.

In the *DeSousa* case, the accused was involved in a fight that resulted in a bystander being injured. The accused had allegedly thrown a bottle against a wall and a fragment of glass had struck the bystander, wounding her in the arm. The accused claimed that section 269 of the *Criminal Code* should be struck down under section 7 of the *Charter* because it contravened the "principles of fundamental justice" insofar as it "put an accused person at risk of imprisonment without the requirement of a blameworthy state of mind." The trial judge agreed with this argument and quashed the indictment against DeSousa. However, the trial judge's decision was later overturned by the Ontario Court of Appeal and the accused's appeal to the Supreme Court of Canada was firmly rejected.

Speaking on behalf of the Supreme Court, Justice Sopinka stated that the principles of fundamental justice, enshrined in section 7 of the *Charter*, were not infringed by the imposition of objective *mens rea* in relation to the offence of unlawfully causing bodily harm:

> One is not morally innocent simply because a particular consequence of an unlawful act was unforeseen by that actor. In punishing for unforeseen consequences the law is not punishing the morally innocent but those who cause injury through avoidable unlawful action. Neither basic principles of criminal law, nor the dictates of fundamental justice require, by necessity, intention in relation to the consequences of an otherwise blameworthy act.

This *mens rea* requirement—of objective foresight of non-trivial bodily harm—also appears in the context of assault causing bodily harm (section 267). For example, in the case of *Dewey* (1999), the complainant had been fighting with another man when the accused came between them and "forcefully shoved the complainant," whose head then struck a jukebox or a corner of the wall as he was falling to the ground. The complainant suffered very serious injuries. At his trial, the accused was convicted of assault causing bodily harm. Dewey appealed to the Alberta Court of Appeal. He claimed that although the offence did, indeed, impose objective liability, it was nevertheless necessary for the Crown to prove that a reasonable person would have foreseen *the particular type of bodily harm that ultimately occurred in this case* (namely, that the victim would fall and strike his head on the jukebox or wall). In dismissing Dewey's appeal, the Alberta Court of Appeal stated that the Crown has satisfied the *mens rea* requirements for assault causing bodily harm if it proves that the reasonable person would have foreseen *any sort of non-trivial bodily harm whatsoever*. It is not necessary for the Crown to prove that the *specific type of bodily harm that was inflicted* could have been foreseen by a reasonable person placed in the same circumstances as the accused. As Justice McClung stated, on behalf of the Court of Appeal:

> The trial judge found that Dewey pushed the complainant more forcefully than would cause a stumble. *It is objectively foreseeable that this action would create a risk of bodily harm which is neither transitory nor trivial.* [emphasis added]

The Offence of Aggravated Assault

Section 268(1) of the *Criminal Code* provides that "Every one commits an aggravated assault who wounds, maims, disfigures or endangers the life of the complainant."

The courts have consistently held that this offence is one that imposes objective liability. For example, in the case of *MacKay* (2004), the accused, who was riding a motorcycle, ran down and seriously injured the victim, Drane, in the parking lot of a fast food outlet. MacKay allegedly told a police officer at the scene of the incident that he had not planned to hurt Drane but rather had intended just to "scare him." MacKay was acquitted at his trial, but the New Brunswick Court of Appeal set aside the acquittal and ordered a new trial. The Court of Appeal held that the trial judge should have instructed the jury that they could also convict MacKay of aggravated assault—if MacKay had threatened to apply force to Drane in his attempt to scare him and if a reasonable person would have "foreseen that in driving his motorcycle in the manner in which he did, a threatening act of force, it exposed Mr. Drane to the risk of serious injury." In delivering the judgment of the Court of Appeal, Justice Ryan said that:

> [I]t would not be necessary for the Crown to prove that Mr. MacKay intended to apply force. The crux of the matter is whether the threat to apply force and the ability to do so, in this case, carries with it the objective foresight of injury if the aggressor miscalculates. The Crown must prove its case, objective foreseeability of serious injury, beyond a reasonable doubt, the charge being that the act endangered the life of the victim.

The Supreme Court of Canada subsequently affirmed the Court of Appeal's decision to order a new trial (*Mackay*, 2005). The Supreme Court held that the jury should be instructed that MacKay could be convicted of aggravated assault if either (1) he deliberately applied force to the victim or (2) he intended to threaten the victim by riding his motorcycle close to him and (3) a reasonable person would have foreseen the risk of serious injury from the application of force or from the threat, as the case may be.

A disturbing example of aggravated assault occurred in the case of *W. (D.J.)* (2012). The accused carried out a circumcision of his four-year-old son

Assault causing bodily harm.

even though he had no medical training. He wished to have the circumcision completed in time for an upcoming religious holiday and could not find a medical professional to undertake the surgery. The procedure caused pain to the child and necessitated emergency surgery at the hospital to prevent disfigurement and functional impairment of his penis. In addition, the accused had caused a "black tar-like Wonder Dust" to adhere to the child's penis and it had to be removed at the hospital.

The accused was charged with a number of offences, including aggravated assault. The trial judge acquitted the accused of aggravated assault but convicted him of other charges. On appeal by the Crown, the B.C. Court of Appeal ruled that the accused should have been convicted of aggravated assault:

> In addition to meeting the requirements to prove assault, aggravated assault requires the mental element of objective foresight of bodily harm. . . . The *mens rea* for aggravated assault is the *mens rea* for assault (intent to apply force intentionally or recklessly or being wilfully blind to the fact that the victim does not consent) plus objective foresight of the risk of bodily harm.
>
> The trial judge in this case found that the accused had objective foresight of the risk of bodily harm to D.J. based upon both his research and his own circumcision. ...
>
> The necessary element of harm required to establish the offence of aggravated assault is made out if the accused's actions disfigured the complainant. It is clear in this case that the accused's actions disfigured D.J., and, as the trial judge found ... that disfigurement required surgery and a general anaesthetic to correct that disfigurement.

The Supreme Court of Canada agreed with the Court of Appeal that the accused should have been convicted of aggravated assault.

Offences Involving Criminal Negligence

Section 219(1) of the *Criminal Code* provides that:

> Every one is criminally negligent who
>
> (a) in doing anything, or
>
> (b) in omitting to do anything that it is his duty to do,
>
> shows wanton or reckless disregard for the lives or safety of other persons.

This definition of criminal negligence is applicable to the following offences: causing death by criminal negligence (section 220), causing bodily harm by criminal negligence (section 221), and manslaughter by criminal negligence (sections 222(5)(b) and 234).

According to the provisions of section 219(1) of the *Criminal Code*, an accused person may be convicted of an offence involving criminal negligence in relation to both positive acts and omissions. Where the gist of the charges is that the accused failed to act, it must first be established that the accused was under a legal duty to act [section 219(2) indicates that "duty" means a "duty imposed by law"]. It should also be noted that section 219 is concerned with the most culpable forms of negligence; indeed, it specifies that, to obtain a conviction, the Crown must establish that, in doing something or failing to do something that it was their duty to do, the accused showed "wanton or reckless disregard for the lives or safety of other persons." As we shall see, this has been interpreted as meaning that the accused will be found guilty of criminal negligence where their conduct (whether it is an act or an omission) amounts to a *marked and substantial departure from the standard of the reasonable person* acting prudently in the circumstances facing the accused.

In the case of *H. (A.D.)* (2013), Justice Cromwell, on behalf of the majority of the Supreme Court of Canada, referred to the words employed by Parliament in section 219 and provided a succinct overview of how it has been interpreted:

> The text of [s. 219] has fueled much debate about the required fault element. The use of the word "negligence" in the name of the offence suggests an objectively defined standard consistent with the meaning of the word "negligence" in the common law of torts. On the other hand, the words "wanton and reckless disregard" could be taken as describing actual knowledge of the risk created by the conduct and therefore a subjective fault element ... Ultimately, the [Supreme Court of Canada] decided [in *Anderson* (1990)] that proof, of intention or actual foresight of a prohibited consequence is not required. Rather, criminal negligence requires a marked and substantial departure from the conduct of a reasonably prudent person in circumstances in which the accused either recognized and ran an obvious and serious risk or, alternatively, gave no thought to that risk.

The decision of the Supreme Court of Canada in the case of *F. (J.)* (2008) is now the most definitive authority with respect to the application of section 219. In this case, the accused was charged with manslaughter by criminal negligence and failure to provide the necessaries of life to his foster son: the basis of the charges was his alleged failure to protect the victim from physical abuse inflicted by his spouse. Section 219 provides that criminal negligence may be established not only by an act but also by a failure to act (an omission). Where there is a failure to act, it must be shown that the accused person failed to perform a "duty imposed by law." In this particular case, the relevant duty was the duty of the accused to provide the necessaries of life to his foster son. The Supreme Court of Canada ultimately entered an acquittal in *F.(J.)*: however, the Court set out very clearly how section 219 should be applied in such cases.

Justice Fish pointed out that when a manslaughter charge is "piggy-backed" on a charge of failing to provide the necessaries of life under section 215 of the *Criminal Code*, the court should take a two-step approach. The first step is to decide whether the accused failed to provide the relevant necessary of life (in this case, the protection of his foster child) and that this failure constituted a "a marked departure from the conduct of a reasonably prudent parent in circumstances where it was objectively foreseeable that the failure to provide the necessaries of life would lead to a risk of danger to the life, or a risk of permanent endangerment to the health, of the child." If the accused is found to have committed the offence under section 215, the second step is to determine whether the accused's failure to protect his foster child represented, in the words of section 219, a "wanton or reckless disregard" for the child's life or safety and whether his failure constituted a significant, contributing cause of the child's death. Justice Fish stated that, to convict the accused of manslaughter by criminal negligence, the Crown has to show that the accused person's omission "represented *a marked and substantial departure* (as opposed to a *marked departure*) from the conduct of a reasonably prudent parent in circumstances where the accused either recognized and ran an obvious and serious risk to the life of his child or, alternatively, gave no thought to that risk."

All crimes that contain objective *mens rea* elements require proof that there was a marked departure from the standard of care expected of the reasonable person acting prudently, and it is clear that, in Canada, the appropriate test is that of modified objective liability. However, crimes based on criminal negligence, which are the most serious of all offences based on objective *mens rea*, require proof of an additional element: namely, that the departure from the reasonable person standard was not only marked but also substantial in nature.

The requirement that there be a "marked and substantial departure from the standard of the reasonable person" in a case of criminal negligence is well illustrated by the tragic case of *L. (J.)* (2006). In this case, the accused had been driving a van, which he had brought to a halt on the street. The victim, who was a friend of the accused, had jumped onto the hood of the stationary van. At this time, the victim was "smiling and laughing." The accused then set the van in motion, but after travelling a short distance, he realized that "what was going on was wrong" and stopped the vehicle. The victim slid off the hood and suffered a fatal head injury. The trial judge convicted L. (J.) of criminal negligence causing death (section 220). The trial judge placed great importance on the fact that the accused had admittedly foreseen the risk of injury to his friend as a consequence of driving the van with him on the hood. Therefore, the trial judge ruled that accused's conduct showed wanton and reckless disregard for the life and safety of his friend and constituted criminal negligence, as defined by section 219 of the *Criminal Code.*

The Ontario Court of Appeal set aside the conviction of L. (J.) and ordered a new trial. The main reason for this decision was the failure of the trial judge to make a specific finding that the accused person's driving conduct amounted to a "marked and substantial departure from the norm." In delivering the judgment of the Court of Appeal, Justice Weiler remarked that "Whether specific conduct should be categorized as criminal negligence is one of the most difficult and uncertain areas in the criminal law." Justice Weiler indicated that the Crown must prove a higher level of misconduct in relation to a charge of criminal negligence than is necessary to prove the lesser offence of dangerous driving: "This higher standard has been described as a marked and *substantial* departure from the standard of care of a reasonable person. ... It is not self-evident that [L. (J.)'s] act of putting the car in gear with a person on the hood satisfies this higher standard."

Justice Weiler concluded that:

> [T]he trial judge committed a palpable and overriding error in finding that the appellant's conduct met the higher standard of criminal negligence without first making a finding regarding the appellant's driving. The trial judge further erred in finding that the appellant was "wanton" or "reckless" without considering all of the circumstances sur-

> rounding the activity including the manner in which [L. (J.)] drove, his youthfulness, the instigation and encouragement of the activity he received from the deceased, and his conduct in trying to help his friend immediately after this tragic event.

This case is significant insofar as it emphasizes that, to establish criminal negligence, the Crown must clear a very high bar to satisfy the *marked and substantial* departure standard.

CAUSING DEATH BY CRIMINAL NEGLIGENCE AND MANSLAUGHTER BY CRIMINAL NEGLIGENCE: IDENTICAL TWINS

The reader will, no doubt, have raised the following question while reading the preceding sections: What is the difference between the offences of causing death by criminal negligence (section 220 of the *Code*) and manslaughter by criminal negligence (sections 222(5)(b) and 234)? The answer is that the elements of each offence are identical. Why, then, are there two separate offences? The answer appears to lie in historical considerations. The offence of causing death by criminal negligence was created in 1955, at least in part as a consequence of the notorious reluctance of juries to convict motorists who killed others while driving their vehicles of the offence of manslaughter. It was felt that juries would be more willing to convict motorists of an offence that did not bear the heavy stigma of manslaughter. The irony is that the critical elements of the two offences, as well as the penalty, are the same in all respects. Significantly, in 1985, Parliament later added two new offences that deal specifically with vehicular homicide; namely, dangerous driving causing death [section 249(4)] and impaired driving causing death [section 255(3)]. The "new" equivalent offences, enacted in 2018, are subsections 320.13(3) and 320.14(3) respectively.

INFANTICIDE

Section 233 of the *Criminal Code* provides that:

> A female person commits infanticide when by a wilful act or omission she causes the death of her newly-born child,[13] if at the time of the act or omission she is not fully recovered from the effects of giving birth to the child and by reason thereof or of the effect of lactation consequent on the birth of the child her mind is then disturbed.

Infanticide is an indictable offence and carries a maximum prison sentence of five years (section 237). It is an offence that may be charged as a stand-alone offence or it may be raised as a partial defence to a charge of murder. A critical question is whether the *mens rea* for infanticide is subjective or objective in nature.

In *Borowiec* (2016), the Supreme Court of Canada ruled that the *mens rea* for infanticide is exactly the same as that for manslaughter: namely, modified objective liability. On behalf of the Court, Justice Cromwell stated that, to establish the offence of infanticide, the Crown must prove the necessary *mens rea* associated with the unlawful act that had brought about the death of the infant and also the *objective foreseeability of the risk of bodily harm to child from that assault*.

Justice Cromwell noted that what distinguishes infanticide from manslaughter is its unique *actus reus*: namely, that "at the time of the act or omission [the accused] is not fully recovered from the effects of giving birth to the child and by reason thereof or of the effect of lactation consequent on the birth of the child her mind is then disturbed." Justice Cromwell also stated that it is not necessary to prove that the act or omission was caused by the accused person's mental "disturbance" and that the "disturbance is part of the *actus reus* of infanticide, not the *mens rea*."

Borowiec had been charged with two counts of second-degree murder after she admitted that she had given birth to two babies in 2008 and 2009 and left them to die in a dumpster. The trial judge acquitted Borowiec of murder and found her guilty of two counts of infanticide, because Borowiec's mind had been "disturbed" as a result of not yet having fully recovered from the effects of giving birth. Both the Alberta Court of Appeal and the Supreme Court of Canada dismissed the Crown's appeal against the verdict.

13. S. 2 defines a newly born child as "a person under the age of one year."

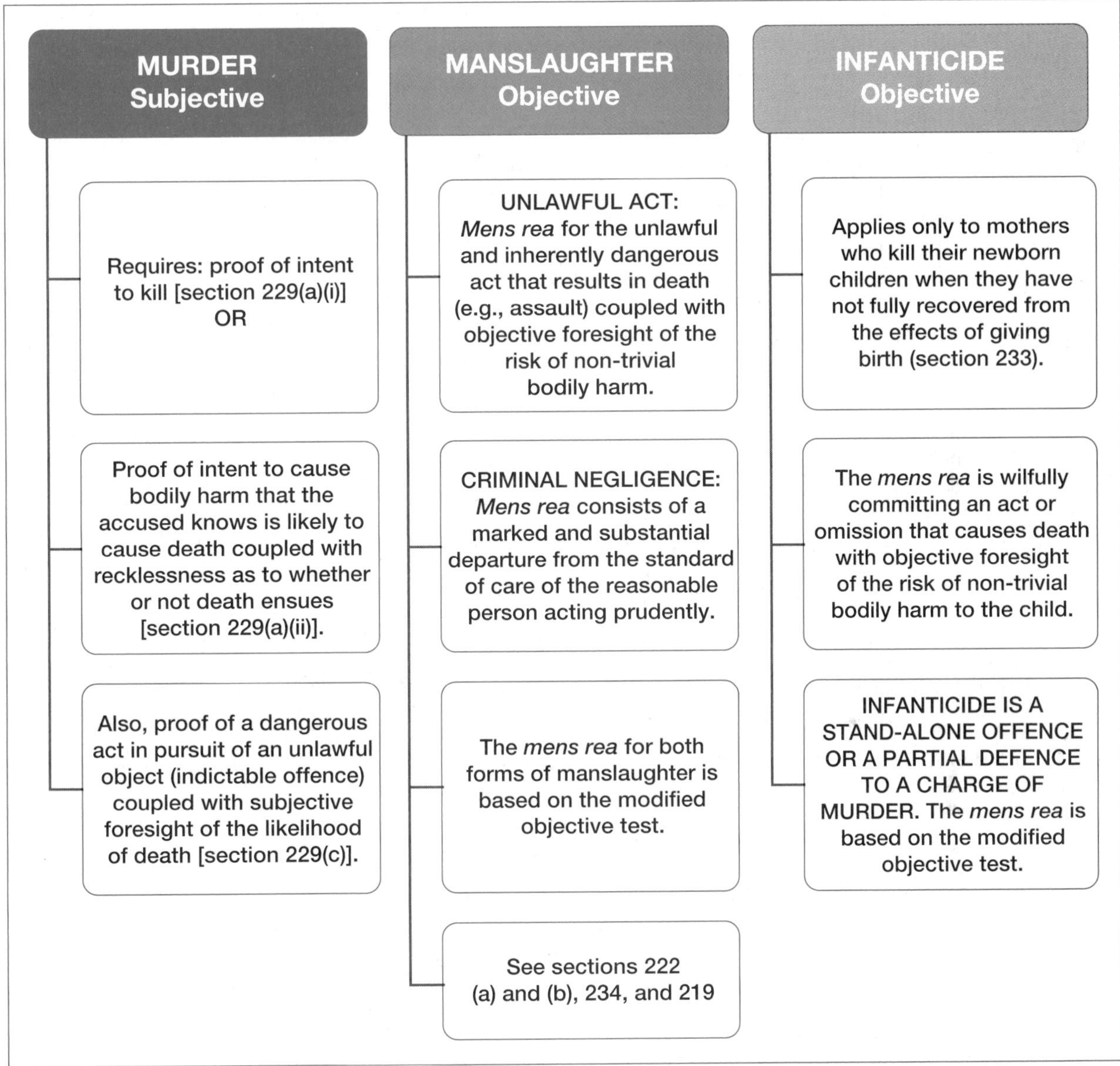

Figure 5-3
Mens Rea *for the Three Categories of Culpable Homicide*

CRIMINAL CODE SECTIONS IMPOSING A SPECIAL STANDARD OF CARE

Where an individual is engaging in activities that are so inherently dangerous as to pose a serious risk to the safety of others, the *Criminal Code* may require them to meet an **elevated standard of care**—the standard of care expected of a reasonable person who has acquired the necessary expertise and training to engage in such activities. Examples of situations in which the *Criminal Code* imposes such an elevated standard of care are sections 79 (possession of explosives), 86(1) (use and storage of firearms), and 216 (administration of surgical and medical treatment). If there is a marked departure from the elevated standard of care, the accused's negligence will justify conviction of the relevant *Criminal Code* offence.

Clearly, these sections all deal with situations in which one would expect the responsible citizen to acquire a reasonable degree of expertise before engaging in conduct that has the potential to be dangerous to the lives and safety of others. Undoubtedly, those who undertake to handle explosives, make use of firearms, or deliver medical care may all be said to be engaging in activities that are inherently fraught with many potential dangers. Therefore, a citizen who, for example, engages in medical treatment is judged by the standard of the reasonable medical practitioner rather than the reasonable person in the street who has no medical training. As Justice McLachlin stated in the *Creighton* case (1993):

> A person may fail to meet an elevated *de facto* standard of care in either of two ways. First, the person may undertake an activity requiring special care when he or she is not qualified to give that care. Absent special excuses like necessity, this may constitute culpable negligence. An untrained person undertaking brain surgery might violate the standard in this way. Secondly, a person who is qualified may negligently fail to exercise the special care required by the activity. A brain surgeon performing surgery in a grossly negligent way might violate the standard in this second way. The standard is the same, although the means by which it is breached may differ.

A striking example of the application of an elevated standard of care occurred in the case of *Lilgert* (2014). The accused was in charge of the navigation of a B.C. ferry, *The Queen of the North*, when it ran aground and sank. Two people were killed. Lilgert was charged and convicted at trial of two counts of criminal negligence causing death. Lilgert's appeal to the B.C. Court of Appeal was dismissed. One of the issues raised in the appeal was whether the trial judge had articulated the appropriate standard of care when she instructed the jury. On this point, the Court of Appeal stated that:

> The body of the evidence would have left the jury with no doubt that they were to compare the appellant's conduct against the standard of a reasonably prudent mariner in charge of the navigation and operation of the vessel. The evidence makes it plain that the task of navigation involves judgment and discretion according to well-established rules of good seamanship …

1. Reasonable Medical Treatment—Section 216

Section 216 of the *Criminal Code* provides that:

> Every one who undertakes to administer surgical or medical treatment to another person or to do any other lawful act that may endanger the life of another person is, except in cases of necessity, under a legal duty to have and to use reasonable knowledge, skill and care in so doing.

This section clearly imposes an elevated standard of liability on those who administer surgical or medical treatment or engage in other lawful activities that may endanger the lives of others. Such individuals are expected to possess the knowledge and skills of the average, competent medical practitioner, etc. This means that although accused persons who administer such treatment may not subjectively appreciate the risk that their conduct is creating, they may still be convicted of an offence under the *Criminal Code* if the reasonable medical practitioner would have appreciated such a risk.

This principle is illustrated by the tragic case of *Rogers* (1968), in which the accused, a former doctor who had been struck from the rolls, was charged with causing death by criminal negligence. Although prohibited from engaging in medical practice, he continued to pose as a doctor and began to treat a little boy who suffered from a skin disorder. Rogers prescribed such an insufficient diet that the boy ultimately died of gross malnutrition. Rogers claimed that he honestly believed that his diet would be beneficial for the boy and that he did not foresee the risk that it might be dangerous. His counsel, therefore, argued that the Crown must prove that his client was reckless (or subjectively aware of the risk) before a conviction could be entered against him. Rogers was nevertheless convicted at trial and his appeal to the British Columbia Court of Appeal was dismissed. The Court of Appeal emphasized that section 216 of the *Criminal Code* prescribes an objective test of criminal responsibility and that the Crown was, therefore, not obliged to establish that the accused subjectively appreciated the risk that his conduct was creating. Since a reasonable doctor would have appreciated the risk created by the inadequate diet,

Rogers was correctly convicted. As Justice Nemetz said in relation to this point:

> Once all of the medical witnesses had testified that the possessors of reasonable medical knowledge would foresee that the taking away of proteins and calories (as was in fact done by Rogers) would probably result in death, it became irrelevant for the trial judge to put Rogers' belief to the contrary to the jury. It was Rogers' duty to have the "reasonable knowledge" that was delineated and which represented the advances in scientific and medical knowledge to this day. If he persisted in this treatment notwithstanding that body of reasonable knowledge he ran the risk of bringing about the unwished result, namely, the death of the child.

In *W. (D.J.)* (2012), discussed above, the accused who had carried out a disastrous circumcision of his four-year-old son claimed that he had

> ... studied circumcision, sought and obtained medical, non-medical, and Rabbinical advice, consulted the Internet, attempted to obtain a hemostat [a device to clamp off a bleeding vein], researched "blood stop powders," purchased "Wonder Dust" and brand new blades, used clean plastic sheets, washed the instruments he intended to use and then boiled them, used a plastic cutting board, and gave D.J. wine to distract him and put him in a cheerful mood before the attempted circumcision.

However, this was irrelevant in light of section 216, and the Supreme Court of Canada pointed out that:

> The trial judge also found that the accused did not have the knowledge, experience, or skill to conduct a circumcision, was aware of the dangers of performing a circumcision on his son, and that his kitchen was not a sterile, or even a sanitary, environment in which to perform a circumcision.

Performing such a circumcision without the necessary medical qualifications and training would amount to criminal negligence in light of section 216, which requires that anyone who performs a medical procedure is "under a legal duty to have and to use reasonable knowledge, skill and care in so doing." Such conduct represents a marked and substantial departure from the standard of care expected of a reasonable medical practitioner, which is the legally required standard.[14]

Similarly, in *Thornton* (1993), the Supreme Court of Canada ruled that a blood donor may be considered to be engaging in a "lawful act that may endanger the life of another person" and is, therefore, placed under a legal duty by section 216 to take reasonable care. Indeed, Chief Justice Lamer stated, on behalf of the Court, that "Section 216 imposed upon [Thornton] a duty of care in giving his blood to the Red Cross. This duty of care was breached by not disclosing that his blood contained HIV antibodies. This common nuisance obviously endangered the life, safety and health of the public."

2. The Duty to Take Reasonable Care in the Handling of Explosives and Firearms—Sections 79 and 86(1)

The *Criminal Code* imposes an elevated standard of care in relation to the handling of explosive substances. Section 79 states: "Every one who has an explosive substance in his possession or under his care or control is under a legal duty to use reasonable care to prevent bodily harm or death to persons or damage to property by that explosive substance."

A similar duty has been imposed on those who handle firearms. Section 86(1) of the *Code* provides that "Every person commits an offence who, without lawful excuse, uses, carries, handles, ships, transports or stores a firearm, a prohibited weapon, a restricted weapon, a prohibited device or any ammunition or prohibited ammunition in a careless manner or without reasonable precautions for the safety of other persons."

In each case, these provisions would be interpreted by the courts as requiring that an accused person meet the standard of care expected of a reasonable person who has taken some training in the safe handling of

14. Since the accused was convicted of the more serious crime of aggravated assault, the charge of criminal negligence causing bodily harm was stayed.

Illustration by Greg Holoboff

Those who handle explosives have to satisfy an elevated standard of care.

explosives and firearms. The standard is not that of the "reasonable novice" who tries their best to cope with explosives or firearms with no knowledge of basic safety precautions. However, as the Supreme Court said in the *Finlay* case (1993), there can be a conviction of an offence under the *Criminal Code* only if the accused person's behaviour can be designated as a marked departure from the standard of care expected of a reasonable person who has the necessary training and skills to deal with explosives and firearms.

Significantly, the Supreme Court has ruled that the elevated standard of care imposed by provisions of the *Criminal Code* such as section 86(1) is that of the reasonable person acting prudently. Naturally, the reasonable person will acquire sufficient knowledge about the use, storage, and transportation, etc., of firearms before undertaking such activity. As Justice McLachlin said in the *Creighton* case (1993):

> Where individuals engage in activities for which they lack sufficient knowledge, experience, or physical ability, they may be properly found to be at fault, not so much for their inability to properly carry out the activity, but for their decision to attempt the activity without having accounted for their deficiencies. The law expects people embarking on hazardous activities to ask questions or seek help before they venture beyond their depth.

However, it is important to bear in mind that the criminal law requires the individual who uses firearms only to meet the standard of care expected of a reasonable person who is acting prudently and has acquired the necessary knowledge to engage in this activity safely. *In other words, the law imposes a "single minimum standard" and does not raise it—or lower it—according to the particular expertise of the defendant in a specific case.* For example, in the *Gosset* case (1993), Chief Justice Lamer suggested that a "police officer trained and experienced in the use of firearms should be held to a higher standard of care in the handling of firearms than the non-police officer." However, the majority of the Supreme Court rejected Chief Justice Lamer's approach. In *Creighton* (1993), Justice McLachlin clearly articulated the rationale for the position adopted by the majority of the justices of the Supreme Court:

> Just as the adoption of a uniform standard of care which is blind to personal characteristics of the accused short of incapacity precludes lowering the standard for deficiencies of experience and temperament, so it precludes raising the standard for special experience or training. Since the criminal law is concerned with setting minimum standards for human conduct, it would be inappropriate to hold accused persons to a higher standard of care by reason of the fact that they may be better informed or better qualified than the person of reasonable prudence. Some activities may impose a higher *de facto* standard than others; brain surgery requires more care than applying an antiseptic. But … this flows from the circumstances of the activity, not from the expertise of the actor.

In other words, a police officer who is charged with an offence of criminal negligence as a consequence

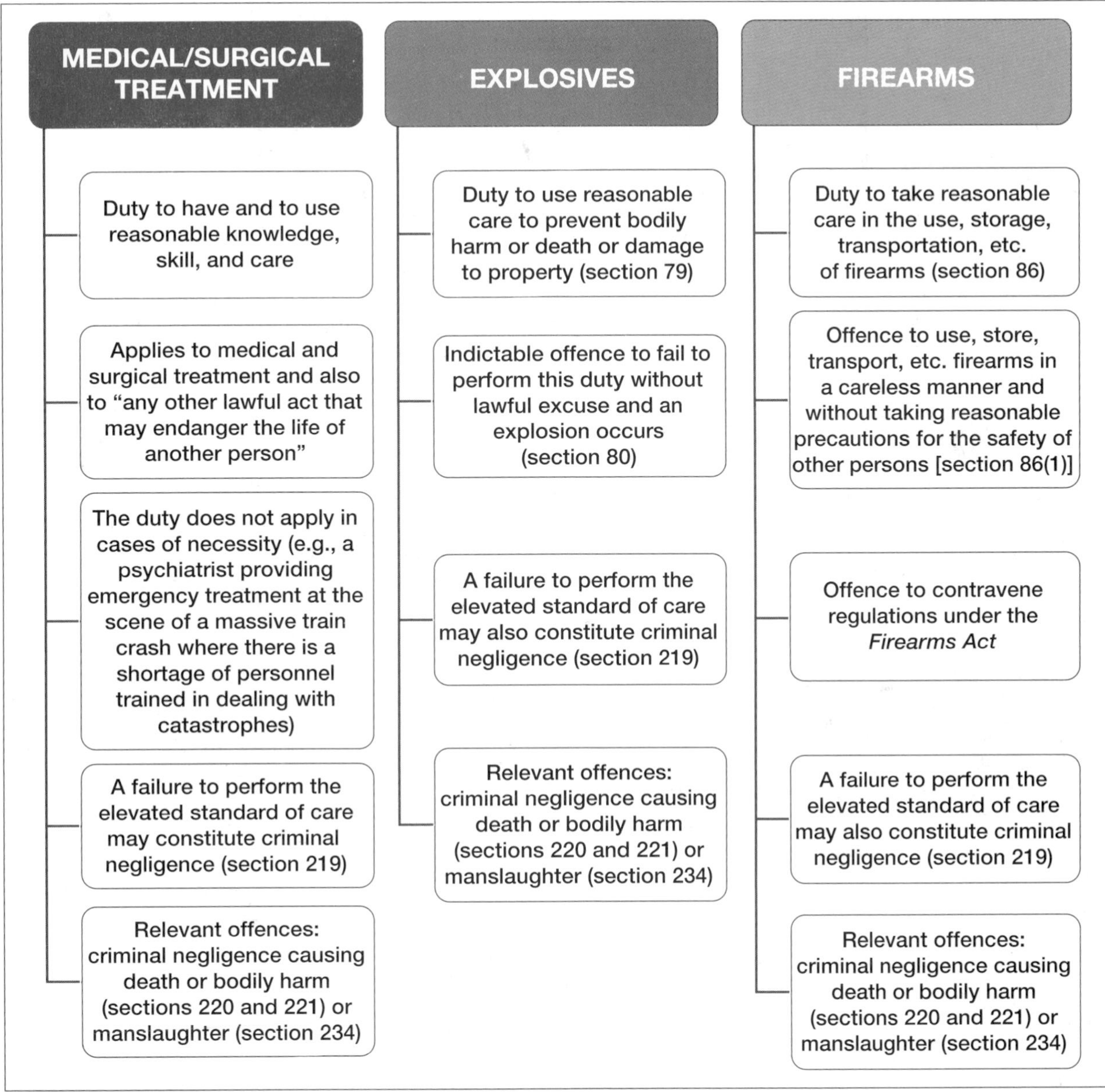

Figure 5-4

Elevated Standards of Care in the Criminal Code

of their misuse of a firearm will be judged by the standard of the reasonable person who uses firearms prudently, and not by the standard of an expert in the use of firearms. The standard of care under section 86(1) is "elevated" in the sense that an individual must acquire a minimum level of knowledge and skill before embarking on such a manifestly dangerous enterprise as dealing with firearms. However, if that individual attains this minimum level of knowledge and skill and acts prudently, then they cannot be found to have been guilty of criminal negligence.

Study Questions

1. Crackit and Winkel are walking on the banks of a fast-flowing river. They are good friends and are laughing and smiling. Crackit decides to "give Winkel a scare" and pushes him toward the river. Crackit believes that he will be able to hold on to Winkel so that he will not fall into the water. Unfortunately, as he pushes Winkel, Crackit slips on some slick grass and fails to maintain a hold on Winkel, who tumbles into the river. Winkel is unable to swim and is rapidly swept away by a strong current. Winkel drowns, and his lifeless body is later found trapped under a rock. Do you think that Crackit would be convicted of a charge of manslaughter or criminal negligence causing death?
2. Nero has a personal grudge against Octavian, a local farmer. In order to exact revenge, Nero decides to set fire to Octavian's barn. The barn burns down before the firefighters can arrive to save it. Tragically, Crassus (a vagrant) had been sleeping in the barn at the time and was killed by the fire. Nero says that he honestly believed there was no one in the barn when he set it alight. What charges, if any, might be laid against Nero?
3. Drummle and his sister, Polly, are looking through the vast quantity of items stored in their grandfather's basement. Polly finds an old-fashioned revolver with a rotating cylinder containing six bullet chambers. She quickly opens the gun and notices that the chamber opposite the firing pin is empty. She points the gun at Drummle, saying, "Bang, bang, you're dead," and pulls the trigger. To her surprise, the gun discharges and Drummle is killed. A gun expert tells the police that when the trigger is pulled on such a revolver, the cylinder containing the bullets rotates. The chamber opposite the firing pin was empty when Polly first looked at the gun, but when she pressed the trigger, an adjacent chamber containing a live bullet rotated into a firing position. Polly claims that she had no idea how revolvers operated and that she honestly believed the gun would not fire when she pulled the trigger; the expert says that this is just the sort of misconception that is quite common among those who are inexperienced with revolvers. The police are thinking of charging Polly with manslaughter. Would such a charge be likely to succeed in a criminal trial?
4. Tiny Tim, who is six years old, is taken for a walk near a wading pool in Aquamarine Park by Fanny, his nanny. Tiny Tim splashes water on Creakle, a man of 28, who has never seen Tiny Tim before. Creakle has just been dismissed from his job without cause by his boss and is infuriated by Tiny Tim's behaviour. Creakle pushes the little boy into the pool. Tiny Tim screams and starts to flounder in the water. Creakle believes that Tiny Tim is "crying wolf" because he assumes that the water in a wading pool must be very shallow. However, Flintwich (the municipal employee responsible for this part of the park) has failed to repair some deep holes that have developed at the bottom of the pool, and at the point where Tiny Tim falls in, the water is more than four feet deep. Tiny Tim cannot swim. Fanny is a former member of the Neptune University swimming team and can easily rescue Tiny Tim. However, Fanny is engaged in conversation with Swiveller, a good friend, and does nothing except wave to the struggling Tiny Tim and urge him to stop playing the fool. Swiveller is also an excellent swimmer. He goes over to the edge of the pond and reaches out for the boy, but Tiny Tim is too far from the edge and Swiveller returns to his intimate conversation with Fanny. Tiny Tim drowns. Creakle, who has already left the scene, does not learn that Tiny Tim drowned until he is visited by the police.

   Consider:

   a. The charges that might be laid in this case
   b. The persons against whom the charges might be laid
   c. The approach that might be taken by defence counsel
5. Barkis drives his truck straight through a stop sign and crashes into a lamppost. Fortunately, no one was injured. Barkis is charged with dangerous driving. He claims that he momentarily lost attention when he was changing the radio station, and when he realized he was close to a stop sign, it was too late to bring his truck to a halt. He also claims that the truck was too heavy to bring to a halt within the few seconds during which he had become aware of the stop sign. Is he guilty of the charge laid against him? Would it make a difference if Barkis stated that he momentarily

fell asleep because the driving conditions had been extremely treacherous (e.g., heavy snow or rain) and he was exhausted? Why or why not?

6. Grewgious is driving his car through a school zone when he suddenly experiences a massive heart attack and loses consciousness. Sadly, his car mounts the sidewalk and strikes a young child, who subsequently dies. Grewgious is charged with dangerous driving causing death. Is he likely to be convicted of this charge? Would it be a relevant consideration that Grewgious had already experienced two heart attacks?
7. Snubbin is driving his pickup truck on a highway. It is a fine, clear day and the driving conditions are excellent. Suddenly, Snubbin's truck crosses the median and collides head on with a car travelling in the opposite direction. The unfortunate driver of the car is Trotter, who is killed as a result of the collision. It appears that Snubbin fell asleep immediately before the accident. Pickwick, a physician who examines Snubbin after the accident, is prepared to testify that Snubbin suffers from narcolepsy (a condition that causes sudden and uncontrollable episodes of deep sleep). If you were Crown counsel, would you charge Snubbin with dangerous driving causing death?
8. Hamlet and Ophelia have a young daughter, Gertrude. They know that Gertrude, who has diabetes, requires regular insulin injections to stay alive. Hamlet and Ophelia are members of a society that organizes séances, and both of them firmly believe in the existence of a "spirit world." Hamlet tells Ophelia that he has experienced a vision in which he saw his father's ghost, who told him that Gertrude was cured of her diabetes and no longer needed injections. Ophelia implicitly believes what Hamlet has told her and they cease giving Gertrude her insulin injections. Gertrude lapses into a coma, and by the time she is taken to hospital, it is too late to save her life. Crown counsel wishes to lay charges of manslaughter against Hamlet and Ophelia. Is it likely that such charges would be successful at a trial?
9. Barnaby Rudge is an adult with a developmental disability who functions at the same mental level as an eight-year-old child. He finds a large rock and decides to go to a bridge that spans a highway. He then drops the rock onto a passing truck, killing its driver. The police wish to lay a charge of manslaughter or criminal negligence causing death against Barnaby. What would you do if you were Crown counsel in this case?
10. Bagstock has three rifles and a large supply of ammunition in his residence. The guns are properly licensed, as required by the *Criminal Code*. However, one day Bagstock leaves one of the rifles in the garage instead of locking it up in a secure cabinet. His 10-year-old nephew, Jo, finds the gun and points it at his friend Oliver. Tragically, the gun is faulty and unexpectedly discharges, wounding Oliver in the leg. Could Bagstock be charged with criminal negligence causing bodily harm?
11. Hippocrates is a plastic surgeon who, for the past 30 years, has specialized in "facelifts" and similar surgical procedures. One day, he is summoned to the emergency room of the hospital and told that since no other surgeon is available, he must operate on Traddles, a man who has suffered major internal injuries in a car accident. Hippocrates realizes that Traddles will die without immediate surgery, so he very reluctantly undertakes to perform the operation. Traddles subsequently dies, and it is suggested that Hippocrates was negligent because he did not know the latest surgical techniques that could have saved a patient who had suffered such devastating injuries as those inflicted on Traddles. If you were Crown counsel, would you charge Hippocrates with manslaughter or criminal negligence causing death?
12. Rosalind is a single mother of very limited means. She lives in a tiny apartment. She has only a living room (where she and her son, Kit, also sleep), a small kitchen, and a bathroom. Kit, who is five years old, frequently plays in the bathroom, where he loves to float some plastic toys in the bathtub. One day, Verges, Rosalind's boyfriend, comes for a visit. Alcohol is consumed and the two adults decide to go to bed. Kit is placed in the bathroom and told to play with his boats in the bathtub. Rosalind locks the bathroom door from the outside. She then engages in sexual relations with Verges. After about half an hour, the adults dress themselves and decide to play with Kit. When they unlock and open the bathroom door, they discover Kit floating face down in the water. Despite the application of mouth-to-mouth resuscitation techniques by Verges and the early arrival of the paramedics (summoned by a distraught Rosalind), Kit cannot be revived. In light of this tragic drowning, Crown counsel is considering laying charges against Rosalind. What charges might reasonably be laid and what defences might be open to Rosalind in light of these charges?

13. Wegg and Snawley are fighting in a bar. Gride angrily throws a beer glass at them to bring the disturbance to an end. The glass unfortunately shatters as it strikes part of the sprinkler system and a large piece of glass is embedded in the arm of Smike, an innocent bystander. Smike is taken to hospital and it requires 47 stitches to close his substantial wound. Gride tearfully tells the police that he never meant to harm anyone and appears to be genuinely contrite. What charge(s) might reasonably be laid against Gride?
14. Mr. Dick has just purchased a quarry that produces limestone. Mr. Dick has no prior experience with the extraction of minerals; indeed, his business experience has been limited to the operation of a large laundry. When Mr. Dick takes over the quarry, he finds two large boxes containing explosives. He decides to transport the explosives to a hut on the other side of the quarry: his reason for this decision is that he believes the explosives may be stolen from their existing location. After he has moved the boxes to the hut, Mr. Dick drives home. Within minutes of his departure, there is a tremendous explosion in the hut. Tragically, two employees at the quarry are killed. A government inspector informs the police that the explosives were perilously unstable and should never have been moved in that condition. A distraught and repentant Mr. Dick says that he is a complete newcomer to the field of explosives and that he had no idea that moving the boxes could trigger a deadly blast. The inspector states that anyone who had even the most elementary knowledge of dealing with explosive materials would never have moved these boxes in light of the dangerous instability of their contents. Is it likely that Mr. Dick would be convicted of manslaughter or criminal negligence causing death?

THE SPECIAL CASE OF REGULATORY OFFENCES:

Strict and Absolute Liability in Canada

CHAPTER 6

Learning Objectives

After reading this chapter, you will understand:

- the distinction between true crimes and regulatory offences;
- the principle that the Crown is required to prove only the *actus reus* elements of a regulatory offence;
- the distinction between absolute and strict liability in the context of regulatory offences;
- how the imposition of absolute liability denies the accused person the opportunity to deny that they were at fault, while the imposition of strict liability allows the accused person to prove, on the balance of probabilities, that they were not negligent; and
- that absolute liability offences will, with few exceptions, be declared invalid under section 7 of the *Charter* if they expose offenders to the possibility of imprisonment.

INTRODUCTION

In Chapter 1, the distinction was drawn between true crimes and regulatory offences, or quasi-criminal law. In this chapter, we examine the special principles and procedures that apply when an accused person is charged with a regulatory offence.

As the Ontario Court of Appeal stated in *Ontario (Ministry of the Environment, Conservation and Parks) v. Henry of Pelham Inc.* (2018), "Public welfare statutes regulate everything from driving to fishing, environmental protection and workplace health and safety." The Court then emphasized that regulatory offences should not be considered as "true crimes":

> ... regulatory offences are not "true crimes"—"conduct that is, in itself, so abhorrent to the basic values of human society that it ought to be prohibited completely." ... Regulatory offences arise in the context of conduct that is otherwise lawful—indeed, conduct that may be encouraged and promoted for the good of society, but which nevertheless requires regulation in the public interest. ... As the Supreme Court noted more recently, "regulatory legislation does not share the same purpose as the criminal law, and it would be a mistake to interpret it as though it did"

A vast number of regulatory offences have been created by the Parliament of Canada and the various provincial/territorial legislatures. In addition, innumerable bylaws have been created by municipalities across Canada, acting on the authority delegated to them by the respective provinces and territories. Many of the provincial offences and bylaw infractions are prosecuted by means of a ticketing system operated by the provinces (tickets for traffic or parking violations, for example, are very familiar to most Canadian adults). Furthermore, approximately 3000 federal regulatory offences, under 20 different federal laws and more than 45 sets of regulations, have been designated as "contraventions" under the *Contraventions Act*, S.C. 1992, c. 47,[1] thereby permitting their prosecution through provincial ticketing systems.[2] Section 4 of the Act states that the purposes of the legislation are:

> (a) to provide a procedure for the prosecution of contraventions that reflects the distinction between criminal offences and regulatory offences and that is in addition to the procedures set out in the *Criminal Code* for the prosecution of contraventions and other offences; and
>
> (b) to alter or abolish the consequences in law of being convicted of a contravention, in light of that distinction.[3]

Many provincial regulatory offences and bylaw infractions will be dealt with out of court by the citizen paying a fine as the result of receiving a ticket. In many cases, fines may be paid online: Ontario, for example, has a "PayTickets" website.[4] In other cases, however, a citizen may be summoned to appear in court. Cases involving regulatory offences will generally be tried in provincial or territorial courts [in most provinces, the Provincial Court; in Quebec, the Municipal Court; in Ontario, the Ontario Court of Justice (municipal provincial offences courts); in Nunavut, the Nunavut Court of Justice;[5] and in the Northwest Territories and Yukon, the Territorial Court].

What are the practical consequences of drawing a distinction between true crimes and regulatory offences? Foremost among these consequences is the fact that, whereas the Crown must prove some form of *mens rea* to obtain the conviction of an offender for a true crime, it generally does not have to do so in the case of a regulatory offence. As we have seen in Chapters 3 and 4, when an accused person is charged with having committed a true crime, the Crown normally has to prove—in addition to the *actus reus* requirements—one or more of the following forms of *mens rea*: intention, knowledge, recklessness, wilful blindness, or criminal negligence (a marked departure from the standard of the ordinary person). However, in the case of a regulatory offence, all that the Crown normally has to prove are the *actus reus* elements. In *Wilson v. British Columbia (Superintendent of Motor Vehicles)* (2015), the Supreme Court of Canada explained the rationale for making it easier for the prosecution to obtain convictions for regulatory offences: "... it has long been recognized that regulatory legislation ... differs from

1. See also Application of Provincial Laws Regulations, SOR/96-312.

2. The Act does not apply to the provinces of Alberta and Saskatchewan.

3. Section 5 provides that:" The provisions of the Criminal Code relating to summary conviction offences and the provisions of the Youth Criminal Justice Act apply to proceedings in respect of contraventions that are commenced under this Act, except to the extent that this Act, the regulations or the rules of court provide otherwise.

4. https://www.paytickets.ca

5. Nunavut has a unified, single-level court. Unlike other territories, Nunavut does not have separate Territorial and Supreme Courts. Judges in the Nunavut Court of Justice hear all types of cases.

Fines for Many Regulatory Offences May Be Paid on the Internet

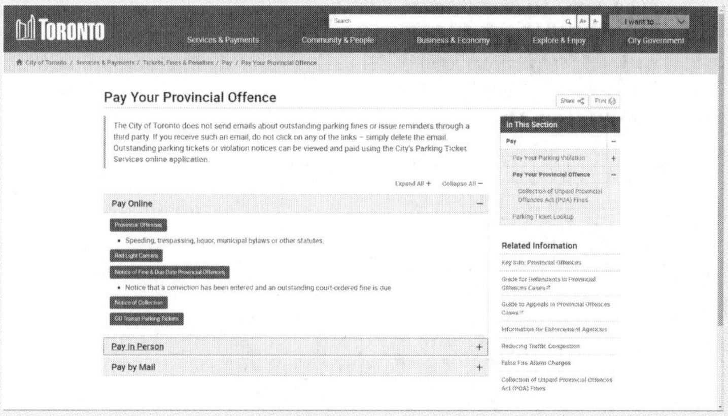

City of Toronto

Increasingly, regulatory offences are being enforced through a ticketing system, and many of the associated fines may be paid online. Not only are many provincial/territorial offences enforced in this manner, but many federal offences may also be dealt with through a provincial ticketing system, by virtue of the *Contraventions Act*, S.C. 1992, c. 47. It is noteworthy that ticketing for these types of regulatory offence has become an efficient method for raising revenue for the governments concerned and significantly reduces the costs of taking offenders through the expensive court process.

A ticketing scheme works by an enforcement officer writing or printing out a ticket that contains the necessary information about the offence and how the applicable fine may be paid. The ticket also indicates that the accused person has the option of going to court and pleading not guilty, should they wish to contest the ticket. The benefit to both the accused person and the taxpayer is that, if the accused does not wish to challenge the ticket, payment of the fine will consume relatively little administrative resources and will avoid the significant costs associated with a prosecution and court trial.

Another great benefit flowing from the designation of *federal* regulatory offences as "contraventions" is that the offender is not encumbered by having a criminal record; such a record will be created if the offender is prosecuted and convicted under summary conviction procedures of the *Criminal Code*. A criminal record may sharply limit potential employment opportunities and an offender's ability to travel outside Canada may be severely restricted. Therefore, the passage of the *Contraventions Act* in 1992 was a very important step taken by the Parliament of Canada to ensure that many federal regulatory offences are not prosecuted in the same way as true crimes.

It is noteworthy that, in August 2013, the Canadian Association of Chiefs of Police passed a resolution in favour of giving police officers the option of handing out tickets to individuals found in possession of small amounts of marijuana. The ticketing process would have been implemented through the federal *Contraventions Act*. It was suggested that the option of giving tickets to individuals possessing less than 30 grams of marijuana would reduce both policing and court costs. The Association also noted that pursuing this path of law enforcement would spare offenders from the handicap of being saddled with a criminal record, which would restrict access to future travel outside Canada, employment, and citizenship. The Association indicated that, in 2007, police reported some 47 000 cases of marijuana possession. What was notable about the Association's resolution was that it suggested extending the ticket process to an offence that had always been treated as a real crime rather than a traditional regulatory offence.

The Association's resolution became moot when Parliament enacted the ***Cannabis Act***, S.C. 2018, c. 16, which came into force on October 17, 2018. This legislation allows, for example, adult Canadians to possess up to 30 grams of cannabis in a public place. However, it is a particularly interesting question of public policy as to whether a ticketing system might be applied to the possession of other drugs currently prohibited by the *Controlled Drugs and Substances Act*, S.C. 1996, c. 19. Would such a step constitute good public policy? Would it encourage individuals who use such drugs to link up with treatment and other supportive services? Would it make sense to forget about a ticketing system and, instead, to decriminalize the possession of small amounts of all drugs and/or to permit physicians to prescribe certain drugs that are currently illegal if the benefits of harm reduction outweigh the risks posed by consuming these drugs?

criminal legislation in the way it balances individual liberties against the protection of the public. Under regulatory legislation, the public good often takes on greater weight."

REGULATORY OFFENCES AND ABSOLUTE LIABILITY

Historically, the courts took the view that defendants who were charged with regulatory offences should not be given any opportunity to argue that they were not to blame for what had happened: indeed, if the Crown could prove the *actus reus* elements of the offence, then the issue of fault was considered completely irrelevant. For this reason, regulatory offences were described in the past as being offences of **absolute liability**.

Ping Yuen (1921) is one of the most notorious cases in which a Canadian court imposed absolute liability on an accused person who had been charged with having committed a regulatory offence. In this case, the accused was a vendor of soft drinks in Moosomin, Saskatchewan. This was in the era of Prohibition, when the sale of alcohol was forbidden. However, "non-intoxicating" beer—with a very low level of alcohol—was permitted and could be sold as a soft drink. A police officer searched the accused's business premises and removed five bottles of soft drinks from his stock. When these bottles were analyzed, it was found that three of them contained beer with a percentage of alcohol in excess of the amount allowed by the Saskatchewan *Temperance Act*, 1917. The accused was charged with a violation of the Act. Under this statute, section 35(1) provided that "In case any person engaged in the business of selling soft drinks or non-intoxicating liquors keeps or has with his stocks of such drinks or liquors or on his business premises any liquor as defined by this Act, such person shall be guilty of an offence." At Ping Yuen's trial, the magistrate found that the accused did not know that any of the bottles contained more alcohol than the law permitted. Furthermore, even the prosecution admitted that it was not possible for the accused to test any of the bottles without destroying their contents for sale purposes; in other words, there was no practical way in which Ping Yuen could have avoided breaking the law! The accused was nevertheless convicted on the basis that, since he was charged with a public welfare offence, the legislature must be taken to have intended to impose absolute liability in relation to the offence. The accused's conviction was subsequently upheld by the Saskatchewan Court of Appeal. In essence, the court ruled that Ping Yuen's offence was not a "true crime" to which any stigma attached. Instead, it was an act prohibited in the public interest under the threat of a financial penalty.

A critical point to bear in mind is the fact that even though Ping Yuen had acted no differently than any "reasonable" retailer would have done in the circumstances, he was nevertheless convicted of the offence. In other words, Ping Yuen was not blameworthy in any sense whatsoever. Nevertheless, his lack of fault was considered to be irrelevant by the courts. Ping Yuen was fined $50. In the Court of Appeal, Justice Turgeon said:

> [I]n the case of beer in this province, it seems to me to be the true intent of the Act that persons who deal in the article are made responsible for it being of a certain quality, namely, not more than 1.13% of alcoholic content, and when they have a too strong alcoholic article in their possession they are liable to the penalty.

In essence, the court seemed to be saying that, to protect the public, the risk of possessing non-intoxicating beer with an excessive alcoholic content was placed solely upon the retailer's shoulders. Since the accused was engaged in the retail business, he must accept such a risk as part and parcel of doing business.

THE ARGUMENTS FOR AND AGAINST ABSOLUTE LIABILITY

Over the years, a number of arguments have been advanced in support of the concept of absolute liability. For example, it was asserted that individuals who engage in activities that may harm the public welfare should be required to meet a high standard of care and attention. Many people believed that, by requiring the Crown to prove *mens rea* in relation to regulatory offences, too many legal loopholes would be created for individuals and corporations to evade their responsibilities to the public. It was argued that absolute liability would remove such loopholes and, thus, would act as an "incentive" for such persons to take precautionary measures, *over and above those that would normally be taken*, to ensure that mistakes and accidents did not occur. The theory was that if an individual or a corporation realizes that there are no legal loopholes to slip through when they are charged with a regulatory offence, then they will take an extraordinary degree of care to avoid committing such an offence.

Another argument advanced in favour of absolute liability was that of administrative efficiency. It was alleged that it would be far too great a burden for the Crown to prove mental culpability in relation to the great number of petty regulatory offences that come before the courts. Since there is a need to process a large number of cases involving regulatory offences, it has been argued that the Crown must have access to a swift and administratively efficient system of law enforcement. It was contended that if the Crown were required to establish *mens rea* in relation to regulatory offences, the whole system of justice would rapidly grind to a halt and, as a result, hundreds of thousands of violators would escape conviction. Therefore, it was argued that absolute liability was a pragmatic necessity if there was to be effective regulation of trade, commerce, and industry in the country.

There are, of course, numerous arguments that militate against the imposition of absolute liability. For example, one of the strongest arguments of this nature is that absolute liability contradicts a deeply ingrained sense of justice since it punishes those who lack any moral culpability. It is a basic notion in our society that an individual who lacks moral culpability should not be convicted of a criminal offence. As the great American Justice Oliver Wendell Holmes once said, "Even a dog distinguishes between being kicked and being stumbled over." Another argument against absolute liability is that it destroys the individual citizen's basic freedom of choice. Indeed, traditional legal theorists have persistently contended that the doctrine of *mens rea* is designed to maximize personal freedom because only the individual who deliberately chooses to break the law is subject to conviction. Absolute liability, of course, would destroy such freedom since it is not based on individual culpability.

In the *Sault Ste. Marie* case (1978), Justice Dickson, of the Supreme Court of Canada, presented a number of convincing arguments against the imposition of absolute liability:

> The most telling is that it violates fundamental principles of penal liability. It also rests upon assumptions which have not been, and cannot be, empirically established. There is no evidence that a higher standard of care results from absolute liability. If a person is already taking every reasonable precautionary measure, is he likely to take additional measures, knowing however much care he takes, it will not serve as a defence in the event of breach? If he has exercised care and skill, will conviction have a deterrent effect upon him or others? Will the injustice of conviction lead to cynicism and disrespect for the law, on his part and on the part of others? These are among the questions asked. The argument that no stigma attaches does not withstand analysis, for the accused will have suffered loss of time, legal costs, exposure to the processes of criminal law at trial and, however one may downplay it, the opprobrium of conviction.

Similarly, in the decision of the Supreme Court of Canada in *Chapin* (1979), Justice Dickson pointed out that "the problems that may be encountered in the administration of a statute or regulation are a very unsure guide to its proper interpretation." Difficulty of enforcement is not *per se* a convincing reason for imposing absolute liability.

THE EMERGENCE OF THE "HALFWAY HOUSE" APPROACH

Whatever the arguments for and against absolute liability may be, there is little doubt that Canadian courts became increasingly uncomfortable with the rigid policy that they had embraced in relation to regulatory offences. Indeed, the courts had left themselves no room to manoeuvre: once they had decided that an offence was regulatory in nature, they would routinely impose absolute liability and thereby deprive the defendant of any defence based on their lack of fault.

Eventually, a more flexible judicial strategy began to emerge in the disposition of cases involving regulatory offences. This strategy was based on the notion that it should be possible for defendants charged with regulatory offences to advance the defence that *they were not negligent*. Very quickly, this was dubbed the **"halfway house" approach** because it finds a middle ground between, on the one hand, requiring the Crown to prove all the *mens rea* elements of an offence beyond a reasonable doubt and, on the other, automatically convicting an accused person merely because they have committed the *actus reus* of a regulatory offence.

When the Crown charges an individual with a true crime, it must establish, beyond a reasonable doubt, all the elements of the *actus reus* and *mens rea* of the offence. In other words, the **primary (or persuasional) burden of proof** in relation to true crimes is nearly always placed upon the shoulders of the Crown. Accused persons are under no obligation to prove their innocence, and it is enough for them to raise a reasonable doubt in order to escape conviction. However, the "halfway house" approach provides that the Crown merely has to prove that the accused committed the *actus reus* elements of the regulatory offence in question. At that point, the burden of proof shifts to the accused to establish their innocence by proving on the balance of probabilities that they were not negligent.

Placing the onus of establishing their innocence upon accused persons is clearly a fundamental departure from the normal rules of criminal law that apply to real crimes. Indeed, the "halfway house" approach gives the Crown a significant advantage when prosecuting individuals for regulatory offences. This advantage is based on the fact that the Crown does not have to prove any mental element in relation to such offences. Unlike the doctrine of absolute liability, the "halfway house" approach *does* permit defendants to advance a defence: however, they must establish this **due diligence** defence on the balance of probabilities in order to escape conviction of a regulatory offence. It is not enough for the accused merely to raise a reasonable doubt as to whether they acted without negligence.

The term **strict liability** has been developed to distinguish those regulatory offences to which Canadian courts apply the "halfway house" approach from those regulatory offences to which the courts still apply the old regime of absolute liability.

THE SUPREME COURT ENDORSES THE "HALFWAY HOUSE" APPROACH: THE *SAULT STE. MARIE* CASE (1978)

In 1978, the Supreme Court of Canada strongly endorsed the "halfway house" approach in the seminal case of *Sault Ste. Marie* (1978). In his judgment, Justice Dickson delivered a strong critique of the various arguments that have been advanced in support of absolute liability. He noted that an increasing number of federal and provincial/territorial statutes were explicitly making provision for a defence of due diligence in the context of regulatory offences. Justice Dickson also pointed out that some Canadian courts were already attempting to apply the "halfway house" approach despite the fact that it had not yet been officially recognized by the Supreme Court of Canada. Justice Dickson then unequivocally expressed the view that the "halfway house" approach should be adopted as part of the criminal law of Canada:

> The correct approach, in my opinion, is to relieve the Crown of the burden of proving *mens rea*, having regard to ... the virtual impossibility in most regulatory cases of proving wrongful intention. In a normal case, the accused alone will have knowledge of what he has done to avoid the breach and it is not improper to expect him to come forward with the evidence of due diligence. This is particularly so when it is alleged, for example, that pollution was caused by the activities of a large and complex corporation. Equally, there is nothing wrong with rejecting absolute liability and admitting the defence of reasonable care.
>
> In this doctrine it is not up to the prosecution to prove negligence. Instead, it is open to the defendant to prove that all due care has been taken. This burden falls upon the defendant as he is the only one who will generally have the means of proof. This would not seem unfair as the alternative is absolute liability which denies an accused any defence whatsoever. While the prosecution must prove beyond a reasonable doubt that the defendant committed the prohibited act, the defendant must only establish on the balance of probabilities that he has a defence of reasonable care.

THE THREE CATEGORIES OF OFFENCES SINCE THE *SAULT STE. MARIE* CASE (1978)

In delivering the judgment of the Supreme Court of Canada, Justice Dickson held that there are now three different categories of criminal offences in Canada:

1. offences in which the existence of *mens rea* must be proved by the Crown beyond a reasonable doubt;
2. strict liability offences, in which there is no necessity for the Crown to prove the existence of *mens rea* (however, defendants may avoid liability by proving that they acted with "due diligence"); and
3. absolute liability offences, in which there is no necessity for the Crown to prove the existence of *mens rea* and in which it is not open to defendants to avoid liability by proving that they acted with "due diligence."

True crimes clearly fall within category 1. Nevertheless, some regulatory offences will also be included in category 1 if the legislature uses words such as "wilfully" or "knowingly," which indicate a clear intent to require proof of full *mens rea*. For example, in the case of *Stucky* (2009), the Ontario

Court of Appeal ruled that the offence of making false or misleading representations to the public, contrary to section 52(1) of the *Competition Act*, R.S.C. 1985, c. C-34, required proof of full *mens rea* because Parliament used the terms "knowingly or recklessly" in the definition of the offence.

However, *the vast majority of regulatory offences will fall within category 2 (strict liability)*. As Justice Wagner stated, on behalf of the Supreme Court of Canada in *La Souveraine, Compagnie d'assurance générale v. Autorité des marchés financiers* (2013), "[regulatory] offences are generally strict liability offences, and strict liability offences do not require proof of *mens rea*." Indeed, in *Kanda* (2008), the Ontario Court of Appeal took the view that, in the *Sault Ste. Marie* case, Justice Dickson had "articulated a presumption that public welfare offences are strict liability offences; accordingly, this presumption must be the starting point in an analysis of a regulatory provision." *Those regulatory offences that do not fall within categories 1 or 2 will be considered*

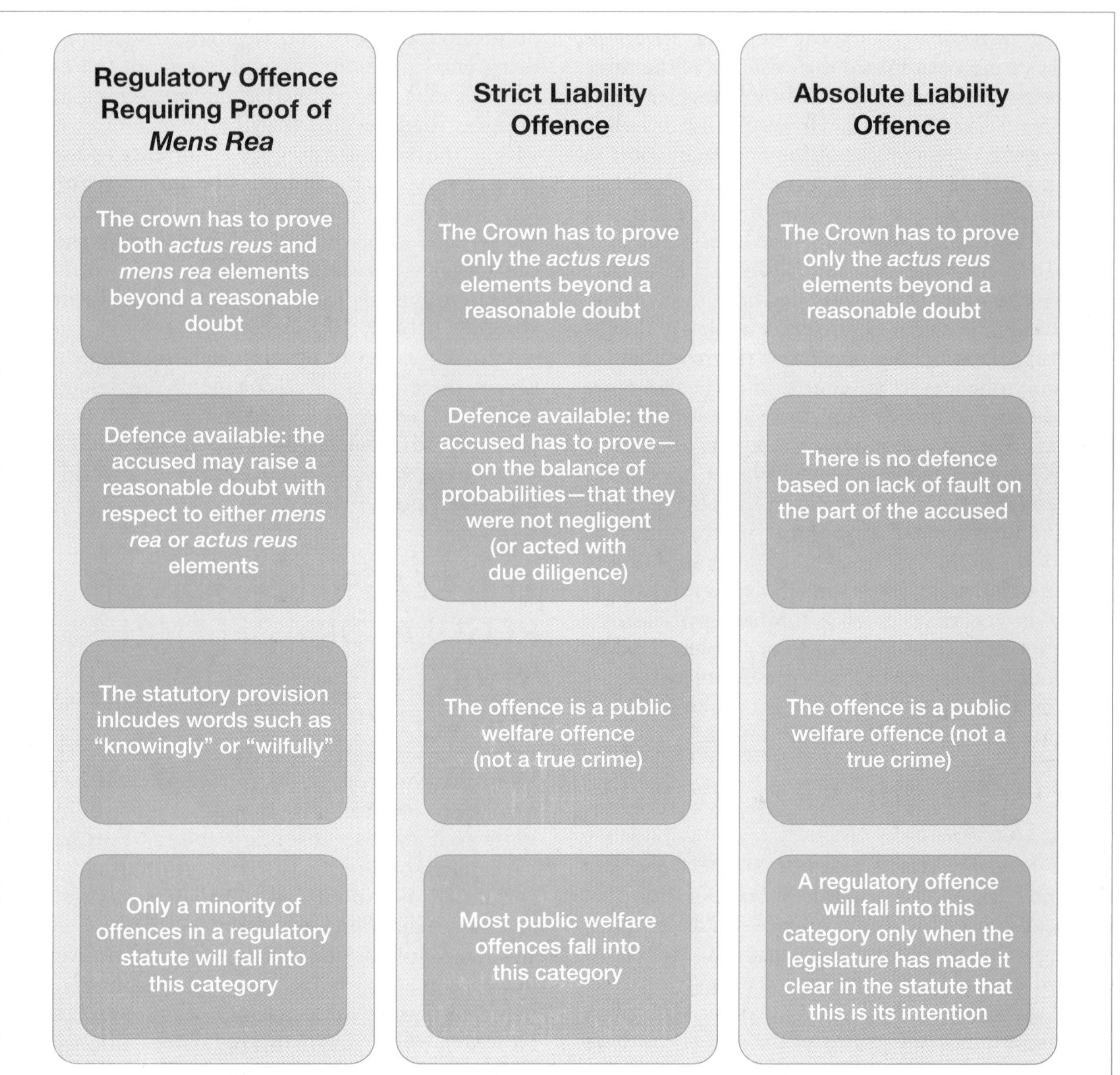

Figure 6-1

Classification of Regulatory (or Public Welfare) Offences

offences of "absolute liability" (category 3). However, Justice Dickson stressed the point that regulatory offences will be placed in category 3 only where the legislature has made it perfectly clear that it intends to impose a regime of absolute liability. In this respect, Justice Dickson said, that "The over-all regulatory pattern adopted by the Legislature, the subject-matter of the Legislation, the importance of the penalty, and the precision of the language used will be primary considerations in determining whether the offence falls into the third category."

It is significant that, almost 30 years later, in *Lévis (Ville) v. Tétreault* (2006), the Supreme Court of Canada strongly reaffirmed the existence of the three categories of offences fashioned by Justice Dickson in the *Sault Ste. Marie* case. However, Justice LeBel, in delivering the judgment of the Supreme Court in *Lévis*, noted that the three categories were "based on a presumption of statutory interpretation." It was not until 1982—four years after the decision in *Sault Ste. Marie*—that the *Canadian Charter of Rights and Freedoms* was enacted and, since that time, the development of a body of *Charter* jurisprudence has undoubtedly had a far-reaching impact on the treatment of regulatory offences by the courts. In particular, as we shall see later in this chapter, the Supreme Court of Canada has ruled that imposing a regime of absolute liability, when conviction of the offence in question may result in the imprisonment of the offender, violates the fundamental principles of justice enshrined in section 7 of the *Charter*. Therefore, both statutory interpretation and *Charter* jurisprudence will have an impact on a court's decision as to whether to classify a regulatory offence as one of strict or absolute liability. As Justice LeBel remarked in *Lévis*, "Absolute liability offences still exist, but they have become an exception requiring clear proof of legislative intent."

THE FACTS IN THE *SAULT STE. MARIE* CASE (1978)

In the *Sault Ste. Marie* case (1978), the facts were that the accused was a municipal corporation that had been charged with the offence of "discharging, causing to be discharged, or permitting to be discharged or deposited materials into a body of water or on the shore or bank thereof, or in such place that might impair the quality of the water," contrary to section 32(1) of the Ontario *Water Resources Act*, R.S.O. 1970, c. 332. The City of Sault Ste. Marie entered into an agreement with a private company for the disposal of all of the city's refuse. The company chose to dump garbage on a site that bordered a creek. Garbage was dumped over a number of freshwater springs that flowed into the creek. After a period, water pollution resulted from this method of garbage disposal. How did the Supreme Court determine into which category the offence charged fell? Was it a true crime requiring proof of full *mens rea* or was it a regulatory offence imposing either strict or absolute liability?

Justice Dickson indicated that "pollution offences are undoubtedly public welfare (regulatory) offences enacted in the interests of public health. There is thus no presumption of a full *mens rea*." Indeed, he said that such a presumption applies only in the case of offences that are "criminal in the true sense." Justice Dickson then decided that the offence charged fell within the second category of offences—namely, offences of strict liability. The major reason for this decision was that, in the legislation that created the offence with which the defendant was charged, the Ontario legislature had not used words that indicated unequivocally that it intended to impose absolute liability. By placing the offence charged within the category of strict liability offences, the Court, therefore, made available to the defendant a defence of acting with "due diligence." A new trial was ordered in which the City of Sault Ste. Marie would have the opportunity to show that it had acted with such "due diligence."

THE CLASSIFICATION OF REGULATORY OFFENCES: STRICT OR ABSOLUTE LIABILITY?

How do the courts distinguish between those regulatory offences that impose strict liability and those that impose absolute liability? Fortunately, Parliament or the provincial/territorial legislature concerned will often make explicit provision for a defence of due diligence in the legislation that creates the regulatory offence in question. Conversely, the relevant legislative body may explicitly state that a regulatory offence is one of absolute liability. However, there are many regulatory offences for which the legislators have made no explicit provision of this type: it is, therefore, left to the courts to decide whether these particular offences impose strict or absolute liability.

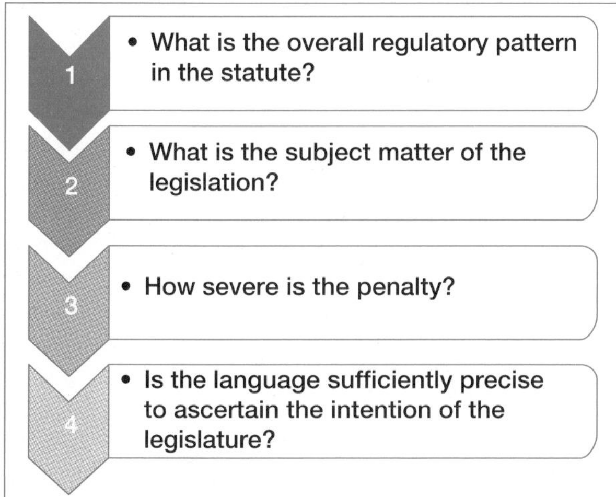

Figure 6-2

Criteria for Distinguishing between Strict and Absolute Liability Regulatory Offences

However, as noted above, the starting point in making this determination is always the presumption that the legislature intended to impose strict liability for regulatory offences. For example, in *Wilson* (2014), the Ontario Court of Appeal was faced with the question of whether section 106(2) of the *Highway Traffic Act*, R.S.O. 1990, C. H-8, which imposed the duty on drivers to wear a seat belt, was an offence of absolute or strict liability. The legislature had not specifically indicated which type of offence it was. However, the Court stated that "there is nothing in the way that the offence is defined that rebuts the strong presumption of strict liability."

It will be remembered that, in the *Sault Ste. Marie* case (1978), Justice Dickson referred to four factors that should normally be considered by the courts when they are faced with the need to classify a regulatory offence as being one that requires proof of *mens rea*, one that imposes strict liability or one that imposes absolute liability: (1) the overall regulatory pattern adopted by the legislature, (2) the subject matter of the legislation, (3) the importance of the penalty, and (4) the precision of the language. These are, by no means, the only factors to be considered: indeed, *Charter* considerations may be a critical element in the decision-making process of the courts. Furthermore, they will always be considered in the context of the "strong presumption" that regulatory offences impose strict liability.

1. The Importance of Examining the Overall Regulatory Pattern in a Statute

In his judgment in *Sault Ste. Marie* (1978), Justice Dickson referred to the "overall regulatory pattern" as an important criterion in making the decision as to whether a particular regulatory offence should be considered one of strict or absolute liability. By this he meant that if a legislature expressly included a defence of due diligence for some offences in a regulatory statute but failed to do so for other offences within the same statute, one may normally conclude that the legislature intended to impose absolute liability in relation to the second group of offences.

In the *Wilson* case (2014), dealing with the classification of the offence of failure to wear a seat belt under the Ontario *Highway Traffic Act*, the Ontario Court of Appeal noted that the Act includes all three categories of regulatory offences. Some sections clearly indicate that the Crown has to prove full *mens rea*: for example, section 104(2.2) provides that "No parent or guardian of a person under sixteen years of age shall authorize or knowingly permit that person to ride a bicycle, other than a power-assisted bicycle, on a highway unless the person is wearing a bicycle helmet as required by subsection (2.1)." The use of the word "knowingly" indicates that the Ontario legislature intended that this offence should be one of those unusual regulatory offences in which the Crown had to prove full *mens rea*. Section 75(4), for example, penalizes motorists who "sound any bell, horn or other signalling device so as to make an unreasonable noise." The Ontario Court of Appeal argued that the imposition of a reasonableness standard indicated that the legislature intended that this regulatory offence should impose strict liability. Finally, Section 84.1(1) penalizes the operator of a commercial vehicle if a wheel becomes detached when the vehicle is on a highway and Section 84.1(5) states that "It is not a defence to a charge under subsection (1) that the person exercised due diligence to avoid or prevent the detaching of the wheel." This clearly indicated that the legislature intended to impose absolute liability. However, the Court of Appeal noted that while the legislature has created a number of offences which clearly fall into one of the three categories, "for most HTA offences, the legislature does not clearly specify the level of fault and it falls to the courts to discern the appropriate level of fault based on the analysis laid down in *Sault Ste. Marie*." For those offences where the legislature has not clearly indicated into which category they fall, the Court will apply the "strong presumption" that they should be designated as strict liability offences. The reasoning of the Court of Appeal in *Wilson* constitutes an excellent example of how the overall regulatory pattern in a regulatory statute can guide the judiciary in determining whether an offence requires proof of *mens rea* or imposes strict or absolute liability. However, as with the other factors identified by Dickson J. in *Sault Ste. Marie*, the overall statutory pattern is a relevant, but not a *decisive* factor.

2. The Importance of Examining the Subject Matter of the Regulatory Offence

The "subject-matter of the offence" is often an important consideration in determining whether a regulatory offence is one of absolute rather than strict liability. In general, it would appear that the greater the threat to the public that is posed by the commission of a regulatory offence, the more likely it is that this offence will be found to impose a regime of absolute liability.

For example, in the *Hickey* case (1977), the Ontario Court of Appeal ruled that the offence of speeding is an absolute liability offence, in large part because of the subject-matter of the offence. Since the subject matter of the offence of speeding is clearly the protection of the public, this factor carried the greatest weight in determining that the offence imposed absolute liability. The Ontario Court of Appeal later re-affirmed that the offence of speeding in Ontario[6] is an offence of absolute liability.[7] In *London (City) v. Polewsky* (2005), the Court stated that "Speed is a factor in many collisions. The overall regulatory pattern adopted by the legislature, the subject matter of the legislation, and the language used suggest that speeding should continue to be interpreted as an offence of absolute liability."

By way of contrast, in *Kanda* (2008), the Ontario Court of Appeal ruled that the offence of driving a vehicle in which a passenger under the age of 16 is not wearing a seat belt is a strict, rather than an absolute, liability offence. The offence is defined by section 106(6) of the *Highway Traffic Act*, R.S.O. 1990, c. H.8.[8] Kanda had been charged with the offence after it was discovered by a police officer that Kanda's eight-year-old son was not wearing his seat belt. Kanda stated that he was unaware that his son had unfastened the belt after he had commenced his journey. The trial judge convicted Kanda, in spite of his explanation, because the offence was one of absolute liability. Upon appeal, however, it was decided that the offence was one of strict liability and that the case should be sent back to the trial judge to allow Kanda to raise a defence of having acted with due diligence. In delivering the judgment of the Ontario Court of Appeal, Justice MacPherson paid considerable attention to the subject matter of the offence:

> Section 106 of the *HTA* requires most people riding in motor vehicles to wear seat belts. The "important statutory purpose" of the seat belt law is "minimizing driver and passenger injuries resulting from car collisions." ... Subsection 106(6) of the *HTA* advances this purpose by making drivers responsible for ensuring that all passengers under 16 years of age use seat belts. The provision is clearly intended to ensure the safety of vulnerable youthful passengers who cannot be relied upon to take responsibility for their own safety.

However, while the offence is concerned with public safety, this does not mean that it necessarily imposes absolute liability. Justice MacPherson asserted that the argument that absolute liability is necessary for effective enforcement does not hold water:

> [T]o regard strict liability as a serious diminution of enforcement capacity is a misconception. Strict liability is what its name implies—a serious commitment to enforcement of the law. In most cases, if a person commits the act proscribed by the law a conviction will follow because establishing the defence of due diligence or reasonable care will not be easy.

Therefore, Justice MacPherson concluded that the subject matter of the offence supported its classification as one of strict liability. This classification struck the right balance between urging drivers to

6. Contrary to section 128(1) of the *Highway Traffic Act*, R.S.O. 1990, c. H.8.

7. Some appellate courts in other provinces or territories have adopted the approach taken in Ontario and have also declared speeding an absolute liability offence: for example, the B.C. Court of Appeal did so in the case of *Harper* (1986), and this case was followed by the Quebec Superior Court in *Director of Public Prosecutions c. Paraie* (2011). However, other appellate courts have refused to do so. For example, in *Williams* (1992), the Appeal Division of the Nova Scotia Supreme Court held that speeding was an offence of strict liability and that the accused, therefore, has the opportunity to advance a defence of due diligence.

8. Now section 106(4).

ensure the safety of children who are passengers in their vehicles and not penalizing those drivers who exercise due diligence in carrying out their duty to ensure that children are properly strapped in with seat belts.

3. The Importance of the Penalty in Determining Whether a Regulatory Offence Imposes Strict or Absolute Liability

The Supreme Court of Canada's decision in *Chapin* (1979) illustrates the principle that, if a severe penalty may be imposed upon conviction of a regulatory offence, it is highly unlikely that the courts will consider such an offence to be one of absolute liability. Ms. Chapin was charged with an offence under section 14(1) of the *Migratory Bird Regulations*, which provided that "no person shall hunt for migratory game birds within one-quarter mile of any place where bait has been deposited." There were a number of significant penalties that could be imposed following a conviction. Indeed, section 12(1) of the *Migratory Birds Convention Act*, R.S.C. 1970, c. M-12, provided that "Every person who violates this Act or any regulation is, for each offence, liable upon summary conviction to a fine of not more than $300 and not less than $10, or to imprisonment for a term not exceeding six months, or to both fine and imprisonment."[9]

Section 22(1) of the Act also provided for a mandatory prohibition, upon conviction, of either holding or applying for a migratory game bird hunting permit for a period of one year from the date of conviction. Clearly, these were relatively severe penalties by any measure, and it was this factor that persuaded the Supreme Court of Canada that the offence should be considered one of strict, rather than absolute, liability.

Justice Dickson pointed out that the normal presumption was that a regulatory offence imposes strict liability and that the Crown must, therefore, advance strong arguments as to why this presumption should be displaced in any given case. Justice Dickson, in delivering the judgment of the Supreme Court, rejected the argument that difficulties of enforcement justified the imposition of absolute liability and focused his attention on the relatively severe penalties that might be imposed upon conviction:

> Difficulty of enforcement is hardly enough to dislodge the offence from the category of strict liability, particularly when regard is had to the penalties that may ensue from conviction. I do not think that the public interest ... requires that s. 14 of the Regulations be interpreted so that an innocent person should be convicted and fined and also suffer the mandatory loss of his hunting permit and the possible forfeiture of his hunting equipment, merely in order to facilitate prosecution.

In the *Chapin* case, the perceived severity of the penalties that might have been imposed led the Supreme Court to conclude that the regulatory offence in question was one of strict, rather than absolute, liability. The *Kurtzman* case (1991) illustrates the converse proposition—namely, that the imposition of a light penalty may be one of the considerations that might persuade a court to rule that the legislature intended to render a regulatory offence one of absolute liability. In this case, the Ontario Court of Appeal ruled that the offence of failing to stop at a red light, in contravention of section 124(16) of the *Highway Traffic Act*, R.S.O. 1980, c. 198,[10] should be considered an absolute, rather than strict, liability offence because, among other reasons, the penalties were relatively trivial. Justice Tarnopolsky pointed out that the penalty for conviction of the offence was a minimum fine of $60 and a maximum of $500. He went on to state that:

> Imprisonment is not a potential penalty except, perhaps, in default of payment. Also, I would agree ... that there is today little, if any, stigma attached to the violation of the *Highway Traffic Act* provisions concerning compliance with traffic signal indicators. I note, too, that suspension or revocation of one's driver's licence is not a penalty which may be imposed upon conviction under s. 124(16) alone.

Since the enactment of the *Charter* in 1982, the nature of the penalty has become a critical factor in determining whether a public welfare or regulatory offence is one of strict or absolute liability. As we shall see later in this chapter, the Supreme Court of Canada ruled, in the *Reference re Section 94(2) of the*

9. This offence is now dealt with by section 14 of the *Migratory Birds Regulations*, C.R.C., c. 1035, issued under the *Migratory Birds Convention Act*, S.C. 1994, c. 22. Imprisonment is still a possible sentence, but the sentencing court is required to take into account, inter alia, "(b) whether the offender was found to have committed the offence intentionally, recklessly or inadvertently; (c) whether the offender was found to have been negligent or incompetent or to have shown a lack of concern with respect to the commission of the offence."

10. See now section 144(18) of the *Highway Traffic Act*, R.S.O. 1990, c. H.8.

Motor Vehicle Act R.S.B.C. (1979) case (1985), that any absolute liability offence that imposes imprisonment as a potential penalty will normally be struck down as an unjustifiable violation of section 7 of the *Charter*: imprisonment of an individual who is without any fault would constitute a deprivation of liberty in a manner that is contrary to the fundamental principles of justice. The consequence of this decision is that courts will take considerable care to avoid declaring a regulatory offence unconstitutional and, therefore, whenever it is possible to do so, they will be far more likely to classify the offence as one of strict, rather than absolute, liability.

An instructive example of the decisive impact of the *Charter* is the case of *Raham* (2010), which involved the categorization of the offence of "stunt driving" (defined as "driving at least 50 km per hour over the speed limit"), contrary to section 172(1) of the *Highway Traffic Act*, R.S.O. 1990, c. H.8. The question for the Ontario Court of Appeal was whether "stunt driving" was an offence of strict or absolute liability. The Ontario legislature did not explicitly state that the due diligence defence is available to an accused person charged with this regulatory offence. Therefore, the Act did not explicitly designate the offence as one of either strict or absolute liability. The Ontario Court of Appeal noted that "stunt driving" was an offence that carried a maximum penalty of six months' imprisonment. If the offence were to be characterized as one of absolute liability, it would be struck down as being in violation of section 7 of the *Charter* because of the potential for a prison sentence. The Court held that there is a presumption that the legislature enacts legislation that is consistent with the *Charter* and, therefore, "stunt driving" should be categorized as an offence of strict liability, thereby providing an accused person with a defence based on due diligence:

> [I]n the post-*Charter* era, the potential for incarceration is much more than simply one of the factors to be considered in categorizing an offence. An absolute liability offence that provides for incarceration as a potential penalty is unconstitutional and of no force and effect, subject to an argument based on s. 1 of the *Charter*. Courts, when interpreting legislation, will presume that the Legislature acted within the limits of its constitutional powers and not in violation of the *Charter*, ... This presumption does not entitle a court to rewrite legislation to avoid a finding of unconstitutionality. It does dictate, however, that if legislation can be reasonably interpreted in a manner that preserves its constitutionality, that interpretation must be preferred over one which would render the legislation unconstitutional. Because of the presumption of constitutionality, it will take very clear language to create an absolute liability offence that is potentially punishable by incarceration.
>
> The Court of Appeal concluded that the presumption that the legislature intended to create an offence that was constitutional was of paramount importance. If a specific offence could reasonably be considered as one of either strict or absolute liability, then the presumption of constitutionality must prevail and the offence must be categorized as imposing strict liability.

4. THE IMPORTANCE OF EXAMINING THE PRECISE WORDING OF REGULATORY LEGISLATION

The specific language used by the legislature has always been considered an important yardstick in determining whether a regulatory offence is one of absolute, rather than strict, liability. Furthermore, since the *Sault Ste. Marie* case (1978), the courts have insisted that a regulatory offence will not be considered one of absolute liability unless the legislature has employed very clear language to categorize it as such. As Justice LeBel stated, on behalf of the Supreme Court of Canada in *Levis (Ville) v. Tétreault* (2006), "absent a clear indication of the legislature's intent, the offence must be categorized as one of strict liability."

For example, in the *Kurtzman* case (1991), the Ontario Court of Appeal paid close attention to the precise wording of the Ontario *Highway Traffic Act* in drawing the conclusion that failing to stop for a red light was an offence of absolute liability. In this respect, Justice Tarnopolsky noted that the "words used in s. 124(16) are mandatory and clearly do not anticipate a defence of due diligence or reasonable care being raised."[11] In his view, the language used in section 124(16) was "mandatory and absolute," and it made no sense to inquire into the "reasonableness of the driver's efforts": "[T]he driver either stops or he does not. In this case, he did not and, therefore, in my view, he contravened the provision."

On the other hand, in the *Kanda* case (2008), the Ontario Court of Appeal held that the wording of another section of the Ontario *Highway Traffic Act*,

11. See now sections 144(18) and (20), *Highway Traffic Act*, R.S.O. 1990, c. H.8.

R.S.O 1990, c. H.8, imposes strict, rather than absolute, liability. In this case, the section in question was section 106(6)[12]:

> No person shall drive on a highway a motor vehicle in which there is a passenger who is under sixteen years of age and occupies a seating position for which a seat belt assembly has been provided unless that passenger is wearing the complete seat belt assembly and it is properly adjusted and securely fastened.

In delivering the judgment of the Court of Appeal, Justice MacPherson subjected the wording of this section to an extensive analysis before concluding that it created an offence of strict liability:

> [T]he *HTA* explicitly creates offences in all three categories of regulatory offences. Subsection 106(6) does not contain the triggering language that would make classification virtually automatic. …
>
> First, the case law does not support the proposition that the language "no person shall" points to absolute liability. …
>
> It is true that some offences employing the "no person shall" or "every driver shall" formulation have been interpreted as absolute liability offences. … However, in those cases the proscribed conduct resulted directly from the person's own action. Section 106(6) of the *HTA*, on the other hand, deals with a situation in which another person—the child passenger—is potentially involved in creating the violation.

Justice MacPherson's second point was that the language of the section concerned did not expressly exclude a defendant from raising a defence of due diligence. The Justice's third point was that the section effectively created an offence of failing to live up to a required standard of care and that it would be "counterintuitive" to suggest that an accused person should be unable to raise a defence of due diligence or having taken reasonable care to avoid committing the offence.

Illustration by Greg Holoboff

The Kanda *case: Not buckling up a child is a strict, not an absolute, liability offence (the importance of examining the subject matter and precise wording of a regulatory offence).*

STRICT LIABILITY OFFENCES AND RAISING THE DEFENCE OF DUE DILIGENCE

Once it has been established that the offence that has been charged is one of strict liability, the onus shifts to the accused person to prove that they acted with "due diligence." As Justice de Montigny, of the Federal Court of Canada, noted in *Mega International Commercial Bank (Canada) v. Canada (Attorney General)* (2012):

> [The due diligence] defence … will be available if it can be established that all reasonable steps to avoid a particular event have been taken. Various courts have noted that it is a heavy burden to meet. … In particular, it will not be sufficient to plead that an error has been made in good faith or that a party had no intention to infringe a statute. … Similarly, the evidence presented to support this defence must relate to the specific offence at issue, and cannot merely establish that the party was generally acting lawfully.

What are the key elements of the defence of due diligence? These were clearly articulated by the Federal Court of Appeal in *Corporation de l'École Polytechnique v. Canada* (2004):

> The due diligence defence allows a person to avoid the imposition of a penalty if he or she presents evidence that he or she was not negligent. It involves considering whether the person believed on reasonable grounds in a non-existent state of facts which, if it had existed, would have made his or her act or omission innocent, or whether he or she took all reasonable precautions to avoid the event leading to imposition of the penalty. … In other words, due diligence excuses either a reasonable error of fact, or the taking of reasonable precautions to comply with the Act.

The Court went on to analyze the type of mistake that would satisfy the requirements of the due diligence defence. The accused person must satisfy both

12. Now section 106(4).

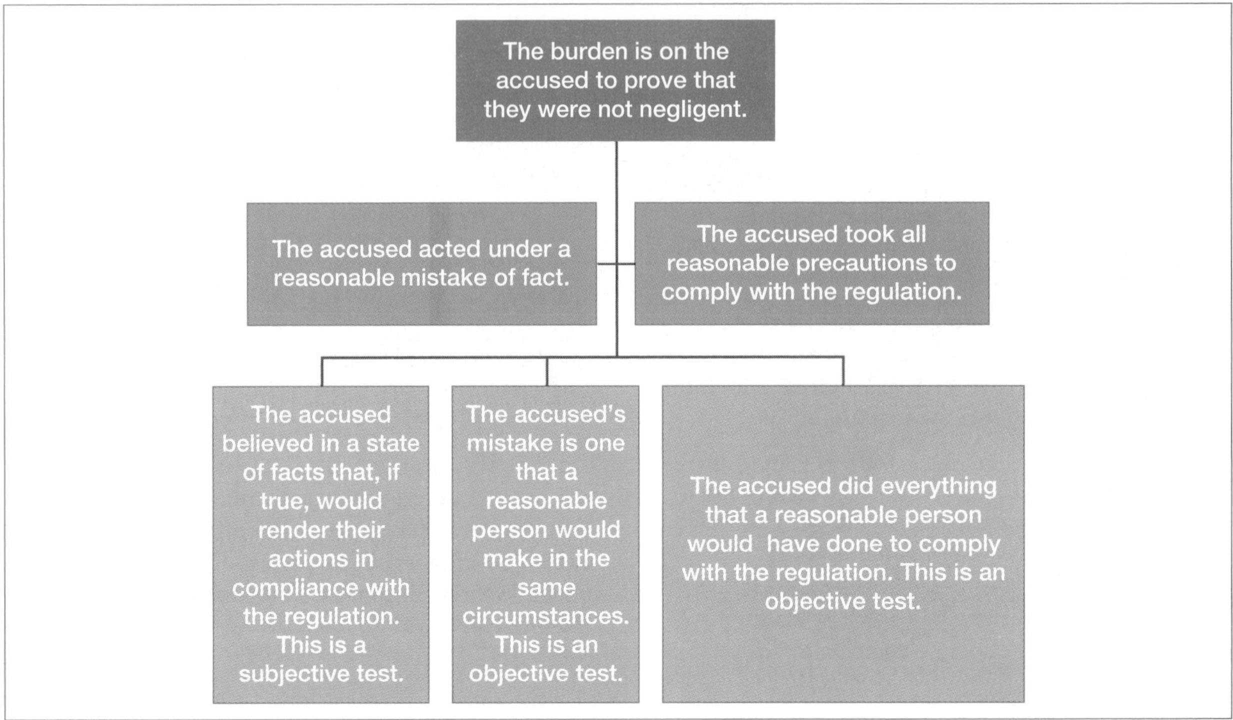

Figure 6-3

The Basic Elements of the Due Diligence Defence

subjective and objective tests. First, they must establish that they were subjectively mistaken with respect to the facts that were material to the definition of the offence. Second, the accused must prove that the mistake they made was one which a reasonable person would have made in the same circumstances.

An instructive example of the application of the due diligence defence is *R. v. Pourlotfali* (2016). This was a case in which the Ontario Court of Appeal ruled that the accused had not established the defence. The Court's ruling concerned the interpretation of section 3(1) of the *Smoke-Free Ontario Act*, S.O. 1994, c. 10 and whether the accused had satisfied the requirements of the due diligence defence that the Ontario legislature had included in section 3(3). The section reads as follows:

> **3** (1) No person shall sell or supply tobacco to a person who is less than 19 years old.
>
> ...
>
> (3) It is a defence to a charge under subsection (1) or (2) that the defendant believed the person receiving the tobacco to be at least 19 years old because the person produced a prescribed form of identification showing his or her age and there was no apparent reason to doubt the authenticity of the document or that it was issued to the person producing it.

Pourlotfali was employed as the manager and store clerk of a convenience store. She sold a package of cigarettes to a young woman who had been sent to "test shop" the store. The shopper produced her Ontario Health Insurance card which indicated that she was only 17-years- old. The Act clearly prohibited the sale of cigarettes to anyone under 19. Pourlotfali looked at the OHIP card and said that she misread the date of birth as 1994 and that she may have been "busy or distracted": apart from these excuses, she could not provide an explanation for why she had sold the cigarettes to an underage shopper.

The Court of Appeal affirmed the trial judge's conviction of Pourlotfali. The accused had perhaps established a subjective mistake, but she certainly had failed to establish on the balance of probabilities that the mistake was reasonable: she had not acted with due care and diligence:

> To interpret s. 3(3) as permitting a defence of honest mistaken belief of fact in the absence of reasonable belief or reasonable care is inconsistent with

Illustration by Greg Holoboff

The need to check ID with due diligence when selling cigarettes

> the statutory provisions read in context and would undermine their legislative purpose, which is to reduce the harm of tobacco by preventing the sale of tobacco products to minors.

The Court of Appeal emphasized that section 3(3) was based on the assumption that the seller of cigarettes would undertake a "careful scrutiny" of any identification that is produced. The accused must prove that she believed the prospective purchaser to be at least 19 after having taken reasonable care to verify their identity and age by reviewing the identification presented. There is no defence when the accused makes an unexplained error when misreading the age of the prospective purchaser that is clearly stated on the identification that is submitted.

Similarly, in *Lévis (Ville) v. Tétreault* (2006), a Quebec-based company (2629-4470 Québec Inc.) was charged under section 31.1 of the Quebec *Highway Safety Code*, R.S.Q., c. C-24.2, with operating a motor vehicle without the necessary registration fees. Tétreault, the driver, was charged with driving a vehicle without a valid driver's licence, contrary to section 93.1 of the *Highway Safety Code*. It was established that both of these offences imposed strict liability, and both the company and Tétreault claimed that they had acted with due diligence. However, the company's defence was based merely on the fact that while it had been informed that it would receive a renewal notice in relation to the registration fees, no such notice was ever delivered. Tétreault's defence turned on his assertion that he had also expected to receive a renewal notice in relation to his licence and that he had mixed up the expiry date for his licence with the due date for payment of the licence fees. The lower courts acquitted the company and Tétreault of the charges against them, accepting their defences of acting with due diligence. However, the Supreme Court of Canada set aside the acquittals and entered convictions because the accused had not proved that they had acted with due diligence. Indeed, the Court emphasized that "passive ignorance" does not constitute a valid defence to charges under regulatory legislation.

On behalf of the Supreme Court, Justice LeBel said:

> In Mr. Tétreault's case, the judgments of the courts below confused passivity with diligence. The accused did no more than state that he expected to receive a renewal notice for his licence and that he had confused the licence expiry date with the due date for paying the fees required to keep the licence valid. He proved no action or attempt to obtain information. The concept of diligence is based on the acceptance of a citizen's civic duty to take action to find out what his or her obligations are. Passive ignorance is not a valid defence in criminal law.

The Supreme Court took a similar approach in relation to the charge against the company. Justice

LeBel ruled that the evidence indicated that the company had failed to establish that it had satisfied the requirement of due diligence. The company knew when the registration fees would need to be paid and that a failure to pay on the specified date would result in the registration becoming invalid. It should have been worried when it did not receive the renewal notice, but it did absolutely nothing. The requirement of due diligence implied that it should have done something to avoid the registration from ceasing to be valid.

Employers are frequently made the target of prosecutions under regulatory legislation, and, of course, they may raise the defence of due diligence if they are charged with an offence of strict liability. In this respect, it is important to remember that, although an *employee* is usually the individual who commits the act that effectively precipitates a prosecution for a regulatory offence, the trial court must nevertheless focus its attention upon the issue of whether the employer acted with due diligence. The court will generally ask whether the employer took *reasonable steps to ensure that their employees carried out their jobs in accordance with the standards set by the regulatory legislation concerned*. For example, did the employer institute an adequate training program for employees, and did the employer maintain an adequate system for monitoring employee performance?

Take, by way of example, the Nova Scotia case of *Sobey's Inc.* (1998), where the employer, a corporation, had been charged with the sale of tobacco or a tobacco product to a person under the age of 19 years, contrary to section 5(1) of the *Tobacco Access Act*, S.N.S. 1993, c. 14. The Nova Scotia Court of Appeal emphasized that the central issue in the case was not whether the employee who allegedly sold the tobacco was "duly diligent," but rather whether Sobey's Inc. acted with due diligence in all of the circumstances. In delivering the judgment of the Court of Appeal, Justice Cromwell quoted the words of Justice Dickson in the *Sault Ste. Marie* case (1978):

> Where an employer is charged in respect of an act committed by an employee acting in the course of employment, the question will be whether the act took place without the accused's direction or approval ... and whether the accused exercised all reasonable care by taking reasonable steps to ensure the effective operation of the system.

IS STRICT LIABILITY A VALID DEVICE UNDER THE *CHARTER*?

The decision in the *Sault Ste. Marie* case (1978) is based on the recognition of a category of regulatory offences that impose strict liability. However, *Sault Ste. Marie* was decided before the enactment of the *Charter*, and a critical question that arises is whether strict liability is constitutionally valid. As we have noted, the very essence of strict liability is the requirement that the accused shoulder the responsibility of proving that they acted without negligence (the defence of due diligence). It might well be argued that requiring the accused to establish their innocence is an infringement of the presumption of innocence guaranteed by section 11(d) of the *Charter* and that strict liability is, therefore, an invalid device that should be struck down. Precisely this argument was advanced in the case of *Wholesale Travel Group Inc.* (1991). However, a majority of the justices of the Supreme Court of Canada rejected this contention and upheld the constitutional validity of strict liability.

The *Wholesale Travel Group Inc.* case was concerned with the offence of false or misleading advertising under the provisions of the federal *Competition Act*, R.S.C. 1970, c. C-23. Under what was then section 37.3(2) of the Act, Parliament made available a defence of due diligence to those charged with false or misleading advertising:

> No person shall be convicted of an offence under section 36 or 36.1, *if he establishes that*
>
> (a) the act or omission giving rise to the offence with which he was charged was the result of error;
>
> (b) he took reasonable precautions and exercised due diligence to prevent the occurrence of such error. [emphasis added]

The majority of the justices of the Supreme Court took the view that placing the onus on the accused to prove the defence of due diligence was not invalid under the *Charter*. Three of the five justices in the majority took the view that strict liability did infringe section 11(d) of the *Charter* but that it was justified as a reasonable limitation under section 1. The other two justices in the majority contended that if one looks at strict liability within the specific context of regulatory offences, it does not violate section 11(d) of the *Charter* and that even if it did, it would be saved by section 1.

Speaking for those justices who took the view that placing the burden of proof on the accused infringed the presumption of innocence but was saved by section 1 of the *Charter*, Justice Iacobucci asserted that Parliament's objective in placing the burden of proof on the accused in cases involving strict liability was of "sufficient importance to warrant overriding a constitutionally protected right or freedom." He concluded that Parliament's objective was to ensure that all those individuals who engage in false or misleading advertising are convicted of these regulatory offences and to avoid the possibility that convictions are not lost because the prosecution is not able to obtain evidence of facts which are peculiarly within the accused's knowledge. This objective was of sufficient importance to justify Parliament's overriding of the presumption of innocence guaranteed by section 11(d) of the *Charter*. Parliament's approach was related to "pressing and substantial" concerns in Canadian society, particularly in light of the principal objective of the *Competition Act*, which was to stimulate "vigorous and fair competition."

Justice Iacobucci also asserted that there was an appropriate degree of proportionality between Parliament's legitimate objective and the means used to achieve that objective (namely, placing the onus on the accused to prove the defence of due diligence). On this topic, Justice Iacobucci stated that:

> [R]egulated activity and public welfare offences are a fundamental part of Canadian society. Those who choose to participate in regulated activities must be taken to have accepted the consequential responsibilities and their penal enforcement. One of these consequences is that they should be held responsible for the harm that may result from their lack of due diligence. Unless they can prove on the balance of probabilities that they exercised due diligence, they shall be convicted and in some cases face a possible prison term. These participants are in the best position to prove due diligence since they possess in most cases the required information. Viewed in this context, and taking into account the fundamental importance of the legislative objective as stated and the fact that the means chosen impair the rights guaranteed by s. 11(d) as little as reasonably possible, the effects of the reverse onus on the presumption of innocence are proportional to the objective.

Justice Cory took the view that strict liability did not infringe section 11(d) of the *Charter* in the first place. In his view, in considering whether section 11(d) was infringed by placing the onus on the accused to prove the defence of due diligence, one must take account of the fact that the context is one of regulatory offences rather than true crimes:

> Criminal offences have always required proof of guilt beyond a reasonable doubt; the accused cannot, therefore, be convicted where there is a reasonable doubt as to guilt. This is not so with regulatory offences, where a conviction will lie if the accused has failed to meet the standard of care required. Thus, the question is not whether the accused exercised *some* care, but whether the degree of care exercised was sufficient to meet the standard imposed. If the false advertiser, the corporate polluter and the manufacturer of noxious goods are to be effectively controlled, it is necessary to require them to show on a balance of probabilities that they took reasonable precautions to avoid the harm which actually resulted. *In the regulatory context, there is nothing unfair about imposing that onus; indeed, it is essential for the protection of our vulnerable society*. [emphasis added]

Indubitably, the *Wholesale Travel Group Inc.* case settled an extremely important question of principle under the *Charter* and has placed the "halfway house" approach, embodied in strict liability, on a firm constitutional basis.

THE *CHARTER* AND ABSOLUTE LIABILITY OFFENCES

The *Wholesale Travel Group Inc.* case (1991) unequivocally established that a regime of strict liability is not invalid under the *Charter*. However, the Supreme Court of Canada has adopted a fundamentally different approach vis-à-vis statutes that create offences of absolute liability. Indeed, the Court has held that, as a general rule, absolute liability offences are invalid under the *Charter—if they may be punished by the imposition of a term of imprisonment.*

The leading authority on this issue is the landmark decision of the Supreme Court of Canada in *Reference re Section 94(2) of the Motor Vehicle Act R.S.B.C.* (1979) (1985), which raised the issue of whether section 94(2) of the *Motor Vehicle Act*, R.S.B.C. 1979 was consistent with the requirements of the *Charter*. Section 94(1) of the B.C. *Motor Vehicle Act* stated that it was an offence for any person to drive a vehicle while they were prohibited or suspended from driving. The penalty for breaching the provisions of this section was, on first conviction, a fine and imprisonment for not less than seven days and not more than six months (in other words, a mandatory prison sentence). Section 94(2) explicitly stated that the offence created by section 94(1) "creates an absolute liability offence in which guilt is established by proof of driving, whether or not the defendant knew of the prohibition or suspension." Not surprisingly, the Supreme Court declared this draconian provision to be contrary to the provisions of the *Charter* and refused to "save" it under section 1. Justice Lamer stated the issue very simply:

> A law that has the potential to convict a person who has not really done anything wrong offends the principles of fundamental justice and, if imprisonment is available as a penalty, such a law then violates a person's right to liberty under s. 7 [of the *Charter*]. ...
>
> In other words, absolute liability and imprisonment cannot be combined.

Significantly, Justice Lamer indicated that it makes no difference whether the imprisonment that may be imposed following a conviction of an absolute liability offence is *discretionary* or, as in the case of section 94(2), *mandatory*: "Obviously, imprisonment (including probation orders) deprives persons of their liberty. An offence has that potential as of the moment it is open to the judge to impose imprisonment. There is no need that imprisonment, as in section 94(2), be made mandatory."

On the other hand, Justice Lamer did not address the critical issue of whether imprisonment, *as an alternative to the non-payment of a fine*, would contravene section 7 of the *Charter* when an absolute liability offence is concerned. In the later case of *Pontes* (1995), the majority of the Supreme Court of Canada expressly left this issue "up in the air." As Justice Cory stated,

> I would leave open for future consideration the situation presented by an absolute liability offence punishable by fine with the possibility of imprisonment for its non-payment in those circumstances where the legislation provides that the imposition and collection of any fine is subject to a means test.

The Ontario Court of Appeal has dealt with this conundrum by taking the view that absolute liability does not violate the *Charter* if there is provision for a review of the accused person's *ability to pay a fine* before there is any consideration of imprisonment for non-payment. For example, in *London (City) v. Polewsky* (2005), the Ontario Court of Appeal ruled that the absolute liability offence of speeding did not violate the accused person's right to liberty under section 7 of the *Charte*r because section 69 of the Ontario *Provincial Offences Act*[13] has put in place a mechanism for ensuring that an inability to pay a fine will not automatically result in imprisonment; therefore, the risk of imprisonment for speeding is "sufficiently remote" as not to engage the accused person's liberty interest under section 7 of the *Charter*.

The decision by the Supreme Court of Canada in *Reference re Section 94(2) of the Motor Vehicle Act R.S.B.C.* (1979) (1985) dramatically illustrates the profound impact the *Charter* may have on the substantive criminal law. In the specific case of absolute liability offences, it is clear that the Supreme Court has greatly reduced the sting of such offences by severely circumscribing the range of punishments that may be imposed. Indeed, the Court has unequivocally stated that if the legislature wishes to give the courts the option to impose a term of imprisonment upon conviction of a regulatory offence, it must ensure that it makes a due diligence defence available to those persons accused of such an offence.

The Supreme Court of Canada revisited this issue in the *Wholesale Travel Group Inc.* case (1991), in which the accused corporation had been charged with the offence of false or misleading advertising under the provisions of the *Competition Act*, R.S.C. 1970, c. C-23. We have already seen that, under what was then section 37.3(2) of the Act, Parliament made available a defence of due diligence to those persons who had been charged with false or misleading advertising. The relevant statutory provisions are as follows:

> No person shall be convicted of an offence under section 36 or 36.1, if he establishes that,
>
> (a) the act or omission giving rise to the offence with which he was charged was the result of error;

13. Provincial Offences Act, R.S.O. 1990, c. P.33, section 69 (15):

> If the justice is satisfied that the person who has defaulted is unable to pay the fine within a reasonable period of time, the justice may,
>
> (a) grant an extension of the time allowed for payment of the fine;
>
> (b) require the person to pay the fine according to a schedule of payments established by the justice;
>
> (c) in exceptional circumstances, reduce the amount of the fine or order that the fine does not have to be paid.

> (b) he took reasonable precautions and exercised due diligence to prevent the occurrence of such error;
>
> (c) he, or another person, took reasonable precautions to bring the error to the attention of the class of persons likely to have been reached by the representations or testimonial; and
>
> (d) the measures referred to in paragraph (c), except where the representation or testimonial related to a security, were taken forthwith after the representation was made or the testimonial was published.

Paragraphs (c) and (d) of section 37.3(2) imposed a positive obligation on the accused to make an *immediate* retraction before they could claim the benefit of the defence of due diligence. This could lead to the result that an individual who did not make such an immediate retraction could be prevented from raising the defence—*even if they acted with due diligence*. For example, an accused person might not discover that they have made a false or misleading statement in an advertisement until sometime after it has been published. Even if the accused person issued a retraction as soon as they became aware of the error, the defence of due diligence would not apply because the retraction had not taken place *immediately after the advertisement was originally published*. In effect, this means that absolute liability could be imposed on a blameless defendant who had, through no fault of their own, failed to make an immediate retraction, and, since imprisonment was a potential penalty under the *Competition Act*, the Supreme Court of Canada ruled that paragraphs (c) and (d) of section 37.3(2) of the Act were invalid in light of section 7 of the *Charter*.

Chief Justice Lamer pointed out that the offence of false or misleading advertising carried a penalty of up to five years' imprisonment and that "it is clear from the developing jurisprudence of this court that the offence must not be one of absolute liability." On the contrary, there must be a "minimum fault requirement of negligence, in that at least a defence of due diligence must always be open to the accused to comply with the requirements of s. 7 of the *Charter*."

According to Chief Justice Lamer, paragraphs (a) and (b) of section 37.3(2) of the *Competition Act* unquestionably provide the accused with a defence of due diligence as that defence had been delineated in the *Sault Ste. Marie* case (1978): "[P]aras. (a) and (b) operate so as to provide a defence to an accused who has taken reasonable precautions to prevent false/misleading advertising and who has been duly diligent in ensuring that advertising is not false or misleading in nature."

However, paragraphs (c) and (d) of section 37.3(2) added an additional requirement to the defence: namely, that there must be a retraction "forthwith" after the false or misleading advertisement has been published. This requirement of "timely retraction" meant, according to Chief Justice Lamer, that the defence embodied in section 37.3 of the *Competition Act* "is considerably more narrow than the common law defence of due diligence." He stated that he agreed with the majority of the Ontario Court of Appeal that:

> [P]aras. (c) and (d) of s. 37.3(2) could have the effect of depriving an accused of the defence of due diligence and could therefore require the conviction of an accused who was not negligent. Paragraphs (c) and (d) make the failure to undertake corrective advertising (a component of false/misleading advertising) an "offence" of absolute liability. Consequently, the constitutionally required fault level is not present in the false/misleading advertising provisions.

In addition to ruling that paragraphs (c) and (d) of section 37.3(2) of the *Competition Act* infringed an accused person's rights under section 7 of the *Charter* because they combined absolute liability with the possibility of imprisonment, Chief Justice Lamer also held that these paragraphs could not be justified under section 1 of the *Charter*. As a consequence, these two paragraphs were declared to be of "no force and effect."

However, it is important to bear in mind that the Supreme Court of Canada did not rule that all absolute liability offences are presumed to be invalid under the *Charter*. In fact, in the later case of *Pontes* (1995), the Supreme Court re-emphasized the point that absolute liability will infringe section 7 of the *Charter* only if it is coupled with the possibility of imprisonment. As was the case in *Reference re Section 94(2) of the Motor Vehicle Act R.S.B.C.* (1979) (1985), *Pontes* was concerned with the offence of driving while prohibited under the provisions of the B.C. *Motor Vehicle Act*, R.S.B.C. 1979, c. 288. Section 92 of the amended Act provided that a person who was convicted of one of a number of serious *Criminal Code* or provincial/territorial motoring offences "is automatically and without notice prohibited from driving a motor vehicle for 12 months from the date of sentencing." Section 94 of the Act made it an offence to drive while prohibited under section 92.

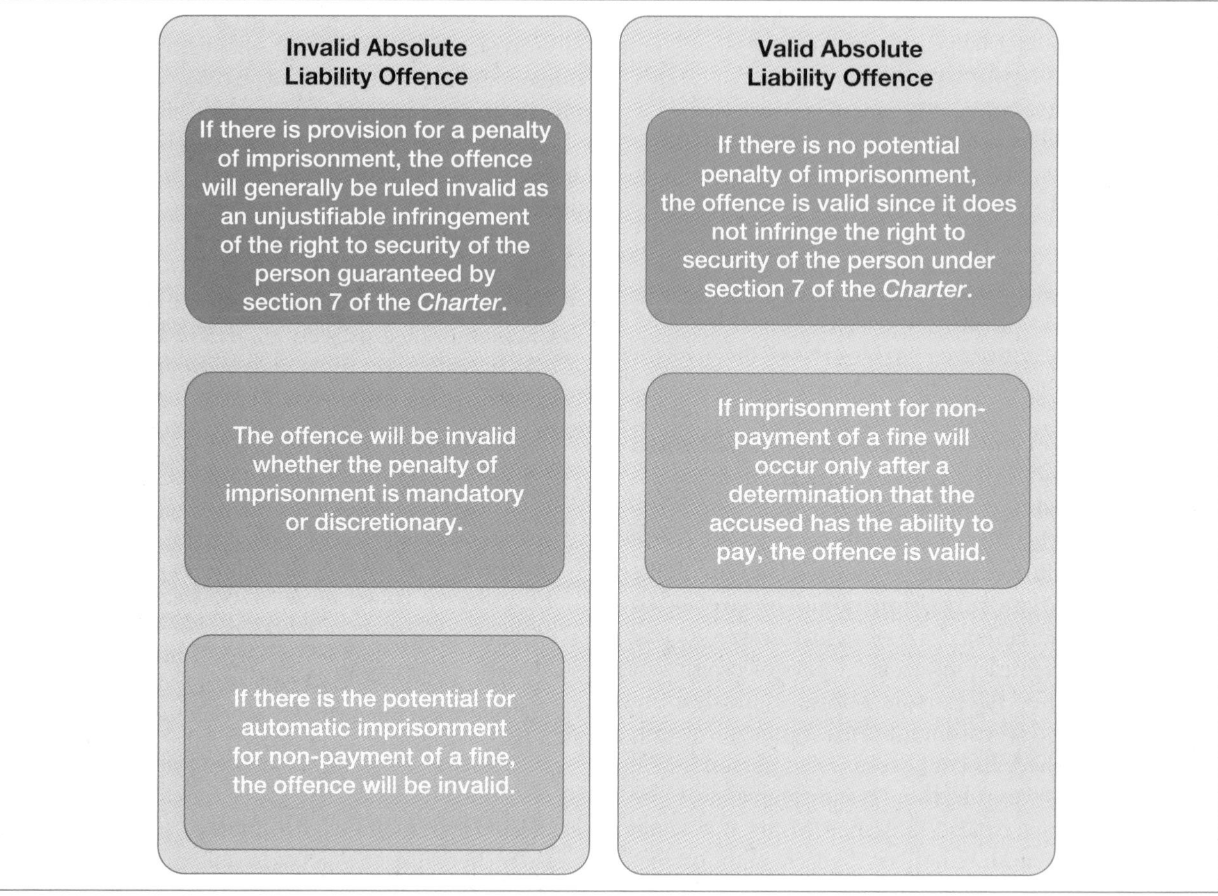

Figure 6-4

The Constitutional Validity of Absolute Liability Offences

Having determined that the offence of prohibited driving under section 94 of the *Motor Vehicle Act* was an offence of absolute liability, the critical issue for the Supreme Court to decide was whether the offence was invalid under the *Charter*. The majority of the Court held that it was not invalid *because there was no potential for imprisonment upon conviction*. This situation was brought about by section 4.1 of the *Offence Act*, R.S.B.C. 1979, c. 305 (amended in 1990), which stated that "no person is liable to imprisonment with respect to an absolute liability offence" under any British Columbia legislation, and by section 72(1) of the *Offence Act*, which stipulated that no person shall be imprisoned for non-payment of a fine. As a consequence of these provisions of the *Offence Act*, Justice Cory stated that the absolute liability offence of prohibited driving did not infringe the *Charter*: "An accused convicted under ss. 92 and 94 of the B.C. *Motor Vehicle Act* faces no risk of imprisonment and there is, accordingly, no violation of the right to life, liberty and security of the person under s. 7 of the *Charter*."

In the case of *1260448 Ontario Inc.; R. v. Transport Robert* (1973) *Ltée* (2003), the Ontario Court of Appeal reached a similar decision in relation to section 84.1 of the *Highway Traffic Act*, R.S.O. 1990, c. H.8, which provided that the owner and operator of a commercial vehicle are guilty of an offence if a wheel separates from the vehicle while it is on a highway. However, section 84.1 also stipulated that the defence of due diligence was not open to a person who is charged with this offence. The penalty to be imposed for this offence is a fine of not less than $2000 and not more than $50 000; however, there is no possibility of imprisonment—even in the event that the defendant should fail to pay the fine.

Furthermore, there is no possibility that the defendant could be sentenced to probation. Although the Court of Appeal recognized that the offence was one of absolute liability, it ruled that section 7 of the *Charter* had not been infringed because, in the absence of any possibility that imprisonment or probation might be imposed, there was no threat to the accused person's right to liberty. The Court also rejected the argument that the accused person's *Charter* right to "security of the person" had been violated by section 84.1 of the *Highway Traffic Act*:

> [W]e are not convinced that a prosecution for the s. 84.1 offence engages the kind of exceptional state-induced psychological stress, even for an individual, that would trigger the security of the person guarantee in s. 7. The offence does not create a true crime, and like most regulatory offences, it focuses on the harmful consequences of otherwise lawful conduct rather than any moral turpitude. ... The s. 84.1 offence focuses on the unintended but harmful consequences of the commercial trucking industry. We reject the proposition that a defendant charged with this offence is stigmatized as a person operating in a wanton manner, heedless of the extreme dangers to life and limb posed by his or her operation. Conviction for the offence at most implies negligence and like the misleading advertising offence considered in *Wholesale Travel*, any stigma is very considerably diminished.

The Court of Appeal also stated that it made no difference that the regulatory offence in question carried a penalty of a significant fine. The threat of a fine of this nature did not subject an accused person to the "kind of serious state-imposed psychological stress that is intended to be covered by security of the person." Indeed, in the view of the Court of Appeal, the right to security of the person, which is protected by section 7 of the *Charter*, "does not protect the individual operating in the highly regulated context of commercial trucking for profit from the ordinary stress and anxieties that a reasonable person would suffer as a result of government regulation of that industry."

Finally, the courts are understandably loath to declare legislation invalid under the *Charter* if they can avoid doing so. Since absolute liability offences that are coupled with the threat of imprisonment will almost always be struck down as invalid under the *Charter*, there is a tendency on the part of the courts to designate a regulatory offence as one of strict, rather than absolute, liability. As noted earlier in this chapter, the courts apply the presumption of constitutionality and, if an offence imposes a harsh penalty, the application of this presumption will most likely lead to a finding that the offence is one of strict rather than absolute liability.

As Chief Justice Lamer, of the Supreme Court of Canada, stated in the case of *Rube* (1992),

> We agree that given the penalties, this is not an offence that could, without offending the *Canadian Charter of Rights and Freedoms*, be one of absolute liability.
>
> On the presumption that Parliament intends its legislation to conform to the exigencies of the *Charter*, we are of the view that the section is one of strict liability and that a defence of due diligence is available to the accused.

Study Questions

1. Assume that a provincial legislature enacts the following provision in its *Retail Sales Act*:
   (a) No retailer shall sell packaged bread without indicating the date of baking on the package.
   (b) Every person who violates subsection (1) is guilty of an offence under this act and is liable to a maximum fine of $5000.

   The *Offence Act* of the province provides that a person may be imprisoned in default of payment of a fine but also stipulates that this penalty should be used only for a person who wilfully refuses to pay even though they have the means to do so.

   Merdle purchases a loaf of packaged bread from the corner grocery store, which is owned by Slackbridge. Merdle notices that the package does not bear a stamp indicating when the loaf was baked, and he complains to the provincial authorities, who charge Slackbridge under the provisions set out above. Slackbridge claims that he purchased the loaf from the Crusty Bakery, which has always stamped its packaged loaves whenever he has obtained bread from it in the past. A spokesman from Crusty states that an inexperienced employee had forgotten to replenish the ink in the date stamp and had not noticed that the stamp was failing to make any impression on the packaging paper. What principles would the court apply in determining whether Slackbridge is guilty of the charge?

2. The Ontario *Liquor Licence Act*, RSO 1990, c L.19 provides as follows:

   30. (1) No person shall knowingly sell or supply liquor to a person under nineteen years of age.

   (2) No person shall sell or supply liquor to a person who appears to be under nineteen years of age.

   61. (3.0.1) Upon conviction for contravening subsection 30 (1), (2), (3), (4) or (4.1),

   (a) a corporation is liable to a fine of not more than $500,000; and

   (b) an individual is liable to a fine of not more than $200,000 or to imprisonment for a term of not more than one year or both.

   How would you categorize the offences under section 30(1) and 30(2)? Are they offences requiring proof of *mens rea*, strict liability, or absolute liability offences? If one or more of the offences are determined to impose strict liability, what do you think the manager of a bar would need to do to establish that they acted with due diligence?

3. Imagine that you have been appointed the manager of a local hockey rink. You know that various safety regulations apply to the operation of a rink of this nature. What steps would you take to ensure that the other employees of the rink observe all the safety regulations? If you were charged with a regulatory offence, would you be able to prove that you had acted with "due diligence"? On the basis of your thoughts about this hypothetical situation, do you believe that the "due diligence" standard is an appropriate one for the courts to apply to most regulatory offences in Canada?

4. Ask your local supermarket manager if they know the difference between strict and absolute liability offences. Also ask the manager what steps they take to ensure that employees meet the requirements of the regulatory statutes that apply to the retail industry in your particular jurisdiction (e.g., hygiene regulations, packaging and labelling regulations, etc.).

5. What arguments may be made to justify maintaining the category of absolute liability offences in Canada? In what circumstances should the courts declare an absolute liability offence invalid under the *Canadian Charter of Rights and Freedoms*?

MODES OF PARTICIPATION IN CRIME AND INCHOATE OFFENCES

CHAPTER

7

Learning Objectives

After reading this chapter, you will be able to understand:

- the various ways in which an accused person may become a party to a criminal offence: being the person who actually committed it ("the principal"); aiding and/or abetting (encouraging) the person who actually committed it; becoming a party by virtue of "common intention"; and counselling an offence that is actually committed by another person;
- the nature and scope of the criminal liability of those who are accessories after the fact to the commission of a crime;
- the basic elements of the three inchoate offences (uncompleted offences) in the *Criminal Code*: (a) counselling an offence that is not committed, (b) attempt to commit a crime, and (c) conspiracy; and
- the principle that one cannot attempt to commit an inchoate offence.

INTRODUCTION

This chapter examines two critical topics in the field of criminal law: (1) the various routes by which an individual may become a party to a criminal offence and (2) the inchoate (or uncompleted) offences of counselling, attempt, and conspiracy.

THE VARIOUS MODES OF PARTICIPATION IN A CRIMINAL OFFENCE

In Canada, an accused person may become a **party to a criminal offence** on the basis that they

- actually committed the offence themselves;
- aided and/or abetted (encouraged) another person to commit the offence;
- **counselled** another person to commit an offence that was later perpetrated by that other person; or
- formed a "common intention" with another person(s) who actually committed the offence.

An accused person who helps a person who has committed a crime to escape justice may be found guilty of the "stand-alone" crime of being an **accessory after the fact** (sections 23, 240, and 463) and does not become a party to the crime itself.

ACTUALLY COMMITTING AN OFFENCE

The most obvious means by which an individual may become a party to an offence is by "actually committing" it. In this respect, section 21(1) of the *Criminal Code* provides:

> Every one is a party to an offence who
> (a) actually commits it.

The **person who actually commits an offence** is sometimes referred to as the **principal** and is, for example, in the case of a murder by shooting, the individual who actually pulls the trigger. There may be more than one principal when an offence is committed: for example, two individuals could both commit the offence of robbery by simultaneously taking money from tellers in a bank.

Principals are, of course, always present when the crime is perpetrated. However, there are some rare situations in which their presence may be "constructive" (or "inferred") rather than "actual." In these situations, the courts may rule that an accused person has committed an offence through the innocent agency of another individual. For example, in the case of *Berryman* (1990), the accused was working as a passport application officer in a passport office. On two occasions, she accepted passport applications knowing that the person from whom they were received was not, in fact, the applicant whose name appeared on the documents. Furthermore, she dishonestly stated,

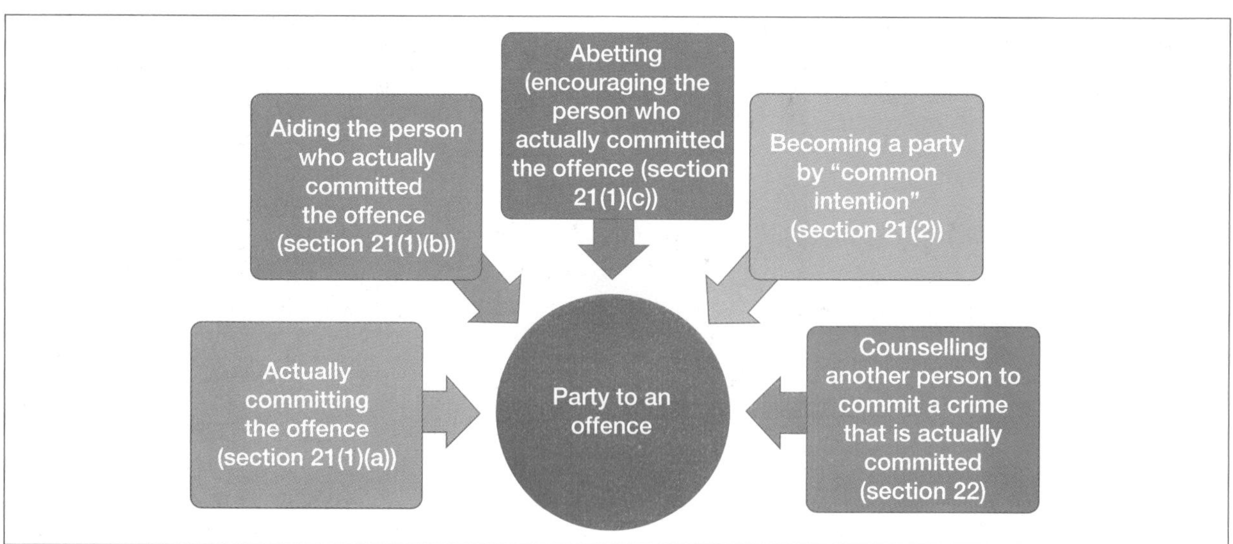

***Figure* 7-1**

Five Ways in Which a Person May Become a Party to a Criminal Offence

in writing, on the front of each application, that the applicant had produced evidence of citizenship and other identification. When the passport documents were completed, Berryman forged the signatures of the purported applicants so as to indicate that the documents had been picked up personally by the persons to whom they had seemingly been issued. She was charged with two counts of forgery of a passport, contrary to section 57(1)(a) of the *Criminal Code*.

However, the Crown was faced with the difficulty that Berryman did not "make" the passport documents herself; they were actually made by another employee who had no knowledge that the information contained in the applications was completely false. Could the accused be convicted of forgery in these circumstances? She was acquitted at trial, but the Crown appealed. The B.C. Court of Appeal ultimately allowed the appeal and entered convictions against the accused. The Court of Appeal held that the accused could be convicted of forgery under section 21(1)(a) even though the *actus reus* of the offence (the actual making of the passports) was carried out by an innocent agent. As Justice Wood pointed out in the judgment of the court, "[A] person who commits an offence by means of an instrument 'whose movements are regulated' by him, actually commits the offences himself."

The passport documents were forgeries in the sense that they were false documents: after all, the information contained in them was untrue in several material respects. The person who made the passports, therefore, committed the *actus reus* of the crime of forgery. However, this person did not have the *mens rea* for the offence because there was no knowledge of the false statements that had been provided by Berryman.

Aiding and Abetting the Commission of an Offence

The second route by which one may become a party to a criminal offence is by aiding and/or abetting another person to actually commit it. To this end, section 21(1) of the *Criminal Code* continues with the following provisions:

> Every one is a party to an offence who …
> (b) does or omits to do anything for the purpose of aiding any person to commit it; or
> (c) abets any person in committing it.

What is meant by the use of the legal terms "aiding" and "abetting"? **Aiding** simply means providing assistance or help to the person who actually commits an offence. **Abetting** means instigating, urging, or encouraging another person to commit an offence. Frequently, a person will both aid and abet another person. However, it is important to bear in mind that one may provide assistance to someone without necessarily encouraging that person to commit an offence: therefore, "aiding" and "abetting" are distinct concepts. For example, Gargery may sell an illegal firearm to Orlick, knowing that Orlick is a professional assassin. Gargery does not encourage Orlick to commit an act of murder, but he does know that Orlick will use the firearm to kill another human being. By providing Orlick with the firearm, Gargery "aids" Orlick but does not "abet" him.

To gain a conviction on the basis of aiding under section 21(1)(b), the Crown must prove that the accused person actively rendered assistance to the person who actually committed the offence (*actus reus*) and did so *with the intent to provide such assistance* (*mens rea*). To obtain a conviction on the basis of abetting under section 21(1)(c), the Crown must prove that the accused person actively encouraged the person who actually committed the offence (*actus reus*) and did so *with the intent to provide such encouragement* (*mens rea*).

In *Briscoe* (2010), the Supreme Court of Canada made a very important point:

> Canadian criminal law does not distinguish between the principal offender and parties to an offence in determining criminal liability. Section 21(1) of the *Criminal Code* makes perpetrators, aiders, and abettors equally liable. … The person who provides the gun, therefore, may be found guilty of the same offence as the one who pulls the trigger. The *actus reus* and *mens rea* for aiding or abetting, however, are distinct from those of the principal offence.

It is clear that, insofar as the matter of criminal responsibility is concerned, section 21(1) of the *Code* places the person who aids and/or abets an offence on exactly the same footing as the person who actually commits it. For example, if the assassins, Brutus and Cassius simultaneously inflict fatal stab wounds on the unfortunate Julius Caesar, they will both be considered to have "actually committed" the crime of murder. On the other hand, if Brutus merely supplies a knife to Cassius and maintains a "lookout" while Cassius stabs Caesar to death, then it is probable that Brutus will be considered to have been a party to the murder on the basis that he aided and/or abetted Cassius (assuming, of course, that he knew that Cassius intended to kill Caesar). However, in

Those who aid or abet others to commit a crime are parties to that crime (sections 21(1)(b) and (c) of the Criminal Code).

both scenarios, Brutus would be convicted of the offence of either first- or second-degree murder. As the Ontario Court of Appeal stated in the *Suzack* case (2000), "[I]t is beyond question that where two persons, each with the requisite intent, act in concert in the commission of a crime, they are both guilty of that crime." However, whether they are principals or aiders and/or abettors depends on "what each did in the course of the common design."

The *Actus Reus* Elements of Aiding and Abetting

The Supreme Court of Canada clarified the nature of the *actus reus* of aiding and/or abetting in *Briscoe* (2010):

> The *actus reus* of aiding or abetting is doing (or, in some circumstances, omitting to do) something that assists or encourages the perpetrator to commit the offence. While it is common to speak of aiding and abetting together, the two concepts are distinct, and liability can flow from either one. Broadly speaking, "To aid under s. 21(1)(*b*) means to assist or help the actor. To abet within the meaning of s. 21(1)(*c*) includes encouraging, instigating, promoting or procuring the crime to be committed."

In general, mere passive acquiescence in the commission of an offence or mere presence at the scene of a crime is not a sufficient condition for the purpose of establishing that the accused aided and/or abetted the principal. However, in practice, it is often exceedingly difficult for the courts to draw a line between passive acquiescence or mere physical presence, on the one hand, and acts or omissions that actually assist or encourage the principal, on the other. This onerous task was attempted, however, by the Supreme Court of Canada in the notorious case of *Dunlop and Sylvester* (1979). These two men were charged with the offence of rape (today, the charge would be sexual assault). The evidence was that there had been a brutal "gang rape" in which some 18 members of a motorcycle club had had forced sexual intercourse with a 16-year-old girl. Dunlop and Sylvester, along with other members of the club, had been present at a bar where the victim and a friend were drinking together; the latter were then taken to a dump site by two other gang members. The victim was, apparently, left alone for a few minutes. She was subsequently attacked and raped by other gang members. Dunlop and Sylvester testified that they had been requested to bring some beer to the dump site for a party and that they had done so. Although the victim claimed that the two accused had participated in the gang rape, Dunlop and Sylvester denied this. In fact, they claimed that, although they saw a woman having intercourse with gang members, they merely delivered the beer and left after a few minutes. At their trial, the accused were convicted, and they launched an appeal.

The issue, which eventually came before the Supreme Court of Canada, concerned the liability of Dunlop and Sylvester as aiders and/or abettors under sections 21(1)(b) and (c) of the *Criminal Code*—in other words, was their admitted presence at the scene of the crime sufficient to convict them of rape? In delivering the majority judgment of the Supreme Court, Justice Dickson said:

> Mere presence at the scene of a crime is not sufficient to ground culpability. Something more is needed: encouragement of the principal offender; an act which facilitates the commission of the offence, such as keeping watch or enticing the victim away, or an act which tends to prevent or hinder interference with accomplishment of the criminal act, such as preventing the intended victim from escaping or being ready to assist the prime culprit.

Justice Dickson then turned his attention to the particular set of circumstances that were alleged to exist in the *Dunlop and Sylvester* case. He pointed out that there was no evidence that Dunlop and Sylvester provided any assistance or encouragement to the individuals who actually committed the rape of the victim. For example, the accused did not shout any encouragement to the principals, nor did they prevent the victim from escaping or hinder any possible rescue. As Justice Dickson noted:

> A person is not guilty merely because he is present at the scene of a crime and does nothing to prevent it. ... If there is no evidence of encouragement by him, a man's presence at the scene of the crime will not suffice to render him liable as aider and abettor. A person who, aware of a rape taking place in his presence, looks on and does nothing is not, as a matter of law, an accomplice. The classic case is the hardened urbanite who stands around in a subway station when an individual is murdered.

The Supreme Court of Canada ultimately allowed the appeals of both Dunlop and Sylvester and directed a verdict of acquittal in respect of each **appellant**.

As Justice Dickson emphasized, it would have been a very different outcome if Dunlop and Sylvester had knowingly provided assistance and/or encouragement to the individuals who committed the various crimes of rape against the victim. For example, in *Briscoe* (2010), discussed above and in Chapter 4, it will be recalled that the accused had driven a group of individuals to a golf course where a young woman, who had been lured into travelling with the group by the false promise of access to a party, was raped and then brutally killed by members of this group. "Throughout the rapes and the killing, Briscoe simply stood by and watched, offering no assistance to either Ms. C. or her assailants." Briscoe was charged with murder, kidnapping, and aggravated assault (on the basis that he had provided assistance to the individuals who actually committed the crimes). The trial judge found that Briscoe had indeed facilitated the commission of these crimes by engaging in the following acts:

> (a) [H]e drove the group to the deserted place where the crimes were committed; (b) he chose the place to stop, the characteristics of which facilitated the commission of the crimes; (c) he opened the trunk of his car and gave a pair of pliers to Laboucan, although they were apparently not used to commit the murder; and (d) he confronted the victim after she had been struck with the wrench and while holding her angrily told her to be quiet or "shut up."

The Supreme Court of Canada agreed with the Alberta Court of Appeal and the trial judge that the *actus reus* of aiding had been proved beyond a reasonable doubt. The issue in *Briscoe* was whether the necessary *mens rea* for aiding had been proved (see the next section).

However, where the accused person has not provided any prior assistance or encouragement, then they cannot be convicted as party to an offence that is committed while they sit or stand passively by. Take, for example, the case of *Nyuon* (2014). The accused was convicted by a trial judge of trafficking cocaine and possession of cocaine for the purpose of trafficking, on the basis that he assisted and/or encouraged a friend to commit these offences. An undercover police officer had arranged to meet Nyuon's roommate in a hotel in Medicine Hat to purchase some drugs. Nyoun had just been lying on his bed and had said nothing except to respond to an introduction to the police officer. The roommate sold the officer some cocaine for $60. Nyuon successfully appealed his conviction to the Alberta Court of Appeal. The Court found that Nyuon had done absolutely nothing to assist or encourage the sale of drugs and, therefore, could not be considered a party to the offence committed by his roommate. Nyoun had merely been present in the hotel room where his friend had conducted the entire drug sale on his own. Nyoun had neither said nor done anything to assist or encourage the transaction.

However, there are certain exceptional circumstances in which a mere failure to act may well constitute aiding and/or abetting within the meaning of sections 21(b) and (c) of the *Criminal Code*. If the accused is *under a legal duty to act and fails to do so*, then—*provided the failure to act is accompanied by the intent to provide assistance or encouragement* to the person(s) actually committing an offence—the accused will become a party to that offence as an aider and/or abettor. For example, a parent is under a duty to provide the necessaries of life to their child (section 215), and this duty includes protecting the child from harm. If a parent knows that their partner is physically abusing their child and does nothing to intervene and/or provide medical attention, then their failure to act could be considered to have aided/abetted the other partner's physical abuse and they will be convicted as a party to the crime.

This horrific situation was considered in *Dooley* (2009). Both the father and stepmother of a seven-year-old boy had been physically abusing him. However, the child died within 24 hours of the infliction of a severe head injury (probably the work of the stepmother). Both father and stepmother were charged and convicted of second-degree murder. The parents blamed each other for the head injury. The Crown did not have to prove which one of them actually inflicted the injury because, under section 21(1), they are both parties to murder whether they actually committed the crime or aided/abetted the other to do so. The Ontario Court of Appeal upheld the convictions of both parents.

The Court of Appeal agreed with the trial judge's view that a parent who stood by and did nothing to protect a vulnerable child from physical abuse would be a party to murder *if they foresaw the likelihood of the child's death as a consequence of such abuse*. The appellate court emphasized that the jury had been clearly informed about the basis on which the "non-perpetrating parent" could be held criminally liable as an aider and abettor of their partner's physical abuse. The "non-perpetrating parent" could be justly convicted (a) if they had failed to perform their parental duty to protect their child from harm; and (b) if this failure had assisted or encouraged the abusive partner to persist in the course of violence, which ultimately led to the child's death. Failing to take steps to protect a child from a partner's abusive conduct can rightly be viewed as a form of providing assistance because the abusive partner is effectively "given a free pass" to inflict violence on a defenceless child. Similarly, the failure of a parent to intervene in order to prevent abuse, when one is under a duty to do so, may be correctly interpreted as providing encouragement to the abusive partner. Of course, the Crown does have to prove beyond a reasonable doubt that there was an *intention to provide assistance or encouragement*.

The *Mens Rea* Elements of Aiding and Abetting

To establish the *mens rea* of aiding and/or abetting, the Crown must provide that the accused intended to render assistance and/or encouragement to the principal when the offence was actually committed. In the words of Justice Charron, in the decision of the Supreme Court of Canada in this change is not necessary. *Briscoe* case (2010):

> Of course, doing or omitting to do something that resulted in assisting another in committing a crime is not sufficient to attract criminal liability. ... The aider or abettor must also have the requisite mental state or *mens rea*. Specifically, in the words of s. 21(1)(*b*),the person must have rendered the assistance *for the purpose* of aiding the principal offender to commit the crime.
>
> The *mens rea* requirement reflected in the word "purpose" under s. 21(1)(b) of the *Criminal Code* has two components: intent and knowledge. For the intent component ... "purpose" in s. 21(1)(*b*) should be understood as essentially synonymous with "intention." The Crown must prove that the accused intended to assist the principal in the commission of the offence. ... "[P] urpose" should not be interpreted as incorporating the notion of "desire" into the fault requirement for party liability. It is therefore not required that the accused desired that the offence be successfully committed. ...
>
> As for knowledge, in order to have the intention to assist in the commission of an offence, the aider must know that the perpetrator intends to commit the crime, although he or she need not know precisely how it will be committed. That sufficient knowledge is a prerequisite for intention is simply a matter of common sense.

In the *Briscoe* case, as was discussed in Chapter 4, the Supreme Court of Canada ruled that *wilful blindness may substitute for actual knowledge*.

The vital importance of identifying the *mens rea* elements of aiding and abetting is particularly evident in those cases where the accused person is alleged to have assisted and/or encouraged another person to commit an act of culpable homicide. It is quite possible for the person who actually committed the homicide to be convicted of murder while other accused parties to the homicide may be found guilty of the offence of manslaughter because they lacked the necessary *mens rea* for murder. This issue was addressed by the Supreme Court of Canada in the case of *Jackson and Davy* (1993). Jackson and Davy had both been charged with first-degree murder following the death of Jackson's employer. On the night of the killing, Davy had driven Jackson to the victim's shop. Jackson admitted that he had killed the victim by striking him with a hammer. It appears that Davy remained near the door to the store and that he heard noises that would suggest that someone was being assaulted. When Davy tried to leave the scene, Jackson forced him to return to the shop and ordered Davy to collect the cash box. The trial judge did not adequately instruct the jury that it would be possible to convict Davy of manslaughter while simultaneously convicting Jackson of murder. Ultimately, Jackson was found guilty of first-degree murder and Davy of second-degree murder. The Ontario Court of Appeal overturned Davy's conviction of murder and ordered a new trial because the trial judge had failed to instruct the jury correctly on the question of Davy's potential liability for the offence of manslaughter in accordance with the requirements of sections 21(1) and 21(2) of the *Criminal Code*.

The Supreme Court of Canada dismissed the Crown's appeal from the decision of the Court of Appeal. The Court noted that the necessary *mens rea*, which must be proved in relation to unlawful act manslaughter, is objective foreseeability of the risk of bodily harm that is neither trivial nor transitory [a rule laid down by the Supreme Court of Canada in the *Creighton* case (1993)]. In the *Jackson and Davy* case (1993), the Supreme Court ruled that this objective test applies equally to a person charged with manslaughter on the basis of having aided and/or abetted someone to kill another person. In the words of Justice McLachlin,

> I conclude that a person may be convicted of manslaughter who aids and abets another person in the offence of murder, where a reasonable person in all the circumstances would have appreciated that bodily harm was the foreseeable consequence of the dangerous act which was being undertaken.

Davy had assisted someone who was ultimately convicted of murder. Nevertheless, the Supreme Court ruled that if Davy lacked the necessary *mens rea* for murder (intent to kill or intent to inflict bodily harm that is likely to cause death and recklessness as to whether or not death ensues), he could still be convicted of manslaughter on the basis that he aided and/or abetted Jackson in the situation where a *reasonable person would have foreseen the risk of bodily harm to the victim*.

In the *Roach* case (2004), the Ontario Court of Appeal stated very clearly that, when an accused person is charged with an offence on the basis that they aided the person(s) who actually committed the offence, then the Crown must prove that the accused acted with intention or wilful blindness; mere recklessness will not be sufficient. Roach was charged with fraud over $5000 and conspiracy to commit fraud. Roach was alleged to have participated in a fraudulent telemarketing scheme, organized by a man called Dube. The victims of the fraudulent scheme were contacted by telemarketers who informed them that they had won valuable prizes in a legal contest. The victims were asked to pay taxes and handling and shipping charges up front to receive their prizes. These charges ranged from US$611 to US$9690. However, the victims were actually sent inexpensive watches and stereos. Dube persuaded Roach to set up a business as a "shipper and receiver" in the telemarketing scheme. Although he testified that he did not know Dube's business was illegal, Roach was convicted of fraud and conspiracy at his trial. The trial judge told the jury that:

> The third element that the Crown must prove beyond a reasonable doubt is that the accused whom you are then considering intended to aid or abet Mr. Dube in committing the offence of defrauding the public. It is not enough that the accused's acts actually aided or abetted Mr. Dube. It must also be proven that the accused knew or intended that his acts would aid or abet Mr. Dube. If the accused knew that his acts were likely to assist or encourage Mr. Dube then you are entitled to conclude that such accused intended to aid and abet Mr. Dube in committing that offence.

The trial judge, when answering questions from the jury, led them to believe that either recklessness or wilful blindness would be sufficient *mens rea* to convict Roach of fraud on the basis that he had aided Dube to actually commit this offence. Roach appealed to the Ontario Court of Appeal, which set aside his convictions and ordered a new trial. The Court emphasized that only an *intention to assist* the person who actually commits an offence or wilful blindness on the part of the accused will suffice for conviction as a party to that offence. As noted in Chapter 4, wilful blindness is treated as being equivalent to actual knowledge by the accused of the nature and consequence of their actions. The Court of Appeal referred to section 21(1)(b) of the *Criminal Code*, which provides that "everyone is a party to an offence who … does or omits to do anything for the purpose of aiding any person to commit it." The person's involvement in the crime even in a secondary capacity makes them a party to the crime. In delivering the judgment of the Court, Justice Borins underscored the fact that Parliament had used the word "purpose" in section 21(1)(b) and held that "purpose is synonymous with intent and does not include recklessness." In summarizing the *mens rea* that must be established for liability as a party under section 21(1)(b), Justice Borins stated that:

> [T]he *mens rea* for party liability is contained in s. 21(1)(b) of the *Criminal Code* that requires that the aid given by the **accessory** to the principal be "for the purpose of aiding" the principal to commit the crime of which the accessory has been charged. To be convicted as an aider, the defendant must not only assist the principal in the commission of the offence, but must intend to do so, although it is not necessary that the aider know all the details of the crime committed. It is sufficient that the aider was aware of the type of crime to be committed and knew the circumstances necessary to constitute the crime that he or she is accused of aiding. … [K]nowledge will include actual knowledge or wilful blindness, but will not include recklessness. This accords with Professor Roach's approach regarding the high level of *mens rea* required for party liability and with the opinions of the other legal scholars that I have reviewed.

Aiding and Abetting in the Context of the Purchase of Illegal Drugs

A significant issue facing the courts is the extent to which persons who provide incidental assistance to those who purchase illegal drugs should be held criminally responsible for their actions. This question was addressed by the Supreme Court of Canada in the case of *Greyeyes* (1997). The accused had been charged with the very serious offence of trafficking in cocaine, on the basis that he was a party to the crime by virtue of aiding and/or abetting. An undercover police officer, Morgan, had asked Greyeyes if he knew where he (Morgan) could obtain some cocaine. Greyeyes indicated that he knew where a source could be found, and he and Morgan went to an apartment building together. Greyeyes identified himself at the door of a particular apartment. An individual inside asked what Greyeyes and his companion wanted; Greyeyes responded with the word "cocaine." When asked how much cocaine was required, Greyeyes looked at Morgan, who indicated "one." Greyeyes relayed this information to the supplier and told Morgan that he would have to pay $40. The person inside the apartment instructed Greyeyes to slide the money under the door. He did so and a small pink flap, containing two-tenths of a gram of cocaine, was passed under the door to him. Greyeyes then gave the drug to Morgan.

The trial judge acquitted Greyeyes on the basis that he had acted only as an agent for Morgan, who was the *purchaser*—not the *seller*—of the cocaine. In effect, the trial judge ruled that Greyeyes had acted only as the mouthpiece for the undercover police officer and had not done anything to assist the vendor in the making of the sale. However, the Saskatchewan Court of Appeal subsequently allowed an appeal by the Crown and convicted Greyeyes of trafficking in cocaine. The Supreme Court of Canada then rejected Greyeyes' ensuing appeal.

It is significant that Justice L'Heureux-Dubé, speaking on behalf of the majority of the Supreme Court, ruled that, in normal circumstances, the purchaser of an illegal drug is not found guilty of *trafficking*, but rather of *possession*. This is a critical difference because the severity of the penalty for trafficking is much greater than for mere possession (a maximum term of imprisonment of life as opposed to a term of seven years). Clearly, this logic should be extended to cover those individuals who have provided "no more than incidental assistance of the sale through rendering aid to the purchaser." Such individuals should be treated as parties to the offence of *possession*, rather than *trafficking*. As Justice L'Heureux-Dubé noted in her judgment, an individual whose conduct was primarily designed to assist a *purchaser* of illegal drugs should "share the culpability and stigma of the purchaser rather than that of the vendor."

In the particular circumstances of the *Greyeyes* case, however, the Supreme Court ruled that the accused had gone far beyond providing assistance to the purchaser, Morgan. Indeed, Justice L'Heureux-Dubé stated that the "facts demonstrate a concerted effort on his part to effect the transfer of narcotics." In her view,

> The appellant located the seller, brought the buyer to the site and introduced the parties. It is clear that without this assistance, the purchase would never have taken place. Moreover, he acted as a spokesperson,

negotiated the price of the drugs, and passed the money over to the seller. He also accepted money for having facilitated the deal. ... [W]ithout the appellant's assistance, the buyer would never have been able to enter the apartment building to contact the seller. *These are not the acts of a mere purchaser, and as a result it is clear that the appellant aided the traffic of narcotics.*

Greyeyes, therefore, was found to be a party to the crime of *trafficking* (as an aider or abettor), because his actions were designed to provide a significant degree of assistance to the *seller* of the cocaine.

It is noteworthy that, in somewhat similar circumstances, the Alberta Court of Appeal ruled that an individual who plays an active role in transferring drugs from a seller to a buyer is actually committing the offence of trafficking and, therefore, it is irrelevant whether that individual was assisting the seller or the buyer.[1] In the case of *Wood* (2007), the accused was charged with trafficking in crack cocaine, contrary to section 5(1) of the *Controlled Drugs and Substances Act*. Undercover police officers requested Wood to obtain a small quantity of drugs for them. Wood used an officer's cellphone to call a seller, who later drove to a rendezvous with Wood. Using an officer's money, Wood obtained crack cocaine from the seller and delivered it to the officers. The trial judge acquitted Wood because he had provided only incidental assistance, he lacked the necessary *mens rea* for trafficking, and his aid was not necessary to the consummation of the purchase. However, upon the Crown's appeal, the Alberta Court of Appeal set aside the acquittal and entered a conviction of trafficking. On behalf of the Court, Justice Côté emphasized that Wood's motive for transferring the drug was irrelevant and that Wood should be convicted on the basis that he had actually committed the offence of trafficking himself:

[K]nowingly and personally committing one of the elements of trafficking in the *Controlled Drugs and Substances Act*, means that one has committed the offence. No resort to s. 21 of the *Code* is then necessary. ...

To phrase that in more general terms, the law of accessories becomes relevant only if the accused has not personally committed the offence. That is elementary law.

Here, [Wood] kept the seller and the buyer separate, and shuttled between the two with the money. I will assume that the accused was not himself a seller (and no one argued in the Court of Appeal that he was). However, it is at least arguable that he "gave" the cocaine to the buying undercover constables. He certainly "transferred" and "delivered" the cocaine. He carried it first across the parking lot, and then part of the distance up 109 Street to the park. And he certainly "offered to do" those things (before and at this time).

Similarly, in the *Mohamed* case (2011), the Alberta Court of Appeal held that a taxi driver who knowingly drove passengers who met with an undercover police officer in order to sell him drugs constitutes "trafficking" within the meaning of the *Controlled Drugs and Substances Act*. The Court upheld the conviction of the taxi driver on a charge of trafficking in cocaine.

To What Extent Must the Aider or Abettor Know the Nature and Scope of the Principal's Plans?

One significant problem that arises in relation to the proof of the necessary *mens rea* for aiding and/or abetting an offence concerns the situation where the accused renders only *incidental assistance* to the principal (the person who actually commits the offence in question). The problem revolves around the issue of the precise extent to which the accused must have knowledge of the principal's plans at the time the accused provides such assistance. It is clear that the accused must know the principal's "general" purpose, but, in many cases, the thorny issue arises as to exactly how far this knowledge must extend to render the accused liable to conviction as an aider and/or abettor.

The nature of the problem is well illustrated by the case of *Yanover and Gerol* (1985). Gerol was charged with the offence of placing dynamite with intent to cause an explosion at a restaurant and disco in Toronto, contrary to what is now section 81(1)(a) of the *Criminal Code*. Gerol had provided the dynamite that was ultimately used by a man called Moon in the creation of the explosion. Gerol asked Moon what the dynamite was for and was told that "my friend asked me to do the job." Apparently, Gerol did not ask Moon what the job was, nor did he inquire as to the identity of the friend. The accused was convicted at trial, but the Ontario Court of Appeal allowed his appeal and ordered a new trial.

1. It is important to take into consideration the very broad definition of "traffic" in s. 2 of the *Controlled Drugs and Substances Act*: "traffic" means, in respect of a substance included in any of Schedules I to IV, "(a) to sell, administer, give, transfer, transport, send or deliver the substance, (b) to sell an authorization to obtain the substance, or (c) to offer to do anything mentioned in paragraph (*a*) or (*b*), otherwise than under the authority of the regulations."

The new trial was ordered because of matters relating to the admission of fresh evidence. However, the Ontario Court of Appeal did take the opportunity to articulate the general principles that should be applied when a trial court has to determine whether an individual in Gerol's circumstances possessed the requisite degree of *mens rea* for conviction of an offence on the basis of aiding or abetting. Clearly, Gerol himself had not been present at the time of the explosion. He was undoubtedly ignorant of the identity of the specific building that was going to be blown up and he did not know anything about its general location. Furthermore, he did not have any knowledge as to when the explosion would take place. However, it does appear that he was fully aware that the dynamite was to be used for the criminal purpose of causing an explosion. In these circumstances, the Ontario Court of Appeal ruled that it would be open to a jury to conclude that the accused was a party to the offence on the basis of aiding and/or abetting [under section 21(1)(b) or (c) of the *Criminal Code*]. As Justice Martin stated, in delivering the judgment of the court:

> For liability to attach under s. 21(1)(b) or (c) it is unnecessary that the person supplying the instrument for the commission of the intended crime know the precise details of the crime intended to be committed such as the particular premises intended to be blown up or the precise time when the offence is intended to be committed, provided that the accused is aware of the type of crime intended to be committed.

Similarly, suppose that Badger assists and/or encourages Weasel to perpetrate an attack against Mole. As a consequence of the assault, Mole suffers bodily injuries that are primarily caused by a stab wound inflicted by Weasel. Is it open to Badger to deny that he was a party to the offence of assault causing bodily harm by claiming that he did not know that Weasel had a knife? The answer would be in the negative because Badger intended to assist or encourage Weasel in the commission of an act that clearly created a very real risk of non-trivial bodily injury. It does not matter exactly how the bodily harm was inflicted on Mole—whether by blows from the fists or by use of a weapon. Badger undoubtedly knew that Weasel intended to inflict bodily harm. He therefore knew the general nature of the offence that was to be committed, and he would be convicted as a party to assault causing bodily harm, even though he might not have known exactly how Weasel would ultimately inflict the injuries in question.

This type of scenario actually unfolded in the case of *Nanemahoo* (2011). The accused was part of a group of young men who attacked the victim. This unfortunate individual "sustained slashes to his face, head and throat that required extensive suturing, and his left ring finger was cut, causing tendon damage." A witness saw the accused kicking the victim but not stabbing him with any weapon. Nanemahoo was charged with aggravated assault. The trial judge believed that, for this crime, the Crown had to prove that Nanemahoo actually stabbed the victim himself. Since there was no such proof, the trial judge convicted Nanemahoo of the lesser charge of assault causing bodily harm. The Alberta Court of Appeal allowed an appeal by the Crown and convicted Nanemahoo of aggravated assault. The Court of Appeal ruled that the trial judge should have considered Nanemahoo's liability as a party to the stabbing committed by other(s). Indeed, the Court of Appeal convicted him of aggravated assault on the basis that he aided the person(s) who actually stabbed the victim [section 21(1)(b)]. The *mens rea* for the offence of aggravated assault is objective foresight of the risk of any sort of bodily harm, and it is obvious that a reasonable person, standing in Nanemahoo's shoes, would have possessed this foresight. After all, Nanemahoo participated in a vicious group attack on a lone victim and it was inevitable that bodily harm would ensue. Furthermore, it was not necessary for the Crown to show that the reasonable person would have foreseen the precise type of injuries that were actually inflicted. As the Court of Appeal noted:

> By virtue of the provisions of section 21(1)(b) of the *Criminal Code*, the appellant need not show that the respondent, as a party to the offence, had any greater *mens rea* than the actual perpetrator and in particular need not establish an objective foresight of the specific wounds resulting from the assault.

Under Section 21(1), the Crown Does Not Have to Establish the Precise Role Played by the Accused

Section 21(1) of the *Criminal Code* was enacted to place those who actually commit an offence and those who aid and/or abet them on exactly the same footing: they all become parties to the offence and may be convicted on that basis. An individual who assists another to commit murder, for example, will be convicted of first- or second-degree murder and the mandatory life sentence will be imposed on them.

This principle was reasserted in the case of Robert William Pickton, who was originally charged with 27 counts of first-degree murder. He was subsequently tried on six counts of first-degree murder and was ultimately convicted by a jury of all six: however, the convictions were for second- rather than first-degree murder. The Crown's case was that Pickton had committed the murders himself and the trial judge had instructed the jury that the Crown must prove that he was the "actual shooter." However, the defence raised the possibility that others may have been involved in the murders and, in response to a question by the members of the jury, the trial judge told them that they could also convict the accused if they found he "was otherwise an active participant" in the killings. In the case of *Pickton* (2010), the defence appealed against the convictions on the basis that the trial judge's revision of his instruction to the jury constituted a miscarriage of justice. However, the Supreme Court of Canada rejected Pickton's appeal because, under section 21(1), Pickton would be equally guilty of murder whether he actually committed the offence or aided/abetted others to do so. As Justice Charron stated, on behalf of the majority of the Supreme Court,

> Nothing would have been gained in this trial by explaining to the jury the distinctions between an accused's participation as principal, co-principal, or aider and abettor. By requiring proof that Mr. Pickton actively participated in the killing of the victims, by acting either on his own or in concert with others, there was no risk that the jury might convict him on the basis of conduct that did not attract criminal liability for the murders. ... The crucial issue is not whether the trial judge properly labelled the nature of Mr. Pickton's liability. ... "The whole point of s. 21(1) is to put an aider or abettor on the same footing as the principal."

Section 21(1) of the *Criminal Code* and the Case of Robert William Pickton: It Is Murder Whatever Part He May Have Played in the Killings

Reuters/Global TV

• • • • • •

Robert William Pickton is one of the most notorious serial killers of modern times. The remains or DNA of as many as 33 women were discovered on his pig farm, and he once boasted to an undercover police officer posing as a cellmate that he had killed 49 women. However, in 2007, Pickton was found guilty of only six counts of second-degree murder. He was originally charged with 27 counts of murder, but the trial judge quashed one of them and ordered that the trial should proceed on only six of the remaining charges. After Pickton was convicted of the six counts of murder, the Crown stayed the remaining 20 charges. One reason for the entry of a stay of proceedings might be that, after his conviction of six counts of second-degree murder, Pickton had already received the highest sentence possible for murder at the time—life imprisonment with no possibility of parole for 25 years. No matter how many more convictions may have been entered against his name, the sentence would have been the same. The *Criminal Code* has since been amended so that, in a case involving multiple murders, the trial judge may impose consecutive periods of non-eligibility for parole (section 745.51). Indeed, in September 2012, Travis Baumgartner, an armed security guard, was convicted of the murders of three co-workers and the attempted murder of a fourth. He was sentenced to life imprisonment with no eligibility for parole for 40 years.[2]

Somewhat surprisingly, the jury convicted Pickton of second- rather than first-degree murder. Presumably, the jurors had a reasonable doubt that the murders were "planned and deliberate." The Crown did not argue that the murders were connected to sexual assaults on his victims. If it had made that argument successfully, under section 231(5) of the Criminal Code, the murder convictions would have been for first-degree murder even if they were not planned and deliberate. There was some evidence of a sexual connection with three murders: a blow-up sex doll containing Pickton's DNA was discovered near the location where the victims' belongings were found. However, this evidence was excluded from the trial because it would be highly prejudicial if

2. *Baumgartner* (2013).

presented to a jury and the remains of Pickton's victims could not provide the necessary proof of sexual assault.

As noted elsewhere in this chapter, the Supreme Court of Canada ruled that the Crown did not have to prove whether Pickton committed the murders himself or whether he aided/abetted others to do so; in either case, Pickton would be convicted of murder. The Supreme Court concluded that "The whole point of s. 21(1) is to put an aider or abettor on the same footing as the principal." Clearly, section 21(1) provides Crown counsel with a valuable tool in the armoury of the prosecution.

The enormous advantage that section 21(1) furnishes to the Crown is also demonstrated by the earlier decision of the Supreme Court of Canada in the *Thatcher* case (1987). This case was unusual insofar as it was possible that the accused either killed the victim himself or paid another person to undertake this deadly assignment.

Colin Thatcher was a former Saskatchewan Minister of Energy and Mines who was convicted of the brutal murder of his ex-wife in 1983. The Crown contended that Thatcher had either killed the victim himself or arranged for someone else to do so and had aided or abetted this person to achieve this result. However, the Crown was unable to specifically identify any other party who may have committed the murder on Thatcher's behalf, if indeed that was the way in which the unfortunate victim met her terrible end. The trial judge instructed the jury that they could convict the accused of murder on the basis either that he actually killed the victim himself or, alternatively, that he was a party to the offence, having aided and abetted another person to carry out the fatal deed. The jury convicted the accused of first-degree murder. His appeal against conviction ultimately went to the Supreme Court of Canada, which ruled that the trial judge's instruction to the jury had been perfectly correct. The Supreme Court, therefore, rejected Thatcher's appeal. The Court also held that it was not necessary for the jury to be unanimous in its verdict as to the question of whether the accused was the actual murderer or whether he aided and/or abetted another person to kill the victim. Indeed, Chief Justice Dickson asserted that this conclusion was implicit in the very wording of section 21 of the Criminal Code:

> [S.] 21 has been designed to alleviate the necessity for the Crown choosing between two different forms of participation in a criminal offence. The law stipulates that both forms of participation are not only equally culpable, but should be treated as one single mode of incurring criminal liability. The Crown is not under a duty to separate the different forms of participation in a criminal offence into different counts. Obviously, if the charge against Thatcher had been separated into different counts, he might well have been acquitted on each count notwithstanding that each and every juror was certain beyond a reasonable doubt that Thatcher personally killed his ex-wife or that he aided and abetted someone else who killed his ex-wife. That is precisely what s. 21 is designed to prevent.

In 2006, Thatcher, who had always maintained his innocence, was granted full parole.

Do you think that the average Canadian appreciates that a person may be convicted of murder—and described as a "murderer" or "killer"—even though that person did not commit the act of homicide themselves but merely provided assistance to the individual(s) who actually killed the victim(s)? Do you think section 21(2) goes too far in spreading the net of liability for murder so broadly, taking into account that there is a mandatory life sentence (with no-parole periods) for all parties convicted under section 21(2)? Should there be a change in the sentencing provisions of the *Criminal Code* to permit the trial judge to recognize the greater or lesser blameworthiness of different parties to a murder?

BECOMING A PARTY TO AN OFFENCE BY VIRTUE OF COMMON INTENTION

The Basic Principles of Liability under Section 21(2)

Section 21(2) of the *Criminal Code* provides:

> Where two or more persons form an intention in common to carry out an unlawful purpose and to assist each other therein and any one of them, in carrying out the common purpose, commits an offence, each of them who knew or *ought to have known* that the commission of the offence would be a probable consequence of carrying out the common purpose is a party to that offence. [emphasis added]

This provision basically codifies the ancient English common law doctrine of **common intention** whereby, if two or more persons set out to execute an unlawful purpose, each of them is equally liable for the consequences of the other's (or others') criminal acts that are committed in pursuit of that common objective. The *Code* imposes an objective test: once the Crown has established the "common purpose," accused persons are liable to conviction for any offence that they either knew or "ought to have known" would be a probable consequence of carrying it out.

Let us suppose by way of example that Steerforth and Crackit agree to rob Micawber's corner store. Steerforth hopes that Micawber will hand over the cash from his till in response to threats rather than actual violence. However, Micawber refuses to hand over the money and Crackit strikes Micawber on the head with a club. Crackit and Steerforth run off with the cash and are soon apprehended by members of the local constabulary. There is no doubt that Crackit and Steerforth are both guilty of *robbery*. However, Steerforth claims that he is not guilty of the offence of *aggravated assault* (section 268 of the *Code*), because not only was it Crackit who actually struck Micawber, but also it was the case that he (Steerforth) intended only to scare Micawber by threats. In spite of his claims, Steerforth would nevertheless be convicted of the crime of aggravated assault by virtue of the application of the principle of common intention, encapsulated in section 21(2) of the *Criminal Code*. Steerforth and Crackit formed a *common intention to commit the crime of robbery "and to assist each other therein*." The Crown would undoubtedly find it relatively easy to prove either that Steerforth *actually knew* or that he "*ought to have known*" that the infliction of non-trivial bodily harm would be a "probable consequence of carrying out the common purpose." After all, the very nature of a robbery is that the victim is exposed to the risk of non-trivial bodily harm.

The application of section 21(2) was considered by the Supreme Court of Canada in the case of *Jackson and Davy* (1993). In this case (discussed above in the context of aiding and abetting), Jackson and Davy were charged with first-degree murder. The theory of the Crown was that Davy drove Jackson to the house of the victim, where they both participated in the killing. The Crown also suggested that the motive for the killing was robbery and that both Davy and Jackson intended to kill the victim during the robbery. However, there was evidence that Davy did not actually participate in the slaughter of the victim, and he testified that he did not form any plan to rob and kill him. Jackson was convicted of first-degree murder and the question arose as to whether Davy could be convicted of murder or manslaughter on the basis of having formed an intention in common to rob the victim. He was convicted of second-degree murder, but the Ontario Court of Appeal granted him a new trial. This decision was later affirmed by the Supreme Court.

In her judgment, Justice McLachlin set out the circumstances in which Davy might be convicted of manslaughter by virtue of the operation of section 21(2):

> On the evidence presented, one of the scenarios available to the jury was that Jackson and Davy had formed a common intention to rob Rae [the victim] and that, in the course of the robbery, Jackson murdered Rae. Even if he did not participate in the murder, Davy could be liable under s. 21(2) in this scenario. If he foresaw that murder was a probable consequence of carrying out the common purpose—in this case the robbery—he would be guilty of second degree murder. On the other hand, if Davy did not foresee the probability of murder but a reasonable person in the circumstances would have foreseen at least a risk of harm to another as a result of carrying out the common intention, Davy could be found guilty of manslaughter under s. 21(2).

The Requirement of Subjective Foreseeability of Death in Murder and Attempted Murder Cases

We have seen that section 21(2) imposes objective liability insofar as accused persons can be convicted of an offence that they "ought to have known" would be a probable consequence of carrying out the common unlawful purpose they have formed with the principal offender(s). However, in the *Martineau* case (1990), the Supreme Court of Canada ruled that, in light of the guarantees provided by section 7 of the *Charter*, accused persons may not be convicted of murder unless they *subjectively* foresaw the likelihood of death ensuing from their conduct. What impact does this principle have in the context of section 21(2)?

In the cases of *Logan* (1990) and *Rodney* (1990), the Supreme Court of Canada ruled that section 7 of the *Charter* requires that the words "ought to have known" in section 21(2) should be struck out, whenever the charge is murder or attempted murder. In other words, where the Crown seeks to obtain a murder (or attempted murder) conviction on the basis of common intention under section 21(2), it must be shown that the accused *actually foresaw* that the death of the victim was a probable consequence of carrying out the common purpose in question.

In the case of *Lévesque* (2013), the Supreme Court of Canada set aside the conviction of the accused and ordered a new trial because the trial judge had not given the jury the correct instruction with respect to

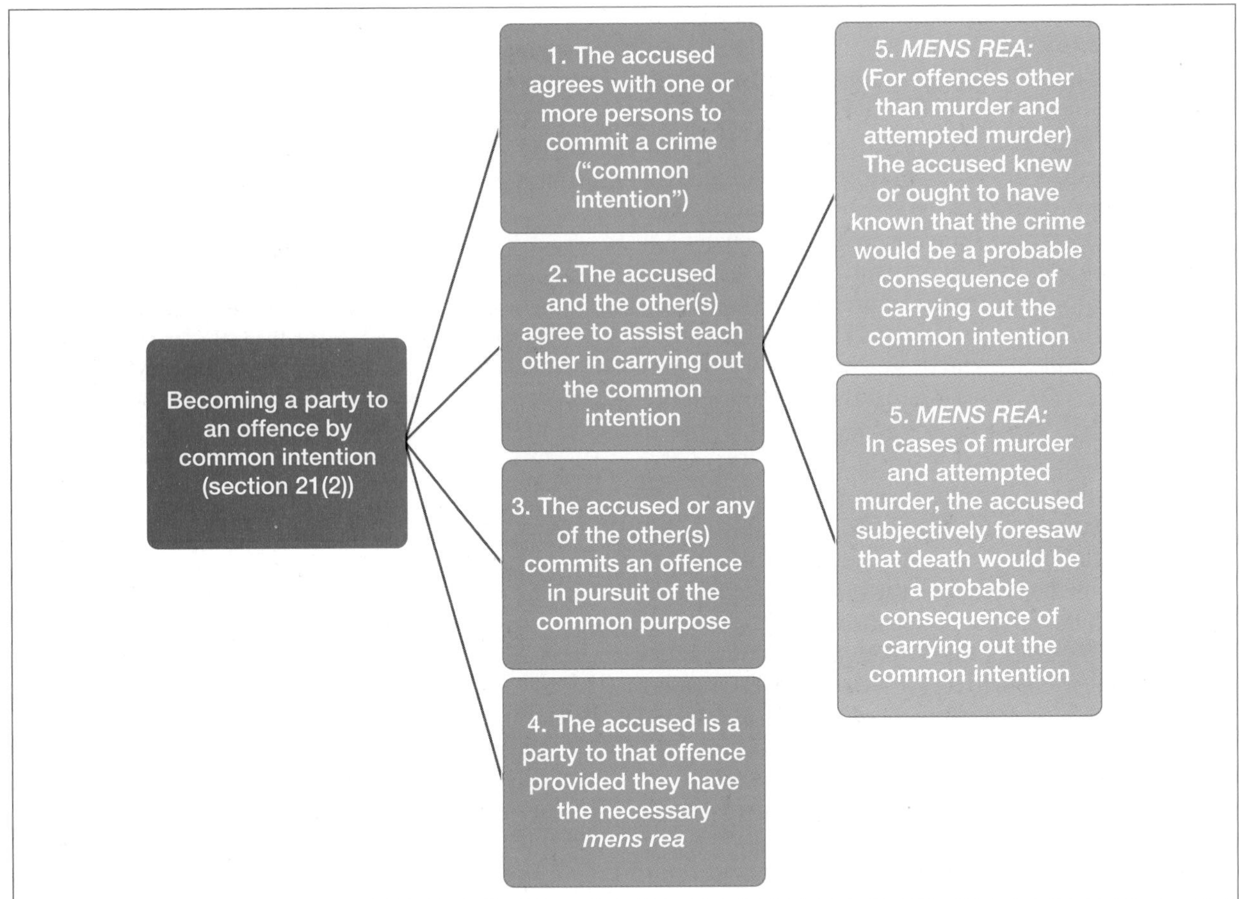

Figure *7-2*

A Step-by-Step Review of the Necessary Elements for Becoming a Party to a Crime by Virtue of Common Intention

the application of section 21(2) to a charge of murder. There had been a home invasion during which two elderly victims had been bludgeoned to death. The trial judge did not make clear to the jury that the individual who did not actually commit the murders could not be convicted of murder on the basis of common intention (the agreement to commit a robbery) unless he subjectively foresaw that the killing of the victims was a probable consequence of carrying out the robbery.

In the *McLellan* case (2018), the Ontario Court of Appeal indicated that the *mens rea* that the Crown must prove in such cases is very specific. McLellan had shot the victim in the course of a robbery committed in the house of a marijuana dealer. Mullen had been convicted of second-degree murder on the basis that he aided and abetted McLellan. His conviction was set aside by the Court of Appeal and a new trial ordered because the original trial judge had not given the correct instruction to the jury. The Court ruled that, in a new trial, the Crown must prove beyond a reasonable doubt that Mullen knew that McLellan "would probably cause the death of the deceased with the intent to cause death, or with the intent to cause bodily harm that the principal knew would likely cause death, being reckless whether death ensued or not" [in other words, with the intent required for murder under s. 229(a)].

Abandonment of the "Common Purpose"

The courts in Canada have long recognized that an accomplice may abandon a common intention to carry out an unlawful purpose and thereby absolve themselves from criminal liability for all acts subsequently committed by their co-conspirators. In the case of *Gauthier* (2013), Justice Wagner, of the

Supreme Court of Canada, identified the reasons that a defence of "abandonment" should be permitted by the criminal law:

> The reasons for recognizing the defence of abandonment in Canadian law bear repeating. There are two policy reasons in criminal law for making this defence available to parties to offences. First, there is a need to ensure that only morally culpable persons are punished; second, there is a benefit to society in encouraging individuals involved in criminal activities to withdraw from those activities and report them.

In the case of *Gauthier*, the Supreme Court of Canada clearly articulated the basic requirements for a successful defence of abandonment. Indeed, Justice Wagner set out the four criteria that must be satisfied before there can be an "air of reality" to the defence:

1. There was an intention to abandon or withdraw from the unlawful purpose;
2. There was timely communication of this abandonment or withdrawal from the person in question to those who wished to continue;
3. The communication served unequivocal notice upon those who wished to continue; and
4. The accused took, in a manner proportional to his or her participation in the commission of the planned offence, reasonable steps in the circumstances either to neutralize or otherwise cancel out the effects of his or her participation or to prevent the commission of the offence.

It is significant that, in the *Gauthier* case (2013), the Supreme Court added a new requirement to the defence of abandonment. The Court held that whether an accused person is alleged to be a party to an offence by virtue of section 21(1) or 21(2) of the *Criminal Code*, the defence may be considered by the trier of fact only *if the accused person shows that they made a reasonable effort to neutralize the effects of their participation or to prevent the principal(s) from committing the offence*. Justice Wagner pointed out that what an accused person has to do to neutralize the effects of their participation or prevent the commission of the offence will depend on the particular circumstances of the case. There may be some cases in which timely and unequivocal notice of withdrawal from the common purpose will be sufficient. However, there will be other cases in which timely communication to the principal offender will not, on its own, constitute "reasonable steps" to "neutralize or otherwise cancel out the effects" of the accused's participation: the accused will be required to take further steps in order to satisfy the requirements articulated by Justice Wagner.

In the *Gauthier* case, the accused, Cathie Gauthier, was charged with being a party—together with her spouse—to the murder of their three children. It was her spouse, Marc Laliberté, who actually killed the children by administering a poisonous concoction of Gravol and oxazepam. The evidence was clear that there had been a murder–suicide pact, according to which the children would be killed, and their parents would commit suicide. Marc Laliberté was also found dead at the scene of the crime, but Gauthier was found alive with a slit wrist that she claimed was inflicted by Marc. The Crown introduced several documents in which Gauthier had set out the couple's intention to kill the children and then take their own lives, using a soporific drug. The Crown also proved that Gauthier had purchased the medication that caused the deaths of the children. Gauthier claimed (without any supporting evidence) that, one day before the tragic deaths, she had notified Marc that she had changed her mind and no longer wished to participate in the common purpose to carry out the murder–suicide pact.

The trial judge refused to put the defence of abandonment to the jury because there was insufficient evidence to give it "an air of reality." Gauthier was convicted of first-degree murder, on the basis of being a party to the murder committed by her spouse [by virtue of section 21(1) of the *Criminal Code*]. Both the Quebec Court of Appeal and the Supreme Court of Canada agreed with the trial judge's decision to withhold the defence of abandonment from the jury and affirmed Gauthier's conviction. However, the Supreme Court stated that even if there had been sufficient evidence to support Gauthier's claim of timely communication to her spouse, the defence would still have failed because she should have taken further steps to "neutralize the effects of her participation or to prevent the commission of the offence." Justice Wagner noted that Gauthier had supplied her husband, Marc, with the drug that caused the death of the children. What further steps should she have taken? According to Justice Wagner:

> For example, she could have hidden or destroyed the medication she had purchased, remained watchful and taken the children to a safe place for the evening, insisted that her spouse give her verbal confirmation of what he intended to do, or simply called the authorities.

Justice Wagner pointed out that the requirements for the defence of abandonment will usually be more demanding when the accused person is charged with being a party to an offence on the basis of section 21(1) rather than section 21(2):

> Aiders and abettors generally do much more than promise their support in carrying out an unlawful purpose in the future. They perform concrete acts to aid the principal offender to commit the offence or to abet him or her in committing it. Their criminal liability and their moral culpability are proportional to these acts and stem from the fact that they have performed them. Thus, merely communicating in unequivocal terms their intention to cease participating in the commission of the offence will not be enough "to break the chain of causation and responsibility."

COUNSELLING AN OFFENCE THAT IS ACTUALLY COMMITTED

An individual may also become a party to a criminal offence as a consequence of counselling a criminal act. Indeed, section 22 of the *Criminal Code* establishes a broad basis for the imposition of criminal liability:

> (1) Where a person counsels another person to be a party to an offence and that other person is afterwards a party to that offence, the person who counselled is a party to that offence, notwithstanding that the offence was committed in a way different from that which was counselled.
> (2) Every one who counsels another person to be a party to an offence is a party to every offence that the other commits in consequence of the counselling that the person who counselled knew or ought to have known was likely to be committed in consequence of the counselling.
> (3) For the purposes of this Act, "counsel" includes procure, solicit or incite.

As a reading of section 22(1) readily indicates, if accused persons counsel an offence that is ultimately committed, they will be convicted of that offence in exactly the same manner as "aiders" and/or "abettors" may be convicted under section 21. Section 22(2) also saddles accused persons who counsel a crime with the responsibility for every other offence that the principal commits as a direct consequence of the counselling. The only limitation placed upon their liability is the requirement that the Crown establish that the accused knew, or *ought to have known*, that such an offence was likely to be committed as a consequence of the counselling. The use of the words "ought to have known" clearly imposes an *objective standard of liability* based upon what the "reasonable" person would have known in the same circumstances as the accused. The only exception to this principle of objective liability would arise where the principal commits the offences of murder or attempted murder. In this situation, the Supreme Court's decision in the *Martineau* case (1990) (see Chapter 4) dictates that, to safeguard the rights of accused persons under sections 7 and 11(d) of the *Charter*, they cannot become parties to these criminal offences unless they had subjective foresight of the death of the victim.

Section 22(3) states that the word "counsel" includes "procure, solicit or incite." Therefore, the term "counselling" covers advising or recommending someone else to commit an offence as well as finding someone to commit an offence, persistently requesting someone to commit an offence, and provoking or instigating someone to commit an offence.

In the case of *Hamilton* (2005),[3] the Supreme Court of Canada set out the basic elements of the offence of counselling. Chief Justice McLachlin stated, on behalf of the majority of the Court:

> [T]he *actus reus* for counselling is the *deliberate encouragement or active inducement of the commission of a criminal offence*. And the *mens rea* consists in nothing less than an accompanying *intent* or *conscious disregard of the substantial and unjustified risk inherent in the counselling:* that is, it must be shown that the accused either intended that the offence counselled be committed, or knowingly counselled the commission of the offence while aware of the unjustified risk that the offence counselled was in fact likely to be committed as a result of the accused's conduct. [emphasis in original]

The *mens rea* requirement articulated by the chief justice includes both an intention that the crime be committed and *extreme recklessness* as to whether or not it will be committed.

An illustrative case involving the counselling of an offence is that of *Soloway* (1975). In this case, the

3. *Hamilton* was a case in which the charge was counselling an offence that was *not* committed, and the facts will be discussed later in this chapter in the section dealing with counselling as an inchoate offence.

accused was convicted by a provincial court judge of a charge that he "did unlawfully steal a driver's licence, registration, and Alberta Health Care Card of a value not exceeding $200." It appears that the victim was invited to Soloway's home by Mrs. Daniels, who was a friend of the accused. The victim felt tired and went to sleep, face-down, on a couch in Soloway's living room. The victim woke up when he felt Mrs. Daniels removing his wallet from his back pocket. He pretended he was still sleeping, because he feared that he might be attacked if he did not do so. There was no money in the wallet. In his evidence at trial, the victim said:

> When [Mrs. Daniels] ... decided that there was nothing in the wallet, she was going to return it ... like I figured common sense would tell them to; and Mr. Soloway says, "No, keep it," ... "It's worth good money, I can sell it at any bar." He says, "You know, there's good money in that sort of thing. You can take strangers around, bop them over the head, and get their wallets. If there is no money you can always make money on the other things that are in the wallets."

The trial judge convicted Soloway as a party to theft on the basis that he counselled Mrs. Daniels to steal the contents of the victim's wallet. Soloway appealed to the Appellate Division of the Alberta Supreme Court, but his conviction was affirmed. Justice Allen crystallized the central issue by stating that:

> [T] he whole point involved in this case is whether the appellant's presence when the wallet was extracted from [the victim's] ... hip pocket and the advice he gave to the woman with respect to keeping the credentials made him a party to the offence of stealing those credentials and thus guilty of the offence of theft.

Defence counsel had contended that Soloway could not be convicted of being a party to theft, because that crime was already complete when Mrs. Daniels removed the wallet from the victim's pocket. Justice Allen rejected this contention. Mrs. Daniels had intended to replace the wallet in the victim's pocket after she discovered that it contained no money. It was only Soloway's prompting that caused her to remove the credentials from the wallet. Viewed in this light, it was clear that the theft of the credentials was not completed until Mrs. Daniels appropriated them with the intention to deprive the victim of them. Therefore, Soloway was properly convicted as a party to a theft he had counselled.

LIABILITY AS AN ACCESSORY AFTER THE FACT

Section 23(1) of the Criminal Code provides that an accessory after the fact "to an offence is one who, knowing that a person has been a party to the offence, receives, comforts or assists that person for the purpose of enabling that person to escape." The *mens rea* and *actus reus* elements, defined by section 23(1), are relatively straightforward. For example, in the case of *Young* (1950), Justice Bissonnette said: "This section obviously admits three constituent elements of the offence: knowledge that a crime had been committed, the desire to help the delinquent to escape and finally a positive act or omission intended to aid him in making his escape."

In the *Young* case, it appears that a man named Douglas Perreault had killed a police constable in Montreal. Perreault's sister, Young, and two other men set out from Montreal to Sheenboro, Ontario, to inform Douglas Perreault's mother of the killing. Not long before reaching their destination, they met a car containing Douglas and Donald Perreault. Both cars stopped, and the Perreault brothers were informed that the police were looking for them in connection with the murder. They also learned that the police knew their names and the licence number of their car. Young offered to hide the Perreault brothers, but his offer was refused. Young was convicted as an accessory after the fact to murder and appealed his conviction to the Quebec Court of Appeal. His appeal was dismissed. Justice Bissonnette addressed the critical issues in the following manner:

> In the present case, there is no doubt that Young knew that a crime had been committed by Douglas and Donald Perreault. ... [T]he information that he furnished ... meant efficacious assistance to the delinquents' escape. To tell them that the police are on their trail is to tell them that they have been identified, when they were still able, at that moment, to entertain the hope that they were not suspected of being the authors of this crime. It was giving them, by this information, immediate and efficacious assistance. The fact that the accused chose, after this information, a method of escape different from that suggested by [the] appellant, does not dispel the efficacy of [the] appellant's intervention.

The requirement that the accused person "know" that an offence has been committed, by the individual to whom they give assistance, is clearly of pivotal importance. However, the courts have emphasized that wilful blindness on the part of the accused will be treated as being equivalent to actual knowledge in the context of section 23(1) of the *Criminal Code*. For example, in *Duong* (1998), the accused was charged with being an accessory after the fact to a murder allegedly committed by Lam. Both television and newspaper reports had linked Lam to two homicides. Lam told Duong that he was "in trouble for murder" and needed shelter. Duong allowed Lam to hide in his apartment for about two weeks before the latter was discovered by the police. Duong knew of the media reports but did not ask Lam any questions about them. He told the police that Lam "just came to me and told me he was in trouble for it but I didn't want to know anything because I knew I would be in trouble for helping him hide, so I didn't want to know anymore." The Ontario Court of Appeal ruled that wilful blindness on the part of the accused would be sufficient *mens rea* for conviction of the offence of being an accessory after the fact.[4] As Justice Doherty noted:

> Wilful blindness refers to a state of mind which is aptly described as "deliberate ignorance." ... Actual suspicion, combined with a conscious decision not to make inquiries which could confirm that suspicion, is equated in the eyes of the criminal law with actual knowledge. Both are subjective and both are sufficiently blameworthy to justify the imposition of criminal liability.

The punishment for being an accessory after the fact is set out in section 463 of the *Code*; it is the same as the punishment for an attempt to commit an offence.

THE IMPACT OF SECTION 23.1 OF THE *CRIMINAL CODE*

Section 23.1 of the Criminal Code stipulates that an accused person may become a party to a criminal offence, even if the person who actually commits it cannot be convicted of that offence: "For greater certainty, sections 21 to 23 apply in respect of an accused notwithstanding the fact that the person whom the accused aids, abets, counsels or procures or receives, comforts or assists cannot be convicted of the offence."

For example, a child under the age of 12 may not be found criminally responsible for their actions (section 13 of the *Criminal Code*). Section 23.1 ensures that, should an adult employ a child under the age of 12 to commit an offence, such as theft, the adult will be found to be a party to the offence regardless of the fact that the child may not be prosecuted. However, section 23.1 is general in its application and is not limited to the case where the principal offender is a young child. For example, in the case of *S. (F.J.)* (1997), the accused had been charged with being an accessory after the fact to murder. Her brother was tried separately in Youth Court for having committed the murder but was acquitted. It was argued on behalf of the accused that she could not be convicted as an accessory after the fact if the alleged principal had been acquitted. However, the Nova Scotia Court of Appeal ruled that, in light of section 23.1 of the *Code*, the accused should nevertheless be convicted of the offence. It is important to bear in mind that the trial judge in the accused's case had found, strictly on the basis of the evidence presented at the accused's trial, that the accused's brother had, in fact, committed murder and that the accused had deliberately tried to cover it up.

In delivering the judgment of the Court of Appeal, Justice Jones noted that section 23.1 had made a significant change to the old common law concerning the liability of accessories:

> It would appear that the provisions of the *Code* were intended to treat parties to offences in the same manner, i.e., that accessories before the fact, aiders and abettors and accessories after the fact would be treated as principals. This is confirmed by s. 23.1 of the *Code*. It is clear from that section and s. 592 of the *Code* it is not necessary to convict a principal in order to convict an accessory.[5] While the language does not refer to the acquittal of the principal, in my view the words "whether or not the principal" is convicted, are broad enough to encompass the acquittal of the principal. Those provisions have changed the common law.

This remarkably expansive interpretation of section 23.1 was later endorsed by the Supreme Court of Canada [*S. (F.J.)* (1998)].

INCHOATE OFFENCES

The final section of this chapter concerns an extremely important topic; namely, the various **inchoate offences** (incomplete or preventive offences) that are defined in the *Criminal Code*. The rationale

4. Duong was ultimately convicted of being an accessory after the fact to manslaughter because, after a successful appeal, Lam was found guilty of manslaughter rather than murder [*Duong* (2001)].

5. S. 592 provides: "Any one who is charged with being an accessory after the fact to any offence may be indicted, whether or not the principal or any other party to the offence has been indicted or convicted or is or is not amenable to justice."

for such offences is fairly obvious in that they permit the police to intervene and prevent the commission of potentially serious crimes. As the Ontario Court of Appeal stated in the case of *Chan* (2003), "[S]trictly inchoate crimes are a unique class of criminal offences in the sense that they criminalize acts that precede harmful conduct but do not necessarily inflict harmful consequences in and of themselves." The Canadian courts have nevertheless emphasized that individuals must not be punished for their malevolent intentions alone: indeed, it is clear that the Crown must prove some overt act on the part of the accused person to justify conviction of an inchoate offence. The inchoate offences to be considered in this chapter are (1) counselling, (2) attempt, and (3) conspiracy.

1. Counselling an Offence That Is Not Committed

Earlier in this chapter, we discussed the criminal liability of individuals who counsel the commission of offences that are ultimately perpetrated; this liability is governed by section 22 of the *Code*. However, section 464 deals with the situation where an individual "counsels" another person to commit an offence that is not ultimately perpetrated:

> Except where otherwise expressly provided by law, the following provisions apply in respect of persons who counsel other persons to commit offences, namely,
>
> (a) every one who counsels another person to commit an indictable offence is, if the offence is not committed, guilty of an indictable offence and is liable to the same punishment to which a person who attempts to commit that offence is liable; and
>
> (b) every one who counsels another person to commit an offence punishable on summary conviction is, if the offence is not committed, guilty of an offence punishable on summary conviction.

It should be remembered that section 22(3) states that, for the purposes of the *Criminal Code*, the word "counsel" includes "procure, solicit or incite." In the *Hamilton* case (2005), Justice Fish, in delivering the majority judgment of the Supreme Court of Canada, provided definitions of these terms:

> In their relevant senses, the *Canadian Oxford Dictionary* (2nd ed. 2004) defines "counsel" as "advise" or "recommend (a course of action)"; "procure" as "bring about"; "solicit" as "ask repeatedly or earnestly for or seek or invite," or "make a request or petition to (a person)"; and "incite" as "urge." "Procure" has been held judicially to include "instigate" and "persuade."

In the *Sharpe* case (2001), Chief Justice McLachlin, on behalf of the majority of the Supreme Court of Canada, emphasized that although the word "counsel" "can mean simply to advise," in the "criminal law it has been given the stronger meaning of actively inducing." In *Hamilton* (2005), Justice Fish, of the Supreme Court of Canada, reiterated this meaning of the word "counsel," noting that "the *actus reus* for counselling will be established where the materials or statements made or transmitted by the accused *actively induce* or *advocate*—and do not merely *describe*—the commission of an offence."

However, it is not necessary for the Crown to prove that anyone was actually influenced by the accused's counselling. This proposition is well illustrated by the case of *McLeod and Georgia Straight Publishing Co.* (1970). In this case, the publishing company and its editor-in-chief were charged with counselling the commission of an indictable offence that was not committed—namely, the cultivation of marijuana, contrary to the provisions of section 6 of the now repealed *Narcotic Control Act*. Under the heading "Plant Your Seeds," an issue of the *Georgia Straight* magazine contained an article that furnished detailed instructions concerning the planting, fertilization, cultivation, and harvesting of the marijuana plant. A woman who had purchased a copy of the magazine appeared as a witness at the trial and admitted she was not influenced by the counselling contained in the article. However, the provincial court judge convicted both McLeod and the publishing company, stating that "if the person bought the paper and the only fair inference is that it was on public sale at the corner of Georgia and Granville Street and if the person bought the paper and read it, they were in fact being counselled to grow marijuana." The defendants appealed to the British Columbia Court of Appeal, which affirmed the company's conviction but set aside McLeod's conviction on the basis that there was "insufficient evidence" to convict him. Justice Maclean made the following significant observations:

> Defence counsel has suggested that "counselling" is not complete unless the person to whom the communication is directed has been influenced by the communication. I cannot accept this submission as in my view there is no justification for assigning such

> a limited meaning to the word "counselling." … In my view, the purchaser of this newspaper was counselled to cultivate marijuana.

Just as it is no defence that the person who was counselled was not, in fact, influenced by the accused's efforts to persuade them to commit an offence, it is likewise not open to an accused person to assert that they should not be convicted of counselling an offence because the accused later repented and renounced their previous actions. Since counselling is, by definition, an inchoate offence, the courts have taken the view that the offence has been irrevocably committed just as soon as the accused has attempted to persuade another person to commit a crime. This principle was strongly articulated in the *Gonzague* case (1983), which involved a charge of procuring the commission of first-degree murder (which was, fortunately, not committed). The accused had incited another individual to murder a business rival. However, when this individual (wearing a body pack recorder provided by the police) later approached Gonzague, the accused told him to forget about the matter and to keep the $200 he had previously paid him in advance. It was suggested that Gonzague had renounced his previous intention of procuring the murder of his rival and that this renunciation should provide him with a valid defence. This suggestion was unequivocally rejected. In the words of Justice Martin, who delivered the judgment of the Ontario Court of Appeal:

> The offence of procuring under s. [464] is complete when the solicitation or incitement occurs even though it is immediately rejected by the person solicited, or even though the person solicited merely pretends assent and has no intention of committing the offence. There is no authority in either the Canadian or Commonwealth decision(s) in support of the view that renunciation of the criminal purpose constitutes a defence to a charge of "counselling, procuring or inciting" under s. [464].

The Supreme Court of Canada has ruled that the *mens rea* required for conviction of counselling is either an intention that the offence actually be committed by the person who is counselled or extreme recklessness with respect to this outcome. In the case of *Hamilton* (2005), the accused had sold computer files and documents to other individuals, using the Internet to do so. These files contained instructions for bomb making and house breaking and a program that generated credit card numbers that might be used for fraudulent purposes. Hamilton was charged with counselling the commission of four offences that were not, in fact, committed: namely, making explosive substances with intent, doing anything with intent to cause an explosion, break and enter with intent, and fraud. At his trial, Hamilton admitted that he had read a computer-generated list of the files concerned but denied that he had actually read the contents of these files. Although he had generated some credit card numbers, he had never used them and there had been no complaints from the bank concerning their misuse. The trial judge acquitted Hamilton of all charges because, in her view, he never intended that these offences should be committed. The Alberta Court of Appeal upheld the acquittals. The Crown subsequently appealed to the Supreme Court of Canada. The pivotal issue before the Supreme Court concerned the *mens rea* elements that must be proved for conviction of the offence of counselling.

In delivering the judgment of the majority of the Supreme Court in *Hamilton*, Justice Fish articulated the *mens rea* requirements for the offence of counselling under section 464 of the *Criminal Code*:

> [T]he *mens rea* consists in nothing less than an accompanying *intent or conscious disregard of the substantial and unjustified risk inherent in the counselling:* that is, it must be shown that the accused either intended that the offence counselled be committed, or knowingly counselled the commission of the offence while aware of the unjustified risk that the offence counselled was in fact likely to be committed as a result of the accused's conduct. [emphasis in original]

Prior to the *Hamilton* case, it had been assumed that only the actual intent that the counselled offence be committed would constitute sufficient *mens rea* for a conviction under section 464. However, the Supreme Court of Canada now appears to have added extreme recklessness as an alternative form of *mens rea* that will be sufficient for conviction of counselling an offence that was not, in fact, committed. Indeed, Justice Fish indicated that if recklessness is to be relied on as satisfying the *mens rea* requirements, the Crown must prove that the accused person was subjectively aware of and consciously disregarded the "*substantial* and unjustified risk inherent in the counselling." It would appear that consciously disregarding a mere *possibility* that the offence may be committed would not satisfy the standard of recklessness developed by Justice Fish. There must be awareness on the part of the accused that there is a *substantial* risk that the offence will be committed. Justice Fish emphasized that the standard of recklessness required for conviction under section 464 is a high one. He expressly rejected the contention that a less rigorous standard should be adopted to combat the potential misuse of the Internet for criminal purposes:

> I would resist any temptation to depart in this case from that relatively demanding standard. The Internet provides fertile ground for sowing the seeds of unlawful conduct on a borderless scale. And, at the hearing of the appeal, Crown counsel expressed with eloquence and conviction the urgent need for an appropriate prophylactic response.
>
> In my view, however, this task must be left to Parliament. Even if they were minded to do so, courts cannot contain the inherent dangers of cyberspace crime by expanding or transforming offences, such as counselling, that were conceived to meet a different and unrelated need. Any attempt to do so may well do more harm than good, inadvertently catching morally innocent conduct and unduly limiting harmless access to information.

The Supreme Court affirmed Hamilton's acquittal on the charges of counselling the commission of the crimes of making explosive substances with intent, doing anything with intent to cause an explosion, and break and enter with intent: in the view of the majority of the justices, the trial judge had correctly found that Hamilton lacked the necessary *mens rea* for conviction of the offence of counselling. However, the Court ordered a new trial on the charge of counselling the offence of fraud. The majority of the Supreme Court concluded that the trial judge should have found that Hamilton did have the necessary *mens rea* for conviction of counselling the commission of fraud. Hamilton had sent an email "teaser" to various individuals in which he advertised software that could generate "valid working credit card numbers." As Justice Fish stated in his judgment,

> [A]s regards the credit card number generator, the trial judge concluded that the documents offered for sale—and sold—by Mr. Hamilton "actively promote or encourage the actions described in them." ... [S]he found that the documents "are likely to incite and are 'with a view to' inciting the offence." ...
>
> Nothing in the evidence suggests that Mr. Hamilton intended these documents to be read in a different manner or that they be used for a different purpose. Moreover, the trial judge expressly found that Mr. Hamilton had "subjective knowledge that the use of false credit card numbers is illegal." ...
>
> [Hamilton] sought to make "a quick buck" by encouraging the intended recipients of his Internet solicitation to purchase a device that generated credit card numbers easily put to fraudulent use.

Justice Fish stated that the trial judge's conclusion that Hamilton had not intended to persuade the recipients of the emails to actually make use of the credit card numbers was not consistent with "the plain meaning of the 'teaser' email" and also with her other findings of fact, including her determination that Hamilton perfectly understood that use of the generated numbers was against the law.

2. ATTEMPT

Section 24 of the Code and Attempt

The rationale underlying the law of **criminal attempt** is undoubtedly the wisdom of preventing crimes before they are committed. It would be absurd if a police officer were required to wait until a robber actually mugged a victim before the officer could intervene and make an arrest. Similarly, it is necessary to punish an individual who has made a serious attempt to commit a crime, because it is highly likely that, if the failed attempt is not sanctioned in some way, the accused will keep trying until they are successful. However, the problem that one immediately encounters is that it is certainly not an easy task to decide when the accused person has travelled far enough along the road toward completion of an offence to justify the intervention of the police and an ultimate conviction of the crime of attempt.

The general provision concerning criminal attempts is set out in section 24 of the *Criminal Code*:

> (1) Every one who, having an intent to commit an offence, does or omits to do anything for the purpose of carrying out his intention is guilty of an attempt to commit the offence whether or not it was possible under the circumstances to commit the offence.
>
> (2) The question whether an act or omission by a person who has an intent to commit an offence is or is not mere preparation to commit the offence, and too remote to constitute an attempt to commit the offence, is a question of law.

The various punishments for criminal attempts are set out in the *Criminal Code* (see Figure 7.4 on page 194).

The *Mens Rea* Relating to Criminal Attempt

Since the major objective of the criminal law relating to attempts is unequivocally preventive in nature, it is scarcely surprising that the courts have emphasized the *mens rea* requirements of criminal attempts. As Justice Laidlaw of the Ontario Court of Appeal commented in the *Cline* case (1956):

> Criminal intention alone is insufficient to establish a criminal attempt. There must be *mens rea* and also an *actus reus*. But it is to be observed that whereas in most crimes it is the *actus reus* which the law endeavours to prevent, and the *mens rea* is only a necessary element of the offence, in a criminal attempt the *mens rea* is of primary importance and the *actus reus* is the necessary element.

Significantly, section 24(1) of the *Code* clearly requires proof of "an intent to commit an offence" as a prerequisite for conviction of any criminal attempt. This requirement of an actual intent to commit an offence undoubtedly implies that the *mens rea* for an attempt may be quite different from that required for conviction of the completed offence. This situation would arise where the *mens rea* for the completed offence falls short of an intention to commit it. Take, for example, the offence of unlawfully causing bodily harm, contrary to section 269 of the *Code*. In the *DeSousa* case (1992), the Supreme Court of Canada ruled that the accused may be convicted of the complete offence of unlawfully causing bodily harm without having the actual intention to cause bodily harm. However, in the case of a charge of *attempt* to unlawfully cause bodily harm, the Crown would be required to prove the intention to cause bodily harm before it could obtain a conviction against the accused. Indeed, this was precisely the conclusion of the Quebec Court of Appeal when it considered this situation in the case of *Colburne* (1991). As Justice LeBel pointed out:

> Even if in certain respects one may find it illogical that the incomplete offence [or attempt] requires a degree of *mens rea* greater than that required for the completed offence, to do otherwise is to transform the attempt into a purely relational offence whose constituent elements would strictly depend on the underlying offence. It exists by itself, although it requires the identification of the underlying offence that the author of the attempt was pursuing. Its distinctive element, in respect of the identification of its mental element, is found precisely in this desire to commit the underlying offence, which corresponds to the notion of specific intent. Section 24(1) makes an attempt a question of intent, of desire of a result and not only, for example, of negligence or gross imprudence, even if that would be sufficient to find the presence of the guilty mind required for the completed offence.

The Supreme Court of Canada emphasized the need for the Crown to prove an actual intent to commit the completed offence in the case of *Ancio* (1984). The accused was charged with attempted murder, and the Crown argued that he could be convicted of this offence if he had the necessary *mens rea* to commit murder in any of the ways for which provision is made in the *Criminal Code*. As mentioned in Chapter 4, an accused person may be convicted of murder even though they lack the actual intent to kill the victim. For example, an accused person may be convicted of murder, under section 229(a)(ii) of the *Criminal Code*, if they cause the death of a human being in the situation where the accused "means to cause him bodily harm that he knows is likely to cause his death, and is reckless whether death ensues or not." Undoubtedly, section 229(a)(ii) provides that the completed offence of murder may be committed by "reckless" defendants who deliberately inflict injuries that they know are likely to cause death. In *Ancio*, the Supreme Court unequivocally ruled that even though it is possible to be convicted of murder without an actual intent to kill, this is not the case for the crime of attempted murder: for conviction of an attempt to commit murder, nothing less than an actual intent to kill will suffice. In the words of Justice McIntyre:

> A reading of s. 24 of the *Code* and its predecessors since the enactment of the first *Code* in 1892 confirms that the intent to commit the desired offence is a basic element of the offence of attempt. Indeed, because the crime of attempt may be complete without the commission of any other offence and even without the performance of any act unlawful in itself, it is abundantly clear that the criminal element of the offence of attempt may lie solely in the intent. …
>
> The completed offence of murder involves a killing. The intention to commit the complete offence of murder must therefore include an intention to kill. I find it impossible to conclude that a person may intend to commit the unintentional killings described in ss. [229 and 230] of the *Code*. I am then of the view that the *mens rea* for an attempted murder cannot be less than the specific intent to kill.

Justice McIntyre also addressed the issue of whether it is illogical to require a higher degree of *mens rea* for the offence of attempted murder than for the completed offence of murder. He stated that:

> The intent to kill is the highest intent in murder and there is no reason in logic why an attempt to murder, aimed at the completion of the full crime of murder, should have any lesser intent. If there is any illogic in this matter, it is in the statutory characterization of unintentional killing as murder.

Earlier in this chapter, it was noted that, in the *Hamilton* case (2005), the Supreme Court of Canada modified the preexisting *mens rea* requirements for the crime of counselling an offence that is not committed. Prior to this case, the law had been that only an actual intent that the counselled offence be committed was sufficient for conviction of this inchoate crime. However, the Court expanded the scope of the *mens rea* requirements for counselling by adding extreme recklessness as a state of mind that would justify conviction of an accused person. It would, perhaps, be logical for the Supreme Court to apply this new approach to the crime of attempt, thereby effecting a significant change in the law. However, it remains to be seen if this development will actually take place in the years ahead.

The case of *Coleville* (1988) illustrates the proposition that the *mens rea* for an attempt may be inferred from the surrounding circumstances. The accused was charged with the attempted theft of a car. He was observed attempting to break into the car on the passenger door side. He and his companion fled when they saw that they had been spotted. They were later apprehended by the police and found to be in possession of a number of items that are frequently used to break into cars, as well as to remove and replace starting mechanisms. The trial judge acquitted the accused on the basis that the evidence did not permit him to ascertain with certainty whether it was the victim's vehicle or its contents that the accused intended to steal. The Crown appealed, and the Quebec Court of Appeal ultimately allowed the appeal and entered a conviction against the accused. Justice Chevalier said that:

> The specific intent of a person found attempting to open a vehicle, while he has in his possession a "slim Jim" or a clothes-hanger is perhaps not totally certain. However, if one finds that in addition he has a tool which can be used to rip out the starting mechanism for the motor ("puller"), for which the intruder does not have the key, and a complete replacement mechanism for the one removed, I consider that one can logically conclude that the purpose of the operation was not to carry out some little search inside the area commonly called the glove compartment. It is only normal to think that it is the automobile and not its hypothetical contents that the intruder was attempting to steal. Even more so, when there is nothing in the evidence indicating that there were some suitable objects within the respondent's view which might have attracted his attention and stimulated his covetous desire.

The *Actus Reus* Requirements Relating to Criminal Attempts

In the case of *Root* (2008), the Ontario Court of Appeal emphasized the rather elusive nature of the *actus reus* elements of criminal attempts:

> In every case of an attempt to commit an offence, the *mens rea* of the substantive offence will be present and complete. In every attempt, what is incomplete is the *actus reus* of the substantive offence. But incompleteness of the *actus reus* of the substantive offence will not bar a conviction of attempt, provided the *actus reus* is present in an incomplete, but more than preparatory way.

Providing a general definition of the *actus reus* requirements of criminal attempts is an extraordinarily difficult task, since such requirements must necessarily vary in relation to the different types of criminal offences that may be attempted. Historically, the courts have discussed the issue of the *actus reus* of an attempt in terms of whether the accused's conduct was too "remote" from the completed offence to justify the imposition of criminal liability. The notorious and intractable problem underlying the law of criminal attempts is that of where to draw the line between acts that are sufficiently "proximate" to the completed offence so as to deserve the imposition of criminal liability upon the accused and acts that are too "remote" from the completed offence to justify any form of punishment. Significantly, section 24(2) of the *Code* provides that the question of whether an act or omission is to be considered "mere preparation to commit an offence, and [therefore] too remote to constitute an attempt to commit the offence" is to be treated as a "question of law" rather than of fact; in other words, in a jury trial, this question must be answered by the trial judge as a matter of legal interpretation rather than by the jury as an issue of fact.

The manner in which judges determine whether the *actus reus* requirements of the attempt have been established by the Crown must necessarily vary according to both the nature of the crime attempted and a number of circumstances peculiar to each individual case. There can be no universal test that will determine the *actus reus* requirements of all criminal attempts. This flexible approach is well illustrated by the leading Canadian case of *Cline* (1956). In delivering the judgment of the Ontario Court of Appeal in this case, Justice Laidlaw articulated a number of principles that have been widely applied by Canadian courts:

> The consummation of a crime usually comprises a set of acts which have their genesis in an idea to do a criminal act; the idea develops to a decision to do that act; a plan may be made for putting that decision into effect; the next step may be preparation only for carrying out the intention and plan; but when that preparation is in fact fully completed, the next step in the series of acts done by the accused for the purpose and with the intention of committing the crime as planned cannot, in my opinion, be regarded as remote in its connection with that crime. The connection is in fact proximate.

Justice Laidlaw then proceeded to specify a number of basic requirements for proof of the *actus reus* elements of the crime of attempt:

> There must be *mens rea* and also an *actus reus* to constitute a criminal attempt, but the criminality of misconduct lies mainly in the intention of the accused. … It is not essential that the *actus reus* be a crime or a tort or even a moral wrong or social mischief. … The *actus reus* must be more than mere preparation to commit a crime. But … when the preparation to commit a crime is in fact fully complete and ended, the next step done by the accused for the purpose and with the intention of committing a specific crime constitutes an *actus reus* sufficient in law to establish a criminal attempt to commit that crime.

The factors in the *Cline* case illustrate the inherent difficulties involved in the task of determining whether the *actus reus* of attempt has been proved. Cline was charged with indecent assault on Peter C., who was 12 years old. Cline was convicted at trial and appealed to the Ontario Court of Appeal, which set aside the conviction of indecent assault[6] and, instead, substituted one for attempt (see section 660 of the *Code*). Cline had approached Peter C., asking him to carry his suitcases for a "couple of dollars." In fact, Cline had no suitcases with him. Peter C. said no and went on his way. The boy testified that Cline had been wearing dark sunglasses that "almost covered his whole face," even though the encounter took place at night. If Cline's conduct had been an isolated act, it is doubtful that the Crown would have been able to establish that an attempt to commit an indecent assault had been committed.

However, evidence was introduced that clearly established that Cline had previously approached a number of other boys in similar circumstances; in at least one of these cases, Cline had actually performed an indecent act without the victim's consent. The Court of Appeal ruled that this evidence was sufficient to establish the *mens rea* of the attempt to commit an indecent assault upon Peter C.: "[E]vidence of similar acts done by the accused before the offence with which he is charged, and also afterwards if such acts are not too remote in time, is admissible to establish a pattern of conduct from which the Court may properly find *mens rea*." The remaining question to be resolved was whether Cline's approach to Peter C. constituted "mere preparation" or whether it could be considered sufficiently "proximate" to the completed offence so as to justify conviction of an attempt; in other words, had the Crown established the *actus reus* of the attempt? In dealing with this issue, Justice Laidlaw stated:

> The appellant intended to commit the crime of indecent assault. He made a plan in detail to carry out his intention. The plan comprised a series of acts which form a clear-cut pattern of conduct, and the accused followed that pattern of conduct on all occasions or the occasion in question, and in precise accordance with that pattern of conduct, he chose a time and place where he might procure a victim necessary for the consummation of the crime. He went to that place at the chosen time. Before or after doing so he put on large sunglasses to disguise his identity. He then waited for the opportunity to pursue his planned conduct to the end. His preparation to commit the intended crime was fully complete. He was ready to embark on the course of committing the intended crime. It was necessary only to lure a victim to a secluded place. … The acts of the appellant from the first moment he approached Peter C. were not preparation. They were not too remote to constitute an attempt to commit the offence of indecent assault.

6. This offence no longer exists. Today, the likely charges would be under s. 151 (sexual interference) or s. 152 (invitation to sexual touching).

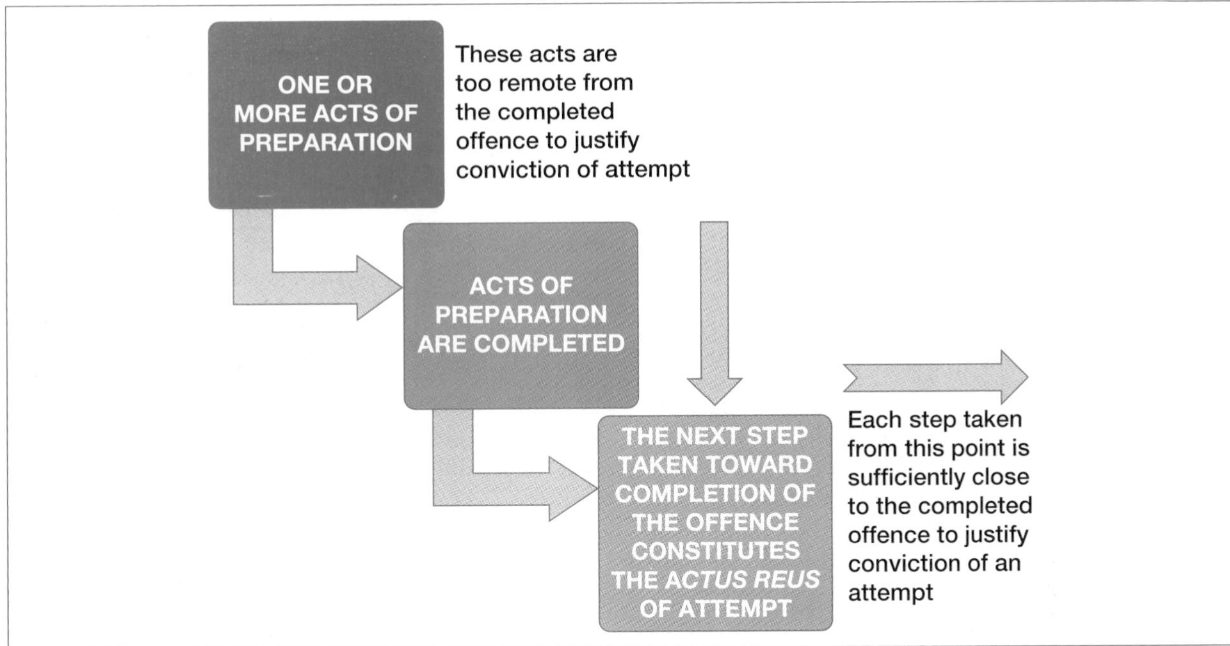

Figure 7-3
The Flexible Approach to Determining Whether the Actus Reus *of Attempt Has Been Committed (the* Cline *Case, 1956)*

In *Boudreau* (2005), the Nova Scotia Court of Appeal furnished a striking example of the application of the principle that, once an accused person has finished their preparations, the next step taken toward completion of the offence that they desire to commit constitutes the *actus reus* of a criminal attempt. Boudreau had recently separated from his wife and arrived at her house in a rage. He was carrying a rifle and told her that he wanted to know what she was "putting him through." He pointed the rifle at his wife with "one hand in the trigger area." On three occasions, Boudreau's wife gestured to him to calm down. Each time this happened, Boudreau told his wife to "back up." However, she eventually escaped. Boudreau followed her to a house across the street and tried unsuccessfully to kick in the door. He told a number of neighbours that he intended to kill his spouse. For some 10 minutes, he remained on the veranda, playing with his gun (it was not clear whether he was trying to load or unload it). He was then arrested and was subsequently charged and convicted of attempted murder. Boudreau appealed against his conviction on the basis that the trial judge had erred when he concluded that Boudreau's actions went beyond mere preparation and constituted the *actus reus* of attempted murder. However, the Nova Scotia Court of Appeal dismissed Boudreau's appeal. The Court agreed with the trial judge's finding that the Crown had proved beyond a reasonable doubt that Boudreau intended to kill his wife. However, the main issue to be decided was whether the *actus reus* of attempted murder had been established. On this matter, Chief Justice MacDonald stated that:

> [T]he trial judge had evidence of the appellant doing the following acts:
>
> - either before entering Ms. Boudreau's kitchen or on Ruby Swaine's veranda, loading the gun with three bullets,
> - carrying the gun from his car to the victim's home with "one hand in the trigger area,"
> - pointing the gun at his victim on at least three occasions,
> - following his victim across the street to Ms. Swaine's home,
> - attempting to kick Ms. Swaine's door open.
>
> These facts provided the trial judge with ample justification to conclude that the *actus reus* had been established. In reaching this conclusion, I am mindful that the appellant's actions did not progress beyond pointing the gun. In other words, the

trial judge found no reliable evidence to conclude that the appellant tried to fire a shot. Yet, there need not necessarily be an attempt to shoot in order to sustain a conviction for attempted murder. Again, there need be only one step following preparation to establish the *actus reus*.

Clearly, in the view of the chief justice, it was not necessary for the Crown to prove that Boudreau had actually attempted to shoot his wife in order to obtain a conviction for attempted murder.

Attempting the Impossible

It will be remembered that section 24(1) of the *Code* provides that an accused person may be convicted of an attempt to commit an offence "whether or not it was possible under the circumstances to commit the offence." This provision may seem a little strange at first sight. However, Canadian courts have generally encountered few difficulties in applying it in practice.

For example, in *Bear* (2013), the accused was charged with aggravated assault. Bear knew that he was HIV positive and he had a cut lip. He deliberately spat into the face of a police officer, after threatening the officer with exposure to HIV. He was convicted at trial of common assault, but the Crown appealed. The Manitoba Court of Appeal set aside the trial decision and substituted a conviction of attempted aggravated assault. Bear could not be convicted of aggravated assault because the Crown would have had to prove that there was a "realistic possibility" that HIV could have been transmitted the police officer and there had been no evidence to support this requirement. However, Bear could be convicted of *attempted* aggravated assault because section 24(1) clearly states that it is immaterial that it was "impossible" for him to transmit HIV by spitting at the officer. His intent to transmit the virus had been clearly established and he had done everything he could to achieve that intent. As Madam Justice Steele stated:

In our case, the accused intended to transmit HIV by spitting. It is immaterial whether he thought his

Illustration by Greg Holoboff

An individual may be convicted of an attempt to commit theft even if the items that they sought to steal are not present at the scene of the crime (one can be convicted of attempting the impossible).

saliva alone was sufficient to do so or he thought that the blood from the cut on his lip mixed with his saliva was sufficient to do so. It is immaterial that it was not a realistic possibility to transmit HIV in this way. His spitting at the police officer coupled with his comments that he had HIV, his threats and his hiding behind the door of the interview room show a completed *mens rea* along with action that was more than preparatory. The criminal element of attempt may lie solely in the intent.

In *United States v. Dynar* (1997), the Supreme Court of Canada undertook an extensive analysis of the so-called question of **impossibility** in the law of criminal attempts and reaffirmed the view that section 24(1) of the *Code* must be given a literal interpretation insofar as it clearly precludes an accused person from raising impossibility as a defence to a charge of attempt. *Dynar* involved an extradition request by the United States. Dynar had been the subject of a failed "sting" operation conducted by the Federal Bureau of Investigation in the United States, and the United States government now sought to extradite Dynar from Canada on charges of attempting to launder money and conspiracy to launder money. Dynar could not be extradited unless it could be established that his conduct would have amounted to a criminal attempt or criminal conspiracy if it had taken place entirely in Canada.

The two relevant money laundering offences under Canadian criminal law arose under section 462.31(1) of the *Criminal Code* and section 19.2(1) of the now repealed *Narcotic Control Act*. At the time that the case first arose, the offences of money laundering under these two statutes required that the Crown prove that the accused laundered money "*knowing*" that it had been obtained by the commission of a designated offence. In fact, the monies involved in the Dynar sting operation were not the proceeds of crime at all, but rather monies belonging to the United States government. This meant that Dynar could not have committed the (completed) money laundering offences because one cannot know something that is not true.[7] However, the critical question was whether he could instead be convicted of *attempting* and/or *conspiring* to commit these offences. The Supreme Court of Canada ultimately rejected Dynar's argument that since it would have been impossible for him to complete the money laundering offences, he had, therefore, not committed any offences known to Canadian law.

In light of the Court's ruling that Dynar could potentially have been convicted of both an attempt and a conspiracy to commit the money laundering offences, he was ordered to be extradited to stand trial in the United States. Justices Cory and Iacobucci stated that "sufficient evidence was produced to show that Mr. Dynar intended to commit the money-laundering offences, and that he took steps more than merely preparatory in order to realize his intention." They pointed out that this was "enough to establish that he attempted to launder money contrary to s. 24(1) of the *Criminal Code*." The Supreme Court essentially held that the issue of impossibility was, by virtue of the wording of section 24(1), totally irrelevant to the determination of whether an accused person is guilty of a criminal attempt. Indeed, Justices Cory and Iacobucci firmly noted that so-called "impossible" attempts "are no less menacing than other attempts":

> After all, the only difference between an attempt to do the possible and an attempt to do the impossible is chance. A person who enters a bedroom and stabs a corpse thinking he is stabbing a living person has the same intention as a person who enters a bedroom and stabs someone who is alive. In the former instance, by some chance, the intended victim expired in his sleep perhaps only moments before the would-be assassin acted. It is difficult to see why this circumstance, of which the tardy killer has no knowledge and over which he has no control, should in any way mitigate his culpability. Next time, the victim might be alive. Similarly, even if Mr. Dynar could not actually have laundered the proceeds of crime this time around, there is hardly any guarantee that his next customer might not be someone other than an agent of the United States Government.

It was clear that Dynar had attempted to engage in activities that, if they had been completed, would have fallen within the definition of crimes that were duly established under the *Criminal Code* and the *Narcotic Control Act*. However, it is noteworthy that the Supreme Court took the opportunity to make it clear that an accused person who attempts to do *something that does not, in fact, amount to a crime* cannot be found guilty of an attempt under section 24(1)—even if the accused fervently believes that they are involved in activity that is criminal. Putting it more simply, there can be no criminal liability for attempting to commit an **imaginary crime**. As Justices Cory and

7. S. 462.31(1) of the *Criminal Code* has now been amended so that it is an offence for a person to launder money "knowing *or believing that* all or a part of that property or of those proceeds was obtained or derived directly or indirectly as a result of (a designated offence)" [emphasis added].

Iacobucci noted in their judgment, there is a critical distinction between "a failed attempt to do something that is a crime and an imaginary crime":

> It is one thing to attempt to steal a wallet, believing such thievery to be a crime, and quite another to bring sugar into Canada, believing the importation of sugar to be a crime. In the former case, the would-be thief has the *mens rea* associated with thievery. In the latter case, the would-be smuggler has no *mens rea* known to law. Because s. 24(1) clearly provides that it is an element of the offence of attempt to have "an intent to commit an offence," the latter sort of attempt is not a crime.

The Supreme Court emphasized that the major purpose of the law of criminal attempts is to discourage individuals from committing subsequent offences. However, this purpose would not be served by punishing attempts to commit so-called "imaginary crimes." As Justices Cory and Iacobucci aptly pointed out:

> [O]ne who attempts something that is not a crime or even one who actually does something that is not a crime, believing that what he has done or has attempted to do is a crime, has not displayed any propensity to commit crimes in the future, unless perhaps he has betrayed a vague willingness to break the law. Probably all he has shown is that he might be inclined to do the same sort of thing in the future; and from a societal point of view, that is not a very worrisome prospect, because by hypothesis what he attempted to do is perfectly legal.

3. CONSPIRACY

The General Principles and Section 465

As is the case with the crimes of counselling and attempt, the *raison d'être* of the offence of **conspiracy** is the prevention of crime. As Justices Cory and Iacobucci noted in their judgment in the Supreme Court of Canada's decision in the United *States v. Dynar* case (1997):

> [T]he rationale for punishing conspirators coincides with the rationale for punishing persons for attempted crimes. Not only is the offence itself seen to be harmful to society, but it is clearly in society's best interests to make it possible for law enforcement officials to intervene before the harm occurs that would be occasioned by a successful conspiracy or, if the conspiracy is incapable of completion, by a subsequent and more successful conspiracy to commit a similar offence.

Police authorities generally regard the offence of conspiracy as an absolutely vital weapon for fighting organized crime, and certainly a considerable number of convictions of individuals involved in organized crime are obtained primarily as a result of proving conspiracies through "wiretap" evidence. However, conspiracy is an offence that is viewed with extreme suspicion by civil libertarians, owing to its vague parameters. Furthermore, the power to charge an accused person with conspiracy is believed to place an unfair advantage in the hands of the Crown; indeed, the offence is sometimes referred to as "the darling in the prosecutor's nursery." Some of the trepidation experienced by civil libertarians when analyzing the nature of conspiracy is reflected in the following passage from Justice Dickson's judgment in the Supreme Court of Canada's decision in the case of *Cotroni and Papalia* (1979):

> Conspiracy is an inchoate or preliminary crime, dating from the time of Edward I, but much refined in the Court of Star Chamber in the 17th Century. Notwithstanding its antiquity, the law of conspiracy is still uncertain. It can, however, be said that the indictment for conspiracy is a formidable weapon in the armory of the prosecutor. According to the cases, it permits a vague definition of the offence, broader standards of admissibility of evidence apply; it may provide the solution to prosecutorial problems as to situs and jurisdiction. ... But the very looseness generally allowed for specifying the offence, for receiving proof, and generally in the conduct of the trial, imposes upon a trial Judge an added duty to ensure against the possibility of improper transference of guilt from one accused to another. There is, I have no doubt, a subconscious tendency upon the part of jurors in a conspiracy case to regard all co-conspirators alike and ignore the fact that guilt is something individual and personal.

The *Criminal Code* provision dealing with conspiracy is section 465, which basically sets out the punishments for conspiracies involving different types of criminal offence but does not define the critical elements of a conspiracy (the penalties are set out in Figure 7.4 It will be necessary to close as "Figure 7.4).").

It is particularly significant that, in general, the penalties for conspiracy are considerably harsher than is the case for criminal attempts. Indeed, the penalties for conspiracy in relation to an indictable offence are normally identical to those imposed where the complete offence has actually been committed; however, in the case of criminal attempts, the penalties for attempting to commit indictable offences are (normally) only one-half of those that may be imposed for committing the complete offence (section 463 of the *Code*). In *United States v. Dynar* (1997), the

Supreme Court of Canada indicated why Parliament has treated conspiracy as constituting such a serious threat to social order. Indeed, Justices Cory and Iacobucci stated that:

> The crime has a long and malevolent history. Conspirators have plotted to overthrow monarchs from biblical times through the time of the Plantaganets (sic) and Tudors. Guy Fawkes conspired with others to blow up the parliament buildings. Today conspirators plot with others to carry out terrorist acts, to commit murders or to import forbidden drugs. Society is properly concerned with conspiracies since two or more persons working together can achieve evil results that would be impossible for an individual working alone. For example, it usually takes two or more conspirators to manufacture and secrete explosives or to arrange for the purchase, importation and sale of heroin. The very fact that several persons in combination agree to do something has for many years been considered to constitute "a menace to society." ... In fact, the scale of injury that might be caused to the fabric of society can be far greater when two or more persons conspire to commit a crime than when an individual sets out alone to do an unlawful act.

The function of the *Criminal Code* provisions concerning conspiracy is, therefore, to prevent conspirators from putting their unlawful plans into execution, that is, to intervene and punish those involved before any serious harm is caused to society. Furthermore, according to Justices Cory and Iacobucci, the severe penalties are necessary to deter the accused persons from repeating their conduct in the future. Curiously, the *Code* does not provide any statutory definition of the elements of conspiracy. As a consequence, Canadian courts have adopted the traditional common law requirements formulated by the English courts. For example, Justice Taschereau, in delivering the judgment of the majority of the Supreme Court of Canada in the case of *O'Brien* (1954), adopted the following definition of conspiracy, which had been fashioned by Justice Willes in the old English case of *Mulcahy* (1868):

> A conspiracy consists not merely in the intention of two or more, but in the agreement of two or more to do an unlawful act, or to do a lawful act by unlawful means. So long as such a design rests in intention only, it is not indictable. When two agree to carry it into effect, the very plot is an action itself, and the act of each of the parties ... punishable if for a criminal object.

In essence, this definition requires *an agreement between two or more persons to commit a crime.* In the decision of the Supreme Court of Canada in the *Dynar* case (1997), Justices Cory and Iacobucci pointed out that the Crown must prove "an intention to agree, the completion of an agreement, and a common design."

What are the *actus reus* and *mens rea* elements of conspiracy? The *actus reus* is the act of agreement, while the requisite *mens rea* is to be found in the intention to enter into an agreement to commit one or more crimes and the intention to carry out the objective of the agreement. The *actus reus* is complete as soon as agreement is reached between the parties. It, therefore, does not matter that no steps are subsequently taken to carry out the objective of the agreement; the parties are guilty of conspiracy just as soon as the agreement is reached with the necessary *mens rea*.

In the case of *F. (J.)* (2013), the Supreme Court of Canada emphasized the fact that the *actus reus* of a conspiracy is the making of an agreement and not any act or acts done in pursuit of its objective. Justice Moldaver, in delivering the judgment of the Court, specifically approved the following statement to this effect:

> The *actus reus* of the crime of conspiracy lies in the formation of an agreement, tacit or express, between two or more individuals, to act together in pursuit of a mutual criminal objective. Co-conspirators share a common goal borne out of a meeting of the minds whereby each agrees to act together with the other to achieve a common goal.

For the purpose of analysis, it may be useful to analyze the offence of conspiracy in terms of three separate elements:

1. an agreement for a common purpose;
2. an agreement between at least two persons; and
3. an agreement to commit a crime.

Element 1: Agreement for a Common Purpose

The necessity of establishing the element of an agreement for a common purpose is well illustrated by the leading Canadian case of *Cotroni and Papalia* (1979). As Justice Dickson of the Supreme Court of Canada suggested, "the facts of the case are bizarre." Cotroni and Papalia were tried in Toronto on a charge that they, together with two men named Swartz and Violi, "unlawfully did conspire together each with the other and with persons unknown to have possession of $300 000, more or less, knowing that the said

$300 000 was obtained by the commission in Canada of the indictable offence of extortion" (also known as blackmail to the layperson). The Crown contended that Swartz and Papalia extracted some $300 000 from Bader and from Rosen (a friend of Bader's in Toronto). The money was paid in response to Swartz's story that Bader would be killed if he did not come up with the cash. Swartz indicated that the threats to Bader's life emanated from Montreal. Both Bader and Rosen believed Swartz's story implicitly. Approximately one year later, two residents of Montreal, Cotroni and Violi, came to believe that their names had been used to extort the $300 000 from Bader. They therefore telephoned Papalia and demanded the **extortion** money for themselves. Papalia indicated that he had received only $40 000 and suggested that they "beat up" Swartz to obtain the rest. Violi told Papalia that this information "[is] gonna save your life."

It was eventually agreed that Violi would come to Toronto to relieve Swartz of the money. The planned meeting in Toronto never took place. Cotroni, Papalia, Swartz, and Violi were all convicted of conspiracy. They appealed to the Ontario Court of Appeal. The appeals of Swartz and Papalia were dismissed, but the appeals of Cotroni and Violi were allowed. The Crown appealed Cotroni's acquittal (Violi having died in the interim period) to the Supreme Court of Canada, and Papalia appealed against the dismissal of his appeal.

The Supreme Court upheld the judgment of the Court of Appeal and dismissed the appeals of both the Crown and Papalia. Justice Dickson pointed out that there was no evidence of any "common agreement" or "common object" among Cotroni, Violi, Papalia, and Swartz. In his view, the evidence established the existence of two separate conspiracies. The first conspiracy involved Papalia and Swartz; its purpose was to have possession of the extorted money. The second conspiracy involved Cotroni and Violi and, possibly, Papalia; its purpose was to obtain, and subsequently to have possession of, a portion of the same money. Justice Dickson also pointed out that the second conspiracy took place solely within Quebec, and therefore the province of Ontario had no jurisdiction in relation to it. Justice Dickson proceeded to conclude that "this is not the conspiracy described in the indictment." He ruled that Papalia was properly convicted of the conspiracy with Swartz. However, he determined that "the only evidence against Cotroni is in respect of a conspiracy not covered by the indictment."

Justice Dickson's judgment casts considerable light on the requirement that there be an agreement for a common purpose:

> The word "conspire" derives from two Latin words, "con" and "spirare," meaning "to breathe together." To conspire is to agree. *The essence of criminal conspiracy is proof of agreement.* On a charge of conspiracy the agreement itself is the gist of the offence. ... The *actus reus* is the fact of agreement. ... *The important inquiry is not as to the acts done in pursuance of the agreement, but whether there was, in fact, a common agreement to which the acts are referable and to which all of the alleged offenders were privy.* ... There must be evidence that the alleged conspirators acted in concert in pursuit of a common goal. ... [I]n order to have a conspiracy, one must have agreement between the co-conspirators. There was simply no evidence of agreement between the four alleged conspirators ... . A common desire to have money cannot create a conspiracy in the absence of a meeting of minds. The facts here show two competing and mutually exclusive objects. Counsel suggested the analogy of four hungry dogs, fighting over a bone. [emphasis added]

Similarly, in *Nicholson* (2018), the Saskatchewan Court of Appeal set aside the convictions of two individuals (Nicholson and Vey) charged with conspiracy to murder their spouses. Vey claimed that he knew that the conversation that he was sharing with Nicholson was being recorded and that he was only pretending to go along with the murder plot to "get back at his wife." In ordering a new trial, the Court of Appeal ruled that the trial judge had not made clear to the jury that they had to be satisfied beyond a reasonable doubt that both accused had a "genuine intention to agree to commit murder." Justice Jackson stated that:

> The crime of conspiracy seeks to prevent the harm caused when two or more people agree to act together to achieve a common unlawful purpose. The Crown must prove both a genuine intention to agree and an intention to achieve the common unlawful purpose beyond a reasonable doubt. There must be a true consensus.

The courts have held that although there must be a "common object" or "common agreement" in order to establish a conspiracy, it is not necessary for the Crown to establish that there is any direct communication between the co-conspirators. For this reason, it is possible to impose criminal liability for participation in so-called "chain" and "wheel" conspiracies. In a "chain" conspiracy, defendant A is in contact with defendant B, B with C, C with

D, and so on. In a "wheel" conspiracy, one or more defendants communicate with each of the other conspirators, thus serving as the "hub" of the conspiracy.

A significant question that may be raised in cases involving the sale and purchase of drugs is whether entering into this transaction also constitutes a conspiracy to traffic in these drugs. If so, a purchaser of drugs may be open to charges not only of possession but also for conspiracy to traffic (which carries a much higher maximum penalty). When large quantities of drugs are sold, a court may well conclude that the parties involved in such large-scale transactions do indeed intend to participate in a broad conspiracy to distribute drugs; in other words, they form a common objective that goes far beyond the confines of the simple sale of the drugs by one party to another.

Take, for example, the case of *Chaulk and DiCristo* (1991), in which the accused had been charged with conspiracy to traffic in a narcotic drug (namely, cannabis resin). Chaulk had picked up at least one package containing cannabis resin from an air cargo depot in the Wabush–Labrador City area. He had also sent at least two packages containing $9000 each to DiCristo in Montreal. Defence counsel raised the argument that a single transaction involving the sale of a drug could not support the conclusion that Chaulk and DiCristo formed the mutual objective to traffic in that drug. However, this contention was rejected at their trial and they were convicted. Their appeal to the Newfoundland Court of Appeal was subsequently dismissed. As Justice Marshall noted:

> Whether or not a single transaction forms the basis of a common design to traffic will depend upon whether the compact pursuant to which the transaction was undertaken is found to transcend beyond a mere agreement of purchase and sale between the dealer and buyer to one establishing an intention by both parties for resale. The scope to be attributed to such an agreement depends upon the individual circumstances.

The Cotroni and Papalia *case (1979): There was no meeting of the minds and no common objective. Instead, the parties involved were like four hungry dogs fighting for the same bone.*

Clearly, a critically important circumstance in this respect is the quantity of drugs involved. In the case of *Chaulk and DiCristo*, the amount of drugs contained in the package was quite inconsistent with the possession for the purpose of purely personal use and, therefore, the inference could be drawn that it was intended for resale. On this basis, the Court of Appeal concluded that "the scope of the agreement of sale and purchase extends beyond transaction between the appellants and extends it to a conspiracy to traffic in the prohibited substance."

Where accused persons are alleged to have joined a *pre-existing conspiracy*, they may not be convicted of the crime of conspiracy unless the Crown can prove that they *adopted the criminal plan as their own and consented to participate in carrying it out*. Merely knowing about the existence of a conspiracy does not render one criminally liable. Take, for example, the case of *Gopie* (2017). The accused was charged with conspiracy to import a narcotic. Ernest Wilson and Tara Fraser agreed to import drugs from St. Maarten, with Fraser acting as the courier. Gopie was present at two meetings between Wilson and Fraser and he was in the car when Wilson handed Fraser $200 for spending money while she was in St. Maarten. Gopie, Wilson, and two other men went to meet Fraser at the Montreal airport when she returned from St. Maarten. However, her luggage had mistakenly been sent to Toronto, where it had been opened by customs officials who discovered it contained cocaine. Gopie later went to the Toronto airport with Fraser and others to retrieve the lost luggage. Gopie waited outside while Fraser went inside, where she was apprehended by the RCMP. Gopie was then arrested in the airport car park.

At his trial, Gopie was convicted of conspiracy to import narcotics. His appeal to the Ontario Court of Appeal was rejected. One of the critical issues at trial was whether Gopie had become part of the conspiracy that had been created by the agreement between Wilson and Fraser to import cocaine. In the Court of Appeal, Justice Gillese stated that the trial judge had correctly instructed the jury on the requirements for convicting Gopie as a member of that conspiracy. The trial judge had emphasized that the Crown had an obligation to prove beyond a reasonable doubt that (1) there was a conspiracy among two or more persons; (2) the conspiracy was to import a narcotic into Canada; and (3) Gopie was a member of that conspiracy. In light of Fraser's own testimony, Justice Gillese noted that the jury could not have had a reasonable doubt as to the existence of a conspiracy between her and Wilson to import cocaine. Therefore, the issue was whether Gopie had joined that conspiracy. At trial, he had argued that the evidence against him was purely circumstantial and that his presence in Montreal was consistent with a simple desire to party there with friends.

Justice Gillese agreed with the trial judge's jury instructions. The trial judge had told the jury that, to convict an individual as a member of a conspiracy, the Crown must prove that they understood the unlawful nature of the plan and "voluntarily and intentionally" made a decision to join it. Furthermore, according to Justice Gillese:

> [The trial judge] stated that, in any case, the person must "actually agree and intend to agree to achieve the common unlawful purpose." He stressed that "mere knowledge" of the common unlawful purpose did not make a person a member of a conspiracy and that "merely being present when something happens, merely acting in the same way as others, or merely associating with others who are said to be members of a conspiracy does not prove that a person has joined in the agreement with knowledge of its nature and purpose."

Justice Gillese concluded that the trial judge had given the jury "the tools it needed" to decide whether Gopie should be considered a member of the conspiracy. Given the various meetings between Gopie, Wilson, and Fraser, and Gopie's active assistance in seeking to retrieve Fraser's luggage both in Montreal and Toronto, the jury evidently were satisfied beyond a reasonable doubt that Gopie was indeed a member of the conspiracy to import cocaine. He was fully aware of the unlawful object of the agreement between Wilson and Fraser, adopted their plan as his own, and willingly consented to being part of it.

In the *O'Brien* case (1954), the Supreme Court of Canada ruled that, in addition to a common agreement or common intention, the Crown must prove that there was "*an intention to put the common design into effect*." In other words, if a party to an alleged agreement does not intend to carry out the common object, that party cannot be convicted of conspiracy. In the *O'Brien* case, the accused was charged with having unlawfully conspired with Tulley to commit the indictable offence of kidnapping. Tulley was not charged and was called as a Crown witness at O'Brien's trial. Tulley testified that he had met with the accused on a number of occasions and that, for the sum of $500, he had agreed to assist O'Brien in the kidnapping of Mrs. Pritchard. Tulley also testified that he received $240 from O'Brien and that the accused had pointed out both the target and her residence to him. However, Tulley insisted that he "never had any intention of going through with this plan, but was just fooling the respondent, or hoaxing him." Tulley then indicated that he had both informed Pritchard of O'Brien's intentions and denounced the scheme to the police. O'Brien was convicted at trial, but his appeal to the British Columbia Court of Appeal was successful and a new trial was ordered. The Crown appealed this ruling to the Supreme Court of Canada, which affirmed the decision of the Court of Appeal.

O'Brien's counsel contended that if Tulley never intended to carry out the agreement to kidnap Pritchard, he could not have been a party to a conspiracy. Since there were no other parties involved, O'Brien must be acquitted because he could not conspire with himself. The Supreme Court of Canada essentially accepted this contention. In the words of Justice Taschereau, who delivered the judgment of the majority of the Court:

> It is, of course, essential that the conspirators have the intention to agree, and this agreement must be complete. There must also be a common design to do something unlawful, or something lawful by illegal means. Although it is not necessary that there should be an overt action in furtherance of the conspiracy, to complete the crime, I have no doubt that *there must exist an intention to put the common design into effect*. A common design necessarily involves an intention. Both are synonymous. The intention cannot be anything else but the will to attain the object of the agreement. I cannot imagine several conspirators agreeing to defraud, to restrain trade, or to commit any indictable offence, without having the intention to reach the common goal.

In the O'Brien's case, there was only one other potential co-conspirator (namely, Tulley), and once it was established that he did not have the intention to put the agreement into effect, it was clear that the accused could not be convicted of the offence charged because it takes at least two parties to hatch a conspiracy. However, as long as at least two parties to an alleged conspiracy do indeed have the intention to carry out the agreement, it does not matter that various other alleged co-conspirators lack such intent. As Justice Lambert of the British Columbia Court of Appeal said in the case of *Miller* (1984):

> [T]he lack of intent of two of the co-conspirators, even if established, does not afford any defence to the other conspirators who have the requisite intent, unless the number of conspirators who have the requisite intent is reduced to one person. At that stage he cannot agree with himself and would be acquitted.

On the other hand, it is important to bear in mind that the courts will normally assume that an accused person who has entered into an agreement to commit an offence does, in fact, intend to carry it out. As the Supreme Court of Canada noted in the *Nova Scotia Pharmaceutical Society* case (1992):

> [T]he Crown must prove that the accused had the intention to enter into the agreement and had knowledge of the terms of that agreement. Once that is established, it would ordinarily be reasonable to draw the inference that the accused intended to carry out the terms in the agreement, unless there was evidence that the accused did not intend to carry out the terms of the agreement.

Illustration by Greg Holoboff

It Takes Two to Tango: There must be at least two eligible conspirators to create a criminal conspiracy.

Becoming a Party to a Conspiracy under Sections 21(1)(a) and (b) and 22(1)

Under subsections 21(1)(b) and (c) of the *Criminal Code*, it is possible to become a party to a conspiracy on the basis of *aiding and/or abetting* the development of the agreement that forms the basis of such a criminal plot. In the case of *F. (J.)* (2013), the Supreme Court of Canada affirmed this view:

> The aiding and abetting of a conspiracy is an offence known to Canadian law. The offence is made out where the accused aids or abets the *actus reus* of conspiracy, namely the *act of agreeing*.

However, the Supreme Court emphasized that becoming a party to a conspiracy by virtue of aiding/abetting the conspirators is strictly limited to acts that assist and/or encourage the act of agreeing:

> Party liability to a conspiracy is limited to cases where the accused encourages or assists in the initial formation of the agreement, or where he encourages or assists new members to join a pre-existing agreement.

In *F. (J.)*, the accused learned from one of two young women that they intended to kill their mother by first drugging and then drowning her in the bathtub. Their strategy was to make this incident look like an accident. The accused gave advice to the two young women with respect to how their plan might be implemented successfully, and he also supplied them with Tylenol 3 tablets that were used along with alcohol to render the victim unconscious. The criminal plot was carried out and the victim was drowned in the bathtub. The trial judge instructed the members of the jury that they could find the accused guilty of conspiracy either as a party (aiding/abetting under sections 21(1)(b) and (c)) or as a principal [under section 21(1)(a)]. The accused was convicted of conspiracy to commit murder and the Supreme Court of Canada ultimately upheld the conviction.

The Supreme Court ruled that the evidence was overwhelming that the accused was a principal (he was a member of the conspiracy) and the trial judge should not have told the jury to consider his liability as a party by virtue of aiding and abetting. The accused did not encourage or assist in the initial formation of the agreement, nor did he assist or encourage other parties to join the preexisting agreement. However, since the accused would undoubtedly have been convicted as a principal, under section 21(1)(a), even if the trial judge had not mentioned liability on the basis of aiding/abetting, the

Court did not set aside the verdict of guilty of conspiracy to commit murder.[8]

An individual may also become a party to a conspiracy by virtue of *counselling* other persons to join a conspiracy [section 22(1) of the *Code*]. For example, in *Bérubé* (1999), the Quebec Court of Appeal held that it is "well-established in jurisprudence that one can be found guilty of conspiracy to commit an indictable offence by encouraging someone to become a member of the conspiracy."

Element 2: Agreement between at Least Two Persons

It is a common-sense proposition that, since an agreement constitutes the essence of a conspiracy, there must be at least two parties. As the Supreme Court of Canada ruled in *O'Brien* (1954), an accused person cannot be convicted of conspiring with themselves. In Canadian criminal law, one of the consequences of this requirement is that a husband cannot be convicted of conspiracy with his wife and *vice versa*.

In the case of *Kowbel* (1953), the Supreme Court of Canada justified this rule on the basis that, historically, spouses have been treated, for the purpose of the law, as "one person." However, it is important to remember that this rule applies only in the situation where the husband and wife are the sole alleged co-conspirators. They can jointly or separately conspire with other individuals within one overall conspiracy and be convicted of the offence.

For example, in *Barbeau* (1996), the accused and her husband were charged, along with three men, of the offence of conspiracy to import cocaine. Both Barbeau and her husband could be convicted of this conspiracy if the Crown proved that each of them had intended to conspire with the three other men. However, Barbeau stated that all she had done was to give—and transcribe—messages by phone and fax because her husband's grasp of English was poor. She said that she had no knowledge of any conspiracy and that she thought the messages related to contraband cigarettes, not cocaine. Although there was no evidence that the accused had met or conspired with the other alleged co-conspirators or that she had agreed with anyone to join a conspiracy, the Crown took the position that she "knew that her husband was involved with others in a conspiracy to import cocaine and that she participated in it by her own acts in furtherance of the object of the conspiracy."

Barbeau was convicted at her trial, but the Quebec Court of Appeal subsequently set aside the conviction and ordered a new trial. The trial judge had instructed the members of the jury that they could find the accused guilty of conspiracy if she had been "wilfully blind" as to the existence and nature of the conspiracy that allegedly involved her husband. In so doing, the trial judge left the impression that the test for *wilful blindness* is an *objective* one—namely, would a *reasonable* person have asked questions in the particular set of circumstances facing the accused? In delivering the judgment of the Court of Appeal, Justice Rothman emphasized that wilful blindness is a form of *subjective*, not *objective*, *mens rea* and that, therefore, it was a serious error for the trial judge to have instructed the jury to consider what a "normal" person would have done in light of the knowledge that Barbeau had of the whole situation:

> The test was not whether the appellant "should" have known or should "normally" have known from the suspicious circumstances that her husband was probably involved in a conspiracy to import cocaine. The question was whether the circumstances were such that she, herself, was in fact, suspicious that this was the case but deliberately refrained from making inquiries so that she could remain in ignorance as to the truth.

Another implication of the "two parties" requirement is that where an undercover police officer or ***agent provocateur*** makes an agreement with *only one other party*, there can be no conspiracy since, as the *O'Brien* case illustrates, the officer or *agent provocateur* will not have the intention to put the common design into effect. In the case of *Root* (2008), the Ontario Court of Appeal referred to a police officer operating in such circumstances as a "counterfeit conspirator"—"not someone with whom the [accused], for that matter anybody else, could conspire as a matter of law." Of course, it is possible that an accused person who is seeking to conspire with an undercover police officer could be convicted, instead, of counselling an offence.

Element 3: Agreement to Commit a Crime

Section 465 of the *Criminal Code* clearly stipulates that it is necessary for the Crown to prove that there was an agreement to commit a crime. More specifically, subsection 465(1)(c) provides that it is an indictable offence to conspire to commit an indictable offence

8. The Court pointed out that, in light of the assistance given by the accused to the sisters and the ensuing death of the victim, he could have been convicted of first-degree murder.

(other than murder)[9] and subsection 465(1)(d) provides that it constitutes a summary conviction offence to conspire to commit a summary conviction offence. However, it is not entirely clear whether it should be possible for the Crown to prosecute individuals for conspiracy to commit absolutely any summary conviction offence that may arise under either federal or provincial/territorial legislation. Many provincial/territorial summary conviction offences might be considered very minor in nature, and it might well be contended that it does not constitute sound policy to charge individuals with a conspiracy to commit a relatively trivial offence, such as jaywalking. On the other hand, section 465(1)(d) does make it clear that a conspiracy to commit a summary conviction offence is itself a summary conviction offence, carrying a relatively lenient maximum penalty.

To obtain a conviction of conspiracy, the Crown must prove that the parties intended to commit a crime that is known to Canadian criminal law. This is the same principle that was discussed earlier in this chapter in relation to the crime of attempt: one cannot either attempt or conspire to commit an imaginary crime. The Supreme Court of Canada firmly underscored this point in the *Dynar* case (1997). As Justices Cory and Iacobucci stated, planning to commit imaginary crimes falls outside the scope of the law: "conspiracy to commit such fanciful offences cannot give rise to criminal liability." However, if the accused do conspire to commit an offence known to the law, then it is irrelevant that, for some reason, it would have been impossible for them to complete the offence. In this respect, the law of conspiracy is identical to the law of criminal attempts. As the Supreme Court of Canada ruled in the *United States v. Dynar* case, the rationale for punishing those who conspire to commit a crime is to punish them *before* their combined efforts cause harm to society. Furthermore, according to Justices Cory and Iacobucci:

> [S]ince the offence of conspiracy only requires an intention to commit the substantive offence, and not the commission of the offence itself, it does not matter that, from an objective point of view, commission of the offence may be impossible. It is the subjective point of view that is important, and from a subjective perspective, conspirators who intend to commit an indictable offence intend to do everything necessary to satisfy the conditions of the offence. The fact that they cannot do so because an objective circumstance is not as they believe it to be does not in any way affect this intention. The intention of the conspirators remains the same, regardless of the absence of the circumstance that would make the realization of that intention possible. It is only in retrospect that the impossibility of accomplishing the design becomes apparent.

It will be remembered that, in the *Dynar* case, the accused would not have been able to complete the offence of money laundering because the funds that he believed were the fruits of crime were actually funds belonging to the United States government. Since the offence, at that time, required proof of *knowledge* that these funds were the proceeds of crime, Dynar could not be convicted of the completed offence of money laundering: he could not "know" something that was, in fact, false. However, as we have already seen, the Supreme Court had no difficulty in stating that Dynar could have been convicted of *attempting* to launder illicitly obtained money, and the very same logic was robustly applied to the offence of conspiracy to carry out this criminal intention.

Can There Be an Attempt to Conspire?

It is an intriguing question whether Canadian criminal law recognizes the existence of an offence of attempting to conspire. In the case of *Déry* (2006), the Supreme Court of Canada unequivocally answered this question in the negative. Déry and Savard had discussed the possibility of stealing some liquor that was being temporarily stored outdoors in some trailers. Their conversations were unexpectedly intercepted in the course of an unrelated police investigation, and, on the basis of these intercepted conversations, Déry and Savard were both charged with conspiracy to commit theft and conspiracy to possess stolen goods. The trial judge acquitted them of the conspiracy charges because it had not been established that they had formed a common intention to steal and possess the liquor. However, instead, the trial judge convicted Déry and Savard of *attempting* to conspire because, in his view, they had gone beyond mere preparation to commit a conspiracy. Déry appealed to the Quebec Court of Appeal, which upheld the convictions, but the Supreme Court of Canada unanimously allowed Déry's appeal and entered acquittals.

In delivering the judgment of the Supreme Court, Justice Fish emphasized that "attempting to conspire to commit a substance offence" had never previously been recognized in Canadian criminal law and that

9. Attempted murder is dealt with under s. 465(1)(a).

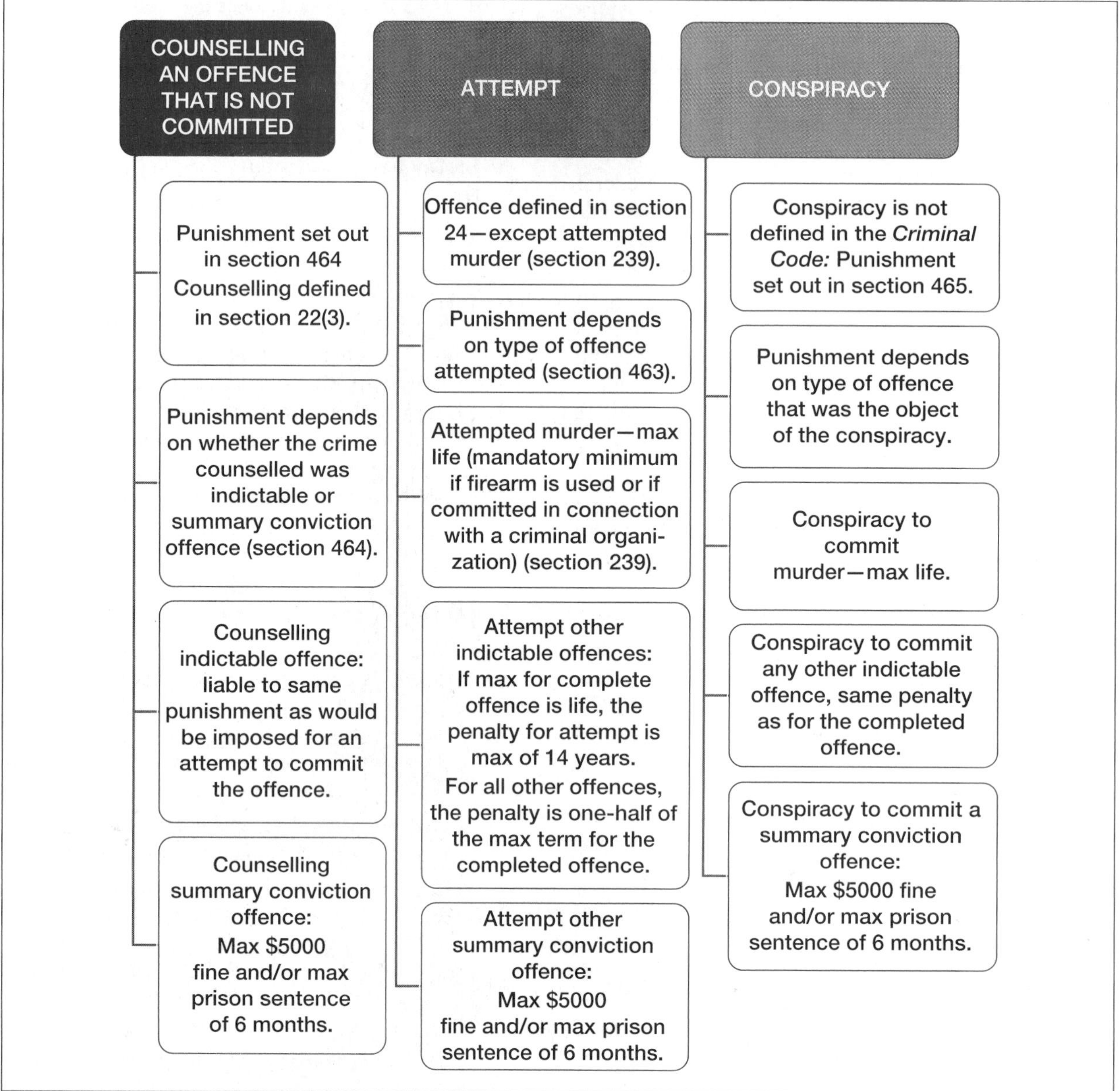

COUNSELLING AN OFFENCE THAT IS NOT COMMITTED
Punishment set out in section 464 Counselling defined in section 22(3).
Punishment depends on whether the crime counselled was indictable or summary conviction offence (section 464).
Counselling indictable offence: liable to same punishment as would be imposed for an attempt to commit the offence.
Counselling summary conviction offence: Max $5000 fine and/or max prison sentence of 6 months.
ATTEMPT
Offence defined in section 24—except attempted murder (section 239).
Punishment depends on type of offence attempted (section 463).
Attempted murder—max life (mandatory minimum if firearm is used or if committed in connection with a criminal organization) (section 239).
Attempt other indictable offences: If max for complete offence is life, the penalty for attempt is max of 14 years. For all other offences, the penalty is one-half of the max term for the completed offence.
Attempt other summary conviction offence: Max $5000 fine and/or max prison sentence of 6 months.
CONSPIRACY
Conspiracy is not defined in the Criminal Code: Punishment set out in section 465.
Punishment depends on type of offence that was the object of the conspiracy.
Conspiracy to commit murder—max life.
Conspiracy to commit any other indictable offence, same penalty as for the completed offence.
Conspiracy to commit a summary conviction offence: Max $5000 fine and/or max prison sentence of 6 months.

***Figure* 7-4**

Overview of the Inchoate Offences

the Court had no intention of doing so at the present time. In the view of the Supreme Court:

> By its very nature … an agreement to commit a crime in concert with others enhances the risk of its commission. Early intervention through the criminalization of conspiracy is therefore both principled and practical.
>
> Likewise, the criminalization of attempt is warranted because its purpose is to prevent harm by punishing behaviour that demonstrates a substantial risk of harm. When applied to conspiracy, the justification for criminalizing attempt is lost, since an attempt to conspire amounts, at best, to a risk that a risk will materialize.
>
> Finally, though Mr. Déry discussed a crime hoping eventually to commit it with others, neither he nor they committed, or even agreed to commit, the crimes they had discussed. The criminal law does not punish bad thoughts of this sort that were abandoned before an agreement was reached, or an attempt made, to act upon them.

Study Questions

1. Bucket, a uniformed police officer, is attempting to arrest Snawley for impaired driving. When Bucket informs Snawley of his intention to arrest him, Snawley starts to strike Bucket with his fists. Cuttle is a bystander who sees the attack by Snawley on Bucket but does absolutely nothing to stop it. Cuttle does, however, yell, "Yippee!" three or four times before Bucket is able to restrain Snawley and place handcuffs on Snawley's wrists. Snawley is convicted of assaulting a police officer in the execution of his duty [section 270(1)(a) of the *Criminal Code*]. Could Cuttle also be convicted of this offence? Bucket will testify that he believes that Snawley understood Cuttle's use of the exclamation "Yippee!" to constitute a form of encouragement for Snawley to continue his attack on Bucket. Would it make a difference to your answer if Bucket had requested assistance from Cuttle in order to make the arrest of Snawley?
2. Magwitch, Merdle, and Murdstone make an agreement to kidnap Guppy, who is the heir to a vast fortune. The three men watch Guppy's movements for a couple of days and Magwitch (the ringleader) then pays Merdle and Murdstone $50 each "for services rendered." Murdstone then exposes the kidnapping plot to the police. He claims that he never really meant to take part in this plan but went along with it only as a means of "learning enough to protect Guppy." Magwitch, Merdle, and Murdstone are charged with conspiracy to kidnap Guppy. Are any (or all) of the co-accused guilty of the offence charged?
3. Perker and Fang decide to rob a store, which is owned by Tulkinghorn. Fang is known to be a very violent person. Perker acts as the lookout while Fang is in the store. However, Perker, who is becoming very fearful, decides to abandon the robbery and runs away before Fang has completed his task in the store. Meanwhile, Fang discovers that Tulkinghorn is surprisingly unwilling to part with the money in his cash register. Fang fatally stabs him and flees the scene, taking some $500 in cash with him. Fang is subsequently killed in a car accident as he tries to make good his escape. However, Perker is later arrested by the police and Crown counsel is wondering whether charges should be laid against him. What charges, if any, could reasonably be laid against Perker?
4. Nubbles and Rudge decide to rob the Tight Fist Bank. They make elaborate plans and purchase some firearms to assist them in their venture. On the appointed day, they drive to a street corner just one block away from the bank; they intend to observe the bank for a while and then undertake the robbery at the most appropriate moment. However, a police cruiser passes by and the two officers notice that Nubbles and Rudge look suspicious. The officers arrest the would-be bandits when they find two sawed-off shotguns and two masks on the back seat of the car. Nubbles and Rudge are subsequently charged with attempted robbery. Are they guilty of this offence?
5. Lancelot decides to steal a valuable diamond ring from Arthur. He goes to Arthur's house and tries to obtain entry by inserting a credit card into the lock on the front door. He is unable to open the door and returns to a bar, where he drowns his sorrows in whiskey. Guinevere, Lancelot's close friend, is disappointed when she discovers that he has failed to fulfill his criminal mission. She therefore travels to Arthur's house, where she manages to obtain entrance by using a set of skeleton keys. However, when she looks in the box in which Arthur usually keeps the ring, she discovers that it is empty. Arthur has taken the ring to a local jeweller for repairs. Merlin, who lives in the basement of Arthur's house, tells the police that he saw exactly what Lancelot and Guinevere had done and that he had heard them talk, on previous occasions, about stealing Arthur's ring. What charges, if any, could reasonably be laid against Lancelot and Guinevere?
6. Madame Mantalini believes that it is an offence to bring a certain type of computer chip into Canada without declaring it (and paying any duty). She arrives at an international airport in Canada, having concealed a large number of the tiny computer chips at the bottom of her suitcase. She attempts to pass through Canada Customs without declaring her hidden cargo. When her luggage is searched, the chips are discovered by a vigilant customs officer. However, the officer informs Mantalini that, owing

to the recent signing of a free trade agreement, this particular type of computer chip can now be imported into Canada without the need to pay any duty. Is Mantalini guilty of a criminal offence? Would it make any difference to your answer if Mantalini had agreed with her partner, Alfred, to smuggle the computer chips on a joint basis?

7. Crisparkle, Dedlock, and Evremonde reach an agreement to rob a bank. They decide that Dedlock should obtain the necessary transportation and drive Crisparkle and Evremonde to and from the bank. Dedlock enters an underground garage and breaks into a powerful sport utility vehicle. Unfortunately, Fezziwig, the owner of the vehicle, sees what is happening and attempts to prevent Dedlock from driving away. Dedlock panics and runs over Fezziwig, killing him instantly. Dedlock is later arrested by the police, and he confesses that he planned to steal the vehicle to use it as a "getaway" vehicle in a bank robbery. Dedlock also tells the police about his agreement with Crisparkle and Evremonde. Crown counsel intends to pursue a charge of second-degree murder against Dedlock. What charges, if any, do you think should be laid against Crisparkle and Evremonde?

8. Wegg has informed a few of his friends that he wishes to hire someone to kill Boffin, who is Wegg's business partner. The local police department is provided with the information that Wegg is searching for a contract killer and Venus, an undercover officer, is assigned the task of contacting Wegg. During a number of telephone calls and a couple of meetings in a bar, Venus repeatedly offers to kill Boffin for $ 10 000, but Wegg is very wary and does not commit himself to any arrangement with Venus. Eventually, Wegg tells Venus. "I accept your offer," and gives Venus information that would help Venus identify Boffin and learn various details about Boffin's everyday activities. However, before Venus has time to reveal his true identity, Wegg says that he has changed his mind and that he does not want Boffin killed after all. At this point, Venus indicates that he is a police officer, informs Wegg of his rights, and places Wegg under arrest. Wegg asserts that Venus was "badgering" him (Wegg) to accept an offer to kill Boffin and that he finally agreed to Venus's proposition because he was feeling harassed by Venus's repeated communications with him. Furthermore, he points to the fact that he quickly changed his mind and told Venus that he had abandoned the idea of killing Boffin. Do you think that a charge of counselling an offence that is not committed (section 464 of the *Criminal Code*) would be successful at Wegg's trial?

9. Blimber and Creakle decide to rob a local bank. They obtain some firearms, some masks, and a copy of the floor plan of the bank that they have chosen as their target. On the day appointed for the robbery, Blimber and Creakle persuade Winkel to drive them to the bank in a stolen vehicle. However, the vehicle breaks down about five blocks from the bank in question. Two police officers notice that Blimber, Creakle, and Winkel are behaving suspiciously and quickly ascertain that their vehicle has been reported stolen. After arresting Blimber, Creakle, and Winkel, the officers discover the firearms, masks, and copy of the floor plan of the bank. Upon further investigation, it is learned that the particular bank that Blimber and Creakle had selected for the robbery had been closed down a week before they were arrested. Indeed, at the time of the arrest, the bank building was empty. Do you think that a charge of attempted robbery would succeed at the trial of Blimber, Creakle, and Winkel?

10. Gradgrind and Krook meet in a bar. Gradgrind tells Krook that he has recently been released from prison and that he is looking for interesting work. Krook suggests that they kidnap Casby, a wealthy stockbroker, and demand a ransom. Krook later invites Gradgrind to his apartment and introduces him to Frank and Margaretta Milvey, who were recently married. Krook, Gradgrind, and the Milveys develop a plan to kidnap Casby at his residence. Krook gives Gradgrind the sum of $1000 for expenses that he may incur in carrying out his designated tasks in pursuit of the kidnapping plot. However, the next day, police officers arrest Krook and the Milveys and reveal that Gradgrind is actually an undercover police officer. Crown counsel realizes that Gradgrind will testify that he never intended to carry out any part of the kidnapping plot and was merely pretending to agree with Krook and the Milveys to lay the basis for criminal charges to be laid against them. Do you think that charges of conspiracy to kidnap Casby would be successful at the trial of Krook and the Milveys? [Note that the offence of kidnapping is defined in section 279(1) of the *Criminal Code*.]

11. Slammer and Provis were cell mates in a provincial prison. When they were released, they immediately decided to carry out an armed robbery at the Twinkling Trinkets jewellery store. They tell their

friend Chivery about the robbery and ask him to join them in this nefarious enterprise: however, Chivery refuses to do so because he has to take a criminology exam on the day set for the robbery. Nevertheless, Chivery vigorously persuades his associate, Barkis, to participate in the robbery and Barkis gleefully agrees to join Slammer and Provis and play a major role in the robbery. Before the robbery can be launched, Slammer, Provis, and Barkis are arrested by the police, who have been keeping them under close surveillance. Crown Counsel is considering charging Chivery with conspiracy to commit robbery (the same charge that will be laid against Slammer, Provis, and Barkis). Do you think that such a charge against Chivery would result in a conviction, should he be tried in a criminal court?

CHAPTER 8

MENTAL IMPAIRMENT AND CRIMINAL RESPONSIBILITY:

The Defences of "Not Criminally Responsible on Account of Mental Disorder" (NCRMD) and Automatism

Learning Objectives

After reading this chapter, you will understand:

- the difference between fitness to stand trial and the defence of not criminally responsible on account of mental disorder (NCRMD);
- the basic elements of the defence of NCRMD under section 16 of the *Criminal Code* and the interpretation of these elements by the courts;
- the various dispositions of not-criminally-responsible accused persons by *Criminal Code* review boards and the courts;
- the defence of automatism, which is based on a lack of voluntariness, and how this defence differs from the NCRMD defence; and
- the special rules relating to the burden of proof that is applied to the defences of NCRMD and automatism and the distinction between the burden of proof and the so-called "evidential burden" that applies to all defences in criminal trials.

INTRODUCTION

This chapter examines the defences of *not criminally responsible on account of mental disorder* (NCRMD) and *automatism*. Both of these defences apply where an accused person has committed the act or omission that constitutes the basis for the criminal charge laid against them but is found not criminally responsible because of a severe impairment of mental capacity.

In the case of the NCRMD defence, it must be established that the accused person had a mental disorder that deprived them of the capacity to *appreciate* the **nature and quality of the act or omission** or to know that it was morally wrong. An accused person who has been found NCRMD is not acquitted of the charge but is held to be not criminally responsible for their actions and may potentially be held in custody in a psychiatric hospital or supervised in the community if it is considered that they pose a significant threat to the community.

The defence of automatism arises when an accused person acts involuntarily because of some form of temporary impairment of their mental faculties, such as clouded consciousness caused by a blow to the head. The defendant who successfully raises the defence of automatism gains an outright acquittal and may not be subjected to any restrictions on their liberty.

THE ISSUE OF FITNESS TO STAND TRIAL

Before proceeding to a discussion of the defences of NCRMD and automatism, it is necessary to distinguish them from the issue of the accused person's fitness to stand trial. The defences of NCRMD or automatism are concerned with the issue of criminal responsibility and are necessarily focused on the state of mind of the accused person *at the time of the alleged offence*. By way of contrast, the issue of fitness to stand trial is concerned exclusively with the state of mind of the accused person at the time of their trial and with the question of whether or not the accused person has the mental capacity to understand the nature and purpose of the trial proceedings and to communicate with their counsel.

Section 2 of the *Criminal Code* defines "unfit to stand trial" as being

> ... unable on account of mental disorder to conduct a defence at any stage of the proceedings before a verdict is rendered or to instruct counsel to do so, and, in particular, unable on account of mental disorder to
>
> (a) understand the nature or object of the proceedings,
>
> (b) understand the possible consequences of the proceedings, or
>
> (c) communicate with counsel.

The courts have interpreted these criteria in a fairly narrow manner and, therefore, it is generally difficult to establish that an accused person is unfit to stand trial. As Justice Sopinka stated, in delivering the judgment of the Supreme Court of Canada in *Whittle* (1994), the *Criminal Code* test for unfitness to stand trial "requires limited cognitive capacity to understand the process and to communicate with counsel." Even if the accused person is experiencing delusions at the time of their trial, this does not necessarily mean that the court will find that they are unfit to stand trial. As the Ontario Court of Appeal held in the case of *Taylor* (1992), "the presence of delusions does not vitiate the accused's fitness to stand trial unless the delusion distorts the accused's rudimentary understanding of the judicial process" or prevents them from recounting to their counsel "the necessary facts relating to the offence in such a way that counsel can then properly present a defence."

Most mentally disordered accused persons will be found fit to stand trial because the limited cognitive capacity test consists of criteria that require only a minimal degree of ability to understand the nature and object of the court proceedings and to provide basic information to defence counsel. Indeed, in the case of *Jobb* (2008), Justice Smith, in delivering the judgment of the Saskatchewan Court of Appeal, emphasized the fact that the threshold for being found fit to stand trial is relatively low in Canada:

> *Many accused persons who are found not guilty by reason of a mental disorder are fit to stand trial. The fact that an accused is not criminally responsible within the meaning of s. 16 does not mean that he or she is unfit to stand trial. If the contrary were true there would be little purpose in providing for the plea authorized by s. 16. Most persons who suffered from the mental disorder defined in the section would be exempted from trial and would not get to plead until they had recovered subsequent to the date of the offence.* [Italics in original]

Justice Smith pointed out that there is a fundamental difference between the test for unfitness to stand trial articulated in section 2 and the definition of the NCRMD defence in section 16. A finding of unfitness to stand trial is based on the existence of a mental disorder and is centred on the accused person's capacity to provide instructions to their counsel and to conduct their defence. However, the test requires only a limited cognitive capacity to understand the trial process and to instruct counsel. Therefore, as long as the accused person has this limited capacity, it is not necessary that they be endowed with the capacity to employ analytical reasoning in reaching a decision whether or not to act on the advice of their lawyer or to make a determination about trial tactics that will ultimately serve their own best interests.

If an accused person is found unfit to stand trial, they may be kept in custody in a mental health hospital or may be supervised in the community until fitness to stand trial is restored.[1] In most cases, an accused person will become fit to stand trial after a relatively brief period of treatment.

THE DEFENCE OF NOT CRIMINALLY RESPONSIBLE ON ACCOUNT OF MENTAL DISORDER

As Justice McLachlin said in the Supreme Court of Canada's decision in the *Winko* case (1999), "In every society, there are those who commit criminal acts because of mental illness. The criminal law must find a way to deal with these people fairly, while protecting the public against further harms. The task is not an easy one."

In Canada, this difficult task is primarily undertaken through the application by the courts of the special defence of **not criminally responsible on account of mental disorder (NCRMD)**. Since our system of criminal law is constructed on the premise that individuals should not be convicted of a real crime unless they deliberately chose to do something wrong, the case of the mentally disordered offender clearly raises some fundamental questions about the appropriateness of applying the criminal law to persons who may not be capable of making real choices because of their mental illness. As Justice LeBel, of the Supreme Court of Canada stated, in the *Bouchard-LeBrun* case (2011):

> According to a traditional fundamental principle of the common law, criminal responsibility can result only from the commission of a voluntary act. This important principle is based on a recognition that it would be unfair in a democratic society to impose the consequences and stigma of criminal responsibility on an accused who did not voluntarily commit an act that constitutes a criminal offence. …
>
> A serious mental disorder constitutes an exception to the general criminal law principle that an accused is deemed to be autonomous and rational. A person suffering from a mental disorder within the meaning of s. 16 *Cr. C.* is not considered to be capable of appreciating the nature of his or her acts or understanding that they are inherently wrong. … The person's actions are not actually the product of his or her free will. It is therefore consistent with the principles of fundamental justice for a person whose mental condition at the relevant time is covered by s. 16 *Cr. C.* not to be criminally responsible under Canadian law. Convicting a person who acted involuntarily would undermine the foundations of the criminal law and the integrity of the judicial system.

However, as we shall soon see, the mere fact that an accused person was mentally disordered at the time of the alleged offence does not automatically excuse them from criminal responsibility. Indeed, only a relatively few mentally disordered persons meet the strict criteria for the successful application of the NCRMD defence.

The NCRMD defence is concerned with the state of mind of the accused person *at the time that the alleged offence was actually committed*. If the accused person concerned could not appreciate the nature or quality of the act or omission in question or did not realize it was wrong (in the sense that it would be morally condemned by reasonable members of society), they will be found not criminally responsible. Nevertheless, it is critical to bear in mind that the NCRMD defence is something of a misnomer. Indeed, it is not really a defence in the true sense of the word because, as section 672.1(1) of the *Criminal Code* clearly states, a verdict of NCRMD is not a finding that the accused "didn't do it" but rather a ruling that "the accused committed the act or made the omission that formed the basis of the offence with which the accused is charged but is not criminally responsible on account of mental disorder." Furthermore, although the defendant is found "not criminally responsible," they are not automatically entitled to walk out of the courtroom as a free man or woman; instead, the accused may well be subjected to restraints on their liberty (including the

1. In those rare cases where an accused person is never likely to recover fitness and is not deemed a threat to public safety, a court may grant that person an absolute discharge.

very real possibility of detention in a secure mental health facility). As Justice McLachlin stated in her judgment in the Supreme Court of Canada's decision in the *Winko* case (1999):

> The NCR accused is to be treated in a special way in a system tailored to meet the twin goals of protecting the public and treating the mentally ill offender fairly and appropriately. Under the new approach, the mentally ill offender occupies a special place in the criminal justice system; he or she is spared the full weight of criminal responsibility, but is subject to those restrictions necessary to protect the public.

THE *M'NAGHTEN* RULES

The foundations of the modern NCRMD defence in Canada were actually laid in the famous English case of *M'Naghten* (1843). In 1843, Daniel M'Naghten shot and killed Edward Drummond (the secretary to Sir Robert Peel, the British prime minister of the day). M'Naghten shot at Drummond under the mistaken impression that he was Sir Robert Peel. M'Naghten believed that Peel and members of Peel's political party were responsible for a systematic campaign of persecution against him. M'Naghten was tried on a charge of murder and had the excellent fortune to be defended by the brilliant Queen's Counsel, Alexander Cockburn. At his trial, evidence was presented that M'Naghten was insane at the time of the shooting and he was acquitted by the jury, who brought in a special verdict of insanity. It was generally felt that the test of insanity that had apparently been applied by the jury went considerably beyond the scope of the existing law. It had been argued that, even though M'Naghten's conduct had to a large extent appeared rational, and even though he clearly knew what he was doing and was capable of telling right from wrong, he nevertheless was suffering from a form of insanity that deprived him of all "power of self-control." The jury's verdict seemed to imply that even though M'Naghten knew what he was doing and that it was wrong, he should be acquitted because his delusions of persecution caused him to lose his ability to control his actions. M'Naghten was subsequently confined in hospital until his death in 1865.

Although M'Naghten was kept in strict custody, there was a public outcry against his acquittal. Even Queen Victoria herself indicated that she definitely was "not amused." As a consequence of this negative public reaction, the House of Lords was asked a series of questions concerning the appropriate test of "insanity" that should be presented to a jury in future cases. Their Lordships' answers to the questions constitute what have become known as the *M'Naghten* Rules. The most important statement was as follows:

> We have to submit our opinion that the jurors ought to be told in all cases that every man is presumed to be sane and to possess a sufficient degree of reason to be responsible for his crimes until the contrary be proved to their satisfaction, and that to establish a defence on the ground of insanity it must be clearly proved that, *at the time of the committing of the act the party accused was labouring under such a defect of reason, from disease of the mind, as not to know the nature and quality of the act he was doing, or, if he did know it, that he did not know he was doing what was wrong.* [emphasis added]

It may well be conjectured that Their Lordships felt that M'Naghten should really have been convicted of murder. After all, the somewhat narrow test of insanity they articulated would almost certainly not have been applicable to the specific facts of M'Naghten's case because M'Naghten did indeed appear to know what he was doing and that it was wrong to kill another human being. It is, therefore, one of the supreme ironies of legal history that the test of insanity, which is still applicable in England, Wales, and (in a modified version) in Canada, bears M'Naghten's name.

The debate over the appropriateness of relying on the *M'Naghten* Rules as the basis for determining the criminal responsibility of mentally disordered accused persons has raged for 175 years. The major criticism levelled against the Rules is that they focus almost exclusively on **cognitive** factors (that is, the accused's reasoning abilities) to the apparent exclusion of *emotional* and *volitional* factors. In particular, the Rules have been criticized for not taking into account the proposition that individuals may be perfectly aware of what they are doing and know that it is "morally wrong" but may nevertheless be utterly incapable of controlling their conduct.

THE MODERN NCRMD DEFENCE IN CANADA

Section 16(1) of the Criminal Code

The basic elements of the *M'Naghten* Rules were incorporated into Canada's *Criminal Code* when it was first enacted in 1892. The present-day version of the rules is articulated in section 16(1) of the *Criminal Code*: "No person is criminally responsible for an act committed or an omission made while suffering from a mental disorder that rendered the person incapable of appreciating the nature and quality of the act or omission or of knowing that it was wrong."

Clearly, this provision of the modern *Criminal Code* bears a close resemblance to the *M'Naghten* Rules of 1843. However, some significant differences must be taken into account. Perhaps the most noteworthy variation between the *M'Naghten* Rules and the version of section 16 originally enacted by the Canadian Parliament in 1892 is the use of the word "*appreciate*" as a substitute for the word "know" in the original phrase "know the nature and quality of the act." In addition, the Canadian Parliament referred to the issue of the accused's "*capacity*" to appreciate the nature and quality of an act or omission or to know that it was "wrong," whereas the *M'Naghten* Rules were concerned only with the accused's actual "knowledge" of these matters. These particular modifications to the *M'Naghten* Rules are still enshrined in today's version of section 16. It is reasonably clear that the Canadian Parliament, by making these modifications in 1892, sought to maintain the basic substance of the *M'Naghten* Rules while expanding their scope in certain critical respects. In 1991, Parliament amended section 16(1) by replacing the stigmatizing word "insane" with the term "mental disorder"; hence, it is now necessary to refer to the NCRMD defence rather than the insanity defence.

How have the Canadian courts interpreted the wording of the NCRMD defence that is now contained in section 16(1) of the *Code*?

The Meaning of "Mental Disorder" in Section 16(1) of the *Code*

Before defendants can successfully assert the NCRMD defence, they must first establish that, at the time of the alleged offence, they were experiencing a **mental disorder**. Section 2 of the *Criminal Code* states that "mental disorder" means "a disease of the mind."

The term **disease of the mind** was used in the *M'Naghten* Rules (1843) and has been extensively interpreted by the courts during the past 170 years. In the case of *Cooper* (1980), the Supreme Court of Canada adopted a remarkably expansive definition of "disease of the mind," as Justice Dickson said in his judgment, "[I]n a legal sense "disease of the mind" embraces any illness, disorder or abnormal condition which impairs the human mind and its functioning, excluding, however, self-induced states caused by alcohol or drugs, as well as transitory mental states such as hysteria or concussion."

This broad definition covers almost any mental condition that a psychiatrist or psychologist would classify as a mental disorder, although it would exclude temporary states of intoxication caused by the voluntary ingestion of alcohol and/or other drugs as well as fleeting mental conditions caused by, for example, a blow to the head. However, it is extremely significant that Justice Dickson immediately added a qualifying statement to this definition: namely, that the NCRMD defence comes into play only if the disease is "of such intensity as to render the accused incapable of appreciating the nature and quality of the violent act or of knowing that it is wrong." In other words, establishing that the accused person suffered from a "disease of the mind" is only the preliminary step toward advancing a successful NCRMD defence. This point was forcefully made by Justice LeBel, in delivering the judgment of the Supreme Court of Canada in *Bouchard-LeBrun* (2011):

> An accused who wishes to successfully raise the defence of mental disorder must therefore meet the requirements of a two-stage statutory test. The first stage involves *characterizing* the mental state of the accused. The key issue to be decided at trial at this stage is whether the accused was suffering from a mental disorder in the legal sense at the time of the alleged events. The second stage of the defence provided for in s. 16 *Cr. C.* concerns the *effects of the mental disorder*. At this stage, it must be determined whether, owing to his or her mental condition, the accused was incapable of "knowing that [the act or omission] was wrong" (s. 16(1) *Cr. C.*). [emphasis in original]

In the *Stone* case (1999), the Supreme Court of Canada emphasized the principle that "disease of the mind" is a *legal*, and not a strictly *medical* term. Although expert medical evidence is necessarily of considerable relevance in determining whether a particular mental condition should be classified as a "disease of the mind," the ultimate decision on this issue must be made by the trial judge. This means that the trial judge may take into account issues of public policy, such as the need to protect the public. For example, an accused person may have a condition that may recur and pose a danger even though a psychiatrist or psychologist may not classify it as a mental disorder. Since an accused person who is found to be NCRMD may be detained in hospital or supervised in the community, the trial judge, in order to protect the public from a possible recurrence of dangerous behaviour, may find that, *as a matter of law*, the accused person had a "disease of the mind." Courts in England and Canada have, for example, classified epilepsy as a "disease of the mind" even though traditionally it has not been regarded by mental health professionals as a mental disorder but rather as a physical condition that causes a temporary malfunctioning of the brain.

Since the designation of a particular mental condition as a "disease of the mind" constitutes a question of law, it is important to clarify the role of the trial judge in this process. In the *Stone* case (1999), Justice Bastarache, of the Supreme Court of Canada, stated that the trial judge is entrusted with the task of deciding "whether the condition the accused claims to have suffered from satisfies the legal test for disease of the mind." However, once the trial judge has made this legal determination, the question of whether the accused actually had a disease of the mind is a *question of fact* to be determined by the trier of fact (the members of the jury, if there is a jury trial, or the trial judge in all other cases). In other words, whether a particular condition, such as epilepsy, should be considered a "disease of mind" for the purpose of section 16(1) of the *Criminal Code* is a question of law that is determined exclusively by the trial judge. However, the issue of whether the accused actually had lived with this condition at the time of the alleged offence is a *question of fact* that is left firmly in the hands of the trier of fact.

In practice, only accused persons who were experiencing a severe mental disorder at the time of the alleged offence are likely to be found NCRMD. In general, it must be established that the accused person had a mental disorder that manifested itself in the form of psychotic symptoms. The American Psychiatric Association's *Diagnostic and Statistical Manual of Mental Disorders, Fifth Edition, or* ***DSM-5***,[2] indicates that schizophrenia spectrum and other psychotic disorders are "defined by abnormalities in the following five domains: delusions, hallucinations, disorganized thinking (speech), grossly disorganized or abnormal motor behavior (including Catatonia), and negative symptoms."[3] Individuals who live with a **psychosis** or a psychotic condition may find it very difficult to distinguish between what is real and what is unreal (they may experience delusions and/or hallucinations), and it is their loss of contact with reality that may render them incapable of appreciating the nature and quality

Illustration by Greg Holoboff

An individual who is experiencing a psychotic episode may not appreciate the nature and quality of their conduct or know that it is morally wrong.

of what they were doing or of knowing that it was wrong. A diagnosis of **schizophrenia spectrum disorder** or some other type of psychotic disorder is, therefore, one of the most likely diagnoses to be made in relation to an NCRMD accused person. In this respect, it is important to note that an individual who has a **major depressive disorder** or **bipolar disorder** (formerly known as manic depression) may experience psychotic symptoms, and their condition may then be diagnosed as **schizoaffective disorder**, which is one of the psychotic disorders listed in the *Diagnostic and Statistical Manual of Mental Disorders (DSM-5).*

In recent years, a particular problem that has faced the courts is whether a psychotic condition that has been triggered by the *voluntary* ingestion of alcohol and/or other drugs should be treated as a "disease of the mind" for the purpose of section 16(1) of the *Criminal Code*. This issue is of paramount importance because, if a "substance-induced psychosis" occurred as a result of an accused person having voluntarily consumed a drug or drugs, they may be denied the benefit of the NCRMD defence and limited instead to the partial defence of intoxication (discussed in Chapter 10). Significantly, the *DSM-5 indicates that the ingestion of* alcohol, methamphetamine, cocaine, and/or cannabis may induce a psychotic disorder in certain individuals (these are classified as "substance/medication-induced psychotic disorders"). How have the Canadian courts dealt with this thorny problem?

2. The American Psychiatric Association. *Diagnostic and Statistical Manual of Mental Disorders, Fifth Edition (DSM-5)*. Arlington, VA: 2013.

3. At p. 87. Catatonia refers to "a marked decrease in reactivity to the environment," while "negative symptoms" refers to "diminished emotional expression," decreased ability to experience pleasure, etc.

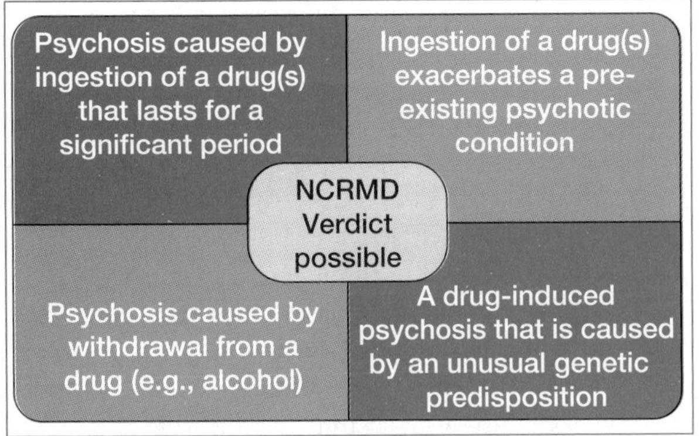

Figure 8-1

The Types of Substance-Induced Psychosis that May Lead to a Verdict of NCRMD [in Light of the Decision in Bouchard-LeBrun (2012)]

In *Bouchard-LeBrun* (2011), the Supreme Court of Canada ruled that the NCRMD defence will not be available to an accused person who experiences only a *transitory* (brief) psychosis as a direct consequence of voluntarily ingesting drugs. On the other hand, the Supreme Court appeared to agree that, if the ingestion of drugs exacerbates a pre-existing psychosis or causes a psychotic condition that endures for a significant period (months rather than days), the accused person may be entitled to raise the NCRMD defence.[4]

Once it has been established that the accused person was experiencing a mental disorder ("disease of the mind"), the next step is to establish either (1) that the accused person lacked the capacity to appreciate the nature and quality of the act or omission that forms the basis of the charge against them or (2) that the accused person lacked the capacity to know the act or omission was wrong. We shall now examine these two "arms" of the NCRMD defence.

The Capacity of the Accused Person to Appreciate the Nature and Quality of the Act or Omission

The Meaning of "Appreciate" in Section 16(1)

It was indicated earlier that, when the *M'Naghten* Rules were incorporated into the 1892 *Criminal Code*, the word **appreciate** was substituted for "know" in the first "arm" of the mental disorder defence. This significant departure from the *M'Naghten* Rules was underscored in the case of *Barnier* (1980). In this case, the accused had shot and killed a woman in an office building and had subsequently taken his gun on the roof and demanded to speak to the prime minister of Canada. It was contended that the accused was experiencing severe delusions. However, at his trial for murder, there was a highly unusual development. All the psychiatrists were agreed that Barnier was incapable of *appreciating* the nature and quality of his act, but the Crown argued that, in law, the word "appreciate" means "know." The two Crown psychiatrists then changed their opinions. They testified that, if "appreciate" means no more than "know," then the accused knew what he was doing and that it was wrong.

The trial judge accepted the Crown's interpretation and Barnier was convicted of murder. The B.C. Court of Appeal allowed his appeal and substituted a verdict of not guilty by reason of insanity. In the view of the court, the trial judge had made a serious error in treating the word "appreciate" as being a mere synonym of the word "know." Although the Crown appealed this ruling, it was ultimately upheld by the Supreme Court of Canada. In delivering the unanimous decision of the Supreme Court, Justice Estey emphasized that Parliament had deliberately employed two different words in the critical portion of section 16(2); namely, "appreciating" (the nature and quality of the act) and "knowing" (that the act is wrong). Therefore, it was obvious that Parliament intended these two words to be given different meanings; otherwise, the "Legislature would have employed one or the other only." In discussing the distinction between the two words, Justice Estey went on to say that:

> The verb "know" has a positive connotation requiring a bare awareness, the act of receiving information without more. The act of appreciating, on the other hand, is a second stage in a mental process requiring the analysis of knowledge or experience in one manner or another. It is therefore clear on the plain meaning of the section that Parliament intended that for a person to be insane within the statutory definition, he must be incapable first of appreciating in the analytical sense the nature and quality of the act or of knowing in the positive sense that his act was wrong.

The Supreme Court of Canada also had occasion to deal with the distinction between the words "know"

4. This issue is discussed more fully in Chapter 10.

and "appreciate" in *Cooper* (1980). In this case, the accused, a man with a long history of hospitalization for mental disorder, had strangled a female patient after a dance. There was medical evidence that although Cooper may have been capable of intending bodily harm and of choking the young woman, he was not capable of intending to kill her. Nevertheless, he was convicted of murder at his trial and the Ontario Court of Appeal subsequently affirmed his conviction. However, the Supreme Court of Canada ultimately allowed his appeal and ordered a new trial. In delivering the judgment of the majority of the Supreme Court, Justice Dickson stated that the person who had drafted the original *Code* had made a deliberate change in language from the *M'Naghten* Rules by replacing "know" with "appreciate" in the first part of section 16(1). This change was made to "broaden the legal and medical considerations bearing upon the mental state of the accused and to make it clear that cognition was not to be the sole criterion." Indeed, Justice Dickson suggested that "emotional, as well as intellectual, awareness of the significance of the conduct is in issue." He went on to declare:

> With respect, I accept the view that the first branch of the test, in employing the word "appreciates," imports an additional requirement to mere knowledge of the physical quality of the act. *The requirement, unique to Canada, is that of perception, an* ability *to perceive the consequences, impact, and results of a physical act.* An accused may be aware of the physical character of his action (i.e., in choking) without necessarily having the capacity to appreciate that, in nature and quality, that act will result in the death of a human being. This is simply a restatement, specific to the defence of insanity, of the principle that *mens rea*, or intention as to the consequences of an act, is a requisite element in the commission of a crime. [emphasis added]

The Meaning of "Nature and Quality of the Act" in Section 16(1)

The Supreme Court of Canada has clearly stated that the phrase "nature and quality" of an act refers exclusively to the *physical* nature and quality of the act concerned. As Chief Justice Lamer said in the *Landry* case (1991), the "first branch of the s. 16(1) test protects an accused who, because of a disease of the mind, was incapable of appreciating the physical consequences of his act."

The Supreme Court's approach to this issue is perhaps best illustrated by the disturbing case of *Kjeldsen* (1981). The accused was charged with the brutal murder of a taxi driver. In the past, Kjeldsen had been found not guilty by reason of "insanity" on charges involving rape and attempted murder and had been detained in a psychiatric hospital. He was on a day pass from the hospital when he first raped and then killed the female taxi driver by shattering her skull with a large rock. All the medical witnesses agreed that Kjeldsen was "a dangerous psychopath with sexually deviant tendencies." The accused, however, was unsuccessful in his attempt to raise what is now known as the NCRMD defence. He was convicted at trial, and his subsequent appeals to both the Alberta Court of Appeal and the Supreme Court of Canada were rejected.

Although it was accepted that Kjeldsen had a form of mental disorder, there was some disagreement between the Crown and defence witnesses as to whether he was capable of appreciating the nature and quality of his violent actions. The expert witnesses for the defence sought to apply a broad test that would require that the accused have the capacity not only to foresee the physical consequences of his actions but also to predict and to understand the *subjective or emotional reactions* of his victim. In the view of the defence experts, a **psychopath** such as Kjeldsen was incapable of experiencing normal or appropriate feelings about the effects of his actions on other people: in short, he could not feel remorse or guilt and, therefore, could not appreciate the nature and quality of his conduct. However, the expert witnesses for the Crown assumed that section 16(1) referred solely to the accused's capacity to understand and foresee the *physical* consequences of his actions and that even a psychopath, such as Kjeldsen, would—in this more limited sense—be able to fully appreciate the nature and quality of his conduct. As Justice McIntyre stated, in delivering the judgment of the Supreme Court of Canada:

> To be capable of "appreciating" the nature and quality of his acts, an accused person must have the capacity to know what he is doing; in the case at bar, for example, to know that he was hitting the woman on the head with a rock, with great force, and in addition he must have the capacity to estimate and understand the physical consequences which would flow from his act, in this case that he was causing physical injury which could result in death.

Justice McIntyre also expressly approved the following passage from the judgment of Justice Martin, of the Ontario Court of Appeal, in *Simpson* (1977):

> I do not think the exemption provided by [section 16(1)] ... extends to one who has the necessary understanding

> of the nature, character and consequences of the act, but merely lacks appropriate feelings for the victim or lacks feelings of remorse or guilt for what he has done, even though such lack of feeling stems from "disease of the mind." *Appreciation of the nature and quality of the act does not import a requirement that the act be accompanied by appropriate feeling about the effect of the act on other people.* ... No doubt the absence of such feelings is a common characteristic of many persons who engage in repeated and serious criminal conduct. [emphasis added]

In rejecting Kjeldsen's appeal, the Supreme Court reached an eminently reasonable result in terms of public policy. After all, the Canadian public would scarcely tolerate a system of criminal justice that released back into the community dangerous individuals who have perpetrated violent crimes, merely because they lacked the appropriate feelings for their victims or did not experience the appropriate pangs of remorse or guilt. Since Kjeldsen appreciated what he was doing and that it was wrong, the Court was fully justified in holding him accountable for his actions. Although Kjeldsen was diagnosed with a **personality disorder** (which the Supreme Court considered a "disease of the mind"), this condition undoubtedly failed to meet the criteria for an NCRMD verdict under section 16(1).

THE CAPACITY OF THE ACCUSED PERSON TO APPRECIATE THAT THE ACT OR OMISSION WAS WRONG

The Meaning of "Wrong" in Section 16(1)

The second "arm" of the NCRMD defence requires that the mental disorder the accused person was experiencing rendered them incapable of knowing that the act or omission was **wrong**. Parliament did not make clear whether the word "wrong" meant *morally* or *legally* wrong. The choice between these two alternatives may nevertheless prove to be the difference between a successful and an unsuccessful defence of NCRMD. Let us suppose that Dorrit kills Crummles, fully appreciating that he is killing the latter and realizing that it is a crime to do so. However, Dorrit, owing to a mental disorder, believes that he has been ordered by God or some other divine being to sacrifice Crummles to save the world from imminent destruction. There is no doubt that Dorrit appreciates the nature and quality of his act, so the first arm of the NCRMD defence does not apply to him. Furthermore, if "wrong" means *legally* wrong, then the second arm of the NCRMD defence does not apply to Dorrit either. However, if "wrong" means *morally* wrong, section 16(1) would be applicable because Dorrit believed that he was acting on the direct orders of "the Almighty" and was, therefore, acting in a manner that would be considered morally justified by his fellow citizens. In the *Chaulk* case (1990), the Supreme Court of Canada finally settled this issue by ruling that "wrong" in section 16(1) means "wrong according to the ordinary moral standards of reasonable members of society."

Chief Justice Lamer, in delivering the majority judgment of the Supreme Court in the case of *Chaulk*, stated that it would be unjust for the courts to find a mentally disordered accused person criminally responsible merely because they knew that their conduct was contrary to the law of the land. In his view:

> A person may well be aware that an act is contrary to law but, by reason of ... disease of the mind, is at the same time incapable of knowing that the act is morally wrong in the circumstances according to the moral standards of society. This would be the case, for example, if the person suffered from a disease of the mind to such a degree as to know that it is legally wrong to kill but ... kills "in the belief that it is in response to a divine order and therefore not morally wrong."

Does the Supreme Court's ruling mean that those offenders who lack basic moral principles will now be acquitted as NCRMD? The answer is clearly in the negative. As the Chief Justice emphasized in his judgment, the Court's judgment provided absolutely no comfort to amoral offenders because, for an NCRMD defence to be successful, *the accused's incapacity to make moral distinctions must be causally related to their mental disorder*. Furthermore, the appropriate test is not whether the individual accused person believes their actions are morally justified, but rather it is *whether they are capable of knowing that society at large regards the conduct as being morally wrong*; in other words, "the accused will not benefit from substituting his own moral code for that of society."

A straightforward illustration of the application of the Supreme Court's definition of "wrong" may be seen in the case of *Landry* (1991). The accused was charged with first-degree murder and admitted that he had killed the victim. However, he advanced a defence of NCRMD. It was accepted that Landry had a severe psychosis that caused him to believe that he was God and the victim was Satan. Landry was convinced that he had to kill "Satan" to fulfill his divine mission to rid the world of the forces of evil. Landry undoubtedly realized that murder was a crime, but the Supreme Court of Canada ruled that he should be found NCRMD because his psychotic mental condition had rendered him incapable of knowing that the **ordinary person** would regard the killing as morally wrong.

A very significant application of the second arm of the NCRMD defence occurred in the case of *Oommen* (1994). The accused had killed a young woman by shooting her as she lay sleeping on a mattress in his apartment, and he was charged with **second-degree murder**. It was generally agreed that there was no rational motive for the killing. The accused had for many years experienced "paranoid delusional psychosis." He came to believe that the members of a local union were involved in a conspiracy to kill him. Tragically, he formed the opinion that the young woman had been commissioned by his enemies to murder him in his own apartment and he became convinced that he had to destroy her before she had the opportunity to kill him. He, therefore, fired 9 to 13 shots at her from a semi-automatic weapon and she subsequently died. A psychiatrist testified that Oommen's mental disorder would not cause him to lose the intellectual capacity to distinguish between right and wrong in the abstract and to know that, in general, killing was wrong. However, his mental disorder would cause him to form an honest belief that the shooting of the young woman was justified under the particular circumstances (namely, that he honestly believed that she was going to kill him, if he did not act first). The trial judge found that the killing was "caused, and indeed, compelled" by Oommen's mental condition and that "subjectively the accused did not believe his act to be wrong." However, the trial judge concluded that Oommen did have the "general capacity to know right from wrong" and ruled that he was not relieved from criminal responsibility under section 16(1).

Ultimately, a new trial was ordered in Oommen's case. The Supreme Court of Canada agreed with the Alberta Court of Appeal that the trial judge had misinterpreted section 16(1). In delivering the judgment of the Supreme Court, Justice McLachlin stated that "the focus must be on capacity to know that the act committed was wrong, and not merely on a general capacity to distinguish right from wrong." In Justice McLachlin's view, "[T]he issue is whether the accused possessed the capacity present in the ordinary person to know that the act in question was wrong according to the everyday standards of the reasonable person." She added that "the real question is whether the accused should be exempted from criminal responsibility because a mental disorder at the time of the act deprived him of the capacity for rational perception and hence rational choice about the rightness or wrongness of the act." In this sense, the trial judge had made a significant error in focusing on Oommen's general ability to distinguish right from wrong instead of concentrating on his capacity to know that the killing of the young woman was right or wrong in the circumstances as he honestly believed them to be. As Justice McLachlin commented, "[S]. 16(1) of the *Criminal Code* embraces not only the intellectual ability to know right from wrong, but the capacity to apply that knowledge to the situation at hand."

The Supreme Court of Canada dealt with the same issue some six years later. In the *Molodowic* case (2000), the accused was charged with second-degree murder following the shooting death of his grandfather. There was no doubt that Molodowic had a serious mental disorder—paranoid schizophrenia—and was affected by visual and auditory hallucinations and delusions of persecution. In short, his mental disorder severely impaired his grasp of reality. The psychiatrists who were called by the defence to testify were agreed that Molodowic did appreciate the nature and quality of his act (namely, that he was killing his grandfather) and that he knew that this was a crime. However, they also expressed the opinion that Molodowic *did not know that his act was morally wrong*. Both of these psychiatrists testified to the effect that Molodowic's "act of shooting was consistent with his mental disorder having caused him to believe that only in so doing could he save himself from further torment." Significantly, the Crown did not call its own psychiatric experts to contradict this evidence.

Molodowic was convicted of murder by a jury, and his subsequent appeal to the Manitoba Court of Appeal was dismissed. However, on a further appeal to the Supreme Court of Canada, the conviction was set aside and a verdict of NCRMD was substituted. The Supreme Court ruled that the jury's verdict was unreasonable in light of the unanimous psychiatric testimony presented at the trial. In delivering the judgment of the Court, Justice Arbour stated that the evidence simply did not support the conclusion that, at the time of the shooting, Molodowic was sufficiently lucid to know that his acts were morally wrong. She went on to state that:

> [T]he totality of the psychiatric evidence did not give rise to the reasonable possibility that the appellant, who laboured under the effects of a severe mental disorder at the time he committed a homicide, and whose moral judgment was impaired as a result, would have had a momentary reprieve from the effects of his disorder, at the critical time, sufficient to provide him with the moral insight necessary to engage his criminal responsibility. …
>
> It is not necessarily easy for a jury to accept that, in lay person's terms, an accused who knows what he is doing and knows that it is a crime, could still genuinely believe that he would not be morally condemned by reasonable members of society for his conduct. In my view, the defence proved this to be the case and, on the evidence tendered at his trial, it was unreasonable to conclude otherwise.[5]

Mock (2016) is a similar, more recent, case in which a jury's conviction of second-degree murder was set aside by the Alberta Court of Appeal and a verdict of NCRMD substituted instead. Mock, who lived with bipolar affective disorder and experienced pervasive delusions, shot and killed his brother, whom he believed to be a clone. Just before he shot his brother, Mock had destroyed his cellphone because, in his delusional state, he believed that the CIA and FBI were using it to conduct surveillance on him. After the shooting and while running naked through a field, Mock tried to kill himself by biting on a rusted pipe and striking himself on the back of the head with a hard object. When the police arrived, Mock was "naked, screaming, crying and incoherent."

At his trial, there was a "glaring disparity between the strength of the expert evidence provided by the Crown and defence." Defence experts, who had interviewed Mock shortly after his arrest, firmly believed that he was in such a blatant delusional state (caused by his psychotic condition) that he was entitled to the benefit of an NCRMD verdict. Two expert witnesses for the Crown denied that Mock had grounds to support a defence of NCRMD, but they did not assess him until 18 months after the killing and long after he had been stabilized by a course of treatment with anti-psychotic medication. Nevertheless, the jury rejected the plea of NCRMD and convicted Mock of second-degree murder. The Alberta Court of Appeal ruled that the jury's verdict was unreasonable. The pivotal issue at the trial was whether Mock was in a psychotic state at the time of the killing and, on that score, the evidence was overwhelming. The Court of Appeal could not understand why the evidence of the Crown experts had not been discounted by the jury. The Court concluded that "… it is our respectful conclusion that the evidence clearly established the defence of not criminally responsible by reason of a mental disorder on a balance of probabilities, and it was unreasonable to have concluded otherwise."

However, it is important to remember that the mere fact that the accused had a severe mental disorder does not automatically lead to the conclusion that the accused lacked the capacity to know that their conduct would be considered morally wrong by ordinary members of society. Furthermore, it is also necessary to bear in mind that accused persons who do raise the NCRMD defence have to prove—on the balance of probabilities—that they lacked the capacity to know that their conduct was blameworthy [section 16(2)]. In *Mock*'s case, his delusional state led him to believe that he was justified in killing "a clone" and the evidence of the defence witnesses had proved the requirements of the NCRMD defence on the balance of probabilities.

The Problem of Irresistible Impulse

An accused person may well say, "I appreciated what I was doing and knew that I was doing something that was wrong; however, because I had a mental disorder, an irresistible impulse came over me and I couldn't help myself." Would such an accused person be entitled to claim the benefit of the NCRMD defence?

In Canada, it is perfectly clear that the so-called irresistible impulse defence is not recognized by the courts. If the accused does not meet the criteria of either of the two arms of the NCRMD defence, set out in section 16(1), the question of irresistible

5. However, in a case in which the psychiatrists who provided expert testimony on behalf of the Crown and the defence, respectively, were *not* unanimous as to whether the mentally disordered accused person had the capacity to know the blameworthiness of his conduct, the Supreme Court of Canada upheld a jury's conviction of that individual on a charge of first-degree murder: see *R. v. Baker* (2010).

Irresistible impulse? Assaulting another man even though two police officers are present.

impulse is absolutely irrelevant. Of course, as the Supreme Court of Canada noted in the *Borg* (1969) and *Abbey* (1982) cases, an irresistible impulse may be a "symptom or manifestation of a disease of the mind," but such a mental condition will not excuse the defendant under section 16(1) unless the other requirements of that provision are met.

Why have the courts taken such a firm stand on the issue of irresistible impulse as the basis for a defence of NCRMD? Perhaps they are understandably reluctant to open the door of the NCRMD defence to individuals who have only a personality disorder or who are classified as psychopaths and claim that they cannot help themselves. This attitude certainly seems to underlie the Supreme Court of Canada's leading decision in *Chartrand* (1976). In this case, the accused had been convicted of killing a police officer. His appeal to the Supreme Court was ultimately rejected. However, the Court's approach to the issue of irresistible impulse is most interesting. It had been contended that the defendant had a psychopathic personality. The medical director of Montreal's Institut Pinel, Dr. Béliveau, stated that Chartrand was

> ... capable of distinguishing between right and wrong—he understands the nature of his actions, and so forth—but that does not mean that there is not an inner pathological process at work that can prompt him to exhibit a form of behaviour that is unacceptable, dangerous, violent and so on, as well as a psychotic process that would be clearly, if you will, obvious in another person.

However, the Supreme Court totally rejected this as a basis for a successful defence under section 16(1) of the *Code*. Indeed, Justice de Grandpré held that "Chartrand was ... able to distinguish between right and wrong, and although he was ill, he was technically sane. What the witness adds on the subject of the inner pathological process cannot be taken into consideration under our criminal legislation, which does not recognize the diminished responsibility theory."

This decision clearly shut the door to the irresistible impulse claim as an independent basis for raising the NCRMD defence in Canada. The Supreme Court's approach clearly underlines the fact that section 16(1) has been interpreted in such a way as to focus on *cognitive*, rather than volitional, factors in determining the issue of whether or not the accused person is NCRMD. It is always difficult to assess the validity of such claims. On the other hand, it may well be argued that there should be some kind of defence open to defendants who can make a plausible claim that they could not control their conduct because of their mental illness. In England and Wales, for example, such individuals may raise the defence of diminished responsibility in such circumstances. This defence operates only in relation to a charge of murder, however, and, if successful, leads to a conviction of manslaughter rather than an acquittal; in other words, it is only a *partial defence*. Whether some form of diminished responsibility defence should be made available in Canada is a matter that has been hotly debated for a number of years and, to date, Parliament has not been willing to introduce it into the *Criminal Code*.

Before leaving the matter of irresistible impulse, it might be useful to consider the possibility that the decision in the *Chaulk* case (1990) might open the door to some defendants' claiming that they suffered an irresistible impulse that caused them to lack the capacity to know that their conduct was wrong according to the ordinary standards of reasonable people. If an accused person living with a serious mental disorder can demonstrate that they were so overwhelmed by an irresistible impulse that they could not, with a reasonable degree of composure, think of the reasons that ordinary persons would view their conduct as right or wrong, such an individual should be acquitted as being NCRMD. It remains to be seen whether the courts will be willing to view such a scenario as one in which the irresistible impulse is a symptom of a mental disorder that excuses the accused under the second arm of section 16(1).

MISCELLANEOUS PROCEDURAL ISSUES

THE POWER OF THE CROWN TO RAISE THE MENTAL DISORDER DEFENCE

Most people assume that the NCRMD defence is an issue raised exclusively by the accused person to avoid being found criminally responsible for their actions. However, in certain, limited circumstances, the issue may be raised by the Crown—even in the face of staunch opposition by the accused person. In the *Swain* case (1991), the Supreme Court of Canada ruled that the Crown may follow this course of action in only two situations: (1) where the accused person puts their state of mind in issue at trial or (2) after the jury or the judge has already concluded that the accused person committed the act or omission that formed the basis for the offence with which they have been charged.

The Supreme Court considered that it was perfectly fair for the Crown to raise the defence of NCRMD where the accused deliberately puts their of mind in issue. For example, if the accused claims that they were in a state of automatism at the time of the alleged offence, the Crown may reasonably assert that the accused's state of mind was the product of a mental disorder and that, instead of being granted an absolute acquittal, the accused should be found NCRMD and subjected to the possibility that restrictions will be placed on their liberty (for example, by being confined in a psychiatric facility). As Chief Justice Lamer said, "[T]he Crown's ability to raise evidence of [mental disorder] is not inconsistent with the accused's right to control the conduct of his or her defence because the very issue has been raised by the accused's conduct of his or her defence." Similarly, the Supreme Court took the view that the accused person's right to liberty and security of the person (guaranteed by section 7 of the *Charter*) would not be infringed if the Crown were permitted to raise the NCRMD defence *after* the accused person has had the opportunity to present their defence. Permitting the Crown to advance the NCRMD defence at the end of the trial ensures that there is no possibility that raising the issue of the mental disorder will prejudice the fact-finding process in cases where the accused declines to put their state of mind in issue. For example, the accused may advance an alibi defence. If this defence is successful, then the jury or judge will grant the accused an absolute acquittal because they did not commit the act or omission with which they have been charged. Allowing the Crown to raise the NRCMD defence before the accused has presented this defence might well prejudice the accused's right to a fair trial. One possibility is that the members of the jury may reason that if the accused is mentally disordered, then they are "just the sort of person" who would commit the offence that has been charged. Given the prejudice that is often shown against individuals living with mental disorders, it is important to ensure that evidence of the accused's mental disorder does not taint the fact-finding process at the time that the jury is considering the question of innocence or guilt.

However, where the accused was clearly suffering from a serious mental disorder at the time of the alleged offence but imprudently refuses to permit their counsel to advance a defence of NCRMD, it may be necessary for the Crown to intervene. Indeed, in these circumstances, one might well argue that the Crown should raise the defence not only in fairness to the mentally disordered accused person but also in the public interest. For example, in the case of *Pietrangelo* (2008), the accused was convicted of aggravated assault and assault with a weapon following attacks on the Mayor of Niagara Falls and his aide. At his trial, Pietrangelo represented himself and steadfastly refused to advance the NCRMD defence. The Crown had considerable evidence that Pietrangelo had been suffering a major mental disorder at the time of the assaults; specifically, a delusional disorder of the persecutory type (paranoid schizophrenia). However, owing to a mistaken interpretation of the law, it did not introduce this evidence after the jury had found Pietrangelo had committed the offences with which he had been charged.

Pietrangelo appealed against his convictions to the Ontario Court of Appeal and, at this time, the Crown finally introduced evidence in support of a defence of NCRMD. The Ontario Court of Appeal set aside Pietrangelo's convictions and substituted a verdict of NCRMD. Justice Sharpe provided the following rationale in support of the Court of Appeal's decision:

> [T]he common law rule allowing the Crown to raise the issue of NCRMD is aimed not only at avoiding the unfair treatment of the accused but at maintaining the integrity of the criminal justice system itself. The accused is not the only person who has an interest in the outcome of the trial; society itself has an interest in ensuring that the system does not incorrectly label insane people as criminals. …

The Burden and Standard of Proof When the Defence of NCRMD Is Raised

Normally, to obtain a conviction, the Crown is placed under the burden of proving all the *actus reus* and *mens rea* elements of a criminal offence. Furthermore, the standard of proof that must be met is "beyond a reasonable doubt." The NCRMD defence constitutes an exception to this general rule. Section 16(3) of the *Criminal Code* states that the party who raises the issue of the NCRMD defence must shoulder the burden of proving it. Furthermore, section 16(2) states that "every person is presumed not to suffer from a mental disorder so as to be exempt from criminal responsibility ... until the contrary is proved on the balance of probabilities." In other words, the party who raises the defence of NCRMD (either the accused or the Crown) must prove that it was more likely than not that the accused was NCRMD at the time of the offence.

In the *Chaulk* case (1990), the Supreme Court of Canada held that placing the burden of proving the defence of NCRMD on an accused person undoubtedly infringes the presumption of innocence that is guaranteed by section 11(d) of the *Charter*. However, the Supreme Court also ruled that sections 16(2) and (3) constituted a reasonable limit on the presumption of innocence and, therefore, these provisions were saved by section 1 of the *Charter*. According to Chief Justice Lamer, Parliament was justified in enacting sections 16(2) and (3) because, otherwise, the Crown would be saddled with the impossible burden of proving that the accused was not NCRMD and accused persons who were not really living with mental disorder would improperly escape criminal responsibility. Of particular importance to the Court was the fact that the Crown has no means of compelling an accused person to cooperate with an examination by a psychiatrist who will testify for the prosecution. If an accused person refuses to cooperate with a "Crown" psychiatrist, the prosecution could be placed in an impossible position if it were required to prove that the accused was *not* NCRMD at the time of the alleged offence. The defence may present testimony from a psychiatrist who has examined the accused firsthand, but the Crown would not be able to do so, and this would place it at a considerable disadvantage before a judge and/or jury.[6] Since the state of the accused's mind at the time of the alleged offence is something that is peculiarly within their own knowledge, it is reasonable, in the view of the Supreme Court, to require them to present evidence on this matter and to prove that the requirements of section 16(1) are met before entering a verdict of NCRMD.

THE DISPOSITION OF NCRMD ACCUSED PERSONS

The defence of NCRMD serves two main functions: (1) it prevents the conviction of individuals whose mental disorder rendered them incapable of making a deliberate choice to do something wrong; and (2) it ensures public safety by imposing restrictions on the liberty of those NCR accused persons who are proved to be dangerous. The second function was explained by Justice LeBel, of the Supreme Court of Canada, in the *Bouchard-LeBrun* case (2011):

> [T]he defence of mental disorder remains unique. It does not result in acquittal of the accused, but instead leads to a verdict of not criminally responsible. That verdict triggers an administrative process whose purpose is to determine whether the accused is a significant threat to the safety of the public, to take any necessary action to control that threat and, if necessary, to provide the accused with appropriate care. A verdict of not criminally responsible on account of mental disorder thus gives effect to society's interest in ensuring that morally innocent offenders are treated rather than punished, while protecting the public as fully as possible.

The *Criminal Code* requires the establishment of **review boards** in each province.[7] These administrative tribunals carry the primary responsibility for deciding whether an "NCR accused person" should be detained and, if so, for how long. However, the trial court may decide to make an immediate

6. However, a judge or jury may draw an adverse (unfavourable) inference against the accused person who refuses to submit to an examination by a psychiatrist appointed by the Crown and would be entitled to take this refusal into consideration when weighing the merits of the accused person's NCRMD defence: see *R. v. McClenaghan* (2010).

7. The review boards that make disposition decisions consist of the Chairperson (a judge or a lawyer who is, eligible to be appointed a judge); a psychiatrist; and a third member, who is usually an individual with expertise in the field of mental health (e.g., a social worker).

disposition of an NCR accused, "if it is satisfied that it can readily do so and that a disposition should be made without delay."[8] In practice, very few trial courts make this decision, leaving it to the review board to determine the appropriate disposition.

The accused may be discharged absolutely or on conditions or, alternatively, may be detained in custody in a hospital.[9] However, any custody order made by a court would be only temporary in nature, being limited to a maximum of 90 days, after which the NCR accused person's case would be considered by the review board.[10] The trial court may also decide to impose a designation of "high-risk accused" (discussed later in this chapter).

Where the court does not make a disposition, then the review board must make such a disposition, normally within 45 days after the verdict is rendered (although this period may be extended to 90 days by the court).[11] In essence, the review boards assume the prime responsibility for making the initial disposition of NCR accused persons, if the court does not do so, and for overseeing the cases of all those individuals who have not been granted an absolute discharge. In the latter situation, the boards are the sole decision-making authorities (except where the NCR accused person has been designated a "high-risk accused").

Right of the NCR Accused Person to Appeal

The *Criminal Code* permits the NCR accused person to appeal to the provincial court of appeal against the disposition made by a court or a board of review.[12]

Criteria for Making Decisions About the Disposition of NCR Accused Persons

Where a court or review board makes a disposition, it must take into account "the safety of the public, which is the paramount consideration, the mental condition of the accused, the reintegration of the accused into society and the other needs of the accused," and it shall "make one of the following dispositions that is necessary and appropriate in the circumstances."[13] As noted above, these possible dispositions are:

1. An absolute discharge (the accused person is released entirely from the criminal justice system);
2. A discharge on conditions (such as living in a designated halfway house and abstaining from alcohol and other drugs);
3. An order to hold the accused person in custody within a hospital (usually a specialized forensic facility).
4. A designation of the NCR accused person as "high risk" (which can be imposed and removed only by a court).

It is important to bear in mind that s. 672.54(a) of the *Criminal Code* states that "where a verdict of not criminally responsible on account of mental disorder has been rendered in respect of the accused and, in the opinion of the court or review board, the accused is not a significant threat to the safety of the public," the court or review board shall "by order, direct that the accused be discharged absolutely." In *Winko v. British Columbia (Forensic Psychiatric Institute)* (1999), the Supreme Court of Canada ruled that *unless the review board or court is satisfied* that the NCR accused person constitutes a significant threat to the safety of the public, then it *must* grant him (or her) an absolute discharge. This means that if the court or review board has any doubts about whether the NCR accused person is a "significant threat to the safety of the public," it must nevertheless grant an absolute discharge.

In delivering the judgment of the majority of the justices of the Supreme Court in *Winko*, Justice McLachlin stated:

> There is no presumption that the NCR accused poses a significant threat to the safety of the public. Restrictions on his or her liberty can only be justified if, at the time of the hearing, the evidence before the court or Review Board shows that the NCR accused actually constitutes such a threat. The court or Review Board cannot avoid coming to a decision on this issue by stating, for example, that it is uncertain or cannot decide whether the NCR accused poses a significant threat to the safety of the public. If it cannot come to a decision with any certainty, then it has not found that the NCR accused poses a significant threat to the safety of the public.

8. S. 672.45(2).
9. S. 672.54.
10. S. 672.47(3).
11. S. 672.47(1).
12. S. 672.72. *R. v. Head* (2016).
13. S. 672.54.

In a more recent decision by the Ontario Court of Appeal, in *Krivicic* (2018), Justice Trotter made the point very succinctly: "Dangerousness is not presumed: it is the other way round." If the review board (or court) concludes that the NCR accused person does indeed pose a significant threat, then it has two choices: it may order that the accused be "discharged subject to the conditions the court or Review Board deems necessary" or "it may direct that the NCR accused be detained in custody in a hospital, again subject to appropriate conditions." Justice McLachlin made it very clear in her judgment in *Winko* that the threshold for justifying the imposition of restrictions on the liberty of the person who has been found NCR is very high: "A "significant threat to the safety of the public" means a real risk of physical or psychological harm to members of the public that is serious in the sense of going beyond the merely trivial or annoying. *The conduct giving rise to the harm must be criminal in nature.*" [emphasis added].

According to Justice McLachlin, "a minuscule risk of a grave harm will not suffice," and, "similarly, a high risk of trivial harm will not meet the threshold." Furthermore, she emphasized that there is no onus on the NCR accused person to prove that they are *not* dangerous—a task that would be extraordinarily difficult to accomplish. It is only if the evidence presented to the review board (or court) establishes that the NCR accused person constitutes a significant threat that restrictions may be placed on their liberty.

As noted above, section 672.54 of the *Criminal Code* provides that an important consideration in determining whether an NCR accused person constitutes a "significant threat to the safety of the public" is the "mental condition of the accused." In the case of *Wodajio* (2005), the Alberta Court of Appeal emphasized that "the 'significant threat' must relate to the [NCR accused person's] mental condition or overall mental state at the time of the hearing" rather than at the time of the offence. As Justice Russell stated in delivering the judgment of the Court:

> The relative importance of the non criminally responsible accused's mental condition to the overall assessment of dangerousness depends on many variables, including the nature of the accused's mental disorder, available treatment, the accused's understanding of his mental condition, and willingness to conform to proposed treatment, and the accused's past and expected success or failure following treatment.

In 2014, the *Criminal Code* was amended to include a statutory definition of "significant threat to the safety of the public":

> For the purposes of section 672.54, a significant threat to the safety of the public means a risk of serious physical or psychological harm to members of the public—including any victim of or witness to the offence, or any person under the age of 18 years—resulting from conduct that is criminal in nature but not necessarily violent.[14]

This definition implies, for example, that the threat of making harassing phone calls to a witness of the offence committed by the NCR accused person might be considered a "significant threat to the safety of the public," even though no violence is involved provided it is likely to cause "serious psychological harm." Making repeated phone calls that might cause a person to reasonably fear for their safety would constitute criminal harassment contrary to section 264 of the *Criminal Code*.

However, the courts have set the bar high for review boards to determine that an NCR accused person constitutes a "significant threat to the safety of the public." For example, in *Sokal* (2018), the NCR accused person had been found NCRMD with respect to two charges of criminal harassment. He had been living with schizoaffective disorder and with the abuse of a number of illegal substances. The Ontario Review Board initially ordered his detention in a secure forensic unit, but he was subsequently permitted to live in the community and, in 2015, the Board granted him a conditional discharge. Among the conditions of his release were reporting to the hospital every two months, abstention from alcohol and non-prescription drugs, and the submission of urine samples on request. Sokal wanted to be given an absolute discharge but, in 2017, the Review Board refused because it believed there was a significant risk that he would engage in substance abuse. This belief was based on the evidence that Sokal had tested positive for cocaine in 2015 and that he had admitted taking crystal meth in 2016—events that occurred considerably before the Review Board's decision.

However, the Ontario Court of Appeal ruled that the Review Board had failed to apply the provisions of section 672.54 of the *Criminal Code* appropriately and granted Sokal an absolute discharge. Sokal had not been violent or aggressive and had lived in the

14. S. 672.5401.

community for three years without any adverse incidents. He was taking his medication as prescribed and had joined a support group for individuals living with schizophrenia. As the Court of Appeal noted, "It was not reasonable for the Board to deny the appellant an absolute discharge in light of the evidence before it." It ruled that Sokal was "entitled to be discharged unless he constitutes a significant threat to the safety of the public" and, in this respect, "the evidence failed to meet the "onerous" standard under s. 672.54."

THE "HIGH-RISK ACCUSED" DESIGNATION

In 2014, Parliament enacted the *Not Criminally Responsible Reform Act*[15] which has given the trial court the power to impose the designation of "**high-risk accused**" when an accused person has been found NCRMD. This designation may be imposed where the NCR accused person has committed a "serious personal injury offence," was 18 years of age or more at the time of the commission of the offence, and (a) the court is satisfied that there is a substantial likelihood that the accused will use violence that could endanger the life or safety of another person; or (b) the court is of the opinion that the acts that constitute the offence were of such a brutal nature as to indicate a risk of grave physical or psychological harm to another person [*Criminal Code*, s. 672.64 (1)].

Upon being designated by a court as "high risk," an NCR accused person will be held in custody in hospital and will not be released by a review board until their designation is revoked by a court. The other consequences of being designated as a high-risk NCR accused include a possible extension by the review board of the period between reviews (up to three years, instead of the usual one), unescorted passes may not be granted to such individuals, and escorted passes may be granted only in narrow circumstances and subject to sufficient safeguards to protect public safety.

This legislation was introduced in response to public concern about a small number of cases in which an individual had committed gruesome murders while in a state of psychosis and had been found NCRMD. One of these notorious cases was that involving Vincent Li, who murdered a fellow passenger on a bus and decapitated him (see further discussion of this case later). Another of these cases involved Allan Schoenborn, who had killed one of his children by repeatedly striking her with a cleaver and two other children by smothering them. In 2010, a trial judge of the B.C. Supreme Court found that Schoenborn had proved that he was not criminally responsible at the time of the killings and brought down a verdict of NCRMD. Subsequently, the Crown attempted to have Schoenborn declared a "high-risk accused." However, in *Schoenborn* (2017), Justice Devlin of the B.C. Supreme Court dismissed the application.

Since the finding of NCRMD in 2010, Schoenborn had been held continuously in the Forensic Psychiatric Hospital of British Columbia and his psychotic condition was in remission, owing to the treatment that he had received in that facility. The Crown nevertheless sought the "high-risk accused" designation and, in addition to referring to the horrific nature of the killings, focused on the evidence that, in the hospital environment, Schoenborn had exhibited anger-management problems, and his aggressive personality had brought him into conflict with other patients.

Justice Devlin concluded that Schoenborn's problems with anger were not related to the episode in Schoenborn's psychotic delusions, which were now in remission because of his psychiatric treatment at the forensic hospital. Therefore, the Judge concluded that he was "not satisfied that there is a substantial likelihood that he will use violence that could endanger the life or safety of another person." Furthermore, Justice Devlin took the view that:

> Given Mr. Schoenborn's current mental condition and course of treatment, particularly the prolonged remission of his psychosis and delusional disorder through antipsychotic medication, I am not of the opinion that the brutal nature of the acts constituting the offences indicates a risk of grave physical or psychological harm as required by s. 672.64(1)(b). I wish to be clear that this is not to say that the offences themselves were not brutal; they were. However, they were committed under fundamentally different circumstances than those in which Mr. Schoenborn currently finds himself, and for that reason I am unable to find him a high-risk accused under s. 672.64(1)(b).

What the *Schoenborn* case suggests is that the "high-risk accused" designation is not really an appropriate disposition for individuals who were in a state of psychosis at the time of the offence which they committed. Such individuals will usually respond to mental-health treatment and ultimately regain the ability to reintegrate peacefully into the community.

15. S.C. 2014, c. 6.

The "high-risk accused" designation is closely related to the dangerous and long-offender provisions of the *Criminal Code*,[16] which are directed at recalcitrant offenders, who are very likely to be identified as psychopaths. It is likely that the courts will, as in the *Schoenborn* case, be unwilling to treat individuals whose offence was committed while in a state of psychosis in the same manner as dangerous psychopaths and keep them in a state of protracted and indefinite custody. Dangerous and long-term offenders committed their offences while they met the criteria for criminal responsibility, whereas those individuals who are found NCRMD were, by definition, not responsible for their actions at the time of the offences with which they were charged.

Mental Disorder as a Partial Defence

There are certain circumstances in which the mental disorder of the accused at the time of the alleged offence does not meet the strict criteria for a successful NCRMD defence under section 16(1) but may nevertheless be sufficient to reduce the severity of the charge laid against them. This situation arises where the mental disorder of the accused prevents them from forming the specific intent required for such offences as murder or robbery. In order to establish the NCRMD defence, an accused person has to *prove it on the balance of probabilities*, but to reduce the seriousness of the charge against them based on the assertion that they lacked the specific intent required because of mental disorder, the accused person only has to *raise a reasonable doubt*. This situation is most likely to occur in the context of a charge of murder where the consequence of raising a doubt about the accused person's intent because of mental disorder is to convict them of manslaughter rather than murder.

For example, in *Reeves* (2017), the accused was convicted of the second-degree murder of his stepfather. Reeves told a police officer over the telephone that the victim had been stealing from him and torturing him and that he "snapped" before stabbing the victim to death. Reeves later told the officer that he had been enduring pain as a result of chips that he claimed had been implanted in his body by the CIA, and he had suffered from sickness caused by satellites passing overhead. In the absence of psychiatric evidence, the trial judge refused to instruct the jury to consider Reeves's mental condition when deciding whether he had the necessary intent for murder.

Reeves appealed his conviction and the B.C. Court of Appeal substituted a verdict of manslaughter. Reeves' mental condition clearly raised a reasonable doubt as to his intent to kill or to inflict serious bodily harm that he knew was likely to cause death and was reckless whether or not death would ensue. The Court of Appeal stated that "The question before the jury on this trial was not could the appellant form

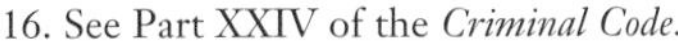

16. See Part XXIV of the *Criminal Code*.

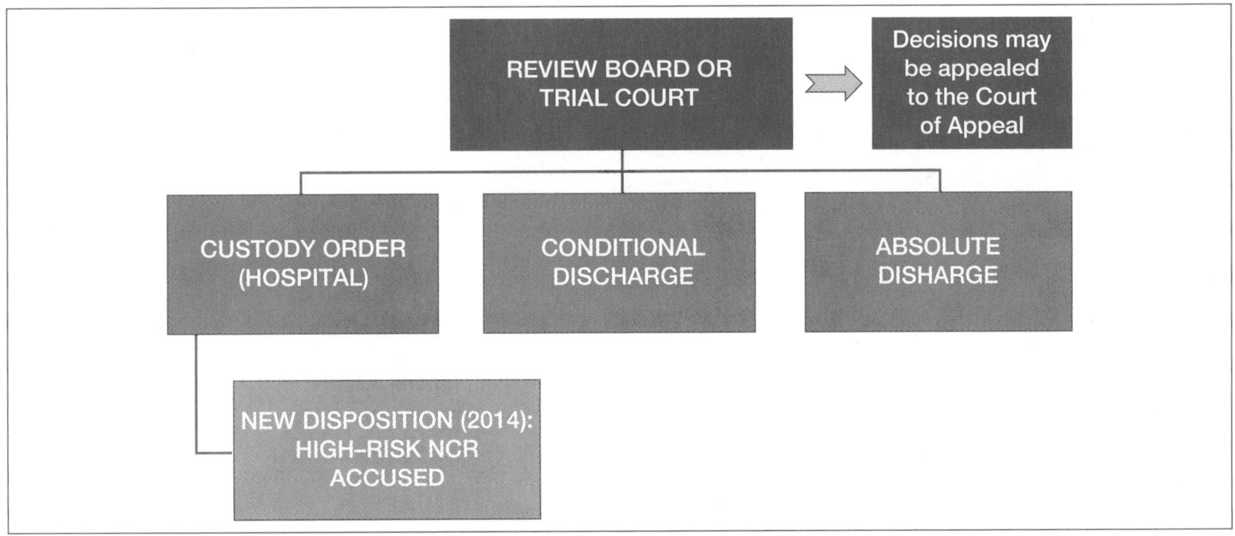

Figure 8-2

The Dispositions That May Be Imposed After a Verdict of NCRMD the intent; it was, did the appellant form the intent? And for that, the jury should have been allowed to consider the appellant's "troubling beliefs" in association with his statement that he snapped."

Clearly, *Reeves* was a case in which the original charge of murder was reduced to manslaughter because the accused had successfully raised a reasonable doubt as whether he had the necessary *mens rea* for murder. This doubt evidently stemmed from Reeves' delusional beliefs and their relationship to his statements that he had just snapped and did not intend to harm the victim. Another way in which to view the *Reeves* case is to consider it as an example of mental disorder bringing about a form of diminished responsibility, with Reeves' deluded mental state reducing the severity of the offence with which he was charged.

In the case of *Jacquard* (1997), the Supreme Court of Canada adopted a similar approach with respect to the key role that evidence of mental disorder may play in reducing a charge of first-degree to second-degree murder. Chief Justice Lamer emphasized that even though evidence of a mental disorder may not be sufficient to raise a reasonable doubt with respect to the accused person's *mens rea* for the crime of murder, such evidence may nevertheless be critical in reducing the charge from first- to second-degree murder:

> It is true that some factor, such as mental disorder, that is insufficient to negative the charge that the accused *intended* to kill, may nevertheless be sufficient to negative the elements of *planning and deliberation*. This is because one can intend to kill and yet be impulsive rather than considered in doing so. It requires less mental capacity simply to intend than it does to plan and deliberate. [emphasis in the original]

However, it is important to bear in mind that being mentally ill is not *necessarily* incompatible with a finding that the accused acted with deliberation and planning. As Justice Martin said, in delivering the judgment of the Ontario Court of Appeal in *Kirkby* (1985):

> Mental disorder may, of course, negative planning and deliberation, but if the murder is, in fact, both planned and deliberate, the existence of mental disorder does not *per se* remove the murder from the category of first degree murder. Mental disorder may or may not negative the elements of planning and deliberation, depending on the nature of the mental disorder and the effects produced by it. The fact that the offender suffers from a mental disorder is not, however, *necessarily* incompatible with the commission by him of … a "cold-blooded" murder. … I do not think that Parliament, by using the word "deliberate," imported a requirement that the offender's previous determination to kill the victim must be the result of reasonable or normal thinking or must be rationally motivated, provided the Crown has established that the killing was planned, and that the act of killing was considered and not the result of sudden impulse.

The Case of Vincent Li

On the evening of July 30, 2008, a truly horrific event took place on a Greyhound bus near Portage la Prairie, Manitoba. A young man, Tim McLean, was for no apparent reason attacked by a fellow passenger, Vincent Li. The victim was stabbed and beheaded. Subsequently, Li ate some of the victim's body parts. On March 5, 2009, Vincent Li was found not criminally responsible for the murder of Tim McLean. Both the Crown and the defence agreed with psychiatrists who found that, at the time of the killing, Li was acting under the influence of an acute psychotic illness (schizophrenia) and that, as a consequence, he was hearing voices that told him that the victim was an alien and that God was ordering him to kill the "alien" or be executed.

Li was found NCRMD and committed to the Selkirk Mental Health Centre. Shortly after arriving at the Centre, he was authorized to take secure walks outside the facility. Many members of the public complained about the walks and about the possibility of Li's eventual release. However, in 2016, Li, now known as Will Baker, was nevertheless released into the community on strict conditions and, in February 2017, he was granted an absolute discharge: since he was successfully taking antipsychotic medication and had fully recovered his mental health, the Manitoba Review Board no longer considered him to pose a "significant threat to the safety of the public."

The gruesome nature of the death of a totally innocent young victim understandably generated a tidal wave of public concern in Canada. Family members urged the passage of "Tim's Law," which would ensure that NCR accused persons such as Li would be incarcerated for life, with no possibility for parole. Many members of the public and certain politicians appeared to sympathize with this approach and, ultimately, legislation was introduced to the Parliament of Canada in 2013. Bill C-54 would have created the special designation of

THE CANADIAN PRESS/John Woods

high-risk NCR accused, which was designed to make it very difficult for such individuals to receive passes to enter the community and would prevent their release until a court removed the designation.

Bill C-54 was not enacted because of the prorogation of Parliament in September 2013. Although it did not go as far as many proponents of "Tim's Law" would have preferred, the provision was reintroduced with the new session of Parliament and, in 2014, the *Not Criminally Responsible Reform Act* was enacted (see the discussion in the text above)

The legislation potentially raises some serious *Charter* issues. In particular, the high-risk designation would appear to be predicated on an assessment of the NCR accused person's dangerousness, based not on their present mental state (after medication) but on the nature of the offence they committed in the past. Indeed, one of the criteria for the designation is that "the court is of the opinion that the acts that constitute the offence were of such a brutal nature as to indicate a risk of grave physical or psychological harm to another person." This approach appears to run afoul of the very clear statement of the Supreme Court of Canada in *Winko* (1999) that the only possible justification for restricting the liberty of an NCR accused person is that they are considered dangerous, *based on a current assessment of their mental condition and potential to create a risk to public safety*. As is the case with Li (now Baker), an individual may commit an appallingly cruel act while experiencing a severe psychotic state, but they may subsequently recover with the administration of medication and other treatment and not be considered dangerous *at the present time*. It may well be argued that restricting the liberty of an NCR accused person who has recovered from their mental disorder and no longer represents a threat to the safety of the public constitutes a violation of section 7 of the *Charter*, even though the act they committed in the past was undoubtedly horrendous.

The Li case indicates the dangers associated with hasty law reform that is fuelled by public outrage. No one would doubt the depth of the suffering experienced by the family members of the victim in this case (as well as the other passengers on the bus and the first responders and police involved at the scene of the homicide). Their experience is almost beyond words to express. However, members of the public may not fully comprehend the nature and extent of an acute psychotic episode, and it might well be argued that no civilized society should hold criminally responsible an individual who commits an act of violence while in that state of utter dislocation from reality. If such an individual is not responsible for their actions, there should be no question of basing their disposition on the punitive considerations that are relevant to the sentencing of offenders who are judged responsible for their actions. Instead, their disposition should be based on the need to protect the public from the risk that they *currently* pose to the public based on their *present mental condition*. In addition, NCR accused persons must be dealt with fairly, with due consideration being given to their need for mental health treatment. As the Supreme Court stated in *Winko*,

> The NCR accused is to be treated in a special way in a system tailored to meet the twin goals of protecting the public and treating the mentally ill offender fairly and appropriately. Under the new approach, the mentally ill offender occupies a special place in the criminal justice system; he or she is spared the full weight of criminal responsibility, but is subject to those restrictions necessary to protect the public.

The evidence is that NCR accused are highly unlikely to commit violent offences after they are discharged. This adds to the argument that the "high-risk" accused designation is a violation of the *Charter* rights of the NCR accused persons who may be targeted by the Crown.

The decision in *Schoenborn* case (2017), discussed in earlier in the text, suggests that the 2014 legislation was misguided insofar as it failed to recognize that those who commit a violent offence while in a state of psychosis should not be treated as though they were culpable for their actions and that treatments for psychosis can be so effective that NCR accused persons no longer pose a threat to anyone. Unfortunately, many members of the public continue to experience fear of the NCR accused which is fuelled by the stigma that surrounds mental illness and a lack of knowledge of the efficacy of current treatments for the psychotic conditions that caused the types of horrific violence committed by NCR accused such as Vincent Li and Allan Schoenborn.

What do you think should be done to assist the victims of such tragic events as the killing of Tim McLean? What programs do you think might be effective as a means of assisting the general public to understand the nature of serious mental health conditions that involve episodes of acute psychosis? How might the public's fear of individuals who live with serious mental illness be reduced? Do you agree with the creation of the "high-risk accused" designation? Do you believe that it infringes the *Charter* rights of NCR accused persons and, if so, is such an infringement justified under section 1 of the *Charter*?

AUTOMATISM

DEFINITION OF AUTOMATISM

Automatism has been defined as "a state of impaired consciousness ... in which an individual, though capable of action, has no voluntary control over that action" [Justice Bastarache, on behalf of the majority of the Supreme Court of Canada in *Stone* (1999)]. Provided the state of automatism did not arise because of a mental disorder or as a consequence of self-induced intoxication, then the individual affected by it is entitled to be acquitted of a criminal charge.

As Justice La Forest, of the Supreme Court of Canada, noted in the case of *Parks* (1992), the defence of automatism is directly relevant to the question of whether the Crown has established that the accused has committed the *actus reus* elements of a criminal offence: "Automatism occupies a unique place in our criminal law system. Although spoken of as a "defence," it is conceptually a subset of the voluntariness requirement which in turn is part of the *actus reus* component of criminal liability."

It would be a serious mistake to confuse automatism with a state of complete unconsciousness. Indeed, as Justice Bastarache pointed out in the *Stone* case (1999), "medically speaking, unconscious means 'flat on the floor,' that is a comatose-type state." Clearly, a comatose individual is not capable of carrying out any actions at all—let alone a crime! Therefore, it is more accurate, Justice Bastarache said, to define automatism as being a form of "impaired consciousness, rather than unconsciousness." Perhaps it is most helpful to think of automatism as constituting a state of *severely clouded consciousness that prevents the accused from acting voluntarily*.

While the NCRMD defence is focused on the negation of the *mens rea* elements of a criminal offence, the automatism defence is concerned with the negation of the *actus reus* elements of an offence. Conceptually, there are at least five separate categories of automatism: (1) automatism caused by "normal" conditions such as hypnosis (which are not considered by the courts to be the result of mental disorder); (2) automatism triggered by an external trauma, such as a blow to the head; (3) automatism that is *involuntarily* induced by alcohol or other drugs; (4) automatism that is voluntarily self-induced by the use of alcohol or other drugs; and (5) automatism caused by a mental disorder (or a "disease of the mind"). However, only those conditions that fall within categories (1) to (3) may lead to the acquittal of an accused person on the basis of the legal defence of automatism.

AUTOMATISM CAUSED BY "NORMAL" STATES SUCH AS SLEEPWALKING

A person who acts in a state of automatism that is associated with a "normal" condition, such as hypnosis or sleepwalking, is entitled to a complete acquittal of any criminal charge. The use of the adjective "normal" is intended to emphasize that these conditions are not the result of a mental disorder. They are conditions that might be experienced by any individual who is subjected to a particular form of stress or process, such as hypnosis.

The commission of criminal offences in such conditions is extremely rare; however, the important case of *Parks* (1992) demonstrates that, in certain circumstances, this category of automatism may result in an acquittal.

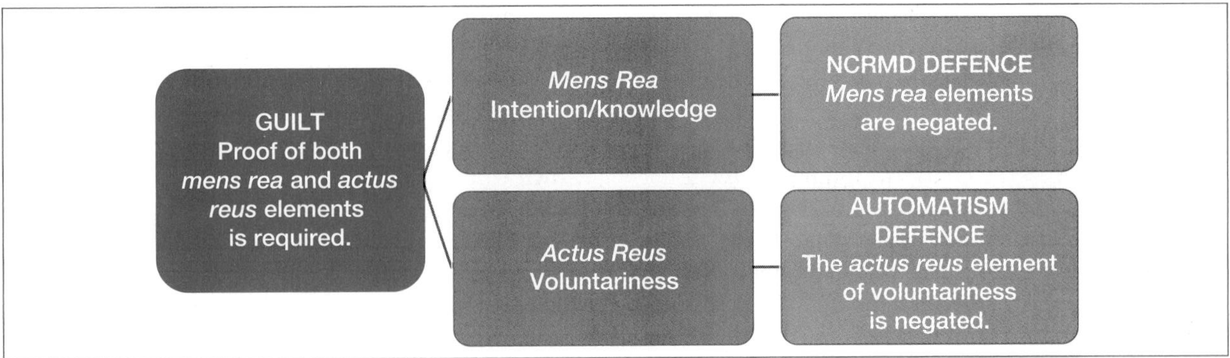

Figure 8-3
Criminal Responsibility and the Defences of NCRMD and Automatism

In *Parks*, the evidence indicated that the accused had apparently fallen asleep and then driven some 23 kilometres to the home of his parents-in-law, where he stabbed and beat them both. His mother-in-law died from her injuries, while his father-in-law ultimately survived his serious injuries. A number of expert witnesses appeared for the defence and supported a defence based on sleepwalking; the Crown, however presented no expert evidence on this issue. Testimony was presented to the effect that Parks had enjoyed "excellent relations" with his parents-in-law prior to the incident in question and that several members of his family had been affected by sleep disorders, such as sleepwalking, adult enuresis (bed-wetting), nightmares, and sleeptalking.

Parks was acquitted at his trial on the basis that he was acting in a state of automatism at the time of the attacks on his parents-in-law. The Ontario Court of Appeal affirmed his acquittal on an appeal by the Crown and underscored the view that sleepwalking is a normal condition. The Crown subsequently appealed to the Supreme Court of Canada, but the Supreme Court agreed with the Ontario Court of Appeal and dismissed the appeal. As Chief Justice Lamer pointed out, the medical evidence had been that "a person who is sleepwalking cannot think, reflect or perform voluntary acts." More specifically, there was expert testimony to the effect that "during the slow wave sleep stage the cortex, which is the part of the brain that controls thinking and voluntary movement, is essentially in coma" and that "when a person is sleepwalking, the movements he makes are controlled by other parts of the brain and are more or less reflexive." Since Parks was sleepwalking at the time of the attacks on his parents-in-law, he was not capable of acting voluntarily; therefore, he could not be convicted of a criminal offence.

It is quite probable that the *Parks* case would be decided differently if it were to come before the courts today. As a result of the decision of the Supreme Court of Canada in *Stone* (1999), there is now a presumption that a state of automatism is caused by a mental disorder and that, if this presumption is not rebutted by the accused person, the only possible outcome for a successful defence is a verdict of NCRMD rather than an acquittal. In *Luedecke* (2008), for example, the Ontario Court of Appeal, relying on the *Stone* case, ruled that a condition of "sexomnia" (in which an individual may engage in sexual activity while asleep) should be considered a mental disorder and that the accused person should be found NCRMD by virtue of section 16(1) of the *Criminal Code*. In light of the change in the law brought about by *Stone*, therefore, it is likely that the courts will now consider sleepwalking a mental disorder and, as a consequence, the *Parks* case may no longer be considered a precedent for acquitting an accused person in similar circumstances.

Automatism Triggered by an External Trauma

Perhaps the classic example of automatism is the situation in which an external blow to the head causes an episode of impaired consciousness, during which the accused engages in conduct that would otherwise be considered criminal. Even though a person who has suffered such a blow to the head may *appear* to be acting normally, they are nevertheless in a state of altered consciousness and are not able to control their conduct. Since the accused person, in these circumstances, acts in a state of impaired consciousness, it is clear that they will be unable to recall any of the events following the trauma to the head; therefore, an important element of the accused's condition is that they experience **amnesia**.

In the case of *Bleta* (1965), for example, the accused and a man called Gafi were fighting in a Toronto street. In the course of the fracas, Bleta fell and hit his head on the pavement. Bleta regained his feet and followed Gafi, who had started to walk away. Bleta then drew a knife and fatally stabbed Gafi in the neck area. Two of the bystanders watching the fight, as well as a police officer, commented that Bleta appeared to be in a "dazed condition" at the time of the fatal blow. Bleta's counsel successfully contended that his client was acting unconsciously and with no voluntary control over his actions at the time of the stabbing. The Supreme Court of Canada implicitly accepted the legitimacy of the automatism defence, although it decided the *Bleta* case on other grounds.

Automatism Involuntarily Induced by Alcohol or Other Drugs

Accused persons who, through no *voluntary* action on their part, become so severely impaired by alcohol or other drugs that they fall into a state of automatism are entitled to be acquitted of a criminal charge because they are incapable of acting voluntarily. For example, suppose that Fanny laces Nell's orange juice with vodka without Nell's knowledge. In these circumstances, if Nell lapses into a state of automatism, she must be acquitted of any criminal charge arising out of her activities while she was in such a condition. Similarly, in the case of *King* (1962), the accused visited a dentist to have two teeth extracted. For this purpose, he was injected with sodium pentothal, a quick-acting anesthetic. The accused claimed that he received no warning that he might subsequently become impaired by the drug and that he was not advised to refrain from driving a motor vehicle. King left the dentist's office, entered his car, and became unconscious while driving it. His car then crashed into a parked vehicle and he was charged with impaired driving. He was subsequently convicted at his trial; however, this conviction was set aside by the Ontario Court of Appeal. The Supreme Court of Canada affirmed the judgment of the Court of Appeal. Although the Supreme Court justices appeared to have different reasons for this decision, there was general agreement that an accused person should not be convicted of an offence if they did not act voluntarily. In the *King* case, it was clear that the accused's impairment was caused by a drug that had been administered by a dentist in the course of a recognized medical procedure and that the effect of the drug was apparently not made known to the accused.

It should be mentioned that the defence that was raised by the accused in the *King* case would be most unlikely to succeed before the courts of today. Hospitals, medical offices, and dentists' surgeries currently require a patient to sign a form prior to any medical procedure that requires the administration of an anesthetic that might impair consciousness. This form generally notifies patients that they must not drive a vehicle and should arrange for other transportation (for example, relatives or a taxi) to pick them up after the procedure. Similarly, it is unlikely that accused persons who have taken prescription drugs would be able to successfully claim that they became impaired involuntarily because of lack of knowledge of the effects of the drugs in question. Indeed, in most parts of Canada, pharmacists routinely place a red warning label indicating that certain drugs should not be mixed with alcohol or specifically warning patients that they should not operate machinery in the event of drowsiness. In short, in contemporary times, it would be very difficult for an individual to claim that they could not have foreseen that a drug or other intoxicating substance could cause impairment of consciousness. If there is *foresight of impairment* and the drug or substance is *taken of the individual's own accord*, then there is absolutely no basis for claiming that the accused acted involuntarily.[17]

Automatism Voluntarily Self-Induced by Alcohol or Other Drugs

The general rule of Canadian criminal law is that accused persons who have *voluntarily* ingested alcohol and/or other drugs and have, as a consequence, experienced a state of altered consciousness are *barred*

17. However, in *Barrett* (2012), the Newfoundland and Labrador Court of Appeal upheld the acquittal of the accused on a charge of impaired driving. The impairment was caused by a pain-killing drug, Tramacet, which he had been prescribed after mouth surgery. The trial judge found that Barrett had not been given any information that would have warned him of the dangers of impairment when taking large dosages. The trial judge took the view that, while Barrett had been negligent, he had not been reckless (the minimum *mens rea* necessary for conviction of the offence).

from raising the defence of automatism. At best, they may be able to raise the *partial defence of intoxication* (discussed in Chapter 10) and, if successful, they will be convicted of a less serious offence rather than given an absolute acquittal. For example, a successful defence of intoxication will lead to the accused being acquitted of a charge of murder and convicted, instead, of the less serious offence of manslaughter.

Traditionally, the courts have assumed that those who *voluntarily* ingest intoxicating substances are *at fault* in so doing and are, therefore, not entitled to the absolute acquittal that follows a successful assertion of a defence of automatism. Such people would be considered to be at fault because it may be taken for granted that every citizen is fully aware that the consumption of intoxicating substances can lead to impairment and that this impairment might cause them to act in a way that might infringe the law. When individuals have ingested such substances of their own free will and with an awareness of the potential consequences of their conduct, then, naturally, the courts will consider that they have voluntarily chosen to run the risk that they might commit an offence of some kind.

However, an accused person may well say, "If I can establish that I was *acting involuntarily at the specific moment that I committed the conduct* in question, then convicting me of a criminal offence for what took place while I was in this state of automatism violates my rights under section 7 of the *Charter*." More specifically, the accused might contend that convicting them in such circumstances constitutes a deprivation of the "right to liberty and security of the person" in a manner that is not "in accordance with the principles of fundamental justice." Is this a valid constitutional argument against the traditional principle of criminal law that bars the accused from pleading automatism when they have become intoxicated voluntarily?

In the *Penno* case (1990), the Supreme Court of Canada was confronted with this constitutional argument in the context of a charge of being impaired while in care and control of a motor vehicle (under, what was then section 253 of the *Code*; now, section 320.14). The accused contended that it was a violation of section 7 to convict him of this charge when he was in such an extreme state of intoxication that he had no awareness of even entering his vehicle. However, the Court firmly ruled that there was no violation of the *Charter* in these circumstances. The Court emphasized the fact that impaired driving offences are quite distinct from other "true crimes" that are to be found in the *Criminal Code* and that individuals accused of committing these serious offences should not be permitted to raise the defence of automatism. In effect, for people accused of an offence under section 253 (320.14) to claim the benefit of the defence of automatism, it would have to be shown that they were intoxicated to such an extreme degree that they were not aware of what they were doing when they assumed care and control of or started to drive a motor vehicle. If such an argument were to lead to an acquittal, it would mean that the more intoxicated such accused persons became, the more likely they would be to gain a total acquittal on the basis of automatism! Obviously, this would fly in the face of the need to protect Canadians from the very real and immediate dangers posed to them by impaired drivers.

In rejecting the contention that highly intoxicated motorists can plead the defence of automatism, Justice Wilson pointed out, in her judgment in the *Penno* case, that Parliament had made impairment an essential element of the *actus reus* of the offences contained in section 253 (320.14) of the *Code* and there is no infringement of the *Charter* when the accused person, in such circumstances, is prevented from raising the defence of automatism. In her view:

> [T]he mental element of the offence under [s. 253] includes the voluntary consumption of alcohol but the *actus reus* requires the voluntary consumption of alcohol to the point of impairment. The distinction appears to make sense in that alcohol consumption to the point of impairment could well negate the intent to have care or control of the motor vehicle and result in the absence of *mens rea* whereas simple consumption might not. The *actus reus* requires impairment by alcohol and not just the prior consumption of alcohol. By making the requirement of impairment an element of the *actus reus* rather than the *mens rea* of the offence, Parliament has avoided the vicious circle which would otherwise be inherent in the offence.

However, when the Supreme Court of Canada addressed a constitutional challenge to the traditional rule excluding self-induced intoxication from the scope of the automatism in a case that fell outside the specific context of impaired driving charges, it adopted a totally different approach. Indeed, in *Daviault* (1994), a case involving a charge of sexual assault, the Court held that, if extreme—albeit voluntarily induced—intoxication produces a state of mind "akin to automatism or insanity," then the accused is entitled to an outright acquittal. The Court held that it would indeed infringe section 7 of the *Charter* if severely impaired persons could be convicted of criminal offences despite the fact that they lacked even a minimal awareness of what they were doing. Justice Cory stated that the "fundamental principles of justice" enshrined in section 7 of the *Charter* would be infringed in such circumstances because the Crown would not be able to establish the voluntariness component of the *actus reus* of the offence charged. Nevertheless, the impact of the *Daviault* case was remarkably short-lived. In 1995, Parliament decided to "trump" the *Daviault* decision by amending the *Criminal Code*. This move was felt to be necessary because many Canadians had expressed their shock at the implications of the Supreme Court's decision for the prosecution of those who, in a state of intoxication, commit violent acts against women and children.

Parliament added a new section, 33.1, to seriously blunt the impact of the *Daviault* case. The effect of the new provision was later summarized by Justice Bastarache when he delivered the judgment of the majority of the justices of the Supreme Court of Canada in *Daley* (2007):

> [Section 33.1] amends the *Code* so that those with a *Daviault* defence will be convicted of the same violent general intent offences they would have been convicted of before the Court's decision. This provision appears to amend the law such that extreme intoxication to the point of automatism or involuntariness is only available for offences that do not include as an element "an assault or any other interference or threat of interference by a person with the bodily integrity of another person."

In light of section 33.1, individuals who voluntarily induce a state of extreme intoxication are clearly precluded from raising the automatism defence if they should be charged with offences involving personal violence. Instead, section 33.1 limits these individuals to raising the *partial defence* of intoxication, which, as we shall see later, is only available in relation to a limited number of offences, known as "specific intent" offences.

Section 33.1, however, only applies to "*self-induced* intoxication." If intoxication is caused *involuntarily*, then the accused person may well advance a successful plea of automatism, resulting in an acquittal. The precise meaning of "*self-induced* intoxication" was considered by the Nova Scotia Court of Appeal in *Chaulk* (2007). The accused had broken into the victim's apartment and threatened him and his children with death. Chaulk also threw a computer and a television onto the floor, removed all his clothes, and grabbed a female neighbour by the blouse. The police were called and Chaulk was arrested. He was "naked, sweating profusely and babbling, vacillating between compliant and combative." The police took Chaulk to the hospital, where the emergency room doctor was of the opinion that Chaulk's condition "was consistent with exposure to chemicals or stimulant-type drugs." Chaulk told another doctor that he had consumed a mixture of "acid, ecstasy and marijuana." However, he later repudiated this statement and claimed that he had not ingested any drugs or alcohol before attending a party, where he drank eight bottles of beer, smoked a marijuana joint, and consumed what he thought was a "wake-up," or caffeine, pill. The trial judge ruled that Chaulk's intoxication was not self-induced and, therefore, section 33.1 did not apply to him. Chaulk successfully raised the defence of automatism/extreme intoxication (as defined in the *Daviault* case) and was acquitted on a number of criminal charges. However, the Crown appealed and the Nova Scotia Court of Appeal ordered a new trial. The appellate court ruled that the trial judge had applied an incorrect test in determining that Chaulk's condition was not self-induced and had failed to address the inconsistency in Chaulk's statements about the nature of the drugs and alcohol he had consumed.

The Court of Appeal articulated the criteria that should be applied when a court is called upon to decide whether the accused person's state of automatism/extreme intoxication was "self-induced' within the meaning of section 33.1. In the words of Justice Bateman:

> I would ... express the test for self-induced intoxication as follows:
>
> (i) The accused voluntarily consumed a substance which;
>
> (ii) S/he knew or ought to have known was an intoxicant and;
>
> (iii) The risk of becoming intoxicated was or should have been within his/her contemplation.

The Court of Appeal also stated that, to establish that the accused person's state of intoxication was self-induced, the Crown does not have to prove that the accused person knew exactly what the substance was that they were taking nor that the accused person's purpose was to "experience its effects."

To date, no appellate court in Canada has addressed the constitutionality of section 33.1 of the *Criminal Code*. Based on the reasoning of the Supreme Court in *Daviault*, it might well be argued that section 33.1 infringes both sections 7 and 11(d) of the *Charter*. However, it might also be asserted that, even if section 33.1 does infringe an accused person's *Charter* rights, it is nevertheless saved by section 1 of the *Charter* as a "reasonable limit." However, in the case of *Bouchard-LeBrun* (2011), the Supreme Court of Canada applied section 33.1 to the facts before it, but did not comment on its constitutionality because the appellant's counsel did not raise this issue. It remains to be seen if there will be a challenge—successful or otherwise—to the constitutionality of this important legislative reform in the years ahead.[18]

AUTOMATISM DISTINGUISHED FROM AMNESIA

It is important to distinguish between *automatism* and **amnesia** (loss of memory). The defence of automatism is concerned with the question of whether accused persons acted voluntarily at the time of their alleged offences. The fact that they have no recollection of what happened does not necessarily mean that they acted involuntarily. For example, it is a common consequence of consuming alcohol that individuals may act *voluntarily and in a conscious, purposive manner*, but still not have any memory of what happened at a certain point after they started to drink. Clearly, such people should not be absolved of criminal liability simply because they cannot remember the crimes they committed while under the influence of alcohol that was consumed voluntarily.

Take, for example, the sad case of *Honish* (1991), in which the accused went to a motel and consumed a large quantity of antidepressant drugs and sleeping pills mixed with alcohol. His intention was to commit suicide. However, one hour later, he was driving his car and was involved in a serious accident; he went through a yield sign and struck another vehicle, causing injuries to three of its occupants, including a small child. Honish drove through the intersection and came to a stop only when he struck a parked vehicle. He was charged with three counts of impaired driving causing bodily harm. However, Honish claimed that he had absolutely no recollection of what had happened between the time he was lying down on his bed in the motel and the moment he woke up in hospital after the accident. Was this state of amnesia relevant to Honish's criminal responsibility? A critical finding of fact made by the trial judge was that Honish was *not acting in a state of automatism* at the time of the accident. There were skid marks, indicating that Honish had attempted to take evasive action, and there was evidence that he had initially climbed out of his car and engaged in "sharp verbal exchanges" with one of the wounded passengers in the car he had struck in the intersection. At that time, Honish also apologized for having hit the people in the other car and admitted he was drunk. The trial judge, therefore, held that Honish had not been in a state of automatism at the time of the accident, and this meant that his state of amnesia was irrelevant. The accused was convicted on all three counts and his appeals to both the Alberta Court of Appeal and the Supreme Court of Canada were rejected. (Incidentally, it is important to note that, even if the cocktail of drugs and alcohol ingested by Honish had indeed produced a genuine state of automatism, he would nevertheless still have been prevented from successfully raising a defence based on his extreme state of voluntarily induced intoxication: see the *Penno* case (1990) and section 33.1 of the *Criminal Code*, discussed in the previous section.)

AUTOMATISM CAUSED BY A MENTAL DISORDER

Where the accused's condition is caused by a mental disorder, they are not entitled to be acquitted by reason of the defence of automatism. Instead, the court must treat the accused's defence as being that of not criminally responsible on account of mental disorder (NCRMD) in accordance with the provisions of section 16 of the *Code* (as was discussed earlier in this chapter).

The courts have drawn a sharp distinction between automatism, which leads to a complete acquittal of the accused, and the NCRMD defence, which leads to a special verdict, under section 672.34, that "the accused committed the act or made the omission but

18. In *Chan* (2018), the Ontario Superior Court of Justice applied s. 33.1 to a case in which the accused had committed murder and other offences while hallucinating, following the ingestion of the drug, Psilocybin. Boswell J. ruled that s. 33.1 infringed both sections 11(d) and 7 of the *Charter*, but was "saved" by s. 1.

is not criminally responsible on account of mental disorder." This distinction is critical because the special NCRMD verdict may result in the accused being kept in custody in a psychiatric facility or being released into the community under far-reaching conditions (section 672.54). In contrast, those defendants who are acquitted as a consequence of the successful assertion of a defence of automatism immediately leave the courtroom without any restrictions whatsoever on their future freedom of action. As Justice Bastarache, of the Supreme Court of Canada, aptly noted in the case of *Stone* (1999), "[T]he determination of whether mental disorder or non-mental disorder automatism should be left with the trier of fact must be taken very carefully since it will have serious ramifications for both the individual and society in general."

THE DEFINITION OF MENTAL DISORDER: PROBLEMS OF JUDICIAL INTERPRETATION

In the past, the courts found it extremely difficult to decide whether certain types of mental condition (such as clouded consciousness associated with a sleepwalking episode or extreme psychological shock) should be placed within the category of "disease of the mind," thereby bringing the accused under the provisions of section 16 of the *Criminal Code*, or whether they should be classified as a form of automatism, thereby laying the basis for an unqualified acquittal, should the accused person's defence prove successful at trial.

How have the courts attempted to resolve the question of whether the accused's condition does—or does not—constitute a "disease of the mind"? In the past, they relied on two major approaches. The first of these involved drawing a distinction between *internal* and *external* causes of a state of automatism. If a state of automatism is precipitated by an *internal* condition (such as epilepsy), then it must be classified as a "disease of the mind." On the other hand, if the state of automatism is induced by an *external* cause (such as a blow to the head or an injection of insulin), then it must be classified as non-mental-disorder automatism. The second approach, which is not necessarily inconsistent with the first, revolves around a determination as to whether the state of automatism is likely to recur—the so-called "continuing danger" theory. The courts took the view that if a condition was ongoing in nature and likely to recur, it constituted sound social policy to classify it as a "disease of the mind": in this way, it would be possible to require that the accused person undergo the treatment that may be necessary to prevent a recurrence of the automatism.

However, in the *Stone* case (1999), the majority of the Supreme Court of Canada adopted the view that judges should not be restricted to the "internal cause" and "continuing danger" theories when they are required to determine whether a specific mental condition constitutes a "disease of the mind" for the purposes of section 16 of the *Criminal Code*. The Supreme Court ruled that judges should also take into account questions of public policy such as whether the alleged state of automatism may be easily feigned and whether acquittal of a defendant on the basis of a particular form of automatism, such as sleepwalking, would open the floodgates to a wave of similar defences in the future. In the *Stone* case, Justice Bastarache stated that the courts should embrace "a more holistic approach" when deciding whether a state of automatism should be categorized as a "disease of the mind." In his view:

> [T]he continuing danger factor should not be viewed as an alternative or mutually exclusive approach to the internal cause factor. Although different, both of these approaches are relevant in the disease of the mind inquiry. As such, in any given case, a trial judge may find one, the other or both of these approaches of assistance. To reflect this unified, holistic approach to the disease of the mind question, it is therefore more appropriate to refer to the internal cause factor and the continuing danger factor, rather than the internal cause theory and the continuing danger theory.

However, it is significant that, in the *Stone* case, the majority of the Supreme Court of Canada stated that there should be a *presumption that any state of automatism is the result of a mental disorder*. Justice Bastarache noted that "it will only be in rare cases that automatism is not caused by mental disorder." In his judgment, he suggests that there should be a

> rule that trial judges start from the proposition that the condition the accused claims to have suffered from is a disease of the mind. ...
>
> They must then determine whether the evidence in the particular case takes the condition out of the disease of the mind category.

Undoubtedly, the *Stone* case signalled an intention on the part of the Supreme Court to reduce the scope of the automatism defence in favour of an approach that results in a finding that the accused is NCRMD—a verdict that leaves the door unequivocally open for the imposition of post-trial restrictions on the accused's liberty (for example, the requirement of treatment).

An example of this new approach was manifested in the case of *Luedecke* (2008). The accused was charged with sexual assault of a stranger. Both the victim and Luedecke had been present at a party and had fallen asleep in close proximity to each other. The victim, who did not know Luedecke, woke up at 5:00 in the morning and, to her horror, found that Luedecke was engaged in an act of sexual intercourse with her. The victim screamed at Luedecke and pushed him away. He raised himself onto his knees and, according to the victim, looked "dazed" and "completely incoherent." She also stated that Luedecke looked like someone who had just been "woken up out of a sound sleep." Luedecke admitted having non-consensual sexual relations but asserted that he was unaware of what he was doing and was acting involuntarily at the time of the incident: specifically, he stated that he was in a state of sexomnia (engaging in sexual activity while asleep). A sleep disorder specialist, whose evidence was not challenged by the Crown, testified that Luedecke "was in a parasomniac state while engaging in sexual activity" with the victim. The expert stated that "parasomnia involves a sudden unexplained arousal from sleep" and "persons may carry out various physical activities while in a parasomniac state." The term "sexomnia" applies to "parasomnias during which an individual engages in some form of sexual activity." According to the expert, "a person who is experiencing a parasomniac episode acts without any volition, consciousness, or capacity to control his or her behaviour."

The trial judge found that Luedecke had acted involuntarily and that parasomnia was not a disease of the mind. He therefore acquitted Luedecke on the basis of non-mental-disorder automatism. The Crown appealed to the Ontario Court of Appeal, which ordered a new trial. The appellate court indicated that, in light of the decision of the Supreme Court of Canada in *Stone* (1999), sexomnia should be considered a disease of the mind, thereby dictating that the accused should be found NCRMD and not given the benefit of an acquittal.

In delivering the judgment of the Court of Appeal, Justice Doherty set out the policy considerations that motivated the categorization of sexomnia as a mental disorder:

> The respondent personifies one of the most difficult problems encountered in the criminal law. As a result of his parasomnia, he did a terrible thing, he sexually assaulted a defenceless, young victim. The reason for his conduct automatism brought on by parasomnia renders his actions non-culpable in the eyes of the criminal law. That very same explanation, however, makes his behaviour potentially dangerous and raises legitimate public safety concerns. An outright acquittal reflects the non-culpable nature of the conduct but does nothing to address the potential danger posed by the respondent's condition. The Canadian criminal law responds to the public safety concerns by treating almost all automatisms as the product of a mental disorder leading not to an acquittal but to an NCR-MD verdict. That verdict acknowledges that the accused committed the prohibited act but is not criminally culpable. An NCR-MD verdict also permits an individualized post-verdict dangerousness assessment of the accused leading to a disposition tailored to the specifics of the individual case. On a proper application of the principles developed in the Canadian case law, the respondent's automatism is properly characterized as a mental disorder and should have led to an NCR-MD verdict.

However, Justice Doherty emphasized that the NCRMD verdict is a *legal* judgment, not a medical or psychiatric diagnosis. Luedecke would not be considered "mentally ill" in the usual sense of that label. However, in the context of the criminal law, a determination that the accused lives with a mental disorder is—to a significant extent—based on the assessment that they represent a potential danger to the public. Unlike an acquittal on the basis of non-mental-disorder automatism, an NCRMD verdict enables the court or a review board to impose appropriate restraints on the liberty of the accused, thereby reducing the risk of any danger to the safety of Canadians.

Psychological Blow Automatism

Prior to the decision of the Supreme Court of Canada in *Stone* (1999), Canadian courts had recognized a form of automatism known as "psychological blow automatism." This version of the automatism defence strongly reflects the influence of the so-called "internal–external test." It is indisputable that a physical blow to the head must be considered an external factor and that, if it causes a state of unconsciousness, the accused is entitled to an absolute acquittal on the basis of automatism. However, what is the situation if the accused claims to have been in a state of dissociation (where the mind does not go with the body) as the consequence of a *psychological* blow? More specifically, should such a blow be considered an external or an internal factor?

Canadian courts have adopted the view that if a psychological blow is alleged to have precipitated a state of automatism, then the question of whether this state should be considered as having been caused by a "disease of the mind" should be answered by determining whether an "average normal person" would have entered into a state of dissociation in the same circumstances. If the particular type of shock alleged would not cause an "average normal person" to enter into a state of automatism, then it may reasonably be concluded that the cause of the dissociation was something internal to the accused—that is to say, a "disease of the mind." For example, if an individual enters into a state of dissociation after witnessing an exceptionally violent attack on a loved one, a court would determine that this reaction is one that might well be experienced by an "average normal person." However, if an individual enters into a state of dissociation and commits a violent crime after discovering that the person for whom they have romantic feelings does not reciprocate them, then a court would be very likely to rule that such an extreme reaction is not one which would be induced in the "average normal person." Such a reaction is so "over the top" that it must have its root in some psychological abnormality on the part of the individual concerned: therefore, the dissociated state should be categorized as a mental disorder in the legal sense of that term.

In the *Stone* case, the Supreme Court of Canada strongly endorsed this approach. Stone was charged with the murder of his wife, whom he had stabbed 47 times. Stone stated that, while travelling with him by car, the victim had insulted and berated him over an extended period. He recounted that he had stopped the vehicle in a parking lot, where the alleged insults continued. According to Stone, the taunts made by his wife included some hurtful comments about his lack of sexual prowess. Stone stated that he had suddenly experienced a "whoosh" sensation that "washed over him from his feet to his head." When he was finally able to focus his eyes again, he found that he was standing over his wife's dead body and that he was holding a hunting knife in his hand. At his trial, Stone claimed that he had been in a "dissociative" state at the time of the killing and sought to rely on the defence of psychological blow automatism. The trial judge ruled that if the accused really had been in a dissociative state, then it had been caused by a "disease of the mind" and the appropriate defence was that of NCRMD under section 16 of the *Criminal Code*. The jury ultimately rejected the NCRMD defence and convicted Stone of manslaughter (accepting the accused's alternative defence of provocation, as defined by section 215 of the *Code*).

The Supreme Court of Canada subsequently rejected Stone's appeal, ruling that, in the circumstances of this particular case, the trial judge had been perfectly correct to refuse to put a defence of psychological blow automatism to the jury. Justice Bastarache, speaking for the majority of the Court, following the "holistic approach" discussed above, ruled that the trial judge had been correct to rule that the dissociated state in which Stone claimed he attacked his spouse was, in the legal sense, a disease of the mind. The internal cause and continuing danger factors, as well as the relevant policy considerations, all pointed to this categorization of Stone's alleged condition at the time of the homicide: "In particular, the trigger in this case was not ... "extraordinary external events" that would amount to an extreme shock or psychological blow that would cause a normal person, in the circumstances of the accused, to suffer a dissociation in the absence of a disease of the mind."

Justice Bastarache emphasized that where an accused person claims to have been suffering from psychological blow automatism, there must be evidence of "an *extremely shocking trigger*," because only such an overwhelmingly powerful event is likely to cause a "normal person" to react by "entering an automatistic state." In *Stone*, the accused could not point to such a severe trigger; indeed, the circumstances of his case suggested that it was more appropriate for Stone to raise the partial defence of provocation (which reduces murder to manslaughter). It is also noteworthy that Justice Bastarache took the view that the "plausibility" of a claim of psychological blow automatism is significantly reduced if a single individual "is both the *trigger* of the alleged automatism and the *victim* of the automatistic violence" (as was the case with Stone's wife); indeed, such a claim should be "considered suspect." This is an important ruling insofar as it ensures that the psychological blow automatism defence may not be raised successfully in cases of alleged provocation. Finally, Justice

Bastarache made some interesting observations about the applicability of the "continuing danger factor" in the context of a psychological blow automatism defence. He noted that the courts should really be focusing their attention on whether the alleged trigger of an automatistic episode is likely to recur: "The greater the anticipated frequency of the trigger in the accused's life, the greater the risk posed to the public and, consequently, the more likely it is that the condition alleged by the accused is a disease of the mind."

All things considered, the decision of the Supreme Court of Canada in the *Stone* case will render it extremely difficult to successfully raise a defence of psychological blow automatism in the future. Only the most extreme forms of shock will be considered to constitute the kind of psychological blow that might cause an ordinary person to enter into a state of dissociation. In the absence of evidence of such an extreme assault on an individual's mind, the courts will hold that the only defence available to the accused is that of NCRMD under section 16 of the *Criminal Code*.

Illustration by Greg Holoboff

An extreme psychological blow could trigger a state of non-mental-disorder automatism.

Automatism and the Persuasional Burden of Proof

A golden thread that runs through the fabric of Canadian criminal law is the presumption of innocence: indeed, this is a principle that is now enshrined in section 11(d) of the *Canadian Charter of Rights and Freedoms*. Before an accused person may be found guilty of having committed a criminal offence, the Crown must first prove all of the *mens rea* and *actus reus* elements of that offence; furthermore, the Crown is required to prove its case "*beyond any reasonable doubt.*" In other words, the **persuasional burden of proof** is placed on the shoulders of the prosecution and the *standard of proof* that must be met is that of proof *beyond a reasonable doubt*.

Nevertheless, in the *Stone* case (1999), the Supreme Court of Canada (by a 5–4 majority) held that where the defence of automatism has been raised, the persuasional burden of proof must be placed on the accused: in other words, the accused has to prove their innocence—a requirement that constitutes a dramatic exception to the general rule that applies to the conduct of criminal trials in Canada. However, the **standard of proof** is not that of "beyond a reasonable doubt" but rather that of "*on the balance of probabilities*" (the same standard of proof that applies in civil trials in Canada). Put more simply, the accused must prove that it was more probable than not that, at the time of the alleged offence, they were in a state of automatism. As Justice Bastarache stated, on behalf of the majority in Stone, "[T]he legal burden in cases involving automatism must be on the defence to prove involuntariness on a balance of probabilities to the trier of fact."

Is it justifiable to require an accused person to prove the defence of automatism, rather than leaving it to the Crown to disprove it? Justice Bastarache reasoned that it is necessary for this exception to be made to the general rule. He took the view that genuine cases of automatism are "extremely rare" and the reality is that it is a condition that may be "easily feigned" by those who attempt to avoid all responsibility for their actions by merely saying, "I don't remember anything about it!" Furthermore, Justice Bastarache stated that most, if not all, of the necessary medical information concerning the alleged condition of automatism rests firmly in the control

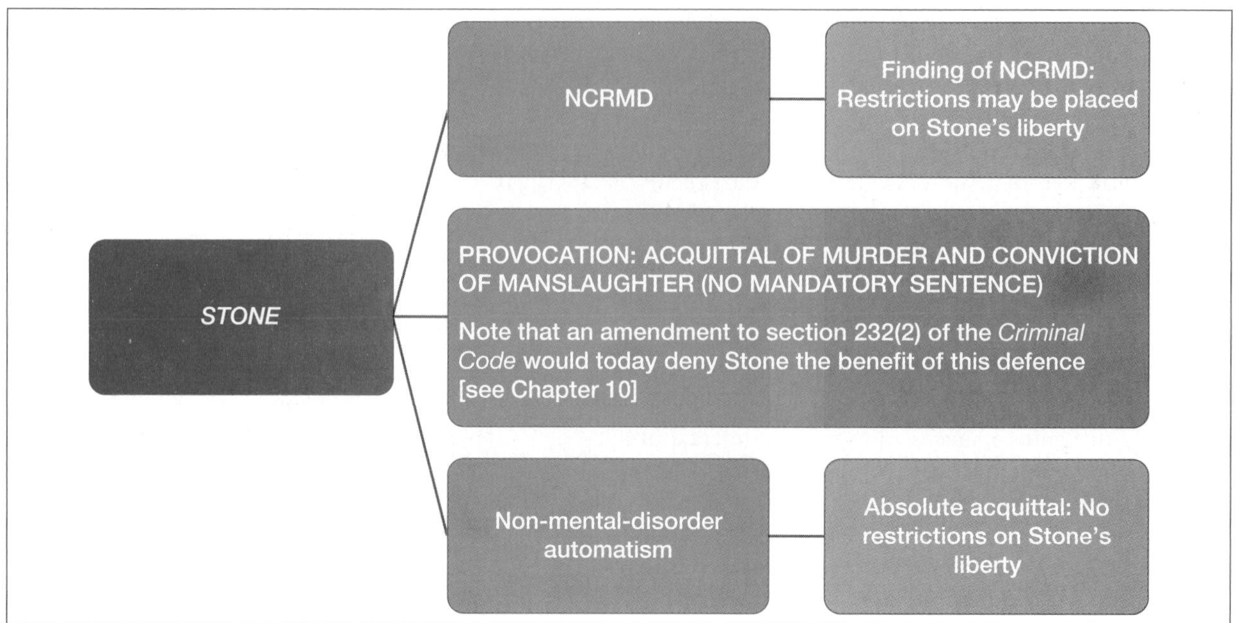

Figure 8-4

The Three Potential Verdicts in the Stone *Case (1999)*

of the accused. Indeed, it would be impossible for the Crown to obtain necessary medical information if the accused should choose to be uncooperative with medical witnesses summoned by the Crown. Therefore, according to Justice Bastarache, it would be totally impractical to "saddle the Crown with the legal burden of proving voluntariness beyond a reasonable doubt." He noted that Parliament had already relieved the Crown of this very burden in relation to the defence of "not criminally responsible on account of mental disorder." Indeed, section 16 of the *Criminal Code* [subsections (2) and (3)] makes it clear that the burden of proof is on the accused to establish the mental disorder defence "on the balance of probabilities." Significantly, in *Stone*, Justice Bastarache fully admitted that placing the onus on the accused to prove the defence of automatism constitutes a violation of the presumption of innocence, guaranteed by section 11(d) of the *Charter*: however, he held that this nevertheless constitutes a "reasonable limitation" that is justified under section 1 of the *Charter*.

Automatism and the Evidential (or Evidentiary) Burden

It is important to bear in mind that every trial judge has the discretion to decide whether to permit a defence to be considered by the trier of fact at the end of a criminal trial. The trier of fact may be a jury or the trial judge, if sitting alone. To prevent entirely speculative defences from being placed before the trier of fact, the courts have developed the notion that accused persons must jump over an initial hurdle: this is known as the **evidential (or evidentiary) burden**. Essentially, this means that defendants must be able to point to evidence that is sufficient to establish that there is "*an air of reality*" to their defence. For practically all the defences that may be raised by an accused person in a criminal trial, the evidential burden is met where the accused can satisfy the trial judge that there is *evidence that is capable of raising a reasonable doubt in the mind of the trier of fact*. If this relatively light burden is not met, then the defence will not be considered at the end of the trial when the judge or jury makes the decision as to whether the accused is innocent or guilty of the charges laid. However, if the evidential burden is met, then the defence is placed before the trier of fact and the onus is now placed on the prosecution to prove—beyond a reasonable doubt—every element of the *actus reus* and *mens rea* of the crime charged. It is critical to recognize that the decision as to whether the evidential burden has been met is one that is made *exclusively by the trial judge as a matter of law* (hence, where there is a jury, the members of that body have no part to play in making this determination).

The Supreme Court of Canada recently summarized the nature and role of the evidential burden in the case of *Mayuran* (2012). In the words of Justice Abella:

> This Court has held that a defence should only be put to the jury if it has an "air of reality." ... The air of reality test imposes two duties on the trial judge: to "put to the jury all defences that arise on the facts, whether or not they have been specifically raised by an accused"; and "to keep from the jury defences lacking an evidential foundation." ... Whether a defence arises on the evidence of the accused or of the Crown, the trial judge must put the defence to the jury if it has an air of reality. ...
>
> In determining whether a defence has an air of reality, there must be an examination into the sufficiency of the evidence. It is not enough for there to be "some evidence" supporting the defence. ... The test is "whether there is (1) evidence (2) upon which a properly instructed jury acting reasonably could acquit if it believed the evidence to be true."

Where the defendant advances a defence of automatism, they are also required to meet the evidential burden before it will be considered a "live issue" at the end of the trial. To meet the evidential burden in a case of alleged automatism, it is clearly not enough for the accused to merely claim that "I don't know what happened ... my mind went blank." Indeed, it is absolutely necessary that the accused point to *some expert psychiatric or psychological testimony* that lends support to the defence. Furthermore, it will generally be required that the accused point to some previous history of automatism or dissociative states. In *Stone* (1999), Justice Bastarache noted that the accused will be more likely to satisfy the evidential burden of proof if there is corroborating evidence from bystanders that "reveals that the accused appeared uncharacteristically glassy-eyed, unresponsive and or distant immediately before, during or after the alleged involuntary act." Furthermore, Justice Bastarache suggested that a claim of automatism is more likely to be credible if there is no motive for the alleged offence: "a motiveless act will generally lend plausibility to an accused's claim of involuntariness."

In the case of *Fontaine* (2004), the accused was charged with first-degree murder. He admitted killing the victim but claimed that he acted involuntarily as a consequence of a psychotic state that had been induced by longstanding abuse of marijuana. Fontaine was alleging that he was in a state of mental-disorder automatism and that he should be found NCRMD under section 16 of the *Criminal Code*. Section 16(2) places the primary burden of proof on the party who is claiming that the accused is NCRMD—in this case, Fontaine himself. Section 16(3) states that the standard of proof is "on the balance of probabilities." However, the critical issue that arose in this case was whether Fontaine had satisfied the evidential burden. The nature of the evidential burden is identical for both mental-disorder automatism and non-mental-disorder automatism: therefore, the decision by the Supreme Court of Canada in the *Fontaine* case is also relevant to cases of non-mental-disorder automatism.

At his trial, Fontaine gave evidence suggesting that he was acting involuntarily, and his testimony was supported by the expert opinion of a defence psychiatrist. However, the trial judge refused to put the defence of mental-disorder automatism to the jury because there was disagreement between the Crown and defence experts and there were contradictions in Fontaine's own evidence. Fontaine was convicted, but the Quebec Court of Appeal allowed his appeal and ordered a new trial because it ruled that the accused had satisfied the evidential burden and was entitled to have his defence put to the jury at the end of the trial. The Supreme Court of Canada affirmed the decision of the Court of Appeal. Justice Fish emphasized that the pivotal issue in the case was the *evidential*, and not the "persuasive," burden:

> ... An "evidential burden" is not a burden of proof. It determines whether an issue should be left to the trier of fact, while the "persuasive burden" determines how the issue should be decided.
>
> ... These are fundamentally different questions. The first is a matter of law; the second, a question of fact. Accordingly, on a trial before judge and jury, the judge decides whether the evidential burden has been met. In answering that question, the judge does not evaluate the quality, weight or reliability of the evidence. The judge simply decides whether there is evidence upon which a properly instructed jury could reasonably decide the issue.

Justice Fish later quoted a passage from the decision of the Supreme Court of Canada in the case of *Cinous* (2002):

> The full question is whether there is evidence (some evidence, any evidence) upon which a properly instructed jury acting judicially could acquit. If there is any or some such evidence, then the air of reality hurdle is cleared. If there is no such evidence, then the air of reality hurdle is not cleared.

Justice Fish then suggested that, "in short, as regards all affirmative defences, I think it preferable to say that the evidential burden will be discharged where there is some evidence that puts the defence 'in play.'" He added that "the defence will be in play whenever a properly instructed jury could reasonably, on account of that evidence, conclude in favour of the accused." In the *Fontaine* case itself, Justice Fish concluded that the accused had met the evidential burden because Fontaine had testified—in considerable detail—as to his state of mind at the time of the homicide and a psychiatrist had also testified that Fontaine "had a serious mental disorder akin to psychosis, which seriously distorted his perception of reality." The defence of mental-disorder automatism should, therefore, have been left to the members of the jury and they should ultimately have been required to decide whether Fontaine had proved it on the balance of probabilities.

Study Questions

1. Gaspard is experiencing a severe form of schizophrenia. He acts under the delusion that Chuzzlewit, his neighbour, has a machine that generates death rays. One day, Gaspard comes to believe that Chuzzlewit is about to turn the death rays in his direction and that, to preserve his own life, he must kill Chuzzlewit immediately. Gaspard breaks into Chuzzlewit's house and stabs him to death with a knife. When the police question Gaspard, it is clear that he realizes that he has killed Chuzzlewit, but he insists, "It was him or me, and I had to get him before he wasted me with those death rays." Gaspard is charged with first-degree murder. Would Gaspard be able to raise the defence of NCRMD with any degree of success at his trial?
2. Sikes brutally rapes Nancy, a young woman. In the course of the attack on his victim, he inflicts several severe injuries with a hunting knife that he used to force Nancy to have intercourse with him. Nancy, fortunately, recovers from her physical wounds, although she has been profoundly shocked by the whole appalling experience. Sikes is charged with aggravated sexual assault. His counsel raises the NCRMD defence. Chalmers, a psychiatrist for the defence, claims that Sikes is suffering from a "psychopathic" personality disorder. Sikes testifies that, because of his mental disorder, he simply could not control his violent impulses and that he could not possibly feel any sympathy for his victim. What is the likelihood that Sikes will be found NCRMD?
3. Duncan, a teller at a local bank, has killed Macbeth, the bank manager. Duncan has bipolar disorder, and at the time of the homicide, he was in a manic state and experiencing delusions. Duncan believed that God had ordered him to destroy Macbeth because Macbeth was an agent of the devil. When he was arrested, Duncan told the police, "I suppose I shall be sent to prison for life." Would Duncan be found NCRMD?
4. Hamlet is charged with the first-degree murder of Polonius. The circumstances are that Hamlet, who has a form of schizophrenia, killed Polonius in the university laboratory where medical research was being conducted on animal subjects. Hamlet later stated that he killed Polonius because the latter was in charge of the laboratory and, as such, was responsible for the "torture of innocent animals." Hamlet also says that animals' lives are more important than those of human beings and that it was, therefore, his duty to destroy Polonius. Would Hamlet's mental disorder furnish him with any defence(s)?
5. Crummles attends a party given by one of his friends, Pumblechook. Crummles accepts Pumblechook's offer of an "upper" (a stimulant) because he is looking for a night of "fun and excitement." Crummles swallows a powder given to him by Pumblechook and, soon thereafter, he experiences hallucinations that cause him to violently assault—and seriously injure—one of the other guests, Buzfuz. Crummles is later charged with aggravated assault. A psychiatrist, Dedlock, is prepared to testify that Crummles had ingested methamphetamine ("crystal meth"), which had produced a toxic psychosis. According to Dedlock, this psychotic condition, which lasted for

only 12 hours, caused Crummles to experience hallucinations that led him to believe that Buzfuz was the devil and that he (Crummles) had to kill "the devil" to save his own life. Crummles claims that he thought that the powder consisted of only a strong dose of caffeine. Would Crummles be able to successfully raise the defence of NCRMD? Would it make any difference to your answer if the toxic psychosis lasted for two months after the ingestion of the methamphetamine?

6. Flintwich suddenly attacks his best friend, Smallweed. There is apparently no reason for the attack. When charged with assault causing bodily harm, Flintwich claims that he has diabetes and was in a hypoglycemic state as a consequence of taking his insulin injection without eating. He says that he has never experienced such an episode before. Does Flintwich have any defence to the charge? Would it make any difference to your answer if Flintwich knew that he could become violent if he did not eat after taking his insulin injection?
7. Arabella is taking some powerful tranquilizers and is aware that she should not ingest alcohol while she is taking them. Unfortunately, she goes to a party and has a few glasses of wine. Subsequently, she leaves the party and enters her car. The police find her in a state of total unconsciousness, sitting in the driver's seat of her vehicle. Arabella later claims that she has absolutely no memory of leaving the party and was not conscious when she entered her car. However, the police wish to lay a charge of being in care or control of a motor vehicle while impaired (section 320.14 of the *Criminal Code*). Would such a charge be likely to succeed at trial? Would it make a difference to your answer if Arabella's physician had told her that it was safe for her to "drink in moderation" while she was taking the tranquilizers?
8. Defarge is walking toward his home when he sees a gang of armed robbers emerging from his local bank. The robbers brutally kill one of the customers, Micawber, who is standing outside the bank between the gang and their getaway car. Upon seeing this distressing scene, Defarge goes into a state of shock and attacks Slammer, one of the robbers, who is trying to give himself up to the police because he disapproves of the killing of Micawber by his colleagues. Slammer is quite seriously wounded by this onslaught. After Defarge is taken to the police station, he claims that he does not remember anything about the attack on Slammer; all he remembers is the brutal killing by the other bank robbers. Does Defarge have any defence to a charge of assault causing bodily harm? Would it make any difference to your answer if Defarge was a "highly nervous" individual and was taking tranquilizers on a regular basis?
9. Tapley is taking a bus journey across the Prairie provinces during a snowstorm. The weather conditions become so severe that he is required to stay overnight in a bus station. During the night, he sexually assaults a young woman, Louisa, who is a fellow passenger. Tapley is forcibly restrained by a security guard. He appears to be confused and unaware of his surroundings. When Tapley is later charged with sexual assault, he claims that he was asleep when the alleged offence occurred and that he has no memory of it. An expert witness is prepared to testify that Tapley suffers from sexomnia (engaging in sexual activity while asleep). What defence(s) might be available to Tapley? Would it (they) be likely to succeed at his trial? Would it make any difference if Tapley had a history of such attacks and was undergoing treatment at a sleep disorder clinic?
10. Dombey takes his four-year-old son, Paul, for a walk in the local park. Once they enter the park, Dombey sits down in a chair and falls fast asleep. Paul wanders away and is killed by a truck as he is trying to cross a busy road on the outskirts of the park. Dombey later states that he suffers from narcolepsy, which is a condition characterized by a frequent—and uncontrollable—desire to sleep. What charges might be laid against Dombey, and, if such charges are laid, what, if any, defence(s) might be available to him?

CHAPTER

MISTAKE OF FACT, CONSENT, AND MISTAKE OF LAW AS DEFENCES TO A CRIMINAL CHARGE

Learning Objectives

After reading this chapter, you will understand:

- the basic elements of the defences of mistake of fact, consent, and mistake of law, as well as the general requirement that the accused must satisfy an evidential burden before a defence may be considered by the trier of fact;
- the underlying rationale for the defence of honest mistake of fact: namely, that the accused lacks the necessary *mens rea* for the offence charged;
- the exceptional requirement in section 273.2(b) of the *Criminal Code* that where an accused person claims a mistaken belief in consent in response to a charge of sexual assault, it must be shown that "**reasonable steps**" were taken to ascertain the consent of the complainant;
- the basic elements of the defence of consent to a criminal charge in the circumstances where the *absence of consent* is a vital element in the case that must be proved by the Crown; and
- the general principle that a mistake of law does not give rise to a valid defence to a criminal charge and the major exceptions to this principle: namely, the defences of "officially induced error" and "colour of right" (although the second exception is only *apparent*, since the Supreme Court of Canada has ruled that it is actually an application of the defence of honest mistake of fact).

INTRODUCTION

In Chapter 8, the special defences of NCRMD and automatism were considered. The remaining chapters in this book explore the other major defences that may be raised in a criminal trial in Canada. It is not possible to consider all the various defences that may be asserted by a person who has been charged with a criminal offence, and those defences that are primarily procedural or technical in nature (such as **entrapment** or **double jeopardy**) have been omitted from the discussion: these latter defences are usually dealt with in works on criminal procedure. It should also be remembered that accused persons may choose to assert their constitutional rights under the *Charter* as a means of defending themselves against a criminal charge. Indeed, we have already examined a number of cases in which criminal charges were dismissed on constitutional grounds (e.g., the *Bedford* decision in 2013, which resulted in a declaration that sections 210, 212(1)(j), and 213(1)(*c*) of the *Criminal Code*, which criminalized certain aspects of the sale of sexual services, were unconstitutional).

This chapter examines the defences of mistake of fact, consent, and mistake of law. Chapter 10 analyzes the defences of intoxication and provocation. Chapter 11 explores the defences of necessity and duress, while Chapter 12 examines the defences of self-defence and defence of property.

It is very important to bear in mind that an accused person is not entitled to raise as many defences as they wish to put on the table at a criminal trial. Indeed, they have to satisfy the evidential burden *before* the trier of fact (whether this is a jury or a judge sitting alone) will consider a particular defence: in the words used by the Supreme Court of Canada in many cases, there has to be sufficient evidence to give an "air of reality" to the defence or to put it "in play" before it will receive any consideration by the trier of fact. This issue was discussed in Chapter 8, but the need to satisfy the evidential burden is a requirement that applies to all the defences discussed in this book.

The defences of **mistake of fact** and consent are considered together in the present chapter because they are frequently (although not exclusively) raised in the context of trials involving charges of sexual assault. Mistake of law is generally not a valid basis for a defence to a criminal charge. However, this chapter examines a number of exceptions that the courts have recognized as a means of minimizing the degree of injustice that might otherwise be inflicted on accused persons should the general rule be applied in an excessively harsh and inflexible manner.

MISTAKE OF FACT

Mistake of Fact: The General Nature of the Defence

The lawyer for a defendant in a criminal trial may well say, "It's true that my client committed the *actus reus* of the offence, but they were nevertheless operating under a serious mistake as to the real facts of the situation. In light of the facts as they honestly believed them to be, they had no reason to believe that they were committing a crime and, therefore, lacked the *mens rea* that the Crown must prove in order to obtain a conviction." Such an assertion may well lead to the acquittal of the client because, as the Quebec Court of Appeal stated in the case of *Charbonneau* (1992), "in offences requiring *mens rea*, honest mistake of fact on an essential factual element is, as a general rule, a defence to the charge."

Take, for example, the strange case of *Mailhot* (1996). The accused was charged with the offence of wilfully doing an indecent act "in a public place in the presence of one or more persons" [subsection 173(1)(a) of the *Criminal Code*]. Mailhot had met a plainclothes police officer in a park and, after engaging in a conversation, the two men went to a spring. After drinking at the spring, the accused and the officer continued talking and, at one point, Mailhot twice asked the officer if he wanted to "see him." The officer did not answer. Mailhot then went to a tree, undressed, and started to masturbate. The officer then revealed his identity and arrested Mailhot. At his trial, the accused was convicted of wilfully doing an indecent act, but, ultimately, the Quebec Court of Appeal set aside the conviction and entered an acquittal. An essential element of the *actus reus* of the offence is that the indecent act was committed in the presence of one or more persons *other than those persons who are engaged in the act itself.* Essentially, Mailhot argued that he mistakenly believed that the undercover officer wished to participate in a sexual act in the sense that he would at least watch the accused. On the facts as the accused honestly believed them to be, he would not be committing an offence because the only person present was a willing participant in the indecent act. In delivering the judgment of the Court of Appeal, Justice Chamberland said:

> In my view, the circumstances in which the events took place do not permit one to find guilty intent on the part of the appellant at the time that he undressed, caressed himself and masturbated. The meeting with the officer, the friendly conversation that they had, their stroll to the spring, the officer's silence when the appellant, twice, revealed his plans, all these elements contributed to leading the appellant to believe that the officer was interested in giving a sexual twist to their meeting. The appellant's mistake involved an essential element required for the existence of the crime prohibited by s. 173(1)(a); the officer's conduct led him to honestly, but mistakenly, believe that the officer would participate in the act that he was preparing to commit, if only by looking at him and by getting emotional or sexual satisfaction from it. In my view, this belief eliminated the blameworthy state of mind which the appellant had to have in order to be guilty of breaching s. 173(1)(a) of the *Criminal Code*.

The *Mailhot* case illustrates the principle that the defence of mistake of fact is really an assertion that the Crown has failed to prove the necessary *mens rea* requirements of the offence charged. This principle may also be applied, for example, to the situation of an accused person who has been charged with sexual assault and asserts the defence of honest, but mistaken, belief in consent. As Chief Justice Lamer stated, in delivering the judgment of the Supreme Court of Canada in the *Davis* case (1999):

> [T]he defence of honest belief in consent is simply a denial of the *mens rea* of sexual assault. ... The *actus reus* of sexual assault requires a touching, of a sexual nature, without the consent of the complainant. The *mens rea* requires the accused to intend the touching and to know of, or to be reckless or wilfully blind as to the complainant's lack of consent. ... In some circumstances, it is possible for the complainant not to consent to the sexual touching but for the accused to honestly but mistakenly believe that the complainant consented. In these circumstances, the *actus reus* of the offence is established, but the *mens rea* is not.

In the decision of the Supreme Court of Canada in the case of *A. (J.)* (2011), Chief Justice McLachlin offered further clarification of the mental elements required for conviction of sexual assault and how the defence of honest mistake may prevent the accused person from forming the necessary *mens rea*:

> A person has the required mental state, or *mens rea* of the offence, when he or she knew that the complainant was not consenting to the sexual act in question, or was reckless or wilfully blind to the absence of consent. The accused may raise the defence of honest but mistaken belief in consent if he believed that the complainant communicated consent to engage in the sexual activity. However ... ss. 273.1(2) and 273.2 limit the cases in which the accused may rely on this defence. For instance, the accused cannot argue that he misinterpreted the complainant saying "no" as meaning "yes."

Must a Mistake of Fact Be Both Honest and Reasonable?

There is no doubt that a mistake of fact must be *honest* if it is to serve as a valid defence to a criminal charge. However, one may also ask whether the mistake of fact must also be *reasonable*—in the sense that it is the kind of mistake that might be entertained by a reasonable person in the same circumstances as those faced by the accused. The answer to this question depends on whether the particular offence concerned requires proof of *subjective* or *objective mens rea*. When proof of *subjective mens rea* is required, the accused person does not have to show that the mistake was reasonable; they have to raise only a reasonable doubt as to the honesty of the mistaken belief. This principle was forcefully stated by Justice Cartwright, of the Supreme Court of Canada, in the classic case of *Rees* (1956): "[T]he essential question is whether the belief entertained by the accused is an honest one and ... the existence or non-existence of reasonable grounds for such a belief is merely relevant evidence to be weighed by the tribunal of fact in determining such essential question."

However, when an offence requires proof of *objective mens rea*, any defence based on a mistake of fact must be one that a reasonable person would make in the same circumstances and with the same knowledge as the accused person. For example, in *Beatty* (2008), Justice Charron, of the Supreme Court of Canada, addressed this legal principle very clearly in the context of a case of dangerous driving, an offence of modified objective liability:

> [A] reasonably held mistake of fact may provide a complete defence if, based on the accused's reasonable perception of the facts, the conduct

> measured up to the requisite standard of care. It is therefore important to apply the modified objective test in the context of the events surrounding the incident.
>
> ... If an accused ... has an honest and reasonably held belief in the existence of certain facts, it may be a relevant consideration in assessing the reasonableness of his conduct. For example, a welder, who is engaged to work in a confined space believing on the assurance of the owner of the premises that no combustible or explosive material is stored nearby, should be entitled to have his perception, as to the presence or absence of dangerous materials, before the jury on a charge of manslaughter when his welding torch causes an explosion and a consequent death.

When an accused person is convicted of an offence requiring proof of *subjective mens rea*, which will usually be the case for more serious offences, the rationale for imposing punishment is that they made a deliberate choice to do something wrong. A person who operates under the influence of a serious mistake of fact in relation to an essential element of the offence charged cannot be considered to have made a choice to do something wrong: for that reason, it would be unjust to convict them of a criminal offence. Even if the mistake is unreasonable, this does not alter the fact that the accused did not deliberately decide to do something wrong. However, as Justice Cartwright aptly pointed out in *Rees* (1956), the reasonableness of a mistake of fact may well be a *relevant factor* in determining the credibility of the accused. In general, the more unreasonable a mistake of fact appears to be, the less likely it is that the judge or jury will believe that the accused is telling the truth. This principle is reflected in section 265(4) of the *Criminal Code*, which applies to all offences involving an assault[1]:

> Where an accused alleges that he believed that the complainant consented to the conduct that is the subject-matter of the charge, a judge if satisfied that there is sufficient evidence and that, if believed by the jury, the evidence would constitute a defence, shall instruct the jury, when reviewing all the evidence relating to the determination of the honesty of the accused's belief, to consider the presence or absence of reasonable grounds for that belief.

Section 265(4) is clearly based on the assumption that the more unreasonable the accused's belief as to consent, the less likely it is that the jury will believe that the accused held this belief honestly. However, this provision does not stipulate that a defence of mistaken belief as to consent will be successful only if the belief was reasonable. It merely requires that the trial judge instruct the members of the jury that they should take into account the reasonableness of the accused's alleged belief as a means of determining the accused's *credibility*. If the members of the jury have a reasonable doubt as to whether or not the accused's alleged belief was honest, then they must acquit the accused—even if they think that such a belief would never have been entertained by a reasonable person.

Although a mistake of fact does not have to be reasonable to serve as the basis for a successful defence with respect to a crime that requires proof of subjective *mens rea*, it is nevertheless important to bear in mind that the defence will be rejected where the Crown proves that the accused was *reckless* or *wilfully blind*. For example, section 264 of the *Criminal Code* defines the offence of criminal harassment and provides a defence to an accused person who honestly, but mistakenly, believes that the complainant is not being harassed: this situation may arise where the accused is following the complainant but honestly believes that the complainant is not aware of the accused's conduct. However, section 264 also states that this defence will fail if the accused acted "recklessly as to whether the other person is harassed." In other words, if the accused subjectively realized that there was a risk that the complainant knew the accused was following them, then the defence of mistake of fact would not be available. In *Briscoe* (2010), the Supreme Court of Canada emphasized that wilful blindness or "deliberate ignorance" is a highly culpable state of mind that is equivalent to actual knowledge of the material elements of the *actus reus* of an offence:

> Wilful blindness does not define the *mens rea* required for particular offences. Rather, it can substitute for actual knowledge whenever knowledge is a component of the *mens rea*. The doctrine of wilful blindness imputes knowledge to an accused whose suspicion is aroused to the point where he or she sees the need for further inquiries, but *deliberately chooses* not to make those inquiries.

1. Where a *sexual* assault is concerned, the defence of mistaken belief in consent must be based on a finding that the accused person took reasonable steps to ascertain consent [s. 273.2(b)]. This special provision is discussed in the next section of this chapter.

How can the courts identify wilful blindness? In *Burnett* (2018), Justice Watt, of the Ontario Court of Appeal, pointed to the type of evidence that might establish wilful blindness. He gave the example of an accused whose evidence divulged "inherently suspicious events characterized by unclear details and at odds with common sense and human experience." He also, very colourfully, indicated that the "evidentiary threshold" for wilful blindness "may also be met by the cumulative effect of several strands of circumstantial evidence from different sources woven together in a mosaic."

Clearly, an alleged mistake of fact cannot be considered honest if the accused person was wilfully blind or deliberately ignorant as to the existence of the essential elements of the offence, and, therefore, such an individual will always be disqualified from relying on it as a defence.

The disturbing case of *Sansregret* (1985) dramatically illustrates the manner in which *wilful blindness* may prevent the accused from raising a successful defence of mistake of fact. The accused was charged with the rape of a woman with whom he had previously been living (today, the charge would be one of sexual assault). The background facts were that, in September 1982, Sansregret had broken into the victim's house during the very early hours of the morning. He was "raging" and terrorized the victim with a file-like weapon that he was carrying. The victim was terrified by Sansregret's conduct and, to calm him down, she held open the prospect of reconciliation and, eventually, they had sexual intercourse. She later reported the incident to the police, asserting that she had been raped; however, no action was taken, largely because the accused's probation officer intervened and asked her not to proceed with her complaint.

In October 1982, Sansregret once again broke into the victim's house in the very early hours of the morning. He was "furious and violent" and threatened her with a butcher knife. He struck the victim and threatened to kill her if the police came. At one point, he tied her hands behind her back. After an hour of enduring this terror, the victim tried to calm the accused down by holding out some hope of reconciliation. After some conversation, they engaged in sexual intercourse. The victim once again complained to the police and, on this occasion, a number of charges, including one of rape, were laid against the accused. Sansregret claimed that he had been operating under an honest mistake of fact as to the consent of the victim. The trial judge acquitted the accused of rape on the basis of this defence, even though she considered that the mistake was totally unreasonable: "No one in his right mind could have believed that the complainant's dramatic about-face stemmed from anything other than fear. But the accused did. He saw what he wanted to see, heard what he wanted to hear, believed what he wanted to believe."

The Crown appealed the acquittal and the Manitoba Court of Appeal allowed the appeal, entering a conviction. The accused appealed to the Supreme Court of Canada, which affirmed the judgment of the Court of Appeal, on the basis that Sansregret had been *wilfully blind* as to the issue of consent and was, therefore, not entitled to rely on the defence of honest mistake of fact. In delivering the judgment of the Court, Justice McIntyre stated that:

> Having wilfully blinded himself to the facts before him the fact that an accused may be enabled to preserve what could be called an honest belief, in the sense that he has no specific knowledge to the contrary, will not afford a defence because, where the accused becomes deliberately blind to the existing facts, he is fixed by law with actual knowledge and his belief in another state of facts is irrelevant.

It is clear that the Supreme Court's ruling was heavily influenced by the fact that the accused had engaged in similar conduct on one previous occasion and that he was aware of the complaint made to the police. In these particular circumstances, he clearly had been alerted to the likelihood that the victim was not giving a true consent to sexual activity with him. In other words, he deliberately closed his eyes to the obvious and, in these circumstances, he was treated as though he actually knew that there was no consent on the part of the complainant. Subsection 273.2(a)(ii) of the *Criminal Code* explicitly stipulates that an honest belief in consent may *not* be raised as a defence to a charge of *sexual assault* if "the accused's belief arose from … the accused's recklessness or wilful blindness."

Exceptions to the General Rule That a Mistake of Fact Does Not Have to Be Reasonable in Order to Excuse the Accused Person from Criminal Liability

As we have seen, the general rule is that a mistake of fact does not have to be reasonable for the accused to raise a successful defence to a criminal charge. However, Parliament has created a number of significant exceptions to this rule. One example of an offence that falls within the category of exceptions is bigamy. Indeed, section 290(2)(a) of the *Criminal Code* stipulates that an accused person has a defence to a charge of bigamy if they believed "in good faith and *on reasonable grounds*" that their spouse was dead.

Perhaps one of the most important exceptions to the general rule concerns those who engage in sexual activity with children under the age of 16 and young persons under the age of 18. In general, it is no defence to a charge of a sexual offence against a child under the age of 16 that the child consented to sexual activity with the accused [section 150.1(a)]. Similarly, consent is no defence to a charge of sexual exploitation of a young person under 18 by abusing a position of trust or authority (section 153), nor is consent a defence to a charge of buying sexual services from a young person under 18 [section 212(4)]. Since consent is no defence to these charges, clearly the accused person's knowledge of the age of the child or young person becomes a critical issue. However, the defence of mistaken belief as to age has been limited to those accused who *take all reasonable steps to ascertain the age* of the child or young person *before* engaging in sexual activity with them [sections 150.1(4) and (5)]. In *George* (2017), Justice Gascon, in delivering the judgment of the Supreme Court of Canada, indicated the rationale for this legislation:

> Sexual crimes are disproportionately committed against vulnerable populations, including youth. The "reasonable steps" requirement in s. 150.1(4) of the Criminal Code ... which requires an accused person who is five or more years older than a complainant who is 14 years of age or more but under the age of 16, to take "all reasonable steps to ascertain the age of the complainant" before sexual contact—seeks to protect young people from such crimes. It does so by placing the responsibility for preventing adult/youth sexual activity where it belongs: with adults. Parliament's allocation of responsibility to adults is crucial for protecting young people from sexual crimes.

Another very significant exception to the general rule concerns the defence of mistaken belief in consent where the accused is charged with *sexual assault*. As we have just seen, where children and young persons are concerned, consent may not be available as a defence to a charge involving a sexual offence. However, in relation to sexual offences involving adults, mistaken belief in consent will normally be a defence that is open to an accused person. Here again, under section 273.2(b) of the *Criminal Code*, Parliament has imposed a duty on those who wish to engage in sexual relations to take reasonable steps to ascertain that the other party is consenting to such activity.

The rationale for restricting the defence of mistaken belief in consent, where the accused engages in some form of sexual activity with an adult, is based on the unique characteristics of the crime of sexual assault.

In the Supreme Court of Canada's decision in the *Park* case (1995), Justice L'Heureux-Dubé presented a convincing analysis of the reasons why the defence of mistake of fact raises unique problems when the accused is charged with sexual assault. She pointed out that, normally, accused persons raise the defence of mistake of fact when they can claim they were under a fundamental misapprehension as to an element of the *actus reus* that is generally not in dispute. She gives the example of a defendant who shoots a man believing he is a deer. There would be no dispute as to the fact that the victim was killed by the accused's gunshot (a death is the key element of the *actus reus* of an offence involving a homicide). The critical issue would then be whether the accused honestly believed that the victim was a deer. However, in cases of alleged sexual assault, a critical element of the *actus reus* is that there was an absence of consent on the part of the victim and there is frequently a fundamental dispute as to whether that particular element of the *actus reus* existed. As Justice L'Heureux-Dubé suggested,

> Assault differs importantly from most other *Code* offences in its interaction with the mistake of fact defence. Under most other offences, mistake of fact will primarily arise in contexts in which the *actus reus* of the offence is beyond dispute. Assaults raise a unique problem that the mental state of another person (i.e., consent or lack thereof) is an essential element that is relevant to both the *actus reus* and the *mens rea* of the offence—an element which almost invariably is materially in dispute.

Furthermore, Justice L'Heureux-Dubé made the critical point that in trials involving charges of sexual assault, the courts face the difficulty that such assaults are not usually witnessed by anyone other than the accused and the complainant and that a conviction may be obtained without the need to prove "visible physical injury to the complainant." These factors render it more likely that there will be a dispute as to the issue of consent.

Justice L'Heureux-Dubé identified another critical reason why the defence of mistaken belief as to consent is so deeply problematic. In her view, there is a "clear communication gap between how most women *experience* consent, and how many men perceive consent." The learned justice noted that part of this gap is caused by "genuine, often gender-based, miscommunication between the parties" and another part is attributable to the "myths and stereotypes that many men hold about consent." Among these myths and stereotypes is the view that "coercive sexuality" is "normal." In light of the inherent danger of reinforcing such myths and stereotypes, the acquittal of accused persons who assert a totally unreasonable belief in consent represents a serious threat to the security of all women.

In line with the concerns expressed by Justice L'Heureux-Dubé, Canadian courts have insisted in recent years that an accused person charged with sexual assault cannot claim that they believed that the complainant's silence amounted to a form of "tacit consent." Indeed, in the decision of the Supreme Court of Canada in *Ewanchuk (*1999), Justice Major, emphasized that "In the context of *mens rea*—specifically for the purposes of the honest but mistaken belief in consent—'consent' means that the complainant had affirmatively communicated by words or conduct her agreement to engage in sexual activity with the accused." Therefore, the accused must point to specific words or conduct of the complainant that they mistakenly believed was an *affirmative communication of consent*, if the defence of mistaken belief in consent is to satisfy the evidential burden and be considered by the trier of fact (judge or jury). Subsection 273.2(c) of the *Criminal Code* has embedded this principle in legislation by stating that the defence is not available to an accused person if "there is no evidence that the complainant's voluntary agreement to the activity was affirmatively expressed by words or actively expressed by conduct."[2]

The unique difficulties created by advancing mistaken belief in consent as a defence to a charge of sexual assault constitute the main rationale for imposing the requirement that the accused *take reasonable steps to ascertain consent*. Therefore, section 273(b) of the *Criminal Code* provides that it is not a defence to a charge of sexual assault that the accused mistakenly believed that the complainant had consented to the sexual activity that constitutes the substance of the charge against them where "*the accused did not take reasonable steps, in the circumstances known to the accused at the time, to ascertain that the complainant was consenting*" [emphasis added].

At the outset, it should be emphasized that section 273.2(b) differs in some important respects from sections 150.1(4) and (5), which define the defence of mistaken belief as to age. Section 273.2(b) reflects the modified objective test, which we encountered when we discussed objective *mens rea* in Chapter 5; more specifically, while the accused must take reasonable steps to ascertain consent, the court must judge the reasonableness of those steps in light of the *circumstances which were known to them at the time of the alleged offence*. The phrase "in the circumstances known to the accused," which clearly imports a *subjective* element into the defence of mistaken belief in consent, does not appear in sections 150.1(4) and (5). Furthermore, while sections 150.1(4) and (5) use the phrase "*all* reasonable steps," section 273.2(b) contains only the words "reasonable steps."

How have the courts interpreted section 273.2(b)? In *Malcolm* (2000), the Manitoba Court of Appeal applied a *modified objective approach*:

> Section 273.2(b) requires the court to apply a quasi-objective test to the situation. First, the circumstances known to the accused must be ascertained. Then, the issue which arises is, if a reasonable man was aware of the same circumstances, would he take further steps before proceeding with the sexual activity? If the answer is yes, and the accused has not taken further steps, then the accused is not entitled to the defence of honest belief in consent. If the answer is no, or even maybe, then the accused would not be required to take further steps and the defence will apply.

What are "reasonable steps" in the context of a defence of honest mistake as to consent? Obviously, the answer to this question will depend on the particular circumstances in each individual case. For example, it may well be the case that an individual who seeks to engage in sexual activity with another person should first seek explicit permission if the individuals concerned are relative strangers to each other. On the other hand, explicitly seeking permission might not be considered a practical (let alone a romantic) option where the parties cohabit and have been routinely engaging in sexual activity with each other.

In *Crangle* (2010), the accused had an identical twin who was involved in a consensual sexual relationship with the victim. The accused engaged in an act of

2. S. 273.2 was amended in 2018 by s. 20 of *An Act to amend the Criminal Code and the Department of Justice Act and to make consequential amendments to another Act*, S.C. 2018, c. 29. Subsections 273.2(a)(iii) and 273.2(c) were added to the *Criminal Code*.

sexual intercourse with the victim, who had been asleep and, when roused, believed the accused was his brother. She asked the accused to cease his activity, and when she turned on the light and discovered his true identity, she reacted with "anger and disbelief." While the victim may have initially agreed to the act of intercourse, she did so only because she believed the accused was his twin brother: she never consented to any sexual activity with the accused as opposed to his twin brother. The accused argued that he acted under an honest, but mistaken, belief that the victim had consented to engage in sexual activity with him. Not surprisingly, the trial judge convicted Crangle of sexual assault and his conviction was affirmed by the Ontario Court of Appeal.

The Court of Appeal agreed with the trial judge that Crangle had not taken reasonable steps to ascertain the victim's consent. It was perfectly clear that he should, at the very least, have made his identity known prior to the initiation of any sexual intimacy. On behalf of the Court, Justice Goudge stated that:

> The jurisprudence makes clear that what is required of an accused in the way of reasonable steps depends on the particular circumstances of the case, and can be more or less, depending on those circumstances, even to the point of requiring an unequivocal indication of consent from the complainant at the time of the sexual activity. …

The trial judge concluded that, in the circumstances of this case, reasonable steps required the appellant to make his identity perfectly clear to the complainant. That conclusion was amply justified on these facts. The appellant knew the complainant had an ongoing consensual sexual relationship with his twin brother, but nothing remotely like that with him. He knew she had gone asleep intoxicated in his brother's bed, as she had done many times before. The bedroom was pitch dark. Nothing about her conduct that night caused him to think that she would ever consent to sexual intercourse with him. The trial judge's conclusion that reasonable steps required the appellant to do more than he did and make his identity perfectly clear to the complainant is fully supported by this evidence.

The Court also pointed out that Crangle was, in any event, reckless or wilfully blind as to the fact of non-consent by the complainant.

The issue of what should be considered "taking reasonable steps to ascertain consent" is particularly important when the complainant has, at some point, indicated a lack of consent to engage in sexual activity with the accused. If the accused claims that they honestly believed that the complainant had changed their mind after an initial refusal, then there is an increased burden on the accused to demonstrate that they took reasonable steps to satisfy themselves that the alleged change of mind was genuine. The accused must point to some evidence that supports the assertion that they held an honest belief that the complainant was affirmatively communicating their consent *at the precise time when the accused resumed their efforts to engage in sexual activity with the complainant.* This situation is well illustrated by *Flaviano* (2014).

The accused was the landlord of a unit that was occupied by the 17-year-old complainant, her step-father, and her mother. Flaviano had entered the unit to repair the dishwasher. Even though he barely knew the complainant, Flaviano asked her to perform oral sex on him. She refused. However, Flaviano persisted and the complainant ultimately engaged in oral and vaginal sexual activity with him. Flaviano was charged with sexual assault. At his trial, he claimed that the complainant had willingly consented to the sexual activity and his fallback position was that, if she had not consented, he nevertheless honestly believed that she was a willing participant. The complainant testified that she did not consent and only submitted to Flaviano's demands because she was scared of him. The trial judge believed the complainant's testimony, but acquitted Flaviano on the basis of the defence of honest, but mistaken, belief in consent. The Crown appealed against the acquittal, asserting that there was no air of reality to the defence of honest, but mistaken, belief in consent and that, therefore Flaviano had not satisfied the evidential burden with respect to this defence.

The Alberta Court of Appeal agreed with the Crown, set aside the acquittal and entered a conviction. The Court emphasized that it is "not sufficient for the accused to have believed the complainant was consenting: he must also take reasonable steps to ascertain consent, and must believe that the complainant communicated her consent to engage in the sexual activity in question." There was no evidence that Flaviano took any steps to find out whether the complainant had changed her mind and could not point to any actions on her part that might indicate that she was communicating a free and voluntary consent to Flaviano's sexual overtures. The Supreme Court of Canada affirmed the decision of the Court of Appeal. Justice Moldaver stated that "there was no evidence that the appellant took any reasonable steps to ascertain whether the complainant was consenting to sexual relations following her initial rejection of the appellant's sexual advances."

In *A.(J.)* (2011), the Supreme Court of Canada applied section 273.2(b) to a somewhat unusual situation. The accused and K.D. were friends of long standing and they had experimented with asphyxiation during sexual relations with each other. On the occasion in question, K.D. had engaged in sexual foreplay with J.A., the accused, and agreed to asphyxiation through choking. K.D. had understood that she could lose consciousness. The accused choked K.D., who lost consciousness for about three minutes. When she regained awareness, she discovered that her hands were tied, and that J.A. was inserting a dildo into her anus. After about 10 seconds had elapsed, J.A. removed the dildo and he and K.D. engaged in vaginal intercourse. Some two months later, K.D. told the police that she had not consented to this sexual activity, but she later recanted, stating that she had made the false allegation because J.A. had threatened to assume full custody of their two-year-old son. The trial judge convicted J.A. of sexual assault, either because K.D. had not, in fact, consented to the insertion of the dildo or, alternatively, that no consent could be given to any sexual activity while the other party was in a state of unconsciousness. The Ontario Court of Appeal allowed the appeal by J.A. and entered an acquittal, but the Supreme Court of Canada restored the conviction, agreeing with the trial judge that no consent could be given to a sexual act that occurred while the other party was insensible and unable to give or withhold consent.

The Supreme Court reviewed the definition of consent with respect to sexual activity that is articulated in section 273.1 of the *Criminal Code*, as well as the limitations on the defence of honest belief in consent contained in section 273.2. Chief Justice McLachlin stated that "Parliament viewed consent as the conscious agreement of the complainant to engage in every sexual act in a particular encounter" and that Parliament had, therefore, "defined consent in a way that requires the complainant to be conscious throughout the sexual activity in question." Advance consent to asphyxiation could not be given because Parliament had enacted a definition of consent that required that the other party should be able to cease the sexual activity at any time, and this could not be done while they were unconscious. With respect to the "reasonable steps" requirement, the Chief Justice said, on behalf of the majority of the Supreme Court justices:

> Section 273.2(b) states that a person wishing to avail himself of the *mens rea* defence must not only believe that the complainant communicated her consent ... but must also have taken reasonable steps to ascertain whether she "was consenting" to engage in the sexual activity in question at the time it occurred. How can one take reasonable steps to ascertain whether a person is consenting to sexual activity while it is occurring if that person is unconscious? Once again, the provision is grounded in the assumption that the complainant must consciously consent to each and every sexual act. Further, by requiring the accused to take reasonable steps to ensure that the complainant "was consenting," Parliament has indicated that the consent of the complainant must be an ongoing state of mind.

Following the *A. (J.)* case, Parliament amended section 273.2 to reflect the central issue in the Supreme Court's decision.[3] Subsection 273.1(1.1) was added to the *Criminal Code:* it states that "Consent must be present at the time the sexual activity in question takes place."

In the *A. (J.)* case, the Supreme Court emphasized that consent must be obtained for each individual sexual act in which the accused engages with another party. This creates a certain degree of uncertainty as to what is expected of individuals who engage in sexual activities with others. Does this mean, for example, that strangers are required to stop and actively obtain consent for each act that is defined as "sexual," ranging from kissing or touching to intercourse of some type? If consent cannot be given in advance, what steps is the reasonable stranger required to take to ensure that consent is being given to each sexual act on an ongoing basis? Where the parties involved have a longstanding sexual relationship, one assumes that the "reasonable steps" requirement will be interpreted very differently. An individual in such a relationship would not be expected to actively obtain consent for each sexual act in which they engage: rather, the individual would be expected to cease any attempt to engage in sexual activity if their partner gives any indication of not wishing to enter on or continue with such activity. As Justice Wood of the B.C. Court of Appeal observed in *G. (R.)* (1994),

3. See s. 19 of *An Act to amend the Criminal Code and the Department of Justice Act and to make consequential amendments to another Act*, S.C. 2018, c. 29.

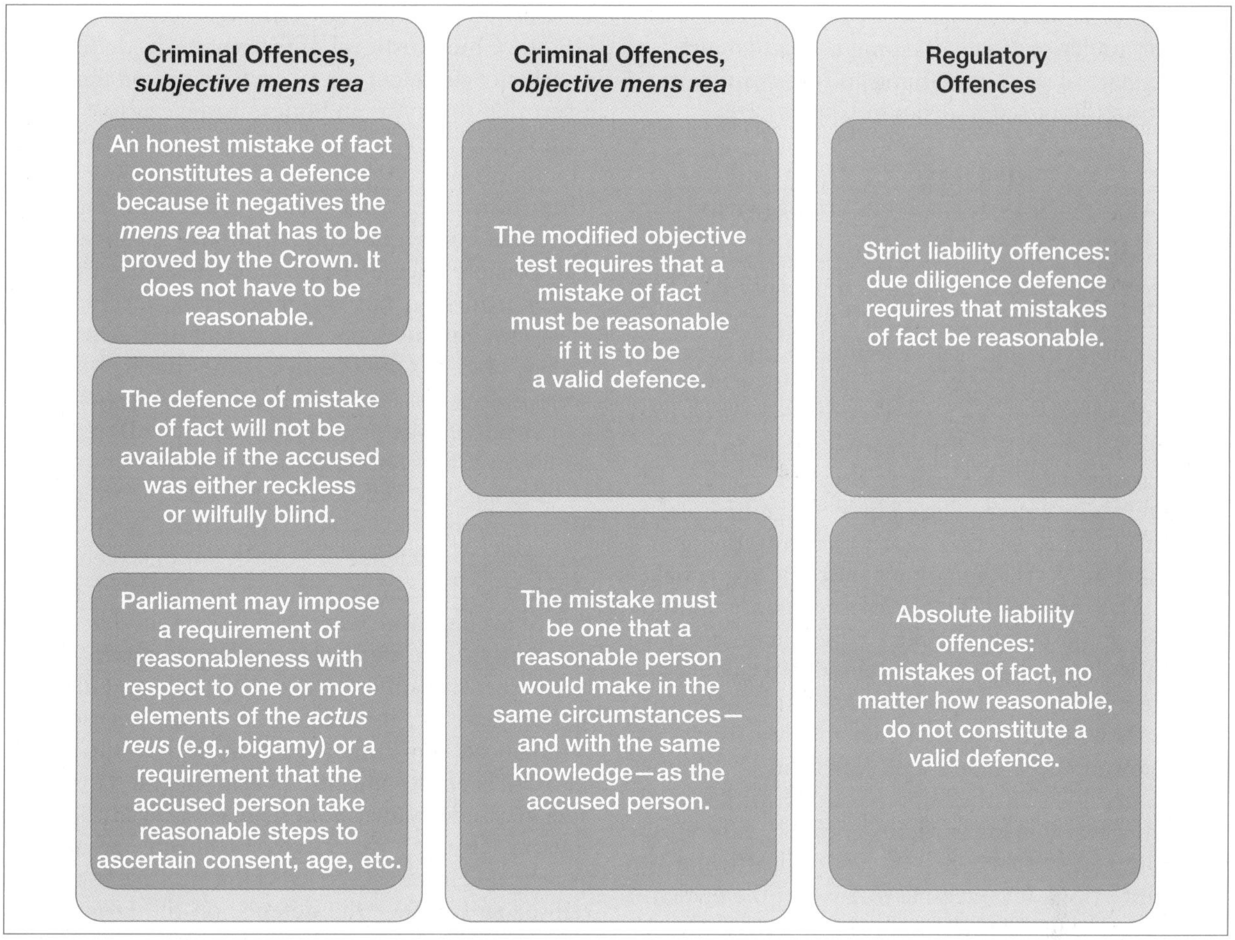

Figure 9-1
Mistake of Fact and Reasonableness as a Requirement for a Valid Defence

section 273.2(b) clearly creates a proportionate relationship between what will be required in the way of reasonable steps by an accused to ascertain that the complainant was consenting and "the circumstances known to him" at the time. Those circumstances will be as many and as varied as the cases in which the issue can arise.

Intoxication and the Defence of Honest Mistake of Fact

May an accused person charged with sexual assault say, "I admit that my belief in consent was unreasonable, but I was so drunk that I nevertheless honestly believed that the complainant consented to sexual relations"? The answer is definitely in the negative, since subsection 273.2(a)(i) of the *Criminal Code* unequivocally states that the defence of mistaken belief in consent is not available if the accused's belief arose from "the accused's self-induced intoxication."

The enactment of this provision in 1992 basically reflects the existing case law on the subject. For example, in *Moreau* (1986), the Ontario Court of Appeal had already ruled that, as a matter of sound legal policy, intoxication should be a valid defence only to a charge of an offence requiring proof of *specific* (as opposed to *general* or *basic*) intent. The offence of sexual assault requires proof only of *general* or *basic* intent and, for this reason, intoxication cannot be raised as a defence. Therefore, in the view of the court, a drunken (albeit honest) mistake as to the victim's consent cannot be considered a valid defence.

Section 273.2(a)(i) applies to only sexual assaults, but the general principle articulated in the *Moreau* case still applies to other offences. An honest mistake of fact in relation to a crime of specific intent may be a defence even if the mistake was caused by intoxication, but a mistake of fact in relation to a crime of basic intent (such as assault or damage to property under section 430) is not a valid defence.

The general rules pertaining to intoxication as a defence are discussed in detail in Chapter 10.

When Can the Defence of Mistake of Fact Be Considered by the Trier of Fact?

The accused person in a criminal trial is not entitled to have *any* defence—no matter how speculative—placed before the trier of fact. Indeed, no defence may be considered by the trier of fact (either the jury or the trial judge sitting alone) until the accused has first satisfied the evidential burden—a legal principle that was discussed in Chapter 8 in the context of the defence of automatism. The defence of honest mistake of fact is certainly no exception to this general principle. As the Supreme Court of Canada held in the *Esau* case (1997), "[B]efore a court should consider honest but mistaken belief or instruct a jury on it there must be some plausible evidence in support so as to give *an air of reality* to the defence" [emphasis added]. It will be remembered from the discussion of the *Fontaine* case (2004) in Chapter 8 that Justice Fish, of the Supreme Court of Canada, defined the evidential burden somewhat differently when he stated that, "[A]s regards all affirmative defences, I think it preferable to say that the evidential burden will be discharged where there is some evidence that puts the defence 'in play.'" He added that "[T]he defence will be in play whenever a properly instructed jury could reasonably, on account of that evidence, conclude in favour of the accused."

Of course, once the accused has satisfied the evidential burden, the defence must be considered by the trier of fact. At the end of the trial, the onus then shifts to the Crown to prove *beyond a reasonable doubt* that the accused was not acting under an honest, but mistaken, belief as to one or more of the essential *actus reus* elements of the offence with which the accused has been charged; after all, the Crown is nearly always placed under the *persuasional burden of proof*. Conversely, if the trial judge should rule that the accused has failed to satisfy the evidential burden of proof, then the trier of fact will not even consider the defence when the time ultimately comes to decide the accused's guilt or innocence.

By way of example, let us examine how the evidential burden of proof is applied in the trial of an accused person who is charged with sexual assault and advances a defence of mistaken belief in consent. In the Supreme Court of Canada's decision in *Davis* (1999), Chief Justice Lamer emphasized that it is clearly not sufficient for an accused person merely to assert that there was an honest mistake as to consent. Undoubtedly, there must be some plausible evidence to support any such contention. According to the Chief Justice, in order for the accused to satisfy the evidential burden of proof, "[I]t must be possible for a reasonable trier of fact to conclude that the *actus reus* is made out but the *mens rea* is not." Only in these circumstances does the defence have "an air or reality," and, as Chief Justice Lamer put it, "[W]here there is no air of reality to the defence, it should not be considered, as no reasonable trier of fact could acquit on that basis."

In general, it will be very difficult for an accused person to convince a judge that there is an "air of reality" to the defence of honest, but mistaken, belief in consent. Indeed, in the case of *Ewanchuk* (1999), the Supreme Court of Canada noted that "cases involving a true misunderstanding between parties to a sexual encounter" arose only "infrequently."

For example, in *Crespo* (2016), the accused had commenced sexual intercourse with the complainant who had been sleeping after a heavy night of drinking. The accused claimed honest, but mistaken, belief in consent, claiming that the complainant had actively participated in sexual activity. However, the trial judge refused to consider the defence on the ground that Crespo had taken absolutely no steps to ascertain whether the complainant was affirming her consent: after all, she was asleep at the time that Crespo initiated sexual relations and the very least step that a reasonable person in Crespo's circumstances should have taken would have been to wake her up and satisfy himself that she was affirming a free and voluntary consent. The Ontario Court of Appeal upheld the conviction, noting that "in light of [the] factual findings, the trial judge was not obliged to consider whether the appellant had an honest but mistaken belief in consent as that defence simply had no air of reality."

How "Honest" Must a Mistake of Fact Be?

Suppose that an accused person makes the following response to a criminal charge: "Owing to an honest mistake, I had no intention to commit the particular offence with which I am charged. It is true that, as a consequence of this mistake, I actually intended to commit a *different* offence. However, I should nevertheless be acquitted since I lacked the necessary

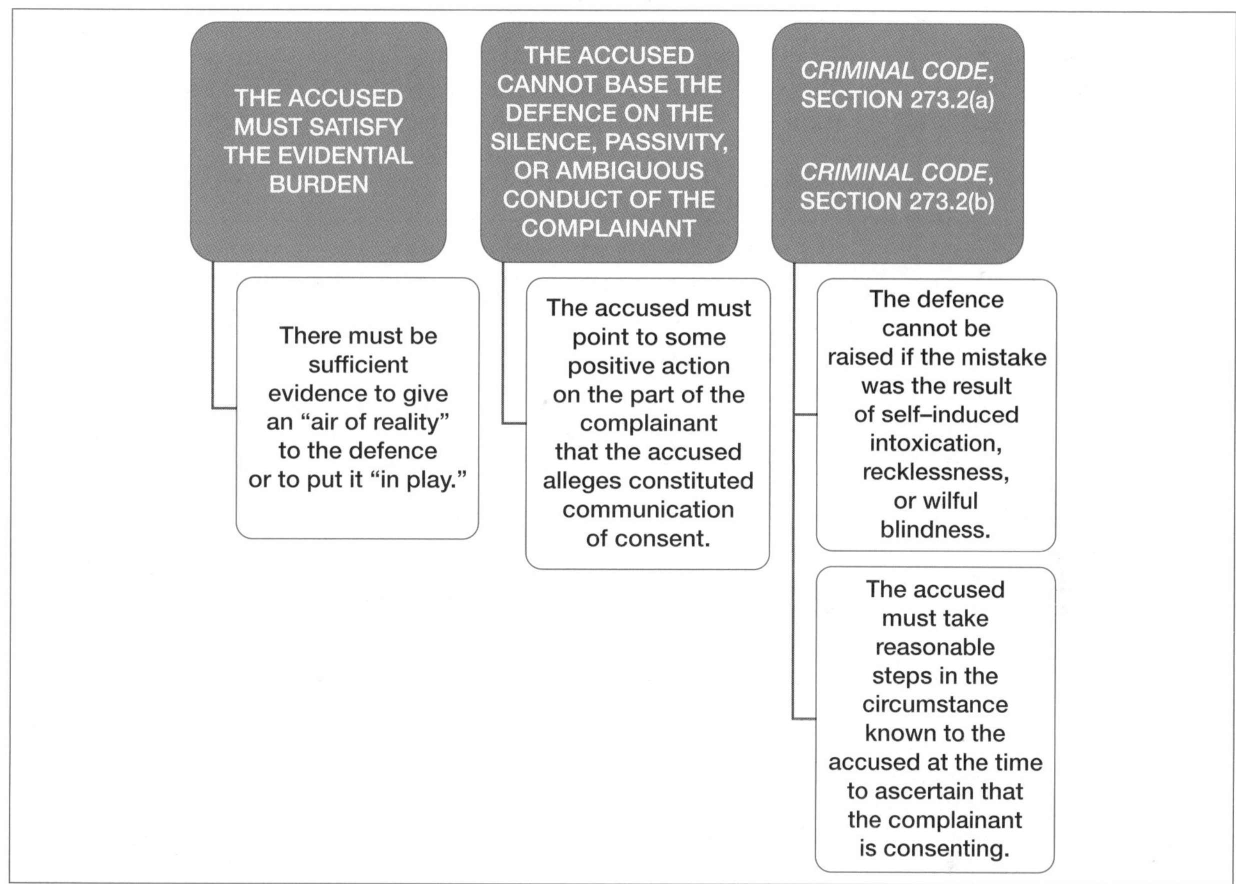

Figure 9-2

The Defence of Mistaken Belief in Consent (Sexual Assault)

mens rea in relation to the specific offence with which I am charged." Can such a defendant escape criminal liability?

The Yukon Court of Appeal addressed this issue in the somewhat bizarre case of *Ladue* (1965), in which the accused was charged with "indecently interfering with a dead human body," contrary to what is now section 182(b) of the *Criminal Code*. The accused either had sexual intercourse or attempted to do so with a dead woman. However, he claimed that, because of intoxication, he did not realize that the woman was dead and instead believed that she was only unconscious. In effect, Ladue claimed that he honestly believed that the woman was alive and, therefore, he clearly lacked the *mens rea* to commit the offence charged—namely, indecent interference with a dead human body. However, if the facts were as Ladue had actually believed them to be, it was clear that he possessed the *mens rea* for rape (an intent to have intercourse without consent). Ladue, therefore, committed the *actus reus* of indecent interference but had the *mens rea* for rape. In these circumstances, the court understandably rejected the defence of mistake of fact. Justice Davey asserted that:

> [I]t would be only in the most exceptional case where the offender might have any doubt whether a body was quick or dead, and in such a case he might defend himself by showing that he did not know the body was dead and that according to his understanding he was acting lawfully and innocently.
>
> That is what the appellant cannot show in this case, because if the woman was alive he was raping her.

Although the *Ladue* decision represents something of a departure from the principle that the Crown must prove that accused persons possessed the specific *mens rea* for the offence with which they are actually charged, the outcome of the case is not objectionable in terms of most people's sense of justice: after all, Ladue intended to commit a *more serious* offence than the one with which he was actually charged. What is

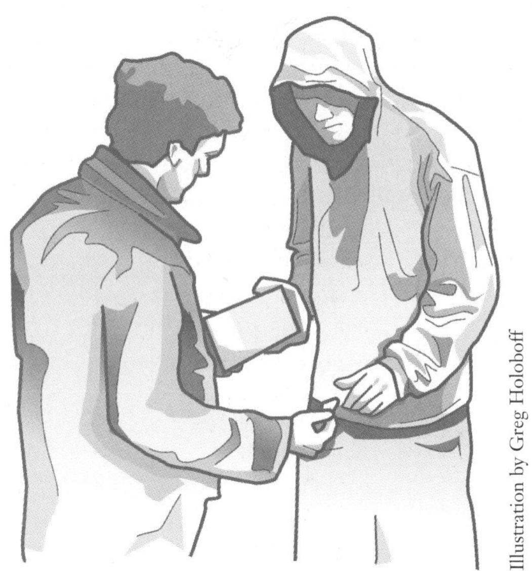

The Kundeus *case: Should he be convicted of attempting to sell mescaline or trafficking in LSD? Is his mistake of fact relevant to his culpability?*

the legal situation where an accused person commits the *actus reus* of a serious offence but, because of a mistake, only possesses the *mens rea* appropriate to a lesser offence? Does the reasoning in *Ladue* also apply here? The Canadian courts have dealt with this issue in the context of legislation relating to the illegal sale of drugs, and they have apparently expanded the reasoning employed in *Ladue*.

In *Kundeus* (1976), the accused had sold what he allegedly believed to be mescaline to an undercover police officer. In fact, the drug was LSD. Kundeus was charged with trafficking in LSD, which was a restricted drug under what was then the *Food and Drugs Act*. The penalty for this offence was a maximum of 18 months' imprisonment (upon summary conviction) and 10 years' imprisonment (upon conviction on indictment). In contrast, mescaline was not a controlled or restricted drug under the provisions of the *Food and Drugs Act*, which was in force at that time. However, it was an offence to sell mescaline under the *Food and Drugs Act* regulations. The penalty for this offence was a maximum of three months' imprisonment (for a first summary conviction), five months' imprisonment (for a secondary summary conviction), and a maximum of three years' imprisonment (for a conviction upon indictment). It is clear that the maximum penalty for the sale of LSD considerably exceeded that which could be imposed for the sale of mescaline. In essence, therefore, Kundeus alleged (in a statement he gave the police) that he believed he was committing the *actus reus* of the *less* serious offence (selling mescaline) but he actually committed the *actus reus* of the *more* serious offence (trafficking in LSD). Nevertheless, Kundeus was convicted of trafficking in LSD despite his alleged mistake of fact, and the Supreme Court of Canada ultimately upheld his conviction.[4]

In *Williams* (2009), the Ontario Court of Appeal applied the general legal principle endorsed in *Kundeus* to a case involving a charge of possession of a loaded, prohibited firearm, contrary to section 95(1) of the *Criminal Code*. Williams claimed that he was mistaken with respect to the length of the barrel of his firearm and, therefore, believed that he was in possession of a "restricted" rather than a "prohibited" firearm.[5] Possession of both prohibited and restricted firearms was dealt with in section 95(1) and the punishment for the offence was the same for either type of firearm. The trial judge acquitted Williams because he lacked the *mens rea* for possession of a *prohibited* weapon, believing, as he did, that he was in possession of a firearm with a longer barrel, which would meet the definition of a *restricted*—not a *prohibited*—firearm. The Court of Appeal rejected this line of reasoning and entered a conviction. The Court adopted the same pragmatic approach that was articulated in the *Kundeus* case:

> To adopt [Williams'] argument that the Crown must prove *mens rea* in relation to the type of weapon specified in the indictment would create an unwarranted hurdle for the Crown. Accused persons could always assert that they had not measured or made any enquiries about the length of the handgun's barrel. Accordingly, regardless of the way in which the charge is framed, the Crown would rarely, if ever, be able to obtain a conviction. ... To give effect to the language and purpose of s. 95(1), and to the intention of Parliament, it is only necessary to give to the *mens rea*

4. Strictly speaking, the majority of the justices of the Supreme Court ruled that since Kundeus did not testify or otherwise adduce evidence at his trial, he had not rebutted the presumption that he intended to sell LSD. However, the evidence of the undercover police officer who purchased the drug clearly established that Kundeus believed that he was selling mescaline. Indeed, when asked to supply "acid," Kundeus told the police officer that he was "all sold out" and offered mescaline instead.

5. S. 84(1) defines prohibited and restricted firearms. The differences between the two types of firearm include the specification of the length of the gun barrel.

> component its common sense meaning: the requisite mental element will be established where the Crown proves that the accused was knowingly in possession of a loaded prohibited or restricted handgun that he or she was not legally entitled to possess. Knowledge that the barrel of the handgun measures 105 millimetres, or more or less than that length—i.e., of whether the handgun is "prohibited" or "restricted"—is immaterial.

The Court of Appeal referred to drug-related cases such as *Kundeus* and applied the practical approach that had been articulated in such cases. The Court stated that there was overwhelming evidence that Williams knew that he had a loaded handgun in his possession and that such possession was contrary to the *Criminal Code*. The assertion that he honestly, but mistakenly, believed that this handgun measured more or less than 105 millimeters was irrelevant. Section 95(1) of the *Criminal Code* creates the offence of possession of a loaded firearm. According to the Court, it does not matter whether the gun was "prohibited" or "restricted." The *actus reus* of the two offences (possession of a banned item) and the *mens rea* (knowledge of the circumstances that rendered it a banned item) "do not relate to different crimes but rather to the same crime in each case."

It is questionable whether the approach adopted by the courts in cases such as *Kundeus* is either consistent with the doctrine of *mens rea* or desirable in terms of its results. It undoubtedly seems somewhat harsh to convict defendants of a more serious offence than the offence they were actually contemplating. Furthermore, there is absolutely no doubt that such an approach flouts the basic principles of the doctrine of *mens rea* in that the Crown is normally required to establish that the accused has the appropriate *mens rea* for the *specific offence(s) charged* before a conviction can be entered. In contrast, some people would argue that those who knowingly deal in illegal drugs should be made to accept the consequences of their actions; after all, their "honest" mistake of fact is tainted by their conscious involvement in an outlawed activity. Similarly, it might well be argued that to permit a defence of honest mistake in such circumstances would "open the floodgates" to conveniently concocted defences; any individuals charged with the sale of a drug that attracts a high criminal penalty for its illicit possession or use would automatically claim that they believed it was a drug that attracted a lesser penalty. It might well be difficult for the Crown to disprove that they really had such a belief.

The decision in *Williams* case, however, does not involve transferring the intent to commit one crime to another, more serious, crime to convict the accused of the latter. Unlike the situation in the *Kundeus* case, the penalties for the possession of the two types of firearm were the same and section 95(1) created only one offence, regardless of whether the firearm was prohibited or restricted. Therefore, the *Williams* case represents a common-sense approach that does not violate the principle that the accused should only be convicted of a crime when they have the *mens rea* for—and commit—the *actus reus* of the same offence.

CONSENT

The General Principles

Let us suppose that Fang visits his dentist, Cruncher, to obtain treatment for an excruciating toothache. Cruncher advises Fang that it is necessary to extract one of his teeth. The latter agrees to this proposition, and Cruncher duly removes the offending tooth. One week later, Fang seeks to have Cruncher charged with assault causing bodily harm and makes explicit reference to the fact that Cruncher used a good deal of force to extract the tooth. Most readers will instinctively exclaim that, of course, Cruncher is not guilty of an assault. However, what is the reason underlying this "common-sense" view? Let us also suppose that Sleary asks Lizzie whether he can borrow her expensive sports car. Lizzie answers in the affirmative and Sleary takes the car onto the highway, where, within a few minutes, he loses control and crashes into a tree. The sports car is completely destroyed, although Sleary emerges relatively unscathed. However, Lizzie now charges Sleary with theft of the car. Is Sleary guilty of this offence? Once again, the "common-sense" answer must be no, but what is the rationale underlying this response?

In each of the cases hypothesized above, the accused individuals cannot be convicted of the offences charged because the *absence of consent* is a vital element of the *actus reus* of the offence that must be proved by the Crown. Section 265 (assault) and section 322 (theft) clearly require that the Crown prove the absence of consent as an essential element of the *actus reus* of the particular offence charged. In a sense, therefore, the plea of "consent" is not really a special defence to a criminal charge; rather, it is an assertion that the Crown has not proved the *actus reus* of the offence charged.

In this chapter, we shall focus on the defence of consent in the context of a charge of assault and, in particular, a charge of sexual assault.

Consent and Assault under Section 265

Section 265 of the *Criminal Code* provides, in part, as follows:

> (1) A person commits an assault when
>
> (a) without the consent of another person, he applies force intentionally to that other person, directly or indirectly;
>
> (b) he attempts or threatens, by an act or gesture, to apply force to another person, if he has, or causes that other person to believe upon reasonable grounds that he has, present ability to effect his purpose; or
>
> (c) while openly wearing or carrying a weapon or an imitation thereof, he accosts or impedes another person or begs.
>
> (2) This section applies to all forms of assault, including sexual assault, sexual assault with a weapon, threats to a third party or causing bodily harm and aggravated sexual assault.
>
> (3) For the purposes of this section, no consent is obtained when the complainant submits or does not resist by reason of:
>
> (a) the application of force to the complainant or to a person other than the complainant;
>
> (b) threats or fear of the application of force to the complainant or to a person other than the complainant;
>
> (c) fraud; or
>
> (d) the exercise of authority.

It is clear from a close reading of section 265 that there are definite limitations to the defendant's plea of consent. Section 265(3) unequivocally states that consent obtained by the application of force or by threats or fear of the application of force or by fraud cannot be considered valid. Furthermore, section 265(3) states that no consent has been given where the complainant submits or does not resist because of the "exercise of authority" by the accused. Section 265(3) applies to all forms of assault, although much of the case law concerning this provision involves charges of sexual assault.

Although it is clear what is meant in section 265(3) by the application of force or threats or fear of the application of force, there is some uncertainty as to the meaning of fraud in the context of a charge of assault. This uncertainty will be examined later in this section. However, it appears that a consensus has emerged that there should be a broad interpretation of the phrase "exercise of authority." If an officer in the Canadian Forces were to order a subordinate to submit to sexual activity, it is perfectly clear there would be no consent because there has been an "exercise of authority." However, section 265(3) may also invalidate an apparent consent even where the accused does not have the right to issue commands or compel obedience. For example, in *Matheson* (1999), the accused was a psychologist who was charged with two counts of sexual assault in relation to sexual intercourse with two of his patients. In delivering the judgment of the Ontario Court of Appeal, Justice Austin held that there was no real consent by the patients because of the power that Matheson had to influence their conduct: "Whether or not the appellant had a right to command or to enforce obedience, he clearly had the power to influence the conduct and actions of others. He also, clearly, exercised that power for his own benefit and interest and against the interests of his patients X and Y."

In *Geddes* (2015), the Ontario Court of Appeal ruled that the phrase "exercise of authority" is not confined to circumstances in which consent is obtained by an individual who is viewed as a "person in authority," whether it be an armed forces officer or a professional person, such as a psychologist. Geddes was a man in his 40s who befriended the victim, a young teenage boy. Geddes regularly invited the victim to accompany him on skiing trips, which Geddes paid for. Geddes also purchased food and various entertainments for the victim. Geddes engaged in sexual activity with the victim for about three years. The victim stated that he never wanted to participate in this activity and only did so because of the persistent requests by Geddes. In addition, the victim asserted that he engaged in this activity because he wanted to obtain the material benefits that flowed from the relationship with Geddes. Geddes was convicted of sexual assault because the trial judge found that any apparent consent on the part of the victim was nullified by "the exercise of authority." The Court of Appeal rejected Geddes's appeal against conviction.

The Court of Appeal held that "An accused stands in a position of authority over a complainant if the accused can coerce the complainant into consent by virtue of their relationship." An important factor in the application of this principle is the existence of a "clear power imbalance" between the individuals in a relationship. If this power imbalance is exploited, then there has been an "exercise of authority" within the meaning of section 265(3)(d). The power imbalance may be based on, for example, a marked disparity in wealth. Geddes used this particular type of power imbalance to manipulate the victim into engaging in sexual activity with him. The Court of Appeal concluded that "[Geddes's] persistence, combined with threats to end the relationship and discontinue the benefits flowing from that relationship, manipulated G.C. into sexual activity which he did not want."

Let us return to the question of the meaning of "fraud" in section 265(3) and examine the uncertainty that surrounds the interpretation of this provision by the courts. Section 265(3) stipulates that any consent obtained by fraud should not be considered a real consent and that an accused may not rely on it as a defence to a charge of assault. Until recently, the only type of fraud that was covered by this provision was fraud as to the actual nature of the act in question and fraud as to the identity of the accused. For example, if physicians engage in sexual activity with patients after having informed them that they are carrying out certain medical procedures, such fraud would render any consent totally invalid. Similarly, if the accused had impersonated the complainant's spouse (in a darkened room, for example), any ensuing consent to sexual activity would be vitiated as a direct consequence of the accused person's fraud. On the other hand, in *Petrozzi* (1987), the British Columbia Court of Appeal ruled that the accused's fraudulent behaviour in promising to pay a sex worker for her sexual services (when he had no intention of doing so) did not render her consent invalid under section 265(3) of the *Code*.

However, in the controversial case of *Cuerrier* (1998), the Supreme Court of Canada expanded the meaning of "fraud" in section 265(3)(c) beyond its traditionally limited scope to include dishonesty that exposes the complainant to a significant risk of serious bodily harm. This case involved an accused person who engaged in sexual intercourse without a condom and without informing his partners that he was **HIV-positive**. These partners would not have consented to such sexual activity if they had known about Cuerrier's HIV-positive status. Justice Cory, speaking for a majority of the Supreme Court, adopted the view that a person accused of concealing or failing to disclose that they are HIV-positive may be found to have committed a type of fraud that vitiates any apparent consent on the part of the victim to engage in sexual activity. As described in Chapter 4, fraud consists of dishonest deprivation (including a risk of deprivation). A reasonable person would consider the deliberate, deceitful non-disclosure of an individual's HIV-positive status to a sexual partner to be "dishonest." As far as deprivation is concerned, Justice Corry stated that "the Crown will have to establish that the dishonest act (either falsehoods or failure to disclose) had the effect of exposing the person consenting to a *significant risk of serious bodily harm*" and the risk that the other party may contract AIDS met this requirement.

Justice Cory rejected the narrow interpretation of the meaning of fraud in section 265(3)(c) that was applied in *Petrozzi*:

> In my opinion, both the legislative history and the plain language of the provision suggest that Parliament intended to move away from the rigidity of the common law requirement that fraud must relate to the nature and quality of the act. The repeal of statutory language imposing this requirement and its replacement by a reference simply to fraud indicates that Parliament's intention was to provide a more flexible concept of fraud in assault and sexual assault cases.[6]

The Supreme Court of Canada ordered a new trial for Cuerrier, who had initially been acquitted of two counts of aggravated assault.

Since the *Cuerrier* case was decided, there have been extremely significant developments in the treatment of **HIV** and **AIDS**. With the widespread use of a cocktail of antiretroviral drugs—known as ART (**antiretroviral therapy**)—HIV is no longer a death sentence. Furthermore, ART has made it possible to reduce the amount of virus in the bloodstream (the **viral load**) to very low or undetectable levels and to significantly reduce the risk of transmitting HIV through sexual activity. Although the risk of transmission cannot be eliminated completely when an individual living with HIV has a very low viral

---

6. This may well mean that, in the future, decisions such as that made in the *Petrozzi* case (1987) may be reevaluated. Falsely promising to pay a sex worker for their services, for example, may be considered a sound reason to invalidate consent on the basis of fraud. After all, no sex worker would consent to sexual activity if they knew that the client had no intention of paying for the services rendered.

load, the evidence is that the reduction in the level of risk may be in the region of 95 percent or more for heterosexual couples.

In light of these dramatic developments, the Supreme Court of Canada revisited the *Cuerrier* decision in *Mabior* (2012). Mabior was charged with nine counts of aggravated sexual assault on the basis that he had failed to disclose his HIV-positive status to nine women with whom he had sexual intercourse. Mabior had been receiving ART and his viral loads were low, thereby reducing the risk of transmission of the virus. The Supreme Court of Canada set out the requirements for conviction of an accused person in Mabior's situation. Chief Justice McLachlin summarized the Court's ruling as follows:

> [T]o obtain a conviction under ss. 265(3)(c) and 273, the Crown must show that the complainant's consent to sexual intercourse was vitiated by the accused's fraud as to his HIV status. Failure to disclose (*the dishonest act*) amounts to fraud where the complainant would not have consented had he or she known the accused was HIV-positive, and where sexual contact poses a significant risk of or causes actual serious bodily harm (*deprivation*). A significant risk of serious bodily harm is established by a realistic possibility of transmission of HIV. On the evidence before us, a realistic possibility of transmission is negated by evidence that the accused's viral load was low at the time of intercourse and that condom protection was used. However, the general proposition that a low viral load combined with condom use negates a realistic possibility of transmission of HIV does not preclude the common law from adapting to future advances in treatment and to circumstances where risk factors other than those considered in the present case are at play.

Ultimately, Mabior was convicted only of the three charges that concerned acts of sexual intercourse that had taken place *without the use of a condom*. Having low viral loads was not considered sufficient *per se* to eliminate "a realistic possibility of transmission" of the virus: to achieve that objective, the accused must also use a condom.[7]

Another example of the expanded concept of fraud vitiating consent is *Hutchinson* (2014). The accused had engaged in sexual relations with the complainant who insisted on the use of a condom in order that she might avoid pregnancy. Contrary to her wishes and unknown to her, Hutchinson had poked holes in the condom and the complainant became pregnant. Hutchinson was convicted of sexual assault because the complainant had only consented to *protected* sexual intercourse.

The Supreme Court of Canada affirmed the conviction, finding that there had been fraud on the part of Hutchinson, as evidenced by his dishonest conduct and the risk of deprivation. Chief Justice McLachlin and Justice Cromwell, delivering the judgment of the majority of the Court, stated that if a complainant has made clear that she does not wish to become pregnant, deceptive behaviour that deprives her of the value of that choice by making her pregnant or laying her open to the risk of becoming pregnant by rendering birth control methods ineffective should be considered a sufficiently serious form of deprivation for the purpose of applying section 265(3)(c), which stipulates that fraud may vitiate consent in the context of a charge of assault, including sexual assault. Hutchinson exposed the complainant to the risk of becoming pregnant by making use of a damaged condom. A condom with pinpricks in it is no longer an effective means of birth control. The Chief Justice and Justice Cromwell took the view that the increased risk of becoming pregnant constituted "a sufficient deprivation for fraud": "We conclude that there was no consent in this case by reason of fraud, pursuant to s. 265(3)(*c*) of the *Criminal Code*. Mr. Hutchinson is therefore guilty of sexual assault."

Special Provisions Relating to the Defence of Consent in Relation to a Charge of Sexual Assault

In 1992, the *Criminal Code* was amended to provide more specific directions to judges and juries required to determine whether the accused may successfully raise a defence of consent when they are charged with sexual assault (under sections 271, 272, or 273). Indeed, section 273.1 of the *Code* states that, in general, consent in the context of a charge of sexual assault means "*the voluntary agreement of the complainant to engage in the sexual activity in question.*"

7. In a companion case, *C.(D.)* (2012), the accused was originally convicted of sexual assault and aggravated assault, but the Supreme Court of Canada affirmed the decision of the Quebec Court of Appeal to enter acquittals because the Crown had not proved beyond a reasonable doubt that a condom had not been worn. Since the accused had a low viral load as a consequence of ART, there was no proof of a "realistic possibility of transmission" of the virus.

The Case of Clato Mabior: HIV and the Criminalization of the Failure to Disclose

iStockPhoto/Thinkstock

Elsewhere in this chapter, the *Mabior* case (2012) was discussed in the context of consent and the circumstances in which consent may be vitiated (rendered invalid) by fraud, by virtue of section 265(c) of the *Criminal Code*. In *Mabior*, the issue was whether non-disclosure of one's HIV-positive status would render consent to sexual intercourse invalid when the other party would not have consented had they known of the accused person's HIV status. The Supreme Court of Canada ruled that non-disclosure would amount to fraud if the accused person knowingly exposed the other party to the risk of serious bodily harm. The Supreme Court held that an accused person must disclose their HIV-positive status if there is a "realistic possibility of transmission of HIV." The Court went on to state that if the accused person (1) has a low viral load (because they are taking antiretroviral drug therapy) and (2) uses a condom, there is no realistic possibility of transmission of the virus.

Mabior was ultimately convicted of three counts of aggravated sexual assault because, although he was taking drug treatment and had a low viral load, he had not used a condom. None of his sexual partners contracted HIV. Mabior finished serving his prison sentence in December 2011 and, in February 2012, he was deported to South Sudan.

The *Mabior* case raises many profound questions. An overarching question is whether it is an appropriate use of the criminal law to punish individuals who live with HIV for engaging in unprotected sexual relations and failing to disclose their HIV-positive status. Chief Justice McLachlin, on behalf of the Supreme Court, clearly took the view that this conduct is an appropriate target of the criminal law. The Court emphasized that such conduct was sufficiently blameworthy to merit designation as a crime:

> The interpretation of fraud vitiating consent to sexual relations should further the purposes of the criminal law, notably identifying, deterring and punishing criminal conduct, defined by a wrongful act and guilty mind. Morality infuses the criminal law. But the law does not seek to criminalize all immorality. The principal objective of the criminal law is the public identification of wrongdoing qua wrongdoing which violates public order and is so blameworthy that it deserves penal sanction. …

> The potential consequences of a conviction for aggravated sexual assault—up to life imprisonment—underline the importance of insisting on moral blameworthiness in the interpretation of s. 265(3)(c) of the *Criminal Code*.

The Supreme Court took the view that engaging in fraud and subjecting the other party in a sexual encounter to a serious risk to their life is blameworthy: "Although it can be controlled by medication, HIV remains an incurable chronic infection that, if untreated, can result in death. As such, the failure to advise a sexual partner of one's HIV status may lead to a conviction for aggravated sexual assault under s. 273(1) of the Criminal Code."

The Supreme Court also stated that failure to disclose infringes basic values enshrined in the *Canadian Charter of Rights and Freedoms*:

> In keeping with the *Charter* values of equality and autonomy, we now see sexual assault not only as a crime associated with emotional and physical harm to the victim, but as the wrongful exploitation of another human being. To engage in sexual acts without the consent of another person is to treat him or her as an object and negate his or her human dignity.

It has been strongly asserted by some that criminalization of the failure to disclose HIV-positive status will have the effect of discouraging individuals living with this condition from seeking testing and treatment. However, Chief Justice McLachlin stated that the Court had not been presented with evidence that would prove this assertion to be true.

Critics of the *Mabior* decision have focused on the lack of certainty as to the precise meaning of "a realistic possibility of transmission" of HIV. The risk of transmission depends on the nature of the sexual act in question. In *Mabior*, the Supreme Court considered only the risk associated with vaginal intercourse. The very complexity of assessing the risk for different types of sexual acts will render it most likely that expert witnesses will disagree in the courtroom. It is also pertinent to ask why, if there is a low viral load, there is also a requirement that an individual living with HIV has to use a condom? Similarly, in the *Mabior* case, the Court did not consider what would happen if a condom breaks during a sexual act. Should this occur, would the HIV-positive individual be required to disclose their HIV status retroactively?

Another potential criticism of the *Mabior* case is that it does not really resolve the uncertainty around which cases of non-disclosure should be prosecuted. For a serious offence such as aggravated assault, it is highly undesirable that there should be an unpredictable variability in patterns of prosecution across Canada. Kari[8] noted that, at the time of the Supreme Court's decision, about half of all the prosecutions for non-disclosure had occurred in Ontario. About 60 per cent of the prosecutions involved heterosexual men and roughly half of these involved black heterosexual men. This statistic certainly raises a question about the potential selectivity of prosecutions, and it remains to be seen whether the *Mabior* decision will enable provinces and territories to set clearer guidelines as to when prosecution for non-disclosure is appropriate.

Significantly, in December 2018, the (then) Federal Minister of Justice and Attorney General of Canada, Jody Wilson-Raybould, issued a set of directives for determining whether to prosecute individuals who failed to disclose their HIV-positive status to their sexual partners. The directives include a statement that prosecutors should not lay charges where the individual living with HIV has maintained "a suppressed viral load" (which is defined as being under 200 copies of the virus per millilitre of blood) because the scientific evidence is that there is "no realistic possibility of transmission" in such circumstances.

The effect of this policy is to remove the requirement, imposed by the Supreme Court of Canada in the *Mabior* case, that a condom must be used *in addition to* maintenance of a low viral load. In this respect, the federal directives undoubtedly recognize the weight of current scientific opinion with respect to the extremely low risk of transmitting HIV, when there is maintenance of a low viral load as a consequence of treatment: in so doing, the directives establish an *evidence-based* approach to prosecution.

The directives also include the statements that there should not be a criminal prosecution where:

> The person has not maintained a suppressed viral load, but used condoms or engaged only in oral sex or was taking treatment as prescribed, unless other risk factors are present.
>
> If a person living with HIV has sought or received services from public health authorities, that must be taken into account when determining whether it is in the public interest to pursue criminal charges.

The federal directives will have a direct effect only in Nunavut, Northwest Territories and Yukon, which fall under federal jurisdiction. In the 10 provinces, decisions about the prosecution of *Criminal Code*

8. Shannon Kari. October 15, 2012. "Rules for HIV Prosecution Unclear Despite SCC Decision." Law Times, p. 15. Lawtimesnews.com.

offences are made by provincial Crown Counsel, under the general direction of provincial attorneys general. Therefore, it will be up to each province to decide if they wish to adopt the federal directives.

In *Mabior*, the Supreme Court did not address the issue of non-disclosure of other sexually transmitted diseases, such as syphilis, gonorrhea, and genital herpes. The risks to life are quite different for each of these diseases and treatment may effect a cure for some of them. Should non-disclosure of such diseases also result in convictions for aggravated assault?

Do you agree that the criminal law should be used to punish individuals who do not disclose their HIV-positive status? What other public health measures might be more effective in reducing the transmission of HIV and other diseases? Do you think the Supreme Court has provided sufficient clarity with respect to the circumstances in which an individual will be convicted of aggravated sexual assault?

In *Hutchinson* (2014), the Supreme Court of Canada ruled that the words "sexual activity in question" refer purely to the physical sex act itself (such as "kissing, petting, oral sex, intercourse or the use of sex toys"). Chief Justice McLachlin and Justice Cromwell stated that "agreement to one form of penetration is not agreement to any or all forms of penetration and agreement to sexual touching on one part of the body is not agreement to all sexual touching."

Subsection 273.1(1.1) states that "Consent must be present at the time the sexual activity in question takes place." This provision, added in 2018, gives legislative recognition to the decision of the Supreme Court of Canada in the *A. (J.)* case (2011), discussed earlier. In addition, subsection 273.1, also enacted in 2018, provides that "The question of whether no consent is obtained under subsection 265(3) or subsection (2) or (3) is a question of law." This subsection is particularly significant because it renders the question of whether a valid consent has been given a decision for the trial judge as arbiter of the law, and not the trier of fact (whether it be a judge or jury).

Subsection 273.1(2) sets out a number of circumstances in which there can be no valid consent to sexual activity:

> For the purpose of subsection (1), no consent is obtained if
>
> (a) the agreement is expressed by the words or conduct of a person other than the complainant;
>
> (a.1) the complainant is unconscious;
>
> (b) the complainant is incapable of consenting to the activity for any reason other than the one referred to in paragraph (a.1);
>
> (c) the accused induces the complainant to engage in the activity by abusing a position of trust, power or authority;
>
> (d) the complainant expresses, by words or conduct, a lack of agreement to engage in the activity; or
>
> (e) the complainant, having consented to engage in sexual activity, expresses, by words or conduct, a lack of agreement to continue to engage in the activity.

Subsection 273.1 makes the important point, "Nothing in subsection (2) shall be construed as limiting the circumstances in which no consent is obtained." Remember that subsection 265(3), which applies to *all* assaults, including sexual assaults, also lists four circumstances in which no valid consent can be given and the subsection has to be read in conjunction with subsection 273.1(2).

Subection 273.1(2)(a) clearly stipulates that no valid consent has been given where a third party purports to give consent to sexual activity on behalf of the complainant. For example, a defendant may not claim the defence of consent where the alleged consent was given by the partner of the complainant.

Subsection 273.1(2)(a.1), added in 2018, emphasizes that a complainant who is unconscious cannot give a valid consent. The *A. (J.)* case (2011) very definitively ruled that a complainant cannot give *advance consent* to sexual activity that might take place while they are unconscious. In that case, the lack of consciousness was caused by choking. However, a more common cause is likely to be the ingestion of alcohol and/or other drugs.

Furthermore, subsection 273.1(2)(b) of the *Code* states that there can be no consent where the complainant "is incapable of consenting to the [sexual] activity for any reason other than the one referred to in paragraph (a.1)" [section 283.1(2)(a.1) refers to a state of unconsciousness].

A complainant who is in a state of acute intoxication would be deemed incapable of giving a valid consent to sexual activity. For example, in the *Daigle* case (1998), the Supreme Court upheld the conviction of the accused where the complainant had been given a dose of PCP without her knowledge or consent. Justice L'Heureux-Dubé agreed with the reasoning of the Quebec Court of Appeal that "[T]he evidence shows that [the complainant], then 15 years of age, who drank in one shot a glass of alcohol in which there was hidden the drug, was not capable of giving a valid consent." Furthermore, in *Randall* (2012), the New Brunswick Court of Appeal affirmed that a complainant has to remain fully conscious in order to be able to give consent to each and every sexual act: in this case, the complainant, who was extremely intoxicated, had had only intermittent periods of consciousness during a series of sexual assaults by the accused. Following the decision of the Supreme Court of Canada, in *A. (J.)* (2011), the Court of Appeal emphasized that the complainant has to remain conscious during the entire period of sexual activity if her consent is to be considered valid. This principle, of course, has been recognized by Parliament in subsection 273.1(2)(a.1).

The Crown does have to prove that the level of intoxication actually impaired the complainant's capacity to consent. In *Al-Rawi* (2018), the Nova Scotia Court of Appeal stated that "Capacity to consent mandates an inquiry as to whether the complainant had the minimal or limited cognitive capacity to understand the nature and quality of the activity, the identity of the person(s) with whom the activity is engaged, and the awareness of choice to agree or decline."

An individual who is so intoxicated that they have lapsed into unconsciousness is, by virtue of 273.1(2)(a.1), deemed unable to consent, but considerably lesser degrees of intoxication may, in many cases, cause an individual to lose the capacity to consent to participation in sexual activities. The Crown will need to address the amount of alcohol and/or drugs consumed and the specific effects that the intoxicants had on the individual complainant concerned. Of course, there are many other reasons why the trier of fact would find that there was no consent. Having the capacity to consent by no means establishes that consent was actually given.

Subsection 273.1(2)(c) provides that no consent has been obtained where the accused has induced the complainant to engage in sexual activity "by abusing a position of trust, power or authority." This provision would potentially cover, for example, situations such as those in which a university teacher engages in sexual activity with a student or a physician becomes physically involved with a patient. To obtain a conviction, however, the Crown would, of course, have to establish that the teacher or physician actually induced the student and or patient respectively to engage in sexual activity by abusing their position of trust in relation to them. For example, in *Snelgrove* (2018), the Newfoundland and Labrador Court of Appeal ordered a new trial in a case in which an on-duty police officer had given a ride home to an intoxicated woman who invited him into her home and the next thing she stated she remembered was that the officer was having sexual relations with her. The mere fact that Snelgrove was a police officer did not automatically invalidate any consent on the part of the complainant. However, Justice Welsh stated that, in a new trial, the jury may consider it relevant that the intoxicated complainant was vulnerable in contrast to the accused on-duty police officer, who was not only in a position of trust or authority to her but was also not impaired by alcohol. It is noteworthy that, in the *Hogg* case (2000), the Ontario Court of Appeal held that, in certain circumstances, a drug dealer may be considered to be in a position of power or authority over an addicted client and that abuse of this position would invalidate any consent that may have been given to sexual activity. As Justice Finlayson said in delivering the judgment of the court,

> The protection of the vulnerable and the weak and the preservation of the right to freely choose to consent to sexual activity is clearly the aim of s. 273.1(2)(c). … I have no doubt that it could have application to the relationship between a drug dealer and an addicted client. However, the relationship is not one of an imbalance of power *per se*. This is not a case of a position of authority or trust, such as in the prototypic doctor/patient, teacher/student relationship, where vulnerability is inherent to the relationship itself. The trial judge should have instructed the jury that they must be satisfied that because the appellant was a supplier of illicit drugs to the complainant, that this relationship created a relationship of dependency that could be exploited by the appellant to vitiate the complainant's consent to engage in sexual activity.

Section 273.1(2)(d) stipulates that no consent is obtained where "the complainant expresses, by words or conduct, a lack of agreement to engage in the activity." This means that a sexual aggressor cannot raise the defence of consent merely because the complainant did not say "no"; if the complainant's *conduct* (e.g., pushing the accused away) expressed a refusal to engage in sexual activity, the accused will be disqualified from relying on the defence of consent. Finally, s. 273.1(2)(e) provides that individuals have the right to withdraw their consent to engage in sexual activity *at any time*, even if they initially gave a valid consent. If the accused refuses to cease such activity at any point after the complainant's consent has been withdrawn, they will be guilty of a sexual assault.

Subsection 273.1(3) indicates that the specific circumstances articulated in 273.1(2)(a) to (e) are not an *exclusive* list of circumstances in which there can be no valid consent: "Nothing in subsection (2) shall be construed as limiting the circumstances in which no consent is obtained."

It is also important to take into account that subsection 273.2(a)(iii), added in 2018, provides that an accused person is barred from raising the defence of mistaken belief in consent where the accused's belief arose from "any circumstance referred to in subsection 265(3) or 273.1(2) or (3) in which no consent is obtained." This provision is of particular importance because, for example, an accused person cannot claim that they were mistaken about the capacity of the complainant to give consent or that they did not realize that the complainant was withdrawing their consent to continue with sexual activity if the complainant had expressed "by words or conduct" their lack of agreement to continue their participation in such activity. Equally, if the accused obtains consent fraudulently, they will not be able to claim mistaken belief in consent as a defence.

Can an Individual Consent to the Infliction of Bodily Harm?

Section 14 of the *Criminal Code* provides that no one can consent to have death inflicted on them and that any consent that may have been given does not affect the criminal responsibility of a person who does inflict death in such circumstances, although, since 2016, there is now an exception for medical assistance in dying (discussed in Chapter 3). For this reason, someone who is not a medical professional who carries out an act of voluntary euthanasia on a terminally ill partner as a so-called "mercy killing" is guilty of murder despite the fact that the partner, while competent to do so, has given an unequivocal consent to this course of action and, indeed, has persistently requested it because they are suffering from extreme pain. However, the *Criminal Code* does not deal explicitly with the question of whether an individual may consent to the infliction of a degree of bodily harm that falls short of death. Should individuals be able to give their consent to the infliction of bodily harm and turn what would otherwise be criminal assaults into lawful actions? In the *Jobidon* case (1991), the Supreme Court of Canada adopted the view that unless there is some overriding social utility that may be identified in relation to the activity in question, consent should not be accepted as a defence to a charge of assault where the accused person intends to cause serious harm and such harm is, in fact, inflicted.

In *Jobidon*, the accused engaged in a fist fight with Haggart. The trial judge found that Jobidon and Haggart had agreed to a fight as a result of a prior altercation between them. Haggart died as a consequence of the blows meted out by Jobidon, and the latter was charged with manslaughter. The theory of the Crown was that Jobidon had committed the unlawful act of assault and, as a consequence, the victim had died; in these circumstances, the contention was that Jobidon was, therefore, guilty of "unlawful act" manslaughter. However, the trial judge found that there had been no assault, and hence no unlawful act. In his view, the victim had agreed to enter into a "fair fist fight" and Jobidon had not intended to exceed the scope of that consent (in the sense that he had no intention to inflict death or grievous bodily harm). In light of this view, the trial judge acquitted Jobidon, but the Crown appealed and the Ontario Court of Appeal substituted a verdict of guilty of manslaughter. The Court of Appeal took the view that where the accused intends to cause bodily harm in a fist fight, the Crown is not required to prove the absence of consent.

Jobidon appealed to the Supreme Court of Canada, which dismissed his appeal. Speaking for the majority of the Court, Justice Gonthier said that *consent should not be a defence to a charge of assault whenever adults intentionally apply force that causes "serious hurt or non-trivial bodily harm to each other in the course of a fist fight or brawl."* According to Justice Gonthier, sound public policy dictates that such an approach be adopted: "Foremost among the policy considerations" is the

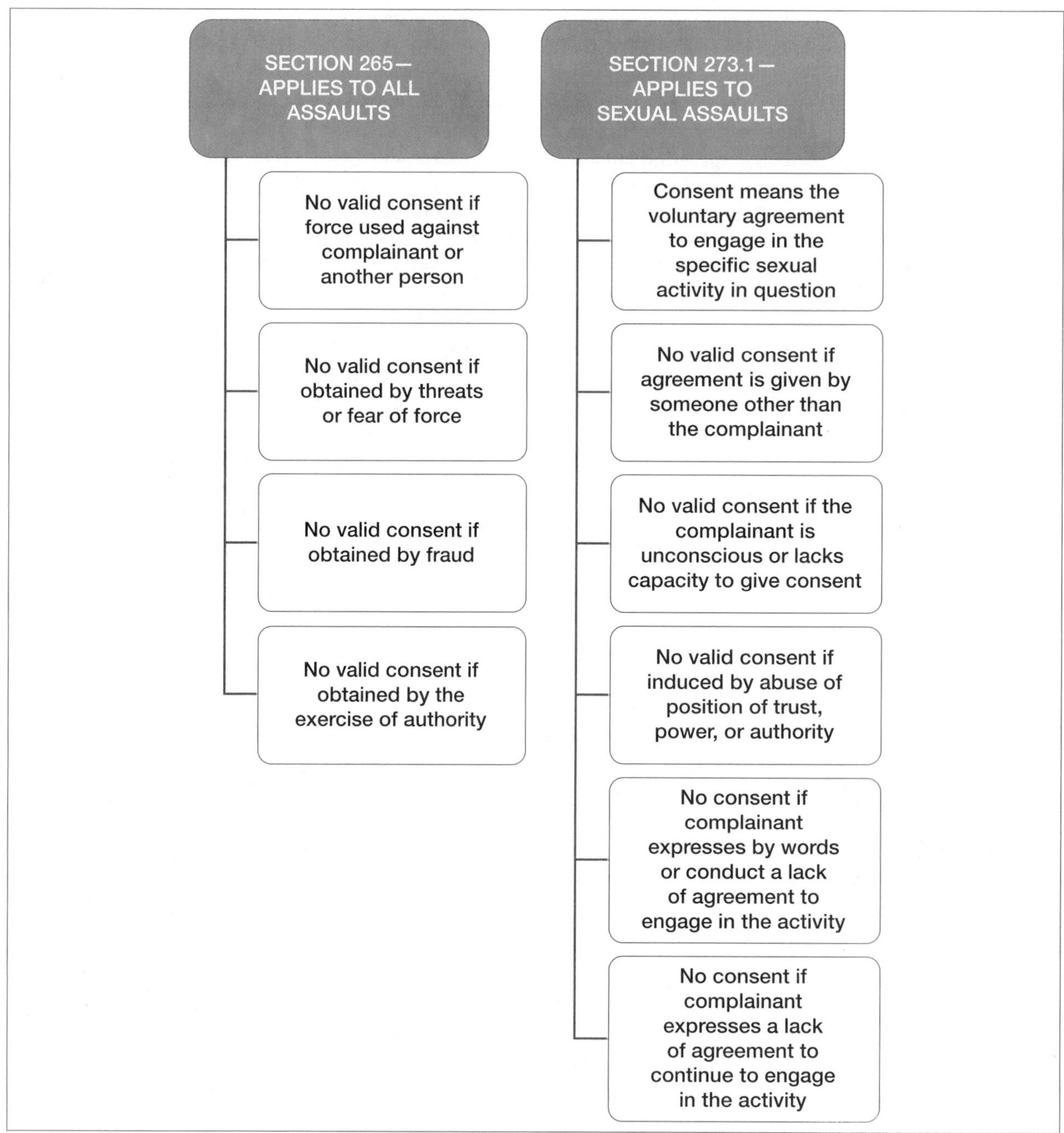

Figure 9-3
Consent in Relation to Charges of Sexual Assault

"social uselessness of fist fights." It is just not in the public interest that adults intentionally cause harm to each other for no good reason. Such fights may lead to tragedy, as in the *Jobidon* case itself, or may result in an even greater brawl if bystanders become involved (which also happened in the *Jobidon* case when the brothers of the protagonists also become involved in a fist fight). Furthermore, if individuals are permitted to participate in consensual fist fights, they may eventually lose their inhibitions against using violence and start to use their fists on their spouses or partners. Finally,

> Wholly apart from deterrence, it is most unseemly from a moral point of view that the law would countenance, much less provide a backhanded sanction to the sort of interaction displayed by the facts of this appeal. *The sanctity of the human body should militate against the validity of consent to bodily harm inflicted in a fight*. [emphasis added]

The Supreme Court of Canada's decision in *Jobidon* does not mean that consent to the infliction of bodily harm will always be considered invalid. It states only that such consent will be invalid where there is no social utility to be gained from the activity in question. Therefore, for example, consent to "bodily harm" would be a defence where medical or surgical treatment was involved or where there was some socially redeeming value to be gained (as in the case of "rough" sports or games). Similarly, if individuals agree to perform stunts in a movie and, as part of that agreement, they consent to participate in "risky sparring or daredevil activities," their consent would be considered valid to a charge of assault should they be injured in the course of these activities; the consent would be valid because those involved in making a movie are creating a "socially useful product."

The Supreme Court of Canada limited the application of its ruling to fist fights between adults. Indeed, Justice Gonthier stated that:

> [T]he phenomenon of the "ordinary" schoolyard scuffle, where boys or girls immaturely seek to resolve differences with their hands, will not come within the scope of the limitation. That has never been the policy of the law and I do not intend to disrupt the status quo. However, I would leave the question as to whether boys or girls under the age of 18 who truly intend to harm one another, and ultimately cause more than trivial bodily harm, would be afforded the protection of a defence of consent.

The *Jobidon* case does not imply that all consensual fist fights between adults necessarily constitute criminal assaults. Indeed, in the case of *Doherty* (2000), the New Brunswick Court of Appeal took the view that the critical issue in such cases is whether the adult combatants *intended* to inflict non-trivial bodily harm on each other. If there is no such intention, then the *consent* of the parties to exchange blows may be effective to absolve them of any criminal liability. On behalf of the court, Justice Drapeau stated that:

> *Even in circumstances where serious harm is inflicted in the course of an altercation*, the injured party's consent to the application of force to his or her person will preclude a finding of unlawful assault against the combatant who stands accused, unless the Crown establishes that such serious harm was intended by the latter's application of force. [emphasis added]

In the *Doherty* case, the facts were that the accused was a bouncer at a strip club. He had expelled Gillan and his friend Boyle because they were drunk and engaging in "intolerable conduct." When Gillan later returned to the club and attempted to hit Doherty, the latter blocked the blow and delivered one punch to Gillan's jaw. Although Gillan later died from a head injury that occurred when he fell to the ground, the trial judge found that Doherty did not intend to cause Gillan any serious injury. The New Brunswick Court of Appeal ruled that Doherty should be acquitted of unlawful act manslaughter because Gillan had *consented to the infliction of force that was not intended to cause non-trivial bodily harm*. In the words of Justice Drapeau:

> There can be no serious challenge to the proposition that, once outside the club premises, Mr. Gillan was bellicose and intent on obtaining retribution for his expulsion by Mr. Doherty. ... I am satisfied that Mr. Gillan's pre-altercation conduct and his physical attack on Mr. Doherty are *outward manifestations of his consent to the application of defensive force* by Mr. Doherty. [emphasis added]

According to the Court of Appeal, Gillan implicitly consented to the use of defensive force by the accused, on the understanding that the latter would not intentionally cause him serious bodily harm. If Gillan's consent was effective in law, then Doherty did not commit an unlawful assault when he punched Gillan on the jaw. Clearly, in these circumstances, Doherty could not be found guilty of unlawful act manslaughter.

In *Paice* (2005), the Supreme Court of Canada also emphasized that *Jobidon* (1991) had decided that consent to a fist fight would be nullified only when (1) the accused person *intended* to cause serious bodily harm and (2) such harm was in fact inflicted on the victim. In *Paice*, Justice Charron clearly rejected the assertion, for example, that a mere intention to cause serious bodily harm would on its own nullify consent to a fist fight:

> [T]he intention to cause serious bodily harm alone cannot serve to negate the other person's consent to the application of force if, in fact, no bodily harm is caused. The activity, a consensual application of force that causes no serious bodily harm, would fall

> within the scope of the consent and not in any way fall with the *Code* definition of assault.

It should be remembered that even if both parties initially give a valid consent to a fist fight, the consent of one of them may subsequently be rendered invalid if the other goes outside the scope of the original consent. As Justice Costigan of the Alberta Court of Appeal stated in *Gardiner* (2018), courts have to ask whether the accused's conduct was "within the ambit of the consent that the two parties gave, or did it materially change the nature of the fight." For example, in *Sullivan* (2011), the accused and the victim agreed to a fist fight, but Sullivan switched to kneeing the victim, whose jaw was broken by the force of Sullivan's knee. The Newfoundland and Labrador Court of Appeal affirmed the conviction of the accused. Justice Wells said:

> Whether consent to a fist fight is explicit or implied, it must be taken to have been given in the expectation that what follows will be a fist fight, carrying with it some risk of serious bodily harm. It is difficult to imagine a fist fight that will not have some risk, however minimal, of serious bodily harm. Employing tactics which will change the nature of a consensual fist fight from an activity having some risk of serious bodily harm to an activity with a significant risk of serious bodily harm makes the fight essentially a fraud.

The Court of Appeal also considered recklessness on the part of Sullivan to be sufficient to satisfy the first *Jobidon* requirement, that there be an actual intent to cause bodily harm if consent is to be rendered invalid. Justice Welsh reiterated the principle that the *mens rea* for aggravated assault is no different from the *mens rea* of assault, namely an intent to intentionally or recklessly apply force to a non-consenting victim (or being wilfully blind as to the absence of consent) plus objective foresight of the risk of bodily harm. How did this principle apply to the case before the Court of Appeal? The Crown did not have to establish that Sullivan intended to break the victim's jaw. Even though this was a "consensual fist fight," aggravated assault will be proved if Sullivan applied force recklessly and that a reasonable person in his circumstances would foresee the risk of serious bodily harm. Justice Welch concluded that "The facts as found by the trial judge lead to the conclusion that Mr. Sullivan acted recklessly in using his knee, particularly making contact with the complainant's face. Serious bodily harm was objectively foreseeable as a result of this action."

It is unfortunate that the *Jobidon* case left many questions unanswered. For example, does the sport of boxing have "social utility" when the argument might be made (although not without considerable opposition) that it supports the values of violence and involves the deliberate infliction of blows that may be extremely dangerous? If it does not have such social utility, presumably participation in boxing amounts to assaultive behaviour. Similarly, the question arises as to what extent an individual may consent to non-essential "surgical" procedures that inflict bodily harm. Presumably, one can consent to body piercing or tattooing because they may have some social utility in terms of giving individuals choices in the area of fashion or enhancing their psychological well-being, but exactly how far may one go in terms of submitting to so-called cosmetic procedures that may conceivably involve the risk of serious injury? All these issues must, no doubt, be dealt with by the courts on a case-by-case basis.

In the case of *Welch* (1995), the Ontario Court of Appeal adopted the view that, on grounds of public policy, an individual cannot consent to the deliberate infliction of non-trivial bodily harm even if they claim that such harm occurred in the course of consensual sexual activity. In *Welch*, the accused was charged with sexual assault causing bodily harm. According to the complainant, the accused had prevented her from leaving his condominium and then had pushed her onto a bed and tied her hands and legs. She also stated that although she protested throughout, the accused then attempted a number of acts of sexual intercourse, beat her with a belt, and inserted an object into her rectum. The complainant suffered extensive bruising to her breast, abdomen, arm, leg, and buttocks, as well as bleeding from her rectum for several days.

The accused claimed that the complainant had unequivocally consented to, and had actually encouraged, what he called "rough sex." The trial judge ruled that even if the complainant had consented to this type of injury, consent was no defence to a charge of sexual assault causing bodily harm. Welch was subsequently convicted by a jury, and the central issue in his appeal to the Ontario Court of Appeal was whether the trial judge had erred in refusing to place the defence of consent before the jury. Speaking on behalf of the court, Justice Griffiths noted that *Jobidon* provided that there was an exception to the rule that a victim cannot consent to the deliberate infliction of bodily harm: namely, defendants who were "acting in the course of a generally approved social purpose when inflicting the harm" would be given the benefit of a complete defence. However, Justice Griffiths pointed out that sexual violence was conspicuously absent from the list of examples furnished by the Supreme Court of Canada when elaborating on the nature of this exception.

According to the Court of Appeal, the facts in *Welch* revealed a course of "sadistic sexual activity" involving bondage and the deliberate infliction of harm on the body and rectum of the complainant. Even if the complainant had consented to this activity, her consent could not have detracted from the "inherently degrading and dehumanizing nature of the conduct." In such circumstances, the "personal interests of the individuals involved must yield to the more compelling societal interests which are challenged by such behaviour." As Justice Griffiths put it, it is arguable that society has the right to "enforce one fundamental residual moral value," namely, that "hurting people is wrong and this is so whether the victim consents or not, or whether the purpose is to fulfil a sexual need or to satisfy some other desire."

Welch was a case in which the level of violence was high and there could have been no doubt that the accused *intended* to—and did—cause bodily harm to the victim. Later decisions by the Ontario Court of Appeal have made it clear that a *willing* partner may give a valid consent to sexual activity that runs the risk of bodily harm occurring *accidentally*—provided that the other party *does not intend to cause bodily harm*. For example, in *Zhao* (2013), the Court said:

> [C]onsent is not vitiated in all circumstances of sexual assault causing bodily harm, but instead only in those circumstances where bodily harm was intended *and* in fact caused. Where the accused did not intend to cause bodily harm, consent is available as a defence, if bodily harm is inadvertently caused.

The problem with the *Welch* case (1995), even with the subsequent clarification by the Ontario Court of Appeal, is that it raises the spectre of state interference with consensual sexual activity that takes place in private. The facts in *Welch* raise serious questions about whether the complainant did indeed consent to what can only be termed brutal treatment. However, there may be some situations in which truly consenting adults, for example, may wish to engage in sexual activity that includes the *deliberate* infliction of some degree of bodily harm in order to enhance sexual pleasure. Take, for example, the practice of (consensual) flagellation, which may well cause bruising on the bodies of the recipient(s). Should the courts use the argument of public policy to invalidate the consent of such adults and turn their sexually oriented activities, which do not harm anyone else, into criminal acts?

Consent to the Infliction of Bodily Harm in the Context of Sporting Activity

The issue of consent to what would otherwise be an assault is frequently raised in the somewhat controversial arena of contact sports. It is indisputable that the very nature of games such as hockey or football requires the intentional application of force to one's opponents. Therefore, it may generally be said that individuals who voluntarily participate in such sports should be deemed to have given **implied consent** to the infliction of a certain degree of force upon their bodies. However, the question will always arise as to exactly where the law should draw the line between legitimate bodily contact and the criminal application of force.

It is clear that the scope of implied consent to bodily contact in sports is not unlimited. In general, a participant in a contact sport may be considered to have consented only to the application of force that occurs within the bounds of fair play and that is reasonably incidental to the sport in question. It may safely be assumed that no hockey or football player would consent to the *deliberate* infliction of serious bodily harm or to the application of force that does not fall within the range of a player's reasonable expectations as to how the game in question should be played. On the other hand, injuries—often of a serious nature—may occur accidentally during the course of normal play, and the doctrine of implied consent will prevent such incidents from being dealt with as criminal offences.

Just how broad is the scope of implied consent in any given sport? In Canada, most of the cases that attempt to explore this issue have involved hockey games. For example, in the *Cey* case (1989), the Saskatchewan Court of Appeal ruled that there can be no implied consent to bodily harm that is *intentionally* inflicted. Furthermore, Justice Gerwing made the important point that "[I]n sporting events ... the mere fact that a type of assault occurs with some frequency does not necessarily mean that it is not of such a severe nature that consent thereto is precluded." Justice Gerwing also stressed the importance of applying *objective criteria* in determining whether the implied consent of sport players to the application of force has been exceeded in any given case:

> Ordinarily consent, being a state of mind, is a wholly subjective matter to be determined accordingly, but when it comes to implied consent in the context of a team sport such as hockey, there cannot be as many different consents as there are players on the ice, and so the scope of the implied consent, having to be uniform, must be determined by reference to objective criteria.

These objective criteria include the setting of the game, the nature of the league in which it is played (e.g., is it amateur or professional?), the age of the players, the conditions under which the game is played (e.g., is protective equipment used?), the extent of the force used, the degree of risk of injury, and the probability of serious harm. In the particular circumstances of the *Cey* case, Justice Gerwing focused on the inherent risk of injury and the severity of the injuries inflicted as being the central issues to be examined in determining the scope of any implied consent: "Some forms of bodily contact carry with them such a high risk of injury and such a distinct probability of injury as to be beyond what, in fact, the players commonly consent to, or what, in law, they are capable of consenting to."

In the case of *McSorley* (2000), the court took the view that deliberately striking another player on the head with a hockey stick clearly fell outside the scope of any implied consent on the part of a professional hockey player in the National Hockey League (NHL). While a professional game was in progress, McSorley had pursued another player and struck him from behind. Swinging his hockey stick as though it were a baseball bat, McSorley hit his victim on the side of the head, causing the latter to suffer a *grand mal* seizure and a serious concussion. Undoubtedly, no player would ever consent to such a violent application of force, and there was no doubt that McSorley's conduct fell far outside the ordinary norms of conduct that apply in professional hockey. McSorley was convicted of assault with a weapon. The Provincial Court judge was satisfied beyond a reasonable doubt that McSorley intended to hit his victim in the way that he did:

> He had an impulse to strike him in the head. His mindset, always tuned to aggression, permitted that. He slashed for the head. A child, swinging as at a Tee ball, would not miss. A housekeeper swinging a carpetbeater would not miss. An NHL player would never, ever miss. Brashear was struck as intended.

Similarly, in *Bertuzzi* (2004), the accused entered a plea of guilty to a charge of assault causing bodily harm. In the course of an NHL game, Bertuzzi skated behind the victim (Moore) and hit him on the right temple with a powerful and unprovoked punch. The victim collapsed on the ice and suffered severe spinal and neurological damage. Bertuzzi was granted a conditional discharge. In passing sentence, Judge Weitzel stated that:

> The confronting of Moore initially may have been within the bounds of the game. To then have the pursuit literally down the ice and then to grab by the sweater in order to get that player to engage in something which it is clear he did not wish to consent to, clearly went beyond the reasonable limits of the game and is an aggravating factor.

The *Bertuzzi* case clearly demonstrates the principle that the doctrine of implied consent has no application when the accused person goes beyond the boundaries of the normal and reasonable expectations of fair play. The victim in this case would never have consented to being "mugged" from behind.

However, the *Leclerc* case (1991) illustrates the proposition that implied consent is not invalidated merely because there has been a serious injury in the course of sporting activity. Leclerc was charged with aggravated assault after he pushed his victim into the boards by striking him in the back or near the neck with his hockey stick. Unfortunately, owing to the speed at which Leclerc was travelling on the ice, his actions caused the victim to collide with the boards and, as a result, the latter was permanently paralyzed from the neck down. The trial judge found that Leclerc's application of force to the victim resulted from his "loss of balance and was part of [his] 'instinctive reflex action,' which had the object of minimizing the risk of bodily harm created by his high speed in close proximity to the boards." Leclerc was acquitted at his trial, and the Ontario Court of Appeal subsequently rejected an appeal by the Crown. Clearly, the outcome would have been very different if the accused had deliberately pushed his victim into the boards with intent to injure him.

Although the principles surrounding the issue of implied consent to the application of force in sporting activities are relatively straightforward, there is no doubt that trial courts have considerable discretion in applying them to the facts of individual cases.

Illustration by Greg Holoboff

Implied consent to the application of physical force in contact sports does not extend to actions that are outside the accepted rules and expectations of the sport in question.

MISTAKE OF LAW

The General Principle: Mistake of Law Is Not a Defence

Section 19 of the *Criminal Code* enshrines one of the most widely known principles of the criminal law: namely, that "ignorance of the law is no defence"; this ignorance is known as **mistake of law**. Indeed, as Justice Lebel, of the Supreme Court of Canada noted, in *MacDonald* (2014), "It is trite law that, except in the case of an officially induced error, a mistake of law is no defence in our criminal justice system." For example, in *Klundert* (2008), the Ontario Court of Appeal ruled that the accused's mistaken belief that the *Income Tax Act*, R.S.C. 1985, c. 1 (5th Supp.), did not apply to him personally was no defence to a charge of tax evasion, contrary to section 239(1) of the Act: "[A] person's mistaken belief that a statute is invalid *or is otherwise not applicable to that person's conduct* … is a mistake of law that is irrelevant to the existence of the fault requirement in s. 239(1)(d)" [emphasis in original]. Similarly, in *Ewanchuk* (1999), Justice Major, of the Supreme Court of Canada, stated that if an accused person believed that "silence, passivity or ambiguous conduct constitutes consent" to sexual contact, then this would be considered a "mistake of law" and would not constitute a defence to a charge of sexual assault.

A dramatic example of the application of section 19 of the *Criminal Code* occurred in the case of *Forster* (1992), where the accused was a commissioned officer in the Canadian Armed Forces who was ordered to report to a new posting. This would have involved moving to Ottawa from Edmonton, where her husband was stationed. Instead of obeying the order to report to her new posting in Ottawa, she attempted to submit her resignation from the Armed Forces.

Such an attempt was ineffective, since she did not follow the prescribed procedures under *Queen's Regulations* for accomplishing this end. She was later charged with being absent without leave, contrary to section 90 of the *National Defence Act*, R.S.C. 1985, c. N-5, and was convicted by a General Court Martial in spite of her defence that she honestly believed that she had effectively resigned from the Armed Forces (i.e., an honest mistake of law). The Supreme Court later ordered a new trial on the basis that the General Court Martial did not meet the requirements of section 11(d) of the *Charter* (specifically, that it be "an independent and impartial tribunal"). However, Chief Justice Lamer pointed out that Forster

> … was mistaken about the legal consequences of her actions, because of her failure to understand that she was under a continuing legal obligation to report for duty notwithstanding her purported resignation by

> letter from the forces. Thus, while she may not have intended to commit an offence under military law, this lack of intention flowed from her mistake as to the continuing legal obligation to report for duty which that regime imposed upon her until properly released from service in accordance with [*Queen's Regulations and Orders*].
>
> It is a principle of our criminal law that an honest but mistaken belief in respect of the legal consequences of one's deliberate actions does not furnish a defence to a criminal charge, even when the mistake cannot be attributed to the negligence of the accused. ... This court recently reaffirmed ... the principle that knowledge that one's actions are contrary to the law is not a component of the *mens rea* for an offence, and consequently does not operate as a defence.

Perhaps the most frequent justification advanced in support of this principle is that it is a practical necessity; indeed, it is contended that the Crown could never successfully shoulder the burden of proving, in every case, that defendants had actual knowledge of the particular law under which they are charged. Furthermore, it has been suggested that if ignorance of the law were to be considered a legitimate defence, this would in effect place a premium on ignorance of the law—a situation that would scarcely be conducive to law-abiding behaviour. However, whatever the justification for section 19 may be, it is incontrovertible that its application may well prove to be extremely harsh in those circumstances where an individual is genuinely ignorant of the law.

The harshness inherent in the application of section 19 is well demonstrated in the case of *Molis* (1981). In this case, Molis was charged with trafficking in a restricted drug (MDMA), contrary to the provisions of section 48(1) of the now repealed *Food and Drugs Act*, R.S.C. 1985, c. F-27.[9] Molis operated a laboratory in which he manufactured a chemical substance known as MDMA (3,4-methylenedioxymethamphetamine, or ecstasy). At the time that he started manufacturing this substance (in August 1975), it was not illegal for him to do so. Unfortunately for Molis, MDMA was later added to Schedule H of the Act and, at that time (June 1976), it became a restricted drug. This amendment to the schedule was brought into effect by a regulation that was duly published in the *Canada Gazette*. Molis, who was unaware of the regulation, continued to manufacture MDMA and was subsequently arrested and charged. The accused was convicted, and his appeals were dismissed by both the Ontario Court of Appeal and the Supreme Court of Canada. Molis contended that there was a significant distinction to be drawn between a mistake of law (that is to say, the wrong interpretation of the law) and ignorance of the existence of a particular penal provision. In the defendant's view, the provisions of section 19 of the *Criminal Code* applied only to ignorance of law in the sense of a mistake of law and not to the ignorance of the very existence of the law. However, Justice Lamer, in delivering the judgment of the Supreme Court, rejected Molis's contention: "Whatever may be the merit of such a distinction ... Parliament has by the clear and unequivocal language of s. 19 chosen not to make any distinction between ignorance of the existence of the law and that as to its meaning, scope or application."

To avoid the harshness of the application of section 19 in certain cases, the courts have shown considerable inventiveness in devising exceptions to the general rule articulated therein. For example, in the case of *Ilczyszyn* (1988), the Ontario Court of Appeal ruled that a mistake as to the legal effect of the civil as opposed to the criminal law may constitute a defence to a criminal charge. The accused was charged with abduction of a child in contravention of the terms of a custody order (contrary to what is now section 282 of the *Code*). The accused knew of the existence of the custody order but believed, on the basis of legal advice, that it was no longer valid after she recommenced habitation with the child's father. The accused's mistake was one of law; she knew the order existed but was mistaken as to its legal effect. The Ontario Court of Appeal nevertheless ruled that the accused had been correctly acquitted at trial. The court stated:

> In most cases, the fact that an accused knew the terms of a custody order and in fact acted in contravention of its terms would be sufficient to persuade a trier of fact beyond a reasonable doubt that he or she intended to do so. However, in an unusual case such as the one before us, where the accused, although knowing of the terms of the order, truly believed on reasonable grounds that it was no longer in existence, there could be no intent to contravene a valid and subsisting order.

It is interesting that the British Columbia Court of Appeal made a similar decision in the case of *Hammerbeck* (1991). This would appear to suggest that Canadian courts are likely to recognize a general principle that a mistake as to the effect of the civil law will provide an effective defence to a criminal

9. See now s. 5 of the *Controlled Drugs and Substances Act*, S.C. 1996, c. 19.

charge. The distinction between a mistake as to a matter of criminal law and a mistake as to a matter of civil law is, therefore, an important one to draw before applying section 19 of the *Code*. However, it is important to bear in mind that there must be reasonable grounds for a mistake as to the civil law before the courts will accept it as a valid defence to a criminal charge. For example, in the case of *Finck* (2003), the Ontario Court of Appeal affirmed the conviction of the accused on a charge under section 282(1)(a) of the *Criminal Code*—abducting a child contrary to the terms of a custody order. The Court of Appeal ruled that he had failed to establish that he had reasonable grounds for his belief that the custody order was no longer in effect. In delivering the judgment of the Court of Appeal, Justice Armstrong noted that the *Ilczyszyn* case (1988) had established that "an objectively reasonable mistake of law might in unusual cases negate the *mens rea* of the offence of parental abduction under s. 282(1)(a) of the *Code*." However, Justice Armstrong stated that, as far as the case of *Finck* was concerned, [T]here simply was no air of reality to the submission that the appellant "truly believed on reasonable grounds" that the custody order ... was "no longer in existence."

The Evolution of a New Defence or "Excuse": Officially Induced Error

There is little doubt that application of the rule that ignorance of the law is no excuse is becoming increasingly problematic in an age when Canadians are faced with a rapidly burgeoning mass of regulatory laws. Legislation at both the federal and the provincial/territorial levels has created a vast body of regulatory offences. What is particularly disturbing is that many of these offences are not contained in the provisions of a statute that is passed in Parliament or the provincial/territorial legislature and readily available to members of the public. Instead, they are incorporated into sets of detailed regulations that may be difficult to locate and their existence may, indeed, be completely unknown to many of the people affected by them.

Many statutes contain provisions that permit the appropriate minister(s) of the Crown to pass regulations into the law, and infringement of them may result in the accused being convicted of an offence. If we take a statute of the province of British Columbia as a typical example, we may see that a significant number of regulations passed under the authority of section 209 of the British Columbia *Motor Vehicle Act*, R.S.B.C. 1996, c. 318, deal with a host of detailed matters that it would be inappropriate to include within the *Motor Vehicle Act* itself (e.g., "prescribing the lights to be carried and displayed on vehicles other than motor vehicles and trailers").[10]

It is clear that such regulations are considerably more inaccessible to the public than acts of Parliament or the provincial/territorial legislatures. Therefore, it may well be contended that it is unfair to apply the principle that ignorance of the law is no defence when the defendant is charged with an offence arising out of the alleged contravention of such a regulation. However, both the (federal) *Statutory Instruments Act*, R.S.C. 1985, c. S-22, section 11, and, for example, the (provincial) *Regulations Act*, R.S.B.C. 1996, c. 402, section 7, provide that if a regulation is duly published in the *Canada Gazette* or the *British Columbia Gazette*, as the case may be, an accused person may be convicted for contravention of such a regulation in spite of the accused's complete ignorance of it. The only weakening of the general rule that precludes ignorance of the law as a defence arises when the regulation has not been published in the appropriate gazette. In such a circumstance, both the *Statutory Instruments Act* and the *Regulations Act* provide that the accused person may not be convicted unless it is proved that, at the time of the alleged offence, reasonable steps were taken to bring the substance of the regulation to the attention of the public in general or, at least, of the persons most likely to be affected by it.

Given the fact that Canadians are faced with a vast array of offences, many of which are "buried" in hard-to-find regulations, should there be any general exceptions to the principle that ignorance of the law is no excuse? It appears that Canadian courts are, indeed, prepared to recognize such an exception, although it is very circumscribed in its nature and application. This new defence is based on the notion of **officially induced error**. More specifically, if accused persons rely on an interpretation of the law made by a public official whose duty it is to provide citizens with advice, then it has been argued that they should be absolved from criminal responsibility if the official's advice proves to be incorrect.

10. S. 209(1)(c), *Motor Vehicle Act*, R.S.B.C 1996, c. 318. There are currently 30 regulations dealing with ""Lamps." *Motor Vehicle Act Regulations, BC Reg 26/58* and 75 separate regulations issued under the Ontario *Highway Traffic Act*, R.S.O. 1990, c. H.8.

The Ontario Court of Appeal unequivocally recognized the existence of the defence of "officially induced error" in the gruesome case of *Cancoil Thermal Corp. and Parkinson* (1986). In this case, there had been an accident at a factory that produced heat transfer coils. An employee had lost the tips of six of his fingers when both of his hands came into contact with a moving blade that was part of the machine with which he was working. The machine in question had originally been equipped with a guard that would have prevented this type of accident, had the guard been in place. Unfortunately for the employee, the guard had been removed on the initiative of both the supervisor and the general manager of the factory. These individuals believed the guard created a hazard since its presence made it more difficult for the operator of the machine to clear away pieces of scrap metal. In addition, it was felt that there was an alternative safety device; namely, a foot pedal that had to be depressed before the blade could be started. As it turned out, while the employee was removing pieces of scrap metal from the machine, he accidentally hit the pedal and, as a consequence, was injured. The accused were charged with a number of offences arising under the Ontario *Occupational Health and Safety Act*, R.S.O. 1980, c. 321.[11]

The trial judge acquitted the accused on the basis of a technical interpretation of the statute. The Crown appealed the acquittal, and the Ontario Court of Appeal agreed that the trial judge's interpretation of the statute was in error. However, the accused raised the defence of "officially induced error" (for the first time) before the Court of Appeal. It was suggested that, two months before the accident, an inspector from the Occupational Health and Safety Division had been informed that the guard had been removed from the machine in question and that he had commented that "[I]t was safe to remove the particular piece of metal in question and that with the machine being operated according to instructions that it was safe to do so."

The Court of Appeal ordered that a new trial be held to deal with this issue. Most significantly, the Court ruled that Canadian criminal law did, indeed, recognize the existence of the defence of "officially induced error." Justice Lacourcière held that it

> ... is available as a defence to an alleged violation of a regulatory statute where an accused has reasonably relied upon the erroneous legal opinion or advice of an official who is responsible for the administration or enforcement of the particular law. In order for the accused to successfully raise this defence, he must show that he relied on the erroneous legal opinion of the official and that his reliance was reasonable. The reasonableness will depend upon several factors including the efforts he made to ascertain the proper law, the complexity or obscurity of the law, the position of the official who gave the advice, and the clarity, definitiveness and reasonableness of the advice given.

This defence of officially induced error has gradually evolved into a basic principle of Canadian criminal law. It has now been recognized as a valid defence by the Supreme Court of Canada and has been applied by a number of provincial appellate courts. In the case of *Jorgensen* (1995), Chief Justice Lamer was the first member of the Supreme Court of Canada to express the view that the defence of officially induced error should be accepted as part of Canadian criminal law. He noted that "[T]he complexity of contemporary regulation makes the assumption that a responsible citizen will have a comprehensive knowledge of the law unreasonable." In his opinion, the very phenomenon of extensive **regulation** "is one motive for creating a limited exception to the rule" that ignorance of the law is no excuse.

Although Chief Justice Lamer stated his belief that the defence of officially induced error would arise most frequently in the context of regulatory offences, he also indicated that the defence could equally well apply to the realm of "true crimes." For example, in the *Jorgensen* case (1995), the accused had been charged with a number of counts of knowingly selling obscene material (contrary to section 163(2)(a) of the *Criminal Code*). The accused operated a video store and was charged after undercover police officers purchased eight videotapes. All these tapes had been approved by the Ontario Film Review Board. Nevertheless, the trial court ruled that three of the tapes were obscene and the accused was convicted. The Supreme Court entered acquittals on behalf of the accused on the ground that he had not "knowingly" sold obscene material. The Crown had not established that the accused "knew of the presence of the ingredients of the subject-matter which as a matter of law rendered the exploitation of sex undue" and, therefore, obscene.

Chief Justice Lamer, speaking for himself alone, took the view that the accused could have been

11. The current version of this legislation is the *Occupational Health and Safety Act*, R.S.O. 1990, c. O.1.

acquitted on the basis of the officially induced error that arose from the board's approval of the films in question. The Chief Justice's summary of the nature and scope of the defence carries a considerable degree of weight, since it was later endorsed by a unanimous Supreme Court of Canada in the case of *Lévis (Ville) v. Tétreault* (2006). According to Chief Justice Lamer:

> [O]fficially induced error functions as an excuse rather than a full defence. It can only be raised after the Crown has proven all the elements of the offence. In order for an accused to rely on this excuse, she must show, after establishing she made an error of law, that she considered her legal position, consulted an appropriate official, obtained reasonable advice and relied on that advice in her actions.

Chief Justice Lamer went on to state that, since officially induced error should be seen as an "excuse" rather than a "justification," it should not lead to a conventional acquittal, but rather to a stay of proceedings by the trial court:

> [T]he accused has done nothing to entitle him to an acquittal, but the state has done something which disentitles it to a conviction ... the successful application of an officially induced error of law argument will lead to a judicial stay of proceedings rather than an acquittal. Consequently, as a stay can only be entered in the clearest of cases, an officially induced error of law argument will only be successful in the clearest of cases.

It is particularly noteworthy that, in the decision of the Supreme Court of Canada in *Lévis (Ville) v. Tétreault* (2006), the Court unequivocally expressed agreement with Chief Justice Lamer's analysis, although it did not apply the defence of officially induced error in the particular circumstances of this case.[12] In delivering the judgment of the Court, Justice LeBel stated that the "analytical framework" articulated by Chief Justice Lamer in *Jorgensen* "has become established" in Canadian criminal law:

> Provincial appellate courts have followed this approach to consider and apply the defence of officially induced error. ... It should be noted ... that it is necessary to establish the objective reasonableness not only of the advice, but also of the reliance on the advice. ... Various factors will be taken into consideration in the course of this assessment, including the efforts made by the accused to obtain information, the clarity or obscurity of the law, the position and role of the official who gave the information or opinion, and the clarity, definitiveness and reasonableness of the information or opinion. ... It is not sufficient in such cases to conduct a purely subjective analysis of the reasonableness of the information. This aspect of the question must be considered from the perspective of a reasonable person in a situation similar to that of the accused.

Neither the company (2629-4470 Québec Inc.) nor the individual (Tétreault) accused in the *Lévis* case had received advice from any officials about their obligations to renew, and pay, for the company's vehicle registration and Tétreault's driver's licence, respectively. Since they had not received any official interpretation of the relevant legislation, the defence of officially induced error was clearly not applicable in this particular case. The accused relied on the argument that they had expected to receive renewal notices in the mail but had failed to do so. However, as Justice LeBel aptly commented in his judgment, "[P]assive ignorance is not a valid defence in criminal law."

Mistake of Law and "Colour of Right"

Officially induced error may provide a defence to a criminal charge in a limited number of circumstances. However, there is one apparent exception to the legal doctrine that ignorance of the law is no excuse. This exception is encompassed by the important principle that what appears to be a mistake of law may constitute a valid defence where it operates to negative the specific intent required by the definition of an offence. For example, in defining theft, section 322(1) provides that the offence is committed only when the accused takes or converts property to their use fraudulently and without **colour of right**. The latter phrase refers to the legal principle that accused persons may not be convicted of theft if they honestly believe that they have a legal right to the property in question. In *R. v. Simpson* (2015), Justice Moldaver of the Supreme Court of Canada relied on the following description of the doctrine:

> The term "colour of right" generally, although not exclusively, refers to a situation where there is an assertion of a proprietary or possessory right to the thing which is the subject matter of the alleged theft. One who is honestly asserting what he believes to be an honest claim cannot be said to act "without colour of right," even though it may be unfounded in law or in fact... . The term "colour of right" is also used to

12. The facts of the *Lévis* case were discussed in Chapter 6.

denote an honest belief in a state of facts which, if it actually existed would at law justify or excuse the act done... . The term when used in the latter sense is merely a particular application of the doctrine of mistake of fact.[13]

In other words, accused persons may be acquitted where they act under an honest mistake of law as to whether or not they have a legal right to such property. In essence, a person who is operating "under colour of right" is mistaken as to a matter concerning their private property rights, and the relevant provisions of the *Code* reflect the view that it would be unduly harsh to convict such a person of a criminal offence. As the Supreme Court of Canada noted, this doctrine is not really an exception to the rule that ignorance of the law is no excuse: *it is, in fact, a very specific application of the defence of mistake of fact.*

A typical example of the "colour of right" defence is provided by the case of *Simpson* (2013), in the Nova Scotia Provincial Court. Simpson had been charged, among other charges, with robbery and using an imitation firearm in a robbery. Simpson had undertaken work for the complainant, who had agreed with Simpson to pay him a fixed amount of money. Simpson, who was in urgent need of payment, came to believe that the complainant was attempting to renege on the agreement. Simpson obtained a starter pistol and threatened the complainant, demanding that he hand over the exact amount of the agreed-upon payment for his work. The complainant paid the money to Simpson and was then asked to leave. Simpson was acquitted of the robbery charges because he had successfully asserted the defence of "colour of right." He had honestly believed that he had a right to the agreed-upon sum of money, even though this claim was not founded in law.

In his judgment, Judge Williams ruled that Simpson had an honest belief that the complainant owed him $300 for 20 hours of work on the basis of terms that had been mutually agreed upon. The Judge noted that Simpson was "neither deceitful nor intended to deceive [the complainant] or to expose [the complainant] to any risks." Even though Simpson knew that the complainant was in possession of considerably more than $300, "he wanted only his fair and proper amount and no more."

This case may usefully be compared with the Canadian decision in *Hemmerly* (1976), in which the accused was charged with robbery after taking some money from his victim at gunpoint. Hemmerly contended that he had acted under "colour of right" because he claimed that the victim owed him money as a result of a prior transaction for the sale of illegal drugs. Hemmerly's conviction of robbery was upheld by the Ontario Court of Appeal because he

13. In this case, the Supreme Court of Canada found that there was no air of reality to the defendant's claim of colour of right, so the Court did not apply the doctrine.

Colour of right: There is a defence to a charge of robbery if the accused honestly believes they have a legal right to the money or other item that is taken from the victim.

knew very well that he would have no claim in *law* to funds arising from the illicit sale of drugs. Justice Martin went on to say that, "[E]ven if the appellant believed that he had a moral claim to the money (which I am far from holding), a belief in a moral claim could not constitute a colour of right." In other words, Hemmerly was not operating under an honest mistake as to his *legal* rights at the time he committed the robbery.

It is important to bear in mind that the defence of acting "under colour of right" applies despite the fact that a court may subsequently find that the accused person concerned did not have the legal right they thought they did. This principle is clearly demonstrated by the case of *Lilly* (1983), in which the accused was a real estate broker who had been charged with the theft of $26 000 that had been deposited in trust with his company in connection with various real estate transactions. It was alleged that the accused had misappropriated the funds in question because he took them out of the trust account *before* the various transactions had been completed. Lilly contended, *inter alia*, that he honestly believed that he had a right to take out his commission from the trust account just as soon as the offers to purchase the various properties had been

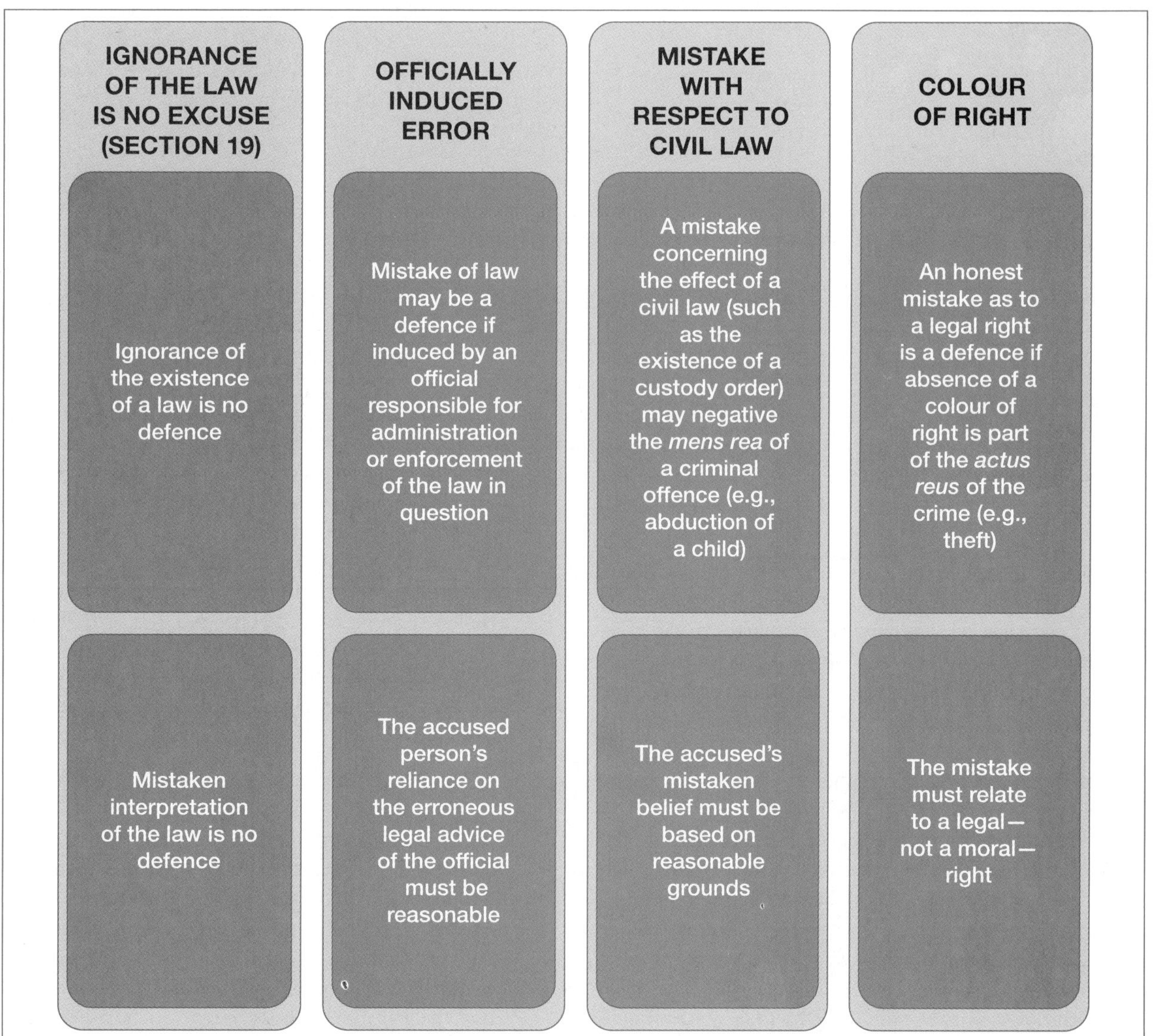

Figure 9-4

An Overview of Mistake of Law as a Defence

accepted by the vendors. Despite this contention, the accused was convicted at his trial. The judge directed the jury that, insofar as the issue of "colour of right" was concerned, the real question was, when did the commission become payable to the accused's company? He also told the jury that it was "up to you to determine if the company, through the accused, had the right to transfer the commission from the trust account" at the time that such transfer was, in fact, made. In effect, the judge was inviting the jury to decide the validity of Lilly's legal claim rather than the question of whether he honestly believed that he had such a right. Ultimately, the Supreme Court allowed the accused's appeal and ordered a new trial. Justice Lamer, speaking for the Court, held that:

> The fate of the accused's defence of colour of right was not dependent upon the jury determining when the commissions were payable. That question was indeed important as relevant to whether the moneys were his or those of his clients. The fact that they still be the property of the client was a prerequisite to his having to raise a defence to the taking or conversion. Rather, the accused's defence was dependent upon whether they, the jury, were satisfied beyond a reasonable doubt that he, the accused, had not, at the time of the transfers, an honest belief that he had the right to that money, and not, as they were told, dependent on what they, the jurors[,] thought his rights were.

The defence of colour of right is not limited to mistakes about ownership of private property. Indeed, section 429(2) of the *Criminal Code* expressly furnishes a defence of acting with colour of right in the context of Part XI of the *Code*, which deals with offences such as *mischief* (destroying, damaging, obstructing, or interfering with the use of property) and *arson*.

Study Questions

1. Perker strikes Snubbin and steals his wallet. Snubbin is seriously injured. Perker is charged with robbery, but he claims that he was only recovering a gambling debt Snubbin owed him and refused to pay. Does Perker have any defence(s)?
2. Minnie Meagles visits her dentist, Dr. Frankenstein, because she has a toothache. Frankenstein tells Minnie that he will have to fill the tooth because parts of it are decaying. While Frankenstein goes to see another patient in an adjoining room, Minnie tells Sairey Gamp, the dental nurse, that under no circumstances can she have an injection of novocaine because she is highly allergic to it. Sairey enters this information in Minnie's file but forgets to tell Frankenstein. While Sairey is tending to another patient, Frankenstein returns to the room in which Minnie is waiting. He tells her to open her mouth and Minnie does so (at the same time, she closes her eyes). Frankenstein says he is going to freeze Minnie's tooth at the same time as he starts to inject her gum with novocaine. Minnie makes a loud noise in protest: however, by the time Frankenstein withdraws the needle, it is too late. Minnie suffers a painful reaction to the anesthetic and has to be treated in hospital. Minnie is so angry about this incident that she goes to the police and asks them to consider charging Frankenstein with assault causing bodily harm. When interviewed, Frankenstein says that he honestly believed that Minnie had consented to the injection and that it was not his fault that Sairey had forgotten to inform him of Minnie's instructions. If Frankenstein were to be charged, would he have a defence? Would it make a difference if Frankenstein routinely required the completion of a written consent form that he believed had already been signed by Minnie (he normally left this task to Sairey Gamp)?
3. Ninetta has an old handgun that has been in her family's possession for many years. She has always considered it to be an "antique collector's piece" and she has been told by Judith, a friend who is an RCMP officer, that she does not need to register it and that a licence is not necessary. In fact, the gun is not an "antique firearm" within the meaning of the definition set out in section 84(1) of the *Criminal Code*; therefore, both registration and licensing are required after all. One day, Ninetta's house is destroyed by fire. A police officer, who is investigating the possibility of arson, finds the gun among

the ashes and is thinking of charging Ninetta with the offence of unauthorized possession of a firearm, contrary to section 91(3) of the *Criminal Code*. If she were charged, would Ninetta have any defence?

4. Blackpool and Clara have been living together for five years in a common law relationship. On a regular basis, they have engaged in consensual sexual activity. They have not been in the habit of seeking explicit permission from each other before proceeding with such activity. On a certain night, Blackpool attempts to initiate a sexual encounter with Clara, but she says that she does not want to have sexual relations with him because she is feeling sick. Blackpool waits for some 30 minutes and then proceeds to engage in an act of sexual intercourse with Clara, who says nothing and remains motionless. Clara wishes to have Blackpool charged with sexual assault. She tells the police that she had definitely not consented to the sexual activity with Blackpool and that she remained silent merely because she was terrified of his losing his temper and subjecting her to physical violence. Blackpool claims that, in light of his previous sexual relationship with his partner, he simply assumed that Clara had changed her mind and was fully consenting to the act of intercourse. If Blackpool were charged with sexual assault, would any defence(s) be available to him at his trial?

5. Ruth Pinch is taken to hospital for an emergency operation to remove her appendix. The operation is successful, and she is brought back to her room, where she falls into a deep sleep. Guppy, her boyfriend, has been waiting in Ruth's room to ascertain her state of health. Guppy and Ruth have been living together for six months, but, the night before Ruth's sudden visit to the hospital, they had engaged in a very heated argument about Guppy's obsession with gambling. Ruth had made it very clear that she did not want him to touch her while they were arguing. Guppy had slept on the sofa and, in the morning, there had been no opportunity for him to resolve the argument with Ruth because she was immediately taken to hospital in great pain. When Guppy realizes that Ruth will remain unconscious in her hospital bed, he takes her head in his arms, kisses her on the lips for a few moments, and leaves. Drummle, a nurse, witnesses this incident, and when Ruth is fully aware of her surroundings, Drummle tells her about it. Ruth says that she did not want Guppy to kiss her and is extremely angry. The police are informed and a detective interviews Guppy, who says that he honestly believed that, in the circumstances, Ruth would consent to his kissing her while she was asleep. Ruth considers Guppy's action to constitute a sexual assault. Crown Counsel is reluctant to lay a charge, but Ruth says that an unconscious person cannot consent to any type of sexual activity and that Canadian criminal law does not recognize advance consent or implied consent in the context of an alleged sexual assault. What advice would you give to Crown Counsel?

6. Nicodemus visits his local bar, where he meets Rosa Dartle, who was previously unknown to him. After consuming a couple of drinks with Rosa, Nicodemus invites her to come to his apartment. Rosa accepts the invitation and accompanies Nicodemus to his building. Once inside the apartment, Nicodemus and Rosa engage in sexual activity. The next day, Rosa travels to the local police station and accuses Nicodemus of having sexually assaulted her. She states that she had been drinking for some time before Nicodemus arrived in the bar and that she had no memory of what happened between the moment when Nicodemus entered the bar and the moment when she woke up next to him in his bed. Rosa is adamant that she would never have willingly engaged in sexual activity with Nicodemus. Nicodemus tells the police that although he realized Rosa had been drinking, he assumed that she knew what she was doing and that she had unequivocally told him that she wished to participate in sexual activity with him. If you were Crown Counsel, would you charge Nicodemus with sexual assault? Do you think that Nicodemus would have any viable defence(s) to such a charge?

7. Cruncher and Slammer are professional hockey players who are playing on opposing teams. As Cruncher is carrying the puck with his stick, Slammer pushes him into the boards along the side of the hockey rink. An altercation develops between them and some punches are thrown. The referee stops play, and after a brief period, the linesmen separate Cruncher and Slammer and lead them toward their respective penalty boxes. However, Cruncher breaks free from his accompanying linesman and skates up to Slammer and punches him in the eye—to the delight of the local fans. Cruncher is 6 feet 5 inches tall and weighs 280 pounds. Slammer is 5 feet 8 inches tall and weighs 150 pounds. The blow inflicted by Cruncher opens a deep cut underneath Slammer's eye and numerous stitches are required to close the wound. Cruncher is charged with assault causing bodily harm. Does Cruncher have any defence(s)?

8. Hippocrates is a medical practitioner who believes that boxing should be banned. In his view, those who participate in boxing are subjecting themselves to an unacceptably high risk of serious brain injury or even death. After a professional boxer dies as a consequence of head injuries inflicted in a fight, Hippocrates approaches Crown Counsel and asks her to lay a charge of aggravated assault against the other protagonist in the fight. What arguments might he use to persuade Crown counsel to proceed with such a charge?
9. To what extent should implied consent be a defence to a criminal charge that arises in the context of the application of force during such contact sports as hockey and football? Should Crown Counsel charge professional hockey players with assault if they engage in fights or inflict serious injuries on the ice? Should football players who deliberately set out to apply extreme force to an opponent be charged with an offence if the latter is seriously injured and unable to continue participating in the game in question? Should Crown Counsel lay criminal charges against professional boxers who injure an opponent? If the object of professional boxing is to knock out an opponent, could it be argued that no one has the right to consent to the deliberate infliction of serious bodily harm and that, therefore, implied consent should not be a defence to a charge of assault against a professional boxer?
10. Smike, a 30-year-old man, meets Henrietta Petowker, a young woman, in a bar. She is drinking alcohol and Smike engages her in conversation for an hour or so. Smike asks Henrietta to come back to his apartment, where they have consensual sexual intercourse. Next day, a police officer comes to the door and escorts Smike to the police station, where he is informed that he is being charged with sexual assault, contrary to section 271 of the *Criminal Code*. It turns out that Henrietta was only 15 years old and had used a forged driving licence to obtain alcohol in the bar. Does Smike have any defence to the charge of sexual assault?

CHAPTER 10

PROVOCATION AND INTOXICATION:

Partial Defences to a Criminal Charge

Learning Objectives

After reading this chapter, you will understand:

- the basic elements of two partial defences to a criminal charge: namely, provocation and intoxication. Provocation reduces murder to manslaughter, while intoxication may reduce a charge of specific intent crime to a **crime of basic (or general) intent** (e.g., robbery to assault).
- the judicial interpretations of the statutory requirements in section 232 of the *Criminal Code* that, to constitute a successful defence, an alleged provocation must be such as would cause the "ordinary person" to lose the power of self-control and that the accused must act on the provocation "on the sudden and before there was time for his [their] passion to cool."
- the three so-called "*Beard* Rules" that determine how the defence of intoxication should be applied: if intoxication causes a "disease of the mind," the accused may be found NCRMD; if the intoxication prevents the accused from forming the specific intent required for establishing a specific intent crime such as murder or robbery, the accused must be acquitted, but may be convicted of a lesser general or basic intent crimes, such as manslaughter or assault, respectively; and if the intoxication affects the accused's ability to control their conduct, as opposed to their intent, there is no defence.

- the ruling of the Supreme Court of Canada, in *Daviault* (1994), that extreme intoxication that produces a state of mind equivalent to mental disorder or automatism is an absolute defence to all criminal charges, provided the accused can prove the defence on the balance of probabilities.
- the enactment by Parliament of section 33.1 of the *Criminal Code*, which eliminates the *Daviault* defence for any crime that involves an element of assault or interference with personal integrity.

PROVOCATION AND INTOXICATION

The defences of provocation and intoxication differ from other defences, such as automatism and mistake of fact, insofar as they are only *partial* defences. In other words, successful defences of provocation and intoxication may reduce the severity of a criminal charge but will not lead to an absolute acquittal. An accused person who successfully pleads provocation will be convicted of manslaughter rather than murder. When an accused person successfully raises the defence of intoxication, they will be acquitted of a more serious offence, such as murder or robbery, and will usually be convicted instead of a lesser crime, such as manslaughter or assault, respectively.

PROVOCATION

THE GENERAL NATURE OF THE DEFENCE AND SECTION 232

As Justice Charron stated in the Supreme Court of Canada's decision in *Tran* (2010), "Provocation is the only defence which is exclusive to homicide." The defence may be raised only in relation to a charge of murder and, if successful, its sole effect is to ensure that the accused is convicted of manslaughter rather than murder. In essence, the defence of **provocation** represents an attempt by the criminal law to show a degree of mercy to individuals who lose their power of self-control in the face of highly stressful circumstances. In Justice Charron's characterization of the rationale for the defence:

> [T]he accused's conduct is partially *excused* out of a compassion to human frailty. While the call for compassion was particularly compelling in times when the alternative was the death penalty, the rationale subsists today, given the serious consequences to the offender flowing from a conviction for murder. …
>
> [T]he requisite elements of the defence, taken together, make clear that the accused must have a *justifiable* sense of being wronged. This does not mean, and in no way should be taken as suggesting, that the victim is to be blamed for the accused's act, nor that he or she deserved the consequences of the provocation. Nor does it mean that the law sanctions the accused's conduct. Instead, the law recognizes that, as a result of human frailties, the accused reacted inappropriately and disproportionately, but understandably to a sufficiently serious wrongful act or insult.

The defence of provocation is defined, in considerable detail, by section 232 of the *Criminal Code*. Therefore, Canadian judges have been somewhat circumscribed in their attempts to develop the law relating to provocation. The provisions of section 232 are as follows:

> 232 (1) Culpable homicide that otherwise would be murder may be reduced to manslaughter if the person who committed it did so in the heat of passion caused by sudden provocation.
>
> (2) Conduct of the victim that would constitute an indictable offence under this Act that is punishable by five or more years of imprisonment and that is of such a nature as to be sufficient to deprive an ordinary person of the power of self-control is provocation for the purposes of this section, if the accused acted on it on the sudden and before there was time for their passion to cool.

(3) For the purposes of this section, the questions

(a) whether the conduct of the victim amounted to provocation under subsection (2), and

(b) whether the accused was deprived of the power of self-control by the provocation that he alleges he received

are questions of fact, but no one shall be deemed to have given provocation to another by doing anything that he had a legal right to do, or by doing anything that the accused incited him to do in order to provide the accused with an excuse for causing death or bodily harm to any human being.

In *Tran* (2010), Justice Charron made the point that the opening words of section 232 make it clear that "the defence will only apply where the accused had the necessary intent for murder and acted upon this intent." Justice Charron also pointed out in *Tran* that Parliament had "carefully limited the application of the defence." Undoubtedly, section 232 sets out a series of formidable requirements for the success of the defence. Therefore, the courts have emphasized that the defence of provocation can never be raised merely because the accused person lost self-control as a consequence of overwhelming anger. This point was strongly emphasized by the Supreme Court of Canada in the case of *Parent* (2001). The accused had shot his estranged wife after she had made a remark that caused him to feel "a hot flush rising." He claimed that, because of this intense anger, he "didn't know what he was doing any more." The trial judge appeared to instruct the jury that intense anger could—on its own account—reduce the charge of murder to manslaughter. However, Chief Justice McLachlin decisively rejected this proposition. Indeed, she stated that although anger may "play a role in reducing murder to manslaughter in connection with the defence of provocation," it cannot be advanced as a "stand-alone defence." More specifically, the Chief Justice asserted that anger may "form part of the defence of provocation [only] when all the requirements of that defence are met": (1) [A] wrongful act or insult that would have caused an ordinary person to be deprived of his or her self-control; (2) which is sudden and unexpected; (3) which in fact caused the accused to act in anger; (4) before having recovered his or her normal control. However, in *Bouchard* (2014), the Supreme Court of Canada agreed with the Alberta Court of Appeal that while the provocative conduct of the victim may not meet the criteria for the defence of provocation under section 232, it may so affect the accused person's mental state that they fail to form the necessary *mens rea* for murder and, therefore, a conviction of manslaughter should be recorded rather than one of murder.

Requirement 1: Conduct of the Victim That Would Constitute an Indictable Offence under This Act That Is Punishable by Five or More Years of Imprisonment and That Is of Such a Nature as to Be Sufficient to Deprive an Ordinary Person of the Power of Self-Control

Requirement 1(A): Conduct of the Victim That Would Constitute an Indictable Offence under This Act That Is Punishable by Five or More Years of Imprisonment

In 2015, Parliament enacted a very significant change to the then-existing section 232 of the *Criminal Code*.[1] Prior to this amendment, section 232(2) stated that "*a wrongful act or insult* that is of such a nature as to be sufficient to deprive an ordinary person of the power of self-control is provocation for the purposes of this section, if the accused acted on it on the sudden and before there was time for their passion to cool."

The 2015 amendment removed the words "a wrongful act or insult" and replaced them with the following: "Conduct of the victim that would constitute an indictable offence under this Act that is punishable by five or more years of imprisonment. ..." This change to the essential requirements for the defence of provocation is particularly important since it signals the intention of Parliament to restrict the availability of the defence to circumstances in which the deceased victim was committing a serious criminal offence. It will no longer be sufficient merely to point to insulting words or actions on the part of the victim. For example, the defence of provocation has historically been associated with the so-called "crime of passion": here, the accused person finds their spouse or partner engaged in a sexual act with another person and kills one or both of them. In light of the recent change to section 232(2), such conduct

1. 2015, c. 29, s. 7.

on the part of the victim(s) would no longer be sufficient to constitute provocation unless it constitutes the background to an assault or other serious offence committed by the victim(s). For example, in Tran (2010), the accused had been separated from his estranged wife. However, he illegally entered her locked apartment and found her in bed with her boyfriend. Tran attacked both his former spouse and the boyfriend. At one point, he took two butcher knives from the kitchen and, in addition to other injuries, cut his spouse's face with a deep slash from the right ear across the entire right cheek. However, his attack on her boyfriend proved to be fatal—he received 17 stab wounds, of which six were lethal. At his trial for second-degree murder, Tran asserted the defence of provocation. Under the pre-2015 version of section 232(2), the trial judge accepted the defence of provocation but, ultimately, both the Alberta Court of Appeal and the Supreme Court of Canada ruled that there was no "wrongful act or insult" because his estranged wife and her male friend were perfectly entitled to engage in private sexual activity. After the 2015 amendment, there would be absolutely no doubt that the defence of provocation would not be applicable since the victim was not committing an indictable offence.

The most common circumstance in which the defence may now be raised is where the victim was committing an assault (section 265 of the *Criminal Code* provides that the maximum sentence for assault is five years of imprisonment). However, other offences that would meet the new requirement in section 232(2) include sexual assault, robbery, extortion, criminal harassment, and uttering threats.

A recent example of the circumstances in which the post-2015 provocation defence is still applicable is the case of *Rasberry* (2017). Following a barbecue, the victim had taken hold of Rasberry and threatened to rape both him and his wife if the victim did not consent to engaging in anal sex with him. Rasberry responded by fatally stabbing the victim with three knives. Clearly, the victim had committed a sexual assault by threatening to rape Rasberry and his spouse.

In order to meet the other requirements in section 232(2), the accused person will generally have to demonstrate that there were *aggravating circumstances* surrounding an assault or other serious crime committed by the victim. For example, the victim may have uttered provocative words or gestures while assaulting the accused (e.g., mocking the accused person's physical or mental disability or boasting about a sexual relationship with the accused person's spouse or partner). Similarly, the victim may have assaulted the accused person against the background of a series of acts that had humiliated the accused

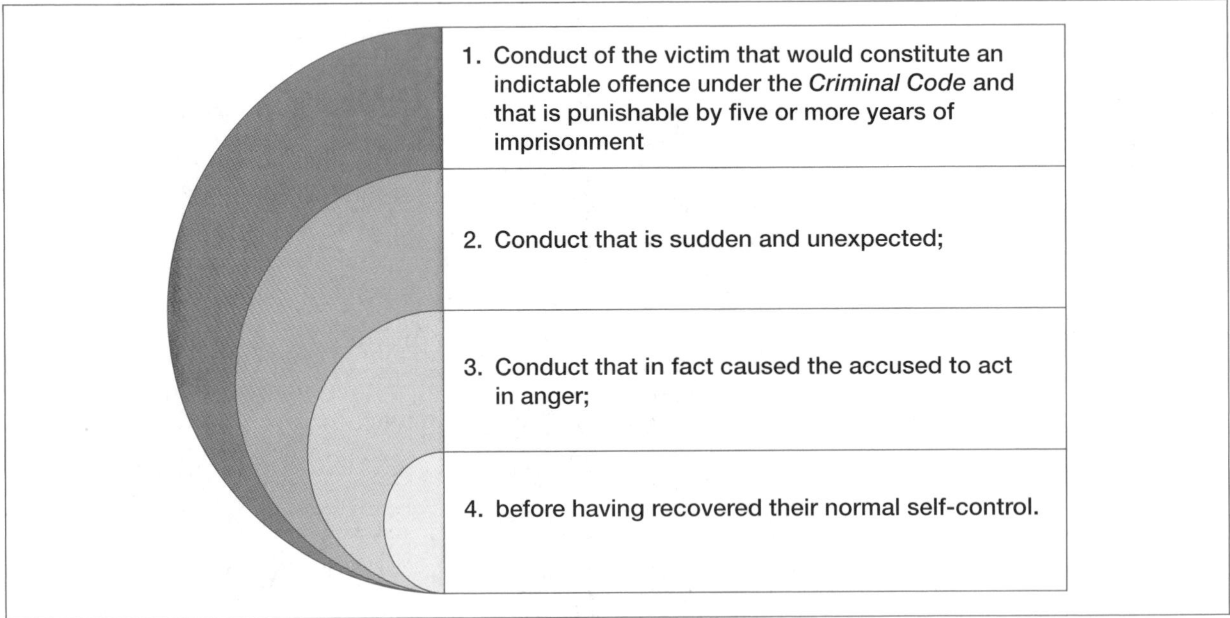
1. Conduct of the victim that would constitute an indictable offence under the *Criminal Code* and that is punishable by five or more years of imprisonment
2. Conduct that is sudden and unexpected;
3. Conduct that in fact caused the accused to act in anger;
4. before having recovered their normal self-control.

Figure 10-1

The Basic Elements of the Defence of Provocation [Modified from the case of Parent (2001)]

person (e.g., the victim had for some time ridiculed the accused person's alleged sexual inadequacies in front of the victim's friends and neighbours).

Requirement 1(B): [Conduct] That Is of Such a Nature as to Be Sufficient to Deprive an Ordinary Person of the Power of Self-Control

Section 232(2) of the *Criminal Code* stipulates that the conduct of the victim that would constitute an indictable offence under this Act that is punishable by five or more years of imprisonment must be *of such a nature as to be sufficient to deprive an ordinary person of the power of self-control.* This requirement is considered to be the *objective component* of the defence. The *subjective component* is the requirement that the accused was in fact provoked. The objective component, based on whether the alleged provocation would be sufficient to cause an "ordinary person" to lose the power of self-control, must be established *before* the subjective component may come into play: in other words, if the accused person cannot establish the objective component, the defence must be rejected. As Chief Justice McLachlin stated in *Cairney* (2013), "By appropriately contextualizing the ordinary person standard, the law on provocation strikes a balance between recognizing human frailties that lead to outbursts of violence, on the one hand, and the need to protect society by discouraging acts of homicidal violence, on the other."

Exactly how the "ordinary person" standard should be applied has posed a particularly difficult challenge for the courts in Canada. A rigidly objective approach would rule out any consideration of the accused's personal characteristics and individual circumstances, and this was the traditional approach adopted by Canadian courts until the 1980s. In *Hill* (1986), the Supreme Court of Canada introduced a more flexible approach in which a limited number of an accused person's individual characteristics, such as age, race, and gender, could be taken into account. These were characteristics that apply to all individuals: therefore, in the words of Chief Justice Dickson, "[P]articular characteristics that are not peculiar or idiosyncratic can be ascribed to an ordinary person without subverting the logic of the objective test of provocation." The Chief Justice argued that "the collective good sense" of jury members will cause them to take into account the racial background of the accused when they are subjected to a racial slur. He also made the important observation that an "ordinary person" does not have a pugnacious personality nor do they act under the influence of alcohol:

> [T]here is widespread agreement that the ordinary or reasonable person has a normal temperament and level of self-control. It follows that the ordinary person is not exceptionally excitable, pugnacious or in a state of drunkenness.
>
> If this were not so, a particularly bad-tempered accused person would have a definite advantage over a "normal" accused person when he or she seeks to raise the defence of provocation.

In the subsequent case of *Thibert* (1996), the majority of the justices of the Supreme Court of Canada appeared to water down the objective component to a much greater extent. Indeed, Justice Cory stated that:

> [I]f the test is to be applied sensibly and with sensitivity, then the ordinary person must be taken to be of the same age, and sex, and must share with the accused such other factors as would give the act or insult in question a particular significance. In other words, all the relevant background circumstances should be considered. In the context of other cases, it may properly be found that other factors should be considered. It is how such an "ordinary" person with those characteristics would react to the situation which confronted the accused that should be used as the basis for considering the objective element.

This statement by Justice Cory plainly demonstrates that, in applying the "ordinary person" test, the jury must consider any particular characteristic of the accused person (other than a pugnacious temperament and drunkenness) *provided only that such a characteristic directly affects the gravity of any taunt or insult that is relied on by the accused as the basis for a defence of provocation.*[2] For example, it may be presumed that the impotence of an accused person should be taken into account, when applying the "ordinary person" test, if the victim taunted the accused with insults relating to this particular form of sexual dysfunction.

However, in the case of *Tran* (2010), the Supreme Court of Canada appeared to retreat a few steps to the more limited approach to the "ordinary person"

---

2. *Thibert* was decided before the 2015 amendment to s. 232(2). Following the change in the law, the victim must have committed a serious indictable offence. A taunt or insult will no longer be sufficient to support a defence of provocation, although a taunt or insult that accompanied a serious offence by the victim, such as an assault, could cause an ordinary person to lose the power of self-control.

test that was advocated by Chief Justice Dickson in the *Hill* case. Justice Charron commented that it is important to limit the type of subjective characteristics that can be taken into account: "Indeed, if all of the accused's characteristics are taken into account, the ordinary person *becomes* the accused." She pointed out that criminal law is concerned with setting standards of behaviour that should be followed by all citizens and that the objective test enacted by Parliament is designed to encourage "reasonable and non-violent behaviour." Indeed, the "ordinary person" test is a means of upholding the standard of "self-control and restraint" that is expected of Canadians.

One of the particular concerns expressed by the Supreme Court of Canada in the *Tran* case was the possibility that some defendants may allege that they have certain cultural beliefs that support extreme and violent responses to any perceived infraction of the rules they claim should govern the relationships between men and women. Such a defendant may argue that the "ordinary person" test should incorporate their *alleged* cultural beliefs and permit them to assert the defence of provocation when they have killed a woman who did not submit to *their* conception of what is appropriate conduct for women. Justice Charron was emphatic in stating that the "ordinary person" test should never be distorted by such claims (which may, in any event, be completely untrue representations of the accused person's cultural background). Similarly, she unequivocally rejected the notion that the "ordinary person" test should incorporate the fact that the accused person is intolerant of individuals with a different sexual orientation from their own:

> [T]he ordinary person standard must be informed by contemporary norms of behaviour, including fundamental values such as the commitment to equality provided for in the *Canadian Charter of Rights and Freedoms*. For example, it would be appropriate to ascribe to the ordinary person relevant racial characteristics if the accused were the recipient of a racial slur, but it would not be appropriate to ascribe to the ordinary person the characteristic of being homophobic if the accused were the recipient of a homosexual advance. Similarly, there can be no place in this objective standard for antiquated beliefs such as "adultery is the highest invasion of property," nor indeed for any form of killing based on such inappropriate conceptualizations of "honour."

In *Tran*, the Supreme Court of Canada did recognize that the context in which the alleged provocation occurs is particularly relevant in the application of the "ordinary person" test. However, it is the objective nature of the context—and not the accused person's subjective response to it—that is important:

> For example, in determining the appropriate objective standard, it will be relevant for the trier of fact to know that the alleged provocation occurred in circumstances where the deceased was wrongfully firing the accused from his long-term employment. This context is necessary to set the appropriate standard. But the standard does not vary depending on the accused's peculiar relationship or particular feelings about his employer or his employment. Personal circumstances may be relevant to determining whether the accused was in fact provoked—the subjective element of the defence—but they do not shift the ordinary person standard to suit the individual accused. In other words, there is an important distinction between contextualizing the objective standard, which is necessary and proper, and individualizing it, which only serves to defeat its purpose.

In the *Thibert* case (1996), for example, the Supreme Court of Canada acknowledged that the objective test should necessarily include some consideration of the "background relationship between the deceased and the accused." As Justice Cory noted:

> [T]he wrongful act or insult must be one which could, in light of the past history of the relationship between the accused and the deceased, deprive an ordinary person, of the same age, sex, and sharing with the accused such other factors as would give the act or insult in question a special significance, of the power of self-control.

The facts in *Thibert* were that the accused's wife had, on a prior occasion, planned to leave him for the deceased, but he had managed to dissuade her from doing so. He apparently hoped to secure a similar outcome when his wife left him on a second occasion. When Thibert was attempting to talk to his wife alone, the deceased took hold of the wife's shoulders "in a proprietary and possessive manner" and moved her around in front of him. The deceased simultaneously taunted Thibert to shoot him, and, ultimately, the latter did inflict a fatal wound.

In approaching the question of whether there was some evidence capable of meeting the requirements of the objective test, the majority of the justices of the Supreme Court held that, in light of the past history that had passed between Thibert and the deceased, a jury might well find that the deceased's actions immediately before his death were "taunting and insulting." Justice Cory went on to state that "It might be found that under the same circumstances, an ordinary person who was a married man, faced with the breakup of his marriage, would have been provoked by the actions of the deceased so as to cause him to lose his power of self-control."

It is important to bear in mind that, to meet the requirements of the "ordinary person" test, the alleged provocation must have a direct relationship to the individual characteristic on which the accused relies. For example, a racist insult would be considered to be of such a nature as to deprive an "ordinary person" of the power of self-control only if that person in fact identifies themselves as a member of the racial group against which the insult is directed. As noted earlier, insulting words or actions will no longer be sufficient *per se* to raise the defence of provocation. However, *if accompanying the commission of a serious crime by the victim*, they may well render the victim's actions just the type of behaviour that would cause an ordinary person to lose the power of self-control.

Requirement 2: A Wrongful Act or Insult That Was Sudden and Unexpected

Section 232(2) provides that, for a defence of provocation to be successful, the accused must have acted upon the alleged provocation "*on the sudden.*" In *Parent* (2001), the Supreme Court of Canada expanded this term so that it means "sudden and unexpected." A person who deliberately initiates the sequence of events that results in the alleged provocation or who, in a calculated manner, places themselves in the situation they claim constitutes provocation is not someone who is entitled to receive the compassionate reduction of a homicide charge from murder to manslaughter. Such a person has a marked degree of control over the circumstances that precipitate the homicide and, in this sense, their conduct contradicts the entire rationale of the defence of provocation—namely, that the accused person has lost the power of self-control. As Justice Charron stated in *Tran* (2010):

> The requirement of suddenness was introduced into the defence as a way of distinguishing a response taken in vengeance from one that was provoked. Therefore, suddenness applies to both the act of provocation and the accused's reaction to it. The wrongful act or insult must itself be sudden, in the sense that it "must strike upon a mind unprepared for it, that it must make an unexpected impact that takes the understanding by surprise and sets the passions aflame."

For example, in *Pappas* (2013), the victim had been blackmailing Pappas for 18 months. One of the threats was against the life of Pappas's mother. Eventually, Pappas felt that he had had enough and went to the victim's house to end the extortion. Pappas took a loaded handgun with him but did not immediately take it out. However, he could not persuade the victim to cease the extortion and the victim renewed his demands, while making an implied threat against Pappas's mother. At this juncture, Pappas claimed that he "snapped." He took out his gun and fatally shot the victim in the back of the head. At his trial for murder, Pappas asserted the defence of provocation and the trial judge allowed it to be presented to the jury. However, the jury rejected the defence, bringing in a verdict of second-degree murder. Pappas's appeals to the Alberta Court of Appeal and the Supreme Court of Canada were rejected.

Chief Justice McLachlin, in delivering the majority judgment of the Supreme Court ruled that the trial judge should never have put the defence of provocation to the jury. There was no air of reality to the defence because the critical requirement of "suddenness," which applies to both the act of provocation and the accused's reaction to it, was entirely missing in this case. The Chief Justice concluded that:

> Viewed in its totality, the evidence suggests that Pappas' mind was prepared for the possibility that [the victim] might reject his pleas to end the extortion, "making [him] do what [he] had to do". His narrative, viewed as a whole, describes a progressive building up of the resolve to kill [the victim]. Accepting Pappas' evidence that he "snapped" as true, this was not the result of a sudden insult striking an unprepared mind. It was simply the final stage of doing what he had come to do—killing [the victim] if that was necessary to stop the extortion and threats.

For these reasons, the Chief Justice ruled that there was no air of reality to the subjective component of the provocation defence.

Requirement 3: A Wrongful Act or Insult That in Fact Caused the Accused to Act in Anger

This requirement is part of the *subjective* component of the defence of provocation. The accused person has first to establish that the wrongful act or insult was sufficient to cause an "ordinary person" to lose the power of self-control (the *objective* component). However, once that first step has been taken, the accused person must next establish they were, in fact, provoked (the *subjective* component). Whereas, for the purpose of the "ordinary person" test, the court may take into account only a limited range of subjective factors that are personal to the accused, all relevant personal factors may be taken into consideration when posing the question, "Did this particular accused person lose the power of self-control?" For example, even factors such as intoxication and an excessively pugnacious and excitable personality will be relevant to answering this inquiry. In *Tran* (2010), Justice Charron addressed the subjective component of the defence in the following manner:

> The inquiry into whether the accused was in fact acting in response to the provocation focuses on the accused's subjective perceptions of the circumstances, including what the accused believed, intended or knew. In other words, the accused must have killed because he was provoked and not because the provocation existed.

The application of the requirement that the accused must establish that they were actually provoked is well illustrated by the case of *Humaid* (2006). The accused had been charged with first-degree murder following the brutal stabbing of his wife. Humaid had asserted that the last words uttered by his wife led him to believe that she had been sexually unfaithful to him. He then called an expert witness who presented evidence concerning the religion and culture that Humaid claimed to espouse. The expert claimed that the culture was male dominated and placed great significance on the concept of family honour. Infidelity, particularly infidelity by a female member of a family, was considered a very serious violation of the family's honour and worthy of harsh punishment by the male members of the family. In spite of this argument, Humaid was convicted of the charge against him: undoubtedly, the jury concluded that the killing was planned and deliberate and not the product of the spontaneous loss of control in response to sudden and unexpected provocation. The Ontario Court of Appeal upheld the conviction and ruled that, in any event, there had been no air of reality to the defence of provocation. The Court of Appeal noted that one of the issues that was fatal to the claim of provocation was the fact that there was no evidence that Humaid had really been provoked and had acted in the heat of passion in response to **sudden provocation**. Rather, Humaid appeared to be suggesting that his culture and religion would, in some way, lead him to believe that killing the victim was an appropriate response to her alleged infidelity. Justice Doherty explained this aspect of the case in the following manner:

> A provocation claim rests on the assertion that an accused in a state of extreme anger lost his ability to fully control his actions and acted while in that state. Provocation does not shield an accused who has not lost self-control, but has instead acted out of a sense of revenge or a culturally driven sense of the appropriate response to someone else's misconduct. An accused who acts out of a sense of retribution fuelled by a belief system that entitles a husband to punish his wife's perceived infidelity has not lost control, but has taken action that, according to his belief system, is a justified response to the situation. ...

Similarly, in *Doucette* (2014), the Ontario Court of Appeal ruled that there was no air of reality to the defence of provocation when it was established that Doucette shot the victim in cold blood, (unsuccessfully) claiming he was acting in self-defence. The Court concluded that:

> ... there is no suggestion in [Doucette's] evidence that he lost control or responded in the heat of the moment to Mr. Batisse's threatening conduct. To the contrary, on [Doucette's] evidence, he had tried to calm Mr. Batisse down, both during the altercation inside the bar and again when Mr. Batisse approached him aggressively on the street. ... [Doucette] testified that he shot Mr. Batisse because he feared for his life, intending only to "get away before I was shot". [Doucette's] evidence effectively negates any suggestion that he had lost control when he pulled his gun and fired in Mr. Batisse's direction.

Requirement 4: The Accused Acted before Having Recovered Their Normal Self-Control

Section 232(2) requires that, to advance the defence of provocation successfully, the accused person must establish that they acted on the wrongful act or insult "on the sudden and *before there was time for their passion to cool.*"

The *Friesen* case (1995) furnishes an excellent example of a situation in which the defence of provocation failed because there had been time for the accused's passion to cool following the alleged

An essential element of the defence of provocation is that the accused person must have acted in response to sudden provocation and before there was time for their passion to cool.

wrongful conduct. Friesen had killed a friend with a builder's nail gun after an alleged act of sexual provocation by the victim. Friesen claimed the defence of provocation when he was charged with first-degree murder. However, the evidence established that, after the alleged provocation, the accused had left the victim and gone to the garage, where he connected a builder's nail gun to a compressor. Obviously, this took a fair amount of time to accomplish. He then returned to the house and shot the victim with "dozens of nails" from the gun. Significantly, at the time of the shooting, the victim was fast asleep. Friesen's conviction of murder was upheld by the Alberta Court of Appeal. In the view of the Court, no reasonable jury could have found that there had been provocation within the meaning of section 232. According to Justice Côté:

> The accused took some time to go upstairs and out to the garage, to rig up the nail gun and all its power sources, and then to deploy them downstairs in the family room next to the victim. So it is very hard to think that that could be "on the sudden and before there was time for his passion to cool." …

"LEGAL RIGHT" IN SECTION 232(3)

Section 232(3) of the *Criminal Code* states that

> no one shall be deemed to have given provocation to another by doing anything that he had a legal right to do, or by doing anything that the accused incited him to do in order to provide the accused with an excuse for causing death or bodily harm to any human being.

This provision imposes an important restriction on the use of the defence of provocation. Undoubtedly, an accused person who engages in legally sanctioned conduct or deliberately incites the commission of an indictable offence, such as an assault, for the specific purpose of providing themselves with an excuse for murder should be barred from raising the defence of provocation. According to Justice Charron in *Tran* (2010), "The phrase "legal right" has been defined … as meaning a right which is sanctioned by law, such as a sheriff proceeding to execute a legal warrant, or a person acting in justified self-defence. …"

One may well ask, in what circumstances are the courts likely to find that the victim had a "legal right" to do what they did within the meaning of section 232(3)? A good example of such a situation is the case of *Louison* (1975), in which the accused was charged with the murder of a taxi driver who had picked him up. The victim had been brutally beaten to death with a hammer. It appears that the accused had pulled a knife on the victim and forced him into the trunk of the taxi. After keeping the victim in the trunk for a couple of hours, Louison decided to give him some air. The deceased hit the accused in the back with a hammer. However, Louison wrested the hammer away from the somewhat enfeebled victim and began to rain blows upon his head. When the body was discovered, the hammer was embedded in the victim's skull.

Provocation does not apply when the victim has a right sanctioned by the law to act in the way they did.

Somewhat surprisingly, Louison advanced provocation as one of his defences, brazenly claiming that he had been assaulted by the victim. The accused was nevertheless convicted, and he appealed to the Saskatchewan Court of Appeal. One of the reasons given for rejecting Louison's appeal concerned the fact that the deceased had been acting in self-defence and, therefore, had a "legal right" to do what he did within the meaning of section 232(3). Chief Justice Culliton stated that:

> It seems to me that in a case of self-induced provocation s. [232] must be given a reasonable interpretation; for example—in an attempted rape, if the victim in resisting the assault should stick her finger in the eye of the assailant causing him injury and severe pain and he thereupon killed her, I think her act in this respect would be construed as something she had a legal right to do and would not be a wrongful act within s. [232]. Similarly, where the pilot of a plane is being held at gunpoint by a hijacker and if he should strike the hijacker with a fist or a wrench whereupon the hijacker shot him, I would not think such action would be considered a wrongful act within s. [232] of the *Criminal Code*.

Predictably, Louison's subsequent appeal to the Supreme Court of Canada was also rejected.

THE DIFFERING ROLES OF JUDGE AND JURY IN CANADA WHEN PROVOCATION IS RAISED

Section 232(3) provides that the determination of certain issues must remain within the exclusive realm of the jury. More specifically, the *Code* states that "whether the conduct of the victim amounted to provocation under subsection (2)," and "whether the accused was deprived of the power of self-control by the provocation that he alleges he received" are questions of fact.

As such, the trial judge must leave such issues to the jury. However, the Supreme Court of Canada has, on a number of occasions, ruled that trial judges still have a duty to determine whether there is sufficient evidence of provocation to justify submitting the issue to the jury: in other words, the accused person has to meet the evidential burden.

The requirements that must be met to satisfy the evidential burden when provocation is raised as a defence were clearly articulated by the Supreme Court of Canada in *Buzizi* (2013). The accused had been convicted of second-degree murder by jury. He had stabbed the victim to death following an altercation during which he stated that he "was angry, mad, upset, 'out of it', scared, afraid, worried, trying to protect himself, and reacting emotionally." The trial judge refused to put the defence of provocation to the jury. The Supreme Court of Canada ordered a new trial because, in the view of the majority of the Court, there had been an "air of reality" to the defence and the trial judge had made an error of law in refusing to instruct the jury to consider the defence of provocation.

The Supreme Court took the view that the jury might not have delivered a verdict of guilty of murder if they had been given the opportunity to consider the defence of provocation. Relying on the previous decision of the Supreme Court of Canada in *Cinous* (2002), Justice Fish stated that "the air of reality test [is not] intended to assess whether the defence is likely, unlikely, somewhat likely, or very likely to succeed at the end of the day." Instead, the correct question is whether the trial record "contains a sufficient factual foundation for a properly instructed jury to give effect to the defence." While appellate courts give considerable degree of deference to trial judges when they are acting in their role as triers of fact, much less deference is accorded to them when they are deciding whether or not to put a defence to a jury because this is a decision on a question of law rather than on a question of fact. Justice Fish said:

> the trial judge is not at all in the "best position" to determine whether a defence has an air of reality, since that is a question of law: "... the interpretation of a legal standard (the elements of the defence) and the determination of whether there is an air of reality to a defence constitute questions of law, reviewable on a standard of correctness."

INTOXICATION

HISTORICAL OVERVIEW OF THE DEFENCE

Until 1996, the *Criminal Code* made no mention of the defence of intoxication. Prior to this date, the development of the defence of intoxication was exclusively a matter of common law; in other words, the nature of the defence was shaped by judges rather than by Parliament.

Historically, intoxication was treated by English courts as being an *aggravating* (rather than a *mitigating*) factor in a criminal prosecution. However, during the course of the 19th century, the English courts gradually started to relax their approach and fashioned a compromise in which intoxication came to be regarded as a partial defence to most of the more serious criminal charges. It was considered a partial defence because it would operate to reduce the severity of the charge against the accused (e.g., from murder to manslaughter or from robbery to assault). Traditionally, the English courts took the view that intoxication should not be available as a *complete* defence to criminal charges. As we shall see, this view was based on the fundamental legal principle that intoxication *may* be a defence to a charge in which the Crown is required to prove *specific intent* in order to obtain a conviction (as in murder or robbery) but is *never* available where the offence concerned is considered to be one in which the Crown has to prove only *general or basic intent* (as in manslaughter or assault).

Until 1994, English and Canadian courts applied basically the same principles when dealing with the defence of intoxication. These principles were generally known as the ***Beard* Rules**, taking their name from the case in which they were first articulated. However, in the case of *Daviault* (1994), the majority of the justices of the Supreme Court of Canada broke away from the traditional approach to intoxication by declaring that there may be circumstances in which intoxication should be considered a *complete* defence, after all. More specifically, they took the view that if a defendant is charged with an offence of *general (or basic)* intent such as sexual assault, intoxication may be a valid defence if it is so extreme as to produce a "state akin to automatism or insanity." This, of course, represented a significant change in the law, because previously intoxication was considered an irrelevant factor whenever the accused was charged with an offence of general (or basic) intent.

In response to the *Daviault* case, Parliament moved, for the first time, to pass legislation dealing with intoxication as a defence to a criminal charge and section 33.1 was added to the *Criminal Code* (coming into force in 1996).[3] Section 33.1 states that intoxication, however extreme it may be, will not be accepted as a defence to a charge of any *general (or basic) intent* offence that "includes as an element an assault or any other interference or threat of interference with the bodily integrity of another person."

In delivering the judgment of the majority of the justices of the Supreme Court of Canada in the leading case of *Daley* (2007), Justice Bastarache provided a succinct overview of the current status of intoxication as a defence to a criminal charge in Canada:

> Our case law suggests there are three legally relevant degrees of intoxication. First, there is what we might call *"mild" intoxication*. This is where there is alcohol-induced relaxation of both inhibitions and socially acceptable behaviour. This has never been accepted as a factor or excuse in determining whether the accused possessed the requisite *mens rea*. Second, there is what we might call *"advanced" intoxication*. This occurs where there is intoxication to the point where the accused lacks specific intent, to the extent of an impairment of the accused's foresight of the consequences of his or her act sufficient to raise a reasonable doubt about the requisite *mens rea*. …
>
> A defence based on this level of intoxication applies only to specific intent offences. …
>
> The third and final degree of legally relevant intoxication is *extreme intoxication akin to automatism*, which negates voluntariness and thus is a complete defence to criminal responsibility. … [S]uch a defence would be extremely rare, and by operation of s. 33.1 of the *Criminal Code*, limited to non-violent types of offences. [emphasis added]

To fully comprehend the somewhat complex nature of the law concerning the intoxication defence in Canada, it is necessary to examine it within an historical context. For this purpose, the analysis of the defence will be undertaken in three sections: (1) the evolution of the *Beard* Rules from 1920 to the present day; (2) the decision of the Supreme Court of Canada in the landmark case of *Daviault* (1994); and (3) the enactment of section 33.1 of the *Criminal Code* and its aftermath.

THE EVOLUTION OF THE *BEARD* RULES: 1920 TO THE PRESENT

The classic authority concerning the defence of intoxication is the English case of *Beard* (1920), decided by the House of Lords. In this case, Lord Birkenhead articulated three rules that rapidly came to be regarded as the authoritative statement of the nature and limits of the intoxication defence. *As modified by subsequent judicial interpretations in Canada*, the three rules may be summarized in the following manner:

1. If intoxication induces a mental disorder ("disease of the mind") and renders the accused "not criminally responsible" within the meaning of section 16 of the *Criminal Code*, they must be acquitted as being "not criminally responsible on account of mental disorder" (NCRMD).

3. 1995, c. 32, s. 1.

2. If intoxication prevents a defendant from forming the intent necessary for conviction of a **crime of *specific* intent** (such as murder, robbery, or theft), they must be acquitted of that crime. However, intoxication can never be a defence to a charge of a **crime of *basic* (or *general*) intent** (such as manslaughter, assault, sexual assault, mischief—wilful damage to property). An accused person who is acquitted of a charge of a *specific intent* offence will nevertheless be convicted of a less serious *basic intent* offence (e.g., manslaughter instead of murder, assault instead of robbery). In this sense, intoxication is only a partial defence.
3. If intoxication falls short of preventing the accused from forming the intent necessary for conviction of a crime of specific intent, it does not constitute a valid defence (in particular, if the accused formed the necessary intent, it is irrelevant that the intoxication made it more difficult for them to control their actions).

The *Beard* Rules were enthusiastically endorsed by the Supreme Court of Canada in the case of *George* (1960) and their authority in Canada was later reaffirmed, without any qualification, in *Leary* (1977). The *George* case furnishes an excellent illustration of the application of the *Beard* Rules to a charge of robbery. The evidence indicated that the accused had visited the home of an 84-year-old man called Averis and demanded money from him. He then beat Averis severely with his bare fists, broke Averis's nose, and caused numerous other serious bodily injuries to the victim. He then stole the sum of $22. The victim indicated that George had threatened to kill him unless he gave him money. George's main defence was that he was in a severe state of intoxication at the time of the alleged offence. At his trial, the judge acquitted the accused on the following

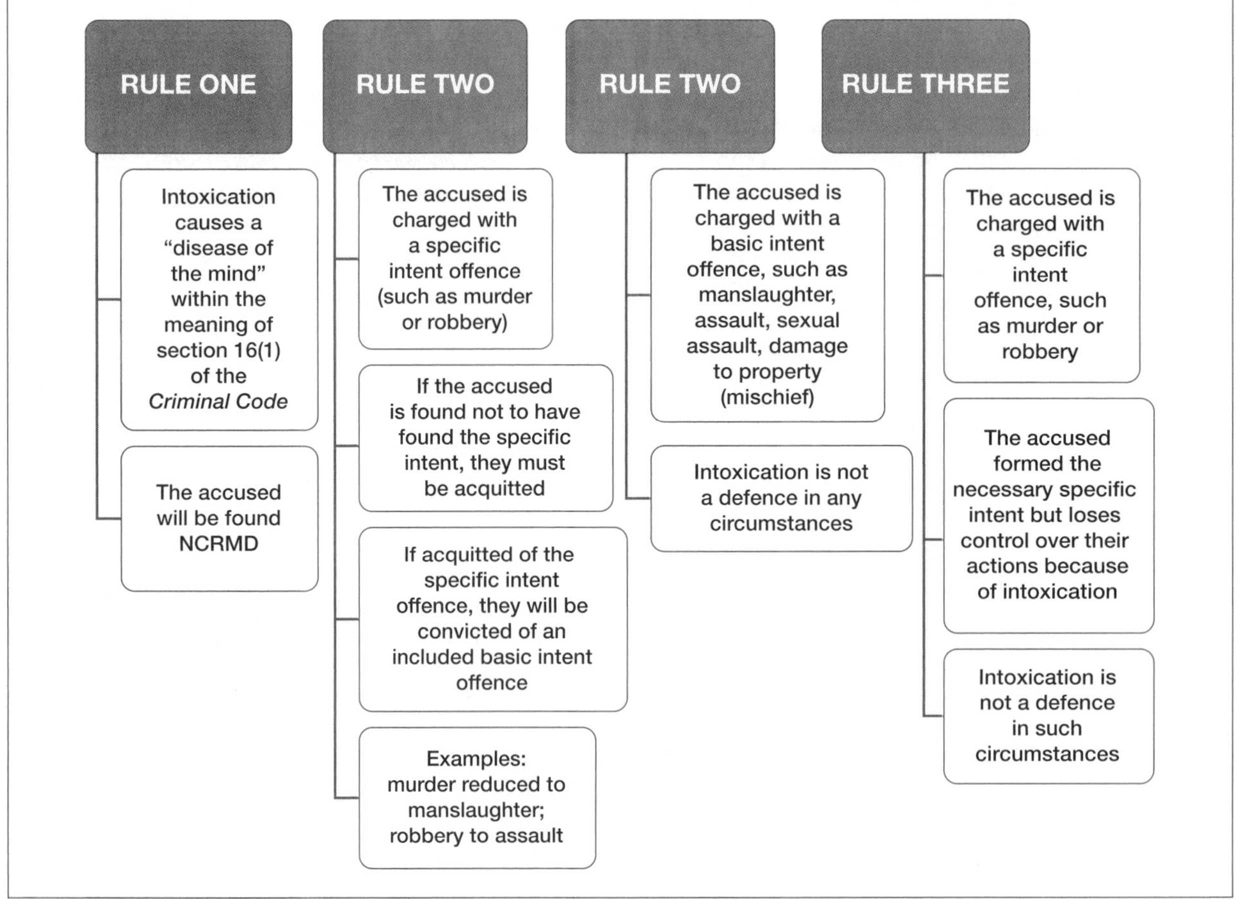

Figure 10-2

How the Beard *Rules Work*

basis: "You are being acquitted not because you didn't do it—there is no doubt in my mind that you did do it—you are being acquitted because I have found that you were so drunk on the night in question that you were unable to form an intent to do it."

The Crown appealed the accused's acquittal. The appeal was unsuccessful in the British Columbia Court of Appeal but was ultimately successful before the Supreme Court of Canada.. Ultimately, the Supreme Court affirmed the accused's acquittal on the charge of robbery. Since robbery is a specific intent offence, drunkenness may be a *partial* defence. Therefore, the Court judged that the accused had been properly acquitted. However, most charges of robbery include a charge of assault (in essence, a robbery normally involves both an assault and a theft), and an accused person may usually be convicted of any lesser offence that is considered to be included in the charge upon which they are tried. The Court pointed out that a simple assault is a crime of *general (or basic) intent* and the *Beard* Rules dictate that drunkenness cannot be a valid defence to such a charge. Therefore, the Supreme Court entered a verdict of guilty of common assault against George.

Justice Ritchie offered an explanation for the distinction the *Beard* Rules draw between basic (or general) and specific intent offences:

> In considering the question of *mens rea*, a distinction is to be drawn between "intention" as applied to acts done to achieve an immediate end on the one hand and acts done with a specific and ulterior motive and intention of furthering or achieving an illegal object on the other hand. Illegal acts of the former kind are done "intentionally" in the sense that they are not done by accident or through honest mistake, but acts of the latter kind are the product of preconception and are deliberate steps taken towards an illegal goal. The former acts may be purely physical products of momentary passion, whereas the latter involve the mental process of formulating a specific intent. A man, far advanced in drink, may intentionally strike his fellow in the former sense at a time when his mind is so befogged with liquor as to be unable to formulate a specific intent in the latter sense.

THE FIRST *BEARD* RULE: INTOXICATION THAT CAUSES A "DISEASE OF THE MIND"

The first *Beard* Rule specifies that if intoxication induces a *"disease of the mind"* and the accused person lacks the capacity to appreciate the physical nature and quality of their actions or to know that it is morally wrong, then they are entitled to raise the defence of NCRMD under section 16 of the *Criminal Code*. When the *Beard* Rules were formulated, at the beginning of the 20th century, the defence of intoxication was focused almost exclusively on the effects of alcohol and it was an alcohol-related condition, *delirium tremens*, to which the first *Beard* Rule was originally addressed. *Delirium tremens* is a condition that occurs when an individual who has a long history of alcohol abuse suddenly ceases drinking. In its most severe form, *delirium tremens* ("the shakes") may induce a psychotic state and an individual may commit violent crimes while under the influence of delusions and/or hallucinations. Since the 19th century, the English courts had recognized that *delirium tremens* may constitute a "disease of the mind" and entitle the accused person to receive the benefit of the NCRMD verdict [see, for example, the reaffirmation of this principle in the Canadian case of *Malcolm* (1989)]. However, by the 21st century, there had been a radical change in the pattern of drug use both in Canada and in many other countries: "simple" alcohol abuse is no longer the central focus of concern for the criminal justice system and the *Beard* Rules. There are now many illegal drugs (such as methamphetamine, known as "crystal meth"; MDMA, known as "ecstasy"; phencyclidine, known as "angel dust"; and "bath salts" that consist of a variety of psychoactive drugs) that, used either on their own or in combination with other drugs and/or alcohol, may produce psychotic reactions and prompt individuals to commit violent crimes. In addition, individuals who purchase street drugs are increasingly unaware of the extent to which what they believe they are buying may actually be adulterated with dangerous drugs, such as the high-strength opioid, Fentanyl. This "new reality" has persuaded the courts to reconstruct the first *Beard* Rule so that a transient psychotic condition that is caused directly by the voluntary ingestion of drugs does not lead to an NCRMD verdict but, rather, is considered within the context of the partial defence of intoxication. In *Bouchard-Lebrun* (2011), the Supreme Court of Canada completed this process of redefining the concept of "disease of the mind" for the specific purpose of applying the first *Beard* Rule to an accused person who has experienced a substance-induced psychosis.

Bouchard-Lebrun and a friend purchased and consumed some ecstasy pills (of a variety known as "poire bleue"). A few hours after taking the drug, they decided to go to the residence of Lévesque, whom they intended to beat up because—strange as it may seem—he was believed to be wearing an "upside down cross." Upon arrival at the building in which Lévesque lived, Bouchard-Lebrun and his companion brutally attacked Lévesque by kicking and punching him many times. A good neighbour, Dumas, saw that Lévesque could not defend himself and intervened. Bouchard-Lebrun grabbed him and threw him down the stairs. As Dumas lay helpless at the foot of the stairs, Bouchard-Lebrun stomped on his head, causing him severe and permanent injuries: indeed, Dumas would have to spend the rest of his days in hospital. Bouchard-Lebrun was charged with two counts of aggravated assault and assault.

Bouchard-Lebrun's defence turned on the fact that, at the time of the violent incident in question, he was in a psychotic state brought on by the ingestion of the ecstasy pills. He argued that he completely lost contact with reality and was acting under the influence of a bizarre religious delusion:

> It was after taking the drug that he became obsessed with the "upside-down cross" supposedly worn by Mr. Lévesque. During the attack, he made statements of a religious nature that, although coherent, were basically absurd. For example, he said that the Apocalypse was coming. At one point, he raised his arms in the air and asked the victims and the helpless witnesses to the attack whether they believed in him. After referring a few times to God and the devil once the attack was over, he blessed Mr. Dumas's spouse by making the sign of the cross on her forehead. Mr. Dumas was still lying on the floor when the appellant then left the scene very calmly as if nothing had just happened.

It was agreed that Bouchard-Lebrun was in a psychotic state brought on by the ecstasy and that the effects of the drug had completely dissipated within four days of the violent incident. He had no history of psychotic illness and he was not addicted to drugs. Bouchard-Lebrun argued that since he was in a psychotic state at the time of the violent incident, he should be found not criminally responsible on account of mental disorder under section 16 of the *Criminal Code*. However, the trial judge ruled that the defence was not available in these circumstances and Bouchard-Lebrun was convicted of the charges. His conviction was upheld by the Quebec Court of Appeal and he then appealed to the Supreme Court of Canada.

The Supreme Court had to decide whether a psychotic state brought on by the voluntary ingestion of a drug constituted a "disease of the mind" for the purpose of section 16(1) of the *Criminal Code*. The Court followed the approach that it had adopted in the *Stone* case (1999), discussed in Chapter 8, when it defined the concept "disease of the mind" for the purpose of drawing a distinction between the defences of mental-disorder and non-mental-disorder automatism. Notably, in *Stone*, the Court had emphasized that "disease of the mind" was a legal, and not a medical, concept (although it was a concept that was "informed" by medical knowledge).

In *Stone*, the Supreme Court had taken a "holistic approach" in which the key elements were whether the accused person's mental state was caused by an *external* as opposed to an *internal* factor (the accused person's psychological or emotional makeup), whether the condition constituted a *continuing danger* to the public, and whether there were compelling *policy considerations* to determine how the condition should be classified. In *Stone*, the Supreme Court had asked the question whether an "ordinary person" might have entered a dissociative state in the same circumstances facing the accused person: if the answer is yes, then the cause of the accused person's mental condition would be considered *external* in nature and, therefore, not a "disease of the mind." If the answer is no, then the cause would be considered *internal* (there must have been something in the accused person's psychological or emotional makeup that precipitated the mental state in question because an ordinary person would not have been affected in this way). In *Bouchard-Lebrun* (2011), the Supreme Court of Canada ultimately ruled that the accused's substance-induced psychotic state was not a "disease of the mind" and, therefore, ruled that he was not entitled to raise the NCRMD defence: his convictions were affirmed.

How did the Supreme Court arrive at this decision? The Court emphasized that Bouchard-Lebrun was not suffering from a psychotic illness before he took the ecstasy pills. He was also not an individual who had been ingesting drugs on an ongoing basis (prolonged drug abuse may cause a mental disorder in certain individuals). The psychotic condition came on immediately after the ingestion of the ecstasy and the symptoms were gone in a matter of a few days. Furthermore, an ordinary person might have reacted in the same manner to this particular drug (the medical evidence given at trial was that a toxic psychosis was a frequent response to ecstasy in the general population). All these considerations suggested that the cause of Bouchard-Lebrun's psychosis was *external* and not precipitated by an *internal* factor, such as an underlying mental disorder. In addition, there was *no continuing danger* to the public because the psychotic condition had dissipated so rapidly. This circumstance also militated against finding that Bouchard-Lebrun's psychosis was a "disease of the mind." As Justice LeBel noted in the judgment of the Supreme Court:

> Provided that [Bouchard-Lebrun] abstains from such drugs in the future, which he is capable of doing voluntarily, it would seem that his mental condition poses no threat to public safety. Although I will not adopt a definitive position on this question, I might have concluded otherwise if [Bouchard-Lebrun] had a dependency on drugs that affected his ability to stop using them voluntarily. The likelihood of recurring danger might then be greater.

Finally, the Supreme Court rounded out its "holistic approach" by canvassing any relevant policy considerations that might be involved in making the determination as to whether the substance-induced psychosis constituted a "disease of the mind." On the policy issue, Justice LeBel was very clear. It would not be sound public policy to permit accused persons in Bouchard-Lebrun's situation to plead NCRMD, particularly in light of the fact that they would have to be given absolute discharges almost immediately if the psychotic state dissipated quickly after the incident that gave rise to the criminal charge. Justice LeBel said, in this respect:

> In light of Dr. Faucher's expert assessment of the frequency of toxic psychosis in circumstances analogous to the ones in the instant case [Bouchard-Lebrun's] position, if adopted, would affect the integrity of the criminal justice system in ways that would be difficult to accept. If everyone who committed a violent offence while suffering from toxic psychosis were to be found not criminally responsible on account of mental disorder regardless of the origin or cause of the psychosis, the scope of the defence provided for in s. 16 *Cr. C.* would become much broader than Parliament intended. These considerations reinforce the conclusion that the toxic psychosis of [Bouchard-Lebrun] in this case is covered by [the *Cooper* case's][4] exclusion of "self-induced states caused by alcohol or drugs."

4. The decision of the Supreme Court of Canada in *Cooper* (1993).

The Supreme Court suggested that each case of substance-induced psychosis must be examined on a case-by-case basis. It would seem that, if intoxication exacerbated a pre-existing psychosis and a psychotic episode resulted, then it would be considered a "disease of the mind" for the purpose of section 16(1). Similarly, if a pattern of sustained drug abuse causes permanent or long-lasting changes to the brain and a psychosis results (e.g., *delirium tremens*), it may also be recognized as a "disease of the mind." However, the Supreme Court emphasized that the type(s) of drug involved will also affect whether a substance-induced psychosis will be treated as a "disease of the mind." If a drug (such as methamphetamine, or "crystal meth") is highly likely to cause a psychotic episode in an "ordinary person," then any psychosis it induces will be considered the result of an *external* cause and, therefore, not a "disease of the mind."

Once the Supreme Court of Canada had decided that the NCRMD verdict was not open to Bouchard-Lebrun, there was no other defence available. Since aggravated assault and assault are basic intent offences, intoxication—no matter how extreme—would not be a defence under the *Beard* Rules. The Court also referred to section 33.1 of the *Criminal Code*, which makes it clear that no defence is available in these circumstances (section 33.1 will be discussed later in this chapter).

Applying the Second and Third *Beard* Rules: The Critical Distinction between Crimes of Specific and General (Basic) Intent

The initial question that must be answered before a court may apply the second and third *Beard* Rules is whether or not the crime charged is one of specific or general (basic) intent. If the crime is one of specific intent, intoxication may be a partial defence, but if the crime is one of general (basic) intent, then intoxication will not in any way absolve the accused of criminal responsibility for their actions. What is the legal distinction between crimes of *specific and general (basic) intent*?

The most recent analysis of this distinction was articulated by the Supreme Court of Canada in *Tatton* (2015). This case involved a charge of arson under section 434 of the *Criminal Code*, which provides that "Every person who intentionally or recklessly causes damage by fire or explosion to property that is not wholly owned by that person is guilty of an indictable offence and liable to imprisonment for a term not exceeding fourteen years." Tatton was responsible for a fire that destroyed the contents of his ex-partner's home. In a highly intoxicated state, he had placed a pan containing oil on the hot burner of a stove and left the house to pick up a coffee. Tatton did not return until 20 minutes later, at which time the house was ablaze. He was duly charged with arson but claimed that the fire was purely accidental. The trial judge ruled that arson under section 434 was a crime requiring proof of specific intent and, therefore, under the *Beard* Rules, Tatton was entitled to raise his intoxication as a defence. He was acquitted at his trial and the verdict was upheld by the Ontario Court of Appeal. The Crown appealed on a question of law (whether arson under section 434 was a crime of specific or basic intent) and the Supreme Court of Canada set aside the acquittal, ordering a new trial. On the question of law, the Supreme Court ruled that the arson offence was a crime of basic intent and, therefore, Tatton would not be able to rely on his self-induced intoxication as a defence, unless it was so extreme as to produce a state of automatism.

In delivering the judgment of the Supreme Court, Justice Moldaver provided an in-depth analysis of the distinction between crimes of specific and general (basic) intent. As in all cases involving charges of a serious offence, the first question to be addressed is what is the mental element? This must be determined by interpretation of the words used by Parliament in the *Criminal Code.* Once this has been determined, the court must decide whether the offence is one of *specific or general (basic)* intent. For many offences, there is judicial precedent that has already settled the issue. However, when there is no settled judicial precedent, how is the distinction to be made? According to Justice Moldaver, the classification must be made on the basis of two factors: the importance of the mental element and the social policy that drives the offence.

As far as the mental element is concerned, the difference between *specific and general (basic)* intent crimes lies in the degree of complexity of the thought and reasoning processes involved. *General (basic) intent* offences involve relatively simple thought processes: assault, for example, requires only an intent to apply force to another person—there is no requirement for the Crown to prove an intent to injure that person. On the other hand, as Justice Moldaver points out, "specific intent offences involve a heightened mental element." These types of offence require not only that the accused person intend to commit the *actus reus* but also that they do so with "an ulterior purpose in mind." Justice Moldaver referred to the example of the crime of assault with intent to resist arrest. The Crown must prove, first of all, that the accused intended to apply force or threaten to do so and, second, that they did so with the ulterior purpose of resisting arrest.

However, *specific intent* offences do not necessarily require proof of an ulterior purpose. They may simply involve the requirement that the accused person's intent to bring about certain consequences is the product of "more complex thought and reasoning processes." Justice Moldaver illustrated this point by referring to the crime of murder [see, for example, section 229, subsections (a) to (c), which articulate three alternative *mens rea* requirements for this appalling crime]. Similarly, the "heightened mental element could take the form of a requirement that the accused have actual knowledge of certain circumstances or consequences, where the knowledge is the product of more complex thought and reasoning processes." For example, section 354 of the *Criminal Code* establishes the offence of possession of property obtained by the commission of an indictable offence. This crime requires the proof of actual knowledge of (or wilful blindness with respect to) the fact that the property in question was obtained by, or derived directly or indirectly from, the commission of an indictable offence. The complex nature of the thought and reasoning processes involved in specific intent offences constitutes the rationale for allowing intoxication as a defence to charges of these crimes. However, general (basic) intent offences require "little mental acuity" and intoxication is unlikely to prevent the accused person from forming the required mental element: therefore, intoxication is no defence to a charge of such an offence.

Justice Moldaver stated that it is only if the analysis of the complexity mental element fails to establish a satisfactory conclusion as to the categorization of an offence as one of specific or general (basic) intent that the court should turn to the issue of social policy. In Justice Moldaver's view, the policy analysis should generally be centred on the issue of whether the use of alcohol is "habitually associated" with the offence in question: if so, it would be poor social policy to permit an accused person to rely on their intoxication as a defence. A good example of this approach would be the offence of sexual assault: "Allowing self-induced intoxication to provide an accused with a defence would be to endorse, if not promote, the very behaviour that has historically proved to be a root cause of the problem." Justice Moldaver also noted that unruly behaviour and damage to property are frequently associated with the abuse of alcohol and that, therefore, it would not be prudent social policy to make intoxication a defence to such offences.

Justice Moldaver suggested that there may well be other social-policy considerations that are relevant to categorizing an offence as one of *specific or general (basic) intent*:

> ... the presence of a lesser included general intent offence in the main offence may be relevant. In such cases, an accused who successfully relies on intoxication to negate the heightened mental element of the main offence can still be convicted of the lesser included offence. Drunkenness will provide no defence to the lesser offence. For example, an accused who successfully raises intoxication as a defence to a charge of assault with intent to resist arrest may still be convicted of the lesser included offence of assault. In these situations, the intoxicated offender will not escape punishment altogether. Consequently, there is less impetus to preclude the accused from advancing intoxication as a defence to the main offence.

Insofar as the offence of arson, contrary to section 434 of the *Criminal Code*, is concerned, the Supreme Court in *Tatton* concluded that the offence could not be considered the product of "more complex thought and reasoning processes." It was relatively straightforward for an accused person to realize that the consequences of a fire would be damage to property: as a consequence, arson would more rationally fit in the category of *general (basic) intent*. In addition, damage to property is frequently associated with intoxication and the social-policy approach would dictate that intoxication should not be a defence to the charge of arson.

The distinction between offences of specific and general (basic) intent has been criticized by many. Indeed, Chief Justice Dickson, in a dissenting judgment in the case of *Bernard* (1988), argued that the distinction should be abolished for the purpose of applying the defence of intoxication. In his view, the distinction serves as "an artificial device whereby evidence, otherwise relevant, is excluded from the jury's consideration." However, the call for the abolition of the distinction has been soundly rejected by the majority of the justices of the Supreme Court in both the *Bernard* and the *Daviault* (1994) cases.

In *Daviault*, Justice Cory, with whom a majority of the justices of the Supreme Court of Canada agreed, curtly stated that "[I]t is now well established by this court that there are two categories of offences ... those requiring a specific intent and others which call for nothing more than general intent."

However, in *Tatton* (2015), Justice Moldaver opined that *Daviault* had not solved the riddle of distinguishing between crimes of *specific and general (basic) intent*: "The general/specific intent dichotomy continues to perplex counsel and trial courts alike. It has been criticized as illogical and as leading to "arbitrary and inconsistent results from court to court, offence to offence and jurisdiction to jurisdiction."

Justice Moldaver suggested that the riddle might be resolved if Parliament were to provide more guidance to the courts with respect to the required mental element for each crime in the *Criminal Code*. He suggested that "legislative intervention was "sorely needed to spell out the mental element of offences and to specify when intoxication short of automatism can be considered." However, without such intervention, the task of interpreting the *Criminal Code* will be left in the hands of the judiciary.

Applying the Second *Beard* Rule to Crimes of Specific Intent

Once it has been established that the offence with which the accused has been charged is a crime of specific intent, the next matter to be considered is the nature of the circumstances in which intoxication may serve as a partial defence to such a charge. In formulating the second rule in the Beard case, Lord Birkenhead stated that "[E]vidence of drunkenness which renders the accused incapable of forming the specific intent essential to constitute the crime should be taken into consideration with the other facts proved in order to determine whether or not he had this intent."

There is a major difficulty with the manner in which the second *Beard* Rule was articulated by Lord Birkenhead. The problem stems from his use of words that focus on the accused's *capacity* to form the specific intent required, rather than the accused's *actual intent* at the time of the alleged offence. Under the second *Beard* Rule, if the accused person's defence raises a reasonable doubt as to their capacity to form the specific intent that must be proved by the Crown, there

The Case of Tommy Bouchard-Lebrun: A Psychotic Reaction Caused Directly by a Drug Is No Defence to a Charge of a Violent Crime

• • • • • •

The case of *Bouchard-Lebrun* (2011), discussed elsewhere in this chapter, is a particularly important one for the development of the criminal law in Canada. It will be recalled that the accused was convicted of aggravated assault and assault following a brutal attack committed while he was in a delusional state. In this case, the Supreme Court of Canada severely limited the opportunity for accused persons to advance the defence of not criminally responsible on account of mental disorder (section 16 of the *Criminal Code*) if they entered a psychotic state following the voluntary ingestion of alcohol and/or other drugs. The decision is significant because, as the *DSM-5* (*The Diagnostic and Statistical Manual of Mental Disorders, Fifth Edition*, 2013) points out, there are many drugs and combinations of drugs that can cause a substance-induced psychosis (including alcohol).

In recent years, medical and mental health professionals have encountered individuals who have entered a psychotic state following the ingestion of certain illegal drugs, such as methamphetamine, phencyclidine, and even cannabis, and have as a consequence lost contact with reality. In this psychotic state, some of these individuals may be prone to commit serious, often violent offences. Should these individuals be held criminally responsible for their actions even if they were "in a different state of reality" and did not realize they were committing a wrongful act?

Severe intoxication may negative the *mens rea* necessary for proof of a crime of *specific intent* (such as robbery or murder) and result in conviction of a lesser crime (assault or manslaughter, respectively). However, since the enactment of section 33.1 of the *Criminal Code*, even extreme intoxication will not provide a defence to an accused person who is charged with a crime of *basic intent* that violates or threatens to violate personal integrity (offences such as assault, sexual assault, manslaughter). In the *Bouchard-Lebrun* case, the Supreme

Court took the view that a psychotic state that is voluntarily induced by the ingestion of a drug does not give the accused person charged with a violent crime an easy means of circumventing section 33.1 by raising the NCRMD defence.

The Supreme Court stated that section 16 of the *Code* applies only where the accused can prove that they had a "disease of the mind"—a legal concept. The Court said that whether a substance-induced psychosis produced a "disease of the mind" must be considered on a case-by-case basis. Following the *Stone* case (1999), the Court stated that a "holistic" approach should be taken, with particular emphasis on whether the psychotic condition was caused by an external factor (the drug(s)) or an internal factor (the psychological makeup of the accused), whether the condition is likely to pose a continuing danger, and policy considerations (such as protecting the public from violence). In *Bouchard-Lebrun*, the accused had no prior history of psychosis and the Court ruled that it was the one ecstasy pill that had precipitated the psychotic state, which dissipated entirely soon after the assault had taken place. Therefore, the Court held that the psychotic state was caused by an *external* factor (the ecstasy) and not any factor related to Bouchard-Lebrun's psychological makeup. Similarly, there was no underlying disease that posed a danger to the public, and this factor also pushed the Court toward finding that the accused was not suffering from a "disease of the mind."

The problem with *Bouchard-Lebrun* is that, although this particular case was fairly cut-and-dried, there are many cases in which it will be extremely difficult for a mental health practitioner to indicate whether a substance-induced psychosis was caused primarily or solely by the drug(s) or by a combination of factors, some internal and some external. For example, an accused person may have a genetic predisposition to a psychotic condition and taking a drug may precipitate a psychotic episode in that individual but not in the "ordinary person." Cannabis, for example, particularly if it is used over long periods, may produce a psychotic condition only in certain individuals who have a predisposition to psychosis, but methamphetamine has the potential to cause a psychotic condition in a large proportion of those who use it (even those who are not otherwise predisposed to a psychosis). It may be very difficult for courts in the future to identify the "cause" of a psychotic state, and the scientific evidence to date may not provide an adequate basis for making these decisions in complex cases. Indeed, the evidence appears to be that the interaction between specific drugs and the human brain is very complex, involving many factors and, in particular, a number of different genetic influences.

The Supreme Court acknowledged that the evidence from two psychiatrists had established that Bouchard-Lebrun was incapable of distinguishing between right and wrong when he was in the psychotic state: "They were in agreement that the appellant had been suffering from 'a severe psychosis that made him incapable of distinguishing right from wrong' at the time he committed the acts in question."

Nevertheless, the trial judge imposed a fairly harsh sentence, particularly taking into account the severe injuries inflicted: five years for aggravated assault and three months for assault, to be served concurrently. Do you agree with the trial judge's reasons (set out below)?

> Some groups want to play down the seriousness of drug use, but it seems to me that it is irresponsible not to consider the disastrous and terrible consequences of drug use. It is neither "preaching" nor "moralizing" to often repeat that the vast majority of offences have close connections to the world of drugs. The case before us is a sad illustration of where drugs can lead, and the person named Patrick Thibeault, who sold those little pills to Tommy Lebrun, is no doubt one of those who will advocate tomorrow for clemency when facing drug trafficking charges.
>
> It has often been said that sentencing is a judge's most difficult task. In this case, it is all the more challenging because the accused is not generally associated with criminal activity, he appears to be a serious worker, and, in particular, he did not premeditate or plan the actions he committed. While it may be less complex to impose a sentence for a serious offence committed by a repeat offender with a significant risk of re-offending, that is not the case here. The accused never premeditated his action and of course never imagined that the state caused by taking psychotropic substances could lead to such results.
>
> But all individuals must take responsibility for any actions they commit. People who drink and drive, thereby causing accidents and injury and/or death, do not deliberately seek out such results. But if they cause injury or death, they must assume the consequences. Here, the accused decided to take drugs, underestimated their effects, which were unknown and evidently dangerous, and did not consider the illegality of possessing these drugs; today, he must take responsibility for the horrible consequences of his actions. ... The social worker was correct to write that "his value system has long been elastic."
>
> See *R. c. Lebrun* [2008] JQ No. 10027 (Court of Quebec (Criminal and Penal Division).

Could Bouchard-Lebrun have foreseen the consequences of taking the ecstasy pill? If not, is it fair to hold him responsible for the terrible consequences that ensued? Would you have imposed such a severe sentence? Courts tend to ask yes or no questions. Could a mental health practitioner state definitively whether a substance-induced psychosis was caused solely, or at least primarily, by the drug as opposed to other factors relating to the specific individual concerned (genetics, psychological makeup, etc.)? If not, what should a mental health practitioner do if asked the yes or no question with respect to the cause of a substance-induced psychosis?

is no question that the accused must be acquitted. However, it by no means follows that an accused person who was *capable* of forming such a specific intent did, *in fact*, form such intent. In light of all the circumstances of the case, there may very well be a reasonable doubt as to whether the accused actually formed the requisite specific intent. Unfortunately, a literal interpretation of the second *Beard* Rule would lead to a conviction of the accused person in such circumstances because the only ground for acquittal mentioned by Lord Birkenhead is the accused's *lack of capacity to form the intent.*

In the case of *Robinson* (1996), the Supreme Court of Canada held that the *Beard* Rules, as written by Lord Birkenhead, violated both sections 7 and 11(d) of the *Charter* because they required a jury to convict an accused person even if they had a reasonable doubt about their actual intent. As Justice Bastarache pointed out in *Daley* (2007), "An accused who was not so intoxicated as to lack capacity to form the intent

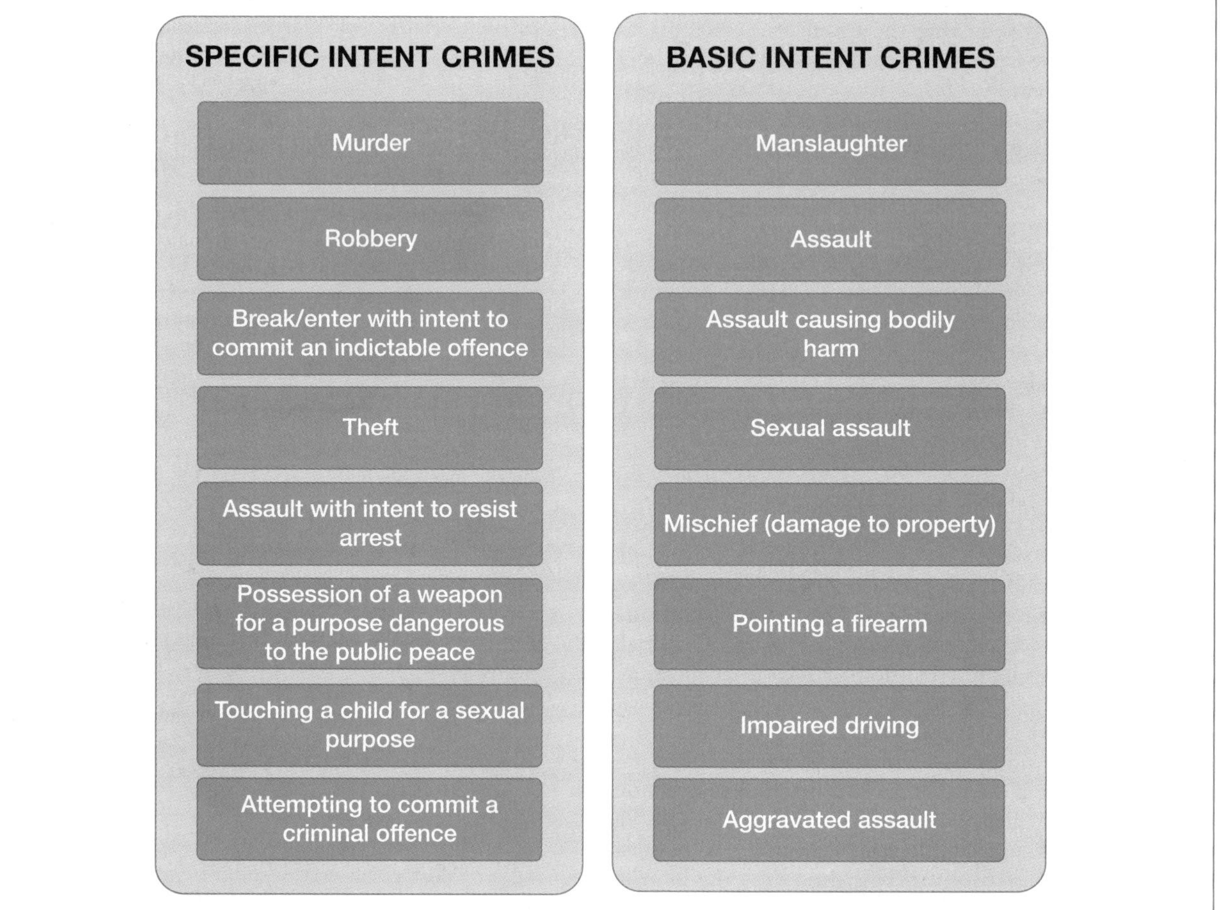

Figure 10-3

Specific and General Intent Offences Identified by the Courts

may nevertheless not have exercised that capacity and formed the specific intent. The ultimate inquiry is always whether the accused possessed actual intent."

In *Robinson*, Chief Justice Lamer clearly articulated the manner in which trial judges should instruct juries in relation to the second *Beard* Rule:

> [B]efore a trial judge is required by law to charge the jury on intoxication, he or she must be satisfied that the effect of the intoxication was such that its effect *might* have impaired the accused's foresight of consequences sufficient to raise a reasonable doubt. Once a judge is satisfied that this threshold is met, he or she must then make it clear to the jury that the issue before them is *whether the Crown has satisfied them beyond a reasonable doubt that the accused had the requisite intent*. In the case of murder the issue is whether the accused intended to kill or cause bodily harm with the foresight that the likely consequence was death. [emphasis added]

In *Lemky* (1996), a case involving a murder charge, the Supreme Court emphasized that, as with any other defence, the accused must satisfy the evidential burden *before* the defence of intoxication may be considered by the trier of fact (whether it be judge or jury). As Justice McLachlin said:

> If the real question is whether the accused was prevented by drunkenness from actually foreseeing the consequences of his or her act, it follows that the threshold for putting the defence to the jury must be evidence sufficient to permit a reasonable inference that the accused did not in fact foresee those consequences. While capacity and intent may be related, it is possible to envisage cases where evidence which falls short of establishing that the accused lacked the capacity to form intent, may still leave the jury with a reasonable doubt that, when the offence was committed, the accused in fact foresaw the likelihood of death.

The correct application of the second *Beard* Rule, following its modification by the Supreme Court in *Robinson* (1996), was well illustrated by the case of *Daley* (2007). The accused was charged with the first-degree murder of his common-law wife. After a night of drinking and partying, Daley returned home in the early hours of the morning to find that his house was locked. His neighbours heard him swearing and attempting to enter both the house and some vehicles that were parked outside. Daley's common law wife was later found stabbed to death and Daley was discovered drunk in a bedroom.

At his trial, Daley claimed that, owing to his alcohol consumption, he had no memory of what happened after he returned to the house at 5 a.m. A pharmacologist testified for the defence and described the effects of alcohol on the "human body, brain functioning and behaviour." His testimony was that one may lose one's memory and experience impaired judgment owing to the ingestion of significant amounts of alcohol, but he also said that one would "still be able to form ideas and carry out complex tasks," describing such a person as being in a state of "alcoholic amnesia." Daley was convicted by the jury of second-degree murder. His appeal against conviction was rejected by the Saskatchewan Court of Appeal and he further appealed to the Supreme Court of Canada, which, by a 5–4 majority, dismissed Daley's appeal.

The crucial question raised in the appeal to the Supreme Court was whether or not the trial judge's instructions to the jury were correct. The trial judge had made it very clear to the jury that the critical issue in the trial was whether Daley had the intent to kill the victim. He told them that:

> Intoxication that causes a person to cast off restraint and to act in a manner which he would not act if sober is no excuse for committing an offence if he had the state of mind required to commit the offence. *Murder is not committed if Wayne Joseph Daley either lacked the intent to kill or the intent to cause bodily harm knowing it was likely to cause the death* of Teanda Manchur.
>
> To prove murder, *Crown counsel must prove beyond a reasonable doubt that Wayne Daley had the intent to kill or to cause bodily harm, knowing it was likely to cause death. To decide whether he had that intent you should take into account the evidence about his consumption of alcohol along with all the rest of the evidence which throws light on his state of mind* at the time the offence was allegedly committed. [emphasis added]

Justice Bastarache found that, viewed as a whole, the trial judge's instructions to the jury were appropriate in the circumstances. The jury were clearly instructed that they must acquit Daley of murder if they had a reasonable doubt whether he actually formed the intent to kill the victim [section 229(a)(i)] or to inflict bodily harm with the foresight that the likely consequence was her death [section 229(a)(ii)]. In particular, the jury would have been very much aware that the critical issue was whether Daley's level of intoxication was so high that it prevented him from foreseeing the consequences of his actions.

Justice Bastarache rejected the suggestion that the trial judge had failed to instruct the jury as to the full implications of the expert witness's testimony. In effect, the expert witness had not clearly stated that Daley did not foresee the consequences of his actions, following his ingestion of alcohol. The expert had indicated that it is possible for an individual to lose their memory of events as a consequence of intoxication, but he also stated that one might "still be able to form ideas and carry out complex tasks." According to Justice Bastarache, "[T]he link between loss of the capacity for judgment and evaluation of appropriateness and loss of the ability to foresee the consequences of one's actions was never clearly addressed" by the expert witness:

> It is questionable whether loss of the capacity to form judgments and judge the appropriateness of one's action equates with loss of the ability to foresee the consequences of one's actions. ... [I]t is hard to accept that a person, here stabbing someone in the side, would not be able to realize such an action could kill. Expert evidence that the intoxication was such that one could not judge the appropriateness of one's actions can hardly be equated to evidence of intoxication sufficient to establish the incapacity alleged to have existed here.

Viewing the trial judge's instructions as a whole and taking a "functional approach" to the task of deciding their adequacy, Justice Bastarache concluded that they were correct and that the jury were directed to consider the appropriate issue—namely, whether Daley foresaw the consequences of his actions when he stabbed his common law wife.

APPLYING THE THIRD *BEARD* RULE

The third rule articulated by Lord Birkenhead in the *Beard* case (1920) reads as follows:

> [E]vidence of drunkenness falling short of a *proved incapacity* in the accused to *form the intent* necessary to constitute the crime, and merely establishing that his mind was affected by drink so that he more readily gave way to some violent passion, does not rebut the presumption that a man intends the natural consequences of his acts. [emphasis added]

Basically, this rule has been interpreted in modern times to mean that, if the accused cannot raise a reasonable doubt as to whether they formed the intent necessary for proof of the specific offence charged, intoxication is no defence. In particular, it is irrelevant that the accused claims that intoxication caused them to lose the power of self-control and engage in behaviour that they would not have committed had they been sober.

The original wording of the third *Beard* Rule raises many difficulties. For example, the use of the words "proved incapacity" might well suggest that the accused is under the burden of proving the defence of intoxication. In the case of *Malanik* (1952), the Supreme Court of Canada ruled that the word "proved" should be dropped from the rule and it should be made clear to the jury that the accused has to raise only a reasonable doubt in order to be successful in advancing the defence. Another difficulty stems from the use of the word "incapacity." As we saw in the previous section, the Supreme Court of Canada ruled in *Robinson* (1996) that the real question is not whether the accused had the capacity to form the specific intent in question but whether they actually formed this intent. Finally, the third *Beard* Rule contains the phrase "does not rebut the presumption that a man intends the natural consequences of his acts." This is problematic because it might suggest to a jury that they should *presume* that every sane or sober person intends the natural consequences of their actions and that there is some onus on the accused to prove that intoxication prevented them from having such an intent. In both the *Seymour* (1996) and the *Robinson* cases, the Supreme Court of Canada took great pains to counter such an interpretation of this element of the third *Beard* Rule. For example, in *Robinson*, Chief Justice Lamer stated on behalf of the Court that he wished to "take the opportunity ... to hold that the presumption of intent to which *Beard* refers, should only be interpreted and referred to as a common sense and logical inference that the jury can but is not compelled to make." Similarly, in *Seymour*, Justice Cory stated on behalf of the Court that:

> Common sense dictates that people are usually able to foresee the consequences of their actions. Therefore, if a person acts in a manner which is likely to produce a certain result it generally will be reasonable to infer that the person foresaw the probable consequences of the act. In other words, if a person acted so as to produce certain predictable consequences, it may be inferred that the person intended those consequences.

However, different considerations will apply where there is evidence that the accused was intoxicated at the time of the offence. The common-sense inference as to intention, which may be drawn from actions of the accused, is simply a method used to determine the accused's actual intent. That same common sense makes it readily apparent that evidence of intoxication will be a relevant factor in any consideration of this inference. It follows that the jury must be instructed to take into account the evidence of the accused's consumption of alcohol or drugs, along with all the other evidence that is relevant to the accused's intent, in determining whether, in all the circumstances, it would be appropriate to draw the permissible inference that the accused intended the natural consequences of his actions.

The question of the common-sense inference embedded in the third *Beard* Rule also became an issue in the *Daley* case (2007; discussed above in connection with the second *Beard* Rule). It was argued on appeal that the trial judge had not made sufficient efforts to ensure that the jury was aware that they were not *required* to draw the common-sense inference. However, Justice Bastarache, on behalf of the majority of the Supreme Court of Canada justices, rejected this assertion. He held that all a trial judge has to do, in these circumstances, is to *link the common-sense inference to the evidence of intoxication*, as required by the *Seymour* case in the passage above. Justice Bastarache took the view that it is usually valuable for a jury to receive instructions about the common-sense inference because this will assist them to understand the process by which they are to determine whether the accused person had the necessary *mens rea*. Justice Bastarache concluded his analysis of this aspect of the *Daley* case by stating that "I do not think the trial judge must take pains to tell the jury they are not bound to draw the inference where there is evidence of a significant degree of intoxication, as this is a matter of common sense." He then indicated his approval of comments made by Justice Huddart of the B.C. Court of Appeal in *Courtereille* (2001):

> [The common-sense inference] does not die with the first drink. The collective common sense and knowledge of life possessed by twelve jurors is of fundamental importance to the unique value of juries. … It is equally good sense and common experience that the effect of alcohol on thought processes is a continuum. … The more intoxicated a person becomes, the greater the likelihood that drink will result first in uninhibited conduct, and ultimately in unintended conduct. It is proper to remind the jury that they may use their common sense with respect to this, even if intoxication is advanced, provided the reminder includes the admonition that the inference is permissive and subject to a consideration of the evidence of intoxication.

The more recent case of *Waite* (2013) furnishes an example of a trial judge's jury instruction that was approved by the Alberta Court of Appeal. It illustrates the typical jury instruction that is now applicable with respect to this aspect of the third *Beard* Rule:

> You may infer, as a matter of common sense, that a person usually knows what the predictable consequences of his actions are and means to bring them about. However, you are not required to draw that inference about Mr. Waite. Indeed, you must not do so if, on the whole of the evidence, including evidence of intoxication, you have a reasonable doubt whether Mr. Waite had one of the intents required for murder. In particular, consider whether this evidence causes you to have a reasonable doubt whether Mr. Waite knew that Mr. David was likely to die. It is for you to decide.

The case of *Courville* (1982) dramatically illustrates the principle laid down in the third *Beard* Rule that if accused persons do form the necessary intent to commit a specific intent offence, they are guilty despite the fact that they were intoxicated at the time. In this particular case, the accused was charged with robbery, but he claimed that he had been suffering from delusions induced by the consumption of drugs and alcohol. The gist of the defence was that the accused's conduct had been caused by "a loss of self-control or an irresistible impulse" that resulted from his state of intoxication. However, the evidence indicated that the accused was fully aware of what he was doing and had formed the specific intent necessary for proof of the crime of robbery. In these circumstances, the Ontario Court of Appeal ruled that Courville should be convicted of robbery despite his intoxication. The Supreme Court subsequently affirmed this decision in *Courville* (1985). The Supreme Court briefly stated that "Loss of self-control or irresistible impulse caused by voluntarily induced intoxication is not a defence to a criminal charge in Canada."

THE DECISION OF THE SUPREME COURT OF CANADA IN THE *DAVIAULT* CASE (1994)

Before 1994, the orthodox approach to intoxication in Canadian courts was to automatically deny the benefit of the defence to *every* defendant charged with a crime of general (or basic) intent. However, in the *Daviault* case (1994), the Supreme Court decisively rejected this approach.

Daviault was charged with the sexual assault of a 65-year-old woman who was partially paralyzed and used a wheelchair. Daviault had apparently consumed some seven or eight beers during the day and then some 35 ounces of brandy on the evening of the alleged assault. He claimed that he did not remember anything between the time that he had a glass of brandy and the point where he woke up nude in the complainant's bed. In other words, he asserted that he had no recollection whatsoever of the events that constituted the alleged assault.

A pharmacologist, appearing on behalf of the defence, stated that if Daviault had in fact consumed the amount of alcohol that he claimed, his blood alcohol level would have been in the region of 400 to 600 milligrams of alcohol per 100 millilitres of blood. In a normal person, this would cause death or coma. However, since Daviault was an alcoholic, he was less susceptible to the effect of alcohol and, in his case, this level of alcohol in the blood might cause him to suffer a "blackout" in which he might enter into a state of dissociation; in such a condition, he would have no awareness of what he was doing and, therefore, would have no memory of the events that occurred.

The trial judge acquitted the accused on the basis that there was a reasonable doubt as to whether he possessed the minimal intent necessary for conviction of the offence of sexual assault. However, the Quebec Court of Appeal substituted a conviction because, in its view, the trial judge had made a fundamental error in holding that intoxication can be a defence to a charge of a general intent offence such as sexual assault. In other words, the Quebec Court of Appeal reasserted the orthodox interpretation of the *Beard* Rules. However, Daviault appealed to the Supreme Court of Canada, claiming that this interpretation of the *Beard* Rules violated his rights under sections 7 and 11(d) of the *Charter*. The Supreme Court agreed and ordered a new trial.

Justice Cory indicated that the distinction between crimes of *specific and general intent* was so deeply entrenched in the fabric of Canadian criminal law that there was no question of abolishing it at this stage of our legal history. However, Justice Cory held that this did not mean that Canadian courts should continue to exclude the possibility of raising the defence of intoxication in cases involving charges of general (or basic) intent crimes; indeed, it was his view, shared by the majority of the Court, that, in certain circumstances, the *Charter* dictates that the accused should have the benefit of the defence of intoxication in relation to crimes of general intent. In essence, the majority of the Court adopted the view that a defence should be available to a person accused of an offence of general intent if, owing to an *extreme degree of intoxication*, they were in a "state akin to automatism or insanity."

Justice Cory ruled that the principle that intoxication can never be a defence to a charge of a crime of *general intent* violated both the principles of fundamental justice guaranteed by section 7 and the presumption of innocence enshrined in section 11(d) of the *Charter*. Indeed, he said that:

> The mental aspect of an offence, or *mens rea*, has long been recognized as an integral part of crime. The concept is fundamental to our criminal law. The element may be minimal in general intent offences; none the less, it exists. In this case, the requisite mental element is simply an intention to commit the sexual assault, or recklessness as to whether the actions constitute an assault. The necessary mental element can ordinarily be inferred from the proof that the assault was committed by the accused. However, the substituted *mens rea* of an intention to become drunk cannot establish the *mens rea* to commit the assault.

Justice Cory rejected the view advanced by many Canadian judges that the voluntary consumption of alcohol is sufficient to constitute the *mens rea* necessary for conviction of the offence of sexual assault. The intent to become intoxicated cannot be substituted for the *mens rea* that the Crown must prove in

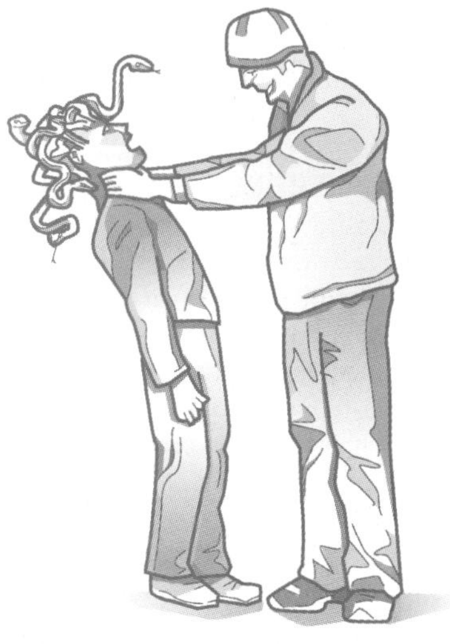

Illustration by Greg Holoboff

The Daviault case: Extreme intoxication that produces a state akin to mental disorder or automatism should lead to an absolute acquittal.

relation to a charge of sexual assault. The so-called "substituted *mens rea*" rule effectively eliminates the minimal mental element required for proof of sexual assault and, in the view of Justice Cory, "*[M]ens rea* for a crime is so well recognized that to eliminate that mental element, an integral part of the crime, would be to deprive an accused of fundamental justice."

On behalf of the majority of the Supreme Court, Justice Cory also ruled that the traditional *Beard* Rules infringed section 11(d) of the *Charter* because, under their provisions, it would be possible to convict an accused person of an offence even if there was a reasonable doubt as to one of the essential elements of the offence:

> For example, an accused in an extreme state of intoxication akin to automatism or mental illness would have to be found guilty although there was a reasonable doubt as to the voluntary nature of the act committed by the accused. ... In my view, the mental element of voluntariness is a fundamental aspect of the crime which cannot be taken away by a judicially developed policy. ...
>
> The presumption of innocence requires that the Crown bear the burden of establishing all elements of a crime. These elements include the mental element of voluntariness.

Justice Cory also rejected the argument that the *Charter* is not violated by the traditional *Beard* Rules because the accused's voluntary decision to become intoxicated renders them "blameworthy." He stated that:

> Voluntary intoxication is not yet a crime. Further, it is difficult to conclude that such behaviour should always constitute a fault to which criminal sanctions should apply. However, assuming that voluntary intoxication is reprehensible, it does not follow that its consequences in any given situation are either voluntary or predictable. Studies demonstrate that the consumption of alcohol is not the cause of the crime. A person intending to drink cannot be said to be intending to commit a sexual assault.

Having ruled that the defence of intoxication should be available to those who are charged with a crime of general intent, the Supreme Court of Canada made it clear in the *Daviault* case that it would be only in very rare and limited circumstances that such a defence would ever be successful. Why did the Court think that this would be the case? According to Justice Cory:

> It must be remembered that those who are a "little" drunk can readily form the requisite mental element to commit the offence. The alcohol-induced relaxation of both inhibitions and socially acceptable behaviour has never been accepted as a factor or excuse in determining whether the accused possessed the requisite *mens rea*. Given the minimal nature of the mental element required for crimes of general intent, even those who are significantly drunk will usually be able to form the requisite *mens rea* and will be found to have acted voluntarily. In reality it is only those who can demonstrate that they were in such an extreme degree of intoxication that they were in a state akin to automatism or insanity that might expect to raise a reasonable doubt as to their ability to form the minimal mental element required for a general intent offence. Neither an insane person nor one in a state of automatism is capable of forming the minimal intent required for proof of a general intent offence. Similarly, as the words themselves imply, "drunkenness akin to insanity or automatism" describes a person so severely intoxicated that he is incapable of forming even the minimal intent required of a general intent offence. The phrase refers to a person so drunk that he is an automaton. As such he may be capable of voluntary acts such as moving his arms and legs but is quite incapable of forming the most basic or simple intent required to perform the act prohibited by a general intent offence.

In addition, the defence recognized in *Daviault* would be extremely difficult to establish in practice because the Supreme Court of Canada placed the primary (or persuasional) burden of proof on the shoulders of the accused. It is not enough, said Justice Cory, for the accused to raise a reasonable doubt as to whether they had the minimal intent required for proof of the general intent offence charged. Instead, the accused must establish *on the balance of probabilities* that they were in a state of extreme intoxication akin to automatism or insanity. No doubt the Supreme Court took this extraordinary step to ensure that the defence of intoxication would not be abused.

After the *Daviault* case, the *Beard* Rules undoubtedly survived, but the second rule was considerably modified by the principle that the defence of intoxication should now be available, in very rare and limited circumstances, to a defendant charged with a crime of general (or basic) intent. Essentially, after *Daviault*, the defence of intoxication will not be available to most defendants charged with a general intent crime because their state of intoxication would not be sufficiently serious to prevent them from forming the minimal intent required for proof of such offences. However, where the intoxication is so extreme as to produce a state akin to automatism or insanity, the accused will be entitled to an acquittal, provided they prove the requirements of the defence on the balance of probabilities.

The Enactment of Section 33.1 of the *Criminal Code* and Its Aftermath

Although the majority of the justices of the Supreme Court apparently took considerable care in *Daviault* (1994) to indicate that it would be in only the rarest of cases that a defendant would be able to escape criminal liability for the commission of general intent offences such as sexual assault, their decision was subjected to a considerable degree of popular criticism. Much of this criticism stemmed from a deep-seated concern for the plight of sexual assault victims and a belief that the *Daviault* defence would permit violent men to avoid taking responsibility for sexual assaults that they committed while intoxicated.

In response to the robust criticism of the *Daviault* decision, Parliament amended the *Criminal Code* by adding a new section dealing explicitly with the issue of intoxication as a defence to a charge of a general intent offence.[5] Section 33.1, which came into effect in 1996, provides the following:

> (1) It is not a defence to an offence referred to in subsection (3) that the accused, by reason of self-induced intoxication, lacked the general intent or the voluntariness required to commit the offence, where the accused departed markedly from the standard of care as described in subsection (2).
>
> (2) For the purposes of this section, a person markedly departs from the standard of reasonable care generally recognized in Canadian society and is thereby criminally at fault where the person, while in a state of self-induced intoxication that renders the person unaware of, or incapable of consciously controlling, their behaviour, voluntarily or involuntarily interferes or threatens to interfere with the bodily integrity of another person.
>
> (3) This section applies in respect of an offence under this Act or any other Act of Parliament that includes as an element an assault or any other interference or threat of interference by a person with the bodily integrity of another person.

In *Bouchard-Lebrun* (2011), the Supreme Court of Canada briefly summarized the circumstances in which section 33.1 would be applicable:

> This provision applies where three conditions are met: (1) the accused was intoxicated at the material time; (2) the intoxication was self-induced; and (3) the accused departed from the standard of reasonable care generally recognized in Canadian society by interfering or threatening to interfere with the bodily integrity of another. ... Where these three things are proved, it is not a defence that the accused lacked the general intent or the voluntariness required to commit the offence.

Section 33.1 does not purport to be a comprehensive statutory treatment of the defence of intoxication. In fact, it deals only with *those offences of general intent that involve an element of assault or interference (or threat of interference) with the bodily integrity of another person.* This means that section 33.1 does not apply to those *general (or basic) intent* offences that do not involve violence or the threat of violence. For example, mischief (damage to property) under section 430(1) of the *Criminal Code* clearly falls outside the ambit of section 33.1 and will still be governed by the Supreme Court's decision in *Daviault* (1994). It is also particularly significant that Parliament did not address the issue of the intoxication defence in relation to *specific intent* offences, and it is clear that, for these offences, the courts will continue to apply the *Beard* Rules.

It should be emphasized that section 33.1 applies to only *self-induced* intoxication. As we saw in Chapter 8, an accused person who becomes intoxicated *involuntarily* is entitled to an absolute acquittal if they act involuntarily in a state of automatism. It will no doubt be remembered that, in *Chaulk* (2007), the suggested criteria for finding that intoxication was self-induced were set out as follows:

- the accused voluntarily consumed a substance which
- she or he knew or ought to have known was an intoxicant and
- the risk of becoming intoxicated was or should have been within her or his contemplation.

Section 33.1 can essentially be viewed as a direct move by Parliament to overturn the Supreme Court's ruling in the *Daviault* case (1994) in those circumstances where the charge against the accused involves an offence *against the person* as opposed to an offence *against property*. However, the enactment of section 33.1 has, unfortunately, caused the law concerning intoxication to become undesirably complex. The present state of the law would appear to be as follows:

1. For crimes of *specific intent*, the second and third *Beard* Rules will continue to apply, and intoxication may be used as a defence where it prevents the accused from forming the *specific intent* that

5. S.C. 1995, c. 32.

must be established by the Crown (e.g., intent to kill, intent to steal).

2. For crimes of *general (or basic) intent*, the situation is somewhat more complicated:

   (a) where the offence involves an element of assault or any other interference or threat of interference with the bodily integrity of a person (e.g., assault, manslaughter, sexual assault), self-induced intoxication can never be a valid defence no matter how severe it may have been at the time (section 33.1);

   (b) where the offence does not involve an element of assault or any other interference or threat of interference with the bodily

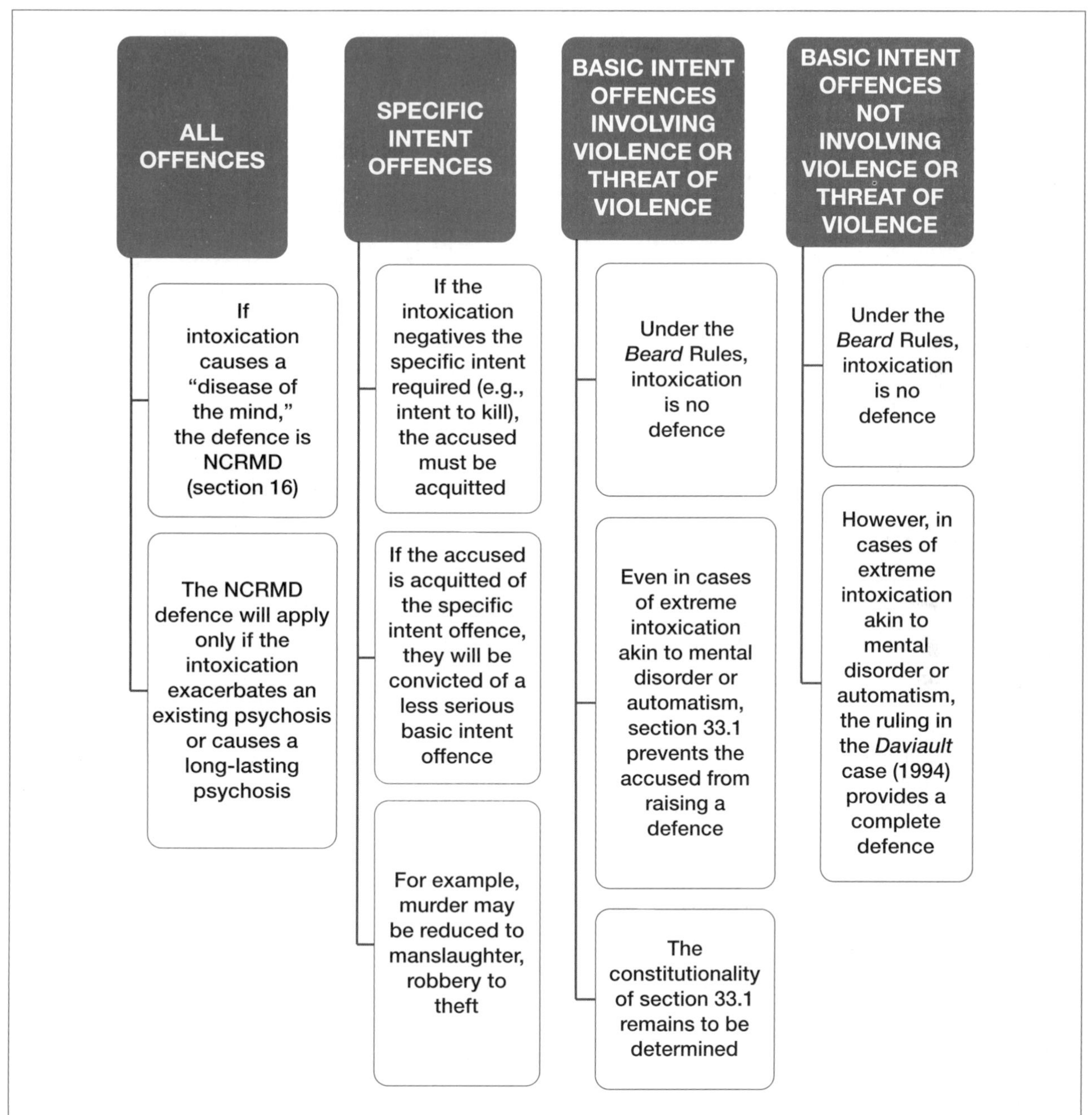

Figure 10-4

An Overview of the Present Law Relating to Intoxication

integrity of a person (e.g., damage to property), then, in those very *exceptional* cases where the intoxication is so extreme as to produce a state akin to automatism or insanity, the accused will have the benefit of an absolute defence (as required by the Supreme Court's ruling in *Daviault*).

A further difficulty with this statement of the existing law is that there are serious questions as to whether section 33.1 is valid under the *Charter*. It could well be argued that section 33.1 flatly contradicts the Supreme Court's unequivocal view, expressed in *Daviault*, that it is a violation of sections 7 and 11(d) of the *Charter* to convict a person who lacks even a minimal degree of *mens rea* at the time that they commit a general intent offence, such as sexual assault. However, it could also be asserted that, even if section 33.1 does infringe an accused person's *Charter* rights, it should nevertheless be declared valid because it constitutes a reasonable limitation that is, in the words of section 1 of the *Charter*, "demonstrably justified in a free and democratic society."

However, even though section 33.1 was enacted as long ago as 1995, no appellate court has yet been called upon to address the constitutionality of section 33.1. In *Daley* (2007), the Supreme Court of Canada referred to section 33.1, but it did not make any comment concerning the question of its constitutionality. In *Bouchard-Lebrun* (2011), the Supreme Court did not refer to the constitutionality of section 33.1 and duly applied the provision to convict the accused of aggravated assault and assault (basic intent offences) even though he was in a substance-induced psychotic state at the time he committed the offences. Indeed, the Court said:

> The self-induced intoxication to which s. 33.1 *Cr. C.* refers is limited in time. It corresponds to the period during which the substance consumed by the accused produced its effects. Section 33.1(2) *Cr. C.* leaves no doubt about this. It provides that a person "is ... criminally at fault where the person, *while in a state of self-induced intoxication that renders the person* unaware of, or *incapable* of consciously controlling, their behaviour, voluntarily or involuntarily interferes or threatens to interfere with the bodily integrity of another person." Section 33.1 *Cr. C.* is intended to prevent an accused from avoiding criminal liability on the ground that his or her state of intoxication at the material time *rendered the accused incapable* of forming the mental element or having the voluntariness required to commit the offence. [emphasis in the original]

The fact that section 33.1 has not been challenged in an appellate court in the 20 years since its enactment would appear to suggest that defence counsel do not consider that a *Charter* challenge is likely to be successful and have, therefore, refrained from launching a constitutional assault on the provision. In theory, the constitutionality of section 33.1 will remain an unresolved issue until the Supreme Court of Canada makes a definitive ruling. In practice, however, the assumption appears to be that a *Charter* challenge would fail, primarily because it is likely that any infringement of sections 7 and 11(d) would be justified under section 1.[6]

6. The Act that added s. 33.1 to the *Criminal Code* contained a lengthy preamble which contained numerous reasons for denying the defence of extreme intoxication with respect to offences involving an "element of assault or any other interference or threat of interference with the bodily integrity of another person." See *An Act to amend the Criminal Code (self-induced intoxication)*, S.C. 1995, c. 32. The use of s. 1 to justify infringements of s. 7 and 11(d) of the *Charter* is illustrated by trial decisions such as *R. v. Vickburg* (1998) in the B.C. Supreme Court; *R. v. Dow* (2010) in the Quebec Superior Court; and *R. v. Chan* (2018) in the Ontario Superior Court of Justice.

Study Questions

1. Pompey meets his friend Elbow in a bar. They start arguing about a sum of money that Elbow owes Pompey. Suddenly, Pompey loses his temper and shouts at the top of his voice, "You're nothing but a slimy jailbird!" Pompey then starts to shake Elbow by the lapels on Pompey's jacket. In response to Pompey's behaviour, Elbow rushes out of the bar and goes to his home, which is just a few blocks away. He retrieves a kitchen knife from his home and returns to the bar, where he stabs Pompey to death. Elbow

had once been incarcerated in a federal correctional institution, but since his release 10 years ago, he has kept out of trouble with the law. With the exception of his wife and Pompey, no one in the local community knew that Elbow had once been an inmate of a prison. Does Elbow have a defence to a charge of murder?

2. Rosaline is married to Moth, but she is having an affair with Costard, Moth's best friend. When Moth discovers the affair, he threatens Rosaline, who decides to leave him. About one month after Rosaline moves out, she and Costard are having a drink together in a public bar. Moth walks in and sees Rosaline and Costard. Moth tells Rosaline that she is a "faithless whore." Costard responds by telling Moth that Rosaline left him (Moth) because he was a "lousy lover" and he roughly shoves Moth in an openly contemptuous manner. Moth then takes out a knife and stabs Costard to death. At his trial for murder, Moth asserts the defence of provocation. Is it likely that this defence would be successful?
3. Winkel is intoxicated and brutally assaults his best friend, Snodgrass. Winkel then steals Snodgrass's cell phone. Winkel is charged with robbery. To what extent, if any, is Winkel's intoxication a defence to the charge of robbery and any other offence that might be included in that charge?
4. Dracula takes a heavy dose of crystal meth (crystal methamphetamine) and becomes extremely violent. He kills his friend Frankenstein. Dracula is charged with second-degree murder, but he claims that he cannot remember anything about the incident. Does Dracula have a defence to the charge laid against him?
5. Cheeryble is in the habit of simultaneously consuming both alcohol and (illicitly obtained) amphetamine drugs. One night, he smashes his way through a window in the living room of Betsey, an elderly woman. When Betsey comes to investigate the noise, she discovers Cheeryble standing in the middle of the room with a large stick in his hand. Cheeryble moves toward Betsey, who is terrified by this encounter and utters a piercing scream. Cheeryble hops out the window and walks slowly down the street. Betsey calls the police, who have no difficulty in arresting Cheeryble on a neighbouring street corner. The Crown wishes to charge Cheeryble with breaking and entering, mischief (damaging property), and assault with a weapon. Cheeryble states that he has absolutely no memory of what happened at Betsey's residence. He states that his last memory was of being in a bar. A blood test reveals that Cheeryble has extraordinarily high levels of alcohol and amphetamines in his bloodstream. Does Cheeryble have any viable defence(s) to the potential charges that might be laid against him?
6. Bagstock has suffered from schizoaffective disorder for almost a decade and has been hospitalized on a number of occasions. He is living in the community and appears to be coping fairly well with his mental health challenges. One night, however, he goes to a bar and a known dealer in illegal drugs offers him some brightly coloured pills. Bagstock immediately ingests a couple of them along with alcohol. The pills contain MDMA (commonly known as ecstasy) and Bagstock rapidly starts to behave in a bizarre manner. He attacks Tapley, the bar owner, with a broken bottle. Bagstock shouts loudly that Tapley is the Devil, who must be "wiped out." Tapley is badly bruised and cut all over his head, and his injuries are life threatening. Fortunately, Tapley survives, but will need many months of intensive rehabilitation. Bagstock is charged with aggravated assault and attempted murder. Bagstock's lawyer asserts that her client was in a psychotic state caused by the MDMA pills and that he was completely divorced from reality at the time of the attack. Both the Crown and defence expert witnesses agree that Bagstock was in a psychotic state and was not capable of knowing that he was doing something that would be considered wrong by ordinary Canadians. What defences (if any) would be available to Bagstock? Which defence, if any, would likely be successful at his trial?

CHAPTER 11

NECESSITY AND DURESS:

Two Excuses Recognized by the Courts as Defences to a Criminal Charge

Learning Objectives

After reading this chapter, you will be able to understand:

- the basic elements of the defences of necessity and duress, which are considered to be *excuses* rather than justifications and are based on the principle of *moral or normative involuntariness*;
- that the common-law defence of necessity requires that the accused demonstrate that the "evil" to be avoided must be greater than the harm caused by the commission of the offence charged; there must be a clear and imminent peril; and there is no reasonable legal alternative;
- that the defence of duress may constitute an excuse where the accused person is forced to commit a crime because their free will is overborne by threats of violence emanating from another person or other persons;
- that the statutory defence of duress, defined by section 17 of the *Criminal Code*, applies only to the person who actually commits the offence while the common-law defence of duress applies to other parties to the offence (e.g., aiders and/or abettors);
- that the Supreme Court of Canada has declared a significant part of section 17 of the *Criminal Code* to be invalid so that the defence of duress, as it applies to persons who actually commit an offence, is an amalgamation of the common law and statutory defences.

THE DEFENCE OF NECESSITY

THE GENERAL PRINCIPLES

The defence of **necessity** arises where the accused can avoid some disaster or calamity only by breaking the law. In advancing the defence of necessity, the accused is basically asserting that the evil that they sought to avoid was greater than the evil inherent in breaking the law. In essence, the accused person asserts that they should be excused from criminal responsibility because the decision to break the law was dictated by necessity and was, therefore, not a free choice. The defence of necessity is not mentioned in the *Criminal Code*. However, as a common law defence, it has been preserved by section 8(3) of the *Code*.

THE RATIONALE FOR THE DEFENCE OF NECESSITY

In the Supreme Court of Canada's decision in *Perka* (1984), Justice Dickson drew a sharp distinction between "justifications" and "excuses." He considered that the defence of necessity constitutes an "excuse" rather than a "justification." Justice Dickson noted that a justification "challenges the wrongfulness of an action which technically constitutes a crime." For example, the police officer who shoots a hostage taker to save the life of an innocent victim is considered to have been fully justified in having used lethal force in these particular circumstances. On the other hand, according to Justice Dickson, an excuse "concedes the wrongfulness of the action but asserts that the circumstances under which it was done are such that it ought not to be attributed to the actor."

In *Ryan* (2013), the Supreme Court of Canada compared both the defences of necessity and duress with self-defence in order to elucidate the distinction between an excuse and a justification:

> Despite its close links to necessity and duress, self-defence, on the other hand, is a justification. ... It "challenges the wrongfulness of an action which technically constitutes a crime." ... In determining whether the defence is available, less emphasis is placed on the particular circumstances and concessions to human frailty and more importance is attached to the action itself and the reason why the accused was justified in meeting force with force. ... [W]hile in a case of duress we excuse an act that we still consider to be wrong, the impugned act in a case of self-defence is considered right.

In *Perka* (1984), Justice Dickson expressed the view that a valid claim of necessity should serve to "excuse" an accused person from responsibility on the basis that they *acted "involuntarily" from a "moral or normative" point of view*:

> The lost Alpinist who, on the point of freezing to death, breaks open an isolated mountain cabin is not literally behaving in an involuntary fashion. He has control over his actions to the extent of being physically capable of abstaining from the act. Realistically, however, his act is not a "voluntary" one. His "choice" to break the law is no true choice at all; it is remorselessly compelled by normal human instincts.

Clearly, the availability of the defence of necessity reflects the willingness of the courts to recognize that it would not be just to punish individuals who, when faced with a dire emergency, chose to break the law rather than risk their own lives or the lives or safety of others: such a choice must be treated as being *involuntary*. According to Justice Dickson, a humane system of criminal law must be based on a "realistic assessment of human weakness" and should not punish those individuals who do not act voluntarily in the fullest sense of that word.

APPLYING THE DEFENCE OF NECESSITY IN RELATION TO LESS SERIOUS CRIMINAL OFFENCES

The assertion of a defence of necessity in a situation where the accused has been charged with the

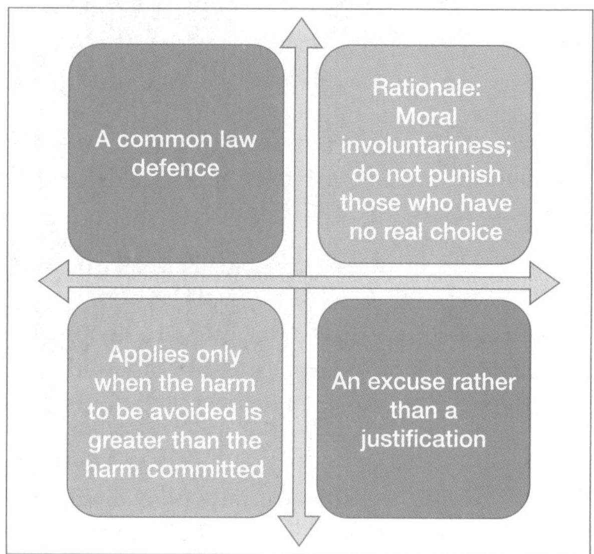

Figure 11-1

The Legal Nature of the Defence of Necessity

commission of a "less serious" offence generally does not create any formidable policy difficulties for the courts. Indeed, there have been a number of cases involving the alleged commission of various traffic offences in which the courts have been prepared to apply the defence of necessity. For example, in *Fry* (1977), the accused was acquitted of a charge of dangerous driving as the consequence of a successful assertion of the defence of necessity. The accused had been clocked at 117 kilometres per hour in a 50 kilometres-an-hour zone in Regina, Saskatchewan. The accused claimed that he had been forced to travel at this speed because the vehicle behind him was tailgating at close quarters. According to the accused, the faster he went, the faster the vehicle behind him went. Judge Boyce acquitted the accused at his trial and stated that:

> [C]ertainly, the accused here endangered the public but I do realize an extremity of circumstance can arise where a choice is made, that is, forced to be made. For example, as I mentioned possibly occurred here, to flee by speed an actual present danger thrust upon him, or to suffer its continuance with its fearsome potential. The way ahead was clear, in fact while I do not commend his judgment, his choice to my mind was not criminal. *He substituted a constructive danger to the public in place of the actual present danger to himself.* [emphasis added]

APPLYING THE DEFENCE OF NECESSITY IN RELATION TO MORE SERIOUS CRIMINAL OFFENCES

When the defence of necessity is raised in relation to "more serious" offences, such as murder, the courts are immediately faced with policy questions of extraordinary difficulty. Indeed, the courts have been extremely reluctant to permit the assertion of such a defence in relation to the most serious criminal offences.

A classic illustration of the traditional reluctance of the courts to recognize the defence of necessity in such circumstances is the somewhat macabre English case of *Dudley and Stephens* (1884). The accused were charged with the murder of a young cabin boy after they had been shipwrecked and were drifting without food or water on the open sea and without any apparent hope of immediate rescue. The defendants had killed the boy and then proceeded to eat his flesh and drink his blood. Had they not done so, it is highly unlikely that they would have survived long enough to be rescued by a passing ship. The defendants' defence of necessity was rejected by the English court. Although the court indicated that it sympathized with the horrific situation in which the defendants found themselves, it was not prepared to acquit the accused on the basis of necessity. One of the major policy considerations that apparently influenced the court was the belief that the recognition of a defence of necessity in such circumstances would open the floodgates to wholesale misuse of the defence by unscrupulous criminals. In the words of Lord Chief Justice Coleridge:

> Who is to be the judge of this sort of necessity? By what measure is the comparative value of lives to be measured? Is it to be strength, or intellect, or what? It is plain that the principle leaves to him who is to profit by it to determine the necessity which would justify him in deliberately taking another's life to save his own. In this case the weakest, the youngest, the most unresisting, was chosen. Was it more necessary to kill him than one of the grown men? The answer must be "No."

Although the court sentenced the accused to death, it clearly anticipated that this sentence would never be carried out. In fact, the sentence was later commuted to six months' imprisonment with hard labour. The court appeared to believe that, in cases such as *Dudley and Stephens*, the firm letter of the law should be upheld but that it was the prerogative of the Queen to grant mercy. Lord Coleridge noted, in this respect:

> There is no safe path for judges to tread but to ascertain the law to the best of their ability and to declare it according to their judgments; and if in any case the law appears to be too severe on individuals, to leave it to the Sovereign to exercise that prerogative of mercy which the Constitution has entrusted to the hands fittest to dispense it.

In Canada, the basis of the modern judicial approach to the defence of necessity in the context of a serious criminal charge is the decision of the Supreme Court of Canada in *Perka* (1984).

THE *PERKA* CASE: THE FOUNDATION OF THE MODERN CANADIAN DEFENCE OF NECESSITY

In the case of *Perka* (1984), the Supreme Court of Canada clearly recognized the existence of a common law defence of necessity—even in relation to serious criminal charges—but it placed very strict limits on the scope of the defence. In *Perka*, the accused were charged with importing and possession of narcotics for the purpose of trafficking. They had been arrested in Canadian waters in possession of a large quantity of cannabis. The accused asserted the defence of necessity, claiming that the load of drugs was originally supposed to have been unloaded in international waters off the coast of Alaska (in other words, the drugs were never intended for delivery in Canada). However, the accused contended that their vessel encountered a number of serious mechanical problems as well as poor weather and that, for the safety of the crew, they were obliged to enter Canadian waters to seek refuge and make repairs. According to the accused, the vessel ran aground in a cove on the west coast of Vancouver Island and started to list; at this point, it was decided to start unloading the cannabis to prevent the vessel from capsizing. However, the police arrived, arrested the accused, and recovered 34 tons of cannabis. The trial judge put the defence of necessity to the jury, who acquitted the accused. However, the British Columbia Court of Appeal allowed the Crown's appeal and ordered a new trial. The Supreme Court affirmed this ruling.

In the Supreme Court, Justice Dickson conducted an exhaustive examination of the nature and scope of the defence of necessity. He expressed his belief that the true rationale for the defence was based on the need to recognize that it is inappropriate to punish actions that are "*normatively involuntary*." In the light of **normative involuntariness**, only those actions that can genuinely be regarded as being involuntary are entitled to the benefit of the "excuse" of necessity. Justice Dickson emphasized that the application of the defence of necessity should be restricted to those cases where the accused has broken the law in "situations of clear and imminent peril when compliance with the law is demonstrably impossible." Only in these types of situations can the accused be considered to be acting involuntarily. He went on to say that "[A]t a minimum, the situation must be so emergent and the peril must be so pressing that normal human instincts cry out for action and make a counsel of patience unreasonable."

For Justice Dickson, one of the most important factors in weighing the validity of a claim of necessity is the question of whether the accused had any *reasonable legal alternative to breaking the law*:

> The question to be asked is whether the agent had any real choice: could he have done otherwise? If there is a reasonable legal alternative to disobeying the law, then the decision to disobey becomes a voluntary one, impelled by some consideration beyond the dictates of "necessity" and human instincts.

Finally, Justice Dickson emphasized that a defendant claiming the defence of necessity should be able to show that there was some degree of "proportionality" between the offence committed and the evil that it was designed to avoid:

> No rational criminal justice system, no matter how humane or liberal, could excuse the infliction of a greater harm to allow the actor to avert a lesser evil. In such circumstances we expect the individual to bear the harm and refrain from acting illegally. If he cannot control himself we will not excuse him.

In the *Perka* case, a new trial was ordered because the original trial judge had not directed the jury's attention to the question of whether any reasonable legal alternatives had been available to the accused.

Illustration by Greg Holoboff

The Perka Case and the availability of a reasonable legal alternative.

In the view of Justice Dickson, the trial judge had incorrectly left the jury with the impression that the only real issue was whether the accused had acted reasonably in heading for the shoreline, together with the cargo of drugs, rather than "facing death at sea." In Justice Dickson's view, this approach did not deal with the critical issue of "whether there existed any other reasonable responses to the peril that were not illegal." For example, a critical question in this respect would be whether the accused should have jettisoned the drugs before entering Canadian waters. Should this drastic course of action be considered a reasonable legal alternative to breaking the law? After all, with the drugs thrown overboard, the accused would have been able to enter Canadian waters without committing a criminal offence.

The question of the availability of reasonable legal alternatives was a pivotal one in *Perka*, but was also central to the decision of the Ontario Court of Appeal in the case of *Carson* (2004). The accused and the complainant, who were both police officers, were engaged to be married and were living together in the complainant's house. Following an altercation, Carson picked up the complainant and carried her to her bedroom. According to Carson, he put the complainant on the bed and, since she was trying to fight him, "he held her down on the bed, lying on top of her, to calm her down and to keep her from hitting him." Carson claimed that he took this action because he was concerned that the complainant would injure herself should she continue to bang her head against the wall. Carson was convicted of assault and appealed to the Ontario Court of Appeal. He asserted that the trial judge had been wrong to reject the defence of necessity. However, the Court of Appeal dismissed the appeal. The Court stated that the defence of necessity was not available to the accused because he had other legal options available to him to ensure the complainant's safety:

> In this case, although the appellant may honestly have believed that he faced a situation of imminent peril, he did not testify that he believed he had no legal alternative open to him. Having regard to the objective component of the test, alternatives were open to the appellant: for example, he could simply have backed away from the complainant and waited to see if she stopped banging her head; alternatively, he could have attempted to place something behind the complainant's head to cushion the blows. Thus, even if the trial judge misapprehended the evidence with respect to the first element relating to the defence of necessity, a requisite component of the defence was not made out.

On the other hand, in *Primus* (2010), the accused was convicted at trial of dangerous driving causing death. Primus claimed that he was driving at high speed to escape shots that were being fired at him from another vehicle containing individuals who had threatened him and made an attempt on his life in the past. In the course of the high-speed chase, Primus's car crashed and his passenger, who was impaled on a fence, died. The Quebec Court of Appeal, applying the criteria set out in the *Perka* case, entered an acquittal because the Crown had not proved beyond a reasonable doubt that Primus was not entitled to the defence of necessity. In particular, there was certainly a reasonable doubt whether a reasonable person in Primus's situation would have found a legal alternative to fleeing at high speed. After all, if Primus had stopped (the only alternative open to him), he and his passenger would almost certainly have been killed.

THE CASE OF ROBERT LATIMER

In *Latimer* (2001), the Supreme Court of Canada further refined the law concerning the necessity defence and did so within the controversial context of a so-called "mercy killing." The facts of the case were undoubtedly tragic. Robert Latimer was charged with the first-degree murder of his 12-year-old daughter, Tracy, whom he had killed by carbon monoxide poisoning. Tracy suffered from severe cerebral palsy and was a quadriplegic. Her disabilities were so severe that she had been bedridden for most of her life. She was described as having the mental capacity of a four-month-old infant and was totally dependent on others for her care. Tracy endured five or six seizures every day, and it was believed that she experienced a considerable degree of pain. Tracy was being spoon-fed and was losing weight because of a lack of essential nutrients. The option of inserting a feeding tube into the stomach had been presented to Tracy's parents. This device would have enhanced the process of providing nutrition and might have permitted more effective pain control. However, this option was rejected by the parents. Tracy had undergone surgery to correct some of her physical problems, but complications had developed that caused her considerable pain and further surgery was planned. However, Latimer had indicated that he regarded such surgical intervention as a form of mutilation. One month before this additional surgery was to occur, Tracy died. Just prior to her death, her father had declined an opportunity to place Tracy in a group home.

The circumstances of Tracy's death were that her father placed her in his pickup truck and inserted into the cab a hose that was connected to the exhaust pipe. Tracy succumbed to carbon monoxide poisoning. At first, Latimer asserted that she had died naturally in her sleep; however, he subsequently admitted to having killed her. Latimer was convicted of second-degree murder, but the Supreme Court ultimately ordered a new trial because of certain irregularities in the conduct of Crown counsel prior to the trial. When Latimer was retried, his counsel tried to raise the defence of necessity, but the trial judge refused to place this defence before the jury because there was no air of reality to the defence:

> What Mr. Latimer saw as a situation that left him no other alternative but to end Tracy's life to alleviate her pain did not create a necessitous situation that the law defines as necessary to advance this defence for this particular crime. *There is no evidence that he had to do what he did to avoid a direct and immediate peril, or that there was no other reasonable course of action open to him.* [emphasis added]

The Supreme Court of Canada unanimously affirmed the decision of the trial judge to refuse to permit the jury to consider the defence of necessity. In its judgment, the Court referred to the decision in the *Perka* case (1984) and reaffirmed Justice Dickson's view that necessity may be raised as a defence only where there was genuine "involuntariness" on the part of the accused. The Court also agreed with Justice Dickson's ruling that the defence of necessity must be "strictly controlled and scrupulously limited" because there is a very real risk that this defence could become "a mask for anarchy."

In its ruling in *Latimer*, the Supreme Court of Canada stated that:

> *Perka* outlined three elements that must be present for the defence of necessity. First, there is the requirement of imminent peril or danger. Second, the accused must have had no reasonable legal alternative to the course of action he or she undertook. Third, there must be proportionality between the harm inflicted and the harm avoided.

It is significant that the Supreme Court held that it is not sufficient for the accused person to assert that they subjectively believed that there was an "imminent peril" and that there was "no reasonable legal alternative." Applying the so-called "modified objective test," the Supreme Court stated that the defence of necessity is available only where the accused person's beliefs are reasonable in light of the particular circumstances facing the accused person and their perception of those circumstances:

> The accused person must, at the time of the act, honestly believe, on reasonable grounds, that he faces a situation of imminent peril that leaves no reasonable legal alternative open. There must be a reasonable basis for the accused's beliefs and actions, but it would be proper to take into account circumstances that legitimately affect the accused person's ability to evaluate his situation. The test cannot be a subjective one, and the accused who argues that he perceived imminent peril without an alternative would only succeed with the defence of necessity if his belief was reasonable given his circumstances and attributes.

However, the Supreme Court stated that the test for the third element, proportionality, is purely objective in nature:

> The third requirement for the defence of necessity, proportionality, must be measured on an objective standard, as it would violate fundamental principles of the criminal law to do otherwise. Evaluating the nature of an act is fundamentally a determination reflecting society's values as to what is appropriate and what represents a transgression. ...

The Supreme Court took the view that it was necessary to adopt a purely objective standard of proportionality because a subjective approach to assessing the competing harms involved would, by definition, focus on the accused person's own appraisal of the situation and such a person is usually concerned with avoiding harm to themselves. An objective standard, on the other hand, would take into account both community standards and constitutional imperatives (such as in the *Latimer* case, the section 15(1) *Charter* equality rights of a disabled person such as Tracy).

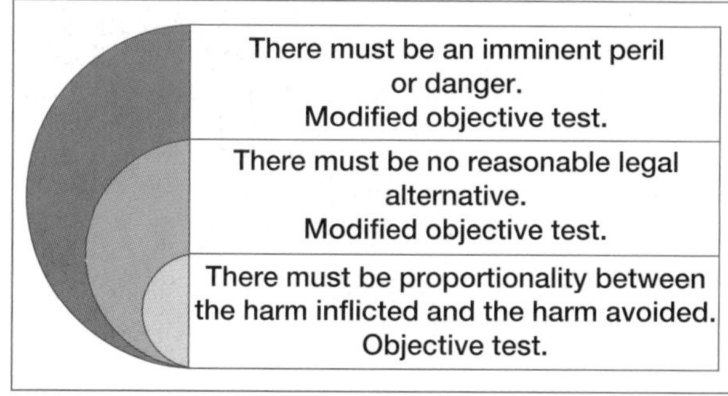

Figure 11-2

The Three Basic Elements of the Defence of Necessity

How did the Supreme Court apply these three basic elements of the necessity defence to the case of Robert Latimer? The Court took the view that the trial judge had acted correctly when he had ruled that there was no air of reality to the defence of necessity. First, the Court held that there was no evidence of an "imminent peril" facing Latimer:

> Acute suffering can constitute imminent peril, but in this case there was nothing to her medical condition that placed Tracy in a dangerous situation where death was an alternative. Tracy was thought to be in pain before the surgery, and that pain was expected to continue, or increase, following the surgery. But that ongoing pain did not constitute an emergency in this case. ... Tracy's proposed surgery did not pose an imminent threat to her life, nor did her medical condition. In fact, Tracy's health might have improved had the Latimers not rejected the option of relying on a feeding tube. Tracy's situation was not an emergency. The appellant can be reasonably expected to have understood that reality. There was no evidence of a legitimate psychological condition that rendered him unable to perceive that there was no imminent peril. The appellant argued that, for him, further surgery did amount to imminent peril. It was not reasonable for the appellant to form this belief, particularly when better pain management was available.

Second, there was no air of reality to Latimer's assertion that he had no reasonable legal alternative to breaking the law. He could have done his best to maintain Tracy's life and alleviate her pain as much as possible. According to the Supreme Court, Latimer could have achieved these goals by permitting the use of a feeding tube to improve her health and reduce her pain through medication. Similarly, he could have accepted the offer of a place for Tracy in a group home. As the Court stated in its judgment:

> The appellant may well have thought the prospect of struggling on unbearably sad and demanding. It was a human response that this alternative was unappealing. But it was a reasonable legal alternative that the law requires a person to pursue before he can claim the defence of necessity. The appellant was aware of this alternative but rejected it.

Third, there was no evidence of proportionality in the sense that the harm that Latimer was seeking to avoid was proportionate to the harm he inflicted. The Court commented that it is difficult to envisage any set of circumstances in which the requirement of proportionality could be met in the case of a homicide. However, even if it could be assumed that necessity could be available as a defence to a charge of murder, the accused would have to point to a harm that was of equal gravity to death. As the Court stated:

> The "harm avoided" in the appellant's situation was, compared to death, completely disproportionate. The harm inflicted in this case was ending a life; that harm was immeasurably more serious than the pain resulting from Tracy's operation which Mr. Latimer sought to avoid. Killing a person—in order to relieve the suffering produced by a medically manageable physical or mental condition—is not a proportionate response to the harm represented by the non-life-threatening suffering resulting from that condition.

In the case of *Nelson* (2007), the British Columbia Court of Appeal emphasized the need to ensure that the modified objective test is applied to the first two criteria articulated by the Supreme Court of Canada in the *Latimer* case. Nelson had a history of engaging in long fasts for the purpose of "spiritual cleansing." He went into the woods and, after a 60-day fast, broke into a house, consumed the homeowner's food, and wrapped himself up in the latter's blankets. The homeowner returned to find Nelson lying on the floor, apparently unconscious. The trial judge acquitted Nelson of the charge of breaking and entering a dwelling and committing mischief therein, contrary to section 348(1)(b) of the *Criminal Code*. The trial judge ruled that the defence of necessity applied because Nelson believed himself to be in a position of imminent peril because of his extreme hunger and state of hypothermia at the time of the break-in. However, the Court of Appeal set aside the acquittal and ordered a new trial because the trial judge had not applied the modified objective test to the particular circumstances in Nelson's case.

The Crown had contended that the situation in which Nelson had found himself was perfectly foreseeable and that, therefore, Nelson could have avoided it. The evidence was that Nelson had fasted on a number of previous occasions and that he knew that, at some point, he would lose control of himself; nevertheless, he decided to engage in another long fast. In the Court of Appeal, the Crown quoted the following passage from the Supreme Court of Canada's decision in *Latimer*: "Where the situation of peril clearly should have been foreseen and avoided, an accused person cannot reasonably claim any immediate peril."

The Crown also argued that Nelson had other legal alternatives open to him than breaking into someone else's home. For example, his original plan was to rummage through garbage cans. He could also have knocked on people's doors to ask for help or called 911. In this respect, the Court of Appeal stated that:

> It is the [Crown's] submission that while the trial judge made reference to other legal alternatives, the judge focused solely on [Nelson's] evidence and applied a subjective test, rather than a modified objective one.
>
> As [Crown] counsel put it, the trial judge erred in law by allowing his analysis to become unmoored from the objective underpinnings of the defence of necessity.

The Court of Appeal ruled that the trial judge had made a significant legal error by failing to ask whether Nelson's perception that he was in a situation of dire emergency and his belief that there were no legal alternatives open to him "had an objectively reasonable foundation." Therefore, a new trial was necessary.

THE DEFENCE OF DURESS

THE RATIONALE FOR THE DEFENCE

The defences of duress and necessity are closely intertwined. As the Supreme Court of Canada noted in *Ryan* (2013), necessity and duress "arise under circumstances where a person is subjected to an external danger and commits an act that would otherwise be criminal as a way of avoiding the harm the danger presents." The Court also pointed out that "in cases of duress and necessity ... the victims of the otherwise criminal act ... are third parties, who are not themselves responsible for the threats or circumstances of necessity that motivated the accused's actions."

As we have seen, the defence of necessity may be raised where external circumstances (such as a violent storm at sea) create an emergent situation in which the accused person is forced to choose between risking a disaster and breaking the law. However, where the defence of **duress** is claimed, the accused is asserting that their power of choice has been overborne by a threat from another human being. The classic example of the application of the defence of duress arises where the accused person is forced—at gunpoint—to break the law. Any humane system of criminal law would provide an excuse to an individual who is faced with the option of submitting to the threat and breaking the law or facing the prospect of death or grievous injury.

It is clear that the underlying rationale for both the defence of necessity and the defence of duress is identical—namely, that it is wrong to punish someone who has not acted in a truly voluntary manner. In the case of *Ryan*, the Supreme Court of Canada reaffirmed the case law that underscored both the common rationale for duress and necessity and the categorization of both defences as excuses rather than justifications:

> The rationale underlying duress is that of moral involuntariness, which was entrenched as a principle of fundamental justice in *R. v. Ruzic* (2001). ... "It is a principle of fundamental justice that only voluntary conduct—behaviour that is the product of a free will and controlled body, unhindered by external constraints—should attract the penalty and stigma of criminal liability." It is upon this foundation that we build the defences of duress and necessity. ... [T]he underlying concept of both defences is "normative involuntariness," in other words, that there is "no legal way out." ... While the test to be met is not dictated by this generally stated rationale underlying the defence, its requirements are heavily influenced by it. ... [D]efences built on the principle of moral involuntariness are classified as excuses. The law excuses those who, although morally blameworthy, acted in a morally involuntary manner. The act remains wrong, but the author of the offence will not be punished because it was committed in circumstances in which there was realistically no choice. ... The principle of moral involuntariness is "[a] concessio[n] to human frailty" in the face of "agonising choice." ... The commission of the crime is "remorselessly compelled by normal human instincts." ... "Morally involuntary conduct is not always inherently blameless."

SECTION 17 AND THE STATUTORY DEFENCE OF DURESS

Although the defences of necessity and duress are based on the same rationale, there is certainly one significant difference between them. Whereas Parliament has chosen not to define the defence of necessity, it has done so in the case of duress. Section 17 of the *Criminal Code* provides as follows:

> A person who commits an offence under compulsion by threats of immediate death or bodily harm from a person who is present when the offence is committed is excused for committing the offence if the person believes that the threats will be carried out and if the person is not a party to a conspiracy or association whereby the person is subject to compulsion,

> but this section does not apply where the offence that is committed is high treason or treason, murder, piracy, attempted murder, sexual assault, sexual assault with a weapon, threats to a third party or causing bodily harm, aggravated sexual assault, forcible abduction, hostage taking, robbery, assault with a weapon or causing bodily harm, aggravated assault, unlawfully causing bodily harm, arson or an offence under sections 280 to 283 (abduction and detention of young persons).

Section 17 undoubtedly imposes a number of strict limitations on the defence of duress:

- The threat made against the accused must be of *immediate* death or bodily harm.
- The threat must be uttered by a person who is *present* when the accused person commits the crime(s) in question.
- The defence may not be claimed where the accused person is a "party to a conspiracy or association whereby the person is subject to compulsion" (e.g., membership of a criminal gang).
- The defence may not be raised in relation to 22 serious crimes (ranging from murder to sexual assault).

In the case of *Paquette* (1976), the Supreme Court of Canada ruled that section 17 applies only to those accused persons who "*actually commit*" a criminal offence—for example, by pulling the trigger in a homicide or striking the victim in a case of assault. The provisions of section 17 do not cover accused persons who become parties to a criminal offence by aiding and/or abetting or by virtue of common intention (e.g., the "getaway driver" in a robbery case): according to the Supreme Court, such accused persons may instead rely on the common law defence of duress (the nature and scope of which will be discussed in the next section of this chapter).

Returning to section 17 of the *Criminal Code*, it is clear that two of the requirements of the statutory defence of duress may deny the benefit of the defence to an accused person who realistically has no choice but to break the law. More specifically, if a threat is made against the accused to inflict death or bodily harm *in the future* (as opposed to a threat of *immediate* death or bodily harm), or if the threat is made by a person who is not *physically present* at the time the accused commits the crime in question, then the accused is precluded from raising the defence of duress. In the case of *Ruzic* (2001), the Supreme Court of Canada ruled that these particular *Criminal Code* requirements are invalid because they infringe the fundamental principles of justice guaranteed by section 7 of the *Charter*.

The facts of the *Ruzic* case provide a clear illustration of the injustice that might occur if the section 17 requirements of a threat of immediate death or bodily harm and the physical presence of the person making the threat are relied upon to deny an accused person the benefit of a defence of duress. In April 1994, Marijana Ruzic, a 21-year-old woman from Belgrade, the capital city of what was then the Federal Republic of Yugoslavia, arrived in Canada by air and was found to be in possession of heroin and a false passport. At her trial, she readily admitted the offences of unlawful importation of a narcotic and use of a false passport. However, she argued that she should not be convicted of these offences because she was acting under duress. She stated that, while she was in Belgrade, she had been systematically intimidated by a "warrior" (a member of a paramilitary group). An expert witness testified that, in 1994, law and order had effectively broken down in Belgrade and the local citizens believed the police could not be trusted to protect them from roaming paramilitary groups that engaged in criminal and "mafia-like activities." The "warrior" subjected Ms. Ruzic to a number of violent assaults (including burning her arm with a cigarette lighter and forcibly injecting her with a substance that was probably heroin). The "warrior" later ordered Ruzic to take three packages of heroin to a restaurant in Toronto. When Ruzic protested, the "warrior" threatened to harm her mother. She then flew to Toronto, via Athens, and entered Canada with the drugs strapped to her body. Ruzic testified that she did not seek the help of the police in Belgrade because she believed that they were corrupt and would not provide her with any assistance. Similarly, she stated that she did not seek help from Canadian authorities because was convinced that the only way she could protect her mother from harm was to carry out the "warrior's" instructions.

Since Ruzic actually committed the offences charged, she would be covered by the provisions of section 17. However, if the "immediacy" and "presence" requirements of section 17 were applied to Ruzic's situation, then she would not be able to claim the benefit of the defence of duress. After all, the threats were of harm that might be perpetrated against her mother in the future and they were made by a man who was thousands of kilometres away when Ruzic entered Canada with the drugs and the false passport. However, the trial judge ruled that these requirements were invalid because they infringed the *Charter* and the jury was permitted to consider the common law defence of duress. Ruzic was acquitted by the jury, and both the Ontario Court of Appeal and the Supreme Court of Canada affirmed this acquittal.

Why did the Supreme Court of Canada agree with the trial judge that the "immediacy" and "presence" requirements of section 17 infringed the *Charter*? In delivering the judgment of the Court, Justice LeBel stated that if these requirements had been applied to the case of *Ruzic*, she could have been convicted of serious criminal offences even though she had no realistic choice but to break the law. However, it is a fundamental principle of justice, guaranteed by section 7 of the *Charter*, that no accused person should be convicted of a crime if they were acting involuntarily:

> Although moral involuntariness does not negate the *actus reus* or *mens rea* of an offence, it is a principle which, similarly to physical involuntariness, deserves protection under s. 7 of the *Charter*. It is a principle of fundamental justice that only voluntary conduct—behaviour that is the product of a free will and controlled body, unhindered by external constraints—should attract the penalty and stigma of criminal liability. Depriving a person of liberty and branding her with the stigma of criminal liability would infringe the principles of fundamental justice if the accused did not have any realistic choice. The ensuing deprivation of liberty and stigma would have been imposed in violation of the tenets of fundamental justice and would thus infringe s. 7 of the *Charter*.

Justice LeBel ruled that since the "immediacy" and "presence" requirements of section 17 were no longer valid, Ruzic was entitled to rely on the more generous provisions of the common law defence of duress. As we shall see, this defence encompasses threats of *future* harm and does not require the presence of the person uttering the threat at the scene of the crime: all that is necessary is that there be a threat of death or serious bodily harm and that the accused reasonably believe it will be carried out if they do not follow the orders of the person who is threatening them. Since Ruzic satisfied the requirements of the common law defence of duress, she was entitled to be acquitted.

In the *Ruzic* case, the Supreme Court of Canada did not rule that every element of section 17 was invalid under the *Charter*. It did not strike down that part of section 17 that prevents an accused person from raising the defence of duress if they became subject to compulsion because of membership in a criminal gang. Furthermore, both in *Ruzic* (2001) and *Ryan* (2013), the Supreme Court expressly left open the question of whether it is an infringement of the *Charter* to deny the benefit of the defence of duress to an accused person who commits one of the 22 offences listed in section 17. This would be a difficult question to address because the offences listed in section 17 are so diverse.

However, in *Willis* (2016), the Manitoba Court of Appeal rejected a section 7 *Charter* challenge to the exclusion of the offence of murder from the benefit of the statutory defence of duress under section 17 of the *Criminal Code*. Willis's life had been threatened by drug dealers over a debt and the dealers told him to kill the victim in order to save his own life. Willis brutally killed a young woman at the behest of the drug dealers. His attempt to raise the defence of duress was rejected both at trial and by the Court of Appeal. Justice Mainella emphasized that the principle of proportionality would always deny an accused person the benefit of the defence of duress. The Justice noted that "murder is a crime like no other" and that "the gap between the harm inflicted and the benefit accrued by the act of murder is cavernous." The crime of murdering an innocent victim could never meet the requirement of proportionality. The only circumstance in which it would be morally acceptable to take a life in order to preserve one's own would be in a situation in which the accused acts in legitimate self-defence.[1]

Of course, the decision in *Willis* applies only to murder committed by the accused. It may well be that a future *Charter* challenge to some of the other offences listed in section 17 of the *Criminal Code* would be successful.

It is significant that the Supreme Court explained that section 17 does not require that the threat in question be directed *at* the accused person him- or herself. Indeed, the threat may be made against a third party (in *Ruzic*, the threat was made against the accused's mother). All that is necessary is that the threat is made *to* the accused person.

In *Ryan* (2013), the Supreme Court of Canada clarified the current status of section 17 of the *Criminal Code* as a consequence of its decision in *Ruzic*:

> ... the Court in *Ruzic* did not leave the statutory defence in place simply stripped of its

1. Even if the *Charter* challenge had been successful, Willis would still have been denied the benefit of the defence of duress because he had a safe avenue of escape (he could have gone to the police for protection or fled the jurisdiction).

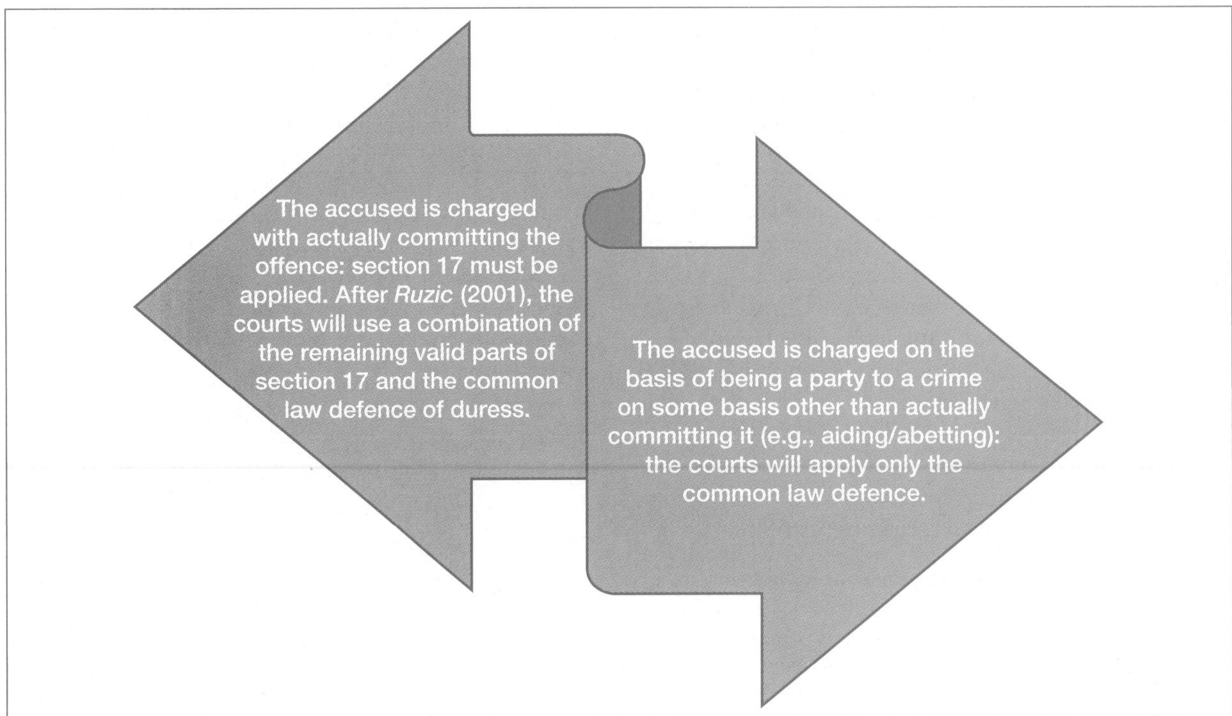

Figure 11-3
The Status of the Defence of Duress after Ruzic *(2001)*

> unconstitutional portions. The Court supplemented the interpretation and application of s. 17 with elements from the common law defence of duress, which it found to be "more consonant with the values of the *Charter*" … . In other words, the Court in *Ruzic* used the common law standard to interpret the affirmative requirements of the statute …

Where ambiguities or gaps exist in the partially struck-down section 17, the common law defence of duress operates to clarify and flesh out the statutory defence.

At this point, it is therefore necessary to analyze the nature and scope of the common law defence of duress.

The Common Law Defence of Duress

In *Ryan* (2013), the Supreme Court of Canada set out the main elements of the common law defence of duress, following its decision in *Ruzic* (2001):

- an explicit or implicit threat of death or bodily harm proffered against the accused or a third person;
- the accused reasonably believed that the threat would be carried out;
- the non-existence of a safe avenue of escape, evaluated on a modified objective standard;
- a close temporal connection between the threat and the harm threatened;
- proportionality between the harm threatened and the harm inflicted by the accused. This is also evaluated on a modified objective standard; and
- the accused is not a party to a conspiracy or association whereby the accused is subject to compulsion and actually knew that threats and coercion to commit an offence were a possible result of this criminal activity, conspiracy, or association.

Each element will be examined in light of the relevant case law.

1. An Explicit or Implicit Threat of Death or Bodily Harm Proffered against the Accused or a Third Person

The threat may be of immediate or future death or bodily harm and may be made either against the accused or against a third party closely associated with the accused (e.g., a child, parent, or spouse). If the threat is made *against* a third party, it still has to be made *to* the accused person if they are to raise the defence of duress successfully. Although the threat may encompass future harm, there must nevertheless be a relatively short interval of time between the threat and the likelihood that it will be carried out. The essence of duress is that the accused person has "no way out," and the longer the period between the threat and its likely implementation, the more opportunities the accused person will have to find alternatives to committing a crime (e.g., by seeking assistance from the police, leaving the area, or removing threatened family members to a safe location).

The threat does not have to be explicit to provide a basis for a successful defence of duress: it may just as well be an implied or implicit threat. This point was strongly affirmed by the Ontario Court of Appeal in the case of *Mena* (1987), in which Justice Martin stated that:

> The threat required to invoke duress may be express or implied. ... [Mena] did not testify that Yee had expressly stated that he would shoot him unless he accompanied Yee but it would be open to the jury to find that Yee, by producing the gun, pointing it at [Mena] and telling him that he was to go with him, had conveyed a threat to [Mena] that if he did not go with Yee he would be shot. [Mena] testified that he believed Yee was going to shoot him.

However, merely "being scared" of someone does not amount to an implicit threat. For example, in *Morningstar* (2017), the accused and two other people were in a triplex unit together with the victim, when one of the other two decided that the victim "has to die." Morningstar admitted to striking the victim on the head with a curtain rod, participating in thrusting the victim to the floor, holding the victim down while the other two people repeatedly stabbed him and himself stabbing the victim three times under instructions from a man called Noel, of whom Morningstar claimed he was "really scared." That individual said to Morningstar, "I need to know that you aren't gonna rat me out." Morningstar was convicted of murder.

In rejecting Morningstar's appeal against conviction, the New Brunswick Court of Appeal agreed with the trial judge that there was no air of reality to the defence of duress in these circumstances. There was no evidence of any threat—explicit or implicit—that Morningstar could reasonably have believed would be carried out. The only threat made to Morningstar was uttered to make him keep his mouth shut about what had happened and was not made to coerce him into committing murder. Morningstar's claim of being frightened of Noel was irrelevant since Noel had not made an implicit threat to force Morningstar to stab the victim.

In the case of *Ryan* (2013), the Supreme Court of Canada emphasized that the threat must be one that is specifically made in order to coerce the accused person into committing a crime. It cannot be raised as a defence in situations where the real issue is one of self-defence. As noted above, both duress and necessity are defences that apply when the victims of the otherwise criminal act are *third parties* who are not themselves responsible for the threats or circumstances of necessity that motivated the accused's actions. In cases involving self-defence, the victim is the individual whose own actions actually precipitated the use of force by the accused person. This critical difference goes a long way toward explaining why duress merely constitutes an excuse and self-defence is considered a justification for the accused person's conduct.

In *Ryan*, the accused, Nicole Ryan, had "been the victim of a violent, abusive and controlling husband. She believed that he would cause her and their daughter serious bodily harm or death as he had threatened to do many times." Nicole had fled the family home but believed that she was in continuous danger from her husband, whom she believed was stalking her. Nicole approached two men and urged them to kill her estranged husband in return for money because she believed that this was the only way she could effectively protect herself and her daughter. Nicole later received a phone call from an undercover RCMP officer who posed as a "hit man," and she eventually offered him \$25 000 to assassinate her husband. She was duly arrested and charged with counselling the commission of an offence not committed, contrary to section 464(a) of the *Criminal Code*. An expert witness at the trial testified that Nicole was a victim of "battered woman syndrome" and saw "no way out" of her hopeless situation. The trial judge found that Nicole Ryan reasonably believed that her husband "would cause her and her daughter serious bodily injury and that there was no safe avenue of escape other than having him killed." He also found that Nicole had been unsuccessful in obtaining any help from the police and other agencies because it was determined that her problems were a "civil matter." The trial judge, therefore, acquitted Nicole Ryan on the basis that she had successfully advanced the defence of duress. The Crown appealed to the Nova Scotia Court of Appeal and, for the first time, raised the argument that the defence of duress was not available to the accused on the facts of the case. However, the Court of Appeal nevertheless affirmed the acquittal. The Crown then appealed to the Supreme Court of Canada, which set aside the acquittal on the ground that duress may be raised only by an accused person who has been compelled by another person to commit an offence against a third party. It does not apply where the accused person seeks to use force themselves or to persuade others to use force against the individual whom they believe poses a threat to them: this situation is one that falls within the scope of self-defence rather than duress. In the words of Justices LeBel and Cromwell:

> Duress cannot be extended so as to apply when the accused meets force with force, or the threat of force with force in situations where self-defence is unavailable. Duress is, and must remain, an applicable defence only in situations where the accused has been compelled to commit a specific offence under threats of death or bodily harm. This clearly limits the availability of the offence to particular factual circumstances.

The Supreme Court, however, did not order a new trial in the *Ryan* case but instead entered a stay of proceedings. The Court ruled that there were doubts about the fairness of a new trial and that the longstanding, severe abuse at the hands of the accused's husband and protracted court proceedings (lasting nearly five years) had taken "an enormous toll" on her: "In all of the circumstances, it would not be fair to subject Ms. Ryan to another trial. In the interests of justice, a stay of proceedings is required to protect against this oppressive result."

The *Ryan* Case (2013): Duress Is Not a Defence to a Charge of Counselling Murder

THE CANADIAN PRESS/Halifax Chronicle-Herald-Brian Medel

The decision of the Supreme Court of Canada in the case of Nicole Ryan has become the leading case that sets the basic ground rules for the interpretation and application of the defence of duress in Canada. The facts of the case are set out elsewhere in this chapter. It will be remembered that the Court ruled that duress may be raised only by an accused person who has been compelled by another person to commit an offence against a third party. It does not apply where, as in this case, the accused person tries to persuade another person to commit a crime.

What is unusual about this case is the fact that although the Supreme Court held that duress was not available as a defence to Ms. Ryan (now known as Doucet), it did not order a new trial. Instead, it entered a stay of proceedings. Six of the justices agreed with Justice LeBel and Justice Cromwell, who stated that:

> The trial proceeded on the basis that duress was available as a matter of law to Ms. Ryan if the facts supported it. She therefore went to trial on the basis that the issues were mainly the factual ones relating to whether she had pointed to evidence capable of raising a reasonable doubt about the various components of duress. Presumably, decisions about the conduct of the defence were made on this basis and might have been made differently had the legal position later adopted by the Crown on appeal, that duress was not open to her in law, been known at the time of trial. There is therefore a serious risk that some of the consequences of those decisions could not be undone in the context of a new trial and this raises concern about the fairness of ordering a new trial. In addition, the abuse which she suffered at the hands of Mr. Ryan took an enormous toll on her, as, no doubt, have these protracted proceedings, extending over nearly five years, in which she was acquitted at trial and successfully resisted a Crown appeal in the Court of Appeal. There is also the disquieting fact that, on the record before us, it seems that the authorities were much quicker to intervene to protect Mr. Ryan than they had

> been to respond to her request for help in dealing with his reign of terror over her. A stay of proceedings is warranted only in the clearest of cases. ... In our opinion, Ms. Ryan's case falls into the residual category of cases requiring a stay: it is an exceptional situation that warrants an exceptional remedy. In all of the circumstances, it would not be fair to subject Ms. Ryan to another trial. In the interests of justice, a stay of proceedings is required to protect against this oppressive result.

Justice Fish was the lone dissenter with respect to the decision to enter a stay of proceedings:

> The criteria for granting a stay—a drastic remedy of last resort—are well-established. ... The Court has made clear that a stay of proceedings is available only in "the clearest of cases." ... These criteria, in my view, are not satisfied in this case.

There has been considerable debate about the appropriateness of entering a stay of proceedings in this case. Some people have taken the view that the Supreme Court of Canada should have found a way to give Ms. Ryan a defence and that, given her dire circumstances, she should have been acquitted. In particular, it has been suggested that Ryan should have been acquitted on the basis of self-defence.

It is significant that the Supreme Court of Canada was very critical of the response of the police ("the authorities") to Ms. Ryan's complaints of violence at the hands of her husband and that their failure to protect her was an important factor in the decision to enter a stay of proceedings rather than to order a new trial. However, on July 10, 2013, the Commission for Public Complaints against the Royal Canadian Mounted Police (2013) issued a report concerning the conduct of RCMP members with respect to the police handling of Ms. Ryan's situation. The Commission chair issued 23 findings and concluded that the RCMP had acted "reasonably." Finding 23 was that "The subject members reasonably demonstrated knowledge of the RCMP's policy regarding relationships, which was followed at all times." The final words of the report are: "This was not a situation where the RCMP refused to assist the parties; on the contrary, RCMP members were responsive to the family's conflicts. I conclude that the RCMP acted reasonably in each of its dealings with Ms. Doucet and her family and did not fail to protect her."

The entry of a stay of proceedings in a case of this nature is undoubtedly questionable. Was it morally and ethically acceptable for Ryan to attempt to hire a contract killer? Is this a legally appropriate manner of acting in alleged self-defence? How extensive should the evidence of alleged abuse be in order to support a plea of self-defence?

After considering the conflicting perspectives on the *Ryan* case, do you think the Supreme Court should have ordered a new trial, in which it would have been open to the accused to advance a defence of self-defence, or do you think the entry of the stay of proceedings was appropriate, given the history of alleged abuse and the potential unfairness of a new trial (as indicated in the judgment of the majority of the Supreme Court)? Since the *Ryan* case was decided, the self-defence provisions of the *Criminal Code* have been completely overhauled. After you have read Chapter 12, you may wish to ask yourself whether the new provisions would make it easier for a woman in Ryan's situation to successfully advance self-defence and obtain an acquittal.

2. The Accused Reasonably Believed That the Threat Would Be Carried Out

In *Ryan* (2013), the Supreme Court of Canada stated that "[T]he accused must have reasonably believed that the threat would be carried out. This element is analyzed on a modified objective basis, that is, according to the test of the reasonable person similarly situated."

If the accused person does not believe that the threat(s) will be carried out, then there is no basis for raising the defence of duress because they would not be deprived of the power of choice. In assessing the reasonableness of the accused person's belief, factors such as their prior knowledge of the person(s) making the threat(s) will be critical. For example, an accused person who has been repeatedly abused by her physically violent partner would very reasonably believe that the latter would carry out a threat of violence if she were to refuse to carry out his order to commit a crime. Similarly, if the accused person knows that the person making the threat(s) is armed and is known to belong to a violent gang, it would be exceedingly reasonable for the accused person to assume that the threat(s) will be carried out. On the other hand, a large and physically fit person would not be expected to take seriously a threat of immediate violence from a diminutive individual who is unarmed.

3. The Non-Existence of a Safe Avenue of Escape, Evaluated on a Modified Objective Standard

A critical consideration when the defence of duress is raised is whether or not the accused could *reasonably* have been expected to take an alternative course of action. If such an alternative were available, then they would be expected to act on it and thereby avoid breaking the law. For example, if the opportunity to escape arises, the accused person must take it; otherwise, they will lose the right to claim the benefit of the defence of duress.

Indeed, in the case of *Keller* (1998), the Alberta Court of Appeal stated unequivocally that where the accused person has a **safe avenue of escape** and fails to pursue it, the trial judge should not even allow the defence to go to the jury:

> Whether there was a safe avenue of escape is a question of fact for the jury. ... However, if on the evidence most favourable to the accused, he had a safe means of escaping the threatened harm without committing the offence, no reasonable jury could possibly acquit on the basis of the defence of duress. *There would be no air of reality to the defence and a trial judge would be obliged to keep the defence from the jury.* [emphasis added]

Why should a defendant who has a "safe avenue of escape" lose the benefit of the defence of duress? In the *Hibbert* case (1995), the Supreme Court of Canada answered this question by referring to the underlying rationale of the defence. In the words of Chief Justice Lamer, who delivered the judgment of the Court:

> An accused person cannot rely on the common law defence of duress if he or she had an opportunity to safely extricate himself or herself from the situation of duress. The rationale for this rule is simply that in such circumstances the condition of "normative involuntariness" that provides the theoretical basis for both the defences of duress and necessity is absent—*if the accused had the chance to take action that would have allowed him or her to avoid committing an offence, it cannot be said that he or she had no real choice when deciding whether or not to break the law.* [emphasis added]

In the case of *Ryan* (2013), the Supreme Court of Canada reaffirmed the principle that the critical question of whether a "safe avenue of escape" was available to the accused person should be determined on a "modified objective basis"; that is to say, would a "reasonable person similarly situated" have appreciated that a "safe avenue of escape" existed? In the words of Justices LeBel and Cromwell:

> The courts will take into consideration the particular circumstances where the accused found himself and his ability to perceive a reasonable alternative to committing a crime, with an awareness of his background and essential characteristics. The process involves a pragmatic assessment of the position of the accused, tempered by the need to avoid negating criminal liability on the basis of a purely subjective and unverifiable excuse.

The critical question becomes whether a reasonable person, standing in the accused person's shoes and sharing the same personal characteristics and experience, would draw the conclusion that there was no safe avenue of escape or reasonable legal alternative. If the reasonable person in this situation would conclude that there *is* a safe avenue of escape, then the accused person would be expected to take it: if they do not, then they cannot rely on the defence of duress because the entire rationale of this excuse is that the accused had no realistic choice but to act as they did.

As the Alberta Court of Appeal stated in the *Keller* case (1998), "[T]he question is whether a reasonable person, with similar history, personal circumstances, abilities, capacities, and human frailties as the accused would, in the particular circumstances, reasonably believe there was no safe avenue of escape and that he had no choice but to yield to the coercion."

It is noteworthy that the Alberta Court of Appeal also suggested that the accused must take reasonable steps to "discover his or her full range of options before deciding to engage in the wrongful conduct."

Naturally, a central consideration in determining whether there was a "safe avenue of escape" is the perceived availability of police protection for the accused. For example, in the *Keller* case, the accused had been charged with trafficking in LSD. The accused argued that he had been threatened with death or bodily harm by a known drug dealer if he (Keller) did not comply with the dealer's instructions. Over a period of four months, he retrieved at least 10 packages of drugs from the Calgary International Airport. Keller claimed that he had not sought the assistance of the police because he was frightened of the drug dealer and his friends and believed the police were incapable of furnishing him with effective protection. The trial judge ruled that there was no air of reality to the accused's defence of duress and refused to put it to the jury. Keller was convicted and his subsequent appeal to the Alberta Court of Appeal was dismissed. The court pointed out that the conduct for which Keller had been charged occurred four months after he was allegedly threatened and that there had been no explicit threats in the interim. Furthermore, the court emphasized that Keller was "not abnormally vulnerable to threats

Illustration by Greg Holoboff

The defence of duress is available only when there is no safe avenue of escape.

of physical violence" and that he had "no reason to think that the police could not give him protection if he reported the situation." Furthermore, Keller had made absolutely no attempt to consider whether he had any legal alternatives open to him: Keller had never contacted the police, even on an anonymous basis, to explore whether they could provide him with protection. Keller did not take any of the steps that a reasonable person would have taken, if they were standing in Keller's shoes and shared his personal characteristics and background.

However, there may be circumstances in which it would be unreasonable to expect the accused person to seek the assistance of the police or other authorities. For example, in the *Ruzic* case (2001), the accused could not seek the protection of the police in Belgrade because, at the relevant time, law and order had apparently broken down and the local citizens could not trust the police to protect them from members of various violent paramilitary groups. Furthermore, Ruzic could not have been expected to seek the protection of the authorities in Toronto because the threats that had destroyed her power of choice were directed not toward her personally but toward her mother, who was thousands of kilometres away in Belgrade. As Justice LeBel noted:

> [T]he law does not require an accused to seek the official protection of police in all cases. The requirement of objectivity must itself take into consideration the special circumstances where the accused found herself as well as her perception of them.

Nonetheless, the issue of the availability of a safe avenue of escape depends on the particular circumstances of each case. For example, in *Foster* (2018), the accused returned from a trip to Jamaica and her plane landed at Pearson Airport in Toronto. Canada Border Services discovered that Foster was carrying 1.2 kilograms of cocaine in her bra. Foster claimed that, while she was in Jamaica, she was threatened by a man who demanded that she take the cocaine to a friend in Toronto. At gunpoint, he threatened to kill her as well as her relatives in Jamaica and her mother in Toronto, if she did not do as he asked. He also told Foster that he had "people" who would watch her on her journey back to Canada and that he knew where she and her relatives lived in the Toronto area. He also claimed that he had connections within the Jamaican police. Foster did not seek the assistance of the authorities at the airport in Jamaica, nor did she disclose that she was carrying cocaine to the flight crew or to the Canada Border Services when she arrived at Pearson Airport.

Foster was charged with importing cocaine, contrary to section 6(1) of the Controlled Drugs and Substances Act, S.C. 1996, c. 19. Foster raised the defence of duress and the trial judge instructed the jury that they had to consider whether "a reasonable person in Ms. Foster's circumstances [would] have believed that there was a safe way to avoid the harm that was threatened, other than by importing cocaine?" Foster was convicted, and her appeal was rejected by the Ontario Court of Appeal. The Court emphasized that Foster's failure to seek any help from customs or police authorities at Pearson Airport was a relevant consideration in determining whether she had the ability to escape the threats made to her in Jamaica if she failed to import the cocaine into Canada. Justice Watt, in delivering the judgment of the Court of Appeal concluded that "Once we accept that the offence of importing was not complete until the appellant and the contraband cleared customs, it follows that a safe avenue of escape was or remained open with the Canadian Border Services Agency or other law enforcement officers at the airport."

The *Foster* case, at first glance, seems to be almost identical to the *Ruzic* case, yet the outcome in each case was very different. The deciding factor in *Ruzic* case seems to have been that the threat to the accused's mother in the former Yugoslavia occurred at a time when law and order had largely broken down in Belgrade. There was, therefore, no safe avenue of escape open to Ruzic in her home country:

she reasonably concluded that she could not seek effective police protection for her mother and that it was a reasonable assumption that the "warrior" who threatened her would carry out the threat to harm her mother if Ruzic did not successfully import the drugs into Canada. In *Foster*, it seems to have been assumed that a reasonable person would have been able to obtain the protection of the police in Jamaica as well as Canada Border Services and the police authorities in Toronto.

4. A Close Temporal Connection between the Threat and the Harm Threatened

In the case of *Ruzic* (2001), Justice LeBel stated, on behalf of the Supreme Court of Canada, that when an accused person raises the defence of duress, the trial judge should nevertheless instruct the jury that there is a "need for a close temporal connection between the threat and the harm threatened"; indeed, the longer the period between the threat and the harm threatened, the less likely it is that the accused may claim that they had no reasonable alternative but to break the law.

In the case of *Ryan* (2013), Justices LeBel and Cromwell articulated the underlying reasons for this requirement in more detail:

> The first purpose of the close temporal connection element is to ensure that there truly was no safe avenue of escape for the accused. If the threat is too far removed from the accused's illegal acts, it will be difficult to conclude that a reasonable person similarly situated had no option but to commit the offence. The temporal link between the threat and the harm threatened is necessary to demonstrate the degree of pressure placed on the accused.
>
> The second purpose of the close temporal connection requirement is to ensure that it is reasonable to believe that the threat put so much pressure on the accused that between this threat and the commission of the offence, "the accused los[t] the ability to act freely," ... It thus serves to determine if the accused truly acted in an involuntary manner.

5. Proportionality between the Harm Threatened and the Harm Inflicted by the Accused

As Justice LeBel said in the *Ruzic* case (2001):

> The common law of duress ... recognizes that an accused in a situation of duress does not only enjoy rights, but also has obligations towards others and society. As a fellow human being, the accused remains subject to a basic duty to adjust his or her conduct to the importance and nature of the threat. The law includes a requirement of proportionality between the threat and the criminal act to be executed, measured on the objective-subjective standard of the reasonable person similarly situated. The accused should be expected to demonstrate some fortitude and to put up a normal resistance to the threat.

In the case of *Ryan* (2013), the Supreme Court of Canada emphasized that the issue of proportionality must be determined on a modified objective basis (as is the case with respect to other elements of the defence of duress). Justices LeBel and Cromwell argued that there are two elements that define proportionality in the context of duress. The first element "requires that the harm threatened was equal to or greater than the harm inflicted by the accused," and the second element "requires a more in-depth analysis of the acts of the accused and a determination as to whether they accord with what society expects from a reasonable person similarly situated in that particular circumstance."

As for the first element, since the only threats that will be considered relevant to a defence of duress involve death or bodily harm, the courts will need to weigh the severity of the crime committed by the accused against the degree of violence threatened by the person(s) who coerced the accused person into committing it. For example, committing the offence of burglary when threatened with death by an armed person would be considered a lesser evil than refusing to carry out the crime and facing liquidation. On the other hand, committing the offence of murder when a threat was made to break the accused person's leg would be considered a greater evil than declining to kill the victim and receiving a painful, but not lethal, injury.

As far as the second element of proportionality is concerned, the courts have taken into account whether the accused person acted with a reasonable degree of fortitude in the face of threats. The legal test applied is whether a reasonable person, in exactly the same situation as the accused, would have been likely to yield to the threats and break the law. For example, a mother who is subjected to threats of violence to both herself and her children by an abusive male partner would not normally be expected to resist these threats, whereas a bouncer at a club might well be expected to resist threats made by a single unarmed male.

It will be remembered that section 17 explicitly excludes 22 crimes from the benefit of the statutory defence of duress. In this respect, Parliament has conclusively determined the issue of proportionality for these offences. In future cases, the Supreme Court of Canada may have to decide whether the exclusion of any or all of these 22 crimes from the benefit of the statutory defence is invalid under the *Charter*. The common law defence does not automatically exclude any crimes from its scope, but it does require proportionality between the crime committed by the accused and the harm that was avoided. Therefore, when applying the common law defence, courts may exclude certain crimes from its scope on a case-by-case basis. However, in *Aravena* (2015), the Ontario Court of Appeal went so far as to say that the defence of duress could apply to individuals who were parties to the offence of murder (by aiding and abetting), although the defence was not actually applied in this case because the accused was part of a criminal organization that he had voluntarily joined.

The Court of Appeal said, in this respect:

> An individual told to "kill or be killed" cannot make a decision that will fully vindicate the right to life, especially if the choice is between the lives of two equally innocent third parties. Whatever the threatened person decides, an innocent life may well be lost. A *per se* rule which excludes the defence of duress in all murder cases does not give the highest priority to the 1-1 sanctity of life, but rather, arbitrarily, gives the highest priority to one of the lives placed in jeopardy.

6. The Accused Is Not a Party to a Conspiracy or Association Whereby the Accused Is Subject to Compulsion and Actually Knew That Threats and Coercion to Commit an Offence Were a Possible Result of This Criminal Activity, Conspiracy, or Association

In *Ryan* (2013), the Supreme Court of Canada observed that both section 17 of the *Criminal Code* and the common law defence of duress deny the benefit of the defence to accused persons who, owing to their involvement in a criminal conspiracy, association, or gang, knew that they were likely to be subjected to threats and coercion. The *Ruzic* case (2001) did not strike down this part of section 17, which will still be applied to accused persons who actually "commit" an offence under the threat of violence. The rationale for denying the defence to members of criminal conspiracies, associations, or gangs is that, since they knowingly accepted the risk that they might be coerced into committing crimes when they joined, they cannot establish the lack of moral voluntariness that is at the very heart of the defence of duress.

In the case of *Li* (2002), the Ontario Court of Appeal stated that the voluntary involvement of the accused person with a criminal organization must be taken into account when determining whether they had a safe avenue of escape. The facts in *Li* were that the three accused persons had been smuggled from China to Canada by a criminal organization known as the Snakeheads. As a consequence, they all owed money to the Snakeheads. Tsang, a member of the Snakeheads organization, later approached the accused persons and asked them to participate in kidnapping three people. Tsang threatened the accused persons and their families with violence if they did not take part in the kidnapping and also told them that their debts to the Snakeheads would be written off should they participate. The accused persons forcibly abducted the victims from their apartment, took them to another location, and held them there for 22 days. The victims were then rescued by the police, who had conducted a surprise raid on the premises. During the period of the victims' captivity, the accused had, for the most part, been left alone with their hostages. For all practical purposes, the accused persons were free to come and go as they pleased: indeed, each of the accused had run errands, such as purchasing food. Furthermore, they had all had an opportunity to make a telephone call to seek the assistance of the authorities, had they wished to do so.

The accused claimed the benefit of the defence of duress at their trial and based their claim on the threats made against them by Tsang, who was acting on behalf of the Snakeheads. However, they were nevertheless convicted on three counts of kidnapping and forcible confinement. The Ontario Court of Appeal dismissed their appeal against their convictions. The Court of Appeal agreed with the trial judge that there was no air of reality to the defence of duress because the accused had a safe avenue of escape open to them. In delivering the judgment of the Court, Justice Finlayson stated that:

> It is undisputed that these appellants knew they were purchasing the services of the Snakeheads before they left China. The appellant Liu even admitted that he previously used the Snakehead

services to gain entry to the United States, and had returned to China before embarking on this effort at getting onto this continent. The appellant Chen testified that he knew the Snakeheads were "smugglers" and that their activity was illegal in China, but added that others use them and so it is perceived as legal. The appellant Li testified that he chose to use the Snakeheads to obtain passage to the United States, despite its high price. None claimed to be surprised on learning of the nature of the Snakeheads organization, nor did any of them claim to have laboured under some belief that it was a benign organization prior to availing themselves of its services. ... *In evaluating the appellants' claim that they had no safe avenue of escape, it is important to take into account their voluntary decision to get involved with the Snakehead organization in the first place. The two concepts are interrelated by the authorities.* [emphasis added]

Justice Finlayson emphasized that, as far as the courts are concerned, it should be recognized that there is a "juxtaposition between a safe avenue of escape and the voluntary assumption of the risk in the first place." For example, when evaluating the accused persons' claim that seeking police protection would have been futile because they were in fear not only for their own lives but also the lives of their families in China, "[T]he court should be reminded of their initiative in approaching the Snakeheads in the first place, and the fact that the threats of

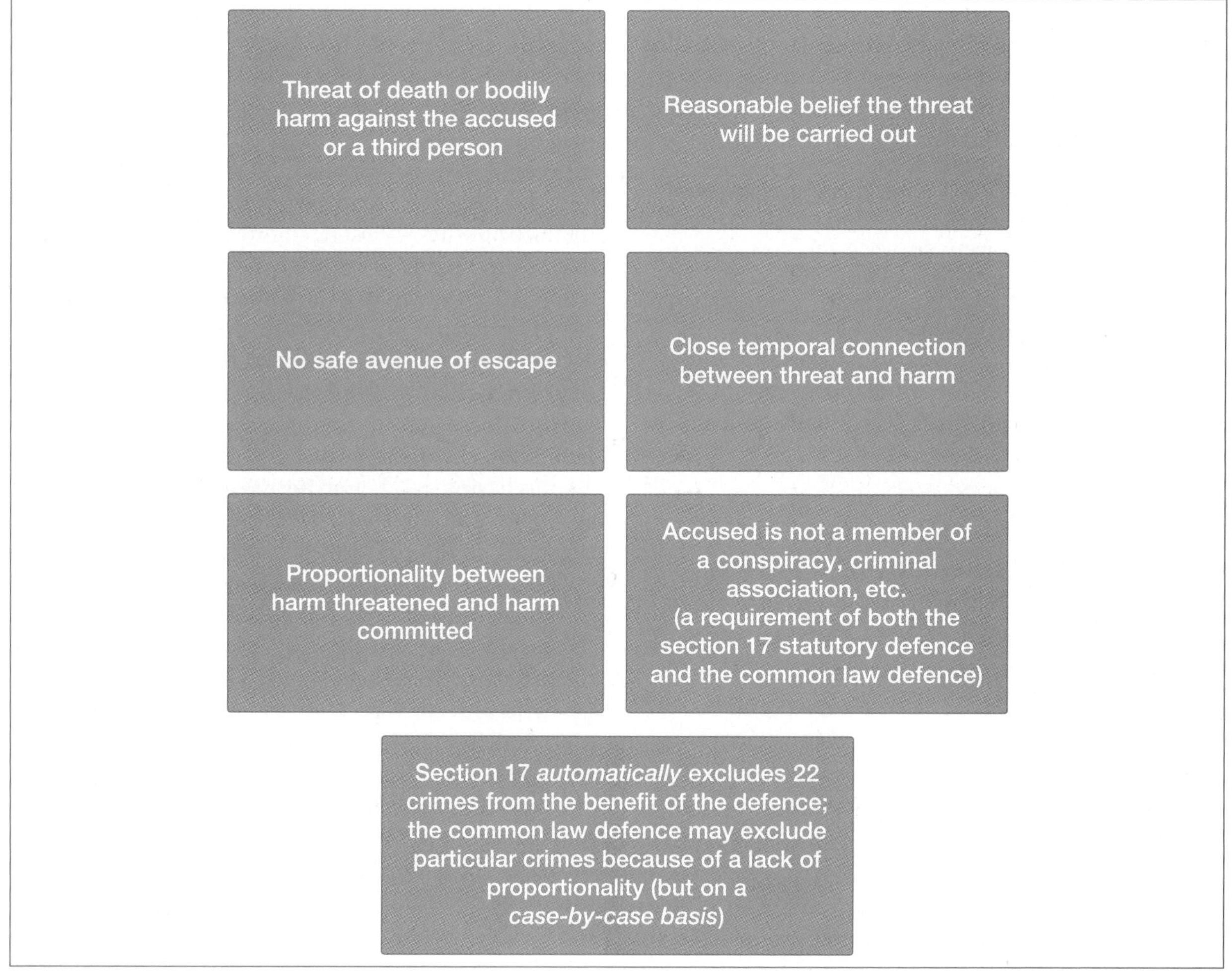

Figure 11-4

Duress: The Basic Requirements of Both the Statutory Defence (Section 17) and the Common Law Defence after Ryan *(2013)*

retaliation against them and their families was sweetened by the inducement of retiring their debts to this organization." In the words of the Court of Appeal:

> There must be an air of reality to the defence of duress before the trial judge can permit it to be considered by the jury. ... However, where as here the proposition put forward by the appellants is that they freely and without coercion placed themselves in the clutches of their alleged tormentors, it would be a mockery of justice to place the issue of the validity of the duress issue before the jury. We have a matter of policy here. The appellants made a deal with the devil and say that they had no alternative than to honour it. They ask this court to place their safety above the liberty and security of their innocent victims and thus encourage the Snakeheads to continue their campaign of extortion through the agency of persons similarly situated to the appellants.

It will no doubt be recalled that the statutory defence of duress, articulated in section 17 of the *Criminal Code*, indicates that the defence may be claimed successfully only if the accused person "is not a party to a conspiracy or association whereby the person is subject to compulsion." In this respect, there appears to be a considerable degree of convergence between the common law and the statutory defence of duress. Significantly, the Supreme Court of Canada did not strike down this particular element of section 17 when it issued its decision in the *Ruzic* case (2001).

Study Questions

1. Wegg is taking part in a wilderness survival course with his friend Dedlock. The two men panic, lose their survival kits, and soon become lost. They wander around a forest for a day and a night without any food, except for the occasional berries they can find on their way. Dedlock says he is exhausted and wants to stay where he is. Wegg presses on alone and comes to a small log cabin. There is no one in the cabin and Wegg breaks down the door. He eats some food that he finds in the refrigerator and also drinks two or three beers. He then takes a truck that is standing outside, using the keys he has found in the kitchen. He drives off at very high speed and, within a minute or two, reaches a town, where he asks for help. Dedlock is later rescued from the forest and soon recovers. The police are contemplating laying the following charges against Wegg: breaking and entering, theft, taking and driving a motor vehicle without the owner's consent, and speeding. Would Wegg have any defence to these charges?
2. The *S.S. Lollipop* sinks in a terrible storm. There are not enough lifeboats and those that are operational are severely overloaded. One lifeboat is commanded by Captain Bligh, who escaped at the last minute from his sinking ship. The lifeboat is so overloaded and so much water is being taken on board that it is obvious the boat will sink within a few minutes. Bligh decrees that all male passengers over the age of 35 must leave the lifeboat and commands that they be "put into the water." The other crew and passengers push the unfortunate "over 35" male passengers into the turbulent sea, where they are unable to hang on to the sides of the boat and they all perish. The remaining occupants of the lifeboat are later saved by a passing ship. Everyone is agreed that if the unfortunate "over 35" males had not left the lifeboat, it is most probable that it would have sunk and everyone on board would have been killed. The Crown is thinking of charging Bligh with murder. Does he have any defence to any charges of murder that might be laid against him?
3. Polonius is a homeless person who has no money. It is a freezing night in the middle of winter, and he is cold and hungry. He is desperate for warmth, shelter, and food. However, since demand far outstrips supply, Polonius is turned away from the only two shelters available for an overnight stay. Polonius sees a restaurant that has been closed for the night. Polonius enters the restaurant by climbing in through a window. He eats some food, consumes one or two soft drinks, and turns on an electric heater to keep himself warm. The police discover Polonius in the restaurant and arrest him for breaking and entering with intent to commit theft. Polonius argues that he would have died from exposure and/or hunger if he had not entered the restaurant, eaten some food, and obtained warmth from the heater. Would Polonius be entitled to a defence of necessity?

4. Chuffey is a guard at a penitentiary. One of the inmates, a man called Murdstone, asks Chuffey to smuggle in some illegal drugs for the use of Murdstone and his cell mates, who are members of a well-known criminal gang. Chuffey initially refuses, but Murdstone threatens to "arrange an accident" for Chuffey if he will not transport the drugs into the prison. Chuffey is terrified by the threat against him and, on Murdstone's instructions, goes to a local bar, where he is given a package by Buzfuz—a very large and intimidating gang member. Chuffey delivers the package to Murdstone, but his actions are observed by another prison officer and he is arrested and charged with trafficking in heroin, contrary to section 5(1) of the *Controlled Drugs and Substances Act*, S.C. 1996, c. 19. Does Chuffey have any defence(s) to this charge?
5. Meagles witnesses a brutal killing that is perpetrated by Bounderby, a local mobster. Bounderby is charged with murder, and Meagles is subpoenaed by the Crown to give evidence at the trial. Before the trial takes place, Meagles receives a number of telephone calls from a man identifying himself as "the Avenging Angel." The gist of these calls is that if Meagles does not have a convenient loss of memory at Bounderby's trial, Meagles's children will be killed. Meagles is too frightened to tell the police and gives false evidence at the trial. As a consequence, Bounderby is acquitted. Crown counsel decides to charge Meagles with perjury under section 131(1) of the *Criminal Code*. Are there any defences available to Meagles?
6. Hamlet is approached by Laertes and Claudius. Hamlet knows these men because he used to be part of the criminal gang to which they still belong. Hamlet severed his relationship with the gang one year previously. Laertes says to Hamlet, "Drive us to the Denmark Bank." When they reach the bank, Laertes orders Hamlet to remain outside in his van. Laertes and Claudius then enter the bank and remove all the available cash from the tellers, who are terrified by Laertes' violent threats. As Laertes is leaving the bank, he fatally shoots the bank manager, who had disobeyed Laertes' command to remain still on the floor. Laertes and Claudius then enter Hamlet's vehicle to escape from the scene of the robbery. However, the police have surrounded the bank and eventually Laertes, Claudius, and Hamlet are taken into custody. Claudius and Hamlet both claim that they acted as they did only because of their overwhelming fear of Laertes, who has previously committed more than one murder. May Claudius and Hamlet claim the benefit of the defence of duress?
7. Cleopatra is a surgeon who has acquired a special expertise in the separation of conjoined twins. She is asked to separate infant twins Hermione and Portia. Tragically, Portia lacks the organs necessary to survive such an operation. The attending pediatricians tell Cleopatra that unless she separates the twins, both of them will die because Portia's bodily needs will eventually overwhelm Hermione's vital organs. In short, Cleopatra is asked to choose between separating the twins and declining to intervene. If she separates them, Portia will immediately die but Hermione will almost certainly enjoy a normal life span. If she does not carry out the surgery, both Hermione and Portia will die in a matter of months. Cleopatra wishes to separate the twins, but she is told that if she does so, she could be charged with the murder of Portia. If this should happen, would Cleopatra have any defence(s) open to her?
8. Lightwood is a 20-year-old man who has a recent-model pickup truck. While he is on his way to work, he brings his vehicle to a halt at a stop sign. Rogue Riderhood, a large man of some 30 years of age, opens the passenger door and occupies the vacant seat in the front of the truck. Lightwood does not know Riderhood and orders him to leave, but Riderhood brandishes a hunting knife and tells Lightwood he will "cut [his] face" if he does not drive him to a farm located just outside the small town in which Lightwood lives and works. Once at the farm, Riderhood orders Lightwood to empty a can of gasoline over some straw in a barn and set fire to it. Lightwood does so and the barn is soon engulfed in flames. The fire brigade is called to extinguish the fire and, unfortunately, one of the firefighters is injured when she is struck by a falling beam. The firefighter is taken to hospital, where her injuries are determined to be relatively minor and she is released the next day. When Lightwood is charged with arson, he strenuously argues that he was forced to set the fire against his will and that he was, at all times, terrified by Riderhood's threat to use the knife on his face. Can Lightwood claim the benefit of the defence of duress? Would his lawyer have any reason to advance an argument based on the *Charter*?

CHAPTER 12

SELF-DEFENCE AND DEFENCE OF PROPERTY

Learning Objectives

After reading this chapter, you will be able to understand:

- the basic elements of the defences of self-defence and defence of property;
- the criteria set out in Section 34 of the *Criminal Code*, which guide the courts in determining whether or not the force used in self-defence was reasonable;
- the circumstances in which the *Criminal Code* specifically precludes the use of the defence of self-defence;
- the meaning of the requirement in Section 35 of the *Criminal Code* that an accused must be in "peaceable possession" of property in order to successfully raise the defence of property; and
- the circumstances in which the *Criminal Code* specifically precludes the defence of property.

SELF-DEFENCE AND DEFENCE OF PROPERTY

Self-defence is one of the most frequently raised defences to charges of assault or homicide. Until March 2013, the *Criminal Code* provisions concerning self-defence and the related provisions dealing with defence of property were extraordinarily complex and, in some respects, contradictory. However, amendments to the *Criminal Code*, which came into effect in 2013,[1] have greatly simplified the law that defines the circumstances in which self-defence and defence of property will be accepted as complete defences to criminal charges.

THE *CRIMINAL CODE* PROVISIONS CONCERNING SELF-DEFENCE

Section 34 of the *Criminal Code* states that a person may use a reasonable amount of force in **self-defence** if they reasonably believe that they or another individual is the target of actual force or that a threat of force is being made against one of them. The section also sets out the factors that the courts must take into account in considering whether an accused person's use of force in self-defence was reasonable in all the circumstances of the case:

> (1) A person is not guilty of an offence if
>
> (a) they believe on reasonable grounds that force is being used against them or another person or that a threat of force is being made against them or another person;
>
> (b) the act that constitutes the offence is committed for the purpose of defending or protecting themselves or the other person from that use or threat of force; and
>
> (c) the act committed is reasonable in the circumstances.
>
> (2) In determining whether the act committed is reasonable in the circumstances, the court shall consider the relevant circumstances of the person, the other parties and the act, including, but not limited to, the following factors:
>
> (a) the nature of the force or threat;
>
> (b) the extent to which the use of force was imminent and whether there were other means available to respond to the potential use of force;
>
> (c) the person's role in the incident;
>
> (d) whether any party to the incident used or threatened to use a weapon;
>
> (e) the size, age, gender and physical capabilities of the parties to the incident;
>
> (f) the nature, duration and history of any relationship between the parties to the incident, including any prior use or threat of force and the nature of that force or threat;
>
> (f.1) any history of interaction or communication between the parties to the incident;
>
> (g) the nature and proportionality of the person's response to the use or threat of force; and
>
> (h) whether the act committed was in response to a use or threat of force that the person knew was lawful.
>
> (3) Subsection (1) does not apply if the force is used or threatened by another person for the purpose of doing something that they are required or authorized by law to do in the administration or enforcement of the law, unless the person who commits the act that constitutes the offence believes on reasonable grounds that the other person is acting unlawfully.

1. 2012, c. 9, s. 2.

WHAT ARE THE ESSENTIAL REQUIREMENTS FOR A SUCCESSFUL DEFENCE OF SELF-DEFENCE UNDER SECTION 34 OF THE *CRIMINAL CODE*?

The new *Criminal Code* provisions state that, to successfully assert the defence of self-defence, the accused person must satisfy three essential requirements. In [*Nur* (2018)], they were summarized as "(reasonable) belief; purpose and (reasonable) response" (see Figure 12-1).

Essentially, the new section 34 requires that, to raise a successful defence, accused persons must at least raise a reasonable doubt that they had a reasonable belief that they or another person were being assaulted and that their actions taken in self-defence were reasonable in all the circumstances of the particular situation in which they found themselves. For example, in *Foster* (2019), the accused became enraged after a verbal confrontation with the victim, which escalated to some physical pushing. Foster then took out an X-Acto blade and slashed the victim "in an act of aggression." Foster was convicted of aggravated assault and his appeal against conviction was dismissed by the Ontario Court of Appeal, which commented that "Acts of

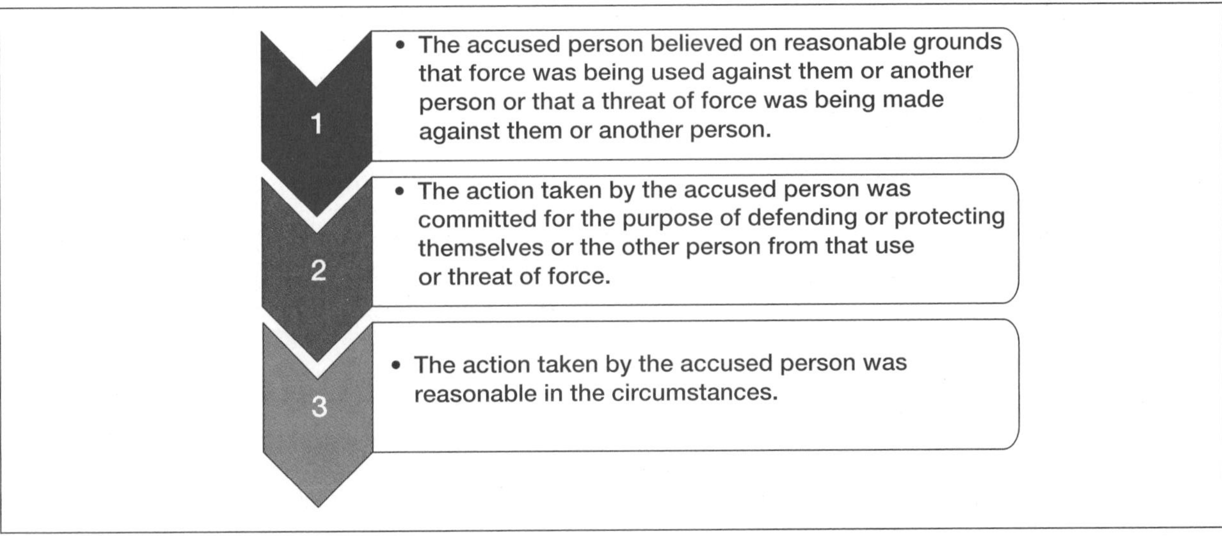

Figure 12-1

The Basic Elements Required for a Successful Defence of Self-Defence [Section 34(1)]

aggression are the antithesis of acts taken for a "defensive purpose," one of the elements of a s. 34 defence." Furthermore, the finding that Foster had become "enraged" belied Foster's "claim that he acted in fear, or based on a perceived need to protect himself or his girlfriend."

Clearly, the reasonableness of an accused person's actions will depend on the nature and extent of the perceived threat to the personal safety of themselves or another person. A bouncer in a bar who is threatened by an unarmed patron would be justified in using only a minimal level of force to subdue the assailant and remove them from the premises. Undoubtedly, the bouncer would not be justified in using deadly force in these circumstances. However, a woman who is threatened or attacked by a male partner who has a long history of inflicting extreme violence on her would be justified in believing that the only way in which she will preserve herself from death or serious bodily harm is to use deadly force (e.g., by deploying a lethal weapon) in self-defence. The requirement that the use of force in self-defence must be reasonably proportionate to the degree of real or perceived force used by the assailant against an accused person has been wittily captured by the phrase that one "cannot use a tank against a chariot."

When interpreting the *Criminal Code* provisions that were in force prior to 2013, the Supreme Court of Canada indicated that there are both *subjective* and *objective* elements in the test that should be applied to determine whether an accused person should be acquitted on the basis of self-defence. The *subjective* element relates to accused persons' subjective perceptions of the circumstances they encountered at the time of the alleged offence. Therefore, it is

Cartoon by Greg Holoboff

One cannot use a tank against a chariot.

necessary to inquire whether the accused persons subjectively believed that they were being assaulted or threatened with an assault and whether they subjectively believed that it was necessary to deploy the degree of force that they actually used to defend themselves. The *objective* element in the test concerns the issue of whether the accused persons' perceptions were based on reasonable grounds. In the *Cinous* case (2002), for example, Chief Justice McLachlin and Justice Bastarache expressed the view that:

> The accused's perception of the situation is the "subjective" part of the test. However, the accused's belief must also be reasonable on the basis of the situation he perceives. This is the objective part of the test. ... [T]he approach is first to inquire about the subjective perceptions of the accused, and then to ask whether those perceptions were objectively reasonable in the circumstances.

The courts have adopted a similar interpretation in the application of the current section 34 of the *Criminal Code*. Figure 12-2 summarizes this approach.

Since the application of the *Criminal Code* provisions relating to self-defence is based on both subjective and objective elements, it is important to bear in mind that accused persons may be mistaken in their perceptions of the circumstances they encounter. However, they may nevertheless be successful in raising self-defence if their mistake is based on reasonable grounds. For example, in *Cunha* (2016), the Ontario Court of Appeal set aside Cunha's conviction of discharging a firearm with intent to wound and aggravated assault and ordered a new trial because the trial judge had failed to consider the highly fraught circumstances in which Cunha had shot a man whom he *mistakenly* believed was armed. Two strange men involved in a drug deal with a tenant in Cunha's house had suddenly appeared in the foyer, one of whom was carrying a shotgun. Cunha believed the second man who started to turn around when Cunha told him to "freeze" was armed and going to shoot him: faced with the need to make a split-second decision, Cunha shot this man in the back and leg. The Court of Appeal ruled that "Overall, the trial judge failed to take account of the

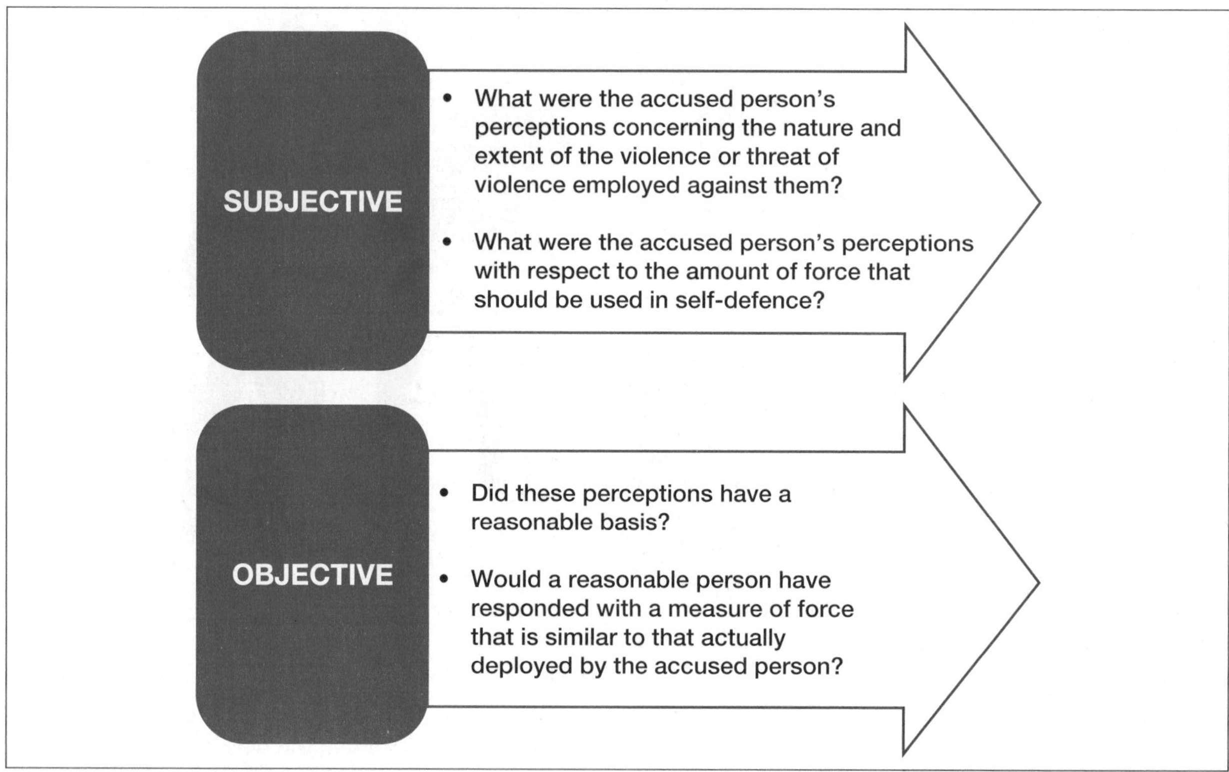

Figure 12-2

The Subjective and Objective Elements of Self-Defence [Section 34(1)]

entire situation from Mr. Cunha's perspective—a frightened home owner suddenly confronted with armed men in his home." The Court noted that "self-defence can be invoked on the basis of reasonable mistakes of fact" and that this "includes mistaking whether the putative assailant was armed as was the case here." The fact that the shot man was in fact unarmed was not fatal to Cunha's defence. It would not have been reasonable to expect Cunha to wait for the intruder to turn around to see if he was armed before pulling the trigger: therefore, self-defence based on a reasonable mistake was still a viable defence for Cunha.

Section 34(2) and the Criteria for Determining Whether the Act of Self-Defence Was Reasonable in the Circumstances

Section 34(2) of the *Criminal Code* specifies a number of factors that the courts should consider when they are called upon to determine whether an accused person's act of self-defence was "reasonable." The wording of section 34(2) makes it clear that this list of factors is not exclusive: other factors may be relevant to the determination of what is reasonable in particular cases. However, the factors that are identified in section 34(2) undoubtedly reflect the key considerations that arise in many of the cases in which the accused person seeks to rely on self-defence in response to a charge of a violent crime. Although the new section 34(2) represents a major change in the law relating to self-defence as an absolute defence, it is inevitable that the courts will place considerable reliance on the large body of case law regarding the interpretation of the self-defence provisions in the *Criminal Code* that were in force prior to 2013. Indeed, this body of case law will greatly assist the courts in assessing whether an accused person's act of self-defence was "reasonable" in all the circumstances and will provide many examples of decisions in which the factors specifically identified in the new section 34(2) played an important role in shaping the ultimate decision with respect to the success or otherwise of the defence.

Each of the factors identified in section 34(2) will be considered in light of any relevant case law that might shed some light on how Canadian courts are likely to assess the reasonableness or otherwise of the accused person's conduct in self-defence. Of course, in practice, the courts will always consider a number of the statutory factors simultaneously as part of a larger picture: for example, "the nature of the force or threat" would always be considered in tandem with the "the nature and proportionality of the person's response to the use or threat of force."

Section 34(2)(a): "The Nature of the Force or Threat"

Clearly, the degree of violence expressed in an attack on the accused person or the degree of menace that is implicit in a threat made against the accused person will play a critical role in determining whether an act of self-defence will be considered reasonable. The greater the degree of violence deployed by the assailant or the greater the menace underlying the threat made by the assailant, the greater the degree of force that might reasonably be used by the accused person in self-defence. The key issues here are, how did the accused person *perceive* the nature and extent of the attack or threat, and were their perceptions *reasonable* in the particular circumstances? For example, in *H. (A.)* (2017), the trial court found that the accused reasonably believed that force was being used against him when the victim reached into his car after having blocked the accused's vehicle with his own car and having previously banged on the accused's car. It did not matter that, in fact, the victim was trying only to remove the accused's car keys.

An accused person does not have to wait until a physical assault is launched against him or her: indeed, the use of force in self-defence may be justified as a response to threatening gestures and/or words. Normally, menacing words unaccompanied by any violent actions or gestures would not justify a resort to defensive force: however, the courts may find that an accused person acted reasonably by using force in response to mere words if there has been a history of violence or abuse by the person making the threats toward the accused person. Indeed, in *Young* (2008), Justice Smith, of the B.C. Court of Appeal, asserted that "[I]n cases of self-defence ... the words of threat must be considered in the context of the history of abuse and the reasonable perceptions of the accused."

Young was a case involving allegations by the accused of domestic violence on the part of the deceased victim. Justice Smith noted that "threatening words" in this context might reasonably cause the accused to "think that she was about to be physically harmed unless she should do something to prevent it regardless of whether she reasonably believed that an actual physical assault was in progress."

Section 34(2)(b): "The Extent to Which the Use of Force Was Imminent and Whether There Were Other Means Available to Respond to the Potential Use of Force"

Section 34(2)(b) identifies two critical factors of considerable importance in determining whether or not the use of force in self-defence was reasonable: (1) the imminence of an attack on the accused person and (2) the availability of alternative means of responding to the threat of an attack.

In many cases, one of the first questions to be asked when self-defence is raised as a defence is whether the accused person was facing or believed on reasonable grounds that they were facing an "imminent" attack. In general, the further in the future an attack is likely to occur, the more likely it is that the accused person will be expected to find a means of avoiding this threat, thereby eliminating the need to use force in self-defence. As Justice Wilson said in the *Lavallee* case (1990):

> The rationale for the imminence rule seems obvious. The law of self-defence is designed to ensure that the use of defensive force is really necessary. It justifies the act because the defender reasonably believed that he or she had no alternative but to take the attacker's life. If there is a significant time interval between the original unlawful assault and the accused's response, one tends to suspect that the accused was motivated by revenge rather than self-defence. In the paradigmatic case of a one-time barroom brawl between two men of equal size and strength, this inference makes sense. How can one feel endangered to the point of firing a gun at an unarmed man who utters a death threat, then turns his back and walks out of the room? One cannot be certain of the gravity of the threat or his capacity to carry it out. Besides, one can always take the opportunity to flee or to call the police. If he comes back and raises his fist, one can respond in kind if need be. These are the tacit assumptions that underlie the imminence rule.

In *Cormier* (2017), the fact that the accused stabbed the deceased, who was coming toward him and was armed with a pipe, gave an air of reality to Cormier's claim of self-defence because of the undoubted imminence of the threat of force being used against him. In this sort of case, the application of the "imminence criterion" creates no difficulties for the courts. However, while the imminence of an attack is, according to section 34(2)(b), an important factor in determining the reasonableness of an accused person's act of self-defence, it is certainly not an absolute prerequisite for the success of the defence. For example, in the *Lavallee* case, the Supreme Court of Canada ruled that the imminence factor should not be given much weight when the accused person is a woman who has been subjected to a pattern of physical abuse by a male partner. Indeed, Justice Wilson asserted that:

> I do not think it is an unwarranted generalization to say that due to their size, strength, socialization and lack of training, women are typically no match for men in hand-to-hand combat. The requirement … that a battered woman wait until the physical assault is "underway" before her apprehensions can be validated in law would, in the words of an American court, be tantamount to sentencing her to "murder by installment" … I share the view … that "society gains nothing, except perhaps the additional risk that the battered woman will herself be killed, because she must wait until her abusive husband instigates another battering episode before she can justifiably act."

The *Pétel* case (1994) serves as an excellent example of the circumstances in which it would be inappropriate to consider the imminence factor in determining the reasonableness of the accused person's act of self-defence. In *Pétel*, the accused was charged with the murder of the companion of her daughter's boyfriend (Edsell). Both Edsell and the deceased (Raymond) had been actively involved in drug trafficking. Edsell and the daughter moved into Pétel's house, and Edsell started to use the premises as a base for his illicit activities. Pétel stated that Edsell frequently threatened her and that he beat her daughter. Pétel was so upset by Edsell's presence in her household that she ultimately moved to another residence. However, her efforts proved to be in vain, since Edsell continued to come to her house to traffic in drugs. On the day of the homicide, Edsell went to Pétel's residence with a revolver, some cocaine, and scales. He told Pétel to hide the gun and then forced her to weigh some cocaine. He then suggested that he would kill Pétel, her daughter, and her granddaughter. Soon afterward, Pétel's daughter arrived with Raymond. Pétel then consumed a small quantity of drugs and went to retrieve the revolver she had hidden. Immediately, she fired the gun at Edsell, who fell down. Raymond lunged at Pétel and she shot him as well. Edsell survived his wounds, but Raymond later died.

At Pétel's trial, she was convicted of murder. However, the Supreme Court of Canada agreed with the Quebec Court of Appeal that there should be a new trial. The trial judge had told the members of the jury that, in making their decision whether Pétel's recourse to deadly force was reasonable, they could consider only the threats made by Edsell *on the same evening as the shooting*: in other words, the trial judge was imposing the requirement of imminence as a *precondition* for the success of Pétel's defence. The Supreme Court ruled that the trial judge had made a serious error when he effectively ruled that Pétel had to show the imminence of an assault in order to establish a valid defence. Indeed, Chief Justice Lamer stated:

> *There is ... no formal requirement that the danger be imminent.* Imminence is only one of the factors which the jury should weigh in determining whether the accused had a reasonable apprehension of danger and a reasonable belief that she could not extricate herself otherwise than by killing the attacker. [emphasis added]

Chief Justice Lamer stated that the various threats made by Edsell during his lengthy period of cohabitation with Pétel were of particular relevance to the jury's determination of whether she had a reasonable apprehension of danger and a reasonable belief in the need to kill Edsell and Raymond. Indeed, the jury needed to consider the threats made *prior to the day of the shooting* to understand exactly how Pétel perceived the circumstances that led to her decision to act in self-defence. The trial judge's direction to the jury to focus their attention only on the threats made on the very evening of the shooting may have led them to "disregard the entire atmosphere of terror" that Pétel said had "pervaded her house." As Chief Justice Lamer concluded, "[I]t is clear that the way in which a reasonable person would have acted cannot be assessed without taking into account these crucial circumstances."

The second factor identified in section 34(2)(b) is the presence or absence of alternative methods of dealing with the use or threat of force against the accused person. If it is possible to choose a course of action that simultaneously protects oneself from harm and avoids the need to resort to violence, then an individual should make that choice even though they have been threatened with the use of force by another party. The objective of any civilized system of criminal law must be to safeguard all citizens from unnecessary harm.

In some respects, the defence of self-defence resembles the defences of necessity and duress. Indeed, a common thread running through the requirements of each is the principle that the accused must take advantage of any less harmful course of action that one would expect a reasonable person to pursue standing in the accused's shoes. Even though an accused person may fear for their life or physical safety, they are expected to accept any reasonable opportunity to escape from the situation rather than inflict deadly force in self-defence. This point was emphasized by the Supreme Court of Canada in the case of *Cinous* (2002). Here, the accused was driving a van with two associates in order to carry out a theft of computers. Cinous contended that he believed that the two associates, who were located in the back of the van, intended to kill him. Cinous pulled into a service station and purchased some windshield washer fluid. He opened the back door of the van and, "seeing his opportunity," he shot one of the associates in the back of the head. The other associate fled from the scene. Cinous was convicted of murder at his trial and the conviction was ultimately affirmed by the Supreme Court. The Court held that there was no air of reality to Cinous's plea of self-defence because there was no evidence to suggest that he reasonably believed that he had no alternative but to kill his associate. As Chief Justice McLachlin and Justice Bastarache stated in their judgment:

> The requirement is that the accused have [*sic*] believed on reasonable grounds that there was no alternative course of action open to him at that time, so that he reasonably thought he was obliged to kill in order to preserve himself from death or grievous bodily harm. In this case, there is absolutely no evidence from which a jury could reasonably infer the reasonableness of a belief in the absence of alternatives. There is nothing in the evidence to explain why the accused did not wait in the service station rather than go back to the van. There is absolutely nothing to explain why he did not flee once he had left the van. Indeed, there is nothing to suggest the reasonableness of his conclusion that he needed to walk back to the van and shoot the victim.

Similarly, in *Grant* (2016), the Ontario Court of Appeal agreed with the trial judge that there was no air of reality to the claim of self-defence when Grant and his companion, Vivian, were robbed of some jewelry and pursued the car which contained the four men who had perpetrated the robbery. Vivian had driven the pursuing vehicle and Grant had fired a handgun which killed one man and wounded three others in the other car. Even though the robbers had taunted Grant and Vivian and one of them had brandished a gun out of the car window, there were other options available to Grant and Vivian than pursuing and shooting the robbers. As Justice Laskin pointed out, "They had several obvious courses of action other than following and shooting at the [robbers' vehicle]. They pursued none of them and gave no explanation why they did not do so."

Grant could have told Vivian to stop the car and turn around or, at the very least, slow down. If he was concerned about the gun that he had seen, Grant could have fired a warning shot. Grant pursued none of those options: instead, he fired 13 shots into the other car with the stated intention of doing as much damage as possible.

However, the courts have articulated a significant qualification to the general principle that one must pursue non-violent options whenever it is feasible to do so. Indeed, it has long been part of the common law that one is not expected to flee from one's home if one is under an actual or reasonably apprehended attack from an intruder. This principle is often encapsulated in the phrase "one's home is one's castle," and it was most recently reaffirmed by the Ontario Court of Appeal in the case of *Docherty* (2012).

In this case, Docherty stabbed and killed a loan shark who had made serious threats of violence against him in the past and, on this particular occasion, had threatened to break Docherty's legs. This incident took place in Docherty's home. Docherty was charged with second-degree murder but was convicted by a jury of manslaughter. The trial judge had informed the jury that Docherty's failure to retreat from his home was a factor to consider when they determined whether Docherty reasonably believed that stabbing the victim was the only way he could preserve himself from death or serious injury. The Ontario Court of Appeal allowed Docherty's appeal and ordered a new trial on a charge of manslaughter. The Court held that the trial judge had made a serious error in suggesting to the jury that they should consider Docherty's failure to leave his home.

Justice Sharpe agreed that self-defence is a defence of "last resort" and will not be accepted if the accused person has other options that may be considered reasonable in all the circumstances of the case. However, he noted that "[D]ifferent considerations apply where a person is attacked in his or her own home." Justice Sharpe referred to the ancient common law "castle doctrine," which supports the legal principle that individuals have the right to defend themselves in their own home and that they are under no duty to retreat from their home:

> The "castle doctrine" rests on the idea that the home provides protection for a person, his family and his possessions and that mandating a duty to retreat would force people to leave the security of their home, leaving their family members exposed to danger and their belongings vulnerable to theft. The castle doctrine also involves the idea that one's home is the last refuge, the last line of self-defence.

Of course, even though one is not required to retreat from one's home when threatened by an intruder, one is nevertheless expected to use no more force than is considered to be reasonable in all of the circumstances.

Section 32(4)(c): "The Person's Role in the Incident"

In judging the reasonableness of an accused person's actions taken in self-defence, the courts will undoubtedly consider the extent to which this person was the aggressor in the events that led to the use or threat of force by the other party or parties to the conflict. The use of force, even in self-defence, should be a last resort in a civilized society, and an individual who initiates a serious assault against another person has effectively made the choice to unleash an episode of violence that could have been avoided by exercising due restraint. Furthermore, the courts will be careful to prevent the situation in which an accused person deliberately provokes the victim to justify inflicting a death blow. As the Nova Scotia Court of Appeal suggested in *Borden* (2017), because of section 34(2)(c), "a protection is hopefully present to prevent self-defence from becoming too ready a refuge for people who instigate violent encounters, but then seek to escape criminal liability when the encounter does not go as they hoped and they resort to use of a weapon."

The greater the degree of violence used by the accused person when initiating a conflict, the less likely it is that they will be able to rely on self-defence when the other party responds with an equal measure of physical aggression. However, having been the aggressor does not necessarily mean that the accused person will be denied the benefit of the self-defence provisions of the *Criminal Code*. If the accused person uses a relatively minimal level of force or makes relatively mild threats against another person and that individual responds with life-threatening force, then the accused person may undoubtedly deploy a reasonable level of force in self-defence: in certain circumstances, a reasonable response may even encompass the use of lethal force.

The *McIntosh* case (1995) raised the question of whether the aggressor in an incident that led to the death of the victim may be entitled to seek the benefit of the self-defence provisions in the *Criminal Code*. McIntosh, who was a disc jockey, gave Hudson some audio equipment with a view to having it repaired. Eight months passed, and Hudson had still not returned the equipment to McIntosh. Although McIntosh made several attempts to recover his property, he failed to do so, and Hudson actively avoided him. On the day of the homicide, McIntosh's girlfriend spotted Hudson working outside and informed McIntosh of this encounter. McIntosh took a kitchen knife and confronted Hudson. Angry words were exchanged and, according to McIntosh, Hudson pushed him, and this led to a struggle between them. Hudson then picked up a dolly[2] and, raising it to head level, moved toward McIntosh, who responded by stabbing Hudson to death.

At his trial, McIntosh was convicted of manslaughter. The trial judge had told the jury that McIntosh could not rely on self-defence if he had provoked the assault on him by Hudson. McIntosh's appeal to the Ontario Court of Appeal was successful and a new trial was ordered. The Supreme Court of Canada subsequently affirmed the decision of the Court of Appeal. While McIntosh clearly initiated the conflict that led to Hudson's death, he was primarily concerned with retrieving his property after months of delaying tactics by the victim and that he used the knife only when Hudson was moving toward him armed with a potentially lethal weapon raised up to head level in a particularly menacing manner. If McIntosh's version of events was to be believed, it might have been possible to view his use of the knife as a reasonable response in desperate circumstances.

Section 34(2)(d): "Whether Any Party to the Incident Used or Threatened to Use a Weapon"

The use or threatened use of a weapon by any of the parties involved in an altercation will certainly constitute a critical factor in the determination as to whether the accused person acted reasonably when using force in self-defence. However, the significance of this factor will depend to a great extent on the specific circumstances of each individual case. For example, in *Mateo-Asencio* (2018), the trial judge considered it to be "significant" that the assailant was unarmed and that the accused used a baseball bat to inflict serious injuries on the assailant. However, the accused was nevertheless acquitted of charges of aggravated assault, assault with a weapon, and possession of a weapon for an unlawful purpose. There was evidence that the assailant, who was apparently intending to use his fists, charged Mateo-Asencio and the trial judge, therefore, decided that the Crown had not proved beyond a reasonable doubt that Mateo-Asencio's actions were unreasonable:

> Mr. Mateo-Asencio reacted instinctively to Mr. McLean's charge by swinging the bat to protect himself from a perceived imminent assault. He swung again, but only after Mr. McLean charged at him a second time.

Discharging a firearm at an unarmed assailant would, in most circumstances, be viewed as an unreasonable act of self-defence. However, as the *Lavallee* case (1990) indicated, it well might be considered a reasonable course of action for a woman to use a weapon against a more powerful male partner who threatens her, following a lengthy period of abuse. If she can establish that she believed on reasonable grounds that using a weapon was the only means of preserving herself from death or serious injury, her claim that she acted in self-defence will constitute a successful defence at her trial even if her partner was unarmed at the time of the shooting.

The use of a firearm as a weapon will generally require that the accused person provide a strong justification for pursuing this option. If a gun is fired directly at another person, the likelihood of the shot proving to be fatal is very high: therefore, the accused person will need to establish that they had reasonable grounds on which to believe that there was no viable alternative to using deadly force. However, a firearm may be used as a means of *preventing* an attack on the accused without the need to fire a shot. Just making an assailant aware that they have a firearm may be sufficient to preserve the accused person from an injury and such an action may be viewed as a reasonable response to the situation and be accepted as valid self-defence. If the assailant has another type of dangerous weapon—such as a knife—and moves slowly toward the accused, the latter may fire a warning shot into the air, and this may be viewed as a reasonable act in self-defence. On the other hand, if the assailant runs swiftly toward the accused person and wields a machete in an aggressive manner, the accused person

2. A dolly is a low platform that sits on wheels or casters and is used to move heavy objects.

may be justified in firing at the assailant because it would be reasonable to judge that this was the only way the accused person could preserve their life.

When the assailant possesses a less lethal weapon than the accused person and does not actually use it, the accused person who responds with deadly force will find it very difficult to make a successful claim of self-defence. For example, in *Cain* (2011), the Ontario Court of Appeal upheld Cain's conviction of manslaughter because his use of a firearm was not in any way proportionate to the threat posed by the victim, who was armed only with a wooden bat.

In assessing whether or not the discharge of a firearm was reasonable, it is important to bear in mind that the courts will focus on the *intentions* of the accused person when the trigger was pulled and not on the *consequences* of their actions. This principle was applied in the tragic *Kandola* case (1993). Kandola's residence was besieged by a group of five men armed with various weapons. These men were making threats against Kandola and the other occupants of the house (including women and children) and were attempting to enter the house. Although the police had been called more than once, they had not arrived at the scene and Kandola decided to fire a warning shot from a handgun with a view to scaring off the attackers. Unfortunately, one of the attackers was accidentally killed by the bullet. The B.C. Court of Appeal ruled that Kandola was entitled to an acquittal on a charge of murder because he had acted reasonably in self-defence. The Court emphasized that "[I]t is important to note that it is the force itself, and not the consequence of the force used, which is justified." Firing a warning shot from a handgun was a reasonable response in the circumstances: the police had not arrived, there was a group of violent men trying to enter the house with a view to assaulting the occupants, and immediate action was necessary to protect them from imminent harm.

Section 34(2)(e): "The Size, Age, Gender and Physical Capabilities of the Parties to the Incident"

Undoubtedly, the relative size, age, gender, and physical capabilities of the parties to a violent incident are critical factors in determining whether the response of the accused may be considered a reasonable act of self-defence. When the accused person is placed at a significant disadvantage in terms of their physical ability to defend themselves from a more powerful assailant, resort to the use of a weapon may be considered reasonable, whereas, if the situation is reversed, the accused person would not be justified in using extreme force in self-defence. For example, as noted by Justice Wilson in *Lavallee* (1990), women may be at a distinct physical disadvantage when they are assaulted by men: "I do not think it is an unwarranted generalization to say that due to their size, strength, socialization and lack of training, women are typically no match for men in hand-to-hand combat." In addition, gender may be a critical issue when a woman has been subjected to sustained abuse at the hands of her male partner: what is considered reasonable in terms of self-defence in this particular circumstance has to be determined in light of a response that may be unique to abused women. As Justice Wilson indicated in *Lavallee*:

> If it strains credulity to imagine what the "ordinary man" would do in the position of a battered spouse, it is probably because men do not typically find themselves in that situation. Some women do, however. The definition of what is reasonable must be adapted to circumstances which are, by and large, foreign to the world inhabited by the hypothetical "reasonable man."

The relative physical characteristics of two men involved in a physical altercation may also be critical to assessing the reasonableness of an accused person's act of self-defence. For example, in *Power* (2016), the accused was a police officer who was charged with assault causing bodily harm. In carrying out an arrest, Power "push-kicked" a homeless man in the abdomen, causing him to fall backwards and injure his head. The victim was a small, frail man, blind in one eye, cognitively impaired and a chronic alcoholic who weighed no more than 120 to 140 pounds. Power was 6-foot-one-inch-tall, weighed about 215 pounds and was "in good physical condition." Significantly, Power had arrested the victim many times previously and was well aware of his poor physical and mental state. The Saskatchewan Court of Appeal restored Power's trial conviction. In rejecting the contention that Power was acting in self-defence, Justice Ottenbreit noted that "factors such as disparity in strength, agility, size and fitness as well as sobriety must be taken into account by the officer in order to respond properly to a perceived threat." In this case, the disparities were overwhelming, and they rendered Power's use of force unreasonable.

Section 34(2)(f): "The Nature, Duration and History of Any Relationship Between the Parties to the Incident, Including Any Prior Use or Threat of Force and the Nature of That Force or Threat"

If there has been a history of violence or threats of violence between the accused person and the individual who attacked or threatened them, it is more likely that a court will judge that the accused person was justified in using force in self-defence. The court may even consider that the accused person was justified in making a so-called "preemptive strike" against such an individual rather than waiting to be attacked and killed or severely injured.

An important example of the significance of a prior record of violence against an accused person who acts in self-defence is the much-discussed case of *Lavallee* (1990). In this case, the Supreme Court of Canada ruled that when a woman kills a persistently abusive partner and raises the plea of self-defence, the trial court may admit expert testimony concerning the so-called **battered wife syndrome**.[3] Such testimony can assist the jury to answer the question of whether the accused believed on reasonable and probable grounds that she had to kill the accused to preserve herself from death or grievous bodily harm.

In *Lavallee*, the accused had been in a battering relationship with a man (Rust) for several years. She had been to hospital several times with serious injuries caused by her partner's violence. She shot Rust in the back of the head as he was leaving her room after he had physically assaulted her and threatened her with death. According to the accused, Rust had given her a gun and told her that he would kill her once all the guests had left the party that was taking place in their residence. Rust then said that if Lavallee did not kill him first, he would kill her. The accused shot him after he had made this remark and turned away to leave the room.

At Lavallee's trial for murder, her counsel argued that Lavallee had acted reasonably in self-defence. The trial judge permitted the defence to call a psychiatrist, who testified with respect to the battered wife syndrome. This evidence was introduced to establish that the accused reasonably apprehended death at the hands of Rust and that she reasonably believed that killing him was the only way of saving herself. The gist of the psychiatrist's opinion was that Lavallee "had been terrorized by Rust to the point of feeling trapped, vulnerable, worthless, and unable to escape the relationship despite the violence." In addition, he suggested that the continuing pattern of abuse by Rust placed the accused's life in real danger. In this respect, he concluded that Lavallee's shooting of Rust should be viewed as "a final desperate act by a woman who sincerely believed that she would be killed that night." Lavallee was acquitted and the Supreme Court ultimately held that the trial judge had been correct to place the evidence of battered wife or abused woman syndrome before the members of the jury.

Justice Wilson, speaking for the majority of the Supreme Court of Canada, noted that the relevant research literature has suggested that abused women experience clearly defined cycles of abuse. She emphasized that, in the case of a woman who has been subjected to such cycles of physical abuse, "[T]he mental state of the accused at the critical moment she pulls the trigger cannot be understood except in terms of the cumulative effect of months or years of brutality." Furthermore, the cyclical nature of abuse means that it becomes possible for the abused woman to make accurate predictions as to the moment when her partner will commence his violent behaviour. Therefore, expert testimony is particularly relevant in such cases because it can point to the accused woman's "heightened sensitivity" to her partner's acts and thereby clarify the question of whether she had a *reasonable* apprehension of death or grievous bodily harm. The critical issue, according to Justice Wilson, is not "what an outsider would have reasonably perceived but what the accused reasonably perceived given her situation and experience." In this light, it is clear that defendants such as Lavallee do not have to experience an actual attack before resorting to self-defence. They do not have to wait "until the knife is uplifted, the gun pointed or the fist clenched before apprehension is deemed reasonable."

The *Lavallee* case is of considerable significance in the development of Canadian criminal law because it clearly recognizes that, when a woman raises the plea of self-defence in response to an attack by a male aggressor, she is not to be judged by the standards of the "reasonable man" but rather by the standards of the "reasonable woman" who finds herself in the

3. **Abused woman syndrome** would be a more appropriate term because it clearly covers *psychological and sexual* as well as physical abuse. In *Malott* (1998), Justice Major, in delivering the majority judgment of the Supreme Court of Canada, used the term "abused woman" when discussing the situations in which evidence of "battered wife syndrome" may be placed before a jury.

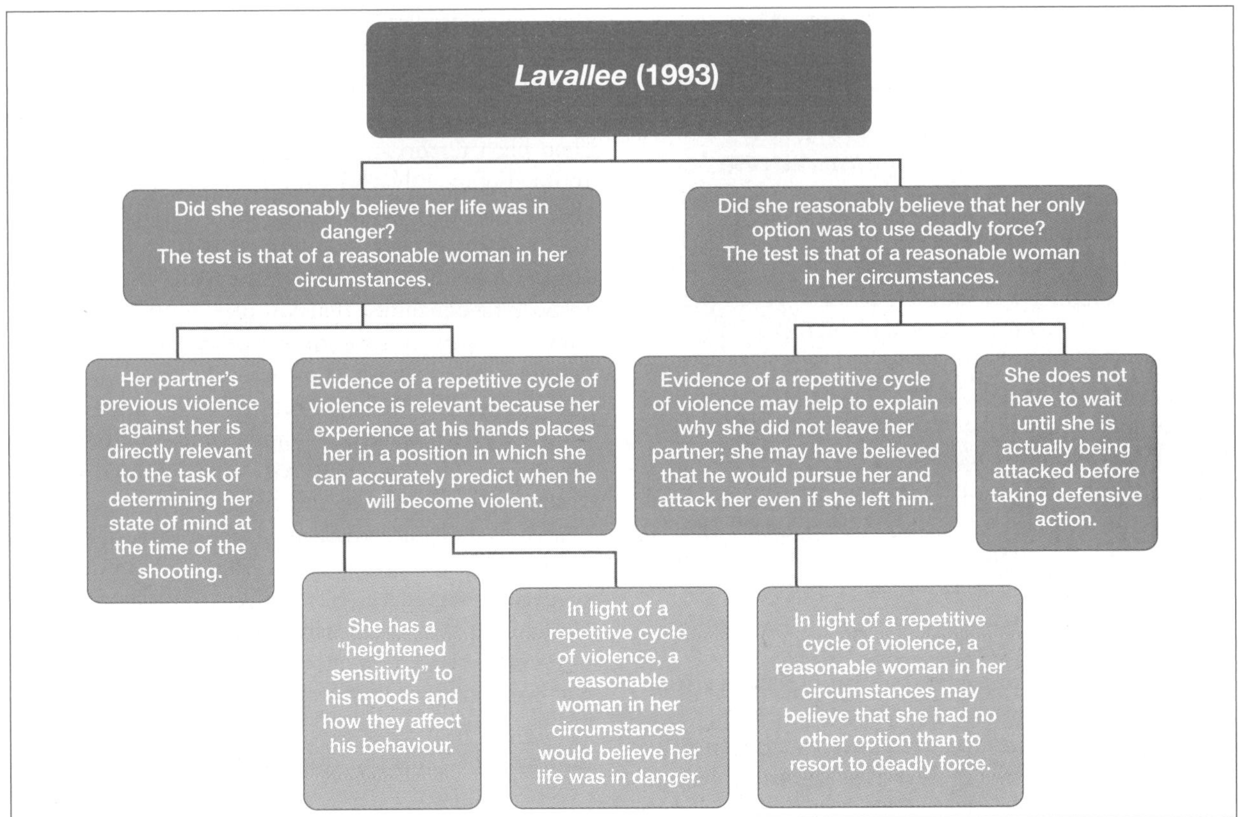

Figure 12-3
The Application of the Principles of Self-Defence in the Lavallee *Case (1990)*

same situation and shares the same experiences as the accused. Expert testimony concerning the abused woman syndrome is not introduced to establish a special defence based on the medical or psychological condition of the accused. On the contrary, it is introduced as a means of establishing the *reasonableness* of the accused woman's beliefs and actions in light of her experience of chronic abuse at the hands of her partner. It is, therefore, important to emphasize that an accused woman does not have to establish that, at the time of the act of self-defence, she possessed all the symptoms of the so-called "battered wife syndrome" in order to gain an acquittal. The evidence concerning the syndrome will be introduced merely to address the ultimate question of the reasonableness of her act of self-defence. In this sense, it would be totally wrong to "pathologize" the defence and to focus on the accused woman's psychological symptoms rather than on the circumstances in which she found herself at the time of the incident in question.

However, it is not enough to establish that the accused woman had been abused and that she wanted to remove herself from the abusive relationship; she must establish that she acted out of genuine fear for her life or safety. Indeed, in *Craig* (2011), the accused had killed her husband by placing a pillow over his face and stabbing him four times in the chest with a butcher knife as he lay in a drunken stupor. Craig claimed that she acted in self-defence because she feared that her husband would become violent when he woke up with a hangover. Although it was established that the husband had engaged in emotional abuse and had publicly humiliated Craig and her son, there was little evidence of physical abuse. The trial judge refused to allow self-defence to be considered because Craig had failed to meet the evidential burden—there was no air of reality to her claim that she feared for her life and safety and that her only resort was to inflict deadly force on her husband. Craig was convicted of manslaughter and her conviction was affirmed by the Ontario Court of Appeal. In the words of Justice Doherty:

> We agree with the trial judge that not every killing by an abused person in response to prolonged abuse

> is justified under the self-defence provisions of the *Criminal Code*. … Self-defence is a justification for what would otherwise be culpable homicide, based on the necessity of self preservation. … A person who kills another to escape from a miserable life of subservience to that person does not act in self-defence absent reasonably perceived threats of significant physical harm and reasonably held beliefs that the killing is necessary to preserve one's self from significant physical harm or death.

Similarly, the courts have been reluctant to expand the *Lavallee* decision to situations that do not involve the imbalance of power that was present in the abusive relationship between Lavallee and her partner, Rust. In *Charlebois* (2000), the Supreme Court of Canada affirmed the second-degree murder conviction of a man who had shot and killed the male victim while he was sleeping. Charlebois had claimed he acted in self-defence because of the "overwhelming fear" of the victim that "he had developed over the course of their long and difficult relationship." However, the Supreme Court was not willing to countenance placing this situation on a par with that which existed in the *Lavallee* case. To accept self-defence in the specific situation that was claimed to exist in *Charlebois* could not be justified either on the facts or in terms of sound legal policy. In this respect, Justice Bastarache stated that "While we have relaxed the requirement of imminency of the threat in the self-defence analysis particular to battered women, on the basis of expert evidence outlining the unique conditions they face, there is no justification for extending its scope further on the evidence presented in this case."

There are undoubtedly other situations in which the existence of a prior relationship involving violence may play a significant role in the court's decision to consider the accused person's act of self-defence to be reasonable. Take, for example, the case of a prison inmate who asserts that they had to launch a preemptive strike against another prisoner who either singularly or as part of a gang poses a realistic threat to the accused person's life and limb. Prisons may be dangerous places to live in, and an inmate who is threatened with violence by other prisoners generally does not have the option of moving away to avoid the risk to their life. This issue was considered by the Supreme Court of Canada in the *McConnell* case (1996). McConnell and others had killed a fellow inmate in a penitentiary. The deceased was apparently a member of a group who had threatened the life of the accused. McConnell started to stockpile weapons (knuckle-dusters[4] and a stick). When the victim walked by, McConnell approached him from behind and repeatedly hit him over the head with some knuckle-dusters while another inmate stabbed the victim in the stomach. The victim died of his injuries, and McConnell was subsequently tried and convicted of manslaughter.

The trial judge refused to place McConnell's plea of self-defence before the jury, stating that McConnell did not believe that he was in imminent danger of death or serious bodily harm at the time of the fatal assault. The Supreme Court of Canada ultimately allowed McConnell's appeal and ordered a new trial. Justice La Forest indicated that he and his colleagues agreed with the views expressed by Justice Conrad in the Alberta Court of Appeal. Justice Conrad had asserted that, for the purposes of a plea of self-defence, an analogy should be drawn between the battered wife syndrome and the so-called "prison environment syndrome," a concept that was raised by an expert witness at McConnell's trial:

> There was evidence from Dr. Weston about inmate behaviour and prison culture and the similarity in the environment to the battered wife syndrome. *There is evidence about the environment in which inmates had to "kill or be killed." Thus a person could believe he or she was being assaulted (a threat with present ability) without it being immediate.* [emphasis added]

In ordering a new trial, the Supreme Court of Canada undoubtedly accepted McConnell's argument that self-defence should be put to the jury because there was some evidence that he reasonably believed both that his life was in danger and that he had no alternative but to employ deadly force in self-defence.

The implications of decisions such as *McConnell* are potentially disturbing since they appear to justify the use of a "preemptive strike" in a prison environment and/or to legitimate the stockpiling of weapons in anticipation of such an act of violence. Certainly, these decisions may prompt one to question not only whether the "law of the jungle" should rule in Canada's prisons but also whether the state is meeting its basic duty to provide safe and humane treatment to vulnerable and powerless inmates.

However, it is important to emphasize that the opportunity to raise self-defence as a justification

4. A knuckle-duster is a piece of metal, usually steel, designed to fit around one's knuckles and used for the sole purpose of fighting. It increases the amount of physical damage to the other combatant while simultaneously protecting the user's own hands from damage.

for violence in the prison setting is severely circumscribed by the requirement that the accused must believe *on reasonable grounds* that they are under the threat of an attack that demands a response in order to preserve their life or to avoid serious injury to themselves. Significantly, in *Primmer* (2018), the Ontario Court of Appeal affirmed Primmer's conviction of assault causing bodily harm because, even though the attack had occurred within a conflicted prison context, Primmer had acted "not in self-defence, but out of anger and a desire to maintain his status."

Section 34(2)(f.1): "Any History of Interaction or Communication Between the Parties to the Incident"

The reasonableness of an act of self-defence will depend to some extent on whether there has been any previous interaction or communication with the person alleged to be the assailant. For example, an accused person who enters into a transaction with a loan shark or a drug dealer may well claim that they had good reason to believe that such a disreputable individual would be likely to use harsh violence should the accused person not pay for any illicit services rendered. Take, for example, the *Docherty* case (2012), in which a new trial was ordered because the trial judge had not made clear to the jury that an accused person does not have to retreat from their home when threatened by an intruder. While in his house, Docherty had stabbed to death a loan shark who had made threats against him in the past and who was, on this particular occasion, threatening to break Docherty's legs on account of an unpaid debt. On a retrial, the generally recognized expectation that a loan shark will employ extreme violence to retrieve money owed on a loan would be particularly relevant to the question of whether it was reasonable for Docherty to grab a knife and stab the loan shark in the neck.

The courts will also pay close attention to any communication that passed between the assailant and the accused person prior to the latter's act of alleged self-defence. For example, in *Young* (2008), the accused had fatally shot her estranged husband and wounded his friend. Prior to the shooting, Young's husband had called her from a bar and, using foul language, threatened to kill her:

> The appellant said he was yelling on the telephone, that I belonged to him and I was his fucking wife and I better get my fucking ass out to the house or he'd fucking hurt me, he would kill me, and I belonged to him and if I didn't get out there, they were comin' to get me.

When the husband encountered Young at the former's residence, he repeated the threat to kill her. Young was convicted of second-degree murder and attempted murder, but the B.C. Court of Appeal ordered a new trial on the charge of second-degree murder because the trial judge had not made it clear to the jury that, given the particular circumstances of the case, verbal threats—even if they were unaccompanied by any physical acts or gestures—could nevertheless lead the accused person to reasonably believe that her life was in danger and that her only option was to use lethal force in self-defence. Justice Smith noted that the telephone call should be an important factor in the jury's decision as to whether Young's shooting her husband could be considered a reasonable act of self-defence:

> The trial judge should have instructed the jury that ... they must consider whether the appellant reasonably believed that she was being assaulted by reason of Mr. Payton's threats uttered in the last telephone call and in the kitchen immediately before his death, including the words, "You're dead, bitch," considered in the context of their previous relationship and the expert evidence of her dependent personality disorder and her conduct manifesting the three-part cycle characteristic of the "battered woman syndrome."

Section 34(2)(g): "The Nature and Proportionality of the Person's Response to the Use or Threat of Force"

Undoubtedly, one of the most important considerations in determining the reasonableness of an accused person's act of self-defence is whether the response was *proportionate* to the nature and scope of the attack or threat directed toward the accused person.

The requirement of proportionality is well illustrated by the case of *Rasberry* (2017), in which the accused had stabbed the victim to death after the latter had threatened both Rasberry and his wife with anal rape. Rasberry argued that he had acted in self-defence. In these circumstances, it was clear that Rasberry met the requirements of sections 34(1)(a) and (b)—namely, that he and his wife were under the threat of force being applied against them and that he used force against the victim both to defend himself and to protect his wife from that very real threat. However, the critical question in this case was whether Rasberry met the requirement in section 34(1)(c) that his use of force had been "reasonable in the circumstances." At Rasberry's trial for second-degree murder, the trial judge ruled that "the crux of the case" turned on the criterion of proportionality articulated in section 34(2)(g). Rasberry used three different knives in his attack on the victim: each of these knives had been retrieved from a block in the kitchen. Two of the knives broke, one within the victim's body. The third knife was bent with part of its blade remaining within the victim. The medical evidence indicated that there were 23 stab wounds and 14 slash wounds. The trial judge found that the degree of defensive force employed by Rasberry was so disproportionate to the nature of the threat presented by the victim that it must be considered unreasonable and, therefore, the claim of self-defence was rejected. However, the trial judge found that there had been provocation and he convicted Rasberry of manslaughter. The Alberta Court of Appeal rejected Rasberry's appeal against his manslaughter conviction. The Court stated that the trial judge's decision was entirely reasonable, considering the nature of the medical evidence:

> Based on the evidence of the medical examiner, it was reasonable for the Trial Judge to infer that the victim would have been largely, if not completely, incapacitated before Rasberry stopped stabbing and slashing him. ... The evidence as a whole provides a basis for his conclusion that Kelloway was disabled before the stabbing ended, and that Rasberry's actions in continuing to stab the victim were unreasonable.

However, the requirement of proportionality is not one that is applied in a strictly objective manner. An accused person may make the kind of mistake that a reasonable person would make in the same circumstances and deploy a level of force that appears to be appropriate at the time but subsequently turns out to be excessive. Such an accused person would nevertheless be entitled to be acquitted on the basis of self-defence. For example, in *Berrigan* (1998), the accused killed an individual he reasonably believed was reaching for a gun but, in fact, was going to take out his cellphone. Of course, there is no objective proportionality whatsoever between killing an individual and retrieving a cellphone, but Berrigan made the kind of mistake that a reasonable person may well have made in the same circumstances (the victim in this case was known both to be violent and to carry a gun).

It is also important to bear in mind that the test of proportionality is directed toward the accused person's *intention* at the time that they use force in self-defence and not toward the *consequences* of the action. The Supreme Court of Canada emphasized this approach in *Kong* (2006). In this case, the accused and his friends were involved in a fight with a group of individuals, one of whom used a bottle as a weapon. According to Kong, when he saw two members of the opposing group running toward him, he took out a knife to protect himself and his friend, who had been hit on the head with the bottle: "He testified he waved the knife as a scare tactic, but when the two kept running towards him, he stepped forward and made a motion with his knife, either swinging or stabbing, to stop Miu and protect himself and John."

Although Kong denied that he stabbed the victim, the jury found he had done so. The trial judge had refused to put self-defence to the jury, stating that there was no air of reality to the defence, and Kong was convicted of manslaughter. The Supreme Court of Canada ordered a new trial in which self-defence should be left to the jury to decide. The Supreme Court agreed with the dissenting judgment of Justice Wittmann in the Alberta Court of Appeal, who made the following comments:

> It was open to the jury in this case to infer that when the appellant drew his knife, his only intention was to apply force to defend himself and prevent what he perceived was an imminent assault from Miu and another member of Miu's group. Miu's death was the unfortunate consequence of this use of force, but that fact, the conflicting testimony about the motion with the knife, and the autopsy evidence should not be used to conclude that he used more force than necessary in the circumstances. ...

Finally, the courts have also recognized that decisions made concerning the use of force in self-defence are usually made in the heat of a highly fraught moment and, as a consequence, they have allowed accused persons a certain degree of leeway with respect to the nature and scope of their response to an attack. The accused person who is the object of an attack may have only a split second in which to react to the threat. Furthermore, it may be very difficult for the accused person to determine the appropriate amount of reactive force that should be deployed if they are face-to-face with an aggressive assailant holding a weapon, such as a large knife. As Justice Martin of the Ontario Court of Appeal said in the *Baxter* case (1975), "[A] person defending himself against an attack, reasonably apprehended, cannot be expected to weigh to a nicety, the exact measure of necessary defensive action."

Section 34(2)(h): "Whether the Act Committed Was in Response to a Use or Threat of Force That the Person Knew Was Lawful"

The final criterion of reasonableness articulated in section 34(2) is whether the accused person knew that they were responding to the use or threat of force by an individual that was legally sanctioned in the circumstances. Unquestionably, such knowledge on the part of the accused will significantly reduce the likelihood of a court finding their act of self-defence to be reasonable. One situation in which this criterion will be extremely important is when a trespasser resists the reasonable efforts of a householder or a landowner to remove the trespasser from their home or land when the intruder is damaging or destroying property in the home: if the trespasser fully appreciates that the householder or landowner has a legal right to engage in their removal in these circumstances and the force used is reasonable, then the trespasser would not be entitled to claim that their resistance was justified. Of course, if the householder or landowner deploys an excessive degree of violence and the trespasser reasonably fears for life or limb, then the trespasser may respond with an appropriate level of defensive force. The right of an individual to employ force in defence of their property is covered by the new section 35, which will be discussed later in this chapter.

Section 34(3) makes it very clear that an accused person may not rely on self-defence if the force used or threatened against them is brought to bear by an individual who is "doing something that they are required or authorized by law to do in the administration or enforcement of the law." For example, a police officer making an arrest or a bailiff removing someone's property under the authority of a court order may use an appropriate degree of force in carrying out their duties, and the individual who is the object of this attention may not resist and claim that they were acting in legitimate self-defence. This *Criminal Code* provision is clearly designed to protect the safety of police officers and other officials who act under the authority of the courts. However, section 34(3) does create an exception to this rule when the individual concerned believes, *on reasonable grounds*, that the police officers or other officials are acting beyond the scope of their legal authority and, therefore, "unlawfully."

The case of *S. (T.A.)* (2016) illustrates the situation in which an accused person uses force in self-defence against assailants who were acting without any lawful authority. The accused was a young female person living in a group therapeutic home. Because they believed that she was suicidal, three youth workers used force to prevent the accused from leaving the home. The accused kicked, punched, and bit one of the workers who attempted to restrain her. She was charged with assault, but she claimed that she acted

Self-Defence and the Use of Force by a Police Officer

Peter Power/The Globe and Mail/CP Images

On July 27, 2013, Police Constable James Forcillo shot and killed 18-year-old Sammy Yatim, who was brandishing a knife with an 11.4-centimetre-long blade in a Toronto streetcar, which he had emptied of passengers. The young man was experiencing a mental-health crisis.

The police officer was responding to an emergency call and his encounter with Sammy Yatin lasted no more than 50 seconds. During this encounter, the officer fired a volley of three gunshots which caused the young man to fall on his back onto the floor of the streetcar. Medical evidence established that this first volley was fatal because one of the bullets had shattered Sammy Yatin's heart.

After about six seconds had passed, the police officer fired a second volley of six shots. Since Sammy Yatin was already dying, this second volley did not in any way contribute to, or accelerate, his death.

Police Constable Forcillo was charged with second-degree murder with respect to the first volley of shots. He was also charged with attempted murder, based on his firing of the second volley. Since one cannot kill someone who is already dead or mere seconds away from death, the charge of attempted murder was applicable because section 24 of the *Criminal Code* states that if one carries out an action with the intent to commit a specific offence (in this case, the intent to kill) that individual may be convicted of an attempt to commit that offence "whether or not it was possible under the circumstances to commit the offence." Attempted murder is charged under section 239 of the *Criminal Code*. This offence carries a maximum sentence of life imprisonment. However, s. 239(1)(a.1) provides for a minimum sentence of imprisonment for four years when a firearm is used in the commission of the offence.

At his trial, Officer Forcillo relied on two defences. Section 25 of the *Criminal Code* provides a justification for a peace officer who "acts on reasonable grounds" and employs "as much force as is necessary" for the purpose of carrying out their lawful duties "in the administration and enforcement of the law." Section 34 provides for the defence of self-defence (as discussed in this chapter).

As far as the first volley of shots was concerned, Constable Forcillo testified that he fired his service gun at Sammy Yatin because he believed that he posed an imminent threat owing to his aggressive behaviour, the fact that he was advancing toward the officer, and his refusal to drop the knife in spite of a warning that he would be shot if he failed to do so. Constable Forcillo's defence with respect to the firing of the second volley of shots was that he mistakenly believed that Sammy Yatim was in a position to rearm himself and was rising up from the floor to continue his assault on the Officer. Video evidence established that, in fact, Sammy Yatim did not raise himself up after the first volley of shots but remained on his back.

On January 25, 2016, the jury acquitted Constable Forcillo of the second-degree murder charge, which was based on the first, fatal volley of shots that he had fired. However, it convicted him of the charge of attempted murder, which was based on the second volley.

On July 28, 2016, Justice Then sentenced Constable Forcillo to six years' imprisonment. The following day, Justice Then rejected a *Charter* challenge to the mandatory minimum sentence of five years' imprisonment. The Judge ruled that section 239(1)(a.1) was not framed too broadly (based on the argument that it should not be applied to police officers) and, therefore, did not infringe the principles of fundamental justice protected by section 7 of the *Charter*. In addition, Justice Then held that the mandatory minimum sentence did not infringe section 12 of the *Charter*, which protects Canadians from "cruel and unusual punishment."

On April 30, 2018, the Ontario Court of Appeal dismissed Constable Forcillo's appeal against conviction and sentence. On December 6, 2018, the Supreme Court of Canada dismissed Forcillo's application for leave to appeal. See *R. v. Forcillo*, [2016] O.J. No. 4024 (Ont. S.C.J.); *R. v. Forcillo* (2018), 361 C.C.C. (3d) 16 (Ont. C.A.); and *James Forcillo v. Her Majesty the Queen*, [2018] S.C.C.A. No. 258.

Section 34(2)(b) indicates that one criterion for determining whether the use of defensive force was "reasonable" is "whether there were other means available to respond to the potential use of force." What "other means" should be considered by a police officer responding to the threat of force against themselves or other people?

Section 34(2)(d) indicates that one criterion for determining whether the use of defensive force was "reasonable" is "whether any party to the incident used or threatened to use a weapon." Since a police officer has special training in the use of defensive force and usually has a number of weapons available to them, how important is it for judges and juries to consider the specific type of weapon in the hands of the assailant?

in self-defence. The Crown relied on section 34(3) but the accused successfully argued that the youth workers had no statutory authority to restrain her. The Judge of the Saskatchewan Provincial Court, therefore, acquitted her of a charge of common assault:

> Because their actions were not authorized by law, T.A.S. was entitled to defend herself from the use of force against her. Having considered the factors set forth in s. 34(2) of the *Criminal Code* and the evidence before me, I find that her actions were reasonable in the circumstances. As a consequence, while T.A.S. intentionally used physical force against Ms. Long in kicking, punching and biting her, I am satisfied that she did so in self-defence.

THE *CRIMINAL CODE* PROVISIONS CONCERNING DEFENCE OF PROPERTY

Section 35 of the *Criminal Code*, which came into force in March 2013, replaced a number of complex provisions relating to the **defence of property** with a more straightforward and coherent articulation of the applicable legal principles:

> (1) A person is not guilty of an offence if
>
> (a) they either believe on reasonable grounds that they are in peaceable possession of property or are acting under the authority of, or lawfully assisting, a person whom they

believe on reasonable grounds is in peaceable possession of property;

(b) they believe on reasonable grounds that another person

(i) is about to enter, is entering or has entered the property without being entitled by law to do so,

(ii) is about to take the property, is doing so or has just done so, or

(iii) is about to damage or destroy the property, or make it inoperative, or is doing so;

(c) the act that constitutes the offence is committed for the purpose of

(i) preventing the other person from entering the property, or removing that person from the property, or

(ii) preventing the other person from taking, damaging or destroying the property or from making it inoperative, or retaking the property from that person; and

(d) the act committed is reasonable in the circumstances.

(2) Subsection (1) does not apply if the person who believes on reasonable grounds that they are, or who is believed on reasonable grounds to be, in peaceable possession of the property does not have a claim of right to it and the other person is entitled to its possession by law.

(3) Subsection (1) does not apply if the other person is doing something that they are required or authorized by law to do in the administration or enforcement of the law, unless the person who commits the act that constitutes the offence believes on reasonable grounds that the other person is acting unlawfully.

The requirements for a successful claim of defence of property under section 35(1) were succinctly summarized by M. Speyer, J. in *Fleming* (2014):

There are now four basic elements to the defence of property, regardless of the type of property. To succeed based on this defence, the accused must raise a doubt that he or she:

had a reasonable belief in the peaceable possession of the property

had a reasonable belief in an actual or pending **trespass**, theft of or damage to it

acted for the purpose of preventing the trespass, theft or damage, *and*

acted reasonably in the circumstances.

The onus remains on the Crown to negate the defence.

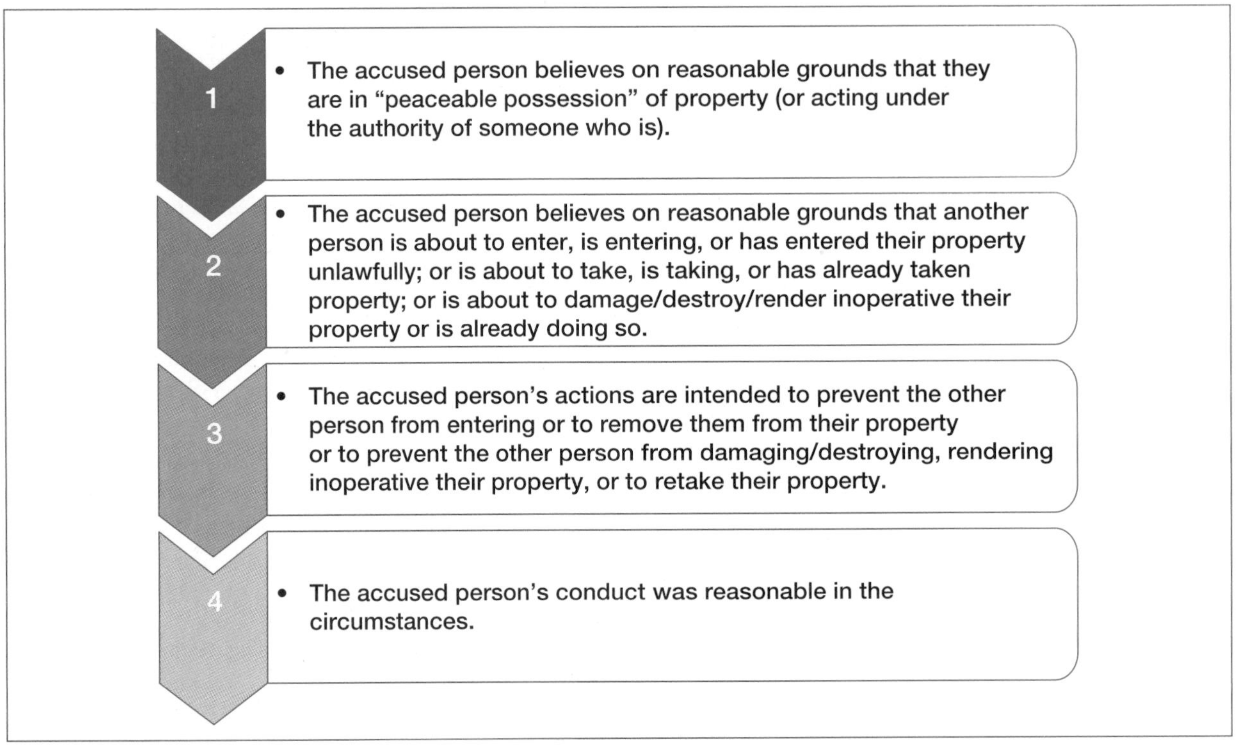

1	• The accused person believes on reasonable grounds that they are in "peaceable possession" of property (or acting under the authority of someone who is).
2	• The accused person believes on reasonable grounds that another person is about to enter, is entering, or has entered their property unlawfully; or is about to take, is taking, or has already taken property; or is about to damage/destroy/render inoperative their property or is already doing so.
3	• The accused person's actions are intended to prevent the other person from entering or to remove them from their property or to prevent the other person from damaging/destroying, rendering inoperative their property, or to retake their property.
4	• The accused person's conduct was reasonable in the circumstances.

The Basic Requirements of a Defence of "Defence of Property" under Section 35 of the Criminal Code

WHAT ARE THE ESSENTIAL REQUIREMENTS FOR A SUCCESSFUL CLAIM OF DEFENCE OF PROPERTY UNDER SECTION 35 OF THE *CRIMINAL CODE*?

The first requirement for a successful claim of defence of property, under section 35(1), is that the accused person believes on reasonable grounds that they are in "*peaceable possession*" of the property in question or that they are "acting under the authority of, or lawfully assisting, a person whom they believe on reasonable grounds is in peaceable possession of property." What is meant by the term **peaceable possession**? Essentially, it means the accused person's possession of the property in question is *not seriously challenged by anyone else*. Clearly, the Parliament of Canada sought to ensure that only individuals who have a reasonably sound claim to property should be entitled to use force to protect it; otherwise, the door would be open to an excessive number of potentially explosive skirmishes over property.

As with each of the requirements for a successful claim of defence of property, section 35 requires that the accused person's belief that they are in "peaceable possession" must be based on "reasonable grounds." As M. Speyer, J. said in *Fleming* (2014):

> The use of the words "reasonable grounds" imparts an objective/subjective test into the analysis. The accused must subjectively believe that he or she has peaceable possession, that the property is at risk and the actions in question must, subjectively, be for the purpose of protecting the property against theft, damage or trespass. However, there is an overarching requirement that the actions be reasonable. This will continue to require a modified objective analysis based on the perspective of a reasonable person standing in the shoes of the accused. The new s. 35 does not enumerate the factors that apply in assessing reasonableness and each case must be assessed on its own unique set of circumstances.

The Meaning of "Peaceable Possession" under Section 35(1)

The application of the "peaceable possession" requirement is well illustrated by the decision in *George* (2000). In this case, the accused was part of a group of protestors who had occupied a provincial park and an adjacent Canadian Forces base. The protestors claimed that they had an indigenous treaty right to both the park and the military base. The accused drove a car at a group of police officers and was subsequently convicted of criminal negligence in the operation of a motor vehicle and assault with a weapon. On his appeal to the Ontario Court of Appeal, George asserted that the trial judge had erroneously failed to consider defence of property as a potential defence. However, the appeal was dismissed. The Court ruled that there had been no peaceable possession of the land in question. Indeed, the police had clearly challenged the protestors in this respect, and the fact that the protestors had stockpiled rocks and sticks "made it clear that any challenge to their occupation could result in violence."

The Requirement under Section 35 that the Act in Defence of Property is "Reasonable in the Circumstances"

Section 35(1) requires that an accused person who claims defence of property in response to a criminal charge must show that they reasonably believed that another person was about to enter, was entering, or had entered their property unlawfully; or was about to take, was taking, or had already taken the property; or was about to damage/destroy/render inoperative the property or was already doing so. In addition, it must be demonstrated that the accused person's actions were intended to prevent the other person from entering or to remove them from their property or to prevent the other person from damaging/destroying or rendering inoperative the property or to retake the property. Once these requirements have been established, the really critical question for the courts is whether the accused person's actions were "reasonable in the circumstances."

The case law that interpreted the pre-2013 *Criminal Code* provisions encompasses some excellent examples of what is considered "reasonable" when an accused person acts in defence of their property. This case law makes a clear distinction between defence of real property (land, houses, apartments, other buildings) and personal property (all property other than real property) because the previous *Criminal Code* provisions dealt with these two types of property in different sections of the *Code*. The new section 35 deals with both types of property in the same section: however, for the purpose of analyzing the case law that examines whether actions taken in defence of property are reasonable, the cases will be divided into those that deal with real property and those that concern personal property.

The pre-2013 *Criminal Code* provisions explicitly referred to those who interfered with the rights of owners of real property as "trespassers." The new section 35(1)(b)(i) does not use this term; it just refers to a "person" who is "about to enter, is entering or has entered the property *without being entitled by law to do so.*" However, since the word **trespasser** is constantly referred to in the pre-2013 case law, it is helpful to define the term. In essence, *a trespasser is someone who violates the rights of others by entering or remaining on their property without any authority to do so.* Thus, a trespasser may be an individual who enters land, a house, apartment, or other building without permission or an individual who originally has such permission but remains after that permission has been withdrawn by the owner or the person acting under their authority. For example, an individual may be given a specific invitation to attend a party. Similarly, a person may enter a store on the basis that members of the public have an implicit invitation to do so. However, it is possible that the invitation to enter or remain on someone else's property as a guest can subsequently be withdrawn. If this occurs, the "disinvited" guest becomes a trespasser if they do not leave within a reasonable period after having been given their marching orders. Can such a trespasser be ejected with the use of a reasonable degree of force? Under the pre-2013 *Criminal Code* provisions, the answer to this question was unequivocally "Yes." However, the current *Criminal Code* provisions do not cover this situation. The new section 35(1)(b)(i) refers only to a person who is "about to enter, is entering or has entered the property *without being entitled by law to do so.*" Read literally, this provision does not cover the disinvited-guest scenario because such an individual would have *entered* the property lawfully. The only situation in which the disinvited guest may be forcibly removed under the current provisions is if they take (or attempt to take) any property on the premises or if they damage or destroy (or attempt to damage or destroy) any property [see sections 35(1)(b)(ii) and (iii)].[5]

This interpretation of the new defence-of-property provisions was applied by P.N. Bourque J. of the Ontario Court of Justice in *R. v. Green* (2017). The Judge ruled that force could not be used to move an individual from a building when he had been invited to attend a meeting from which he was later ordered to leave. When the complainant refused to go, he was "pulled and shoved and manhandled" out of the building. Two of the individuals who had evicted the complainant were convicted of assault. As far as section 35(1)(b) was concerned, there was "no air of reality to the assertion that [the complainant] was about to "take property" or "damage the property." Therefore, since the complainant had been invited to the meeting in the building, the two accused had no right to use force to remove him. The Trial Judge rejected the argument that the complainant had "lost any and all right he had to remain" at the very instant he was ordered to leave the building and that this fact entitled the accused to forcibly eject the complainant:

> That does not fit with the words of the section [35(1)(b)]. The defendants would have had to take this action on the edge of the territory as the section speaks of being "about to enter" or "has entered the property without being entitled by law to do so". The defendant was already on the property, when they purported to revoke this right.

The leading pre-2013 case dealing with the reasonableness of a property holder's use of force against a trespasser who entered the property *unlawfully* is *Gunning* (2005). This case concerned the fatal shooting of Chester Charlie, an uninvited person who came into Gunning's home during a party. Shortly before the shooting, Gunning found Charlie sitting on the edge of his bed going through the bottom drawer of his night stand. [This circumstance would be an important fact under the current section 35(1)(b)(ii) because it might cause a reasonable person to believe that Charlie was about to steal one or more items of Gunning's property, thereby permitting Gunning to remove him, using a reasonable degree of force]. Gunning asked Charlie to leave, but the latter refused and assaulted Gunning, who picked up a loaded shotgun to "intimidate or scare" Charlie into departing from the premises. According to Gunning, the gun discharged accidentally, and Charlie received a fatal wound to the neck. Gunning was charged with second-degree murder and was convicted at his trial. Gunning's conviction was upheld by the British Columbia Court of Appeal, but the Supreme Court of Canada later set aside the conviction and ordered a new trial.

5. A trespasser who refuses to leave may be committing a *provincial or territorial* offence. Therefore, the householder could call the police and the recalcitrant trespasser may be arrested. (See, for example, the trespass legislation in British Columbia and Ontario: *Trespass Act, R.S.B.C.* 1996, c. 462; *Trespass to Property Act, R.S.O.* 1990, c. T.21). In *D.L.M.* (2018), the B.C. Supreme Court allowed the accused's appeal against conviction of assaulting a police office and entered an acquittal. The accused had withdrawn her consent to the officers being in her unit and they were, from that point, *not acting in the execution of their duties*: "the police actions, though well intended, egregiously interfered with the appellant's privacy rights, property, dignity, and her right not to be interfered with."

The Supreme Court held that the trial judge should have instructed the jury to consider the issue of defence of property. Gunning did not claim that he intentionally shot Charlie in self-defence. Instead, he asserted that the shooting was accidental. The Supreme Court noted that Gunning was in possession of his house, that the possession was peaceable, and that, after he had been asked to leave, Charlie was undoubtedly a trespasser (although the request to leave was not the critical factor in the case since Charlie had never been invited to the party in the first place and had not entered the house lawfully). The only question that needed to be addressed was whether Gunning used a reasonable amount of force in the circumstances of the case. The jury may well have concluded that it was reasonable for Gunning to retrieve a firearm for the sole purpose of scaring or intimidating Charlie into leaving Gunning's house. As Justice Charron indicated, "[A]ll of the events preceding the shooting had to be taken into account in determining whether Mr. Gunning had used reasonable force in his attempt to eject Mr. Charlie." At the new trial ordered by the Supreme Court, the jury would be required to determine whether Gunning had acted reasonably in defence of his home. The focus of inquiry would be on Gunning's intentions at the time he made use of the firearm. If he did indeed merely intend to scare or intimidate Chester Charlie so the latter would leave Gunning's house, the jury may well consider his conduct reasonable in light of Charlie's assault on Gunning. If the gun discharged accidentally, then the fatal consequence of Gunning's conduct would not disqualify him from the benefit of the defence.

The *Gunning* case illustrates the willingness of the courts to show some degree of sympathy to individuals who resort to the use of force when threatened by a violent intruder in their own homes. However, conduct taken in defence of property should always constitute the least violent response that a reasonable person would consider necessary in the particular circumstances. The *Jamieson* case (2002) furnishes a good example of an act taken in defence of an individual's home that was manifestly unreasonable in terms of the excessive violence that was inflicted on the intruder. Jennings was consuming illegal drugs (GBH and crystal meth) in Jamieson's home and was behaving erratically. Jamieson told Jennings to leave, but the latter refused. Jamieson then threw acid over Jennings, even though Jennings had "made no threatening gestures or violent movements": "Jennings was taken to hospital and treated. His injuries, third degree burns to his face, scalp, ear, neck and chest, were grievous and he endured a significant period of hospitalization and several surgeries, including skin grafts, leaving him seriously disfigured."

Jamieson was convicted of aggravated assault and the British Columbia Court of Appeal agreed with the trial judge that throwing acid over a trespasser who refuses to leave is, in no way, a proportionate or reasonable response to the mere refusal of a trespasser to leave one's home.

An instructive example of a situation in which the accused person acted unreasonably in defence of his *personal property* is the case of *Szczerbaniwicz* (2010). The accused was a lieutenant-colonel in the Canadian military. He had separated from his spouse of 30 years but had invited her to spend the night with him in the house they had formerly occupied together. The couple discussed the removal of Ms. Szczerbaniwicz's personal possessions from the house, but the discussions escalated into a heated altercation. Ms. Szczerbaniwicz removed her husband's mounted university diploma from the wall and threw it onto the floor. Szczerbaniwicz pushed his wife into the staircase, causing bruising to her back, legs, and elbow. She discovered the next day that her finger was broken.

Szczerbaniwicz was charged with assault causing bodily harm and, in his defence, maintained that he was justified in using force to protect property

Cartoon by Greg Holoboff

Section 35: What is a reasonable level of force when one wishes to remove a trespasser from one's property?

that was valuable to him. At his court-martial, the trial judge agreed that there was an air of reality to the defence but found that Szczerbaniwicz used a disproportionate measure of force and, therefore, convicted him. Szczerbaniwicz's appeal ultimately reached the Supreme Court of Canada, which affirmed his conviction. Applying the *Criminal Code* provision then in force, the Supreme Court took the view that the key issue was whether the use of force was "reasonable in all the circumstances." As Justice Abella stated, on behalf of the majority of the Court:

> The reasonableness of "all the circumstances" necessarily includes the accused's subjective belief as to the nature of the danger or harm, but the objective component of the defence is also required: the subjective belief must be based on reasonable grounds. ...
>
> This is a case about a husband who lost his temper in an argument and pushed his wife with such force that she landed on the staircase and sustained extensive bruises. He used force because his wife threw to the floor a framed and easily replaced piece of paper of sentimental value. The trial judge found the use of this force in these circumstances to be disproportionate. This conclusion is eminently justified based on the legal and factual contexts.

Similarly, in *Reddick* (2018), the Nova Scotia Court of Appeal affirmed Reddick's conviction of aggravated assault and possession of a weapon for a dangerous purpose. The Court agreed with the trial judge that Reddick had no basis for claiming that he had a defence under section 35 because he was trying to recover medication which he claimed had been stolen by the victim. The Court of Appeal observed that Reddick had violently attacked an unarmed man, breaking his cane over the victim "in a vicious onslaught" and ruled that, even if the victim had stolen his medication (an allegation rejected by the trial judge), "Mr. Reddick's use of force was excessive."

It is important to remember that section 35(2) states that, even if individuals reasonably believe that they are in "peaceable possession" of property, they are not entitled to an acquittal based on defence of property if they do not have a "claim of right" to the property (an honest belief that they have a legal right to the property) and the person who is entering, taking, etc., the property in question does, in fact, have a legal right to its possession. This means that the famous saying "possession is nine-tenths of the law" is certainly invalid in this context. An individual who is in possession of property may not defend it against another person who is, in fact, legally entitled to it, *unless* one has an honest belief that one has a *legal right* of some kind to the property in question. For example, a thief who has stolen a cellphone may not use force to prevent the lawful owner from repossessing it—even if the thief has been using it quietly for some time and has not previously been challenged by anyone.

Section 35(3) parallels section 34(3) (dealing with self-defence) insofar as it prevents an individual from using force in defence of property if the party entering, taking, etc., the property is "doing something that they are required or authorized by law to do in the administration or enforcement of the law." The only exception arises if that individual "believes on reasonable grounds that the other person is acting unlawfully." For example, this provision protects a bailiff acting under a court order to seize property for payment of a debt from forcible resistance by the person in whose possession the property currently resides. Seizing a car or a television from an individual creates a situation in which emotions may run high and it is imperative that the criminal law not provide any encouragement for that individual to resort to violence when a bailiff executes their duty under clear legal authority. In this respect, it is significant that Parliament has made it clear that even if an individual honestly believes that the bailiff or other official is acting beyond the scope of their authority, it must be shown that this belief was based on *reasonable grounds;* otherwise, there is no basis for a claim of defence of property under section 35(1).

In *Woolridge* (2017), the accused was being admitted to a correctional facility and bit the thumb of a correctional officer who was attempting to take some medication and an inhaler from Woolridge before he was taken to his cell. Woolridge suffered from seizures and asthma and was adamant that he needed to take these items to the cell with him. He was told that if he needed any medication, medical staff would prescribe it for him. Woolridge was charged with assaulting a peace officer acting in the execution of his duties and thereby causing him bodily harm. He argued that he honestly believed that he was entitled to defend his property and that the correctional officer had no authority to take it from him. The Provincial Court Judge rejected this defence, referring to section 35(3): "I am satisfied that Mr. Woolridge knew he was at the Lockup and was dealing with correctional officers. It would have been unreasonable for Mr. Woolridge to believe that Correctional Officer Barnes was acting unlawfully."

In any event, the defence was not available because biting the officer was a wholly disproportionate response and, therefore, unreasonable. After all, Woolridge could simply have engaged in "passive resistance."

Study Questions

1. Martini invites Highball to a party, which is held in Martini's apartment. Highball becomes quite obnoxious and insults Martini's girlfriend, Tequila. Martini tells Highball to leave the premises "forthwith," but despite repeated requests to remove himself, Highball refuses to do so. Martini then attempts to throw his unwelcome guest out the front door. Highball resists very strenuously and starts to punch Martini in the face with a marked degree of force. Martini grabs a metal bar and strikes Highball on the head until the latter "falls limp" and Martini deposits the dazed Highball outside his apartment, in the corridor. Some other tenants spot Highball and take him to the Cocktail Hospital, where he is treated for concussion and lacerations of his scalp. He subsequently recovers without any permanent damage. If Martini were to be charged for his role in this sordid affair, would he have any special defence(s) open to him?
2. Hermia has lived with Lysander for 10 years, during which he has, on various occasions, subjected her to physical assaults, some of which have caused serious injuries (such as extensive bruising to the body, a broken nose, and concussion). One night, Hermia returns home late from an evening meeting and Lysander becomes furious with her. He yells that he is "going to fix her once and for all." However, he is so drunk that he passes out on the couch. Hermia goes to the kitchen and picks up a large knife. She then returns to the room where Lysander is sleeping and stabs him to death. Would Hermia be able to raise a successful plea of self-defence if she were charged with murder or manslaughter?
3. Elbow is an inmate in a prison that has gained an unfortunate reputation for its brutal atmosphere. Most of the prisoners have been convicted of violent offences, and there is a widespread belief that inmates are likely to survive only if they act on the maxim "kill or be killed." Pompey, a notoriously unpredictable and violent inmate, approaches Elbow and tells him that his "time is up." Elbow interprets this as a death threat and acquires a knife for self-protection. When Pompey is taking a shower, Elbow approaches him from behind and stabs him to death. When charged with first-degree murder, Elbow claims that he was acting only in self-defence. Is Elbow likely to be successful in raising the defence of self-defence at his trial?
4. Creakle is drinking in a bar when he is accosted by a group of young men, who are evidently part of a gang. He refuses their demands for money and runs out into the parking lot. However, five or six of the gang members pursue him, threatening to beat him up. Creakle turns around and pulls out a knife, which he waves horizontally in the hope that his pursuers will stay away from him. Smike, one of the gang members, nevertheless moves toward Creakle, and Smike's throat is cut when he walks into the knife. Smike dies within a few minutes. Creakle is charged with manslaughter. He strongly denies any intent to wound Smike. Would Creakle be able to successfully raise a defence of self-defence?
5. Magwitch has been separated from his wife, Betsy, for six months. When they separated, Magwitch had taken with him a number of items that Betsy believed belonged to her. Betsy goes to Magwitch's apartment to retrieve these items. Unfortunately, they engage in an acrimonious argument. Betsy takes hold of a trophy that Magwitch had won in a hot-dog-eating contest and says she will hang on to it until Magwitch agrees to return all the items that she claims belong to her. Magwitch considers the trophy to be of great sentimental value, and when Betsy refuses to hand it over, he angrily attempts to snatch it from her hands. After a brief struggle, Betsy releases the trophy, but, in doing so, she falls backward and hits her head on an iron hat stand. Betsy suffers a mild concussion and a laceration to the back of her head that requires 10 stitches at the emergency room of

the local hospital. Magwitch is charged with assault causing bodily harm. Is there any relevant defence he could raise in response to this charge? If so, is it likely that he would be acquitted at his trial?

6. Cruncher is the bouncer at a popular downtown bar. Buzfuz has consumed an excessive amount of alcohol and is pestering other customers. Cruncher asks Buzfuz to leave. Buzfuz refuses, but Cruncher manages to escort him out of the bar. A few minutes later, Buzfuz returns with a group of his friends and, at the entrance to the bar, angrily demands readmission. Cruncher rebuffs Buzfuz, who then yells obscenities and threatens to knock out Cruncher's teeth. When Buzfuz raises his fist and aims a blow toward Cruncher, the bouncer parries it with his arm and then gives Bufuz a hard push away from the door. Unfortunately, Buzfuz slips and, while falling to the ground, hits his head on a concrete step. Buzfuz suffers a severe brain injury, lapses into unconsciousness, and dies in hospital a few hours later. The Crown is considering charging Cruncher with manslaughter. What, if any, defences might Cruncher be able to rely on to avoid conviction should the Crown decide to proceed with this charge?

7. Nadgett accompanies his good friend, Snubbin, to the emergency department of a large hospital. Snubbin lives with bipolar affective disorder and has just run out of his usual medication for control of this condition. It is after midnight and Snubbin realizes that it is too late to obtain a prescription from his regular physician or at a walk-in clinic. Snubbin has to wait for three or four hours before he is seen by Dedlock, an emergency department physician. When he meets with Dedlock, Snubbin is angry about having had to wait for so long and he shouts loudly at Dedlock. Instead of writing a prescription, Dedlock, who has no expertise in psychiatry, says that he is going to sign a certificate that will cause Snubbin to be involuntarily committed to the psychiatric ward of the hospital. Snubbin refuses to cooperate and Dedlock enlists the aid of two security guards to force Snubbin to go to the psychiatric ward. Snubbin yells to Nadgett to help him. Nadgett believes that Dedlock has no authority to deprive Snubbin of his liberty because Snubbin is just angry and not exhibiting symptoms of acute mental disorder. Nadgett struggles with the security guards and one of them suffers a broken wrist. Snubbin is eventually taken to the psychiatric ward but is released next day by Gradgrind, a psychiatrist. Nadgett is charged with assault causing bodily harm. Does he have a defence to this charge?

APPENDIX

A Brief Note on the Canadian Criminal Court System

To assist the reader in acquiring a rudimentary understanding of the role of the courts mentioned in the text, this appendix offers a brief overview of the system of criminal courts in Canada. However, it should be emphasized that, at best, this overview paints a skeletal picture and the reader should be aware that there are numerous variations on the basic model as one moves from one province or territory to another.

All criminal cases enter the judicial system through the various *provincial or territorial courts*, where a provincially or territorially appointed judge sits without a jury.[1] However, although the majority of criminal cases are completed within the provincial courts, some cases must later move on to other courts for trial. All summary conviction offences are dealt with in the provincial or territorial courts, but whether an indictable offence will be tried there depends on the seriousness of the offence and, in some cases, on the choice of the accused person. Generally, the more serious criminal cases will not be tried in the provincial or territorial courts; instead, they are tried in the superior court of criminal jurisdiction of the various provinces and territories.

1. In Yukon and Northwest Territories, there are territorial courts. However, in Nunavut, the Nunavut Court of Justice combines the powers of the superior court of criminal jurisdiction with those of the territorial court. This permits the same judge to hear all criminal cases that arise in the territory. Such an approach is necessary given the fact that many communities in Nunavut are small and isolated: consequently, a judge has to travel to such communities to hear criminal cases.

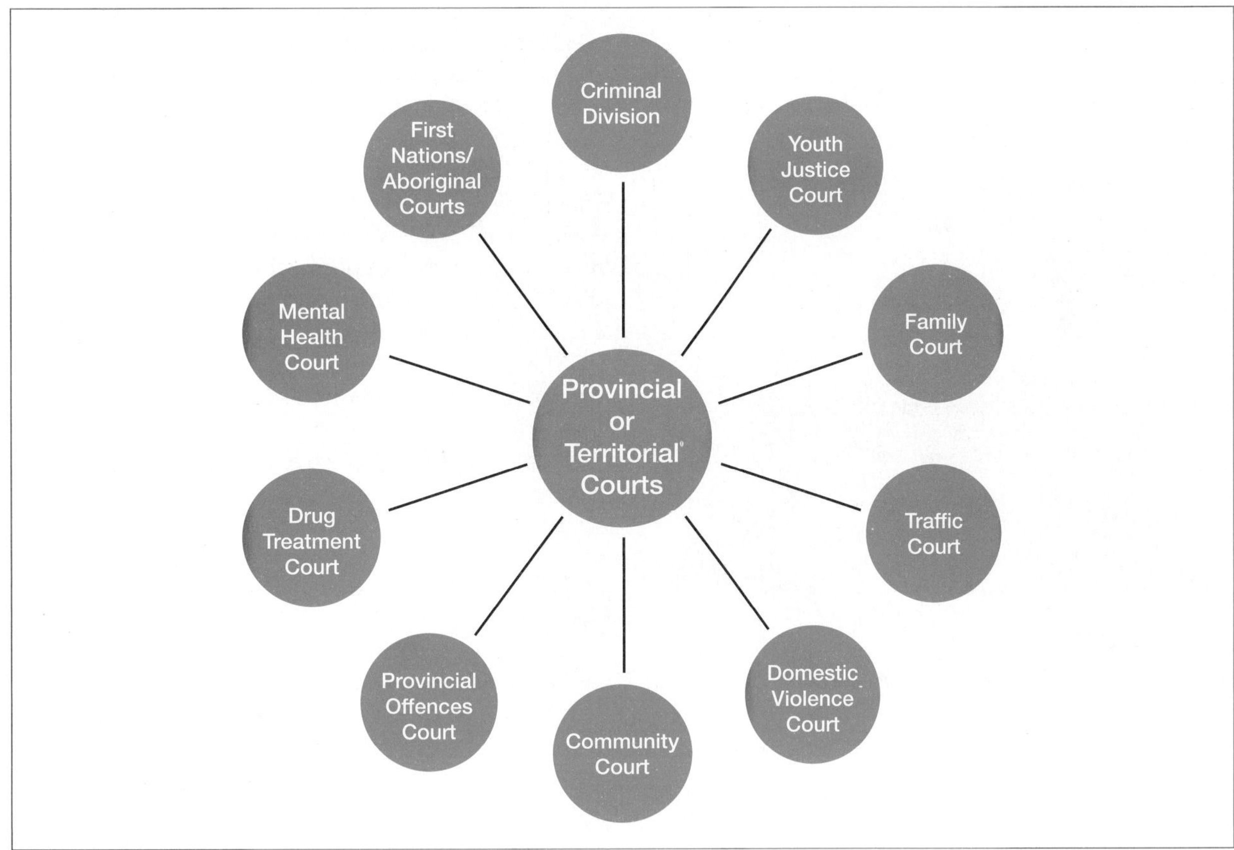

Figure APP-1

Organization of Provincial and Territorial Courts. The Specific Divisions Vary from One Province/Territory to Another.

Provincial and territorial court judges are appointed and paid by their respective provinces and territories. [In Ontario, the name for this level of court is the *Ontario Court of Justice*; in Quebec, it is known as the *Court of Quebec (Cour du Québec)*]. The provincial or territorial courts may be organized in different divisions, such as the Criminal Division, Youth Justice Court, Family Court, Provincial Offences Court, or Traffic Court. In recent years, there has been a trend toward the establishment of specialized provincial courts in certain urban jurisdictions; for example, First Nations Courts in British Columbia, Alberta, Saskatchewan, and Ontario; Drug Treatment Courts in Vancouver, Calgary, Edmonton, Regina, Winnipeg, Toronto, London (Ontario), Durham (Ontario), and Ottawa; Domestic Violence Courts in Ontario (53 jurisdictions), Manitoba, Alberta, and the Yukon; a Community Court in Vancouver; and Mental Health Courts in Ottawa, London (Ontario), Toronto, Kenora (Ontario), Montreal, and Saint John (New Brunswick).

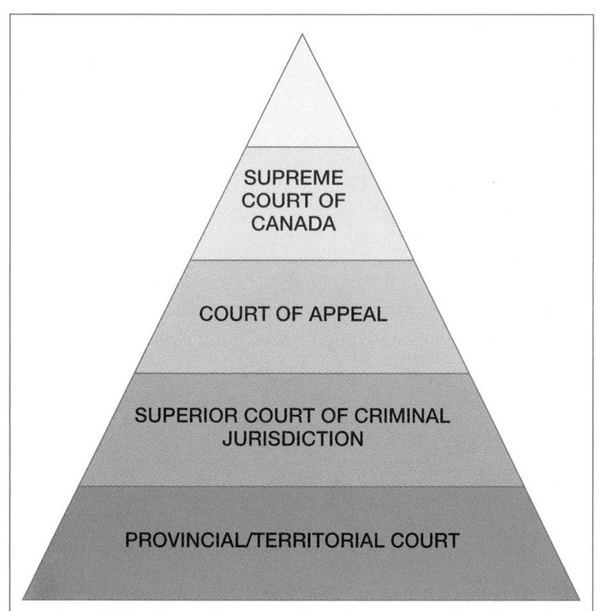

Figure APP-2
Hierarchy of Canadian Criminal Courts

In each province and territory, there is a *superior court of criminal jurisdiction*. The name of this court is not identical in each province. It is known as the *Supreme Court* in British Columbia, Yukon and Northwest Territories, Nova Scotia, Prince Edward Island, and Newfoundland and Labrador; the *Court of Queen's Bench* in Manitoba, Saskatchewan, Alberta, and New Brunswick; the *Superior Court* (*Cour Supérieure*) in Quebec; and the *Nunavut Court of Justice* in Nunavut. In Ontario, this court is known as the *Superior Court of Justice*. Although the superior court has a broad jurisdiction to try criminal cases, in practice it tries only the more serious types of criminal offence. The superior court judge may try cases either sitting alone or with a jury. In certain circumstances, the superior court may hear appeals from the decisions of provincial courts in relation to summary conviction offences. Judges in the superior courts are appointed and paid by the federal government.

Above the superior court of criminal jurisdiction in the judicial hierarchy is an appeal court, known as the *Court of Appeal* (the *Appeal Division of the Supreme Court* in Prince Edward Island). The courts of appeal hear appeals directly from the decisions of the courts that have tried indictable offences and act as the second line of appeal in the case of summary conviction offences.

The highest tier in the hierarchy of courts in Canada is occupied by the *Supreme Court of Canada*, which hears appeals from the various provincial and territorial courts of appeal. The Supreme Court of Canada is the highest court in the land and is the final stage in the appeal process.

For further information, see the following:

Department of Justice Canada, *Canada's Court System* (2013):
https://justice.gc.ca/eng/csj-sjc/ccs-ajc/

Canadian Judicial Council, *Canada's Court System* (2013):
http://www.cjc-ccm.gc.ca/english/resource_en.asp?selMenu=resource_courtsystem_en.asp

GLOSSARY

abetting: Section 21(1)(c) of the *Criminal Code* provides that an individual becomes a party to a criminal offence if they abet another person to actually commit this offence. In the context of section 21(1), abetting means instigating, procuring, or promoting a crime to be committed, or encouraging another person to actually commit an offence. (page 161)

absolute liability: This form of liability may be imposed in relation to the less serious offences arising under regulatory legislation (either federal or provincial/territorial). The Crown may obtain a conviction for a violation of such legislation without having to prove ***mens rea*** on the part of the accused persons concerned. Furthermore, these accused persons are denied a defence even if they can prove that there was no negligence on their part. As a general rule, absolute liability may not be imposed where imprisonment is a potential penalty. Most regulatory offences impose strict, rather than absolute, liability (see **strict liability**). (page 140)

abused-woman syndrome: See **battered-wife syndrome**. (page 329)

accessory: An individual who is involved in the commission of a crime in a secondary capacity. (page 166)

accessory after the fact: This term refers to a person who, knowing that an individual has been a party to a criminal offence, gives the latter comfort or assistance with the intention of enabling them to escape justice. (page 160)

accused: The person against whom a criminal charge has been laid. (page 2)

acquittal: An official discharge from prosecution, usually after a verdict of not guilty. (page 28)

active euthanasia: See **euthanasia**. (page 54)

actus reus*:** This term can be understood only in light of the concept of *mens rea*. ***Mens rea refers to the various mental elements (other than voluntariness) that are contained in the definition of a particular criminal offence. *Actus reus* refers to all the other elements of the offence that must be proved (including voluntariness) before an accused person may be convicted of the particular offence in question. (page 21)

agent provocateur: An individual (usually undercover police officer or paid informer) who, for law enforcement purposes, associates with members of a group in order to incite them to commit an offence. (page 192)

aiding: Section 21(1) of the *Criminal Code* provides that an individual becomes a party to a criminal offence if they aid another person to actually commit that offence. "Aiding" means actually providing assistance with the intention of providing such assistance. (page 161)

AIDS: Acquired immune deficiency syndrome. This transmissible disease is caused by the human immunodeficiency virus (**HIV**). (page 247)

"air of reality" test: See **evidential (or evidentiary) burden**. (page 228)

amnesia: The partial or total loss of memory. For the purposes of the criminal law, specific attention is paid to amnesia that occurs in connection with the commission of the ***actus reus*** of a criminal offence. ***Retrograde amnesia*** refers to memory deficits in relation to events that occurred *prior* to the incident in question. ***Anterograde amnesia*** refers to memory deficits in relation to the incident itself and to events following the incident. ***Retrograde amnesia*** is not relevant to an accused person's criminal responsibility. However, an accused person with ***anterograde amnesia*** may have been in a dissociative state at the time of the alleged crime and, therefore, may be entitled to the benefit of a defence of **automatism** or **NCRMD**. Dissociative disorders are "characterized by a disruption of and/or discontinuity in the normal integration of consciousness, memory, identity, emotion, perception, body representation, motor control, and behavior" (See ***DSM-5***, 2013). (page 220)

antiretroviral therapy (ART): This treatment consists of a combination of drugs that act to suppress the **HIV** virus and reduce the risk of its transmission to others. (page 247)

appellant: The party who appeals from the decision of a "lower court." In Canada, either the Crown (the prosecution) or the accused may appeal such a decision (in accordance with certain limitations defined in the ***Criminal Code***). (page 163)

appreciate: Section 16(1) of the *Criminal Code* provides that an accused person must be found **NCRMD** if, at the time of the alleged offence, they were suffering from a mental disorder that rendered them "incapable of appreciating the nature and quality of the act or omission." In this context, "appreciate" means something more than simple awareness of one's conduct: the accused must have the capacity to "perceive the consequences, impact, and results of a physical act." (page 204)

assault: In criminal law, an assault arises when an individual applies force intentionally to another person or attempts or threatens to apply force to another person (section 265 of the *Criminal Code*). There are three categories of assault: assault; assault with a weapon or causing bodily harm; and aggravated assault. (page 22)

assisted suicide: It is an offence under section 241(a) & (b) of the *Criminal Code* (as amended in 2016) for a person who is not a medical professional or a nurse practitioner to counsel (encourage) or **assist** another person to commit suicide. The most common form of assisted suicide is the ingestion of a lethal dose of drugs provided by another person for this specific purpose. Assisted suicide performed by a physician or nurse practitioner in conformity with the requirements of the **Medical-Assistance-in-Dying (MAID)** provisions of the *Criminal Code* is legal in Canada. (page 56)

automatism: A state of impaired consciousness that renders a person incapable of controlling their behaviour while in this state. A person in such a state cannot be said to be acting voluntarily and, therefore, cannot be held criminally responsible for their conduct. If the condition is caused by a mental disorder ("disease of the mind"), the correct defence is **NCRMD**. If not caused by a mental disorder, the accused is entitled to an acquittal. (page 218).

battered-wife syndrome: A condition that may appear among women who have been physically and/or mentally abused by an intimate partner over an extended period. It is also called *battered-woman syndrome*. Among the major symptoms are intense fearfulness and feelings of helplessness. Where an accused person has killed or inflicted grievous bodily harm on her partner, she may raise the defence of **self-defence** under section 34 of the *Criminal Code*. Evidence of battered-wife syndrome may be introduced to establish whether the accused person reasonably believed that her life was in danger and that she could preserve herself only by using deadly force. A more appropriate term is "abused-woman syndrome," since this takes into account the significance of emotional or psychological, as well as sexual, abuse. (page 329)

***Beard* Rules:** These judge-made rules define the circumstances in which an accused person may successfully raise the defence of intoxication. The rules are as follows: (page 279)

1. If intoxication induces a mental disorder and renders the accused "not criminally responsible" within the meaning of section 16 of the *Criminal Code*, they must be acquitted as being "not criminally responsible on account of mental disorder" (**NCRMD**). (page 199)
2. If intoxication prevents a defendant from forming the intent necessary for conviction of a crime of specific intent, they must be acquitted. However, intoxication can never be a defence to a charge of a crime of **general** (or **basic**) intent. (page 279)
3. If intoxication falls short of preventing the accused from forming the intent necessary for conviction of a crime of specific intent, it does not constitute a valid defence. (page 290)

bigamy: The offence of bigamy is committed when a person goes through a form of marriage while still married to another person; goes through a form of marriage with another person knowing that this other person is still married to someone else; or goes through a form of marriage with more than one other person simultaneously (section 290 of the ***Criminal Code***). (page 22)

bipolar disorder: A mental disorder characterized by alternating episodes of mania and depression. Mania may be defined as an abnormally elevated, expansive, or irritable mood. Bipolar disorder was previously known as manic-depressive disorder. (page 203)

blackmail: See **extortion**. (page 272)

bona fide: In good faith. That is to say, a party has acted without any dishonesty or fraud. (page 81)

burden of proof: This indicates which party is responsible for proving certain facts in a trial. Since the Crown is asserting in a criminal trial that the accused has committed an offence, the **persuasional (or "primary") burden of proof** is normally on the Crown to prove all the ***actus reus*** and ***mens rea*** elements that constitute the offence charged. The **standard of proof** that must be met by the Crown is that of "*beyond a reasonable doubt*." In the rare cases where the accused is placed under the burden of proof to establish a particular fact (e.g., that they were not criminally responsible because of mental disorder or were in a state of automatism), the standard of proof is ***"on the balance of probabilities."*** (page 14)

bylaw: Legislation enacted by an inferior body that acts under delegated authority, such as the laws passed by a municipal council that has been granted authority under provincial government legislation. (page 8)

Canadian Charter of Rights and Freedoms*:** The ***Charter is part of the ***Constitution*** of Canada. It was enacted by the *Constitution Act, 1982* (UK) c. 11 and proclaimed in force on April 17, 1982. The ***Charter*** guarantees certain rights and freedoms considered of great importance to Canadians. The *Charter* is one of the most important statutes in Canada, since the courts may declare invalid any federal or provincial/territorial laws that infringe the rights or freedoms guaranteed by the ***Charter***. (page 7)

***Cannabis Act*:** The *Cannabis Act*, S.C. 2018, c. 16 permits legal access to the drug Cannabis while regulating and controlling its production. An important objective of the Act is to eliminate the black market for the drug and to impose severe penalties on individuals who deal with the drug outside the approved legal framework established by the Act. In addition to imposing safety and quality requirements with respect to Cannabis, a major goal of the Act is to prevent young persons from accessing the drug. (page 139)

care or control: Section 253 of the *Criminal Code* provides that it is an offence to have the "care or control" of a motor vehicle or vessel while one's ability to operate the vehicle or vessel is impaired by alcohol or another drug or while having a blood alcohol level of more than 80 milligrams of alcohol in 100 millilitres of blood.

In *Boudreault* (2012), the Supreme Court of Canada stated that: (page 28)

> "[C]are or control," within the meaning of s. 253(1) of the *Criminal Code*, signifies (1) an intentional course of conduct associated with a motor vehicle; (2) by a person whose ability to drive is impaired, or whose blood alcohol level exceeds the legal limit; (3) in circumstances that create a realistic risk, as opposed to a *remote possibility*, of danger to persons or property.

In the *Toews* case (1985), the Supreme Court of Canada ruled that "acts of care or control" are "acts which involve some use of the car or its fittings and equipment, or some course of conduct associated with the vehicle which would involve a risk of putting the vehicle in motion so that it could become dangerous."

In 2018, the enactment of the *Cannabis Act*, S.C. 2018, c. 16, which legalized the possession of cannabis for recreational purposes, elicited considerable public concern with respect to the possibility that users of the drug may find themselves in care or control of, or impaired while driving, a motor vehicle. New provisions were added to the *Criminal Code*, permitting the promulgation of regulations that set prescribed limits for the amount of a drug (such as cannabis) which is found in an individual's blood and which approve the methods (devices) that may be used by the police to make the necessary measurements. (Chapter 2) (page 28)

careless driving: Careless driving, or driving without due care and attention, is an offence under provincial or territorial legislation. The offence may be proved by establishing that the accused person's driving conduct fell—even to a minor extent—below the standard of care expected of a reasonable driver acting prudently in the circumstances facing him or her. (page 114)

carelessness: Conduct that falls below the standard of care expected of a reasonable person acting prudently in the circumstances facing them. (page 110)

causation in fact: See **factual causation**. (page 50)

causation in law: See **legal causation**. (page 50)

circumstances: Circumstances always constitute an essential element of the **actus reus** of a criminal offence. The relevant, or "material," circumstances that the Crown must prove are those contained in the definition of the offence. For example, when the accused person has been charged with sexual assault, a material circumstance that the Crown must prove is that there was no consent to sexual activity on the part of the **complainant**. (page 22)

civil law: If the entry, civil law system, is deleted, then this whole sentence should be deleted. However, this is not my preference.

I would like the entries for both civil law and civil law system in the sixth edition to be restored. The term, civil law system should no longer be in bold face and the "(see below") should be deleted. The following entry, civil law system, can just be included in the entry on civil. The term "civil law" primarily refers to the body of laws that deals with the relationships between private citizens. For example, an individual citizen may bring a legal action for compensation on the basis that their neighbour's negligence has caused some degree of harm. The goal of the civil law action is solely to compensate the citizen for the loss caused by the neighbour. In contrast, the criminal law is primarily concerned with punishing a convicted person for the wrong done to the state by the latter's misconduct. The criminal law trial is a proceeding between the Crown and the accused, whereas the civil law action initiates a proceeding between private citizens. (page 110)

cognitive: Relating to a person's knowledge and reasoning abilities as opposed to the emotional factors that may influence their behaviour. (page 201)

colour of right: Accused persons who act under the influence of an honest, albeit mistaken, belief that they have a valid *legal* right are considered to be acting under colour of right. In certain circumstances, such persons may have a defence to a criminal charge. For example, they may have a valid defence to a charge of theft where they honestly believe that they have a valid right to the property in question, even though it subsequently turns out that this right is not recognized by a court of law. (page 263)

common intention: Section 21(2) of the *Criminal Code* provides that an individual may become a party to a crime committed by another person by virtue of having formed a common intention with this person. Common intention exists where two or more individuals agree to commit a crime and to assist each other in carrying out this agreement. If one of these individuals subsequently commits another offence in the course of carrying out the common intention, then each of the other individuals concerned will be found to be a party to that other offence, provided they either knew or ought to have known that the commission of this other criminal offence "would be a probable consequence of carrying out the common purpose." When the charge is murder or attempted murder, the words "or ought to have known" must be deleted from section 21(2): the accused must have had *subjective* foresight of the likelihood that death would be a probable consequence. (page 170)

common law: A term with at least two meanings. The term is used to denote a legal system inherited from England in which judges decide cases by applying the legal principles embodied in **precedent** cases decided in the past. The doctrine of *stare decisis* requires courts to apply principles from the cases highest in their court hierarchy. In a related sense, common law also means the law common to all of England. As cases were decided by courts in England, over time judges in various regions drew upon the rulings of those deciding cases elsewhere, eventually resulting in a common body of law. The common law system is predominant in England and Wales, the Canadian provinces and territories (with the exception of Quebec), the American states (with the exception of Louisiana), Australia, and New Zealand. (page 10)

complainant: A person who makes a complaint to the authorities that they have been the victim of a criminal offence. (page 25)

conduct: A voluntary act or omission constituting the central feature of a criminal offence. (page 22)

consequences: The Crown usually has to prove that the accused person's conduct caused a certain consequence as an essential element of the ***actus reus*** of the criminal offence with which the accused person has been charged. However, there are a number of exceptions to this principle. For example, to obtain a conviction of the offence of perjury, the Crown does not have to prove that the accused person's lies were believed by anyone. (page 22)

conspiracy: An agreement by two or more persons to commit a crime. (page 186)

***Constitution Act*, 1867:** Canada's foundational constitutional document. It establishes Canada as a federal state and contains the provisions that delineate the spheres of responsibility for each of the two levels of government. It also contains provisions pertaining to the structure of Canada's court systems and a variety of provisions pertinent to the union of the former colonies into confederation. (page 2)

constitutional exemption: A potential remedy under the *Charter*. Instead of declaring a provision of the *Criminal Code* invalid, a court may rule that it is unconstitutional only in its application to a particular individual in exceptional circumstances. For example, in the *Latimer* case (2001), the accused was found guilty of second-degree murder as a consequence of an act of so-called "mercy killing." Section 745 of the *Criminal Code* prescribes a mandatory sentence of life imprisonment (with no eligibility for parole for at least 10 years) for second-degree murder. The trial judge recognized that the Supreme Court of Canada had ruled that section 745 does not constitute "cruel and unusual punishment" contrary to the requirements of section 12 of the *Charter*. However, he ruled that life imprisonment *in Latimer's very unusual circumstances* would be "grossly disproportionate" (hence, "cruel and unusual punishment" within the meaning of section 12 of the *Charter*) and he granted Latimer a constitutional exemption from the imposition of the mandatory sentence. Instead, Latimer was sentenced to one year in prison, followed by a one-year period of probation. The Saskatchewan Court of Appeal later ruled that Latimer was not entitled to a constitutional exemption and sentenced him to life imprisonment without eligibility for parole for 10 years. The Supreme Court of Canada upheld the decision of the Court of Appeal in *Latimer* (2001). (page 90)

contempt of court: Under section 9 of the *Criminal Code*, courts have the power to convict a person of criminal contempt of court. The term "criminal contempt" covers any wilful conduct on the part of the accused that tends to interfere with the proper administration of justice or to bring it into disrepute. It includes, but is not limited to, the deliberate defiance or disobedience of a court order in a public manner. (page 11)

counsel: In Canada, the term refers to the lawyer representing a party in a trial. In criminal cases, Crown Counsel represents the Queen (that is to say, they are the prosecuting lawyer), whereas defence counsel represents the accused. (page 17)

counselling: Section 22(1) of the *Criminal Code* provides that a person who counsels an offence that is actually committed by another person becomes a party to this offence. Section 464 provides that an individual is guilty of the inchoate offence of counselling if they counsel another person to commit an offence that is not ultimately perpetrated. The *Criminal Code* states that "counsel" includes "procure, solicit or incite." (page 160)

crime: A crime consists of conduct that is prohibited, because it is considered to have an "evil or injurious or undesirable effect upon the public," and a penalty that may be imposed when the prohibition is violated. (page 2)

crimes of specific and general (or basic) intent: According to Justice McIntyre in the case of *Bernard* (1988), a **specific intent offence** is "one which involves the performance of the *actus reus*, coupled with an intent or purpose going beyond the mere performance of the questioned act." Examples are murder (section 235 of the *Criminal Code*); assault with intent to wound (section 244); and breaking and entering with intent to commit an indictable offence [section 349(1)(a)]. According to Justice McIntyre, a **crime of general (or basic) intent** "is one in which the only intent involved relates solely to the performance of the act in question with no further ulterior intent or purpose." He noted that "the minimal intent to apply force in the offence of common assault affords an example." Another example is the crime of wilful destruction or damage of property (mischief) (see section 430). See also Justice Bastarache's summary of the distinction between specific intent and general (or basic) intent cases in *Daley* (2007): "[S]pecific intent offences require the mind to focus on an objective further to the immediate one at hand, while general intent offences require only a conscious doing of the prohibited act." (page 279)

criminal attempt: Section 24 of the *Criminal Code* provides that it is a crime to attempt to commit a criminal offence. To gain a conviction of criminal attempt, the Crown must prove that the accused actually intended to commit an offence and that they did or omitted to do "anything for the purpose of carrying out his (or her) intention." The accused must have gone beyond "mere preparation" to commit an offence, and it is no defence that it would not have been possible to commit the offence in the circumstances. (page 179)

***Criminal Code*:** The *Criminal Code*, R.S.C. 1985, c. C-46 (first enacted by the Parliament of Canada in 1892), is the most important source of criminal law in Canada. This statute is divided into 28 major parts and deals with both substantive criminal law as well as the procedural law relating to criminal matters. (page 7)

criminal law: The area of the law that delineates the rules and principles of culpability for acts and omissions deemed by the state to be crimes. (page 2)

criminal negligence: According to section 219(1) of the *Criminal Code*, a person is criminally negligent if in "doing anything" or "in omitting to do anything" that it is their "duty to do," they show "wanton or reckless disregard for the lives or safety of other persons." This definition is applicable to the offences of causing death by criminal negligence; causing bodily harm by criminal negligence; and manslaughter by criminal negligence. These are offences that impose **objective *mens rea*** and require proof of both a marked and substantial departure from the standard of care expected of a reasonable person acting prudently in the same circumstances and with the same knowledge as the accused person. (page 38)

criminal procedure: This term refers to legislation that specifies the procedures to be followed in the prosecution of a criminal case and defines the nature and scope of the powers of criminal justice officials. (page 7)

dangerous driving: Section 320.13(1) of the *Criminal Code* creates the offence of dangerous driving or, more specifically, operating "a conveyance in a manner that, having regard to all circumstances, is dangerous to the public." The Supreme Court of Canada has ruled that the Crown must prove that the accused person's driving conduct constituted a marked departure from the standard of driving care expected of a reasonable driver acting prudently in the particular circumstances facing the accused. The *mens rea* of the offence is objective, but the courts must apply the modified objective test. The accused must be acquitted if they can raise a reasonable doubt as to whether a reasonable person, with the same knowledge of the circumstances facing them, would have appreciated the nature of the risk created by their driving conduct. The *actus reus* of the offence consists of driving conduct that is dangerous to the public in light of the particular circumstances of the case (such as the nature of the street or highway and the amount of traffic that might reasonably be expected at the time of the alleged offence). Section 320.13(2) creates the offence of dangerous operation causing bodily harm and section 320.13(3) creates the offence of dangerous operation causing death. Sections 320.13(1) and 320.13(2) are hybrid offences, but section 320.13(3) may be tried only on indictment and carries a maximum penalty of life imprisonment. (page 113)

defence of property: In certain circumstances, an accused person has a defence to a criminal charge that has been laid against them because they used force in defence of their property (including the act of removing a trespasser from the property). Section 35 of the *Criminal Code* sets out the requirements for the defence: (1) the accused person believes on reasonable grounds that they are in "peaceable possession" of property; (2) the accused person believes on reasonable grounds that another person is about to enter, is entering, or has entered their property unlawfully; or is about to take, is taking, or has already taken property; or is about to damage/destroy/render inoperative their property or is already doing so; (3) the accused person's actions are intended to prevent the other person from entering or to remove them from their property or to prevent the other person from damaging/destroying, rendering inoperative the property or to retake the property; and (4) the accused person's conduct was reasonable in the circumstances. (page 335)

defendant: In a criminal trial, the defendant is the person against whom a criminal charge has been laid and who is, therefore, placed in the position of defending themselves against such a charge. (page 26)

direct intention: This concept refers to the situation in which an accused person engages in conduct with the unequivocal desire to bring about the consequence(s) prohibited by the criminal law. (page 88)

disease of the mind: See **mental disorder**. (page 202)

double jeopardy: This term refers to the ancient doctrine of the criminal law that accused persons may not be placed twice in jeopardy for the same incident. Therefore, if they are charged again in relation to this incident, they may plead their previous conviction or acquittal as a complete defence to the second charge. The special pleas in question are known as *autrefois convict* and *autrefois acquit*. (page 233)

***DSM-5*:** *Diagnostic and Statistical Manual of Mental Disorders, Fifth Edition*. Arlington, VA: American Psychiatric Association, 2013. (page 203)

dual offence: See **hybrid (or dual) offence**. (page 3)

due diligence: When an accused person is charged with an offence of **strict liability,** they may raise the defence that they acted with due diligence. To gain an acquittal, the accused must prove this defence on the balance of probabilities. Generally, the accused must establish that they exercised all reasonable care and took reasonable steps to ensure that the standard of care required by the law was met. (page 142)

duress: The common law defence of duress may be raised where the accused person has committed an offence under the threat of death or serious bodily harm by another person. The accused person may be excused from criminal responsibility if they had no real choice but to break the law. In *Ryan* (2013), the Supreme Court of Canada identified the six basic elements of the common law defence of duress: (1) an explicit or implicit threat of death or bodily harm made against the accused or a third person; (2) the accused reasonably believed that the threat would be carried out; (3) the non-existence of a safe avenue of escape; (4) a close temporal connection between the threat and the harm threatened; (5) proportionality between the harm threatened and the harm inflicted by the accused; and (6) the accused is not a party to a conspiracy or association whereby the accused is subject to compulsion and actually knew that threats and coercion to commit an offence were a possible result of this criminal activity, conspiracy, or association. (page 305)

elevated standard of care: Where an individual is engaging in activities that are so inherently dangerous as to pose a serious risk to the safety of others, the *Criminal Code* may require them to meet an "elevated standard of care": the standard of care expected of a reasonable person who has acquired the necessary expertise and training to engage in such activities. Examples of situations in which the *Criminal Code* imposes such an elevated standard of care are possession of explosives, use and storage of firearms, and administration of surgical and medical treatment. (page 129)

entrapment: This occurs where law enforcement authorities (usually through the agency of undercover officers or paid informers) instigate others to commit criminal offences (primarily those offences involving the sale of illegal drugs) for the purpose of prosecuting them. Although the police are entitled to use undercover methods of investigation, they are not entitled to persuade an individual to commit an offence that they would not have committed but for the persistent pressure by the police to do so. If entrapment of this type takes place, an accused person may be granted a stay of proceedings (a direction by the court that criminal proceedings be suspended). (page 233)

euthanasia: The literal meaning of euthanasia is "a good death." The word is derived from Greek (*eu* = "well or goodly" and *thanatos* = "death"). There are two major categories of euthanasia for the purposes of the criminal law. **Active euthanasia** is the deliberate use of a painless method of death (such as a fatal injection) to end the suffering of another person. Active euthanasia by any individual who is neither a physician nor a nurse practitioner is prohibited in Canada and the person who engages in this practice is guilty of murder. Active euthanasia by a physician or nurse practitioner that conforms to the **Medical-Assistance-in-Dying (MAID)** provisions of the *Criminal Code* is legal in Canada. **Passive euthanasia** consists of withdrawing medical treatment with the clear understanding that taking this step will accelerate the onset of death from a pre-existing illness. Passive euthanasia has always been considered an appropriate medical practice, provided that it is carried out with the *consent* of the individual concerned and that they are considered *competent* to make such a decision. (page 58)

evidential (or evidentiary) burden: This term refers to the requirement that an accused person point to some evidence in order to have a defence considered by the **trier of fact**. The term refers primarily to the simple requirement that before a defence (such as mistake of fact) may be put to the trier of fact, the trial judge must be satisfied that the accused has introduced sufficient evidence to give an "**air of reality**" to the defence or to "put the defence in play." As the Supreme Court of Canada held in the case of *Cinous* (2002), "[T]he full question is whether there is evidence (some evidence, any evidence) upon which a properly instructed jury acting judicially could acquit. If there is any or some such evidence, then the air of reality hurdle is cleared. If there is no such evidence, then the air of reality hurdle is not cleared." The evidential burden merely requires that the accused introduce some evidence capable of raising a reasonable doubt as to the issue in question. The onus placed on the accused in such circumstances is a light one and is primarily designed to prevent them from raising totally speculative defences that have no support in any of the evidence presented to the court. Once the defence is put to the trier of fact, the Crown must normally prove beyond a reasonable doubt that it does not apply (e.g., that the accused was not operating under a mistake of fact). This is referred to as the "**persuasive burden of proof.**" In *Fontaine* (2004), the Supreme Court emphasized that "An 'evidential burden' is not a burden of proof. It determines whether an issue *should be left to the trier of fact*, while the 'persuasive burden' determines *how the issue should be decided*." (page 228)

extortion: A person commits the offence of extortion (section 346 of the *Criminal Code*) where they, without reasonable justification or excuse and with the intent of obtaining "anything" (e.g., money or property), induce or attempt to induce another person to "do anything or cause anything to be done" by means of "threats, accusations, menaces or violence." In popular terminology, this offence is sometimes called blackmail. (page 188)

factual causation (or causation in fact): According to the Supreme Court of Canada in *Nette* (2001), factual causation "is concerned with an inquiry about how the victim came to his or her death, in a medical, mechanical, or physical sense, and with the contribution of the accused to that result." (page 50)

federal criminal law power: Under the *Constitution Act, 1867*, the Parliament of Canada has exclusive jurisdiction in the field of "criminal law and the procedures relating to criminal matters." (page 2)

first-degree murder: Section 231 of the *Criminal Code* indicates the circumstances in which murder will be considered first-degree, as opposed to second-degree, murder. In general, first-degree murder is murder that is both **planned and deliberate**. There are also certain exceptional circumstances in which a murder will automatically be classified as first-degree murder, whether or not it is planned and deliberate (e.g., murder of a police officer or murder committed in the course of a sexual assault). The penalty for first-degree murder is life imprisonment, with no eligibility for parole for 25 years. Where an accused person has been convicted of multiple murders, committed after December 2011, the trial judge may impose *consecutive* periods of non-parole eligibility (section 745.51). (page 60)

foreseeability (of prohibited consequences): If the consequences of one's actions are foreseeable, it is relatively simple to conclude that there is a causal link between these actions and their consequences. The requirement of foreseeability in criminal law ensures that an accused person's responsibility for their actions is not unlimited: they may be punished only for prohibited consequences that could reasonably have been foreseen. (page 51)

fraud: Section 380 of the *Criminal Code* creates the general offence of fraud, which consists of the dishonest deprivation of another person's property. The Crown does not have to prove that the accused person's conduct caused any actual loss to the victim. It is enough that there was "prejudice or risk of prejudice to the economic interest of the victim." (page 81)

fraudulently: Section 322(1) of the *Criminal Code* provides that, to obtain a conviction for theft, the Crown must prove that the accused took another person's property "fraudulently." This means that the accused must take the property intentionally, under no mistake, and with knowledge that it belongs to someone else. Where the accused takes the property as a prank, the court may hold that they did not act fraudulently, although this is a very unusual defence. (page 78)

crimes of specific and general (or basic) intent: According to Justice McIntyre, a crime of general (or basic) intent "is one in which the only intent involved relates solely to the performance of the act in question with no further ulterior intent or purpose." He noted that "the minimal intent to apply force in the offence of common assault affords an example." Another example is the crime of wilful destruction or damage of property (mischief) (see section 430). See also **crimes of specific and general (or basic) intent**. (page 269)

"halfway house" approach: See **strict liability**. (page 141)

high-risk accused: In 2014, Parliament enacted The *Not Criminally Responsible Reform Act* (S.C. 2014, c. 6), which has given the trial court the power to impose the designation of "high-risk accused" when an accused person has been found NCRMD (see Chapter 8 for details). The consequence of this designation are as follows: (1) upon being designated by a court as high risk, an NCR accused would be held in custody and could not be considered for release by a review board until the designation is revoked by a court; (2) a high-risk NCR accused could potentially have their review period extended up to three years; and (3) such an individual would not be entitled to unescorted passes and could obtain an escorted pass only in narrow circumstances and if a structured plan is in place to address any undue risk to public safety. (page 214)

HIV: Human immunodeficiency virus—the virus that causes acquired immune deficiency syndrome (**AIDS**). (page 247)

HIV-positive: This means that an individual has had a positive reaction to a test for **HIV**. (page 247)

hybrid (or dual) offence: An offence that may be prosecuted as an indictable or summary conviction offence, at the discretion of the Crown. (page 3)

imaginary crime: An accused person cannot be convicted of attempting or conspiring to commit an imaginary crime. If the accused person attempts or conspires to do something that does not in fact constitute a crime, while nevertheless believing that what they have attempted or conspired to do is indeed a crime, then they have attempted or conspired to commit an imaginary crime. (page 185)

implied consent: In certain circumstances, the existence of *implied* consent may be a defence to a charge of assault. Individuals who voluntarily participate in contact sports are automatically deemed to have given implied consent to having a certain degree of force inflicted on their bodies. However, a participant in a contact sport may be considered to have consented to only the application of force that occurs within the bounds of fair play and that is reasonably incidental to the norms of the sport in question. (page 257)

impossibility: It is not a defence to a charge of criminal attempt or conspiracy that the offence the accused was attempting or conspiring to commit would have been impossible in the circumstances. For example, it would not be a defence to a charge of criminal attempt that the accused attempted to steal money from a wallet that turned out to be empty. (page 185)

improper medical treatment: Improper medical treatment that is not administered in good faith may sever the chain of causation between the wounding of the victim and the victim's ultimate death. In such a case, the accused person would not be considered to have caused the death of the victim. (page 65)

inchoate offences: The criminal law does not punish individuals for thinking about committing a crime, but once they start on a course of conduct designed to achieve a criminal goal, they may, in certain circumstances, be convicted of an offence even though that goal is never achieved. These offences are known as inchoate because the accused persons concerned do not complete the crimes they originally had in mind. The three inchoate offences recognized in Canadian criminal law are (1) attempt, (2) conspiracy, and (3) counselling an offence that is not committed. (page 176)

indictable offence: Indictable offences are, generally, the most serious criminal offences. Furthermore, those indictable offences considered particularly serious in nature may be tried only in the superior court of criminal jurisdiction. An indictment (from which the indictable offence takes its name) is a formal document that sets out the charge(s) against the accused and is signed by the Attorney General or their agent. (page 2)

indirect intention: This concept refers to the situation in which an accused person does not desire to bring about the consequences prohibited by the criminal law but is nevertheless considered to have intended them. (page 88)

infanticide: According to section 233 of the *Criminal Code*, "A female person commits infanticide when by a wilful act or omission she causes the death of her newly born child, if at the time of the act or omission she is not fully recovered from the effects of giving birth to the child and by reason thereof or of the effect of lactation consequent on the birth of the child her mind is then disturbed." In section 2 of the *Code*, a "newly born child" is defined as "a person under the age of one year." Infanticide may either be a defence to a charge of murder or manslaughter or a stand-alone crime. The maximum sentence on conviction of infanticide is five years' imprisonment (section 237). (page 121)

intention: According to Justice Dickson in the *Lewis* case (1979), intention means "the exercise of a free will to use particular means to produce a particular result." (page 22)

***inter alia*:** Among others. (page 7)

intervening act: In certain circumstances, an intervening act may sever the chain of causation between the defendant's original wounding of the victim and the latter's subsequent death. Where this occurs, the defendant will not be held responsible for having committed a culpable homicide. However, even if there is an intervening act, the Crown may still obtain a conviction if it can be shown that the original wound inflicted by the accused was "operative" (or continuing to have some impact) at the time of the victim's death. (page 61)

legal causation (or causation in law): According to the Supreme Court of Canada in *Nette* (2001), legal causation "is concerned with the question of whether the accused person should be held responsible in law for the death that occurred." See also **factual causation**. (page 50)

major depressive disorder: According to the American Psychiatric Association's *Diagnostic and Statistical Manual of Mental Disorders, Fifth Edition* (2013), the essential feature of this mental disorder is "a period of at least two weeks during which there is either depressed mood or the loss of interest or pleasure in nearly all activities." (page 203)

manslaughter: Generally, this offence involves the commission of an unintentional homicide. The ***mens rea*** for the offence is generally objective in nature: the Crown must establish either that the accused's conduct amounted to a "marked and substantial departure from the standard of care expected of a reasonable person acting prudently" (manslaughter by criminal negligence) or that the accused killed the victim in the course of committing an offence (such as an assault) that a "reasonable person would have foreseen as being likely to cause non-trivial bodily harm" (**unlawful act manslaughter**). The successful use of the defence of provocation (section 232 of the *Code*) may result in an accused being convicted of manslaughter rather than murder, even though they intended to kill the victim; this is an exception to the general rule that manslaughter involves the commission of an unintentional homicide. (page 38)

marked departure test: When the *Criminal Code* imposes objective liability for offences such as dangerous driving or criminal negligence causing death or bodily harm, the Crown must prove that the accused person's conduct constituted a marked departure from the standard of care expected of a reasonable person acting prudently in the particular circumstances facing the accused person. In the case of offences requiring proof of criminal negligence, the departure must be both marked and substantial. (page 111)

medical assistance in dying (MAID): Parliament enacted Bill C-14, the *Medical Assistance in Dying Act*, which became law on June 17, 2016. This legislation made various major changes to the *Criminal Code*, which permitted physicians and nurse practitioners, in highly regulated circumstances, to engage in active euthanasia of patients or to provide them with a medically assisted suicide if they are suffering from a serious, incurable disease and their "natural death has become reasonably foreseeable." See Chapter 3. (page 55)

***mens rea*:** This concept refers to those mental elements (other than voluntariness) contained in the definition of any particular criminal offence that the Crown must prove before an accused person may be convicted of that offence. (page 21)

mental disorder: According to section 2 of the *Criminal Code*, this means "a disease of the mind." The Supreme Court of Canada approved the following definition in the *Rabey* case (1980):

> Any malfunctioning of the mind having its source primarily in some subjective condition or weakness internal to the accused (whether fully understood or not) may be a 'disease of the mind' if it prevents the accused from knowing what he is doing, but transient disturbances of consciousness due to specific external factors do not fall within the concept of disease of the mind.

Section 16 of the *Criminal Code* provides that an accused person will not be found criminally responsible if, as a consequence of a mental disorder, they lack the capacity to appreciate the nature and quality of their conduct or to know that the average person would regard the conduct as morally wrong. When an accused person claims a state of non-mental-disorder automatism, the Supreme Court of Canada in *Stone* (1999) ruled that a "holistic" approach should be taken to determine if a mental condition is to be considered a "disease of the mind" and considered under section 16. This approach includes looking at the "internal-external" and "continuing danger" factors as well as policy considerations. *Stone* also decided that there is a presumption that a state of automatism is caused by a "disease of the mind." In *Bouchard-Lebrun* (2011), the Supreme Court ruled that a self-induced psychotic state may not be considered a "disease of the mind," justifying a verdict of NCRMD, unless it meets the requirement that the psychosis can be seen as being caused by an internal factor (such as a pre-existing psychosis or a genetic abnormality). See Chapter 8. (page 202)

mistake of fact: An accused person will generally be entitled to an acquittal if they operated under a mistaken belief as to one or more of the material circumstances surrounding the alleged crime. Where the accused person honestly believes in a state of facts that, if true, would not constitute an offence, then they lack the **mens rea** necessary for the crime with which they have been charged. (page 233)

mistake of law: Section 19 of the *Criminal Code* makes it clear that ignorance of the law is no defence to a criminal charge. Neither a mistaken interpretation of the law nor complete ignorance as to the existence of a particular law is a valid defence. However, the courts have ruled that section 19 applies only to mistakes concerning the criminal law; mistakes as to the civil law may give rise to a valid defence (e.g., a mistake as to whether a custody order is valid). **Officially induced error** is an *apparent* exception to the rule that mistake of law is no defence. (page 259)

modified objective test: The courts have ruled that certain offences, such as dangerous driving, criminal negligence causing death or bodily harm, and manslaughter, impose objective liability on an accused person. The Crown must prove that the accused person's conduct amounted to a marked departure from the standard of care expected of a reasonable person acting prudently. However, the Supreme Court of Canada has ruled that the test is not purely objective in the sense that the courts must take into account the particular circumstances facing the accused person and their perception of those circumstances. The modified objective test requires that the court ask whether a reasonable person, with the knowledge the accused person had of the relevant circumstances, would have realized the risk that their conduct created and would have refrained from taking such a risk. (page 110)

motive: The reason for, or explanation of, a person's conduct. Generally, the **mens rea** requirements for conviction of criminal offences do not include any reference to the accused's motive. For example, a non-medical practitioner or non-nurse practitioner may intend to kill another human being, and thereby commit the crime of murder, even though some people might consider that there is a laudable motive for killing the victim (e.g., so-called "mercy killing"). (page 89)

murder: This offence involves the commission of a homicide by a person who intends to kill their victim or who subjectively foresees that their conduct is likely to cause death. Section 229 of the *Criminal Code* indicates that murder is committed where (1) the accused intends to kill; (2) the accused intends to inflict bodily harm that they know is likely to cause death and is reckless whether death ensues or not; or (3) the accused, for an unlawful object, does anything that they subjectively know is likely to cause death and does thereby cause death notwithstanding that they wish to achieve the unlawful object without causing death or bodily harm. (In this context, unlawful object refers to "the object of conduct, which, if prosecuted fully, would amount to a serious crime that is an indictable offence requiring ***mens rea***.") There are two categories of this offence: **first-degree murder** and **second-degree murder**. (page 96)

nature and quality of the act or omission: Section 16(1) of the *Criminal Code* provides that an accused person must be found **NCRMD** if, at the time of the alleged offence, they had a mental disorder that rendered them "incapable of appreciating the nature and quality of the act or omission." "Nature and quality of the act or omission" refers exclusively to the *physical* nature and quality of the act or omission. (page 199)

NCRMD (not criminally responsible on account of mental disorder): The common abbreviation of the verdict of "not criminally responsible on account of mental disorder" (section 672.34 of the *Criminal Code*). To be found NCRMD, the accused must prove that the criteria established in section 16(1) of the *Code* have been met. According to section 672.1 of the *Code*, a verdict of NCRMD "means that the accused committed the act or made the omission that formed the basis of the offence with which the accused is charged but is not criminally responsible on account of mental disorder." (page 200)

necessity: The common law defence of necessity arises where the accused can avoid some imminent disaster or calamity only by breaking the law. In advancing the defence of necessity, the accused is basically asserting that the evil that they sought to avoid was greater than the evil inherent in breaking the law. In essence, the accused person asserts that they should be excused from criminal responsibility because the decision to break the law was dictated by necessity and was, therefore, not a free choice. The defence will not be successful if the accused had a reasonable legal alternative to breaking the law. (page 299)

negligence: In criminal law, negligence is a form of objective ***mens rea.*** A person is negligent when their conduct falls below the standard of care expected of a reasonable person acting prudently. Negligence may be a sufficient form of *mens rea* to convict an accused person of certain *Criminal Code* offences, but only if that person's conduct amounts to a marked departure from the standard of care expected of a reasonable person facing the same circumstances as the accused. Only the most serious incidents of negligence will justify the accused's conviction of a **true crime**; such negligence may be called criminal (or penal) negligence. (page 39)

normative involuntariness: The rationale underlying the defences of **duress** and **necessity** is that the accused person had no real choice but to break the law. The Supreme Court of Canada has referred to this rationale as "normative involuntariness"—the notion that, in a moral sense, the accused person acted involuntarily. (page 301)

not criminally responsible on account of mental disorder: See **NCRMD.** (page 200)

Oakes test: The test, developed by the Supreme Court of Canada in the *Oakes* case (1986), to establish whether a limit placed on a *Charter* right or freedom can be justified under section 1 of the *Charter*. The test consists of two parts. The first requirement is that the objective of the impugned legislation imposing a limit on a right or freedom must be of "sufficient importance to warrant overriding a constitutionally protected right or freedom." In this respect, the legislative objective must "relate to concerns which are pressing and substantial in a free and democratic society before it can be characterized as sufficiently important." Second, the means chosen to implement the legislative objective must be "reasonable and demonstrably justified." This involves a "form of proportionality test": are the means chosen proportional to the objective that the legislation seeks to implement? (page 13)

objective *mens rea*: Offences requiring proof of objective *mens rea* impose on the Crown the burden of establishing that a reasonable person would have appreciated the risk created by the accused's conduct and would have chosen not to take that risk. Objective *mens rea* is not concerned with what actually went on in the accused's mind at the time of the alleged offence, but rather with what the reasonable person would have known if placed in exactly the same circumstances. The fault of the accused lies in the failure to direct their mind to a risk the reasonable person would have appreciated. (page 75)

officially induced error: As a general rule, a mistake of law is not a valid defence to a criminal charge. However, a defence may be available in the case of "officially induced error." This defence may be raised successfully where the accused person has been charged with a violation of a regulatory statute and has reasonably relied on the erroneous legal opinion or legal advice of an official who is responsible for the administration or enforcement of the law in question. (page 261)

omission: The general principle in Canadian criminal law is that an accused person may not be convicted on the basis of a mere omission (a failure to act) unless they are under a prior (legal) duty to act. (page 33)

ordinary person: To establish the defence of **provocation,** it must be shown that the homicide victim was committing a serious indictable offence and that any provocation flowing from that offence was "of such a nature as to be sufficient to deprive an ordinary person of the power of self-control." In the *Thibert* case (1996), the Supreme Court of Canada held that "the ordinary person must be taken to be of the same age, and sex, and must share with the accused such other factors as would give the act or insult in question a particular significance." However, in *Tran* (2010), the Court emphasized that "the objective test enacted by Parliament is designed to encourage 'reasonable and non-violent behaviour'" and also that "the ordinary person standard must be informed by contemporary norms of behaviour, including fundamental values such as the commitment to equality provided for in the *Canadian Charter of Rights and Freedoms.*"

The term "ordinary person" is also used when courts are required to determine whether a particular mental condition should be designated a "disease of the mind" for the purpose of section 16(1) of the *Criminal Code*, which defines the **NCRMD** defence. If an ordinary person, for example, would have entered a dissociative state in response to a specific psychological blow, the mental condition of the accused person would not be considered a "disease of the mind" because the cause was *external* to the accused person: they would, therefore, be acquitted of a criminal charge on the basis of the defence of non-mental-disorder automatism. However, if an ordinary person would not have entered into a dissociative state in response to the same psychological blow, then the cause of the mental condition would be considered a factor that is *internal* to the accused person (a psychological/neurological/genetic disorder): in these circumstances, the accused person's condition would be categorized as a "disease of the mind" and they would be restricted to a defence of **NCRMD**. (page 207)

palliative care: Drug or other medical treatment designed to alleviate pain, without curing the condition that causes the pain. The term is most commonly applied to the treatment administered to patients who have terminal illnesses. (page 54)

partial defence: Some defences operate to reduce the severity of the charge of which the accused is ultimately convicted, instead of absolving the accused of all criminal responsibility whatsoever. For example, a successful plea of **provocation** merely reduces the charge of which the accused is convicted from one of **murder** to one of

manslaughter. By way of contrast, if the accused successfully argues **self-defence** under section 34 of the *Criminal Code*, they are entitled to be absolved of all criminal responsibility; in this sense, self-defence is a complete defence. (page 87)

party to a criminal offence: There are a number of ways in which an individual may become a party to a criminal offence: (1) actually committing an offence; (2) **aiding** and/or **abetting** an offence committed by another person; (3) becoming a party to an offence by virtue of **common intention**; and (4) **counselling** an offence that is actually committed by another person. (page 160)

passive euthanasia: See **euthanasia**. (page 55)

peaceable possession: In certain circumstances, section 35 of the *Criminal Code* permits an individual who is in "peaceable possession" of property to use force in defence of this property. In this context, "peaceable possession" means possession "that is not seriously challenged by others." (page 337)

***per se*:** In or of itself. (page 34)

person who actually commits an offence: Section 21(1)(a) of the *Criminal Code* states that a person is a party to a criminal offence if they "actually commit it." This person is sometimes referred to as the **principal** or the perpetrator of the offence. They will nearly always be physically present at the scene of the crime but, in exceptional circumstances, may act through an innocent agent. For example, the accused person may have persuaded a small child to administer a fatal dose of poison to the victim. The accused person would be considered to have actually committed the offence of murder through an innocent agent (the child). (page 160)

personality disorder: A form of mental disorder in which the affected individual maintains a "good grip on reality" but whose behaviour and ways of thinking about their environment are considered abnormal or deviant. In the context of criminal behaviour, the most relevant of these disorders is the antisocial personality disorder. According to the American Psychiatric Association's *Diagnostic and Statistical Manual of Mental Disorders, Fifth Edition* (2013), the essential feature of antisocial personality disorder is a "pervasive pattern of disregard for, and violation of, the rights of others, occurring since age 15 years." Such conduct may bring an individual affected by this disorder into conflict with criminal justice authorities. (page 206)

persuasional (or primary) burden of proof: See **burden of proof**. (page 227)

planned and deliberate: Section 231(2) of the *Criminal Code* states that first-degree murder is murder that is "planned and deliberate." This term means that the accused must act on a previously formulated plan and that their conduct must not be impulsive. (page 78)

primary (or persuasional) burden of proof: See **burden of proof**. (page 141)

primary source of law (or main sources of criminal law): A main source of law, including statutes and case law in the Canadian legal system. (page 5)

principal: This term refers to the person who "actually commits" a criminal offence as opposed to individuals who become parties to the offence on some other basis (such as **aiding** and **abetting**). (page 160)

provocation: Section 232 of the *Criminal Code* provides that culpable homicide that would otherwise be murder may be reduced to manslaughter if the accused person who committed the homicide did so "in the heat of passion caused by sudden provocation." The defence requires that the homicide victim was committing a serious indictable offence and that any provocation flowing from that offence was "of such a nature as to be sufficient to deprive an ordinary person of the power of self-control." It must be shown that the accused person acted on the provocation "on the sudden and before there was time for his [or her] passion to cool." (page 270)

psychopath: An individual who shares many of the characteristics of individuals who suffer from antisocial personality disorder. Although there is considerable debate as to the precise nature of psychopathy, psychopaths may be characterized by a lack of sound judgment, an inability to learn from previous experience, a lack of remorse or guilt for anything that they do in violation of the rights of others, and a lack of capacity to understand how others see them. However, a psychopath does not lose contact with reality in the sense that a person who has schizophrenia may do and, therefore, is not likely to be found **NCRMD**. (page 205)

psychosis: A mental disorder characterized by profound disturbances in a person's thoughts, emotions, and ability to perceive reality (e.g., schizophrenia). (page 203)

quasi: Seeming; not real; halfway; almost as if it were; analogous to. (page 4)

quasi-criminal law: **Refers to regulatory offences as opposed to true crimes.** (page 4)

reasonable steps: Section 273.2 of the *Criminal Code* states that a person who is charged with sexual assault may not raise the defence of mistaken belief that the complainant consented to sexual activity unless the accused person can raise a reasonable doubt that they took "reasonable steps in the circumstances known to the accused at the time, to ascertain that the complainant was consenting." Reasonable steps are the steps that a reasonable person acting prudently would take in light of the specific knowledge of the surrounding circumstances that the accused person had at the time of the alleged offence. (page 232)

recklessness: A form of **subjective *mens rea***. It arises where the accused subjectively knows that their conduct creates a risk that certain prohibited consequences will occur but nevertheless persists in this course of conduct when a reasonable person would not do so. (page 94)

regulation: Subordinate legislation, usually promulgated by a Cabinet minister under the authority of a statute granting the authority to create such legislation. (page 262)

regulatory offence: An offence arising under regulatory legislation (federal, provincial/territorial, or municipal). Such legislation deals with the regulation of inherently legitimate activities connected with commerce, trade, and industry or with everyday matters such as driving, hunting, fishing, and so forth. Regulatory offences are, generally, not considered to be serious in nature and usually result in the imposition of only a relatively minor penalty. (page 3)

respondent: Literally, this is the party who "responds" when an appeal is launched against the decision of a lower court by the other party to a criminal case (who is known, formally, as the **appellant**). (page 124)

review board: The special tribunal that has been established in each province (under Part XX.1 of the *Criminal Code*) to make or review decisions as to what should happen to those who have been found **NCRMD** ("not criminally responsible on account of mental disorder"). The dispositional alternatives available to the review board are an absolute discharge, a conditional discharge, or an order that the NCR accused person be held in custody in a psychiatric facility. (page 211)

safe avenue of escape: When an accused person raises the defence of **duress,** it must be established that they did not have an "obvious safe avenue of escape." If a reasonable person—with the same knowledge that the accused had of the surrounding circumstances—would have taken the opportunity to escape, then the defence would fail. (page 312)

schizoaffective disorder: A mental condition in which there are symptoms of both schizophrenia (see below) and an affective (or mood) disorder, such as depression or mania. (page 203)

schizophrenia spectrum disorder: Refers to a group of severe mental disorders in which an individual may experience incoherence in thought and speech, hallucinations, delusions, and inappropriate emotional responses. (page 203)

second-degree murder: Murder that is not **first-degree murder** is second-degree murder [section 231(7) of the *Criminal Code*]. Where an individual is convicted of second-degree murder, the automatic penalty is life imprisonment [section 745(c)]. Section 745.4 of the *Code* provides that the trial judge may set a period of non-eligibility for parole ranging from a minimum of 10 years to a maximum of 25 years. If the accused has previously been convicted of murder, then the penalty is life imprisonment with no eligibility for parole for 25 years [section 745(b)]. Where an accused person has been convicted of multiple murders, committed after December 2011, the trial judge may impose *consecutive* periods of non-parole eligibility (section 745.51). (page 207)

self-defence: The *Criminal Code* provides that, in certain circumstances, an individual may justifiably use force in self-defence. The most important provision that defines the defence of self-defence is section 34. Under this provision, an accused person may claim self-defence if (1) they believe *on reasonable grounds* that force is being used against them or another person or that a threat of force is being made against them or another person; (2) the act that constitutes the offence is committed for the purpose of defending or protecting themselves or the other person from the use or threat of force; and (3) the accused person's conduct was *reasonable* in the circumstances. (page 320)

specific intent: According to Justice McIntyre in the case of *Bernard* (1988), "one which involves the performance of the ***actus reus***, coupled with an intent or purpose going beyond the mere performance of the questioned act." Examples are murder (section 235 of the *Criminal Code*); assault with intent to wound (section 244); and breaking and entering with intent to commit an indictable offence [section 349(1)(a)]. See also **crimes of specific and general (or basic) intent**. (page 87)

standard of proof: See **burden of proof**. (page 227)

strict liability: In the context of criminal law, this form of liability may be imposed in relation to various regulatory offences arising under both federal and provincial/territorial regulatory legislation. The Crown may obtain a conviction for a violation of such legislation without having to prove ***mens rea*** on the part of the accused. However, the accused may avoid liability by proving that they acted with "due diligence" in all the circumstances. Strict liability is sometimes referred to as the "halfway house solution" to the problem of finding an efficacious, yet fair, method of prosecuting regulatory offences. (page 142)

subjective *mens rea*: Offences that require proof of subjective *mens rea* impose on the Crown the burden of establishing that the accused actually intended the consequences of their conduct or that, knowing of the probable consequences of such conduct, the accused proceeded in reckless disregard of that risk, or that the accused was wilfully blind. Subjective *mens rea* is concerned with what actually went on in the accused's mind. (page 75)

substantial and integral cause: The special test of causation that applies exclusively to first-degree murder, under sections 231(5) and (6) of the *Criminal Code*. (page 61)

substantive criminal law: This term refers to legislation that defines the nature of various criminal offences (such as murder, manslaughter, and theft) and specifies the various legal elements that must be present before a conviction can be entered against an accused person. The term also refers to legislation that defines the nature and scope of various defences (such as **provocation, duress**, and **self-defence**). (page 7)

sudden provocation: The defence of **provocation** may be raised only where the accused person responds to sudden provocation. If the accused person initiated the process that preceded the fatal altercation with the victim, the defence will fail. (page 276)

summary conviction offence: Generally, summary conviction offences are less serious in nature and may be tried only before a provincial court judge. These offences may be created by both federal and provincial/territorial legislation. (page 2)

transferred intent: Where A intends to strike B but misses and strikes C, they may be convicted of assault on the basis of the doctrine of transferred intent. A intends to commit the ***actus reus*** of assault, but actually commits the ***actus reus*** of assault in a way other than they intended (i.e., by striking the "wrong" victim). The ***mens rea*** for the ***actus reus*** of the assault that did not happen (the assault of B) is transferred to the ***actus reus*** of the assault that did occur (the assault of C). The doctrine applies to a number of offences (such as murder and the various types of assault in the *Criminal Code*), but it operates only within the confines of the same offence. For example, an intention to wound an animal cannot be transferred to the ***actus reus*** of assault of a human being, when the accused aims to strike a dog but instead strikes a person. (page 92)

trespass: The unlawful interference with another's property, person, or rights. (page 336)

trespasser: A trespasser is one who unlawfully enters another person's land, residence, or any other building. Section 35 of the *Criminal Code* provides that a person in **peaceable possession** of property may use force to protect their property from a trespasser (including preventing a trespasser from entering on the property and removing a trespasser from it)-provided the accused person's conduct is *reasonable* in the circumstances. (page 338)

trier of fact: The party responsible for deciding the facts in a trial. In the case of a jury trial, the members of the jury are the triers of fact and the judge is responsible for making decisions about the applicable law. Where the trial judge sits without a jury, then they are the trier of fact as well as the ultimate arbiter of the law. (page 91)

true crimes: While **regulatory offences** are concerned with the regulation of inherently *legitimate* activities, true crimes are offences that represent a serious breach of community values and are considered both "wrong" and deserving of punishment. In general, true crimes consist of those offences contained in the *Criminal Code* as well as the serious offences contained in the *Controlled Drugs and Substances Act* (which is concerned with the punishment of those involved with the use of illegal drugs). (page 3)

unlawful act manslaughter: See **manslaughter**. (page 120)

unlawfully causing bodily harm: This offence is defined by section 269 of the *Criminal Code*. The ***actus reus*** consists of unlawful conduct that causes bodily harm. The unlawful conduct must amount to an offence under either federal or provincial legislation. The ***mens rea*** is objective in nature: the Crown must prove that a reasonable person, facing the same circumstances as the accused, would have foreseen the risk of non-trivial bodily harm. (page 124)

viral load: A measurement of the amount of HIV in the blood. A low viral load reduces or may even eliminate the risk of transmission of the virus. (page 247)

voluntariness: This concept refers to the basic requirement of the criminal law that an accused person's conduct be the product of their own free will. It is a fundamental requirement of the ***actus reus*** of an offence: where there is no *voluntary* action (e.g., because the accused is in a state of automatism), there is no *actus reus* and the accused must be acquitted. In addition, the issue of voluntariness may be particularly relevant to the establishment of certain defences. For example, the assertion that the accused was not able to make a genuinely free choice as to whether or not to break the law may constitute valid grounds for raising the defences of **duress** or **necessity** (here, the criminal law makes reference to **normative involuntariness** as the basis for recognizing these defences). (page 46)

wilful blindness: In *Briscoe* (2010), the Supreme Court of Canada stated that "the doctrine of wilful blindness imputes knowledge to an accused whose suspicion is aroused to the point where he or she sees the need for further inquiries, but *deliberately chooses* not to make those inquiries." This form of ***subjective mens rea*** exists when an accused chooses to be "deliberately ignorant" that particular circumstances exist (for example, that goods are stolen). The Crown must establish that the particular accused person had become subjectively aware of the need to make an inquiry as to the relevant circumstances but deliberately refrains from making the inquiry because they do not want to know the truth. Wilful blindness is treated as being equivalent to *actual* knowledge. (page 98)

wrong: Section 16(1) of the *Criminal Code* provides that an accused person must be found to be **NCRMD** if, at the time of the alleged offence, they were suffering from a ***mental disorder*** that rendered them incapable of knowing that the act or omission in question was "wrong." In this context, "wrong" means morally wrong or "wrong according to the everyday standards of the reasonable person." (page 206)

Additional Terms (Not Referenced in the Text, but Frequently Used in Decided Cases that You may Read)

absolute and conditional discharge: When an accused person has been found **NCRMD**, the court or board of review may order that the NCR accused person be held in custody in a psychiatric facility. However, the court or board of review may also grant an **absolute discharge**—an outright release with no restrictions on the liberty of the NCR accused person—or a **conditional discharge**—a release that is subject to various conditions, such as residence in a particular location and attendance for treatment.

appeal: A formal proceeding by means of which the Crown or the accused may request a review of a decision by a "higher court." For example, the provincial/territorial Court of Appeal is a higher court than the Superior Court of Criminal Jurisdiction or the Provincial Court, whereas the Supreme Court of Canada is, in turn, a higher court than the Court of Appeal.

circumstantial evidence: Evidence of a series of circumstances that may lead the **trier of fact** to draw an inference of guilt when no direct evidence is available (evidence is "direct" when a witness testifies as to what they actually observed by sight, hearing, etc.).

civil law system: This term (distinguished from civil law, above) refers to a legal system based on the approach of Roman law and usually characterized by the existence of a comprehensive code. This system of law is predominant in continental Europe, Scotland, and (as far as the **civil law** is concerned) Quebec.

code: A collection or system of laws. In a **civil law system**, a code would ideally be a complete system of law, logically arranged according to basic principles and promulgated by the appropriate legislative authority. The origins of the **civil law system** are to be found in the collection of laws made by the Roman Emperor Justinian and referred to as "The Code." In France, for example, the *Code Civil* (originally promulgated in 1804 and at one time known as the *Code Napoléon*) contains the **civil law** of that country.

***Controlled Drugs and Substances Act*:** The *Controlled Drugs and Substances Act*, S.C. 1996, c. 19, regulates "controlled drugs and substances," such as narcotics (including heroin and cocaine), amphetamines, LSD, and barbiturates. Among the most important offences under this Act are possession, trafficking, possession for the purpose of trafficking, importing and exporting, and production of a controlled substance.

***de facto*:** In fact.

injunction: A court order prohibiting or requiring action of some kind.

***intra*:** Within; inside.

***intra vires*:** Within the jurisdictional power of.

precedent: A previous decision or judgment of a court (usually, an appellate court) that is referred to as an authority that should be followed by a judge in a similar factual situation.

***prima facie*:** At first sight; on the face of it. A *prima facie* case is literally one that will suffice until contradicted and overcome by other evidence.

re: In the matter of; with reference to.

sources of criminal law: The primary sources of criminal law are (1) legislation and (2) judicial decisions that either interpret such legislation or state the **common law**.

***ultra vires*:** Beyond the jurisdictional powers of.

INDEX OF CASES

Gauthier (2013), 298 C.C.C. (3d) 277 (S.C.C.): 172–174
Geddes (2015), 322 C.C.C. (3d) 414 (Ont. C.A.): 246–247
George (1960), 128 C.C.C. 289 (S.C.C.): 280
George (2000), 145 C.C.C. (3d) 405 (Ont. C.A.): 337
George, [2017] 1 S.C.R. 102: 237
Gonzague (1983), 4 C.C.C. (3d) 505 (Ont. C.A.): 178
Goodwin v. British Columbia (Superintendent of Motor Vehicles), 2015 SCC 46, [2015] 2 S.C.R. 250: 9
Gopie (2017), 356 C.C.C. (3d) 36 (Ont. C.A.): 189–190
Gordon (2009), 241 C.C.C. (3d) 388 (Ont. C.A.): 92
Gosset (1993), 83 C.C.C. (3d) 494 (S.C.C.): 132
Grant (2016), 342 C.C.C. (3d) 514 (Ont. C.A.): 325–326
Greyeyes (1997), 116 C.C.C. (3d) 334 (S.C.C.): 166–167
Guess (2000), 148 C.C.C. (3d) 321 (B.C.C.A.): 88–89
Gunning (2005), 196 C.C.C. (3d) 123 (S.C.C.): 338–339

H. (A.) (2017), O.J. No. 1427, 2017 ONCJ 201 (Ont. C.J.): 323
H. (A.D.) (2013), 295 C.C.C. (3d) 376 (S.C.C.): 37–38, 94, 126
H. (P.) (2000), 143 C.C.C. (3d) 223 (Ont. C.A.): 27
Hamilton (2005), 198 C.C.C. (3d) 1 (S.C.C.): 174, 174n, 177, 178–179, 181
Hammerbeck (1991), 68 C.C.C. (3d) 161 (B.C.C.A.): 260–261
Harbottle (1993), 84 C.C.C. (3d) 1 (S.C.C.): 60–61, 61n
Harper (1986), 53 C.R. (3d) 185 (B.C.C.A.): 146n
Hatfield (1997), 115 C.C.C. (3d) 47 (Ont. C.A.): 32
He (2008), 237 C.C.C. (3d) 1 (B.C.C.A.): 80
Head (2016), 341 C.C.C. (3d) 488 (N.L.C.A.): 212n
Hemmerly (1976), 30 C.C.C. (2d) 141 (Ont. C.A.): 264–265
Hibbert (1995), 99 C.C.C. (3d) 193 (S.C.C.): 312
Hickey (1977), 30 C.C.C. (2d) 416 (Ont. C.A.): 146
Hill (1986), 25 C.C.C. (3d) 322 (S.C.C.): 273, 274
Hinchey (1996), 111 C.C.C. (3d) 353 (S.C.C.): 89
Hogg (2000), 148 C.C.C. (3d) 86 (Ont. C.A.): 252
Holland (1841), 174 E.R. 313 (Assizes): 67, 68
Honish (1991), 68 C.C.C. (3d) 329 (Alta. C.A.), affirmed (1993), 78 C.C.C. (3d) 96 (S.C.C.): 223
Humaid (2006), 208 C.C.C. (3d) 43 (Ont. C.A.): 276
Hundal (1993), 79 C.C.C. (3d) 97 (S.C.C.): 115–117
Hutchinson, [2014] 1 S.C.R. 346: 248, 251
Hydro-Québec (1997), 118 C.C.C. (3d) 97 (S.C.C.): 6

Ilczyszyn (1988), 45 C.C.C. (3d) 91 (Ont. C.A.): 260, 261
Irwin (1998), 123 C.C.C. (3d) 316 (Ont. C.A.): 94

Jackson and Davy (1993), 86 C.C.C. (3d) 385 (S.C.C.): 165, 171
Jacquard (1997), 113 C.C.C. (3d) 1 (S.C.C.): 87, 216
James Forcillo v. Her Majesty the Queen, [2018] S.C.C.A. No. 258: 335
Jamieson (2002), 166 C.C.C. (3d) 501 (B.C.C.A.): 339
Jeffers (2012), 280 C.C.C. (3d) 54 (B.C.C.A.): 91
Jobb (2008), 239 C.C.C. (3d) 29 (Sask. C.A.): 199–200
Jobidon (1991), 66 C.C.C (3d) 454 (S.C.C.): 253–255, 256
John (2018), 366 C.C.C. (3d) 136 (Ont. C.A.): 13n
Jordan (1956), 40 Cr. App. Rep. 152 (C.C.A.): 65–66
Jorgensen (1995), 102 C.C.C. (3d) 97 (S.C.C.): 262–263
K. (S.) (1995), 103 C.C.C. (3d) 572 (B.C.C.A.): 26–27, 26n
Kanda (2008), 227 C.C.C. (3d) 417 (Ont. C.A.): 143, 146, 148–149
Kandola (1993), 80 C.C.C. (3d) 481 (B.C.C.A.): 328
Keller (1998), 131 C.C.C. (3d) 59 (Alta. C.A.): 312–313
Keshane (2012), 356 D.L.R. (4th) 649 (Alta. C.A.): 9–10
Khawaja (2012), 290 C.C.C. (3d) 361 (S.C.C.): 92n
King (1962), 133 C.C.C. 1 (S.C.C.): 220
Kirkby (1985), 21 C.C.C. (3d) 31 (Ont. C.A.): 216
Kitching and Adams, [1976] 6 W.W.R. 697 (Man. C.A.): 61–63
Kjeldsen (1981), 63 C.C.C. (2d) 161 (S.C.C.): 205
Klundert (2008), 238 C.C.C. (3d) 6 (Ont. C.A.): 259
Kong (2006), 211 C.C.C. (3d) 1 (S.C.C.), overruling (2005), 200 C.C.C. (3d) 19 (Alta. C.A.): 333
Kowbel (1953), 110 C.C.C. 47 (S.C.C.): 192
Krivicic (Re.) (2018), 362 C.C.C. (3d) 490 (Ont. C.A.): 213
Kundeus (1976), 24 C.C.C. (2d) 276 (S.C.C.): 244–245, 244n
Kurtzman (1991), 66 C.C.C. (3d) 161 (Ont. C.A.): 147, 148

L. (J.) (2006) 204 C.C.C. (3d) 324 (Ont. C.A.): 127–128
*La Souveraine, Compagnie d'assurance générale v. Autorité des marchés financ*iers, [2013] 3 S.C.R. 756: 143
Ladue, [1965] 4 C.C.C. 264 (Yuk. T. C.A.): 243–244
Laine (2015), 327 C.C.C. (3d) 67 (Ont. C.A.): 120
Lamb v. Canada (Attorney General), 2017 B.C.S.C. 1802, 5 B.C.L.R. (6th) 175 (B.C. Supreme Court): 58n
Landry (1991), 62 C.C.C. (3d) 117 (S.C.C.): 205, 206–207

INDEX

B

C

D

J

K

L

M

N

O

P

Q

R

S